He Also Spoke as a Jew

Parkes–Wiener Series on Jewish Studies

Series editors: David Cesarani and Tony Kushner

ISSN 1368-5449

The field of Jewish Studies is one of the youngest, but fastest-growing and most exciting areas of scholarship in the academic world today. Named after James Parkes and Alfred Wiener, this series aims to publish new research in the field and student materials for use in the seminar room, to disseminate the latest work of established scholars and to re-issue classics that are currently out of print.

The selection of publications reflects the international character and diversity of Jewish Studies; it ranges over Jewish history from Abraham to modern Zionism, and Jewish culture from Moses to post-modernism. The series also reflects the inter-disciplinary approach inherent in Jewish Studies and at the cutting edge of contemporary scholarship, and provides an outlet for innovative work on the interface between Judaism and ethnicity, popular culture, gender, class, space and memory.

Other Books in the Series

HE ALSO SPOKE AS A JEW
The Life of James Parkes

HAIM CHERTOK

Foreword by
Irving Greenberg
Founding Director, Holocaust Memorial Museum,
Washington, DC

VALLENTINE MITCHELL
LONDON • PORTLAND, OR

First published in 2006 in Great Britain by
VALLENTINE MITCHELL
Suite 314, Premier House, 112–114 Station Road,
Edgware, Middlesex HA8 7BJ

and in the United States of America by
VALLENTINE MITCHELL
c/o ISBS, 920 NE 58th Avenue, Suite 300
Portland, OR 97213-3786

Website: http://www.vm.books.com

British Library Cataloguing in Publication Data

Chertok, Haim
    He also spoke as a Jew : the life of James Parkes. –
    (Parkes-Wiener series on Jewish studies)
    1. Parkes, James William, 1896–   2. Theologians – Great
    Britain – Biography   3. Christianity and other religions –
    Judaism – History – 20th century   4. Judaism – Relations –
    Christianity – History – 20th century
    I. Title
    261.2'6'092

ISBN 0 85303 644 6 (cloth)
ISBN 0 85303 645 4 (paper)

Library of Congress Cataloging-in-Publication Data
A catalog record has been applied for

Typeset in 11/13pt Palatino by Vitaset, Paddock Wood, Kent
Printed in Great Britain by MPG Books Ltd, Bodmin, Cornwall

Contents

List of Plates

Acknowledgements

The Parkes Papers and Library are housed among the Special Collections in the Hartley Library at the University of Southampton whose archives were, for three extended periods between 2000 and 2004, my burrow, my retreat, and my second home. Without the material support of the Hartley Institute and the ongoing encouragement of Professor Tony Kushner, Director of the James Parkes Centre for the Study of Jewish/non-Jewish Relations) and Dr C. M. Woolgar, Director of Special Collections of the University Library, this work could never have been undertaken. In addition, I wish to thank the friendly, highly professional, at times forbearing library staff, most notably Karen Robson and Jenny Ruthven who daily accommodated the vagaries of the visiting Israeli researcher, and Chris Pilcher who always greeted him with a smile. The author is grateful to the University of Southampton Library for permission to use items from the Parkes Collection.

In the course of researching, writing and editing this work, no one could have been more dedicated and invaluable than Maggie Davidson Chertok, to whom this work is lovingly dedicated. I wish to thank my publisher Frank Cass of Vallentine Mitchell for his faith in this project and his highly professional staff including Mark Anstee, Toby Harris and Lisa Hyde.

Others have at various stages of the project been generous of their time and ever forthcoming in offering assistance: Professor Edward Alexander (Seattle), the Rt. Hon. Tony Benn (London), Jane Brock (Guernsey), Lucy Brouard (St Peter Port), Reverend Richard Cole (Geneva), Richard and Ursula Dunn (Barley, Hertfordshire), Alison Elias (Cambridge), Joseph Emanuel (Jerusalem), George Fletcher (New York), Shalom Freedman (Jerusalem), Elliott A. Green (Jerusalem), Irving Greenberg (New York), *The Guernsey Press*, Ian Jack (London), The Jewish Historical Society of England, Ethelea Katzenell (Beersheva), John Krivine (Sde Boker, Israel), Uri Lebowitz (Geneva), Rochelle Mancini (New York), Steve Mauger (Guernsey), Peter Pannett (St Peter Port), Abraham Rabinovich (Jerusalem), Dr Phil Rankilor (St Peter Port), Professor Colin Richmond (Woodbridge, Suffolk), Patrick Rolleston (Dublin), Ellen Roth (London), Moshe Roth (Beersheva), Jess Seewald (Beersheva), Myer Steinberg (Melbourne), Tsila Stern (Beersheva), Richard Sweeney (Bloomsburg, PA), Michael Terry (New York), Debbie Unger (Miami Beach), Professor Bernard Wasserstein (Chicago), Dr Jean-Marc Weinstein (Lahavim, Israel), Ruth Edith Weisz (Cambridge), Ruth Weyl (Northwood, Middlesex), Professor Zvi Werblowsky (Jerusalem), Doris and Sam Wilkinson (Barley, Hertfordshire), and Robert Wolfe (Netanya). In matters both great or small, I thank each and every one of you for your timely assistance and steadfast encouragement.

Foreword

This book is a remarkable portrait of a remarkable human being. James Parkes (1896–1981) was a pioneer, nay a revolutionary, in one of the great religious reformations of all time – the recasting of Christian Jewish relations. The movement – now in full force – seeks to reverse nineteen hundred years of hostility and fratricide, rooted in theology and liturgy (a tradition which has been summed up in Christianity as the Theology of Contempt).

Since the contempt and the negative stereotypes on which the Christian false witness against Jewry was based were reflected on, hermeneutically developed and imaginatively articulated over the course of centuries, since they involve the very sacred scriptures and sources of both religions, the complexity and difficulty of such a new understanding is extraordinary. The classic Christian claims that the Jews forfeit their calling by God by dint of refusing to accept Christ – which refusal was driven by arrogant obduracy and consequent spiritual blindness – were articulated in fundamental holy texts, then repeated and elaborated by some of the greatest thinkers and religious authorities in the history of the tradition. The dogma was radicalized and made even more poisonous by scriptural assertions that the Jews were deicides. This moral degradation was translated into the later horrifying libel that Jews were well poisoners, plague spreaders, host desecrators, child torturers who went beyond the pale by slaughtering children and baking Judaism's sacred foods with the blood of the innocents. These claims were so widely diffused and accepted that an alleged victim, Simon of Trent, was canonized as a saint. Even in the nineteenth century, channels within the Catholic Church disseminated such a malicious report, and mainstream Vatican authorities hesitated to disown or condemn such allegations.

Now, impelled by the recognition of the horror of the Holocaust (which illustrates the ultimate consequence of hatred unchecked) and by the incredible encounter of Jews and Christians in a democratic society, the barrier of scorn and misunderstanding is brick by brick being dismantled. So powerful a force was the guilt and trauma of the Holocaust that even a Pope as theologically conservative as John Paul II (who felt the lash of the Shoah) extended this revision dramatically even as he fought against the liberalization of the Catholic Church in other doctrinal areas.

Imagine then, if one can, a man who decades before the Holocaust, and long before the full effects of mixing with Jews were felt, grasped the extent of the historic acts of injustice of Christians toward Jewry and determined to atone for them by ending them. Imagine how in his incredible capacity for empathy, he was able to penetrate through layers and layers of denigration and centuries of hardening the heart in order to feel the Jews' pain and victimization. Imagine the power of discovery that enabled him to internalize the message and fate of Judaism as well as the intellectual daring that enabled him to apply these insights to the reformulation of the classic Christian faith in which he was so deeply rooted. This is the man – Ecce Homo – James Parkes, stunningly and sympathetically portrayed in the book before you.

Haim Chertok has drawn a humanly touching, deeply insight-ful portrait of the whole man. James Parkes went forth as a paladin for a hitherto excluded and mistreated people but he was no simple white knight. He was a flawed and paradoxical creature who rose to intellectual and spiritual greatness as he fought for justice for Jews and Judaism. How an 'introspective, hyper-sensitive, chronically ill, frequently forlorn' child grew into a religious leader, path breaking thinker and brilliant performer at the lectern is richly depicted in this beautifully written volume. How a not-too-prepossessing clergymen given to self-pity, how an insecure reverend given to offset his handicaps by romancing his life story, matured into a scholar 'great in conscience and mag-nificent in compassion' is superbly delineated. How Parkes became 'a man of feeling not given to tears alone but to decisive, effective action' is traced accurately and with feeling by an author who has achieved just the right mix of sympathy and objectivity, stirred with compassionate feeling and understated wit.

Using myriad pieces of evidence and conceptual analysis, always with an eye to the telling detail, Chertok takes us through the peregrinations of this life without a misstep. Chertok describes Parkes unfolding from the discovery of the pathology of anti-Semitism to the understanding of the Christian problem, from the amassing of knowledge and insight about Judaism to the recog-nition of the contradictions and the reformulation of the Christian narrative. The writer explains the objections Parkes encountered, the resentments he aroused and the setbacks that left him feeling under-appreciated, bypassed and much aggrieved. The author captures well the intellectual growth and philosophical courage that enabled Parkes to reformulate the relationship of Christianity and Judaism and to understand in a new way God's plan for creation (as well as the parallel and joint role, which by God's will, the two faiths were intended to play). Chertok communicates the dilemma and the pain of a man penalized economically by his battle for the dignity of Jewry, who accepted subsidies from Jewish friends, although this provided grist for his detractors and enemies. Chertok portrays the mix of idealism and ambition in Parkes, both his capacity for selfless devotion to the cause of the Jews and his self-interested, constant push for recognition and appreciation of his accomplishments.

One cannot praise enough the author's ability to read a person's life so poetically, so accurately, so contextually. Chertok relates biography and theology so skillfully as to shed new light on an important but neglected thinker and his original thinking. He lets us 'taste' the richness of Parkes' imagination and the incredible achievement of a person, deeply rooted in one faith achieving insight into another faith, the insight equivalent to an insider. The author portrays the Parkesian unyielding insistence that Christianity 'reform itself, abjure itself, and confess itself', and the Parkesian optimism that challenged Karl Barth's radical Christian pessimism as he battled to liberate the Church from its incubus of Jew hatred and enlighten it with Judaic insight. In the end, Chertok has made a strong case for his claim that Parkes was 'the most steadfast and effective defender of the Jewish people to emerge from Gentile ranks in the twentieth century'.

This book is admirable more than just for its loving recovery of the life and thought of an overlooked theologian. It has significant implications that go beyond its doing justice to one unjustly treated thinker. Chertok shows us how Parkes entered into an intense, unmediated encounter with another faith, passed through the crucible of white hot acknowledgement of sins and injustices inflicted on another faith's practitioners, yet emerged a deeper, better Christian. As Parkes said: the shocks, the recognition, the rethinkings had not 'made me wish to deny or modify one single positive aspect of my traditional Christianity'.

Parkes' achievement is of enormous importance as role model and precedent. We live in a time when the human encounter between religionists followed by theological reformulations has led to bewilderment and confusion. When the absolute claims of various religions were broken by this new encounter, for many believers this led to syncretism and/or relativism. In turn, these phenomena have led to a fundamentalist backlash (and even violent jihad) to stem the erosion of faith commitments and traditional values. Parkes' life and work point to the alternative, better way – to a principled pluralism, to a new role for religion as a healer and source of values in a post-modern society. Parkes shows that activists need not dispense with thought, nor should passionate commitment lead to the use of force and suppression of the Other (or of the internal antagonist.) Thanks to Chertok's yeoman research work and writing, Parkes leads us toward the contemporary reconnection of Judaism and Christianity in a manner that carries extraordinary moral power and cultural significance.

Parkes was a soldier in the First World War who came back from life in the trenches having been gassed at Flanders to resume Her Majesty's service and then went on to labor in the vineyard of the Lord. But, as this book makes manifest, his greatest heroism was on the battlefield of religion, theology and society. There he marched through miasmas of hatred, bore the slings and arrows of outraged traditionalists, broke through the barriers of ignorance, stereotype and sanctified contempt. The young boy who lost his mother, brother and sister to death and felt lost and homeless came to understand and support the wandering Jews' desire to come home to their ancient land (Zionism). Similarly, the gadfly who could have slipped into the role of alienated outsider within, actually came to be at home with two faiths. Christianity he practiced faithfully. Although scrupulous about maintaining distinctions vital to the integrity of adherents of both faiths, for the other, Judaism, he developed the capacity to speak *also* as a Jew. That is, he spoke 'on the basis of believing Judaism also to be true – as true as Christianity. Both religions are true. Neither is simply an incomplete form of the other and I do not desire to see either disappear, even by conversion to the other' (Parkes, *Judaism and Christianity*, Chicago, IL: University of Chicago Press, 1948, pages 18–19). For this illuminating and ultimately inspiring portrayal, for this book of rare quality, we are all indebted to Haim Chertok.

Now, dear reader, let the feast begin!

Irving Greenberg
New York, April 2005

PART 1
THE MATTER OF GUERNSEY

1

Homecoming

On a clear day, the wandering eye squinting eastward towards France, either from Miellette Bay at the northern end of the island of Guernsey's eastern shore or from Jerbourg Point at its southernmost extremity, can easily discern the grey outline of the Cotentin Peninsula's thrust into the sea. Guernsey, in fact, is a geological extension of Cotentin. With the ominous imposition of what is today Cotentin's most prominent landmark – the nuclear reactor at Flamanville – the scene is identical to what James Parkes as a young boy peering over the water viewed more than a century ago. This Norman shoreline is thirty-eight miles from Guernsey, second in size and population of the Channel Island group. Invisible on the horizon, the southern coast of England, historical and cultural counterweight to France, pokes out of the water some eighty miles to the north. Paying allegiance to the English crown since the time of the Norman Conquest, these anomalous, largely self-governing, detached chunks of the mainland are Britain's oldest dominions.

Comprising altogether twenty-five square miles, little Guernsey is barely larger than the island of Manhattan; together with the nearby islets of Alderney, Sark, and Herm, the administrative bailiwick of Guernsey comprises in all some thirty square miles. However with a long southern leg and a shorter eastern one converging at a right angle, the island is topo-graphically quite varied. At forty-five square miles, the island bailiwick of Jersey, twenty-five miles to the southeast, is the giant of the Channel Island group, and it supports a proportionately larger population. At the onset of the last century Parkes' island was home to around 40,000 people, most of whom worked in agriculture: dairying and cultivating tomatoes, flowers and vegetables for export to England. To a lesser extent, fishing and quarrying granite were also important occupations. Today, many island residents consider that its pastoral character has been compromised irretrievably. Actually a rise in population of about fifty per cent to nearly 60,000 inhabitants does not seem such dramatic growth in the course of a century. To the casual visitor, for at least nine months of the year Guernsey retains its predominantly rural charm. However, international banking and tourism have displaced farming as major industries and, especially during summertime and holidays, swarms of visitors swell Guernsey's twisting roads and clog the narrow sidewalks of St Peter Port, the island's only town.

At the outset of 'Boyhood in Guernsey', the opening segment of Parkes' exploration into his island origins, he celebrates 'pre-tourist Guernsey' as 'a most gorgeous place in which to be young'. Visualizing himself as a free spirit wandering over a verdant, unspoiled paradise, Parkes broadly sketches a fairly conventional, romanticized version of what comprises an idyllic, rural boyhood: 'I explored every cliff path and bay, every rock and cranny in its long coast line, knew it in summer calm and winter storm, revelled in all the colours of sea and land, discovered all its flowers, was familiar with all its butterflies, was passionately devoted to its fascinating and amusing history, and immensely admired the adventurous and pioneering spirit of the islanders.'[1]

Overshadowed by this effulgence, later only grudgingly surfacing at all, is the *causa sine qua non* that enabled young Parkes to indulge his enthusiasm for his native island's topography and natural history with such avidity: he was so chronically weak and febrile that as a matter of course he was excused from school games. In fact he was frequently absent from the classroom for weeks at a time. Although his lamentable physical constitution lent ample scope for discontent, Parkes prefers to remember that he was a happy, indeed exuberant, boy. 'My one complaint against life,' he recalls, 'was that I was not of full Guernsey descent.'

But this statement is misleading, for in actuality Parkes could not claim even partial descent from the island's native stock. Nevertheless, the youth's solitary exploits along Guernsey's cliff paths and in its insular crannies inspired heady fancies of a lineage far more precious than what seemed to him the far too prosaic direct line of English Parkeses. In fact Parkes pulls out all the stops to try to transform his father's decampment from England for the Channel Islands in the waning years of the nineteenth century into a kind of glorious Parkes family reunion.

However flimsy or far-fetched, through his father Parkes appro-priates every tie that might serve to support the fantasy of a glorious homecoming in which he too might play a vicarious role.

Although not a word is squandered on the birthplace of his mother, we are given portentous notice that his great-grandmother had lived 'for some time' on the island of Jersey. Or again, during the Napoleanic period, so that the British fleet might shield tiny Alderney Island from French incursions, we are informed that his grandfather was placed in charge of constructing the island's naval harbour. Inordinately proud of this antecedent, a civil engineer who was awarded the Treford Premium – a major professional prize – for designing harbours in India, Parkes takes pains to dissociate his grandfather from the 'asinine design' of Alderney's harbour which, we are given to understand, had been foisted upon him by the Admiralty. One stormy day, leaving scarcely a trace, the Treford laureate's creation sank ignobly beneath the waves.

Even less consanguinity or trace of irony may be discerned when, vainly bolstering his boyhood conceit of significant family ties to Guernsey itself, Parkes resuscitates two great-great-great aunts who apparently had resided in St Peter Port for a short period during the early nineteenth century. For Parkes as an adolescent, these distant links served to cushion the plain, cold fact that Henry Parkes, a trained engineer like his father before him, was simply an immigrant to Guernsey from Staffordshire, around Lichfield.[2] Even sixty years later, the white heat of all this spurious propinquity still warmed the imagination of the Guernseyman while he was composing his life story. As for Parkes' mother, the dearth of detail about her origins leads one to infer that prior to immigrating with her husband to Guernsey, neither she nor any of her forebears could claim any link to these island specks in the Gulf of St Malo.

After the first flush of enthusiasm for war had worn off, in 1916 military conscription was imposed in England. It was not, however, automatically applicable to the Channel Islands. Indeed, the only outright obligation of the Guernsey Militia, 'Royal' since having been granted the title by William IV in 1831, was to defend an endangered British sovereign. Nevertheless, in time of war a high proportion of islanders has always volun-teered for British military service, and the *jurats*, or legislative

councils of the bailiwicks of Guernsey and Jersey made their
forces available for overseas duty. Thus, under the command
of a Guernseyman, Major-General Sir Beauvoir de Lisle, was
born a new regiment of the British Army – the Royal Guernsey
Light Infantry. This unit 'suffered such losses at Paschendaele,
Cambrai, and Lys that they were withdrawn from the front
and detailed for guard duties at the G.H.Q. until the end of
the war'.[3]

That so many Guernsey families suffered grievous wartime
losses on the killing fields of Paschendaele may help to account
for Parkes' taciturnity when he returns briefly to the deaths of
his siblings at the end of 'Boyhood in Guernsey':

> David had joined up immediately after war was declared.
> He had become a private in the Artists' Rifles (28th London)
> and soon after was given a commission in the South Stafford-
> shire Regiment. He went to France in the first months of the
> war, reached a captaincy, and was killed in the winter of
> 1917 at Paschendaele. Molly went to Cheltenham, I think,
> in 1913, and was there until 1918 when she was lost in the
> torpedoing of the S.S. *Leinster* in the Irish Sea. She had had
> measles and, as by that time we had no home, a school
> friend who had also had measles invited her to convalesce
> with her family in Ireland.[4]

For a youngster who had fabricated family ties to 'a homeland'
out of odd scraps and bare bones of family legend and who fifty
years later would still be rhapsodizing over its native soil and
local history, the flat offhandedness of '... by that time we had
no home ...' bears particular note. The demise of Parkes' mother
during his early adolescence and the loss in rapid-fire succession
of both his siblings meant that what had once seemed a permanent, natural, secure configuration – father, mother, brother,
sister, and himself – established in a regular, fairly typical home
had suddenly vanished. Moreover, if his father as a widower had
at first provided a simulacrum of 'a proper home', could never
quite be viewed as a normal one.

The condition of homelessness, here so closely connected
to these three family deaths, goes far to account for Parkes'
reticence in examining darker corners of his distant past. Even
at half-a-century's remove from what at the time were tragically

commonplace events, one senses that Parkes' reserve carries a heavier emotional burden than he feels comfortable uncovering and probing let alone broadcasting to the world on his voyage of self-discovery. It was not a dearth of feeling but an overload that deterred him from offering direct commentary on the enormity of his personal loss. His muteness betrays both the suddenness and poignancy of the trauma that Parkes underwent. It also points forward, resonating both emotively and intellectually with what would later become Parkes' powerful, instinctive empathy with a perennially homeless people.

Throughout Parkes' very early years, the possibility of such drastic change had been unimaginable. In fact at the time of his birth on 22 December 1896, Guernsey could have been a byword for immutability. Prior to his years of retirement, one of Parkes' rare allusions to the pre-1914 island was delivered before a Jewish audience at a conference in Toronto in September 1968. The Guernsey of that era, he declared, was 'a world of stable currency and falling prices'. It had enjoyed 'dominion status from England since the thirteenth century. A member of the European Decimal Union, Guernsey used impartially the francs of France, Belgium and Switzerland, the liras of Italy and the drachmas of Greece, all of which were equal and worth precisely nineteen American cents. At the same time it was, however, also a world of comforting public values.'[5]

Yet in the very year he was composing his memoirs, Parkes elsewhere was emphasizing that his boyhood island was 'a stable *but not a static world*' (emphasis supplied). It was, he explained,

> similar to what Tennyson described
> '... as a great society
> with freedom broadening slowly down
> From precedent to precedent.'
> The problems of poverty, sickness and unemployment had been targeted by the government. Empire was just ceasing to be a competition of grab and despoil, and feeling about Kipling's famous 'white man's burden' [was] based on an implicit sense of effortless superiority.[6]

Trumping Tennyson with Kipling, how aware was Parkes that his reflections on his original homeland were actually conflicted? Apparently, not in the least. Parkes recalls with warmth and evident approval that this vanished world, his primal home, was imbued both with comforting stability and with a Tennysonian vision of the melioration of society. After all, for the young boy his agriculturalist father, who prided himself in employing advanced greenhouse methods, could have been a very embodiment of Tennyson's spirit of progress. At the same time, a more mature sensibility records that its 'effortless superiority', a phrase that defines an attitude which Parkes would assimilate as a personal value, was complicit with the Victorian imperialism and racism which also help define the spirit of the era. Together with his personal losses, these two retrospective slants on turn-of-the-century Guernsey engendered an ambivalence that subverted Parkes' capacity to come to terms with his early past.

Two years after delivering his remarks in Toronto, in an interview that repeats the sound bite about 'stable currency and falling prices', Parkes introduces a note that was entirely absent in the account of his Guernsey youth in *Voyage of Discoveries:* 'I was a politically-conscious adolescent.'[7] In fact, as the above remarks suggest, precious little supports Parkes' claim of precocious political awareness, and, as we shall see later, much indicates quite the opposite. This cryptic statement may possibly be attributed to the uneasiness and consequent revisionist impulse of the septuagenarian when recalling the naiveté of young Jimmy Parkes.

'In the centre of the island of Guernsey is the parish of St Andrew. At the eastern end is the Manor of Rohais. My father was the falconer of the Manor, and I was born at *Les Fauconnaires* in December 1896.'[8] In such deceptive guise does Parkes launch himself into the world. All that is otherwise lacking for a traditional, formulaic passage into the genre of fairy tale is 'Once upon a time …' Parkes' embrace of archaism is uncontrived, indeed perfectly natural; in this fashion he makes 1896 sound very long ago and very far away.

Parkes recalls no monetary transaction ever taking place between the falconer of the Manor and the Seigneur of Rohais. However, 'the Manor itself was on the *Fief le Comte,* and the Count of Isles was the Duke of Normandy – that is, the King of England. Him we owed five chickens and two sacks of corn, but he refused to receive it in kind, so my father had to argue annually with the appropriate official as to the values of corn and poultry.'[9] What is evoked is the regnant feudalism of a magical outpost still heavily suffused with the graceful trappings of Christian medievalism as well as earlier brutish pagan survivals with which it coexisted but rarely intersected. 'Ghosts and witchcraft,' Parkes lets drop laconically, 'were normal accompaniments of life in the Channel Islands.'[10]

A suggestive black-and-white image appears among a fascinating collection of photographs redolent of Old Guernsey. Captioned 'Jousting tournament staged at Delancey Park in the early 1900s', it depicts what appears to be a score or more of armoured cavalrymen at rest. Under gorgeously plumed hats, they sit in a field in front of what looks like a large, old farmstead. Like spectral crusaders, four of the chevaliers, topped by helmets and resplendent in white cloaks and capes, sit astride horses also bedecked in white, their cloths prominently marked above their haunches by dark crosses. One would-be champion menacingly points his lance at a sixty-degree angle towards heaven.[11]

The entire scene adumbrates an uncompromising, unapologetic antiquarianism that evidently was fostered, indeed revelled in, by a considerable number of the turn-of-the-century islanders. At the very least, the tableau argues that a highly suggestible Guernsey lad of the era could easily have imbibed an intoxicating brew of medievalism, one wholly pervasive on an island removed from mainstream currents, where feudal forms and titles were still part of the negotiable currency of the realm. Whether as a boy Parkes actually witnessed these staged jousting tournaments or similar spectacles is uncertain. It seems hardly accidental, however, that a groundbreaking historian of the medieval period, who once commented that many aspects of medieval society merited 'honour and approbation',[12]

> ... would wield a proud plume and a vigorously polemical quill. The brooding mystery, of course, is that when he eventually took to his mount he would ride as the Paladin of the Jews!
>
> Seven decades later, in the memories of surviving old-timers this was a precious era of irretrievable innocence.

Inadequate transport contributed towards the grouping of Guernsey people into 'town and country folk'. St Peter Port, with its kitchen maids and society uppercrust, spoke fair to good English. Thanks to an efficient tram service, in Parkes' youth St Sampson and Vale, the eastern parishes that range north from St Peter Port, were integrated into the greater town set. Further afield, but still enjoying relatively easy access to St Peter Port by horse and wagon, were St Martin parish to the south and the central agricultural parishes including Parkes' St Andrew. Then there was 'the Far West' where, beyond a line that could be drawn from Vazon Bay in the north to Le Gouffre on the southern shoreline, *les habitants* lived in a nether region. From this Gallic third of the island, at whose heart were St Saviours and Torteval parishes, standard Guernsey English was infiltrated by phrases such as 'a la prochaine' and 'caw damme'.[13]

The same memoirist warmly recalls the social matrix into which Parkes was born and scenes similar to those he must have witnessed on many occasions.

> It was an extraordinary situation in such a small island, but understandable when it is pointed out that if you lived in St Peter in the Wood or Torteval and couldn't afford a horse and trap, you would be in the majority ... Saturdays provided the only opportunity to spend a few hours shopping in St Peter Port for those who lived within walking distance of the bus route, or could beg a lift in a van bound for the markets.
>
> Market Square was the Picadilly Circus of the town in those days. The pedestrian had to pick his way between horse and vehicle over the whole area. Guernsey bonnets topped the fashion parade *en route* to the stalls, where home-made butter was displayed on a cabbage leaf, each pound bearing the stamp of the individual farm. The 'West' graced the town once per week with their presence and hard-won produce. The west coast storepots had been raided to load the stalls with chancres, lobsters and crayfish. Other vans brought vegetables and grapes carefully laid in trays to ensure that the bloom survived intact.[14]

The only time when Parkes' recollections of boyhood impinge on such everyday social material occurs when he evokes his family's summer vacations in the island's western reaches. Equally telling, although he began his schooling in the lower school of Elizabeth College, which is prominently located on the heights of St Peter Port, and continued attending the college for the next eleven years, the island capital itself, fulcrum of the poona ascendency, is entirely neglected. This is consistent with the introspective loner's defensive isolation from the society of his peers. Although caution should be taken not to exaggerate his boyhood self-immersion in a private, alternative world, there is no question that he had few if any close friends among his contemporaries.

Another memoir supplies additional inferential evidence of Jimmy Parkes' alienation from his peers: 'A huge crowd attended the annual Rocquaine and St Peter Port Regattas in August 1905 to mark L'Entente Cordiale between France and the Channel Islands.'[15] The event passed unnoted by Parkes. Then there was the royal visit of Prince Albert on 23 September 1905 for which 'people turned out in their thousands' and the races at L'Ancresse Common on 23 July 1908, which attracted 'an enormous crowd'.[16] Again, almost certainly because he did not attend, these events also left no impression. Where was young Parkes during the all-day fete of 20 July 1911 to mark the coronation of King George V?[17] Evidently, elsewhere.

In sum, Parkes' personal seclusion and general isolation from the ordinary island communal life enjoyed by his contemporaries may be safely inferred from the absence of any allusions to major events which all other Guernsey memoirists recall with relish. Moreover, seeking and finding solace and sanctuary in church rectories, on island cliffs and inside caves, in flowers and poetry, and in kitchens and parlours, Parkes' early disinclination to play with children his own age after his mother's death seemed to freeze him into a fixed attitude of withdrawal. Aside from being cultivated by several 'honorary aunties', the introverted youngster appears typically to have been solitary, and were it not for ordinary interaction with his sister and brother, a prototypical loner.

Years later, ostensibly describing the existential dilemma of 'Man as [a] person', Parkes seems to have drawn upon unconscious intimations of that bereft, alienated, painfully shy adolescent back on Guernsey:

> ... however close his relations with other persons, there has always remained one chamber within his heart of which he

can give the key to no one, one chamber in the heart of those whom he loves most dearly to which he is still denied access. He is at once infinitely gregarious and infinitely lonely; and until he comes to terms with himself and finds some solution which accepts this paradox, both the presence of others and their absence can be agony to him.[18]

As Parkes' narrative would have it, in addition to his appropriation of Guernsey's unspoiled natural landscape as an expression of the contours of his youthful imagination, he imaginatively projected himself into the inner fabric of a romanticized version of the island's past, fancifully embellishing family ties so as to intensify his fragile sense of self and ties to a homeland. Yet at the same time that Parkes professed to have loved his native island extravagantly, we notice that he kept aloof from social intercourse with flesh and blood islanders, notably those of his own age, and maintained distance from public celebrations of Guernseytude, as if sensing that they threatened the integrity of Guernsey as an idealized, imaginative construct.

The resulting paradox is that the more diligently the memoirist laboured to portray an Edenic childhood on his lost island paradise, the more clearly flaws on the surface or outright falsification highlight the introspective, hypersensitive, chronically ill, frequently forlorn little outsider that Jimmy Parkes actually was. The distortions feel far from intentional. In his mind, the old man had negotiated a second homecoming, one no more substantially grounded in actuality than his first. It is of course true that almost everyone's natural inclination is to gloss over or repress utterly memories that recall childhood unhappiness. In Parkes' case, however, the tendency seems more intense and compulsive than normal. It serves to put us very much on our guard.

NOTES

1. James Parkes, *Voyage of Discoveries: Autobiography* (London: Victor Gollancz, 1969), p. 9, ff.
2. Ibid., p. 68.
3. Peter Johnston, *A Short History of Guernsey* (St Peter Port: Guernsey Press, 1994), p. 90.
4. James Parkes, *Voyage of Discoveries*, p. 25.
5. James Parkes, 'Jews, Christians, and the World of Tomorrow', University of Southampton, Parkes Archives, File 60/8/12.

6. Parkes Archives, File 60/35/1.
7. Abraham Rabinovich, 'Expert on the Poison Gas of Anti-Semitism', Interview with James Parkes, *Jerusalem Post*, 24 April 1970.
8. James Parkes, *Voyage of Discoveries*, p. 9.
9. Ibid., p. 24.
10. Ibid., p. 11.
11. Nick Machon, *More Guernsey As It Was* (St Peter Port: Guernsey Press, 1987), p. 42.
12. James Parkes, *God at Work In Science, Politics and Human Life* (London: Putnam, 1952), p. 103.
13. Leo Hamel, *The Musings of Memory* (St Peter Port: Guernsey Press, 1981), p. 75, ff. A corruption of 'God damn me'.
14. Ibid., pp. 75–76.
15. Nick Machon, *More Guernsey As It Was*, p. 38.
16. Ibid., p. 45.
17. Marie de Garis, 'St. Pierre du Bois: The Story of a Guernsey Parish and Its People', *Guernsey Herald*, St Peter Port, 1990, p. 125.
18. James Parkes, *God at Work In Science, Politics and Human Life*, pp. 23–24.

2

St Annie

But what of James Parkes' mother? Behind what interior façade, what heavily brocaded, psychological tapestry has she been sequestered? Parkes' presentation of her is enigmatic. On the one hand, he serves up conventional sentiments of filial devotion; on the other, he provides exceedingly little concrete information upon which to base them. As opposed to some marginal or eccentric *dramatis personae* who bulk large as they strut through youthful portions of Parkes' memoir – the eccentric Seigneur of Sark, the headmaster of Elizabeth College, even a nameless pair of litigious French-speaking peasants – Parkes' mother hardly features. The result is a silhouette, barely a sketch, an under-exposure redolent of meaningful evasiveness.

Not only, for example, are his mother's sister, parents and other antecedents unnoted but so is her given name! Annie Katherine Bell Parkes was born in Surbiton (at the time in Middlesex; later, after a shift in county boundaries, in Surrey). Her parents are listed as James Bell and Catherine Annie Lister.[1] Moreover, while owning that his mother was 'a charming water colourist, both of landscape and of buildings',[2] her professional writer son neglects mentioning that, albeit a minor talent, she too was a published author. So before ruminating upon the perennial mysteries of fathers and sons, *seigneurs* and falconers, let us attend to some abiding vacancies of sons and mothers.

At the age of forty-three, after an extended illness, Annie Parkes died on 23 March 1911.[3] Her departure left her younger son, then fourteen, bereft not only of his spiritual bulwark but, amidst shifting alignments within his nuclear family, of his emotional anchor as well. Had he been five or eight years old at the time, perhaps memory could be faulted for gaping deficiencies of detail or incident, but while adolescence may be a period of notorious turbulence, it is hardly a memory-occluded zone. Nevertheless, Parkes' excursion into his past yields no word, no smile or expression, not a single concrete or treasured image of the loving mother that might fortify him against grief or the erasures of time.

Where, then, can we find her traces? Parkes devotes all of two sentences to her reanimation: 'She was deeply religious, and yet had a very independent mind. Though I was young when she died, she left a powerful influence on me, and I owed an enormous amount both to her regular lessons on Sundays and to her remarks at odd moments'.[4] Behind a series of intensifiers – *deeply, very, powerful, enormous* – Annie Katherine Bell Parkes registers simply as an integer.

Catching the spirit, the author of the only study dealing with Parkes to date modestly upgraded Parkes' sententious assessment of his mother from 'a powerful influence' to '...a most important influence in his life, particularly in regard to his religious outlook'.[5] Obviously guided by an awareness that little Jimmy would grow into the Reverend James Parkes, this observer settled comfortably for the plausible but unearned conclusion that the influence of Parkes' mother on his development was more profound than his father's, for which no parallel assessment is ventured. Laying aside for the moment those regular Sunday sessions of moral instruction, the jejune sketchiness of this maternal apparition gives one considerable pause for thought.

Of course, it is Parkes himself who insists that his mother exerted a powerful influence on his life but his only evocation of Annie Parkes doing this is disappointingly bland: he alludes to 'her regular lessons on Sundays'. How spectacularly convenient would have been a recollection of her saying, 'Son, you must never forsake God's chosen people – the Jews'. But we are left to infer that Parkes probably had in mind the sort of universal apophthegms any Christian mother undergoing a fatal, lingering illness might pronounce over her impressionable son, remarks such as 'Always make me proud of you' or 'I will always be with you' or simply 'God loves you'. How much really can be made of the impact of remarks passed 'at odd moments' when not one is fondly recalled? These are thin rations indeed, in contrast to the feast served up in a parallel section of a justly celebrated memoir by a celebrated poet, Parkes' exact contemporary:

> My mother used to tell us stories of inventors and doctors who gave their lives to the service of humanity, and poor boys who struggled to the top of the tree, and saintly men

who made examples of themselves. And the parable of the king who had a very beautiful garden which he threw open to the public ... [I recall] three sayings and a favourite story of my mother's: 'Children, I command you, as your mother, never to swing objects around in your hands. The King of Hanover put out his eye by swinging a bead purse.' And again, 'Children, I command you, as your mother, to be careful when you carry your candles upstairs. The candle is a little cup of grease'. And, 'There was a man once, a Frenchman, who died of grief because he could never become a mother'.[6]

We recognize, of course, that James Parkes did not possess the imaginative powers of Robert Graves; still, merely for the sake of minimal credibility, how could he have failed to provide the minimal specificity any attentive reader would anticipate? In its absence, again one wonders how he could have expected readers to absorb or even fully to credit that he 'owed an enormous amount' to Sabbath lessons of which not one gets lovingly recounted.

To a lesser degree, Parkes' guardedness extends to his brother and sister. His recollections about his siblings are charged with less emotional intensity than even the comic embarrassment he felt about his grandfather's queer design for Alderney harbour.[7] 'I was the middle one of three children. David was eighteen months older than I; Molly was equally younger. Both were killed in the first war. We were a very united family, and I do not remember any serious quarrels.'[8]

David and Molly, whose given name was actually Mary Katherine,[9] are evoked primarily in conjunction with youthful frolicking along Guernsey's rocky coast and beaches, an association that gives a vital clue as to the whereabouts of the missing person in the text. In the absence of direct testimony, might not we too profitably discern her presence in the emotional texture of images dislodged out of the family's summer holidays along Guernsey's primeval, western coast? Obliquely but insistently, these are linked with the memory of Annie Parkes. As Parkes zestfully recounts:

When my mother was alive, we always spent three weeks of August in a cottage, first at Rocquaine, then at Vazon.

We used to descend on the cottage with a van full of beds, tin baths, cooking pots and what-not, while its regular occupants gave over to us their great canopied bed, their kitchen and their parlor.[10]

Throughout those carefree summer days, David, Jimmy and little Molly scampered over the rocks and shoreline of Roquaine Bay and along the tidal basins of the enchanting western region of Vazon. The children gathered shrimps and prawns from the exposed tidal pools, and Parkes particularly delights in recalling how he uncovered and dispossessed small octopi from their kingdom under the rocks. It was, however, mainly a solitary activity because his brother and sister '... adored bathing, and became first-class swimmers, but I was such a skinny little creature that I became blue in five minutes, and was willingly hauled out of the sea.'[11]

Liberated from the pretence of loving to bathe in the sea, Parkes indulged his passion for architecture, and spent endless hours constructing immensely detailed to-scale castles and cathedrals in the sand. Not the cold, dangerous sea but the shoreline was his natural element. Though the nipping sand fleas were ubiquitous, the beaches of that innocent time and place, unstained by tar and oil slicks and free of litter and debris, fostered an illusion of pristine perfection that joined them in Parkes' memory with Annie Parkes. In the end, of course, the devouring sea relentlessly advanced upon the shore, and, just as the boy reluctantly yielded his intricate, medieval creations to the inexorable tide, eventually sharp, clear memories of his mother too were flattened and effaced.

The Parkeses' closest neighbors were local farmers, M Sarre at Rocquaine and M de Garris at Le Gelée. On Sundays the two boys passed up the nearby, French-speaking Torteval Church in Cobo, preferring instead to negotiate the quiet, twisting lanes behind le Gelée to join worshippers at the English service at St Savour's.[12] 'From the contemporary point of view,' Parkes recalls, 'the amazing thing is that, during the three weeks involved, we regarded these now tumultuous bays as our private property, and hardly ever saw a stranger trespassing in them.'[13] Not only the grandeur of the sky and the sea but also the virginal insularity of Rocquaine Bay, an inviting concavity at the western end of the island, is confirmed by a contemporary's

breathily naïve but charming account of seaside holidays from the same era.

> The pull to the top of the island was low and ponderous, then, at Les Caches, the pace quickened, taking us at a cracking pace through the dip at Les Cornu. The Forest then Torteval Roads rumbled away below to a rolling, swaying motion of the vehicle, jolting as the iron-shod wheels slipped off smooth projecting stones in the water-bound road surface. Would the journey ever end?
>
> Clip-clop, clippity-clop, clippity-clop, exchange a wave with a woman in a Guernsey bonnet; enjoy the flowers she was attending in her front garden; draw deep on virgin air from the sea carrying the aroma of gorse from the nearby cliffs ... Just we and the horses spanning the hard stony roads on the way to the Imperial ...
>
> The first sight of the sea from the heights above Rocquaine Bay was always a thrill. Soon the brakes would be applied as we reached the descent to the coast. A light sea breeze thrummed into the ears, mixing the scents of the land with those of a rocky shore rich with the foliage of the sea ... [This was] a different world, a world where the grass looked and smelt fresher; where the sand was whiter and finer than on my beach haunts 'back home' ... At the sea wall I renewed acquaintance with the glorious sweep of Rocquaine Bay which, when considered with the very long journey from St Peter Port, was certain evidence of the great size of the island.[14]

Would anyone guess from such an account that the actual journey from St Peter Port to Rocquaine amounts to barely eight miles? From Parkes' point of embarkation in St Andrew parish, nearer to the island's epicentre, it would be 'a very long journey' of around five miles. Except for these exhilarating weeks of August, the growing boy did not enjoy many opportunities to experience the freedom and excitement of either travel or the seashore. When the blue of the bay first broke into view, the overflowing emotion felt by Jimmy, the country lad were surely very much the same as they were for the cosmopolitan from St Peter Port.

Although not executed with anything like the lyric vitality of 'Fern Hill', the emotional impulse informing Parkes' recollection

is in similar vein to Dylan Thomas. Parallel memory traces rise
and coalesce to a crescendo of exultation:

> It was a wonderful time for us children: the farms, the
> fishermen, the little shops, and the French *patois* which all
> the country people then spoke were enchanting as the
> lovely bays, the rock pools, and their varied life. Shrimp teas
> from our own nets, fish that had been caught by one of our
> fishermen friends the night before, and a three pound pot
> of apricot jam were special treats associated with those
> joyful days.[15]

Which returns us to our initial puzzlement. It is most striking
that a text so enthusiastically expansive, over-brimming with
concrete images of the natural setting, provides such mad-
deningly little detail about the woman who was always on or
near the scene and who purportedly exerted such critical influence over the direction of Parkes' future. Was the wound of
emotional dismemberment at his mother's death still so raw
sixty years later that an inner censor struck every allusion to her
name, occupation, antecedents, appearance and age? Not only
have incident and conversation been suppressed, but, save for
the sensual freight of smell and taste carried by jam, tea, and
fish, scar tissue also conceals every obvious sign of the boy's
emotional wreckage.

It is clear that the ageing historian had neither the desire to
depart from his lifelong script nor the capacity to improvise on
the theme of the lost, ethereal mother. Rather than the pain of
genuine recollection, we encounter pat, long-held common-
places and set piece clichés. Most importantly Parkes, growing
up in a household whose religious configuration resembled that
of the boyhood home of Saint Augustine,[16] something he could
not have overlooked when he eventually read the *Confessions*,
held fast to the reassuring truism that he surely was cast more
in the mould of his pious, Christian mother than of his agnostic
father. All the more overwhelming, then, the impact of an understated allusion to the event which spelled an end to innocence:
'Holidays on the bays ceased after my mother's death.'[17]

When, after a lingering illness, his mother was wrenched from
him, it was as if everything joyful and good died with her. The
richness and specificity of those natural images of Guernsey

argue that Parkes came to habitually associate the island of his childhood with an unspoiled garden, a prelapsian, unfallen Eden inhabited by a fair field of uncorrupted folk and presided over by the imago of Saint Annie. It is the natural island itself, therefore, which bears the weight of the otherwise suppressed, displaced filial feeling that was submerged beneath a burden of grief. How better to account for Parkes' disinclination to explore or even acknowledge any intrinsic tension between his mother's religiosity and her 'independent mind'? In sum Parkes' cursory treatment of his mother and recoil from the burden of excavating this painful corner of his past is rooted in an incapacity *even after sixty years* to confront the depth of the despair and anger that tormented him at the time of her untimely death. Only intimations of deep-seated pain and unresolved mourning can adequately account for Parkes' reticence.

In this connection, curious but instructive parallels may be drawn between Parkes and two contemporaries. A decade older, David Herbert Lawrence was born in 1885. As boys both were frail, solitary and sickly which taken together stimulated their bookishness. Both viewed their fathers as powerful, natural antagonists. Both underwent religious upbringings, Lawrence's strict and Parkes' earnest. Both competed disadvantageously for maternal favour against stronger, healthier, more virile older brothers, but both exploited their own weaknesses, transforming them into strengths. Fate then operated in complicity with their guilt-ridden, repressed wishes. When Lawrence was sixteen, his older brother died; David Parkes was killed in the war when James was twenty. Fate also exacted a very heavy price for these 'victories'. Both of their mothers also died young: Lydia Lawrence succumbed to cancer in 1910; a year later, Annie Parkes died of complications resulting from a combination of pancreatic malfunction and heart failure.[18] Internalizing both grief and guilt, for the rest of their lives the two younger sons idealized their stricken mothers, each embracing a romanticized vision appropriate to his vastly different ideological and spiritual commitments.

Their most conspicuous point of departure? Whereas Lawrence rebelliously donned the colours of a pre-industrial, primeval community, one aligned with an instinctual order wherein men and women fulfilled themselves through self-assertion and perpetual struggle,[19] Parkes, fixated by an etherealized, frozen image of womanhood, would sublimate his sexuality by championing an oppressed, still vibrant traditional community the potency of whose covenant with God was, he insisted, undiminished by time or circumstance. Overriding this critical disjunction however, we discern a salient convergence: both men were driven to realize a higher mission. Inevitably, society exacted a heavy toll for such chronic nonconformism, not the least part of which was that each was constrained to live in straitened circumstances.

In counterpoint, Parkes' lonely, unsociable school years and strong attachment to his mother evoke quite a different figure, a younger contemporary who would also become an ardent Christian Zionist. (Lawrence was, in his way, far too socially conventional to have much truck with Jews.) General Charles Orde Wingate's background demonstrates both the waywardness of the paths of philo-Semitism and the potency of the impulse. At his public school he too totally shunned games, and he too was shunned in turn by his mates. His, however, was suffering with a contrary spin: whereas Parkes would have given a great deal to romp with the other boys on the playing fields, young Wingate's Calvinist upbringing forbade him to play games, regarding them as frivolous and sinful. Because he acted out of conviction, even as a youngster Wingate never lacked self-esteem.[20] The sober, God-fearing boy on Guernsey, on the other hand, was so unassertive and timid that, as he puts it, 'had you asked [me] in 1913 to say Boo! to a goose, I think I would have been uncertain of my ability to do so'.[21]

Wingate was so drawn to Jews and the Zionist cause that when on active duty in Palestine in the late 1930s he secretly trained squads of kibbutzniks to take the offensive on nightly raids against the Arabs. In effect, he became a living embodiment of the romantic hero rising in defence of the Jews on the field of battle. On the other hand, Parkes' field of activity was, for the most part, intellectual: he took up the pen instead of the sword. To this day Wingate is a rarity: he surpassed even General Edmund Allenby and Arthur Balfour, a British hero in the annals of contemporary Israel, with streets, a forest, even a settlement named in his honour. Indeed, he and Parkes had so much in common that, had their paths ever crossed, one imagines they would surely have been intensely drawn to each other.

Marshalling the slim evidence, let us now try imaginatively to resurrect Annie Parkes, long religiously at odds with her

husband, quietly reading her Sunday morning texts to her three
children. It may safely be assumed that she leaned heavily upon
traditional stories from the Old Testament. It is easy to imagine
David (actually, after his father, *Henry* David) warming to the
heroic exploits of his dashing biblical namesake, a warrior king
who was also a great poet and lover. In fact, Parkes later provides
strong inferential grounds for this hypothesis:

> While we were still at *Les Fauconnaires* and I shared a
> bedroom with my elder brother, David, I remember coming
> back from church full of rage at the meaningless and
> unacceptable psalms which we had been singing. David was
> always a good conservative, and at once defended the
> psalms on the grounds that we had always had them, and
> I replied that we had had the psalms of David long enough,
> and it was time we had the psalms of James![22]

Later in life Parkes would have much to say about James the
Just, leader of the Jerusalem Church, who fell as Christianity's
first martyr.[23] In this first show of boyish petulance, however, it
is unlikely that young Jimmy actually associated himself with
the brother of Jesus. On the other hand, the fraternal wrangle
over the authorship of the psalms plainly points towards the
more deep-seated rivalry between the brothers. It is probable
that the sensitive youngster would have seen much of himself in the classic biblical role, so prominent in his mother's tales
from the Book of Genesis, of the clever younger son who is
unfavoured – even disfavoured – by the exacting, severe father.

At some point in the course of these boyhood Sundays, either
Parkes' own study of Greek or his mother startlingly revealed to
him that James was actually the Greek form of Jacob. It must
have struck him with the very force of revelation, a stunningly
fortuitous linkage of the Bible hero to which he felt most drawn
with himself. With antecedents far predating the seventeenth
century, by his own lights he, Jimmy Parkes, was a kind of latter-
day 'Jacobite'. To the boy's shaping imagination, the tale of Jacob
and Esau inevitably attached to Henry Parkes the seal, cord and
staff of blind, old Isaac-the-Patriarch who, to his younger son's
consternation, outrageously and unfairly preferred the
physically more proficient but less worthy Esau-cum-David over
Jacob-cum-James.

For the youngster, the best part of the story surely came when, with the active encouragement and collusion of his mother, young Jacob outwitted both older brother and father to claim the inheritance his true worth merited. Annie Parkes had no need to gloss her text: it spoke directly and intuitively to her delicate, quick-witted younger son. Moved to counteract her husband's flagrant preference for their first-born,[24] she tactfully made Jimmy aware not only that she loved him well and (he felt) best but that she perceived and appreciated his special abilities and merit. Taking care not to distress David, in the family dynamic Annie Parkes, an overcompensating Sarah or Rebecca figure, was complicit in favouring her younger son. Sheer surmise? To a degree, but later events in Parkes' life powerfully confirm that suggestive aspects of this story deeply embedded themselves in his psyche. As we shall in fact see, they prefigure the trajectory of his affective life with remarkable force and uncanny accuracy.[25]

Did Parkes' strong, childhood bonding with an Old Testament hero also contribute to his later sense of vocation as a defender of the Jewish people? For the present it is enough to note that among major biblical protagonists Jacob was not a random choice. Upon successfully negotiating a probationary period, confirmed by a change in name, he is traditionally identified both as the actual father of the Jewish people and the eponymous progenitor of the Jewish peoplehood. It goes without saying that Annie Parkes would have been astonished had anyone suggested that her younger son's wholehearted love for her would, displaced on to their island paradise and overlaid by symbolic associations, eventually metamorphose into a symbiotic embrace of the Jewish people. But there is no reason to think that she would have been dismayed.

To sum up, the stark psychological contrast between the exuberance of Parkes' imaginative attachment to Guernsey, upon which he lavishes a surfeit of emotional currency, and the paucity of specific detail about his beloved mother argues for a depth of ambivalence that his voyage into the past never plumbs. Subsuming its nourishing, life-enhancing role as an idyllic backdrop for youthful, sensual exploits, we perceive a murkier Guernsey, one functioning as a multidimensional symbol upon which Parkes projected all the extravagance of his repressed grief and unconscious feelings of abandonment. The lad who had once dislodged octopi from under rocks was the memoirist who refrained from uncovering, dislodging or probing memories that, were he to relax his lifelong habit of vigilance, would throb afresh. To still his hurt, boyhood grief had been frozen and anesthetized: a lifetime later, it still had not thawed.

The negative evidence of *Voyage of Discoveries* argues strongly that at the age of fourteen major areas of Parkes' emotional development were permanently stunted or deformed. Filling the void, stanching the wound, Guernsey itself was appropriated as a substitute matrix, an emotional surrogate whose importance in Parkes' psychological, emotional and even intellectual economy can scarcely be exaggerated. Prematurely ejected from Eden, the bereft son was not merely predisposed but overdetermined to transfer and attach his grief and floating love for his mother to an idealization of his lost island paradise whose rustic natives sustained a primeval, explicitly pre-English social order. It is in this transfigured, symbolic key that we concur with the judgment that the impact of Annie Parkes on the life of her son was paramount. For the present we leave open the question whether Parkes' struggle to resolve his stormy relationship with his father proved more urgent, and in the end more critical, in the shaping of his character and personality.

It is, I believe, of more than passing interest that although Parkes reveals no sign of conscious awareness of the efficacy of this aforesaid psychodrama, he nevertheless was thoroughly familiar with the Freudian mechanisms of projection, transference and displacement. In order to explain the dynamics of the psychopathology of antisemitism,[26] in an investigation of the aetiology of the animus against Jews and the hostility to Judaism in recent centuries, in 1945 Parkes elucidated their interaction in considerable detail.[27]

NOTES

1. Greffe Registry at the Royal Court, St Peter Port, Guernsey.
2. Parkes, *Voyage of Discoveries, Autobiography* (London: Victor Gollancz, 1969), p. 52.
3. Greffe Registry.
4. Parkes, *Voyage of Discoveries*, p. 13.
5. Robert A. Everett, *Christianity Without Anti-Semitism: James Parkes and the Jewish–Christian Encounter* (Oxford: Pergamon, 1993), p. 1.
6. Robert Graves, *Good-bye To All That* (New York: Anchor, 1989), pp. 30–31.
7. *Vide* Chapter 1.

8. Greffe Registry.
9. Parkes, *Voyage of Discoveries*, p. 12.
10. Ibid.
11. James Parkes, 'Holidays in My Childhood', *Guernsey Society Journal*, St Peter Port, August 1976, p. 5, Parkes Archives, File 60/33/92/81.
12. Ibid.
13. Parkes, *Voyage of Discoveries*, p. 12.
14. Leo Hamel, *The Musings of Memory* (St Peter Port: Guernsey Press, 1981), pp. 32–33.
15. Parkes, *Voyage of Discoveries*, p. 12.
16. *Vide* Augustine, *Confessions*, translated and introduced by R. S. Pine-Coffin (Harmondsworth: Penguin Classics, 1982), pp. 11, 45.
17. Parkes, *Voyage of Discoveries*, p. 13 ff.
18. That Parkes' brother was killed six years after his mother died displaces but does not significantly alter the psychological nexus.
19. Jeffrey Meyers, *D. H. Lawrence: A Biography* (New York: Random House, 1992), pp. 63–67.
20. Christopher Sykes, *Orde Wingate* (London: Collins, 1959), p. 30, ff.
21. Parkes, *Voyage of Discoveries*, pp. 15–16.
22. Ibid., p. 223.
23. *Vide* Chapters 7, 10, 21, 25, and 26.
24. *Vide* Chapter 6.
25. *Vide* Chapter 18.
26. After 1933 Parkes, recognizing the inaccuracy and potentially pernicious connotations of *anti-Semitism*, consistently rendered it *antisemitism*. Later, Emil Fackenheim followed suit: 'The spelling out to be antisemitism, i.e. without the hyphen, thereby dispelling the notion that there is an entity "Semitism" which "anti-Semitism" opposes.' Fackenheim, 'Post-Holocaust Anti-Jewishness', in *World Jewry and the State of Israel*, ed. Moshe Davis (New York: Arno Press, 1977), p. 11. I have followed the same practice.
27. James Parkes, *An Enemy of the People: Antisemitism* (Hammondsworth: Penguin, 1945), pp. 85–87.

3

A Most Improbable Isle

Guernsey must surely be one of the least likely splinters of
Europe from which one would expect a scholar and activist with
the interests, passions and expertise of James Parkes to emerge.
As noted by one observer, 'Parkes' reputation as an expert on
Jewish issues is such that it is difficult to imagine him ever
accepting the traditional stereotypes of Judaism. Yet there was
nothing in his background to prepare him for the role he was to
play in the effort to revise Christian ideas about Judaism.'[1] This
superficially reasonable view was echoed by the keynote speaker
at a symposium at the University of Southampton in 1996,
marking the centenary of Parkes' birth: '... nothing in James
Parkes' early biography explains why he should have come to
be devoted to the study of the Jews'.[2]

Parkes himself lent explicit grounds for this judgment,
implying that his initial curiosity, his growing appreciation,
and ultimately his obsession with Judaism emerged, as it were,
ab nihilo:

> I knew nothing special about Jews, and my knowledge of
> Judaism came from the normal equipment of an Oxford
> trained theologian. I had been taught that post-Christian
> Judaism was an arid and meaningless legalism; I had seen
> no reason to waste time studying it. In consequence, when
> I started in Geneva [in 1928] I knew nothing of the post-
> Biblical history of the Jews or of Judaism.[3]

Later he pinpointed 1929, when he was already well into his
thirties, as the period that '... saw the beginning of my real
involvement with the Jewish question'.[4]

But is it really tenable that the parochial origins of the man
who in his lifetime published more than twenty historical studies
delineating Christian-inspired hatred and injustice visited upon
Jews and Judaism – several of them groundbreaking and many

influential – may be viewed as entirely irrelevant to the obsessive concern of his adult life? Should it be granted so readily that in his youth the measured voice and partisan pen that touched off what has become a revolution in religious thought and attitudes among thinking Christians of the Western world enjoyed no significant contact with a single living, breathing Jew? May we not discern in those Guernsey years any manifestations that translated into a particular interest in Jewish history or concern for the Jewish people?

To rest content with the teasing paradox that the twentieth century's most dedicated and effective Christian advocate for the Jewish people should emerge from sea-girt, effectively *Juden-rein* Guernsey feels highly unsatisfactory. Although observers may be technically correct, the melancholy theme of homelessness that surfaces in the first chapter of *Voyage of Discoveries* opens the door to the possibility that, including Parkes himself, they all may just have been grievously astigmatic about this matter.[5] Far from laying the question to rest, Parkes' heuristic disclaimer in fact prods us toward its more negotiable restatement. What we really want to identify are those factors which contributed to moulding Parkes into the kind of man who, when confronted directly by the irrationality and viciousness of antisemitism, would be so personally repulsed that as a matter of course he would respond with extraordinary sympathy, persistence and passion.

Obviously, Parkes' equivocal position as an anaemic middle child sandwiched between more robust but ultimately doomed siblings within the family constellation is a matter of signal psychological importance. Before directing our attention decisively away from his island home, however, with an eye towards establishing the grounds for its pertinence and particular aptness in the development of its broad-minded native son, we shall shift our focus from Guernsey's geography to its history. Notwithstanding Parkes' frequent disavowals, it transpires that his youthful enthusiasm for his mother island and his identification with its native sons played a pivotal, if not determinative, role in the shaping of his mental economy as regards the seemingly unrelated matter of the Jewish people. Remarkably, for the rest of his life Guernsey would strike a potently symbolic, subterranean 'Jewish' chord in Parkes' sensibilty, one that marked him indelibly. But in what ways was Guernsey 'Jewish'?

Aside from *Voyage of Discoveries*, the motif of the chivalrous champion battling for justice in the name of the oppressed emerges in one of the very few references to family background to be found in Parkes' writings. In a personal essay reminiscent of the style of Charles Lamb, Parkes refers to a pamphlet published in 1821 by Joseph Parkes, his first cousin at the remove of four generations. A constitutional lawyer in Birmingham, Parkes' political reformer cousin propounded the daring proposition that Jews be granted unrestricted admittance to all public places in England and Wales. Noting that, in spite of having burned Servetus in the time of Calvin, Presbyterians enjoyed this dispensation, the lawyer held that the same privilege should be extended to Jews who had killed Jesus in the time of Pontius Pilate.[6]

Suppressing the rueful impulse to comment on the uncritical aspersion of Jewish deicide, one which on other occasions he would have hotly contested, Parkes responded warmly to the main drift of his distant cousin's argument: 'I am proud to be the second member of my family to engage in the battle for justice for the Jews.'[7] Just as Byron, Joseph Parkes' contemporary, adopted the cause of Greek freedom as his own, with something of a latter-day Byronic sensibility James Parkes would adopt 'Justice for the Jews' as his lifelong escutcheon. Although it is impossible to determine precisely when Parkes first encountered his cousin's essay, it could have been earlier than is generally thought, a possibility which challenges the easy assumption that Parkes' youthful isolation from matters and persons Jewish was virtually complete. The essay's very existence encourages a closer examination of the matter and a modest historical excursus.

In 1277 a London Jew named Abraham is recorded as originating in 'La Geinseye'.[8] However Edward I's edict expelling the Jews from England in 1290 also applied to the Channel Island group, an intrinsic part of his realm. Wedged between Edward's fiat and the Edict of Expulsion promulgated by Charles II of France in 1289, only very few Jews would have taken refuge on these islands, and they would have been secret adherents to their faith. Nevertheless, as in England itself,[9] we may reasonably assume that a sprinkling of low profile, anonymous Jews did somehow contrive to reside in the Channel Islands throughout the Middle Ages.

We observe that in 1482 Edward Brampton, a converted Portuguese Jew, was appointed governor of Guernsey, the last indication of any Jewish presence until the second half of the eighteenth century. A very small Jewish community was established in St Helier (Jersey) in the middle of the nineteenth century. It survived for about thirty years, and a Jersey Jew named Krichefski, born in 1916, served for a time as a senator on the island. Inasmuch as Parkes himself was a contributor to *Encyclopædia Judaica* (1971 edition), we may presume that he too gleaned what little there was to harvest from that authoritative source about the Jewish presence in his boyhood islands.

However, the law does not necessarily define the situation on the ground. It was, after all, not until the close of the Second World War that Jews would be declared eligible to be chosen by the States of Election, the lower house of the island's legislative assembly, for office in the *jurat*, a judicial and legislative body of twelve persons holding office for life.[10] Yet Roman Catholics and Freethinkers (along with brewers and publicans) faced identical legal restrictions, and no one can doubt that they were well represented among the inhabitants of the island.

Given the efficiency of the expulsion, however, it is fair to conclude that at most a minuscule number of Jews unofficially resided in England between the date of their legal banishment in 1290 and official Jewish readmission in 1656 under Oliver Cromwell. By the era of Parkes' boyhood, a sprinkling, perhaps even a heavy sprinkling, of low-profile Jews did indeed reside on Guernsey. For example, six centuries after island sources alluded to a 'London Jew named Abraham', a local resident recalled that one of the food stalls at Les Halles of St Peter Port was run by a Mrs Abraham;[11] a not unreasonable conjecture is that she too was a Jewish vendor.

Even more suggestive, consider the following passage by a lifelong Guernsey resident:

> One morning in the 1880s a couple of little Jewish brothers, Tommy and Henry James arrived at the White Rock and trudged to St Peter in the Wood with all their worldly possessions contained in a big red handkerchief carried on sticks on their shoulders. They took lodgings at La Madeline and found employment as postmen. Tommy subsequently married a local girl. He bought a house at Le Longfrie which

became the parish post office. He collected the mail daily
from St Peter Port perched aloft on the horsedriven high red
mail-cart. His post office was also a general shop where one
could buy anything from a gallon of paraffin to a ha'penny
stick of black liquorice. Once a week a doctor's surgery was
held in a back room of the shop. In all these activities Tommy
was helped by his unmarried daughter, Mary. When he died
and his elder son according to the law, took possession of
the dwelling, Mary moved to a house, then called Beaulieu,
near the Sion Chapels, which she renamed Roseneath,
taking the post office and the shop with her.[12]

This homely citation provides illuminating sidelights on the pace
and character of rural Guernsey life in a district adjoining the
one in which James Parkes lived. He surely would have warmed
to its authenticity. The writer unequivocally identifies the
brothers James as Jews, and her tone does not in any way suggest
that Jewishness served as a mark of dishonour or disability.

That Henry and Tommy did not bear a typically Jewish
surname argues all the more strongly that other Jews had quietly
settled on both Guernsey and Jersey. Except perhaps for his
adaptability, nothing in Tommy James' experience augers anything stereotypically Jewish. Moreover, save for the peculiarity
that a in a Norman-French parish someone not conversant with
le Guernesiais should be hired as a postman, of all things, there
seems no reason to doubt her identification of the brothers as
Jews. Although Henry disappears from her narrative, Tommy's
career offers an exemplary instance of total immersion and full
assimilation into indigenous Guernsey society, an attainment for
which native-born Jimmy could only yearn.

If not with Tommy James or Mrs Abraham, it nevertheless
begins to seem more plausible that Jimmy Parkes did come into
passing contact with a small number of itinerant or resident
Guernsey Jews. Even so it remains unlikely that he would have
been aware of it at the time. Had any chance encounter with an
identifiable, flesh-and-blood Jew been somehow meaningful or
piqued his curiosity, given its retrospective import we should
naturally have expected that Parkes would have recorded it
among his island memories. Moreover, it is probable that Parkes
as a boy would not have been sensitive to the exact ethnicity
of any obvious stranger. In short, the impact of these hypothetical

Jewish encounters on Parkes' consciousness would have been nugatory.

Thus far, aside from the high probability that, as a professional historian from Guernsey with a fixation on Jewish matters, Parkes himself covered much the same ground we have just traversed, the historical yield seems conspicuously meagre. Guernsey still appears to be a most improbable point of departure for the life journey of one of the last century's most philosemitic Christians until, that is, we suddenly perceive that a germane affinity underlies all this seemingly specious surmise about Jews and their conjectural encounters with a youngster named Jimmy. It is an affective link whose intimations the historian in his prime surely sensed powerfully.

It has already been underscored that Parkes' droll admission that he was 'not of full Guernsey stock' points to his outsider's boyish yearning to attach himself more intimately and wholeheartedly to his homeland. Although too withdrawn, self-conscious and irredeemably English to attend Sunday services at a nearby French-speaking church in Cobo when vacationing on the island's western reaches or to seek out French-speaking playmates,[13] by cultivating members of the household of one of Guernsey's most established 'old families', Parkes gradually positioned himself in a comfortable and comforting social niche. Christine Ozanne, nearly a decade older than Parkes, was the daughter of the Rector of St. Martin's Rectory, a country parish church. Tellingly, upon becoming an intimate of the Ozannes, Parkes and Christine proclaimed their 'attachment' by publicly declaring each other 'cousins'.[14]

Let us recall that Parkes' native St Andrew parish lay very near the fault line between the predominantly English-speaking, socially superior, progressive eastern side of Guernsey and the Norman-French population that dominated the culturally and socially 'backward' west. As late as the 1930s,

> the everyday language of the *St Pierrais* inhabitants of St Pierre du Bois parish was still *Guernesiais* at home, on the farm, in the greenhouses and the shops. Although from 1930 church services on the island were held in English, local chapels still held theirs in French. Parish notices in the press were also printed in French. When in 1936 a reporter was selected to interview aged Mrs Mary Galienne, he had to

be a *Guernesiais* speaker for not only the old lady but her son as well understood not a word of English.[15]

In Parkes' boyhood, then, the local *Guernesiais* culture and language were still vibrant and competitive; although their future might be bleak, they had not yet been decisively superseded by a tide of Anglophones. These considerable reserves of *Guernesiais* vitality stamped Parkes' psyche with the template of a viable, native people who, exploiting their natural wit and wits, ingenuity and disingenuousness, could not only survive but occasionally score significant victories in their ongoing *Kulturkampf* against the dominant settler culture. This adversarial dynamic played itself out in every aspect of Guernsey society. Young Parkes observed, acknowledged the resilience of and empathized with the stubborn heroism of that besieged native culture.

The parallels between the social, economic and political position of the Norman-French of Guernsey and the historic defensive stance of the Jews vis-à-vis the encroaching, triumphal cultures of Christendom are self-evident. The recalcitrance of *les Guernesiais* adumbrated what would in time be Parkes' primal intuition as a young theologian: the essential and positive role of the Jewish people in God's covenantal economy was still viable, it had not been terminated with the establishment of Christianity, and most importantly, it was not and never would be superseded by its daughter religion. Over time how could this salient parallel between *le Guernesiais* and Jewish cultures vis-à-vis their would-be supplanters not impress itself upon Parkes? We are confronted by a massive irony: far from its celebrated irrelevance to Parkes' choice of vocation, picturesque, unreconstructed Guernsey could have been a most apt place for nurturing one of the century's most creative revisionist Christian theologians and its foremost Christian champion of the Jews. The following chapter delineates Parkes' positive affinity to *les Guernesiais* in detail and aims to demonstrate how it equipped him with the paradigm which years later would translate into his radical, daringly heterodox embrace of the Jewish people.

A final fillip: if culturally Guernsey is as marginal a European backwater as one could possibly imagine, from a different angle it can appear almost cosmopolitan. Then or now, how many British youngsters have grown up among speakers of French or with a warm familiarity and close identification with a competitive European culture? The quaint dialect Parkes heard spoken as a boy turned out to be intimately related to the tongue he spoke and heard during his six-year sojourn in Geneva, the furthermost point from Guernsey in the span defining the Gallic sphere of European influence. From this paradoxical perspective, Parkes' provincial childhood may be cited as having uniquely prepared him for his future role as an active player on the international scene.[16]

NOTES

1. Robert A. Everett, *Christianity Without Anti-Semitism: James Parkes and the Jewish–Christian Encounter* (Oxford: Pergamon, 1993), p. 161.
2. Nicholas de Lange, 'James Parkes, A Centenary Lecture', in *Cultures of Ambivalence and Contempt: Studies in Jewish–Non-Jewish Relations*, eds. Jones, Kushner and Pearce, (London: Vallentine Mitchell, 1998), p. 31.
3. James Parkes, 'Christendom and the Synagogue', *Frontier* (London), Vol. 2, No. 4 (Winter 1959), pp. 271–72.
4. James Parkes, *Voyage of Discoveries* (London: Victor Gollancz, 1969), p. 111.
5. *Vide* Chapter 1.
6. James Parkes, 'I Walk Round My Library', February 1977. Typescript version in Parkes Archives, File 60/9/19/20, pp. 11–12.
7. Ibid.
8. *Encyclopædia Judaica*, Jerusalem: Keter, 1972, Vol. 5, pp. 334–35.
9. James Shapiro, *Shakespeare and the Jews* (New York: Columbia University Press, 1996), pp. 62–76.
10. Charles Cruickshank, *The German Occupation of the Channel Islands: The Official History of the Occupation Years* (Guernsey: Guernsey Press, 1975), p. 3.
11. G. W. J. L. Hugo, *Guernsey As It Used To Be*, (St Peter Port: Guernsey Star and Gazette, 1933), p. 27.
12. Marie de Garis, *St Pierre du Bois*, p. 130.
13. *Vide* Chapter 2.
14. Parkes, *Voyage of Discoveries*, p. 19.
15. de Garis, p. 136.
16. Geoffrey Chaucer, who in addition to Middle English and Italian spoke Parisian French, would likely have found *le Guernesiais* little changed over the centuries, quaintly familiar, and reminiscent of the Anglo-Norman dialect spoken by the Prioress in *The Canterbury Tales*. *Vide* Donald R. Howard, *Chaucer, His Life, His World, His Work* (New York: Dutton, 1987), pp. 21–24.

4

The Aptness of Guernsey

Parkes assigns his birthplace to the parish of St Andrew, a designation evocative of the heritage of the past. At first glance it may seem an affectation that an ecclesiastic should indicate his birthplace by parish name; in this instance it is a simple matter of accuracy. Guernsey resembles other formerly French-speaking outposts around the world, retaining, despite changes, a residue of their Gallic heritage.[1] The island, which today has utterly transformed itself from the agricultural economy that prevailed in Parkes' day, is divided into ten parishes. Some of them popularly bear English names, others French, and others both.

At the turn of the century, approximately half of the islanders spoke *Guernesiais* as their native tongue.[2] Considerably more comprehended it. These included not only the island's Gallic peasantry but also prestigious, long-established, landed families such as the Ozannes, Careys and De L'Isles, the cross-over social French element 'of full Guernsey descent' whose romanticized exploits from past centuries were the stuff of young Parkes' day-dreams. Unlike the upstart English settlers who dominated the social life of St Peter Port, the older families were rooted primarily in the countryside.

The island at that time was still of course primarily agricultural. Almost every day young Parkes witnessed aspects of the primitive, labour-intensive, exploitative rural economy which based itself upon a French-speaking peasant class kept in thrall to *les Anglais*. What did he actually behold on a typical day? Parkes is stingy with such particulars, but a contemporary of his, another long-lived islander, paints the following scene from the parish of St Pierre du Bois:

> Corn was still mainly broadcast by hand and cut at harvest with a serrated sickle. The sheaves were tied with long bramble runners or bands of twisted corn stalks. When it

was being gathered in, tithe and cambert sheaves were set aside for collection later by the license-holder of these dues. Care was always taken that these particular sheaves were those with the most ragwort and other noxious weeds ... In the old days threshing was done by hand; the sheaves were hit against a wooden horse in the granary to dislodge the ears of corn. The grain was then placed in a big circular wooden frame, or fan, covered with cowskin and thrown in the air to separate the husks.[3]

At the time *le Guernesiais*, a Guernsey-French subdialect, predominated in St Pierre du Bois. Fronting the western coast at Rocquaine Bay, it was a more traditional parish than St Andrew; nevertheless, both parishes embraced the practices of Guernsey's agricultural heartland, and resemblances far outweighed divergences.

Contrary to what people imagine our country roads were quite busy although certainly quieter than they are at the present time. There was a constant stream of traffic moving along them: children on the way to or from school, cattle being led to the fields or to the nearest public watering-trough, a farm-cart rumbling along and the heavy clop-clop of the horse drawing it. Occasionally a funeral procession, headed by the rector and undertaker wended its solemn way churchward. Also there were three covered baker's vans delivering bread round the parish, each on certain days of the week ...[4]

Manifestly, these same country roads brought young Parkes into frequent contact with the island's Gallic native stock. Much like Kipling, whose books he devoured as a youngster,[5] Parkes grew up in a society where social and mercantile intercourse reflected patterns of cultural imperialism that are typically imposed upon the natives by enterprising settlers. Still, the young Parkes admired the stubborn pride, independent spirit and perseverance of these French-speaking outsiders, fellow outsiders in their own land. He felt imaginatively and even spiritually drawn to this indigenous element. At the same time, however, the English boy found their ways amusing and on occasion doubtless he too patronized *les Guernesiais*.

More than merely entertained by Gallic folk traditions, the young boy, strongly susceptible to supernatural agencies, consciously appropriated many of them. 'There certainly were witches on the island,' he assures us on several occasions, 'some of considerable power.'[6] This serves as prologue to his recounting a number of droll legal disputations in which the wily French peasant culture, pitted against the more sophisticated, colonialist legal system of the British usurpers, emerges triumphant. Somewhat enigmatically, his memoir devotes greater attention to two seemingly ephemeral legal cases – exemplars of the traditional sort embodying the comic failure of the two cultures to engage – than to incidents involving his mother, brother and sister. This queer disproportion prompts our closer scrutiny. Both of these court proceedings pivot around the collision between Guernsey 'witches' and the island's modern legal system.

The account of the case which Parkes thought 'extraordinary' purports to be a direct transcription of litigation between 'Farmer A' and 'Farmer B' before an Anglophone, French language-challenged jurist. 'B' accused 'A' of bewitching his cattle. 'A' then compounded his alleged transgression by sending 'B' threatening letters, an offence for which 'B' claimed his opponent should be liable under the law. Parkes observes:

> But neither was really interested in the letters. They were concerned with the witchcraft which could only be discussed and explained in *patois* – and the case was tried before a Bailiff who was indeed an islander, but did not know the *patois*. At one point the Bailiff tried to estimate the extent to which the plaintiff had been frightened.
>
> 'What did you feel like when you received the letters?' asked the Bailiff.
>
> 'I was troublesome,' he replied.
>
> 'What do you mean "troublesome"?' asked the Bailiff.
>
> 'I was afraid of the wicked men in the house,' the plaintiff responded.
>
> 'But how many people were there in your house beside your family?'
>
> 'How was I to know?' responded the plaintiff.[7]

Now we translate the key words into *patois*: 'troublesome' is the English cover word for *ensorcelled* – bewitched; 'wicked men' is the cover word for *mauvais gens* – evil spirits. And

how could the poor man tell how many evil spirits were
infesting his house and tormenting and terrifying his cattle,
as they certainly *were* doing? … At this point the bailiff
wisely adjourned for lunch, when someone could explain
to him what it was all about.[8]

This account raises a number of interesting issues. First, in
what sense could Parkes possibly have 'remembered' these
events? There exists only the remotest likelihood that young
Jimmy had actually been present in the courtroom to witness
the proceedings, and even if unaccountably he had been, could
not possibly have rendered them with such precision from
memory. So what Parkes 'remembers' was probably a recollection
of hearing or overhearing one or more embellished versions of
this courtroom 'entertainment' from adults after the event.[9] Parkes
here draws upon collision-of-cultures island anecdotes and tall
tales that were staples of the turn-of-the-century Guernsey oral
tradition. His courtroom recordings ultimately derive from the
bank of shared cultural memory of an Anglo community so
confident of its ascendancy that, without feeling the least threat,
it could indulge in these exercises in self-deprecation. Moreover,
there must have existed powerful, overriding reasons for this
most meticulous of historians not only to gloss over the fuzzy
provenance of his 'island tales' – pastoral equivalents of 'urban
legends' so much commented upon by sociologists in recent
decades – but, seemingly unawares, to perpetrate the innocent
pretence that he had actually borne witness to the recorded
events.
   Beyond that, one wonders why in his 'autobiography', of all
places, Parkes should regale us with two such tales – however
'amusing' or 'extraordinary' he might have thought either of
them – merely in order to exemplify the collision between the
folkways of the natives and the English legal system. A single
anecdote might have been viewed as a decorative, innocent
diversion, but the recounting of the second one, analysed in detail
in the following chapter, constitutes a telling deviation from
expectation. It suggests that, lodged deeply in Parkes' virtual
memory, these anecdotal accounts assumed a significance that
went beyond either their sheer piquancy or their function as tales
that illustrated subdued tensions or open hostility between the
native French and the supplanting English island cultures.[10]

What is plain is that Parkes' emphasis on the importance of the language and culture of the original island stock is retrospectively associated with the more pristine values of the uncontaminated, pre-tourist island in which he came to invest so much filial feeling. This Old Order, or original dispensation, carried curious baggage: the static, superstitious, essentially pagan beliefs and practices of Guernsey's surviving Norman stock.

Theoretically, of course, by the waning of the Victorian era popular belief in ghosts and witches, normative in Shakespeare's day, should have ebbed, yielding its sway to a more progressive or rational world-view, or to the kind of liberal Christianity which Parkes himself embraced. On Guernsey, however, these antiquated vestiges, with their medieval survivals and ritualistic fragments, had never really been confronted by modernism. Instead, the two maintained parallel, discrete patterns of uneasy coexistence. Neither as boy nor man did Parkes doubt for an instant that the New Order, despite its obvious strengths, did not, indeed could not, arbitrarily annul the Old Order's access to vital, primal powers.

In the above anecdote of the farmers, there can be little question which culture and belief system exercised a greater claim on young Parkes' sympathies. Nevertheless, matters are not entirely clear-cut. As an upper classman at Elizabeth College, a period in his development when his loyalties were fluid, Parkes did not hesitate to align himself with 'the English element', snobbishly despising any classmate who spoke the imperial tongue with 'a good Guernsey accent – always exemplified by the solecism of asking "Where's he to?" instead of "Where is he?" Guernsey English is as quaint at times as Guernsey *patois*.'[11]

It was in 1898, when Parkes was barely two, that the first of a series of measures designed to replace French with English as Guernsey's official language was introduced in the States of Election. Fiercely resisted, it passed by nineteen to thirteen votes.[12] It would take another twenty-eight years for English definitively to supplant the Norman *patois* as the single official language of the courts and the States of Election as well as for 'the franc [to be] dropped as official currency in favour of the English pound. The two currencies had been used side by side for many years.'[13]

After the Norman Conquest, French was the language of the ruling class, and for several centuries England was a bilingual nation. The original Norman French came to have a 'colonial' character ... During the thirteenth century ... the French spoken in England became further differentiated [from Anglo-Norman] into a dialect called Anglo-French, the subject of much mirth and condescension in France.[14]

Almost a thousand years after the invaders from Normandy had established their political and cultural hegemony over England, on the Guernsey of Parkes' boyhood history played itself backwards through an inverted mirror; a full-cycle reversal of that process was well underway.

The island's linguistic friction accurately reflected the cultural tug-of-war. Plainly, behind a veil of cordial relations, throughout the period that Parkes' was growing up, tension between the island's competing cultures was endemic. Victory to the English, however, was foreordained: ever since the first years of the last century, the erosion of Norman-French dialect in both public and private spheres on Guernsey has been inexorable, and its official standing has been constantly undermined. In the most recent census, only 4,068 Guernseyites stated that they still spoke some *Guernesiais;* of these, no more than 1,262 might be classified as fluent. As for passive comprehension, the figure rises to some 6,300, or some ten per cent of the island's current population.[15]

In short, while a stubborn remnant of what Parkes as a boy viewed as plucky island yeomanry still proudly adheres to its cultural heritage, over the past century, except during the Second World War when the German occupiers actually favoured the use of local French dialect, pressure to conform and assimilate has been unremitting and losses have mounted steadily. For the future historian, however, born and raised at that time and in that place, native speakers of what has now become an endangered ethno-linguistic species were part and parcel of the organic fabric of an Edenic universe with which he powerfully empathized. They were an essential constituent of the 'homeland' to which his heart paid allegiance, a vital, abiding presence in his primal mythos of identity. As broached in the preceding chapter, at a later stage in Parkes' intellectual development the template of the Norman-French under cultural siege would transmogrify stunningly, breeding unforeseen, idiosyncratic consequences: Parkes' displaced feelings of attachment would project themselves upon another people who, in roughly parallel circumstances as the Norman-French, had discovered the means and the strength to survive.

To clarify this point further, I return to the opening lines of 'Boyhood in Guernsey': 'In the centre of the island of Guernsey is the parish of St Andrew. At the eastern end is the Manor of Rohais. My father was the falconer of the Manor, and I was born at *Les Fauconnaires* in December 1896.' In case the innocent reader should invest 'the Manor of Rohais' with unearned grandeur, Parkes *qua* historian dutifully informs him that the Seigneur of Rohais was actually a chap named Mr Bainbrigge. 'In principle,' Parkes writes, 'Bainbrigge could ring us up and tell us he was going hawking that afternoon, and request us to provide their feudal obligation, falcons.' Extending the same anachronistic principle, Parkes adds 'the Parkes family would have resisted by going down on their knees at the front gate and raised the *Clameur de Haro* had Bainbrigge tried to expel them'.[16]

Hearkening back to the early Norman period, *le Clameur de Haro* is an archaic legal formula unique to Guernsey and neighbouring Alderney. Tradition assigns its origins to a plea for justice delivered directly to Rollo, the Viking Duke of Normandy. Coextensive with contemporary legal procedures, this anachronistic residue of the island's medieval heritage remarkably enough still provides ordinary men and women with a sanctioned recourse with which, at least temporarily, to thwart what they perceive to be an autocratic abuse. Theoretically, a common citizen could fall to his knees and, kneeling before two witnesses, declare that a wrong had been committed. He is then supposed to loudly intone the Lord's Prayer in *Le Guernesiais*. If he recites *le Clameur* before the bailiff within twenty-four hours of the alleged offence, any demand he deems arbitrary or unjust is automatically suspended until a legal investigation has been undertaken and a judgment rendered by a magistrate.

By the early part of the nineteenth century this practice had fallen into disuse, but it seems to have enjoyed a modest revival during Parkes' youth. Another memoirist recalls a further instance of its efficacy:

[The] *Clameur de Haro* was not, as far as I remember, availed of until my early manhood, when Mr H. Turner revived its use in connection with a house in Mill Street and [*sic*] which he feared would injure his business premises. The protest was effectual and matters were arranged to Mr Turner's satisfaction. Twice since then, the *clameur* has been made use of to good purpose ... In my youth, it seems to me, the *clameur* was referred to only as an oldtime privilege.[17]

In sum, although those seeking redress by means of *le Clameur*'s special authority have always been few, this histrionic final appeal, so symbolically charged not only with feudalistic but also incipiently democratic weight, has never been abrogated. Moreover, whenever invoked it seems to prove remarkably efficacious. For example, *le Clameur* was most recently invoked on 30 March 2000 when, before a packed conveyancing court Paul Moed, an island insurance broker with no shortage of *chutzpah*, successfully blocked a property sale he claimed was detrimental and prejudicial to his rights. Prior to this occasion, in recent times its guerilla practitioners ambushed the regular legal establishment in Guernsey in 1997 and once again in Alderney in 1998.[18]

Parkes' ostensible purpose in raising his hypothetical *clameur* at the very outset of his memoir now seems manifest: although *virtu* still paid homage to some archaic forms of feudalism, in reality it was lip service. Henry Parkes and neighbour Bainbrigge, the Lord of the Manor, were both transplanted English melon growers under the skin. Neither was keenly conscious of his feudal 'station' nor entertained the remotest prospect of exercising any of its prerogatives. Subsuming this motif of superficial egalitarianism, however, we detect an extremely durable subcurrent. Although the 'advanced' and educated segment of the social order recognized that it was all just a bit of a charade, during Parkes' youth this creaky holdover from the religio-medieval world view, along with accommodation of notions such as resident ghosts and witches, still survived, especially, of course, among the original stock. Moreover, like the unsupplanted *Guernesiais* tongue, *le Clameur* was not only formally but still operationally accessible.

Many other cultural residues that elsewhere had succumbed to antiquated, picturesque irrelevance were still notably vigorous on the island. Until the late Victorian era this was a time-defying realm whose official coinage was neither the shilling nor the franc but *le livre Tournois,* a mythical coin that based itself upon the value of a certain amount of corn in the fourteenth century. Parkes comments that in lieu of monetary payments to the Seigneur of Rohais, his father annually owed his liege – that is the Duke of Normandy, or the English sovereign – five chickens and two sacks of corn. Annually, its monetary equivalent was rendered to an island official and duly recorded in the island ledger. 'We also owed annual *rentes* to a curiously vague collection of people, all of whom could claim an annual sum as heirs of the original Vavaseur de Jersaï who had been awarded the farm after the battle of Creçy in 1345.'[19]

The battle of Creçy in 1345! The resilience of such feudal traces impacted powerfully upon the imagination of the sickly lad who was so touchingly zealous in seeking to ratify the authenticity of his island roots. One surmises that 'the skinny little creature' who used to turn blue after five minutes of splashing in the sea was revitalized and nourished by these living shards of medievalism. He built splendidly intricate castles out of sand and created fabulous scenarios of heroism and chivalry in which to situate himself: in his mind's eye he saw himself as a knight errant, a champion of the tournaments and a defender of the weak.

At least as much as his military or university experiences, then, it was Guernsey, spiritualized and transformed by youthful romantic musings, that armed Parkes for the adult world. His boyhood constitutes a field of triumph for the shaping imagination over mere genetics and the drabness of everyday reality. Against the banality of the commonplace, Parkes rendered judgment in favour of both Farmers 'A' and 'B' against the edicts of their colonial oppressors. Before exploring ramifications emerging from what is probably the most resonant vestige out of that antique past, we rest content for the moment with the image of the young boy riding across the sands as a white knight of Christian *virtu* and, with the raising of *le Clameur de Haro* in *Guernesiais,* the theme of *le Fauconnaire*'s licensed resistance to the authority of *le Seigneur,*[20] two richly apposite leitmotifs for any man's heroic leave-taking on a voyage of self-discovery.

NOTES

1. Unlike all other American states Louisiana is today still politically subdivided into parishes rather than counties.
2. Harry Tomlinson, author of *Étude Grammaticale et Lexicale de Parler Normand de L'ile Guernsey* Edingburgh: (University of Edinburgh, 1981), conversation with Philip Rankilor, October 2002.
3. Marie de Garis, *St Pierre du Bois: The Story of a Guernsey Parish and Its People* (St Peter Port: The Guernsey Herald), 1990, pp. 123–24.
4. Ibid., pp. 133–34.
5. James Parkes, *Voyage of Discoveries, Autobiography* (London: Victor Gollancz, 1969), pp. 16, 22.
6. Ibid., p. 11.
7. Ibid., pp. 11–12.
8. Ibid.
9. Although when writing as a historian or about biblical narrative Parkes exactly weighs the credibility of his sources, it is plain that as a memoirist he is relatively elastic about some important issues. Anna Akhmatova seems especially relevant here: 'Every attempt at a continuous narration in memoirs is a falsification … The human memory is constructed like a projector that throws light on individual moments, while leaving the rest in impenetrable darkness.' Cited in *Anna Akhmatova: Poet and Prophet*, Roberta Reeder (New York: Saint Martin's Press, 1994), p. 501. *Vide* also Chapter 36.
10. For a fuller discussion of this point, *vide* Chapter 5.
11. Ibid., p. 14.
12. de Garis, *St Pierre du Bois*, p. 129.
13. Peter Johnston, *A Short History of Guernsey* (St Peter Port: Guernsey Press, 1994), p. 91.
14. Donald Howard, *Chaucer, His Life, His World, His Work* (New York: Dutton, 1987), p. 21.
15. Official Guernsey Census: *Report on the Census of Population and Households for 2001* (St Peter Port: States of Guernsey, 2002), p. 61.
16. Parkes, *Voyage of Discoveries*, p. 9.
17. G. W. J. L. Hugo, *Guernsey As It Used To Be* (St. Peter Port: Guernsey Star Gazette, 1933), pp. 62–63.
18. *Vide* 'Guernsey' on Internet website in October 2002. Unrecorded is whether Moed, a Jewish immigrant from South Africa whom the author encountered on a visit to St Peter Port in 1995, recited the Lord's Prayer in English, French, *Le Guernesiais*, Afrikaans, or at all.
19. Parkes, *Voyage of Discoveries*, pp. 23–24.
20. In Jewish tradition resides a fascinating if rarely embraced practice, which there is no evidence Parkes had ever heard of, that closely parallels central aspects of *le Clameur de Haro*. During a synagogue service, when a Torah scroll is opened for reading aloud, any congregant who feels deeply aggrieved, for whatever cause, may come forward and, pounding his fist upon the lectern, demand that the public reading be halted for as long as it takes for him to register his protest before the discomfitted congregation. Like it or not, the congregation is constrained to listen. An instance of this occurred in Israel during the Cold War: a pious scholar, outraged when the State of Israel agreed to extradite Harry Sobel, an American Jew who sought political asylum in Israel when he was accused of spying for Russia, created turmoil when, at the synagogue attended by the Minister of the Interior, he halted the Torah reading on Shabbat in order to dramatize his protest. Cited by Haim Be'er in *The Pure Element of Time* (Hanover, NH: University Press of New England/Brandeis, 2003), p. 27.

5

Les Droits de Seigneur

Keeping in view the strong possibility that Guernsey's bi-
culturalism was instrumental in implanting the seed of Parkes'
attachment to the Jewish people that would germinate and surface later in his life, let us again return to the point of embarkation for *Voyage of Discoveries*. Equipoised in exquisite opposition,
in his mind's eye Parkes sees two figures: his father, *le Fauconnaire* and Mr Bainbrigge, *le Seigneur*. 'In principle Mr Bainbrigge
could ring us up and tell us he was going hawking that afternoon, and request us to provide the falcons.'[1] In the following
discussion our focus will shift between the bifurcation of the
two figures and, both in principle and in practice, the reciprocal
nature of their relationship.

For Parkes, the above feudal relationships along with their
atavistic formal entitlements did not operate primarily as picturesque window dressing. Parkes invests his hypostatic medieval
tableau with an oft-rehearsed dream-vision of the unified Parkes
family on their collective knees genuflecting, as it were, as they
chant *le Clameur de Haro* in unison. Utilizing feudal privileges
accruing to them by virtue of their vassalage, their aim is to avert
being exploited by the imperious *Seigneur*. At this primary level,
the main thrust of the fantasy features the adolescent youngster
acting in concert with his father, a figure with whom, in fact, he
was temperamentally out of sync and not infrequently at odds.
(In Parkes' symbolically charged vision, the other siblings in the
tableau at best play marginal, secondary parts.)

Suffusing the scene is an overriding religious dimension. Just
as for this believing Christian the prerogative of God to choose
incarnation in the person of the son of an itinerant Galilean car-
penter was an unassailable option, it was incontrovertible in
principle that *le Seigneur* might choose immanence through the
unlikely vessel of plain old neighbour Mr Bainbrigge. On the
spiritual level, then, for the same reasons that Parkes' natural
sympathies were aligned foursquare with Farmers 'A' and 'B',

whose tongue and ways were fundamentally incomprehensible to the English-speaking magistrates, Parkes' deepest loyalties and affections were in principle invested to a greater degree in the persona of *le Seigneur* than in his own father.

Especially when viewed decades later through the prism of Parkes' transforming imagination, Bainbrigge-the-Englishman's hypothetical performance in the role of God-the-Father appears emasculated, inauthentic, effete, and pretentious. In consequence, any ritualistic demands issuing from him might legitimately be parried from within the indigenous, medieval-Christian, Norman-French tradition; that is, they may be thwarted by timely recourse to a *Clameur de Haro*. However, as if uneasily conscious that Bainbrigge had been grievously miscast for his part in this psychodrama, Parkes reiterated its essential elements by spinning yet another anecdotal recollection from boyhood, one incorporating a more potently symbolic face of *le Seigneur*. This second, more authentically regal avatar bears incisively on the issue of the sovereignty of God-the-Father.

When Parkes was twelve, in the course of recuperating from an extended illness, he spent an entire summer on the tiny, tradition-bound Island of Sark.

> I stayed with two delightful old ladies, Laura and Patty Hale, at the head of the Dixcart Valley. It was in the days of the old Seigneur who was, to put it mildly, extremely eccentric. The year I was there the most surprising thing was that every windowsill on the ground floor was painted a brilliant yellow … I naturally asked, 'Why?'
>
> 'The Seigneur' was the answer.
>
> Apparently an Englishman had bought a *quarentaine* – one of the forty farms into which Sark was subdivided – and had disputed seigneurial rights with regard to his purchase. After careful consideration as to how he could impress the pestilent Englishman with the fact that he was *le Seigneur*, he had gone over to Guernsey, bought an immense pot of yellow paint, and walked around the island, his duck gun as usual under his arm, and had painted every window sill he could reach, daring anyone to stop him.[2]

Sark, to this day a remarkably unspoiled place, was peopled by Parkes' imagination with strong-minded old ladies, quaint

customs and its own distinctive *patois*. It was, in fact, more
prototypically Old Guernsey than Guernsey itself. The very stuff
of romantic legend, at the time of his sojourn it was governed
by an eccentric but artistic *Seigneur* who, wielding his paint-
brush like a sceptre, was splendidly typecast for the part of the
Supreme Creator of the universe. In this Eden he still maintained
intimate, caring relations with his subjects and all the aspects of
his domain that we find in the Genesis account. Both for
outsiders and any would-be usurpers of his sovereignty, the act
of painting the island's windowsills a brilliant yellow made a
conspicuous statement of his sublimity and heliocentric powers.[3]
In all likelihood, for Parkes this activity was suggestive of God's
command to the Hebrew slaves in Egypt in the Book of Exodus.
If they were prepared to abandon their bondage for authentic
freedom and wished to be passed over by the Angel of Death,
they should smear blood over the lintels and door posts of their
houses, in such wise making as dramatic a statement as the
yellow sills of Sark.

This leitmotif of the *Seigneur* demanding his due with which
Parkes, probably unwittingly but certainly tellingly, decorates the
opening pages of his autobiography and later revisits in a Sarkian
key, springs from a deep layer of his psyche. Many years later,
shortly after his marriage, when he wished to introduce his new
wife to these islands, Parkes recounts that he 'took Dorothy for
an unforgettable spring holiday in Sark.'[4] Rather than Guernsey,
it was Sark to which he resorted because this smaller island, super-
intended by its Prospero-like *Seigneur*, still exuded a primeval,
magical, mystical aura.

A cluster of images embracing the bailiff, English law and
language, his own father, and the usurpation of native authority
stands in clear opposition to this recalcitrant Sarkian blend of
tradition-laden natural images and values. From an early age
these countervailing symbolic constellations exercised immense
power and authority over Parkes' imagination. Viewed from the
perspective of his mature commitments, the latter was infused
with powerful overtones emanating from the Lord of the Universe, the God of Creation, the living God of the Old Testament,
and of His abiding love for the never-abandoned children so that
they may live. As the 1920s darkened into the desperation of the
'30s and '40s, Parkes' commitment as a Christian would again
and again mandate his return to the field as a knight errant in

the service of *le Seigneur's* chosen people whom Hitler, apotheosis of the principle of usurpation, had chosen for destruction.

We are now equipped to deconstruct the text of those court cases from the preceding chapter and to excavate their subtext. In both instances, the overriding point was that the instrumentality of ghosts and witchcraft – indigenous Guernsey phenomena – could not possibly be adjudicated in the English language or exclusively according to the strictures of English law. Disingenuously confounding the bailiff, Farmers 'A' and 'B' implicitly bested English hegemony simply by speaking in their natural voices, *le patois*. In one court case, cultural dissonance is revealed specifically through linguistic impenetrability. In the second, the incommensurability of the two cultures is more generalized.

Parkes claims 'to remember' that this second case involved a magistrate,

> … new to the island background … gaily hearing evidence of illegal activities of which an old lady had certainly been guilty, when a jurat … spotted what was happening. He hastily sent the magistrate a note reminding him that the only statute dealing with witchcraft was that of Elizabeth I, and asking him whether he intended to have the old lady burned! The magistrate wisely adjourned for lunch.[5]

We may plausibly infer that at Parkes' deeper strata of consciousness a more fundamental confrontation subsumed the comic courtroom dissonance.

As in the episode of the Sarkian *Seigneur*, so with the witchcraft cases let us superimpose the agency of an Original or Old or First Dispensation. For 'English jurisprudence', the triumphalism of the New Dispensation may be substituted. Justice in both of these courtroom dramas depends upon an ironic reversal: it is witchcraft, a projection of the primitive or primal order of nature that flourished prior to the New Dispensation, that embodies the realm of spirit. Neither Farmer 'A' nor Farmer 'B' was really interested in the threatening letters, for which we may confidently substitute 'the letter of the law'. Both were actually concerned with the realm of spirit, or spirits. Paradoxically reversing expectations, it is Christian law, or the New (English) Dispensation whose representatives, playing the part of stereotypical Pharisees, comically miss the real point of

the legal quarrels. It is this – the cluster embracing the New
Testament – that functions as the 'the dead letter'. That is why,
in context, it is both literally and metaphorically 'out to lunch'.[6]

Neither in the idiosyncratic histrionics of the Sarkian sovereign
nor in the incomprehensibility of both the judges and defendants
in the two court cases that he resurrects, is it likely that Parkes
even remotely apprehended the network of implication subsuming the anecdotal narrative fragments. What is far more salient
is his intuitive sympathy with the ongoing validity of the Old
Order, and that his appreciation for the absurdity of the situation wherein the workings of the Old Order should be judged
by the standards of the New. In any event, it is clear-cut that at
this deeper stratum the legal proceedings adumbrated in these
boyhood anecdotes prefigure Parkes' later theological insights as
to how God's plan for the healing of Creation, or *tikkun olam*,
depended upon the symbiosis of Judaism and Christianity. In
due course, this complex matter will be addressed at considerably greater length.[7]

'Nothing in James Parkes' early biography,' we recall Nicolas
de Lange averring, 'explains why he should have come to be
devoted to the study of the Jews.'[8] On the contrary, to conclude
with de Lange, Robert Everett and others that this mélange of
droll anecdotes out of Parkes' island boyhood – including ghostly
antics which we shall shortly investigate[9] – have nothing to do
with the philosemitic persona that Parkes slowly developed and
later assumed with such enthusiasm seems fallacious. These
recollections at first may read like an assemblage of discrete trivia,
but when one grasps the three-tiered society of Parkes' island
home, the transformed fragments are infused with symbolic
weight.

In retrospect, it may justly be said that Parkes' idyll on
Guernsey actually reached its apotheosis on Sark. As a youngster,
although he butted his head against the impenetrable *patois*, he
still gave his heart to the otherness and irreducible impermea-
bility of the Norman-French culture. Only as an adolescent did
he succeed in penetrating the more cultivated, assimilated segment of native Guernsey society. A parallel pattern would assert
itself in Parkes' maturity when he engaged a far more illustrious
people, one whose religious and national culture, contrary to
expectations, proved not only accessible but even receptive as
they themselves warmly welcomed Parkes' advances. Indeed,

because as a scholar he insistently viewed Jesus as the Jew he of course was and because as a Christian he felt he could legitimately acknowledge and appropriate the living residue of that Jewishness, as an adult Parkes would never have grounds to complain, as he had on Guernsey, that he was not 'of full native stock'. Indeed, from the start of his public mission, his stock with *these* natives has always been high.

Later in life, Parkes' painstaking research would disclose the depth and tenacity with which the taproot sin of antisemitism had insinuated itself into the texture of the Gospels, the very heart of the religion in which he had taken holy orders. Nineteen centuries of Christian calumny had produced a primordial, irrational and brutal hatred of Jews. Almost at once Parkes' conscience informed him to what end he should devote the rest of his life. His central mission, which had come to him like a gift from God, constituted not alone an ethical but a psychological and metaphysical imperative. At this juncture, twin, reciprocal paths opened up before him: out of living remnants of medievalism Parkes would realize his boyhood daydream of knight errantry by taking up his lance in a personal crusade in defence of the people of *le Seigneur*, shielding them at times from their most savage enemies. Simultaneously, Parkes would begin his other grand undertaking: the extirpation of antisemitism from the maw of Christianity.

In sum, as an inveterate outsider and loner, young James Parkes responded profoundly to the organicism of the lives of the natives of Guernsey, most of whom still lived in intimate, vital contact with their usable past and maintained the rich heritage of the primal *Seigneur*. For Parkes the deeply ingrained, apparently merely picturesque traditions of the island's Norman-French stock – embracing both the peasant base and acculturated older families such as the Ozannes – eventually would merge with the seemingly superseded, superficially fossilized, communal traditions of the Jewish people first under attack, later under siege, and ultimately under threat of extermination.

It is clear that Parkes himself perceived the nature of the debt he owed to his Guernsey heritage imperfectly. He preferred to ascribe his heterodox love for the Jewish people and radical theological slant on Judaism entirely to his having drawn the inevitable moral conclusions from his research into classical and medieval sources. As he observed in 1952, he was 'more than

ever convinced by ... [his] work as a historian that Judaism
survives because it is the will of God that it should survive, and
that the divine truth which it mediates to man is not displaced
by that of Christianity'.[10] His first close involvement with individual Jews in the early 1930s substantiated and reinforced this
perspective.

Elsewhere Parkes attributed his radical theological outlook
entirely to 'intellectual honesty' which 'compelled him to
abandon the belief that post-Christian Judaism was a collection
of niggardly and unspiritual legalisms ... '[11] Yet underlying these
intellectual constructs lay, as argued above, a critical psycho-
dynamic dimension. In the crucible of Parkes' spiritual imagination, the Norman-French and their cognates, the Jewish people,
occupied overlapping symbolic terrain. Drawing upon the same
emotional fund of sympathetic identification, they ultimately
coalesced. If *les Guernesiais* served unconsciously as the Jews
of his youth, in later years the Jews functioned as emotional
surrogates for *les Guernesiais*. Were Parkes less psychologically
armoured and had he at the age of seventy-two a somewhat
different agenda, the opportunity to revisit his past in tranquillity occasioned by the composition of *Voyage of Discoveries*
might have led him to similar conclusions. Self-reflection, however, was never his special strength.

Although mainstream Christian theologians could readily
accommodate the hypothesis that the survival of the Jewish
people had been the will of God, for several decades exceedingly
few would endorse Parkes' conclusions that the divine truths
embodied by Judaism and the eternal favour of God had not
been and would never be supplanted by those embodied by
Christianity. Moreover, a quarter of a century after the publication of *God At Work*, the gap between Parkes' appreciation
for Judaism and for normative Christianity had, if anything,
widened:

> As I studied the post-Christian growth of Judaism I realized
> that what I was hearing about was a religion different
> from Christianity, with a different discipline of living.
> Unquestionably, it is this which has been responsible for the
> survival of the Jewish people, not, as [Arnold] Toynbee once
> asserted, just as a fossil, but as an extremely dynamic and
> adaptable society ... This challenged and indeed overthrew

my previous acceptance of the spiritual development of
society as being a christocentric-human relationship.[12]

Yet even for Parkes a full acknowledgement of the enormity of
Christian responsibility for the emergence of Nazism and the
direct complicity of millions of professing Christians in mass
murder would not necessarily have led to taking the field as a
great Christian champion of the Jewish cause – combating anti-
semitism and defending the establishment of a Jewish homeland
in Palestine – had it not, I submit, so powerfully conformed to
the contours of the sensibility shaped on his childhood island.

Both large and small, the differences between peoples as
disparate as the Norman-French and the Jews scarcely require
detailing, but for Parkes these were readily eclipsed by profound
parallels. Guernsey and his attachment to *les Guernesiais* provided him with the proleptic model which later, in a vastly
different key, accounts for the depth and strength of his affinity
for the Jewish people. In effect, Parkes' natal land had been more
than half-populated by figurative Francophone 'Jews'. Neither
in its court of law nor in the hearts of the people had the English
dispensation replaced the alternative, older order.

Finally, unlike his inner need to establish a consanguine
attachment to Guernsey through the likes of putative great-
great-great-aunts, Parkes never had to stretch a point to assert
an intimate connection to Judaism or its people. They were part
and parcel of his faith as a Christian. Nevertheless, later on
another distant relation arises, one who links him even more
urgently to his Old Testament roots. Unexpectedly, Parkes
resurrects the family legend of the original dispossession of the
Parkeses from 'the land on which they had lived for generations
near Dudley [not far from Birmingham] because ... he [John
Parkes] disliked his relations. But he, and he alone, knew that
every inch of it was coal, and the purchase of it started the
fortunes of I forget which earl'.[13]

This primal family myth, redolent of humankind's aboriginal
temptation, greed and the banishment from Eden, adumbrates
the inner dread that afflicted Parkes throughout his youth. In his
manhood Parkes would never again endure the metaphorical
displacement he had suffered as a solitary youngster, either the
actual homelessness that ensued upon the fracture of his family
or the acute sense of metaphysical homelessness that – at times

as cause, at other times as effect – accompanied his periodic physical and emotional breakdowns. Championing *les droits* of the Jewish people for *le Seigneur*, however, enabled Parkes to repossess his family's original, pre-Guernsey heritage: a Blakean vision of England as Jerusalem, like Guernsey itself a formerly Edenic realm of natural goodness unbesmirched by coal-black covetousness and greed.

As in the beginning, in the end it was Christianity that anchored Parkes' spiritually. Nevertheless, it was the Jewish people and the Jewish faith that afforded him the safe and capacious harbour he needed for emotional nourishment and healing. An understanding of Parkes' heart and full insight into his thought requires due recognition of the importance of this other crucial homecoming.

NOTES

1. James Parkes, *Voyage of Discoveries: Autobiography* (London: Victor Gollancz, 1969), p. 9.
2. Ibid., pp. 12–13.
3. Iconographically, Christians in the medieval period associated the colour yellow with negative characteristics such as jealousy, heresy, treachery and, inevitably, Jewishness. It was the colour of the badge that in pre-expulsion England proclaimed Jewish identity. If the actual old Seigneur of Sark would not necessarily have been aware of this connection, both as a historian of the period and from his projection of *le Seigneur* into his symbolic role as the Deity, Parkes certainly was. Windowsills painted yellow could be viewed as a flag confirming that *le Seigneur*, still bound by the conditions of his contract, would be starring as the God of the Jews in a long-run production that gave no hint of closing in the foreseeable future. *Vide* Ruth Mellinkoff, *Outcasts: Signs of Otherness in Northern European Art of the Later Middle Ages*, 2 vols (Berkeley: University of California, 1993), Vol. 1, pp. 35–36.
4. Parkes, *Voyage of Discoveries*, p. 215.
5. Ibid., p. 11.
6. *Vide* Chapter 4, Endnote 8.
7. *Vide* Chapters 19 and 29.
8. *Vide* Chapter 3.
9. *Vide* Chapter 8.
10. James Parkes, *God at Work in Science, Politics and Human Life* (London: Putnam, 1952), p. 7.
11. James Parkes, 'Christendom and the Synagogue', *Frontier* (London), Vol. 2, No. 4 (Winter 1959), p. 172.
12. James Parkes, 'Judaism and Christianity', *European Judaism*, Vol. 13, No. 1 (Autumn 1979), p. 36.
13. Parkes, *Voyage of Discoveries*, p. 158.

6

'Poor Father'

In the centre of the island of Guernsey is the parish of St Andrew. At its eastern end is the Manor of Rohais. My father was the falconer of the Manor, and I was born at Les Fauconnaires in December 1896.[1]

All beginnings are both formative and informative. The above reprise of the opening lines of Parkes' record of his wayward voyage through life provides a less than perfectly secure handhold for his readers' parallel expedition through some of the knottier, more matted strands of implication at the deeper reaches of Parkes' psyche. At the outset we take note immediately of three distinct but dynamically entwined, plastic motifs: the island, the manor, and, the father.

Having penetrated the thickets of the island as close to the heart of the matter as we might, before focusing on his father we turn our attention if only briefly to Parkes' childhood home, *Les Fauconnaires*.

> [It was] a gloomy house facing north, overshadowed by huge ilex trees, surrounded by ancient outbuildings. [Its] dry granite walls were three feet thick. The boys could hear, lying in bed, the rats collecting apples from the loft and rolling them bump, bump down through the dry walls.[2]

Gloom, ilex trees, rats – *Les Fauconnaires* feels more like a stagy backdrop for a melodramatic, late eighteenth-century tale of Gothic terror than the buoyant, Victorian childhood Parkes set out to relate. Yet, as recounted earlier, as long as the home was presided over by his mother, the Queen of Light who swept away all shadows, despite being marked by chronic illness, Parkes' childhood under its roof seems to have been happy enough.

The knell of *Les Fauconnaires* is, however, the cue for Henry Parkes, standing in the wings rehearsing his scowls and silences, to make his initial entrance playing 'the heavy' in his son's theatre of memory. But first, lest one misconstrue the coloration of 'falconer of the Manor' or the nasalized atmospherics of *Les Fauconnaires*, Parkes tempers them with his professional historian's allegiance to homely data: 'In actual fact,' he amends, 'my father was an Englishman and a civil engineer, who had come to Guernsey to grow tomatoes and melons. But then, so too had the Seigneur of Rohais.'³ In these introductory lines Parkes speaks in contrapuntal voices: he is the meticulous scholar who deeply respects the integrity of fact and the primacy of accurate data, but at the same time he displays the distinctive markings of an unreconstructed romantic.

The rhetorical strategies employed by Parkes in *Voyage of Discoveries* often result in his conscious intentions being at odds with his pen. In the introductory segment it is less manifest content than stylistic oddity that hints at opacity and points towards concealment. As noted earlier, whenever Parkes tried to engage the sources of his sensibility, he was significantly blind-sided by sentiment and psychological defensiveness. Especially when he alludes to the fabric of strained relationships within his family, critical aspects of the dynamic are revealed only obliquely. That is, while the larger design is clear enough, details and nuance often need to be elicited inferentially.

One voice, for example, blandly assures the reader that 'we were a *very* united family, and I do not recall any serious quarrels'. That sounds very sunny indeed until a few moments later, after alluding to some lengthy boyhood illness, it drops a brick about the untimely demise of his mother without missing a beat. Then, somewhat shockingly, Parkes records not that her death left Henry Parkes very sad, disconsolate, or crestfallen but rather curiously, '[it] ... left my father *very* poor'. At the start illness, then, death and poverty all play a part in Parkes' jollified childhood narrative. Before we have a chance to absorb the ramifications of the family's altered situation, as though it were purposely shifting the spotlight elsewhere, the narrative voice offers a seeming *non sequitur*: Henry Parkes then 'became a *very* good cook ...'⁴ (original emphasis).

Anyone acquainted with Parkes' typically measured style would be disconcerted with the sheer banality of the above. Elsewhere in his mature work we rarely encounter such an over-kill of intensifiers, their presence all the more prominent when juxtaposed with the precision and vivacity of the memoirist's retrieval of young Jimmy Parkes in the act of exploring '… every cliff path and bay, every rock and cranny in its long coast line …' and his immense admiration for 'the adventurous and pioneering spirit of the islanders'.[5] As noted earlier, whenever the focus shifts to the flora or fauna of his natal island or to its natives, Parkes' descriptive powers are characterized by a lyrical warmth and an exactitude of detail that expel all doubt about the authenticity of feeling. In sharp contrast, instead of brilliant patches of recollection, images of Parkes' father, mother and siblings float past like well-worn set pieces or ill-focused, impressionistic swashes of colour.

Parkes' adverbial excesses argue that even in old age, when recalling his boyhood presumably in tranquillity and much disposed to viewing it as an idyll, he simply could not banish the elegiac mists of chronic illness, poverty, emotional displacement, solitude and death. In short, Parkes' version of his early years is unreliable. For example, details surrounding the demise of his mother do not confirm that the Parkes family may be adequately described either as very united or very poor. While there is no reason to question Henry Parkes' gradual acquisition of culinary skill, that he 'developed into a very good cook' most probably serves as a psychological screen for the youngster's deep-seated ambivalence. If, in the above locution, we provisionally substitute 'father' for 'cook,' even though this seems to extol his father, the effect is to pry into a painfully ambiguous relationship that was, in its way, at least as formative as Parkes' love for his mother.

Parkes' gradual resolution into a smooth weave of the tangle of incompatible strands issuing from his ill-matched parents closely parallels that of two other eminent products of the Victorian era, D. H. Lawrence (discussed earlier)[6] and Thomas Hardy. Rather than the specific details, it is the process that is salient.

> Like D. H. Lawrence, Hardy was exceptionally close to parents of markedly different temperament. Lawrence possessed all his mother's fierce repressive Puritanism, as well as his father's zest for living. Hardy's father had a passive, contemplative nature, his mother a canny initiative and an iron will. Their eldest son inherited both tendencies,

in all the measure of a genius. And as Lawrence's stories reveal more directly than his novels the two biological sides of his nature, Hardy's too have the same tendency. They encapsulate in miniature ... both the bleak, close determination of his being, and its tender, vulnerable passivity.[7]

In a letter to the editor of a journal dedicated to island nostalgia, Parkes reported that his father came to Guernsey in 1894 or 1895, around a year before he himself was born, in order to grow melons and tomatoes.[8] Aside from 'an adventurous spirit', satisfactory reasons for Henry Parkes quitting England are never delineated. We may reasonably infer, however, that although he had followed his father, the prize-winning engineer, into the same profession, it was with notably less success. This would argue that, undeterred by hard work or the costs of nonconformity, his middle-of-the-journey abandonment of homeland and profession was fostered not alone by the prospect of self-sufficiency within a pristine setting but also by a desire to put distance between himself and *his* father.

Tomatoes, still popularly called 'love apples', had been introduced into Guernsey in the 1860s 'as a supplementary crop to the cultivation of grapes', at the time still a major island export.[9] These were raised in greenhouses, but even after tomatoes had largely supplanted the grapes, these small farming establishments were still called 'vineries'. To this day many old island greenhouses are rife with vines, and even where the greenhouses have been abandoned, vines can be seen wildly proliferating nearby. The same pattern occurred with the island's fig culture.

Greenhouse construction was a boom enterprise in the early decades of the century; Henry Parkes 'bought Gorseland Vineries and *Les Fauconnaires* from a Miss de Jersey (who had built more than a dozen greenhouses)'.[10] What lent the elder Parkes' operation its cutting edge was neither mechanization nor labour-saving practices; on the contrary Gorseland Vineries was, if anything, labour-intensive. In those days 'heating was provided by an anthracite-fueled boiler and cast iron pipes which carried hot water between the rows of tomato plants. At the end of the short season – most tomatoes were pulled up and a second planted – jobbing labourers helped the regular staff to prepare the soil, digging by hand.'[11]

Henry Parkes' newfangledness, on the strength of which he wagered the wellbeing of the young family, uprooting them from the Midlands,[12] lay in his novel method of sorting and grading his fruit with the result that the tomatoes at the bottom of the pile could be counted upon to be as firm as the fruit on the top. On the face of it, young James roundly admired his father's risk-taking boldness, a trait that allied him with the 'adventurous and pioneering spirit of the islanders'. He might even have appreciated that in a place where vestigial feudal allegiances were still honoured and some ancient practices maintained, Henry Parkes' innovation could bear the burden of a progressive, democratic parable: if tomatoes on the bottom looked and tasted as good as the ones on the top, then falconers (i.e. recent island immigrants) were as good under the skin as seigneurs of the manor or long-time Guernsey inhabitants.

On the other hand, a serf-like drudgery prevailed in these vineries, and throughout their childhood the three Parkes children were constrained to spend '… countless hours separating "specials" – tomatoes perfect in size and shape – from As, Bs, Cs and irregulars'.[13] At the time, Henry Parkes' tomato revolution probably afforded greater satisfaction to the father than to the children. Nevertheless, pride undiminished by the passage of sixty years, Parkes does note that London's Covent Garden always welcomed produce marketed under the logo of Parkes' Gorseland.

Parkes recalls that, paying the foreman twenty-five shillings a week and ordinary workers between eighteen and twenty-two shillings, his father employed eight men in all. Even by the standards of the day, the wages he paid were hardly munificent. 'In those early years of the twentieth century,' one veteran Guernseyman recalls, 'a family of husband and wife with two or three children could get by fairly easily on a wage of £1 weekly, especially if they grew their own vegetables and kept a pig and a few hens.' It was not until 1939 that labourours' wages reached the level of £2 a week.[14] Another old Guernseyman's recollection of the prevailing pay scale for labourers is even more astringent: 'With few exceptions servants' wages at the time ranged from £8 to £16 per annum. The £1 equalled 24 francs at the period. Charwomen earned 2 francs a day, I think, 4 francs was the usual pay of gardeners.'[15]

It is virtually certain that the three Parkes children were not paid for sorting the tomatoes. This, of course, is hardly unusual in a rural, family business; nor does it necessarily suggest that the children felt exploited. Still, when we recall Parkes' otherwise seemingly gratuitous remark that he '... was a politically conscious adolescent',[16] his suspiciously perfect recall of what others earned for their drudgery is suggestive. As an adult Parkes affected the superior bearing and manner of, say, a 'special' Gorseland tomato; his political instincts, nevertheless, were progressive and egalitarian, and unlike his father he would be a lifetime supporter of the Labour Party.

Parkes also notes that he earned half-a-crown a week tutoring a neighbour's sons for two hours, six nights a week as well as 'quite an amount as a bookbinder' and a shilling an hour teaching Latin to an adult six miles away. 'It seemed,' he adds, 'fabulous wealth.'[17] As before, the exact sums as well as the distance that he walked on foot – six miles was halfway across the island – and the fact he tutored adults as well as children are recorded with considerable pride. It is quite likely that his older brother, who in his free time led an active social life, did not contribute as much to the family economy. Further, 'Molly and I used secretly to supplement his [their father's] housework while he was doing the shopping'.[18] The picture that emerges is of a youngster who exerted himself unstintingly to earn a good word from his father. Yet no matter how hard Jimmy tried, 'the very good cook' favoured his more vigorous offspring, especially David.

'Father,' Parkes concludes, 'stopped tomato growing several years before World War I. In these years his average income was considerably less than £500.'[19] This sum included income from a small inheritance. Still, however much young Parkes may have felt his father had become 'very poor,' to whatever depths Henry Parkes' income actually sank, we may be certain that it still dwarfed the annual income of Guernsey's peasant labourers, servants and charwomen. The net effect of even harsh times was to lower the genteel, immigrant English family's status relative to the island's native gentry. It would never have occurred to Henry Parkes to compare his estate to that of Guernsey's genuinely poor and, more pertinently, neither did it occur to his younger son.

Among the belt-tightening measures taken by *les nouveaux pauvres*, the most dramatic was the dismissal of the family retainer, an outward sign of the family's fall in social status.

Many decades later Parkes still characterizes this as 'courageous ... Rather than keep up public appearances and scrape for every penny behind the scenes, he [his father] would be comfortable.'[20] Courageous seems rather inflated rhetoric for 'plumping for comfort'. To be sure, Parkes seems to endorse his father's choice, but what a falling away is this brand of courage from the medieval chivalric tradition, the pioneering exploits of the islanders, or even the degree of risk-taking in which Henry Parkes himself had indulged in the 1890s.

Despite his earnest application of 'scientifically progressive' Victorian principles, in the end Henry Parkes had not genuinely revolutionized island agriculture. True, for a time Gorseland unquestionably enjoyed success and, as Parkes concludes with perhaps a fine shade of irony, his father had been '... a pioneer in grading of tomatoes, ahead of his time in growing melons'.[21] Still, after more than a decade of toil in the vineries, when in 1910 tomato prices severely plummeted, Henry Parkes abandoned the enterprise in which he had invested so much of his life. His main channel of ambition blocked, nothing comparable ever replaced it.

In taking the measure of his father's life, Parkes aimed at generosity. Even though the sale of Gorseland Vineries spelled the end of tomato sorting, Parkes' emphasis is less on liberation than the disappointment that clouded his widower father's later years. Good in the kitchen, he was 'a spotty housekeeper'. When he sold *Les Fauconnaires* and with the proceeds repurchased a corner lot of the property, he constructed a less pretentious dwelling for his family. Adept with his hands, in reduced circumstances the elder Parkes also took to carving and building model yachts. The new house was vulnerable to draughts and occasionally gusts from all directions, yet unlike *Les Fauconnaires*, it was also was very sunny. In fact 'the bungalow' may be viewed as an embodiment of Henry Parkes himself: on the one hand decisive, resourceful and somewhat unconventional, after his wife's demise he cut a more chastened, withdrawn, diminished figure. It is far from clear that his children appreciated his virtues as much as sharing an irrational, unarticulated sense that their downward slide would not have occurred had their mother not departed from the scene.

After the death of Annie Parkes, darkness increasingly governs the narrative. We learn that throughout boyhood Parkes suffered

grievously from debilitating headaches. Indeed, he was considered too sickly, frail and lachrymose to play games at school.
He missed months of classes at a stretch. For at least one period,
this comprised an entire school term.[22] He simply was not 'a
regular chap', and inevitably his schoolmates considered him
something of a milksop. In his least discreet statement about his
flawed relationship with his father, Parkes reveals, 'it was not
that there was enmity between my father and myself, but he was
much more interested in my brother and my sister, who played
games, did not constantly go to bed with appalling headaches,
did not write poetry, or know where every flower that grew in
the island was to be found'.[23]

Frustrated by his father's aloofness, the bookish, rather sissi-
fied, often solitary adolescent found an emotional outlet outside
the home. 'I was very fortunate after her death in that a friend
of hers, Christine Ozanne, daughter of the Rector of St Martin's,
spotted me looking miserable at a party – I loathed parties – and
invited me to the Rectory.' Parkes was soon spending nearly all
his free time in the company of Christine Ozanne, friend and
stand-in for his departed mother, in what became his second
home. This relationship would set a pattern: in later life Parkes
repeatedly attracted the attentions and affection of somewhat
older women. The Ozanne connection unsheathes open criticism
of his father: '… [I] certainly had many more serious discussions
of everything under the sun [at the Ozannes] than I ever had
with my father.'[24] If not open enmity, father and son plainly
shared a mutual, silent recognition not merely of disaffinity but
of outright disaffection. With the passing years, their emotional
estrangement would only deepen.

Sublimating his loneliness, he found another outlet with
which to rechannel his adolescent angst: intense absorption in a
number of collections. He would in fact develop into a lifelong
collector, wedded to an inveterate habit of mind whose psychological and symbolic significance will later be addressed in
detail.[25] His earliest enthusiasm was for ancient coins, especially
the early coinage of Guernsey 'which had the most wonderful
monetary system until 1919', so wonderful that decades later he
could not restrain himself from boasting about his 'perfect
collection of all issues' of five franc coins that Guernsey had
purchased after they had been withdrawn from circulation in
France, or bombarding the reader with its marvellous intricacies.

Parkes' earliest ambition was in its way predictive: to work in the Coin Department of the British Museum. Then, at the age of nine, he made the cardinal error of announcing a revised life plan to his father: instead of becoming a functionary in that great repository of ancient currency, he would train as an architect. He wanted to be a builder of great churches. Henry Parkes' precise response goes unrecorded, but its effect was withering. His father, Parkes notes,

> ... as a Victorian civil engineer, viewed architects with contempt, so that I had to abandon that idea. But I still loved architecture, and began to collect books and photographs, mostly post-cards. By the time I was fourteen, though I had never seen a cathedral, I knew the dimensions and building dates of every English cathedral, and could identify any photograph I was shown, even of minor details.[26]

Who could not be struck by the insensitivity of a parent who so summarily tramples his young child's benign interests or harmless ambitions? Parkes' tenacity in the face of his father's opposition bespeaks considerable inner strength. After all, the sensitive boy's consciousness that his father thought him fundamentally a misfit had to be acute and extremely hurtful. At the same time, its effect seems to have been salutary: it steeled the boy's determination to resist domination. Some years later, once again to the silent consternation of his father, a similar dynamic would promote Parkes' decision to take orders in the Church of England.

Particularly from the perspective of Parkes' antiquarianism, his youthful passion for ancient coins and stately churches clearly adumbrates his eventual vocational choices as an historian and Anglican clergyman. One can easily visualize the sickly, socially dysfunctional, stubborn boy, already evidencing a scholarly disposition, seated at his desk or the kitchen table. With self-conscious obduracy, for untold hours he would pore over his growing collection of ancient five franc pieces and his picture gallery of churches and cathedrals. The phenomenal growth in particular of the latter collection argues remarkable inner resolution. For in order to accumulate thousands of postcards and photographs of English churches, the lad from the remote island had to dispatch abroad a vast number of solicitations. One imagines the boy's heart beating with anticipation at the arrival of the postman and his joy at examining and sorting his day's harvest. These treasures were all the more precious precisely because they were so devalued by his father.

Henry Parkes, of course, was more than merely a trained engineer and former tomato grower; he was also a professed agnostic, that most doctrinaire of persuasions which, in a late Victorian backwater, could be notoriously dour. Not unaware that his son craved his love or at least his approbation, he mainly ignored the boy's stubborn dedication to his several collections. At times, however, employing either ungentle sarcasm or a passing scowl, he conveyed his desire that Jimmy not waste time and energy on stuff and nonsense like ancient coinage and picture postcards of churches. Inevitably, on occasion his disparagement was interpreted as encompassing his son's religious commitment. This is not to say that, in his fashion, Henry Parkes did not feel some pride or affection for his younger son. However, it was always highly qualified, and its display was neither overt nor very frequent.

With the war's erasure of other family members, on their own James and Henry Parkes could barely maintain cordial relations. Except for very brief interludes, after the summer of 1919 they would never again share the same quarters. Until his dying day Parkes neither forgot nor forgave the sting of paternal disappointment and apparent indifference that he suffered as a boy. He records no instance of his father conferring praise on any of his books, no instance of any acknowledgement of the many accolades bestowed upon him, nor, with a single exception,[27] of any manifestation of even token pride in his many achievements. Aside from passing mention, the only time his father resurfaces significantly in Parkes' memoir is on the occasion of his death in the waning days of the Second World War.

Yet, in spite of their being at such odds, as a boy Parkes never ceased to try to earn the approval that was never freely extended. In the end, he paid his father the compliment of unconsciously emulating his qualities of independence of thought and action. Regardless of the general run of opinion or the disagreeable consequences, both Henry and James Parkes stuck fiercely to their beliefs and principles. Unattached to any parish, unaffiliated to any university, the son, like his father, resolutely chose to be a freelancer. Paradoxically, the boy who had been so inordinately shy, so habitually withdrawn from other children, and so uncertain of his abilities grew up to be as resourceful and stubborn as his father as well as far more gregarious.

Never articulated, the inner dimensions of the Parkes family dynamic stand out in bold enough relief. They constitute unyielding, subterranean lines of force in what Parkes, with unconscious irony, decades later insisted upon construing as his 'very united family'. Whatever unity there once had been was early on fragmented by sibling rivalries and illness and later swept away by war and death. Where once there had been five, only two remained, the two least bound together by ties of affection. Of the three children who once had played along the summer strand on the rocky coast of Vazon, only Jimmy had come through. Chance or Providence or God had willed it. Imbued with meanings he could not fully fathom, some of them psychologically censorious and painful to his conscience, the unpredictable turn of events led the surviving son to conclude that his life should be, or rather must be governed by some special purpose.

NOTES

1. James Parkes, *Voyage of Discoveries: Autobiography* (London: Victor Gollancz, 1969), p. 9. Also *vide* Chapter 36.
2. James Parkes, 'The Bungalow Ghost', Publication of *La Société Guernesiaise*, St Peter Port, September 1965.
3. Parkes, *Voyage of Discoveries*, p. 9.
4. Ibid., p. 10.
5. Ibid., p. 9.
6. *Vide* Chapter 2.
7. John Bayley, 'The Two Hardys', *The Power of Delight, A Lifetime in Literature: Essays 1962–2002* (New York: W. W. Norton, 2005), p. 48.
8. James Parkes, *Guernsey Magazine*, St Peter Port: 11 May 1977.
9. Peter Johnston, *A Short History of Guernsey* (St Peter Port: Guernsey Press, 1994), p. 91.
10. Parkes, *Guernsey Magazine*.
11. Nick Machon, *Guernsey As It Was*, St Peter Port: Guernsey Press, n.d., p. 23.
12. Parkes, *Voyage of Discoveries*, p. 158.
13. Parkes, *Guernsey Magazine*.
14. Marie de Garis, *St Pierre du Bois: The Story of a Guernsey Parish and Its People*, St Peter Port, *Guernsey Herald*, 1990, p. 134 ff.
15. G. W. J. L. Hugo, *Guernsey As It Used To Be*, St Peter Port, *Guersney Star and Gazette*, 1933, p. 27, p. 63.
16. *Vide* Chapter 1.
17. Parkes, *Voyage of Discoveries*, p. 10.
18. Ibid.
19. Parkes, *Guernsey Magazine*.
20. *Vide* Chapter 8.
21. Parkes, *Guernsey Magazine*.
22. Parkes, *Voyage of Discoveries*, p. 10.

23. Ibid., p. 14.
24. Ibid.
25. *Vide* Chapter 22.
26. James Parkes, 'My Collection of Architectural Photographs', 1975, unpublished,
    Parkes Archives, File 60/9/19/1.
27. Parkes, *Voyage of Discoveries*, p. 18.

7

Swots and Swats

Upon completing the first grade at a dame school, young Parkes was transferred to Elizabeth College, founded in the 1560s by Elizabeth I. Its benefactress charged it with a dual mission: 'to educate Channel Islanders in English and Anglican ways and to protect them from the influence of continental [Calvinist] Protestantism'.[1] Three hundred years later, these rather insular aims still served as the school's guidelines and fairly adequately defined its underlying ethos.

Surrounded by a tall, metal-tipped fence, the imposing, stone, central building, through whose portals Parkes passed daily for eleven years, was constructed between 1826 and 1829. Set near the crest of the hill overlooking St Peter Port's harbour, it was then and remains something of a castellated, Victorian pastiche. The two-storey Romanesque restoration structure is agreeably topped by a Gothic-revival tower that stands out as one of the dominant features of the town's skyline. The large, airy, square classrooms are illuminated by means of high, narrow windows. A century ago a gymnasium stood in front of the main building, obscuring the façade, but it was replaced in the 1920s.[2] Also gone is the small porter's lodge that stood by the main gate from where a watchful eye could be kept on the comings and goings of the pupils.[3] Overall, however, the general impression of the complex is much the same today as it was in the Parkes' time.

In September 1914, with the outbreak of hostilities, the older boys, among them David Parkes, went off to France to defeat the Hun. A great many would never see Guernsey again. At that time Jimmy Parkes was sixteen and just entering upon his final year at Elizabeth College. Somewhat surprisingly, he was chosen to serve as senior prefect, a position David had held two years earlier. The choice of Parkes for this prestigious post raises a number of questions. For a start, as memorably portrayed by Parkes' slightly older contemporary E. M. Forster,[4] schools of the period were rife with cliques and infested by a veritable cult of games. There is no reason to suppose that Elizabeth College was significantly unlike 'Sawston School,' pseudonym for Tonbridge which the novelist actually attended. In such a climate, success at sports was the broadest, surest road to status and prestige. The selection as senior prefect of a timid, reclusive scholar who shunned games absolutely – a chap assuredly not one of the 'bloods' – registers oddly.

According to a past historian of the college, the headmaster, upon consultation with his deputy and some senior teachers, has always appointed the senior prefect.[5] Yet as Parkes makes abundantly clear, if relations between him and headmaster William Penney began poorly, they only skid further downhill thereafter. The two headstrong figures cordially despised one another. Perhaps, then, David's popularity and effectiveness as prefect had been instrumental in the appointment of his younger brother to the post. Parkes himself, perhaps with a nod to humility, attributes his elevation to the departure of all the older boys, but since he surely was not the only sixteen year-old in the senior class, that only begs the question. He also mentions that he had been 'an inoffensive lance-corporal in the O.T.C.' [Officers' Training Corps] and 'a complete little "swot"'.[6]

The current headmaster at Elizabeth helps to contextualize the issue by placing strong emphasis upon Parkes' strong academic record, commenting that 'his surprise would seem to spring from modesty rather than lack of merit'.[7] Although none of the aforesaid fully demystifies the matter, Parkes' emphasis on his 'inoffensiveness' is suggestive. If other potential candidates were associated with one or another rival social cliques, which seems not improbable, then in addition to academic excellence Parkes may have represented a compromise choice.

Had the 'complete little swot' not served as senior prefect, then his inability to maintain a technically decent relationship with the headmaster of Elizabeth College would have been a matter of no special account. However they frequently had to confer and soon were openly antagonistic. Parkes remembers Penney as lazy and, curiously enough, something of a hypochondriac, traits that mirror his father's image of his younger son. At the same time, these represented Penney's view of his young scholar: chronic sickliness easily translates into hypochondria and 'laziness' attached itself to any boy who for whatever reason refused to compete in school games. Parkes' warfare

with Penney adumbrates an aggressively adversarial, even
bellicose, pattern that would assert itself in a number of Parkes'
future relationships with figures in positions of authority in the
military, academe and the Church, many of whom he came to
perceive as undisciplined, negligent or corrupt.

In any event, if the headmaster had believed that Parkes'
accession to power would raise little controversy, he could not
have been more mistaken. Sensing that his young, inexperienced
junior prefects were 'timid in exercising authority' and that,
for some unclear reason, the school was 'visibly disintegrating',
Parkes concluded to his own satisfaction that 'everything
depended upon him'.[8] This was not the last time he would
come to view himself as 'the indispensable person'. Such blatant
immodesty and arrant vanity argue a powerful need for self-
assertiveness and perhaps self-justification. One saving grace is
that Parkes in his seventies clearly did appreciate that his ego-
ridden self-evaluation sometimes rendered the senior prefect
insufferable. Moreover, although it led young Parkes at times to
exceed his authority outrageously, a day would come when his
inflated self-assessment would be apt enough.

Parkes dubs the period between September 1914 and December
1915, when he enlisted in the Army, as 'unquestionably the most
formative' of his life.[9] What he really means is transformative.
Suddenly a new side of his personality had emerged full-blown:
Parkes the martinet. Unused to exercising authority over others,
Parkes recast himself as a robust dictator. The best that can be
said for this taxing period is that it was not very protracted.
Walking the length of the second-floor corridor today, a visitor
passes a gated-off section of hallway that looks as though it
might store janitorial supplies. In Parkes' day this semi-secluded
space served as a kind of pen where, menacingly removed from
public view, younger pupils caught breaking school regulations
were administered corporal punishment.[10]

Transmogrified into a perfect horror, 'refusing to overlook
any breach of discipline', Parkes became 'violently unpopular'
with the other boys. He remarks consolingly,

> My classical and literary scholarship came to my aid, and I
> modelled myself on all the forgotten heroes of literature and
> antiquity. Taking as my mottoes two Latin tags, *Oderint dum
> metuant* – let them hate me so long as they fear me – and

populus vult decipi, decipiatur – the vulgar like to be deceived, deceive them – I sailed into battle with a stern front and panic inside I was determined not to show.[11]

Upon soundly thrashing two sixth formers 'from the city' who had not observed some petty regulation, 'the country boy' triumphantly recalls being held in awe by all the other students. Although in later life Parkes would disavow those Latin tags as his *modus vivendi,* charging into other polemical frays – political, theological and scholarly – he never ceased to model himself inwardly on classical and chivalric heroes.

Just as he strove to outperform his older sibling, then off fighting in foreign fields, Parkes deliberately and decisively distanced himself from his former, weak self. Less openly acknowledged was his desire to supplant David in his father's affections. A further sign of Parkes' embrace of his new persona may be discerned in the tentative, experimental shift in loyalties in the youngster who at one time had yearned to be 'of full Guernsey descent'. Now we hear that 'we were horrible little snobs in the Elizabeth College of those days. We represented very much the English element on the island ...'[12] Elizabeth I surely would have been gratified that, even centuries later, her goal of fostering Anglophilia in her Channel Island possessions was so uncompromisingly in the ascendant in the academy she had established.

Until fairly recently, little marked a true English gentleman more unmistakably than his dexterity with Greek and Latin. Parkes' high proficiency in these tongues strongly reinforced his personal realignment from the 'country boy' to the 'English lad'. As he proudly recollects, he was,

> ... the last boy to receive a full Victorian education in the classics. From the age of thirteen I had only one period a week each of English, Scripture, Essay and History. The whole of the rest of the week was spent in learning Latin and Greek, both of which languages I had, of course, begun well before I was thirteen. When I left I could write Latin and Greek as fluently as I could English ...'[13]

At this juncture in his life, Parkes' latent antagonism towards his father began to attach itself to his headmaster who in telltale ways is portrayed as an alter ego of his hostile father. Henry Parkes, for example, had once been the island's premier promoter of progressive tomato and melon cultivation; William Penney, in turn, had 'once been a brilliant [educational] pioneer', one 'who had stayed on too long'.[14] Of equal significance with such verbal echoes is the vastly disproportionate space Parkes devotes to his running feud with Penney. This confirms that the headmaster bulked very large in the psychic life of the sixteen-year-old prefect serving as a screen upon which the youth might safely project his submerged animosity towards his father.

In sharp contrast, at this time Parkes established the sort of supportive relationship he wished he could have enjoyed with his father with his first form master, Mr Goodman, who appears to have been Parkes' first close adult male companion. Like his student, Goodman was an inveterate collector, and the two of them spent 'many out-of-school hours arranging and classifying his varied collections'.[15] On afternoons after school one can easily envisage the older and younger numismatists seated side by side in Goodman's study, examining and commenting upon rare or curious coins.

Parkes' tense relations with William Penney almost surely provided amusing grist for their social intercourse. Although Goodman sensed the deep-seated tension that prevailed between his late afternoon visitor and his father, it is unlikely that the man was openly discussed. If, however, Henry Parkes was too sensitive a topic for open discourse, sallies directed at the headmaster of the college, the young scholar's nemesis, would have been relatively unthreatening; in fact, as they tenderly sorted and handled Goodman's treasures, it is inconceivable that the two did not exchange wry witticisms about counterfeit, nicked or otherwise devalued pennies.

Parkes also established close relations with William Rolleston, his history master, '… who discovered me one Easter holiday solemnly dusting and cleaning books, and repairing broken bindings. He joined me, and between us we cleaned and catalogued the whole [school] library.'[16] The Elizabeth College library impressively occupies a circular turret high in the central tower of the college and affords a splendid view of St Peter Port in every direction. Many of its volumes are old and valuable. It is hardly surprising that young Parkes was drawn to it. What could be more commendable than voluntarily to devote the

better part of one's holiday to dusting, cleaning and repairing books in the college library? On the other hand, what better
than the image of the orphaned scholar alone in the tower
kneeling over stacks of books, duster in hand, touchingly to
disclose the extent of young Parkes' characteristic solitude and
the full measure of his alienation from the far messier, more
boisterous and gregarious lives of most his schoolmates? No
wonder Rolleston was instantly won over.

In a similar vein, as mentioned earlier, Jimmy and Molly used
secretly to supplement their father's slipshod house work.[17]
Whether in the school library or on the kitchen floor, it is difficult
to imagine sweeping and dusting occupying a place of honour
in the memoirs of any other Englishman of high accomplishment. Even Parkes' protective self-irony does little to disguise
how much these activities betray a striving for, if not an obsession
with orderliness akin to prissiness that he would never outgrow.
Nevertheless, after years of associating almost exclusively with
protective, older women for whom the precocious, mother-
less adolescent exerted irresistible appeal, his friendships with
Goodman and Rolleston, Parkes' first adult male role models,
mark a significant psychological milestone, clearly signalling an
important stage in his maturation.

In addition to forging bonds with teachers, Archie Campbell
and William Spiller now came on the scene. These seem to be
Parkes' first close companions among his contemporaries. They
served their senior prefect well, protecting him from reprisals
from boys he had disciplined and acting as his deputies whenever he was incapacitated by one of his blinding headaches, a
vestige of his vulnerable past that would not stay banished.[18]
Parkes notes that the three friends communicated with one
another by means of telepathy, something he accepts in the
same prosaic spirit as shortly he will exhibit in reporting the even
more extraordinary exploits of 'the Bungalow Ghost'.[19]

So, around the advanced age of sixteen, Parkes abruptly catapulted from a socially dysfunctional caterpillar into something
of a butterfly, one capable of displaying great stores of natural
charm. In fact from this time forth he always seemed able to
attract friends and admirers with relative ease. Now too for the
first time Parkes took a tack that promised not merely to equal
a mark set by his older brother but to surpass it. In 1914 David
had garnered the Channel Island Scholarship to Pembroke

College that has long been annually allotted by Oxford to an Elizabeth College scholar. To Penney's consternation, Parkes now utterly disdained applying for this award; instead, he insisted upon competing for an Open Scholarship to Hertford College. Superficially praiseworthy, Parkes' real motivation did not do him quite so much honour. Not only did he wish to broadcast his real worth as loudly as possible, but, in the disputatious style that would characterize much of his professional life, his real aim was to deflate his headmaster:

> Mr Penney was always boasting that he was a scholar at Hertford College. It was foolish of him to deny that I had brains ... but, as he did deny it, I intended to put before him the dilemma of either stopping to boast [*sic*] of his Open Scholarship, or of admitting my intelligence.[20]

Foolishly, Penney attempted to enlist Parkes' father in a campaign to derail his young scholar's plans, but he blundered when he mentioned that transportation to Oxford to sit for the Open Scholarship would entail an expenditure not easily afforded. This allusion to Henry Parkes' reduced station in life was counterproductive. Not merely insulted, the former agriculturist was also conscious that, if only temporarily, the burden of his son's animus had transferred from himself to Penney. In a rare instance that proved the rule, the father now supported his younger son.

Nevertheless, Penney dug his heels in all the more. Every bit as petty and tyrannical as his senior prefect, he actually forbade the College's classics master, E. W. Hickie, from preparing Parkes for the competitive examination. Especially since Hickie had grown close to Parkes – master and prefect served as President and Vice-President respectively of the School Debating Society[21] – this was an absurd directive which was easily circumvented. In due course Parkes was awarded the first Open granted an Elizabeth College pupil in twenty-five years. Setting a standard for mean-spiritedness, Penney withheld extending congratulations to his school's outstanding scholar until a quarter of a century later when, upon coming across an announcement of Parkes' marriage in an island newspaper, he sent felicitations to his former adversary.

After many months of sparring with Penney and swatting younger scholars, Parkes' long-brewing emotional crisis would no longer be repressed. Midway through his final term at school, the scholarship affair behind him, Parkes awoke one day to discover that his Greek, about which he so proudly boasted, was everything but Greek to him. Discovering his young protégé reduced to gibberish, Hickie called on Christine Ozanne, 'rightly guessing,' Parkes interpolates, that 'my father would have no idea what to do'.[22]

Under siege, in dire need of rescue, Parkes was undergoing a complete nervous breakdown. He himself attributes it to pressures emanating from longstanding hostility with Penney. This is at best a partial, largely self-serving diagnosis. As with John Stuart Mill, an earlier figure famously equipped with a splendid command of Greek and a mother who plays a suspiciously negligible role in his *Autobiography*, surely Parkes' early breakdown may also be traced to a cold, overbearing father and to the painful loss of his mother. In any event, his collapse led directly to the reestablishment of an idyllic ménage consisting of surrogate mother and stationary juvenile. As Parkes recalls, Ozanne first collected her younger friend,

> ... then borrowed a lovely old farmhouse above Petit Bot, installed herself in it, and put me to bed. My memory of what followed is a little vague, and I think I had quite a long time before I was able to get up again; but I spent a very happy convalescence on the cliffs and in the lovely garden of the farm.[23]

The erstwhile senior prefect had been put to bed by his 'cousin'. Parkes' relationship with Ozanne points towards another recurring, psycho-emotional pattern in his life: competitive, even aggressive with men, Parkes characteristically displayed an ingrained passivity in his relationships with women, especially older women by whom he not infrequently contrived to be taken into tow and even, on occasion, put to bed.[24]

Parkes' psychological turmoil is curiously reminiscent of the bibilical Jacob's nocturnal wrestling match with 'the man', or 'the angel' at the River Jabbok. The identity of this contestant is obscure, but it surely encompasses aspects of Jacob's own personality that needed to be confronted and overcome in preparation for his long-delayed encounter with his elder brother Esau, favourite of his father, whom Jacob had slyly supplanted.

At bottom, Parkes' assumption of his brother's roles at home and school together with his provisional appropriation of Penney's despotic, alien personality were simply too much for the young man to accommodate. At the cost of a permanently wounded heel, uncanny precursor of permanent injury to Parkes' foot that would be sustained during the war, Jacob prevailed after one long night of struggle. For Parkes, however, this necessary prologue for breaking through to a higher level of psychological integration would take considerably longer.[25]

Meanwhile, it took many months for the maternal ministrations of 'Cousin' Christine to prove efficacious and for Parkes to recover his health and Greek sufficiently 'to go back to the battle'. The context this time was not his feud with Penney but once again the recalcitrant behavior of the students of 4B 'who were making life hell for their temporary master'.[26] The martial metaphor is instructive, confirming the hypothesis that Parkes' breakdown may be largely attributed to his assumption of an inauthentic, authoritarian personality which, as he admitted, had made him 'violently unpopular'. This pattern prefigures the course of Parkes' future military experience. Moreover, it would not be the last time that Parkes' agonistic proclivities would erupt in inappropriate circumstances.

With uncommon, uncharacteristic insight into himself, Parkes remarks that the effect of his deep, open hostility towards Penney 'did more to let my character develop' than any superficial friendship possibly could have.[27] He does not explicitly pay his father a similar compliment, but in their stubbornness and egoism, William Penney and Henry Parkes were much alike. Each in his own way activated correspondingly unfavourable sides of Parkes' personality. When, for example, the senior prefect found good occasion to whack a scion of the island's patrician Carey clan, he was severely chastised by his headmaster. Decades later, however, Parkes was still basking in the glow of his audacious behaviour, bragging how, when called to account by the headmaster, he had demonstrated that technically he had followed rules formulated by Penney himself. The frustrated headmaster was constrained to concede the point.[28]

The deeper structure of this incident offers a suggestive parallel to an earlier ritual contest and foreshadows Parkes' future path. The prefect canes an insubordinate son of a prestigious island English family. Then, echoing the manner in which Farmer

'A' arraigned before the English bailiff had adhered to a *patois*, which had totally confounded the judge, Parkes bamboozles Penney by demonstrating how he had disingenuously adhered to the precise letter of Penney's own regulations. Farmer 'A' was dismissed; Parkes was exculpated. Like the farmer in his confrontation with 'the judge', Parkes plays the hair-splitting grammarian, or the stereotypical Pharisee and proverbial 'Talmudic Jew', the very role his mature scholarship would rehabilitate with fresh vision and appreciation.

> [The Pharisees] were the sole authentic heirs of the line of development which opens with the Babylonian Exile and the return, and which is still giving the world the worship of the synagogue, church and mosque, the conception (at any rate in the Western world) of the Holy Scriptures, whether Old and New Testament or the Quran, as well as making a substantial contribution to both education and law.[29]

Sharply distinguishing himself from Paul and later classic Christian expositors, Parkes came to roundly respect the Pharisaic method of interpretation and continual reinterpretation of the Law. Was Parkes' skilful appropriation of a prototypical Jewish role in his confrontation with his headmaster, whose ego had prevented him from acknowledging the young scholar's talents, a matter of chance? Rather it perhaps reflected a natural strain of his character and sympathy, one that anticipated his future willingness to reevaluate and revise received Christian wisdom about the supposed self-serving deviousness of the Pharisees.

In the affair of the caning of young Carey we note yet another droll twist. Penney, overcome by 'gargantuan laughter,' adroitly turns the tables on his young adversary: he predicts that the proud scholar 'would in the course of time undoubtedly be hanged,… and that meanwhile I had provided him with perfect material for belabouring the Careys for interference in the just punishment of their wicked offspring'.[30] In effect, the Machiavellian schoolmaster, a survivor of many previous battles, was repositioning himself so as to stand strategically in league with his upstart prefect whose diabolical cleverness he would exploit to fend off the self-righteous interference of island aristocrats.

James Parkes, who matter-of-factly confessed to a belief in powers exercised by Guernsey's ghosts and witches, would hang! This is redolent of the statute from the time of Elizabeth I that would have burned the old *Guernesiais*-speaking lady as a witch. Lying in the balance is whether it would be for his heterodox views and for his stubborn pride that Parkes would be hanged. Either way, Parkes never forgot or completely discounted Penney's heavy malediction.

In fact, Penney has, unawares, presciently linked Parkes both to the messianic principle and its discipular antithesis, the figure upon whom Christian exegetes of the Gospels would project their hatred of the Jewish people for the next two millennia. The tasks of reformulating the former and of demythologizing the latter would preoccupy Parkes for much of his lifetime. There would be times when not a few of Parkes' theological or political adversaries would have relished seeing the fulfilment of Penney's curse. Fortunately, as prefigured in the judicial business of the island farmers, the magistrate would adjourn for a seventy-year recess.

In his own precincts, however, Penney proved correct, but poetic justice may yet defeat his ends. Nowadays, although general awareness of James Parkes at Elizabeth College or elsewhere on Guernsey is virtually non-existent, high on a wall behind a stairwell corridor on the ground floor of the main building of Elizabeth College, among other undusted plaques commemorating the outstanding academic achievement of past Elizabethans, one hangs in obscurity. It declares that James William Parkes was the outstanding scholar of the class of 1914–1915. Occasioned by this writer's second visit to the island, however, a full-page story about Parkes appeared in the island's weekly paper.[31] As far as can be determined, so far these comprise the only tokens of public recognition the world-renowned scholar has been accorded on the island of his birth.

NOTES

1. Robert A. Everett, *Christianity Without Anti-Semitism: James Parkes and the Jewish-Christian Encounter* (Oxford: Pergamon, 1993), p. 2.
2. Nick Machon, *Guernsey As It Was* (St Peter Port: Guernsey Press, n.d.), p. 15.
3. Nick Machon, *More Guernsey As It Was* (St Peter Port: Guernsey Press 1987), p. 8.
4. E. M. Forster, *The Longest Journey* (London: Penguin edition, 1907), pp. 151–230.

5. Keith Bichard in conversation as reported by Philip Rankilor, January 2003.
6. James Parkes, *Voyage of Discoveries* (London: Victor Gollancz, 1969), p. 16.
7. Nick Angell, current headmaster, as reported by Philip Rankilor, January 2003.
8. Ibid.
9. Ibid.
10. Conversation between two senior prefects, the author and Maggie Davidson conducted at Elizabeth College, 1 September 2000.
11. Parkes, *Voyage of Discoveries*, p. 16.
12. Ibid., p. 14.
13. Ibid., p. 13.
14. Ibid., p. 14.
15. Ibid.
16. Ibid., p. 15.
17. Ibid., p. 10.
18. Ibid., pp. 17–18.
19. *Vide* Chapter 8.
20. Parkes, *Voyage of Discoveries*, p. 18.
21. *The Elizabeth Annual*, St Peter Port: 1915, p. 126.
22. Parkes, *Voyage of Discoveries*, p. 19 ff.
23. Ibid.
24. Petit Bot belonged to the Baronne de Coudenhove (aka the painter Elsie Henderson). Like Christine Ozanne, on an earlier occasion La Barronne, almost a decade older than Parkes, had also once 'rescued' Jimmy Parkes from 'being bullied by a damsel at eight or nine'.
25. For Parkes' lifelong identification with Jacob-the-Patriarch, *vide* also Chapters 2, 10 and 25.
26. Parkes, *Voyage of Discoveries*, p. 20.
27. Ibid., p. 19.
28. Ibid., pp. 20–21.
29. James Parkes, *The Foundations of Judaism and Christianity* (London: Vallentine Mitchell, 1960), p. 133.
30. Parkes, *Voyage of Discoveries*, p. 22.
31. Peter Pannet, 'Searching for the Man Who Hitler Feared', *Guernsey Press*, 16 September 2000, p. 4.

8

The Father, the Son and the Bungalow Ghost

A man who wishes his tale believed does himself no service by speaking of the supernatural ...[1]

In 1910 the widower Parkes, strapped for ready cash, sold *Les Fauconnaires* and built a new house for himself and his three children. It was a very different house from *Les Fauconnaires* which, we recall, was gloomy and rat-infested.[2] The family's new home – a sun-swept bungalow – was far less lugubrious, and yet paradoxically it, and not *Les Fauconnaires*, would serve as the backdrop for Parkes' encounters with a rather whimsical ghost. As if challenging readers to make of it what they will, Parkes served up the sequence of episodes that comprise 'The Bungalow Ghost', adapted from a previously published article,[3] as a separate five-page addendum to 'Boyhood in Guernsey'. It is in fact a curious way of dealing with a recalcitrant business.

Without displaying any real awareness of the apparition's significance, without even wondering aloud just why a ghost story should occupy so prominent a place in the story of his life, Parkes details three early, other-worldly appearances out of dozens of sundry manifestations that amused and bedevilled members of his family during two distinct time frames: regularly between 1910 and 1915 and much less frequently from 1919 until a final command performance in 1928. These three episodes repay close attention.

Each supernatural incursion features an 'elemental', a term Parkes borrowed from Elliott O'Donnell, a self-professed authority in the field of paranormal phenomena whose expertise about the causes and taxonomy of spectral appearances Parkes valued highly. According to O'Donnell's handbook,[4] an elemental specializes in impersonation; that is, it plays what appear to be pointless, mischievous pranks upon its victims. Although an elemental may assume a variety of shapes and forms, the 'Bungalow Ghost' took particular pleasure in acting the part of members of the Parkes family. It is clear that Parkes took all of this at face value; we recall that earlier he had laconically confessed his belief in 'ghosts and witchcraft [which] were normal accompaniments of life in the Channel Islands'.[5]

Much of a lifetime spent as a professional historian in no way disabused Parkes of his childhood belief in supernatural manifestations which, in fact, requires no great leap of credibility for anyone with strong religious convictions. Nevertheless, he introduces this most exotic segment of his narrative with a prologue that serves as an apologia for readers of a rationalist turn of mind.

> I am recalling events of forty to fifty years ago, which we never wrote down at the time. But I must in fairness to us all add that we viewed any manifestation of the ghost with the utmost scepticism, cross-examined the member of the family who had heard or seen it, and tried the most far-fetched explanation to discount it ... We were all, every one of us, involved in its visitations.[6]

Striving for verisimilitude, Parkes then adds a detail which, if only marginally, logically weakens the case for the reality of the ghost: 'two of us might hear it at the same time, but I don't remember two of us seeing it simultaneously'.[7]

Aware that for sceptics this diversion will do the rest of his narrative little service, Parkes earlier had already declared himself a lifetime subscriber to the reality of ghostly phenomena. With little to lose, his rhetoric of forthrightness persuades the reader that only truly well-founded instances of incursions by the uncanny could possibly have persuaded him to jeopardize his trustworthiness with further chatter about ghosts. Paradoxically, therefore, the more Parkes dares, the more successfully does he induce a suspension of disbelief.

In *The Turn of the Screw*, published in the year of Parkes' birth, Henry James gives the reader leave ultimately to reserve judgment about the objective authenticity of Peter Quint. Not so for the Parkes' ghost, whose activities extended over a period of eighteen years. The validity of each manifestation, we are given to understand, was addressed from every possible angle by a sternly non-committal family committee that fulfilled its mandate in the manner of a Roman Catholic committee appointed to investigate the authenticity of a 'miracle'. Wherever possible, the Parkeses assigned naturalistic grounds to account for seemingly preternatural phenomena. Only those hard-core instances utterly resistant to rational explanation were declared ghost-driven.

In the initial episode, Parkes reports seeing his father holding a milk can. Dismounting his bicycle, he called out 'All right Dad, I'll fetch the milk', but, apparently not hearing, his father disappeared around the corner of the bungalow. Although the distance between the two should have been easily negotiable, Parkes was unable to move rapidly enough to catch up with this apparition of Henry Parkes. In the second visitation David, upon returning home from school, heard their sister playing the piano from within. When he entered the house, the music abruptly ceased, and the room turned out to be empty. In a final interlude, James returned home from a school play. Upon seeing him by the back door, his father entered the kitchen to make him a cup of cocoa. But the boy was neither in the dining room nor anywhere in the house. In fact, he arrived home half an hour later.[8] Is it not clear that each of these failed encounters reflects estrangement between father and son?

Perhaps because it played upon expectations, hopes or anxieties, a particularly favourite ghostly caper was to impersonate the Parkeses' postman who came to call bearing what seemed to be an encrypted message. Inexplicably, it seems never to have occurred to any of the family members that the spectral postman could have been bearing a message from the recently deceased Annie Parkes. Her son notes,

> Only once did it make our hair stand on end, at tea time on a sunny afternoon. It had successfully deceived all of us, one after another, and our realization that 'we had had the ghost again' was greeted with peal after peal of very unpleasant laughter from the empty field.[9]

One is reminded here of William Penney's collapse into 'gargantuan laughter', and perhaps led to wonder about Parkes' unswerving belief in the power of evil and mockery to impinge upon the everyday world and of the apparent inefficacy of religious faith to counteract them.

We do well to bear in mind that all three of Mrs Parkes'
children were regular churchgoers but rarely as an ensemble.
Whereas David was drawn to St Stephens, which was High
Church, Jimmy 'loved the country parishes',[10] a preference that
in a way prefigured his later appreciation for the democratized,
decentralized structures of mainstream Judaism.

> The nature of the [rabbinic] academy was significant to
> him because it was so unlike the Christian tradition. The
> academy was made up of people from all occupations of
> the community and from all economic classes. There was
> neither professional clergy nor clerical authority. The
> strength of this organizational pattern, Parkes held, lay
> principally in the fact that the affairs of the people were
> discussed and determined by the 'experience of the com-
> munity as a whole'.[11]

Since French-speaking Calvinists generally officiated at most of
these country parishes,[12] young Parkes had to go to considerable
lengths to ferret out an English-speaking rural congregation.

   In the religious sphere, the family's odd man out was, of
course, Henry Parkes. Although some of his forebears had been
Unitarian, on Sunday mornings the declared agnostic engaged
in secular pursuits. Especially when Annie Parkes was still alive,
it is difficult to imagine the children ever directly confronting
their father about his non-belief or that they were ever seriously
affronted by him. Then, almost immediately after her death,
the Bungalow Ghost began its career as family impersonator.
Was this a coincidence? Lacking Elliott O'Donnell's expertise in
spectral phenomena, save to underscore that the ghost's initial appearances coincided with the period when the agnostic
widower would obviously have been most vulnerable to some
sort of spiritual intercession, one can only say that perhaps it was.

   Adopting logical and methodical procedures that would have
recommended themselves to Conan Doyle, the children and
their father, making something of a ritual out of their enthusiastic, exhaustive examination of evidence, viewed each fresh
visitation from every conceivable angle. 'Only if the incident
survived this scrutiny did we put it down to the ghost'.[13] This
meticulous sifting and weighing of available evidence adumbrates Parkes the future scholar: it reminds one of nothing less

than the dispassionate, disinterested tone he adopts in his historical and theological studies. What further seems clear is that the high significance Parkes descries in this eighteen-year 'interlude', implicit in the prominence he attaches to such an extended sidebar, rests little upon a fascination with ghostly phenemona as such.

Compared to Henry Parkes, this show of open-mindedness cost the three siblings little. After all, if on a particular occasion the ghost were declared inauthentic, that meant only that it was 'disqualified' that one time. On the other hand, although it probably went unsaid, each of the four Parkeses surely appreciated that every newly validated ghostly manifestation served to repudiate the cornerstone of Henry Parkes' philosophy. How this professed agnostic squared his rationalism with what increasingly seemed irrefutable evidence of incursions of a ghost into their lives goes unrecorded, but the disparity is so vast and elementary that it could not help being immediately apprehended by the supporting cast of 'dear Watsons'. In short, these doings afforded young Parkes and his siblings repeated opportunity to challenge the world-view of their father. Therefore, although these mock-serious, semi-formal family courts of inquiry were often amusing or even downright jolly occasions, their implicitly adversarial subtext lent them an air of subdued tension.

The publication of the earlier version of 'The Bungalow Ghost' in an island journal sparked an exchange of letters between Parkes and a doctrinaire sceptic named Lambert who, for all one may tell, could have been an 'elemental' impersonating Henry Parkes, some twenty years dead. After an opening volley, Parkes entered the fray with a withering rejection of Lambert's initial hypothesis – that the bungalow might have been affected by the action of tides. Found wanting, Lambert rejoined that earth tremors may have been the true source of the ghost. 'One cannot help feeling that some obscure event triggers off a perceptual experience, and that the "impersonation details" are supplied, unconsciously of course, by the person who sees the apparition.'[14]

To this Parkes parried,

> I regard my hypothetical elemental as being as 'natural' as your 'impersonal causes' in that I regard it as simply a

mental equivalent to the dinosaurs or whatnot in the physical evolutionary process – a failure or misfit which is very likely almost extinct … I suspect such 'misfits' may be becoming rarer … dying out … The idea of an evolutionary misfit seems to me the most natural and reasonable explanation of many stories of angels, pucks, goblins, etc. Some are good, some are bad, some are commonplace. I do not know of any 'scientific' argument which denies the possibility of such an explanation, and I find it more 'scientific' than most of the attempts to explain the manifestation away.[15]

This thrust displays Parkes' polemical metal admirably, both the seductiveness of his measured style and its concealed bite. More pertinent to him than confirming the authenticity of the ghost qua ghost was that the agency of this 'hypothetical elemental' tended to confirm the presence of a 'mental equivalent' or spiritual aspect of reality rather than Lambert's or his father's rigid materialism. Moreover, sixty years after the ghost's retirement, the balance of power had shifted decisively from Henry Parkes to the talebearer, his memoirist son. As much as the ghost's multiple appearances over a stretch of eighteen years, it was Parkes' telling the ghost story in print, first in 1965 and then retelling it in 1969, that yielded him one of his sweetest fruits – a posthumous victory over his father.

Granting that the working premise of an elemental force from the netherworld meddling in the lives of the Parkeses is at least as persuasive as many other explanations, the above hypothesis leads us to suspect a source for those spectral impersonations. Theoretically, it could have been an emanation from Annie. As mentioned above, it is curious that at no point did any of the Parkeses conjecture that she was implicated in the strange happenings at the bungalow or that the ghost might be connected to her untimely departure. Or rather, if any suspicion of the sort occurred to any of the family, in keeping with Parkes' profound reserve about his mother, nothing hints at it. In fact Parkes offers an entirely different rationale to account for those ghostly japes.

One afternoon at tea with Edith Carey, an island historian and pillar of the well-established clan, indeed a stalwart among his brigade of 'aunties', Parkes raised the possibility that the bungalow had been accidentally constructed upon the site of an ancient Celtic cromlech, a tomb or stone circle, 'though there is not the slightest trace of its existence'. He then recounted one of the most recurrent experiences: fearful of cows wandering into the garden, Parkes was awakened one night by the sound of what seemed to be the movement of cows. Realizing that the pasture was empty, he thought at the time that it might have been the wind rustling through the long grass near the veronica hedge. In the end he concluded that it had to have been the ghost as 'footsteps swishing through the long grass were unmistakeable'.[16]

Cross-examined by Carey, Parkes recalled that the falconer's field of Gorseland was called *Le Jaonnêt,* a common name on the island. Checking her 'amazing collection of old island records', Carey discovered that '… in the sixteenth century it was called *Le Jaonnêt du Trepied* – the Gorseland of the Cromlech'.[17] Parkes rests comfortably with Carey's findings, obviously treating them as persuasive. And indeed, if one is not inclined to credit a causal relationship between the recently departed wife and mother and these supernatural happenings, Carey's is perhaps the best of all available explanations to resolve the mystery. Except perhaps for some rural districts of Ireland or the further reaches of the Hebrides, nowhere more in the formerly Celtic British Isles did such a syncretic amalgam of early Christian and pagan belief in the supernatural coexist so congenially as in the Channel Islands.

Equally strange is that Parkes seems never to have made a conscious association between these atavistic, pre-Christian agencies and a number of superstitious vestiges lodged within the fabric of Christian supernaturalism. The legend of the head cloth of Saint Veronica, for example, conflates pagan origins with a medieval overlay. At one point earlier in his memoir, however, he did effect an explicit synapse between the Holy Ghost and the *spiritus mundi.* Recounted presumably as a rollicking example of the misalliance between Guernsey's bilingual cultures, a French-speaking, Calvinist country pastor who was invited to address an English-speaking congregation in St Pierre du Bois parish 'mounted the pulpit and gave out the text: "the Ghost truly is wishful, but the meat is poorly"'. Elsewhere, much restrained, Parkes comments: 'I hope the rest of the sermon kept up the standard!'[18]

With its congenial accommodation to a world-view premised upon the unimpeded immanence of the spiritual world, the special prominence Parkes attaches to the Bungalow Ghost warrants attention from yet another angle. Henry Parkes believed that, at considerable cost, he had secured a corner of a field upon which to build a bungalow free of all feudal entitlements.[19] For Parkes, then, the impersonator's repeated spectral irruptions bespeak a miscalculation, one testifying to the likelihood of a flaw or inadequacy in his father's legalistic mode of understanding. Although the family never could fathom just what the putative Ghost of the Cromlech actually desired of them, it could be said that, rather than having liberated a corner of his field from feudal obligation, Henry Parkes was still unknowingly in thrall to a set of traditional values and obligations that were now demanding their due. The ghost was demanding its equivalent of five chickens and two sacks of corn.

In his theological writings Parkes, a smiling impersonator in his own right behind the pseudonym of 'John Hadham', repeatedly urged Christian thinkers to de-emphasize the Christo-centricity of the Church and to pay greater attention to the other two 'channels' – a term he much preferred to 'persons' – of divine activity.[20] Of course the Holy Spirit, or Ghost, traditionally reflects the third mode of the Godhead, one which Parkes associated specifically (but not exclusively) with the scientific revolution, and the creative spirit of humanism.[21] In the context of Guernsey and in view of the extraordinary prominence of the Bungalow Ghost in Parkes' evocation of his youth, such an interpretation seems rather out of joint. Whatever our private views, if we take Parkes' beliefs seriously, an entirely different dynamic would prevail.

It was suggested earlier that the Old Order on Guernsey appertained to an amalgam of the traditions of the original Norman-French native stock together with agglomerations of medieval atavisms and superstitious appurtenances. The New Order, on the other hand, more narrowly embraced Anglo-Saxon and/or rationalist components. For Parkes religious belief, and in particular his Anglican faith, served to bridge these two domains. Extrapolating from this dichotomy, although as an adult Parkes departed Guernsey and entered upon the world scene, we have already ventured our belief that in the recesses of his consciousness the exotic Norman cultural survival he had observed (aspects of which he had absorbed) later coalesced with a plangent, richer, far more prominent phenomenon: the parallel mystery of the survival of the Jewish people. Not only had both the Norman-French and Jewish cultures survived against all odds into contemporary times, but both peoples, each frequently consigned to oblivion, still displayed remarkable residual vitality. In short, the ground for Parkes' powerful attraction to the Jewish people had been ploughed and sown by his boyhood on Guernsey.

The Bungalow Ghost, an 'elemental' lodged in a subterranean level of consciousness, arose from Old Celtic, pre-Norman origins to haunt the site of a cromlech. However, what in Parkes' boyhood had been 'the Old Order' was itself later supplanted not only by the English ascendancy but by an even more ancient 'order', one that would soon take permanent possession of Parkes' imagination. From this angle, the bungalow, ironically built by an agnostic Englishman, functioned instrumentally as an allegorical representation of the house of Christianity, as the Church still 'haunted' by restive Jewish antecedents and their living descendants: ongoing representatives of an unresolved past that refuse to be put to rest theologically or destroyed utterly by the two faiths that it fathered.

Impersonations, after all, are not merely cheeky jests; they have everything to do with identify and authenticity. To the best of his understanding, Henry Parkes thought he had fulfilled all of the feudalistic conditions governing his land purchase to the letter. This led him mistakenly to believe that he could buy and actually own that cromlech. At least in the early years of the ghostly intromission into their collective lives, the Parkes family in concert exhaustively debated the provenance of each ghostly manifestation, but they never appeared to consider perhaps the most relevant point: the basis of the original land purchase. The ghost might have been implicitly challenging the right of the Parkeses to inhabit its site because, on grounds as intelligible to them as the reasoning of the farmers was for the English magistrates, they were forbidden, unworthy or otherwise incapacitated from purchasing exclusive rights to it.

True, with a single noted exception, the ghost apparently never aimed to frighten the family, an act that might have been directly interpreted as an effort to eject them as interlopers. Nevertheless, the fundamental, indeed the elemental reason memories of the Bungalow Ghost haunted Parkes all his life was his unarticulated but gnawing awareness that the purchase by his father had been misconceived and that the cromlech's original occupants had never acquiesced in their displacement. In a transposed key, Parkes came to appreciate and to advocate the idea that the Church's historic claim of exclusive right to the truth was its original sin, a cardinal error that had engendered terrible consequences. The bill for past payment of chickens and corn was long overdue.

According to Parkes, the ghost stopped appearing in 1928. In July that year Parkes arrived in Geneva to begin a lengthy sojourn working as a staff member of the International Student Service. At an ISS conference earlier that year in Chartres, he had tabled a recommendation that a conference be organized to bring together nationalist and Jewish student organizations that had come to violent blows on campuses throughout the Continent.[22] This proposal represented Parkes' first public involvement with Jewish issues. There is no indication that the 'coincidence' of the ghost's retirement from the scene and of Parkes' 'coming out' on the Jewish Problem ever occurred to him or that he viewed them as linked in any way.

Recalling that Lambert was neither the first nor the last to get bloodied crossing polemical swords with James Parkes, it seems politic not to discount or disparage Edith Carey's explanation, one which Parkes himself implicitly endorsed: the spirit was an emanation from *Le Jaonnêt du Trepied*. Indeed, it carries the seeds of a more adequate solution to the mystery. Let us postulate, however, that those two occurrences of 1928 were in fact connected. Furthermore let us postulate that, in Parkes' subconscious, the years of spectral sightings touched the very same chord that accounted in considerable measure for his extraordinary empathy with the Jewish people. Indeed, in a fashion Parkes' lifelong devotion to the Jewish people can be understood precisely as a displaced repayment of an old, outstanding debt, one he was determined, probably even felt predetermined to redeem. In this case it is entirely explicable why, when Parkes ultimately heeded his inner, inchoate promptings, the Bungalow Ghost declared a truce. Parkes had put paid to its eighteen-year campaign of haunting. It may even be said that, in its way, the ghost had achieved its real objective. Complementing our earlier discussions,[23] Parkes may then be conceived as disposed to empathizing not only with Guernsey's Norman-French but, in his maturity, with the Jewish people, eternal targets of the sort of marginalization and oppression by Christendom that he himself endured as a youngster. This intimate, emotional nexus between Jews and native Guernseyites would permanently mark Parkes' imagination.

Given the space and the opportunity, Jews can and do live out Jewish lives with supreme indifference to the claims or needs of Christianity, but given their origins, Christians can never long remain indifferent to Jews or Judaism. Transposing his inborn deficiency into a new key, prodded by manifestations of the spirit and the spirit world, Parkes set off on an idealistic quest that may be characterized as a pilgrim's regress: Earnest Christian's exploration of the descent of his faith from a minor branch of Judaism. In his early thirties the Nazi menace impelled Parkes to acknowledge, to delve into, and ultimately to re-evaluate, the historic knot of pain and guilt that binds Christianity to its mother faith, Christians to Jews. Along with symbolic pressures exerted by memories of his mother and his original island home, this new awareness coalesced into a tide of admiration and respect for the Jewish people that led Parkes in the end to identify closely with them. In this wise the deep structure under-lying the many appearances of the apparition Parkes called the Bungalow Ghost could well have been instrumental in effecting an algorithmic shift in his way of thinking about the relationship of Christianity to Judaism.

NOTES

1. Peter Carey, *Illywhacker* (London: Faber and Faber, 1988), p. 194.
2. *Vide* Chapter 6.
3. James Parkes, 'The Bungalow Ghost', St Peter Port: *Publication of La Société Guernesiaise*, September 1965.
4. Elliot O'Donnell, *Family Ghosts and Ghostly Phenomena* (London: Dutton, 1934).
5. *Vide* Chapter 1.
6. James Parkes, *Voyage of Discoveries* (London: Victor Gollancz, 1969), p. 26.
7. Ibid.
8. Ibid., p. 27.
9. Ibid., pp. 26–27.
10. Ibid., p. 23.
11. James Parkes, 'Christendom and the Synagogue', cited by Robert Everett, *Christianity Without Anti-Semitism: James Parkes and the Jewish–Christian Encounter* (Oxford: Pergamon, 1993), p. 180.
12. Robert Everett, *Christianity Without Anti-Semitism*, p. 1.
13. Parkes, *Voyage of Discoveries*, p. 26.
14. Lambert, letter to Parkes, 25 September 1965, Parkes Archives, File 60/33/83.
15. James Parkes, letter to Lambert, ibid., October 1965.

16. Parkes, *Voyage of Discoveries*, p. 30.
17. Ibid.
18. Ibid., p. 13.
19. Ibid., p. 24.
20. James Parkes, *God at Work In Science, Politics, and Human Life* (London: Putnam, 1952), p. 64.
21. Ibid., p. 138 ff.
22. Parkes, *Voyage of Discoveries*, p. 111.
23. *Vide* Chapters 3 and 5.

PART 2
WAR AND ITS AFTERMATH

9

To the Front

'Carry on there,' said a young officer at the head of his company. Something in his eyes startled me. Was it fear; or an act of sacrifice? I wondered if he would be killed that night. Men were killed most nights on the way through Ypres, sometimes a few and sometimes many. One shell killed thirty in one night, and their bodies laid strewn, headless and limbless, at the corner of the Grande Place. Transport wagons galloped their way through, between bursts of shellfire, hoping to dodge them, and sometimes not dodging them. I saw the litter of the wheels and shafts, and the bodies of the drivers, and the raw flesh of the dead horses that had not dodged them. Many men who were buried alive in Ypres, under masses of masonry where they had been sleeping in cellars, were awakened by the avalanche above them. Comrades tried to dig them out, to pull away great stones, to get down to those vaults below from which voices were calling; and while they worked other shells came and laid bodies above the stones which had entombed their living comrades. That happened, not once or twice, but many times in Ypres. There was a town major of Ypres. Men said it was a sentence of death to any officer appointed to that job. I think one of them I had met had had eleven predecessors.[1]

In January 1916 James Parkes underwent another sea change: he left off being a schoolboy senior prefect and became a soldier. He exercised little if any choice in the matter. As he informs us, 'the College expected me to join the Army, and told me my scholarship would be kept for me'. We may be certain that his father expected the same as indeed did the young man himself. As Parkes states, he 'intended to join the Army, as all my contemporaries were doing. In actual fact, I do not think that I had ever heard of pacifism or conscientious objection, and had, in consequence, not given the idea any thought.'[2]

At the time, exceedingly few young men of Parkes' generation had ever seriously entertained pacifist ideas. Conformity prevailing in the provinces, it would be a mistake to imagine that in the early months of 1915 it was any different in Oxford.

The city, like the rest of England, was now plastered with
recruiting posters ... and dons and clerics were still doing
their best to justify the War and turn it into England's Holy
Crusade. A pamphlet by Professor Gilbert Murray, called
'How Can War Ever Be Right?' had a good sale and was
discussed with approval, but the pacifist bias which modi-
fied its conclusion that war is occasionally justified was far
from appearing in the belligerent utterances of some of his
colleagues.[3]

Parkes, then, seems to have given no thought to pacifism and
also precious little to what he actually did think about enlistment
and going off to war. 'Patriotism', 'Honour', 'Country' were
virtually writ in gold upon the escutcheon of every public
school in England. For the most part, in spite of those mysterious
early stirrings of political consciousness,[4] Parkes simply fulfilled
expectations and marched off on the heels of his older brother.
    In marked contrast were other voices, representative of a tide
of urgent idealism and genuine youthful passion, here expressed
in a letter from a young man to the woman he was engaged to
marry.

Everything here is always the same. The same khaki-clad
civilians do the same uninspiring things as complacently as
ever. They are still surprised that anyone should be mad
enough to want to go from this comfort to an unknown
discomfort – to a place where men do not merely play at
being soldiers ... It is summer – but it is not war; and I dare
not look at it. It only makes me angry with myself for being
here – and with the others for being content to be here.
When men whom I have once despised as effeminate are
being sent back wounded from the front, when nearly
everyone I know is either going or has gone, can I think of
this with anything but rage and shame?[5]

Parkes, whose matter-of-factness is at such variance with the
importunate tone of anguish expressed above, was assuredly not
tortured by anger, rage or shame. One feels he would not have
objected too strenuously had he been entirely overlooked by the
military machinery. Like the other young man, however, neither
patriotism nor England's Holy Crusade affected his attitude

about going off to war or the prospect of dying in battle. Both responded from a personal perspective. Like some of those alluded to above, feeling himself vaguely effeminate and generally ambivalent about soldiering, Parkes' chief concern was with acquitting himself reasonably well in battle. With his older brother already at the front, Parkes entered the Army unresistingly, determined not to betray inner uncertainties, and all the while fatalistically preparing himself, if perish he must, to perish honourably.

Parkes reports that, with all of Henry Parkes' children in military service, his widower father left the ghost to its playful devices, shut up the bungalow and moved to London.[6] This is somewhat misleading: throughout the war years the bungalow was in fact inhabited by another island family.[7] For its own reasons, the ghost did not bother haunting the new occupants. For the duration of the war Henry Parkes would do his patriotic bit by working for the government as a draughtsman and factory designer.

Looking back, Parkes applies an explicitly Manichaean taxonomy to his Army experiences, recalling them as 'an astonishing series of alternatives of extreme black and white'.[8] Since in time of war popular propaganda relentlessly debases the enemy while simultaneously celebrating its own brave hearts, such one-dimensional thinking is commonplace enough. However, Parkes' *bête noire* was not the German combatant who, in fact, is scarcely mentioned. As with so many soldiers both before and after, the major campaigns of Parkes' war as he remembers it were mounted against the traditional bureaucracy, the encrusted brass and other anti-democratic bastions of privilege and class embedded within the military structure. Again and again he rages against the ingrained, self-serving egoism of Army professionals who exploit their authority to pad their pockets and to cushion themselves from discomfort or serious danger.

One wryly recalls that only a few months before embarking upon active service the erstwhile senior prefect himself, for the sake of maintaining good order, might fairly have stood accused of aligning himself over-enthusiastically with the violent, darker forces of public school repressiveness. Perhaps too generously, this strutting about in the vestments of the schoolboy autocrat may be viewed as an uncharacteristic interlude, a misguided experiment in adult role-playing fuelled mainly by an inner drive to fill his brother's shoes. That it culminated in a nervous break-down argues strongly that the shoes were a tight squeeze, the entire masquerade a temporary aberration. At the same time, his protracted campaign of opposition to the autocratic, small-minded headmaster could be viewed as rigorous training for engaging and triumphing over the many avatars of Penney whom Parkes would encounter during his three and a half years in uniform. Indeed, he himself filed most of his experiences as a soldier as extensions of battles with the lunacy engendered by pennyweight pettiness and egoism.

Ever in pursuit of his brother, Parkes joined David's old regiment. The Artists' Rifles was a unit that attracted public school-boys and men in the professions with whom Parkes always felt most comfortable. His initiation into military life was surprisingly auspicious: although the ferry ride from Southampton to Rouen proved a terrible ordeal for most of the newly recruited Artists, it was not so for the Channel Islander in their midst.

'Being accustomed to being sea-sick, I spent twenty-four hours looking after those who were not accustomed, with the result that I was one of only four who were not sea-sick on the voyage!' Being one of the four who were not sea-sick out of three hundred recruits seemed a meaningful portent to Parkes, so notoriously sickly as a schoolboy. Parkes suddenly stood confidently among the ranks of the strong and healthy, quite capable, he imagined, of surviving the perils of both war and the British brass.

Upon arrival at the quayside of St Omer, Parkes was uncere-moniously thrust back into the ranks of the plebes by a bloody-minded adjutant – the very incarnation of Parkes himself as senior prefect – who greeted the new arrivals in typically 'black' wise: 'You think you are a lot of bloody gentlemen, and I'm a bloody ranker. Well, now you're a lot of bloody privates and I'm your bloody adjutant, and we'll see how you like it.'

Parkes had abruptly rejoined the ranks of the déclassé. After seventeen days of maltreatment, however, he was still holding his own, standing tall among the healthy few: '… we who had been 300 on arrival, were only 146 when we entrained for St Omer, the HQ where the Artists were doing guard duty. Five were dead and the rest in the hospital.'[9]

Five young soldiers had already been fatally wounded while skirmishing in Parkes' other war, the one behind the lines. It strikes a most chilling note. 'Whiter' treatment awaited Parkes and the other 145 survivors in Rouen where a considerate QM permitted the recruits to sort themselves into four companies, and a generous sergeant major distributed ample stores of food from his stockpile. 'If after these two experiences I did not know how to treat men when I myself became an officer, I could have no one but myself to blame!' Here Parkes contemplates alternative models of how to comport oneself in a position of authority, but foregoes no self-criticism about his own recent style of leadership at Elizabeth College.

In 1914 David had served for a time with the Battalion Scouts. Predictably, Parkes was now invited to join the same regiment which, as if he were following a script, he duly proceeded to do. The Scouts were, he noted,

> a picked lot; we paraded quite separately from the rest of the men; did long route marches; became fit enough to do several miles at a double with full packs; trained in map reading, sketching and other special competences – and, alas, became expert navigators of the canals round St Omer in the heavy canal boats of the region.[10]

A familiar, deep-seated ambivalence informs the above. Although Parkes ever fancied himself an enemy of unearned privilege and a champion of the oppressed, at the same time he took no small pride in being asked to join 'a picked lot'. Throughout his life he would accept the prerogatives usually associated with class as his proper due. While disporting himself as a kind of natural aristocrat, Parkes' broader, democratic sympathies were accommodated as a superior form of noblesse oblige which tempered an unaddressed, never resolved conflict between Parkes' personality and his conscience. This papered-over polarity from time to time erupted into small crises that periodically triggered nervous breakdowns.

Parkes' brilliant start as a soldier ran into a serious snag at a St Omer café popular with his elite unit. A waiter served him with *un citron au vin blanc* diluted with untreated canal water. He fell dangerously ill, and was immediately sent to hospital where he remained for three months, his condition complicated by the effects of a recent inoculation against typhus. 'All the glands of my neck and head swelled up until I could not open my mouth ... I more or less lived on aspirin and three daily doses of medicine.'[11]

Raised a teetotaller, the future fancier of rare and pricey vintages claims that, until informed by an amused nurse, he was entirely unaware that his chief medication consisted of slugs of straight port. The interlude felt like a regression to his boyhood bouts of infirmity and weakness that would be followed by extended periods of recuperation. In fact, it became the prototype for the forty odd months of Parkes' career as a soldier.

Notwithstanding the restorative qualities of the remedy, Parkes underwent what sounds like a devilish time in the army hospital. Denied nourishment until his condition could be diagnosed conclusively – an exercise at which three doctors laboured fruitlessly for three weeks – the regime almost did him in. 'On the whole I was much more nearly killed by the RAMC than I ever was by the Germans.'[12] This blackish spell serves Parkes as a handy example of the inflexibility of Army regulations and the military's intrinsic incapacity to question, reevaluate or reinterpret procedures that may once have served a purpose but later entail more harm than good.

This period of hospitalization, the first of many,[13] constitutes a standing indictment of uncritical reliance on cumbrous traditions. Traditionally, in contrast to the mode of thought characteristic of Jesus, Christian exegetes have labelled this sort of inflexible thinking 'Pharisaical'. Remarkably, no hint of such tendentiousness distorts Parkes' mature thought. Instead, turning this potentially pernicious association on its head, Parkes developed a warm appreciation for the analytical methodology practised by the Pharisees in the Talmud. In the future Pharisees will be displaced from their conventionally reactionary niche by Parkes' hidebound opponents within the Anglican hierarchy. This is prefigured in this period of his life by his confrontation with 'pharasaical', narrow-minded, self-serving military apparatchniks.[14]

Later that spring Parkes convalesced in high style for three months at Maxstoke Castle in Warwickshire as the houseguest of the Reverend David Lee-Elliott, a newly acquired friend. The contrast to wintering at the muddy front in Flanders could not have been greater. It recalls Parkes' idyllic convalescence on the magical island of Sark when he was twelve and again later in his teens, after his nervous breakdown at Elizabeth College, of his willing enthralment to 'Cousin' Christine in that 'lovely old farmhouse above Petit Bot'. In doing battle with the world's ills, whenever he physically or emotionally overextended himself, Parkes – handsome, precocious, highly intelligent – was adept at attracting somewhat older and well set-up protectors and rescuers.[15]

With Guernsey inconveniently distant and the bungalow rented to the West family, Parkes spent most of his short leaves at fourteenth-century Maxstoke, with its sixteen staircases and nineteen bedrooms, as Lee-Elliott's guest. Unsurprisingly Parkes' romantic sensibility found it 'an enchanting place', a country seat that fairly resonated with the aura of the Middle Ages.[16]

The idyll soon faded, however. In the summer of 1916 Parkes was ordered to Denham where he joined the Officer Cadet Battalion and afterwards transferred for training to a former staff college at Camberley, not far from Sandhurst. His clearest memory of this period occurs when his commanding officer's wife, a distant cousin, invited him to tea. Never really well off, Parkes was well connected. In December he was awarded his commission and was attached to the Queen's Royal West Surrey Regiment.[17]

> A few weeks later the Devil came to Ypres. The first sign of his work was when a mass of French soldiers and coloured troops, and English, Irish, Scottish and Canadian soldiers staggered through the Lille and Menin Gates with panic in their look, and some foul spell upon them. They were gasping for breath, vomiting, falling into unconsciousness, and, as they lay, their lungs were struggling desperately against some stifling thing. A whitish cloud crept up to the gates of Ypres, with a sweet smell of violets, and women and girls smelt it, and then gasped and lurched as they ran and fell.[18]

After crossing to France, Parkes' regiment advanced first to the abominable 'Bull Ring' at Etaples, then to a village in the southern sector of the infamous Ypres Salient. In the depths of that miserable winter of 1917, Parkes was quartered about ten miles south of Paschendaele.[19] Here, although each of the other young officers shared 'a batman', Parkes manoeuvred to obtain one exclusively for himself, a dependable older soldier who, he figured, could do with a lighter job. Grateful to his young officer, Sergeant King would serve Parkes loyally and efficiently.

Anyone who has ever been in combat would readily confirm that those days, months or years remain etched indelibly in one's consciousness. Occasionally misplaced, they are never dislodged or truly forgotten. The recollections of battle cited above, however, do not issue from Parkes' pen. Dating from March 1915, two years before Parkes himself was dispatched to virtually the identical sector, they were recorded by a distinguished journalist of the period. But why the necessity to resort to a surrogate for a taste of Parkes' battlefront experiences? The Guernseyman himself provides an answer: 'The life of an infantry subaltern in the Ypres Salient has been described so often,' he remarks with studied casualness, 'that I have nothing fresh to add to it.'[20]

This reticence is uncharacteristic. Parkes mentions the endless staircases and bedrooms of Maxstoke Castle in detail, yet, presumably to save his readers from the tedium of *dejà vu*, every trace of his months at the front is suppressed or expunged, as if they had no real bearing on the man he would become. Of course, it is not inconceivable that the seventy-three-year-old memoirist really felt he had nothing fresh to add to the myriad personal accounts of the boredom, the fighting and the dying in the trenches. But one wonders how he could simply skip over those four months when agony, horror and self-sacrifice comprised his daily fare. Surely those images left lasting impressions, possibly untreated wounds that festered in the psyche of the twenty-year-old officer. Did he imagine that his readers would be incurious about his feelings, uninterested in his thoughts and uncaring about his performance under fire? It is insupportable that Parkes truly concluded that all of this was of little significance and would be of little or no interest to his readers.

In addition to the heat, fear and gore of actual battle, Parkes also chose not to delineate how his war experiences confirmed, shook or otherwise affected his belief in God or in Christianity, a singular omission. Was Parkes' response as a man of faith to the wartime butchery curiously muted? This is conspicuously at odds, in fact, with what we encounter in the revulsion and confusion of many other sensitive young men who went marching off to battle as Christian soldiers.

> God and Christianity raised perplexities in the minds of simple lads desiring life and not death. They could not reconcile the Christian precepts of the chaplain with the

bayoneting of Germans and the shambles of the battlefield. All this blood and mangled flesh in the fields of France and Flanders seemed to them – to many of them, I know – a certain proof that God did not exist, or if He did exist was not, as they were told, a God of Love, but a monster glad of the agonies of men.[21]

Parkes would have us infer that his inner confidence in the relevance of Christianity was never seriously buffetted by the enormity of waste and the pointlessness of the sacrifices that he encountered daily. But perhaps his stubborn refusal to replay his life in the trenches reflects just the opposite. Perhaps under constant assault his faith in the edifice of Christianity had indeed wavered. Under the circumstances, who would cast any blame? For Parkes, however, such a dose of doubt and uncertainty could well have precipitated an emotional or psychological collapse. This perhaps enables us not to accept but at least to grapple intelligently not only with what, as we shall see, may fairly be characterized as Parkes' abnegation at the front but also, sixty years later, with his egregious evasiveness with his pen. Had Parkes confessed that his faith had teetered even momentarily, it would have helped us to comprehend just how and why he later never directly addresses 'the perplexities of [other] simple lads' in trying to square Christian precepts with the reign of the bayonet.

Another noteworthy omission in his account of front line service is any reference to the disturbing physical and emotional detachment of Anglican chaplains from the heat of the battle. The war's most famous English-language chronicler of the butchery in the trenches was born barely a year before Parkes, a brief gap that translated into nearly two additional years of slogging in the trenches. As before, it falls to Robert Graves,[22] Everyman's normative guide to the thoughts and feelings and doubts and failings of soldiers of the Great War, to introduce what must have been for Parkes a deeply troubling moral concern. From every angle, the Church of England did not have a good war.

For Anglican regimental chaplains we had little respect. If they had shown one-tenth the courage, endurance, and other human qualities that the regimental doctors showed, we agreed, the British Expeditionary Force might well have started a religious revival. But they had not, being under orders to avoid getting mixed up with the fighting, stayed behind with the transport. Soldiers could hardly respect a chaplain who obeyed these orders, and yet not one in fifty seemed sorry to obey them. Occasionally, on a quiet day in a quiet sector, the chaplain would make a daring afternoon visit to the support line and distribute a few cigarettes before hurrying back ... Sometimes the Colonel would summon him to come up with the rations and bury the day's dead; he would arrive, speak his lines, and hurry off again ... The colonel in one battalion I served with got rid of four new Anglican chaplains in four months; finally he applied for a Roman Catholic, alleging a change of faith in the men under his command. For the Roman Catholic chaplains were not only permitted to visit posts of danger but definitely enjoined to be wherever fighting was, so that they could give extreme unction to the dying. And we never heard of one who failed to do all that was expected of him and more.[23]

The abjectness of an Anglican chaplaincy that studiously avoided coming under fire was particularly galling when contrasted to the unhesitating risk-sharing of the Catholic priesthood. If not outspoken at the time, should Parkes not at least have noted the dereliction later? Yet, as if it never registered, this future Anglican cleric lets it all pass without comment. Later in life, of course, Parkes not only confronted pusillanimity and wrong-headedness within the Anglican clergy but impatiently scoured long-sanctified errors from Christian doctrine. This early, wilful silence bespeaks the distance Parkes had yet to traverse before he had fashioned a mature, self-confident Christian faith, one capable of not flinching when struck full in the face by inconvenient truths. It conveys a sense of wordless shame and a deep embarrassment.

Judging from the dozens of anecdotes and episodes recounted elsewhere in his memoir, it is a virtual certainty that had Parkes scored any notable coups at the front or somehow distinguished himself, we would have heard about it. In the end, the curtain of silence that Parkes drops over the Ypres Salient is not merely vexatious but profoundly telling. One concludes that his profession of solicitude for his reader's need for novelty conceals considerably more than he cares to admit. This black hole, raising the suspicion that his reluctance to recall events or feelings afresh cloaks shafts of squeamishness, embarrassment or possibly even shame, will be addressed in the next chapter.

> I think the worst time was after the counter-attack, when we lay in that trench all day surrounded by the dead. I still had Longstaffe by my side, though his expression changed after death. The look of surprise faded. And we listened to the wounded groaning outside. Two stretcher-bearers volunteered to go out and were hit as soon as they stood up. Another tried later. After that I said, 'No more, everybody keep down.' By nightfall most of the groaning had stopped. A few of the more lightly wounded crawled in under cover of darkness and we patched them up as best we could. But one man kept on and on, it didn't sound like a human being, or even like an animal, a sort of guttural gurgling like a blocked drain.[24]

Finally, an illuminating approach to the Parkes' psyche under stress may be gleaned from poet Charles Simic's childhood memory of a school trip to a museum in Belgrade where he viewed an exhibition of photographs of atrocities.

> As terrifying as the details were, they tend to blur in my mind except for a few details. A huge safety pin instead of a button on the overcoat of one of the victims; a shoe with a hole in its sole that had fallen off the foot of a man who lay in a pool of blood ... it was like seeing hard-core pornographic images for the first time and being astonished to learn that people did such things to one another. I could not talk about this to anyone afterward.[25]

Traditionally, young manhood is tried in three arenas: the playing field, the battlefield, and the bedroom. All are stages where performance is sorely tested and critically evaluated. None of these are arenas wherein Parkes could really distinguish himself. What Simic underlines is that unbridled violence and sexuality may be viewed as correlative excesses, that brutality may be subsumed as a type of pornography or debauchery. Later Simic alludes to a book of photographs of the First World War compiled by a German photographer. It depicts '... wrecked and plundered churches, obliterated villages, torpedoed ships, soldiers in death agonies, corpses putrefying in heaps, close-ups of soldiers with huge facial wounds ...' [26]

It is of course understandable that, while peering out from the corner of the eye, one should wish to avoid gazing directly upon such lurid images. However, to shut the door so resolutely upon the scenes of war and battles in which one has been engaged seems of a piece with the unacknowledged prudery that Parkes prefers to disown. Though not brooked by Parkes, we dare not scant it. No less than the minute recording of the past, the silences speak both loudly and eloquently.

NOTES

1. Philip Gibbs, *Realities of War*, Vol. I (London: Hutchinson, 1938), p. 87.
2. James Parkes, *Voyage of Discoveries* (London: Victor Gollancz, 1969), p. 30.
3. Vera Brittain, *Testament of Youth, An Autobiographical Study of the Years 1900–1925* (London: Virago, 1978), pp. 126–27.
4. *Vide* Chapter 1.
5. Brittain, *Testament of Youth*, pp. 125–26.
6. Parkes, *Voyage of Discoveries*, p. 25.
7. Ibid., p. 53.
8. Ibid., p. 31, ff.
9. Ibid., p. 32, ff.
10. Ibid., pp. 32–33.
11. Ibid., p. 33.
12. Ibid.
13. *Vide* Chapter 11.
14. *Vide* discussion of Parkes, *Jesus, Paul and the Jews*, in Chapter 23 and John Hadham's BBC religious broadcast in Chapter 25.
15. *Vide* Chapter 7, Endnote 23.
16. Parkes, *Voyage of Discoveries*, p. 34.
17. Gibbs, *Realities of War*, pp. 83–84.
18. Parkes, *Voyage of Discoveries*, p. 34.
19. Ibid., p. 35.
20. Ibid.
21. Gibbs, *Realities of War*, p. 131.
22. *Vide* Chapter 2.
23. Robert Graves, *Good-bye To All That* (New York: Anchor, 1989), pp. 189–90.
24. Pat Barker, *The Ghost Road* (New York: Dutton, 1995), pp. 194–95.
25. Charles Simic, 'Archive of Horror', *New York Review of Books*, Vol. L, No. 7, 1 May 2003, p. 8.
26. Charles Simic on Ernst Friedrich's 1924 Collection *Krieg dem Kriege!*, Ibid., p. 9.

10

Overdose in the Trenches

A hundred years ago, his grandfather had volunteered and been shipped out to France with his regiment. A year or two later he had come back, invalided with trench foot. Absolutely nothing of his time there had survived ... And this lack of the slightest souvenir was complicated by another layer of mistiness, of concealment. He knew, or thought he knew, or at least had believed for half his life, that his grandfather would talk freely about his enlistment, training, departure for France, and arrival there, but beyond this point he would not, or could not, go on. His stories always stopped at the front line, leaving others to imagine frantic charges across the cloying mud towards a merciless greeting. Such taciturnity had seemed more than understandable: correct, perhaps even glamorous. How could you put the carnage of that time into mere words? His grandfather's silence, whether imposed by trauma or by heroic character, had been appropriate.

But one day, after both his grandparents were dead, he had asked his mother about her father's terrible war, and she had sapped his convictions, his story. No, she had said, she didn't know in France where he had served. No, she didn't think he had been anywhere near the front line. No, he'd never used the phrase 'over the top'. No, he hadn't been traumatized by his experiences. So why, then, did he never talk about the war? His mother's answer had come after a lengthy pause for judgment. 'He didn't talk about it because I don't think he thought it was interesting.[1]

James Parkes served in Flanders from January until early June of 1917. During his final weeks at the front he assumed command of his company '... for the simple reason,' he states matter-of-factly, 'that I was the only officer still alive'.[2] This self-deprecation reminds us of Parkes' disingenuous comment when he was selected as senior prefect: 'all the older boys had left to join the Army'.[3] In this present circumstance, however, it cost Parkes something to admit, if only implicitly, that his tardy elevation to a command post actually did attest to his superiors' low evaluation of his leadership skills. One senses that, like the smallest kid on the block who is the last one selected when a group of boys choose sides to play a street game, it was no accident that Parkes was, of all the officers in his unit, considered a last resort.

In this context games are suggestive, reminding us that 'the only officer still alive' was merely months away from the frequently sick and bed-ridden swot, the loner who avoided boisterous antics and all contact sports. True, Parkes was skilled in attracting the sympathetic attentions of his elders, whether artistic 'aunts', bachelor teachers, or hearty ministers. Yet his military career, which had commenced on a floodtide of good health and high spirits, very soon turned dodgy. Parkes understood that a combination of martial prowess and selflessness were the qualities needed to inspire others to charge unhesitatingly, again and again, into the shadow of the Valley of Death. Although the imagination of the boy growing up on Guernsey had gorged on virtuous and just knights battling the foe, the gap between the idealized self-image he had nurtured and the figure he actually cut as a commanding officer caused Parkes considerable anguish. An unbridgeable gap yawned between the knowledge and the performance.

Little if any blame accrues to this. Upon considering the pervasiveness of the disorder, the confusion and the carnage, the very ordinariness, futility and normalcy of the violence especially after the passage of almost a century we do well to pause long and hard before casting any aspersions upon a combatant who distanced himself from what Robert Graves tersely designated 'all that'. Nevertheless, perhaps too cosily for his own self-esteem, it appears that shortly after his elevation to new responsibilities, Parkes manoeuvred to temper his anxieties in the way he knew best: by reassuming the all-too-familiar role of the convalescent.

At least in part, Parkes' want of ability as a field commander may be attributed to over-habituation to the pleasures of his own privileged company; he was too aloof, too self-contained, too much the would-be gentleman, and surely too prissy to be really admired and fully respected by his men. It was not that Parkes could not or did not respond to the suffering of his troops or earn a measure of their affection. As one observer put it: 'What an Englishman is hopeless at, but James Parkes was good at, is putting himself in the place of someone else: principally Jews in the case of Parkes.'⁴ But all that still lay ahead, in the coming years of the decade when his affective life would ripen markedly. Meanwhile, coiled like a restless serpent within was the unspoken source of his turmoil.

A stunningly handsome subaltern named Geoffrey, a 'reticent idealist with visions of a clerical career', makes a cameo appearance in one the most enduring memoirs of the war. 'He hated war, and though the role of a poor curate would probably have made him as happy as anyone of his Franciscan temperament could be in a materialistic and self-seeking world, as an officer with the trenches in prospect he became uncertain of his own courage and felt profoundly miserable.'[5] Parkes rings true to type save that, unlike Geoffrey, for the most part he grimly concealed his inner apprehension and his fear of disgracing himself. At the front when he was not too exhausted to think at all, these insecurities and anxieties haunted Parkes' waking hours far more than the fear of dying.

That the 'swot' did not command his men with panache or the sublime brilliance bred of hundreds of hours of adolescent imaginings was a disappointment, but that is not to say that he did not perform dutifully. A brief, sardonic jotting alludes, for example, to how he did not win a Military Cross for his exploits on 'an immensely successful trench raid in which we captured a loaf of bread with only about 80 casualities'.[6] Like Geoffrey, however, Parkes was not a natural leader on the field of battle, something his men and his superiors sensed instinctively. We look again to Robert Graves for a measure of further insight into what Parkes himself perceived as a failing.

While convalescing from a severe case of bronchitis in hospital in Oxford, Graves recalls that he sorely missed the company of his comrades at the front and felt guilt and ambivalence at being separated from them. The affection that welled within him at the very thought of them was irrepressible and transparent. In contrast, when in the latter half of 1917 Parkes was convalescing in the rear, nothing of the sort was said. Later, in March of 1918, after Parkes had been permanently reassigned in England, the German 'Great Push' began along the entire front in Flanders. Augmented by a thirty per cent increase in forces transferred after the collapse of the Eastern Front in the wake of the Russian Revolution, the Germans temporarily engulfed Allied positions in the Ypres Salient where Parkes had served and his brother had been killed.[7] Parkes in England fixedly averted his gaze from images of the battlefield and, from all the evidence, restricted his thoughts to immediate tasks at hand.

We may infer further Parkes' standoffishness from another of

Graves' tableaux: a brothel used by soldiers in Bethune, outside the Ypres Salient.

> The Red Lamp ... was around the corner in the main street. I had seen a queue of a hundred and fifty men waiting outside the door, each to have his short turn with one of the three women in the house. My servant, who had stood in the queue, told me that the charge was ten francs a man – about eight shillings at that time. Each woman served nearly a battalion of men every week for as long as she lasted. According to the Assistant Provost Marshal, three weeks was the usual limit: 'after which she retired on her earnings, pale but proud'.[8]

Graves pauses to describe the queue at The Red Lamp not because he himself was a habitué. Quite the opposite; even when on leave in England, the future devotee of goddesses did not attend dances, flirt, or sleep with available young women. Neither did he so comport himself with available young men. As he explains, in his fashion he was exercising fidelity to one of the younger boys at Charterhouse School to whom he had a sentimental attachment. While in Flanders, Lieutenant Graves ' ... was always being teased because I would not sleep even with the nicer girls; and I excused myself, not on moral grounds or on grounds of fastidiousness, but in the only way that they could understand: I said I didn't want a dose'.[9]

It is quite impossible to imagine James Parkes taking his place in a queue of a hundred and fifty at the sign of the Red Lamp or his coming down with a dose of the clap. When he too was baited for his abstinence, as he must have been, Parkes surely expounded upon sexual restraint as a moral choice rather than as a prophylactic expedient. In fact, as recollected by Parkes in his retirement, not the faintest scent of prurience attaches itself either to his schoolboy exploits or to the recreational choices of the young subaltern on leave behind the lines. To all intents and purposes, he could have been a monk. It is not very remarkable that Lieutenant Parkes was elevated to a front line command only *faute de mieux*.

He could not have helped but notice that others cut in his mould had indeed risen to the occasion, risen ... and fallen. In sum, we conclude that Parkes' truncated, hermetic version of the life of an infantry subaltern in the Ypres Salient issued far less from solicitude for his reader than from a gnawing awareness of his youthful inadequacies and a powerful resistance to under-mine or destabilize the terms of the truce he had long ago reached with himself. The core of the issue is not modest self-effacement but disinterested self-appraisal. It is manifest that Parkes performed his routine military duties meticulously, but, as we shall see, no more than most young men was he particu-larly well suited to play the hero, to inspire flagging troops, or to execute his part as commanding officer of troops under fire with special flair. His time of heroism would come, but only later and on an entirely different field of honour. Like his namesake and alter ego, the wily young Jacob in the Old Testament tales he heard as a child, James would first have to confront and vanquish his ghosts.[10]

Before we presume to pass critical judgment upon Parkes' performance under fire, it behoves us to refamiliarize ourselves with just how ghastly normalcy in the trenches really was. Extensive citation is mandated precisely because Parkes chose not to recall, replay and relive scenes of the injured, the dying and the dead. Contextualization, in short, is absolutely essential.

> We went up to the corpse-strewn front line. The captain of the gas-company who was keeping his head, and wore a special oxygen respirator, had by now turned off the gas-cocks. Vermorel-sprayers had cleared out most of the gas, but we were still warned to wear our masks. We climbed up and crouched on the fire-step, where the gas was not so thick – gas, being heavy stuff, kept low. Then Thomas arrived with the remainder of A Company, and with D we waited for the whistle to follow the other two companies over. Fortunately at this moment the Adjutant appeared. He was now left in command of the Battalion, and told Thomas that he didn't give a damn about orders; he was going to cut his losses and not send A and D over to their deaths until he got definite orders from the Brigade. He had sent a runner back, and we must wait.
> ... My mouth was dry, my eyes out of focus, and my legs quaking under me. I found a water-bottle full of rum and drank about half a pint; it quieted me and my head remained clear. Samson lay groaning about twenty yards

beyond the front trench. Several attempts were made to
rescue him. He had been very badly hit. Three men got
killed in these attempts; two officers and two men wounded.
In the end his own orderly managed to crawl out to him.
Samson sent him back, saying he was riddled through and
not worth rescuing; he sent apologies to the Company for
making such a noise.

We waited a couple of hours for the order to charge. The
men were silent and depressed; only Sergeant Townsend
was making feeble, bitter jokes about the good old British
Army muddling through, and how he thanked God we still
had a Navy. I shared the rest of my rum with him, and he
cheered up a little. Finally a runner arrived with a message
that the attack had been postponed ... At dusk we all went
out to rescue the wounded, leaving only sentry in the line.
The first dead body I came upon was Samson's, hit in seventeen places. I found that he had forced his knuckles into his
mouth to stop himself crying out and attracting any more
men to their death ... We spent all that night getting in
the wounded ... The Germans behaved generously. I do not
remember hearing a shot fired that night; though we kept
on until it was nearly dawn and we could see plainly; then
they fired a few warning shots, and we gave it up.[11]

Whether eloquent, tactical or shameful, an accurate record of
the past must pay heed to Parkes' silences. Even decades after
the war, upon hearing the wife of a close friend mention that
her father had served in the trenches as a seventeen-year-old
German infantryman, Parkes turned sullen. 'The horrors of
the war,' she continued, 'were with him still, and he still had
nightmares.' She could, of course, have been describing Parkes
himself. While guarded, his response was revealing enough: 'I
don't want to talk about any of that because if I do I won't sleep
tonight.'[12]

Anyone attempting to take the measure of the man has
forfeited the prerogative of not talking about all that. To review,
during the first half of 1917, Parkes served in the trenches of the
Ypres Salient. It was a period of nightly attrition, periodic
military feints, general deadlock and increasing tension. Neither
the British nor the Germans would launch a significant attack
until the final weeks of spring, some time after Parkes had

assumed a command position. What was the general military situation? Beginning on 21 May, a major British advance was preceded by a heavy nightly bombardment that aimed to soften the German lines. On the 7 June the Second British Army under General Plumer launched an assault at Messines Ridge from the southern end of the Ypres Salient, the very sector where Parkes was stationed. The bombardment intensified after 7 June. Plumer's attack would be one of the few clear-cut British victories of the entire war,[13] but Parkes did not take part in the assault because by the end of the first week of June, he had already been evacuated.

Having soldiered at the front long enough to have borne laconic witness to the death under fire of all the other subalterns in his regiment, Parkes had outgrown his initial eagerness to tread in his brother's footsteps, a trail he now knew led to near-certain death. In his final weeks as commanding officer, Adjutant Parkes had certainly been informed that preparations were underway for an imminent major offensive. On or around 21 May, he was exposed to mustard gas which initially went undetected. Some days after returning from the line, while on parade Parkes suddenly went blind.[14]

Unlike chlorine, which was introduced by the Germans in 1915, or phosgene, its successor gas of choice, mustard gas is almost entirely odourless. First used in 1917, it causes both internal and external blistering. Because of the increasing effectiveness of protective procedures, however, by the time Parkes reached the front mustard gas claimed far fewer casualties than it had in the first years of the war. 'Even so, gas victims often led highly debilitating lives once they were discharged from the army.'[15] That Parkes' sudden blindness occurred several days after his exposure suggest he received a relatively mild dose of gas. Nevertheless, rather puzzlingly at first, he was evacuated from the front and then moved from hospital to hospital. He ended up in hospital in London during the zeppelin raids of the autumn of 1917 and was never shipped back to France.

As well as causing temporary blindness, Parkes' small dose seems also to have conveniently blinded him to some of his own motivations. Perhaps he had good grounds for not recollecting them in detail more than fifty years later, but he certainly cannot be accused of examining them in depth. We never learn, for example, whether Parkes, self-described as a 'half-way pacifist',[16]

ever fired his rifle with the intent to kill, whether he did in fact
ever kill anyone, or whether this was an issue of conscience at
all. What we do learn is that, along with the light case of mustard
gas poisoning, Parkes suffered not from the light but respectable
wound for which many soldiers on the line nightly prayed but
from a different and notoriously debilitating infirmity. As though
it had slipped his mind, Parkes neglects to mention until later
that a case of trench foot contributed to his removal from the
front line.

It is only when he recalls being admitted for treatment in a
hospital in Britain that Parkes remarks, 'during my time in the
Ypres Salient I had once spent a week in water without taking
my boots off. When I took them off at last, I took most of the
skin of the soles of my feet with them.'[17] In consequence, in one
foot Parkes developed an unusual, incurable condition known as
Dupuytren's contracture which is often hereditary and generally
attacks its victim's palms and fingers.[18] In the middle of an operation to relieve the excruciating pain of the contracture, Parkes
actually 'died' under general anaesthesia. He revived only when
towels dipped in boiling water were flicked all over his body.[19]
Upon his recovering consciousness, the attending doctor spoiled
Parkes' 'rebirth' by crassly sharing the intelligence that '... he
couldn't possibly live more than three years'. Parkes claims that
he paid little heed to this jaundiced prognosis, but in fact it left
an indelible impression; in the coming years he referred to it on
more than one occasion.[20]

Given the clammy condition of the Allied positions, trench
foot was endemic:

> Because the enemy was on the high ground, and our men
> were in the low ground, many of our trenches were wet
> and waterlogged, even in summer after heavy rain. In
> winter there were bogs and swamps ... The enemy drained
> his water into our ditches when he could, with the cunning
> and the science of his way of war, and that made our men
> savage.[21]

Nevertheless, like frostbite, trench foot is eminently preventable.
In no way could it be viewed as the equivalent of 'an honourable
wound'. Graves speaks of it thus:

In a good battalion … men were bent on going home either with an honourable wound or not at all. In an inferior battalion, the men would prefer a wound to bronchitis, but not mind the bronchitis … In a really good battalion, like the Second when I first joined it, the question of getting wounded and going home was not allowed to be raised. Such a battalion had a very small sick list. During the winter of 1914–15, the Second reported no more than four or five casualties from 'trench feet' [*sic*], and in the following winter no more than eight or nine; the don't-care battalions lost very heavily indeed.

'Trench feet' seemed to have been almost entirely a function of morale. It occurred in spite of the formulaic lecture NCOs and officers repeated time after time to their troops: Trench feet was not caused by tight boots, tight puttees, or any other clothing calculated to interfere with the circulation of blood in the legs. Trench feet was caused, rather, by going to sleep with wet boots, cold feet, and depression. Wet boots, by themselves, did not matter. If a man warmed his feet at a brazier, or stamped until they were warm, and then went to sleep with a sandbag tied around them, he took no harm. He might even fall asleep with cold, wet feet, and find that they had swelled slightly owing to the pressure of his boots or puttees; but trench feet developed only if he did not mind getting trench feet, or anything else because his battalion had lost the power of sticking things out.[22]

'… Going to sleep with wet boots, cold feet, and depression' – Graves writes with considerable authority on the matter. So what might one make of Parkes' temporary oversight, his telling neglect even to mention the onset of trench foot at the time of his evacuation? Plainly he would have us infer that the exigencies of beastly weather, rotten terrain, horrific front-line duty and the 'normal' bloody wartime contingencies of command conspired to keep him on his feet or, at least, in his wet boots for days on end, that is, his trench foot was an understated, permanently painful emblem of devotion to duty under hellish conditions. Given Parkes' strong sense of responsibility and a history of working himself into a state of exhaustion, this sounds plausible enough until we recall that it is inconceivable that Adjutant James Parkes was uninformed about the perils of trench foot or that he could have forgotten the conditions leading to its onset.

We already know that the British offensive in Parkes' sector of the front did not commence until 7 June. Especially during a protracted attack, one well might imagine that free moments to attend to one's person would be hard to come by. However by 7 June Parkes had almost certainly already been evacuated. He had served as the commanding officer of his unit in the trenches during a period of merely 'routine' horror and misery. This was ghastly enough, what with the relentless round of nightly patrols, nocturnal shelling, and, worst of all, the screams of the wounded begging to be rescued or, more likely, put out of their misery. All this was certainly agonizing to supervise and to endure, but still the mystery abides. Could it be that Parkes' dedication to duty and his men was so exhaustive and exhausting that in the course of a full week he could not dutifully spare fifteen minutes in order to remove his boots, to massage and to warm his wet feet? Upon considerable reflection, one concludes that such blatant absentmindedness seems out of character and is, on balance, improbable.

Hence, self-reproach and a shaky conscience almost surely play major roles in accounting for the opaque curtain that Parkes drapes over his four months on the front lines. Furthermore, deep-seated ambivalence over his performance as a combat officer best explains why, in recounting the events leading to his evacuation to England, he spotlights a relatively minor dose of gas poisoning, a passing condition, rather than trench foot, which led to a far more disabling and long-lasting one. The mother in the above epigraph was either mistaken, or she was protecting her father, the narrator's grandfather, from disgrace. Parkes did indeed contract trench foot while serving in the perpetually damp trenches, but at the same time is it far less likely that he thought the fighting 'uninteresting' than that something happened that he would rather obliterate from memory.

To reiterate, like untold thousands of combatants, James Parkes left the front lines in psychological distress, emotionally scarred and in severe physical pain, but he did not, at least not in the customary sense of the word, ever sustain a wound. That he suffered all his life from bad conscience about equivocal aspects of his wartime service is underscored by the manner in which he permitted it to be described for consumption back at home: 'No. 3121, Parkes, James William ... Brother of No. 3099 ... Served in France 1916–17. Wounded. Medal, Victory Medal.'[23]

This misrepresentation of his wartime affliction would persist: in accounts appearing in both Guernsey dailies a few years later, a passing reference to Parkes' military service mentions again that he had been 'wounded' in the war.[24] Since Parkes was out of the country at the time, it is clear that the source must have been his father. At worst, the falsification may be viewed as harmless, a mild distortion which could only have been of marginal interest to other readers of those papers. However one conjectures that, upon Parkes' return to Guernsey, nothing struck him quite as forcibly in those newspaper accounts than that 'mild distortion'.

By the time Parkes served as a commander in the trenches, he had borne witness to the deaths not only of many of the troops whom he had commanded but also of every one of his predecessors. Given the execrable conditions, the toll on his nerves was incalculable. Graves lays special emphasis upon the ubiquity of depression and the low morale among many of the front-line units. It is probable that, in addition to severe pain from his physical afflictions, Parkes suffered from frayed nerves, if not full-blown depression. This hypothetical 'half-way pacifist' may once have imagined himself as a dashing knight; however, with his history of constitutional debility, including a number of physical collapses and at least one complete nervous breakdown, is it surprising that after several months in the trenches Parkes reached the point when he inwardly knew all too well that he could not carry on any longer as the commanding officer of his company?

As mentioned above, in the same year that Parkes was evacuated to a hospital in London, Graves was hospitalized in Oxford. Upon the latter's release, he too was permanently reassigned. Unlike Parkes, however, Graves could state openly what Parkes had suppressed: he 'liked to believe that [he] would still be alive when the War ended'.[25] Of course Parkes shared this sentiment, but now there was no 'saviour' in the form of Christine Ozanne or the Baronne de Coudenhove[26] to come to his rescue. Given the meaninglessness and absurdity of the wholesale slaughter in the trenches, one concludes that in desperation Parkes decided to save himself by acting on his own behalf. He would, of course, never bring himself actively to desert his post, but could he not passively cooperate with circumstances that would lead in time to his evacuation? Like Hemingway's *Tenente* Frederic Henry, like so many others, first in his mind and then with his feet, James Parkes too bid a private farewell to arms by breaking his appointment with an early death. At the point when he reached his limit, he acquiesced to a ready means of opting out. Given that the trenches were little more than a charnel house, who could condemn him outright for choosing to live?

In sum, it would be not merely unsympathetic but entirely unjustifiable to state as a conclusive fact that Adjutant James Parkes contracted a case of trench foot as a well-considered tactic in order to have himself shipped off the line. On the other hand, it does not seem unreasonable to surmise that, with a considerable degree of awareness, Parkes sensed an opportunity and, notwithstanding inner qualms, in the end embraced it. Colluding with his physical infirmities, he seems to have acquiesced to coming down with trench foot, one which for the rest of his life would serve, both physically and psychologically, as an equivocal, chronically painful emblem, in part of inadequacy and self-betrayal but in equal measure of the life-force. Even though the memoirist in his seventies circumvented testifying directly about his experiences under fire, he could scarcely have repressed the knowledge that it was his 'dose of trench foot' that almost certainly saved his life.

NOTES

1. Julian Barnes, *Cross Channel* (London: Picador, 1996), pp. 205–206.
2. James Parkes, *Voyage of Discoveries* (London: Victor Gollancz, 1969), p. 35.
3. Ibid., p. 16.
4. Colin Richmond, 'Parkes, Prejudice, and the Middle Ages', in *Cultures of Ambivalence and Contempt: Studies in Jewish–Non-Jewish Relations*, eds Jones, Kushner and Pearce (London: Vallentine Mitchell, 1998), pp. 225–26.
5. Vera Brittain, *Testament of Youth, An Autobiographical Study of the Years 1900–1925* (London: Virago, 1978), pp. 202–203.
6. Taken from the back of a photo of Parkes' Commanding Officer along with 'This is the man I won the MC for', Parkes Archives, File 60/34.
7. B. H. Liddell Hart, *The Real War, 1914–1918* (Boston: Little, Brown, 1930), p. 388.
8. Robert Graves, *Good-bye To All That* (New York: Anchor, 1989), p. 122.
9. Ibid.
10. *Vide* Chapter 7.
11. Graves, *Good-bye To All That*, pp. 157–59.

12. Ruth Weyl interviewed by the Author and Maggie Davidson in Rehovot, Israel, 26 October 2003.
13. Liddell Hart, *The Real War*, pp. 330–31. Albeit to a lesser extent than General Edmund Allenby, another British military hero of the First World War, Plumer is better remembered in Israel than in Great Britain. Between 1925 and 1928 he served as Palestine's third high commissioner, and a prominent square in Jerusalem is named in his honour.
14. Parkes, *Voyage of Discoveries*, p. 35.
15. Michael Duffy, 'Weapons of War', website for *First World War*, April 2003, p. 5.
16. Parkes, *Voyage of Discoveries*, pp, 40–41.
17. Ibid., p. 39.
18. 'Trench Foot', website of *Indiana Hand Center*, May 2003.
19. Parkes, *Voyage of Discoveries*, p. 39.
20. James Parkes in a letter to Margaret Bell, a cousin, 1978, Parkes Archives, File 60/16/52.
21. Philip Gibbs, *Realities of War*, Vol. I (London: Hutchinson, 1938), p. 78.
22. Graves, *Good-bye To All That*, pp. 172–73.
23. *Elizabeth College Register*, edited by Brigadier General D.H. Drake-Brockman, Volume II, 1874–1911, St Peter Port: The Star and Gazette, 1931, p. 268.
24. *Guernsey Star* and *Guernsey Evening Press*, St Peter Port: 29 April, 1935. Also *vide* Chapter 20.
25. Graves, *Good-bye To All That*, p. 245.
26. *Vide* Chapter 7, Footnote 23.

11

Down the Rabbit Hole

The attitude to gas has changed. It's used more and feared less. A few of the men are positively gas happy. OK, they think, if a whiff or two gets you back to the base and doesn't kill you, why not? It's become the equivalent of shooting yourself in the foot and a lot harder to detect.[1]

In hospital, Parkes had time enough to reflect upon his inglorious deliverance from the jaws of death. After retracing David's footsteps first as senior prefect and a holder of a scholarship to Oxford, then as a member of the Artists' Rifles and the Battalion Scouts, like his brother he had found himself fighting in the trenches of Flanders. At some point during the autumn of 1917 Parkes received official notice that Captain Theodore David Parkes, dispatched to France in the early months of the war, had fallen in battle on 5 October in Polygon Wood.[2] Five miles south of Paschendael and five miles east of Ypres, this is the area where Parkes had been gassed earlier in the year. Except for passing mention, and that out of its time frame, Parkes' memoir does not allude to his reaction upon learning of the fall of David Parkes in battle, a telling omission one might be tempted to attribute to the restraint or self-discipline natural to the British character. More relevant, however, was probably its intimate association with a personal dereliction so long hidden from light that Parkes chose to keep it under wraps.

While lying on his back during that painful period of recuperation, Parkes ruminated endlessly upon his months at the front. When not performing his round of duties creditably enough fighting off fatigue, that he might follow his older brother into an early grave must have clouded his every waking moment. Yet, looking back, this Anglican cleric never recounts that he rendered thanks to his Creator; nor did this brilliant classicist praise Tyche or Fortuna; nor did this agnostic's son acknowledge the actions of Providence. How could he have been so unreflective?

Parkes, in short, was conscious of having acted surreptitiously. While at times feeling guilty for merely being alive, at other moments he appeased his conscience with the soothing rationalization that he had done his best, that all men had a limit and that he had reached his. In his obituary notice, David Parkes was remembered as 'one of the most popular Elizabethans of recent years'.[3] Even discounting the latitude extended to eulogists, one credits its general validity and senses all the more that a similar encomium would not have been composed about his younger brother.

On release from hospital, Parkes was posted to Sittingbourne, a huge base that accommodated three principal groups of officers: the permanent party, those in training for front-line duty, and their counterparts – those who had for a variety of reasons been reposted from the Continent to England.[4] Whereas the outgoing contingent felt they were marked for early death – a depressingly just assessment – those plucked whether for well-earned or equivocal reasons out of harm's way were acutely conscious of enjoying a reprieve. In transit, they were like voyagers on escalators that noiselessly glided in opposite directions. Descending or ascending, doomed or saved, the passengers could have reached out and touched those passing on the adjoining track; but each of these ghostly bands remained starkly ephemeral for the other. Such was the etiquette that prevailed in this purgatorial way station. As for Parkes, just as he expresses no rancour towards the Germans who gassed him, neither does he evince compassion for the poor souls slated for slaughter.

Instead, as if overcompensating for the niggardliness of his recollections of actual combat, in recounting his experiences in the rear he becomes positively profligate. His animus against that third echelon at Sittingbourne, the permanent party that supervised the flow of human traffic to and from the zone of death, is untempered by the passage of time. Indeed, as with repetitive tales typically told by garrulous old soldiers, while the telling may be cathartic, the listening can be stupefying. Parkes resurrects a series of incidents principally in order to excoriate 'an utterly detestable upper crust of individuals ... few of whom had been to France, and who monopolized all the extra-pay positions in the battalion without either the will or the competence to do any of the work for which extra pay was intended'.[5]

There is no reason to doubt his testimony that 'all the training work of the battalion was done by temporary officers like myself; none of us ever got promotion, and, even when we were offered staff jobs (as we were, for we were an efficient lot), "they" usually managed to have them cancelled'.[6] Such compulsive grousing, the raw, undigested stuff of Parkes' real campaigns, matched the feckless, hollow, small-minded brass against the dutiful, devoted, deserving staff. However, unlike the routine, fatigue, boredom and gore in the Salient, which finally undid him, at Sittingbourne Parkes found himself on a field of battle upon which he could perform with high distinction. He labelled this behind-the-lines conflict as the war of 'black versus white', that is, a metaphorical chess game. These mock-epic battles comprise the fodder for Parkes' private stock of 'war stories'.

Enthusiastically immersing himself in his new duties, Parkes performed so well in the Northern Command Gas School's anti-gas training course that he was temporarily attached to the Brigade Gas School. This was presided over by Captain Trend, a rare exception to the general run of incompetents Parkes encountered on the home front and one of the exceedingly few for whom he has a good word. His frank admiration was reciprocated. When Trend officially requested that the young officer be attached to the regular staff, however, his order was countermanded by Parkes' commanding officer, the very incarnation of the petty-minded Penney who once had forbidden the classics master to tutor his insubordinate senior prefect. Were Parkes even to communicate with Trend, he was informed, the young second lieutenant would be subject to arrest.

As in similar skirmishes, Parkes proved crafty enough to uncover means to thwart whatever he considered unjust, 'blackish' designs upon his interests. When Trend himself was appointed adjutant, Parkes, though among Sittingbourne's most junior officers, was parachuted ahead of others to become his successor as the head of the Gas School. There he forged a working staff consisting of two assistant gas officers, four to six NCOs, and some 'store men' into a highly competent team capable of effectively training three to four thousand men at a time.[7] Parkes takes justifiable pride in his long hours, devotion to detail and pedagogic originality, the same triad of qualities he would exhibit in post-war years as an activist in international student organizations. Reminiscent of his untold childhood hours spent sculpting castles on the beaches of western Guernsey, for example, he took great pains to enliven his lectures by using scale-model reconstructions of the terrain of Flanders. However he does not recall that his zeal in the performance of his duties bore a subterranean connection with the salving of a wounded conscience.

In spite of his excellent performance as a gas-officer, Parkes soon discovered that an assignment in the rear areas was something like falling down the rabbit hole – everyday logic was illusory. Entitled to a captaincy by virtue of his level of responsibility, Parkes was frozen in his second lieutenancy '… while a totally inefficient and unqualified captain played bridge and billiards with the colonel, wore the green tabs, and enjoyed the extra pay'.[8] Parkes scorned the games and the players at Sittingbourne as much as he had at Elizabeth College. His outrage over the inequity of his situation was rivalled only by his resentment at the loss of the extra pay, something that mattered to the young officer who, not for the first time in his life, was conscious of feeling 'poor'.

One might perhaps feel tempted to sympathise. However at the very time when across the Channel hundreds of thousands were being butchered, Parkes' groans and remonstrations about mistreatment soon become exceedingly tiresome. It is also worth recalling that although Parkes' adversaries – the bridge and billiards set – actually were empty vessels of privilege and idleness, Parkes himself was not averse to comfort or privilege; he relished, for example, his periodic sojourns under the leisurely eaves of Maxstoke. Futher, while it is undeniable that most of Parkes' superiors do seem an altogether reprehensible lot, at the same time Parkes' self-satisfaction with his own awesome competence and superior abilities are off-putting. His smugness constituted a standing challenge to his superiors. In Sittingbourne he was a recalcitrant Alice negotiating the hills and dales of Wonderland. It was neither the first time nor, one hastens to add 'Thank God', would it be the last that he would not or could not simply 'get along'.

In good time the vagaries of Army regulations would permit the aggrieved Guernseyman a measure of personal revenge:

> [It was] the spring of 1918, at the time of the breakthrough which brought the Germans almost to the coast. I was

working fourteen hours a day, often training and fitting men by moonlight, when I succumbed to the influenza epidemic. There was nobody available to take my place for I alone of my staff was entitled to certify that a man was fully trained ... I sometimes had to lecture three hours on end with a temperature of 104. When I was not lecturing, I was carried out to my parade ground where I would have anything up to twenty squads doing different training.[9]

Acting strictly by the book, the medical officer pronounced that he could not render treatment until Parkes was properly put to bed, a directive the colonel was of no mind to issue. 'By the second week I was in a lovely mental condition. The gas-officer remained 100% efficient. The personal "me" was completely delirious.'[10] In this feverish state Parkes, in front of the assembled troops, berated a major who had had the effrontery to trespass on his parade ground. If he were not to cashier his invaluable gas officer, the colonel was driven to interpret Parkes' audacity as a sign that he had lost his senses and therefore indeed should go on leave the very next day. But this was far too long for Parkes to wait. Throwing the colonel a jaunty salute, he smartly pivoted and marched right out of sight.[11]

In this lively recollection, Parkes portrays himself as being as stiff-necked and daft as the colonel. With a temperature of 104, he could simply have reported himself ill. Instead, even if it meant his death, he would inflict 'revenge' upon the system which had deprived him of rightful rank and pay. At the same time it had extended him immunity from retribution through a 'Mock Turtle' technicality: as the only official gas officer, he alone was authorized to certify trainees. In short, the infuriated colonel positively required the services of his insubordinate subordinate. Parkes was of course fully aware that he was insulated from serious reprisal.

Moreover, one cannot overlook the fact that his position afforded him a number of highly desirable perks. During that spring and summer of 1918, for example, he enjoyed 'weekends in the gorgeous Kentish countryside, often ending up with a Sunday in Canterbury Cathedral'.[12] Although Parkes does not directly allude to Thomas à Becket, so prominently depicted in the stained-glass windows of the edifice that drew him repeatedly to the first seat of Anglicanism, the theme of martyrdom powerfully echoes his indulgent appraisal of his own position versus vested authority throughout this period. Later on, the dedication of England's first popular saint to the highest ideals surely fortified a tendency toward self-sacrificing idealism that the young lieutenant would manifest upon returning to civilian life.

In the end, Parkes was constrained by poor health reluctantly to reject his belated appointment to the post of commanding officer of the gas school and the rank of major. After nine months of duty as gas-officer – the average tenure was only four – many hours in the testing chamber had overexposed him to chlorine which in turn led to a violent attack of dry pleurisy. This time the medical officer insisted not only that Parkes resign his post but also that he reject two subsequent, attractive-sounding offers of postings to even damper climates. Eventually, a more suitable assignment did come through, and Parkes made his escape from the topsy-turvy regimen of blackish Sittingbourne.

Quite ill upon arrival at his new post in the 'bracing climate of the East Coast', Parkes was met with a firm, friendly handshake. He had 'again passed from a black to a white'.[13] In civilian life his new adjutant, Captain E. S. Hall, was a distinguished architect, a profession long close to Parkes' heart. Hall reciprocated Parkes' admiration and appointed him his assistant adjutant right from the start. Rather than playing cards or billiards, Hall and his staff spent their duty time helping to resolve difficulties of soldiers under their command. Parkes wondered how to account for such obvious 'whiteness'.

> My first Sunday morning, when I went to the 8 o'clock service in the great parish church of Lowestoft, I discovered part of the answer. The Second-in-Command, the Adjutant, most of the Battalion Orderly Room, several of the Company Commanders, and a fair sprinkling of NCOs and privates were all regular communicants.[14]

It is understandable, under the circumstances, that at the time Parkes felt he had discovered 'the answer'. However it is a little unnerving that not an iota of irony borne of later experience colours his explanation.

Unexpectedly finding himself in a congenial milieu, Parkes was then confronted by a new kind of challenge. Although as a result of his Dupuytren's condition he still could not walk without intense pain, the Colonel insisted that Parkes accompany him as a mounted officer on his rides. In spite of his upbringing as a countryman, Parkes avers he had never mounted a horse in his life, a seemingly dubious claim until we recall just how sickly he had been as a youth. Yet, just as on his first Channel crossing Parkes turned out to be an unexpectedly fine sailor, so he now proved to be a natural equestrian,[15] in a way this was only appropriate for the future Christian knight errant.

Parkes was ultimately placed in charge of the sensitive and complicated task of transferring men to other Army units and, later on, of demobilization. As he was intensely aware, being an Oxford scholar he himself qualified for one of the highest priorities for early discharge; but Parkes acceded to Hall's plea that he first complete his assigned task. At the very of the end of the war, long after Hall's release from active service, the long-languishing Parkes, finally elevated to an adjutancy, would still be on active duty.

It was in his new capacity that Parkes pulled off a caper that still warmed his heart many decades later, a more telling tale than he seemed to realize. When the Commanding Officer of Company A took a month's leave on urgent private business, he prevailed on Parkes to assume command in his absence. In the following episode, Parkes plays the judge. A sick soldier who should not have taken a walk before eating breakfast had fainted. Unaware that Parkes was acting in both of his capacities – as adjutant and as temporary commanding officer, hence technically his own superior – the medical officer issued a complaint about the neglect of the CO. Parkes then proceeded to compose,

> ... a very aggrieved letter to myself as adjutant, regretting Private X having fainted, but protesting that I could not be held responsible. I then returned to the orderly room, wrote to myself and accepted my explanation. That done I replied to the MO, requesting him 'before he made such serious complaints against my officers, to pay more attention to the facts'.[16]

As if a generation of soldiers had not been slaughtered wholesale just across the Channel, Parkes' recollections of his military years once again shifted to the farcical key of *Catch-22*, or Lieutenant James Parkes versus the bureaucratic blackguards. This anecdote also transports us back to the innocent world of French-speaking litigants testifying before befuddled Guernsey magistrates and of Parkes' hoisting Penney on his own legalistic petard. Such rhetorical razzle-dazzle was the very stuff of Parkes' whimsical mental universe wherein he was the cleverest man in Christendom. It also points in the direction of Parkes, the future admirer of proto-Talmudics. Like an underground operative, Parkes was now deeply embedded within the interstices of a system that, while he lambastes it mercilessly for its inherent creakiness and corruption, is one that he learned to play to his own advantage for all it was worth.

A final example of his capricious idealism: in 1919, when the Provost Martial Office covertly urged Parkes to be 'quicker with courts martial … since a conviction would mean a consider-able economy to the country' (those convicted forfeited their military bonuses), Parkes disdained to act as an accomplice to injustice. In fact as a 'magistrate' he chalked up a perfect record: not one single conviction.[17] Of passing note: it was at this point in addition to witty sallies that Parkes also composed his first article. Like the memoir that would be published precisely fifty years later, 'Demobilization' resolutely turned its back upon scenes of war and the slaughterhouse that was Flanders.[18]

Thereafter Parkes suffered yet another physical collapse, this time from the aftereffects of cumulative exposure to gas. Upon recovery, having completed his assigned task with such admir-able thoroughness that, conscience laved, he felt he could retire honourably from the field, Parkes upgraded his own personnel folder to a category that he rightly anticipated would presently lead to his own demobilization. Who could blame Parkes for taking pride in his Colonel's final evaluation? 'Mine was the only form in which he had said that one of his officers was capable of rising to any rank, that he was a good battalion officer, and that he could also rise to any rank in staff work.'[19] It was a just but also highly ironic judgment. Beyond his sensitivity to injustice, Parkes' sense of the ridiculous was far too developed for him ever to have survived in the regular Army. His evalua-tion safely in hand, 'before [the] astonished eyes of the demobilization officer' Parkes himself signed the rest of the requisite forms.

After more than three years in uniform, in the spring of 1919 Parkes returned to civilian life. From his army years he reports retaining two lifetime habits: poking his toes out of the bottom of the bedclothes and shaving in the tub. More rewarding was a third habitual activity which he would cultivate and enjoy for the rest his life: like both of his parents and his Aunt Annie (his father's eldest sister), he had developed into a skilled draughtsman. Filling many sketchbooks when he served in France and Flanders, he grew adept at sketching views of the countryside, houses, churches and villages. Spicing his artistic pursuits was an awareness that depicting 'military terrain' in such manner was strictly forbidden.

In the end, the schematic, Manichaean dichotomy of 'black and white' governing Parkes' remembered account of his army years served as a paradigm for many future confrontations with various ecclesiastical, social service and academic bureaucracies. When earlier in life he had crossed lances with Penney, he had been energized primarily by an acute sense of his own intellectual worth. Aside from expiation, in the army the dominant motivating impetus was more a need to align himself with the forces of rationality, justice, fairness and simple decency. Militarist and patriotic cant are conspicuously absent. Nothing better enabled Parkes to think well of himself than to dissociate himself from the institutional bridge and billiards set and, within calculated limits, to expose and defeat them. This went far to prepare him for the main mission in his life: the struggle against institutional Christianity's vitriolic attitude and historical acts of injustice perpetrated against the Jewish people.

Within a week of his re-entry into civilian life Parkes, who was always pleased to call himself a Guernseyman, had returned to his native island. It lay, he imagined, as distant as possible from the cruelties perpetrated by the Queen of Hearts at the front or the rationalized inanities of mad tea parties in the rear areas. He was out of harm's way, but after more than three years in uniform, readjustment to the rhythms of civilian life took time. Understating his emotional distress and psychological imbalance, Parkes remarks,

I was in no state to go straight to Oxford when I was demobilized. I spent a long and lazy spring and summer at Maxstoke and in the Island, spending time in both Jersey and Alderney, and building up a collection of pastels of the cliffs, bay, and old forts and castles of all the islands.[20]

This lyrical, recuperative interlude, much occupied by sketching and the re-establishing of ties with old friends was not unalloyed. Carefree hikes along the island's pathways and shoreline could no longer be undertaken spontaneously on his sensitive feet. Moreover, Guernsey turned out to be more of a combat zone than he had anticipated – his long-simmering troubled relations with his father were unresolved.

The reunited but much-diminished 'Parkes family' shared quarters in the reoccupied bungalow, leaving the tenants, 'who had looked after it during the war, in possession of the kitchen and the rooms at the end of it in return for Mrs West doing the cooking for us'.[21] Although 'bungalow' evokes an image of snugness, in fact this left the Parkeses with a drawing room and no fewer than five bedrooms. This certainly sounds like quite enough space in which two adult men might knock around without colliding. However when James proposed combining two of the rooms into one larger space that might serve as a sitting room, he and his father clashed.

> My parent was completely uninterested in anything but the cheapest and most efficient way to get a required result. Shelves were cheaper than chests of drawers or cupboards. Linoleum was easier to sweep than carpets – and so on. His lack of interest in possessions extended to any possessions I was rash enough to leave at home while I was at Oxford. I was a born collector, but was likely to find he had given away books or other things I had acquired on a previous vac. This was particularly trying with old family possessions.[22]

One of the heirlooms in which Parkes had invested particular sentiment was an Irish damask tablecloth. Upon discovering it in his absence, his father cut it up into tea and floor cloths. His father's insouciance with possessions and his galling lack of respect for his wishes, vexed Parkes greatly. This rudeness said less about Henry Parkes' general attitude towards material possessions than his low assessment of a son who could never replace in his affections the one who had fallen in the trenches of Flanders. More than by the supporting details, the depth of

Parkes' acrimony and estrangement is pungently conveyed by his chillingly impersonal labelling of his father as 'my parent'.

Suddenly, however, as if newly realizing that rehearsing a bill of indictment of the sins of his long-dead parent would not redound to his credit, Parkes strains to recall at least a few of his father's attainments: in his day Henry Parkes had been a composer of amusing limericks, some of which had been collected and published. (In fact his grandfather, the civil engineer, had also produced similar sorts of books.) Predictably, this line of propitiation soon sputters to a halt when, as Parkes damningly recollects, after he had 'with considerable difficulty' gathered together all of his father's and grandfather's books, while he was at Oxford his parent 'had burnt or given away the lot, as he wanted the space to keep tools in!'[23]

Young Parkes could not elude the horns of Joseph Heller's catchy dilemma merely by flushing himself out of the bowels of Wonderland. When living at Oxford, Parkes masochistically persisted in 'testing' his father by periodically 'forgetting' to take one or more of his treasured possessions back to college. It was a game James Parkes could neither lose nor 'win': confirming expectations, Henry Parkes, destroying or disposing of anything and everything left by his son, came out 'black' every time.

NOTES

1. Pat Barker, *The Ghost Road* (New York: Dutton, 1995), pp. 180–81.
2. Commonwealth War Graves Commission, website, spring 2003.
3. *Guernsey Evening Press*, St Peter Port, 13 October 1917.
4. James Parkes, *Voyage of Discoveries* (London: Victor Gollancz, 1969), p. 35.
5. Ibid.
6. Ibid., pp. 35–36.
7. Ibid.
8. Ibid., p. 37.
9. Ibid., pp. 37–38.
10. Ibid., p. 38.
11. Ibid., pp. 38–39.
12. Ibid., p. 40, ff.
13. Ibid., p. 41.
14. Ibid., p. 42.
15. Ibid., p. 43.
16. Ibid., p. 45.
17. Ibid., p. 47.
18. James Parkes, 'Demobilization: The Situation Made Clear', *Punch*, 26 February 1919.
19. Parkes, *Voyage of Discoveries*, p. 51.
20. Ibid., p. 53.
21. Ibid.
22. Ibid.
23. Ibid., p. 54.

12

'Holy James' at Oxford

Nearing twenty-three, in October 1919 Parkes embarked upon his war-delayed undergraduate education at Oxford. The impact of a war in which millions of soldiers and civilians had been mindlessly slaughtered was incalculable. If for many too old to have fought themselves the pre-war social order seemed still intact, in fact it was a cold simulacrum, a husk whose inner kernel had shrivelled. The vital centre had sustained a crashing blow, coming undone for those whose belief had been shattered. Virtually everyone of Parkes' generation shared a strong consciousness that the First World War marked a watershed. Its self-confidence blasted, the pretensions of European, Christian civilization to superiority were exposed as hollow.

At the same time, those who had 'come through' viewed themselves as the last and the best of 'the old school', superior beings who loved virtue, ethics and the classical heritage and who aimed for the highest standards of achievement. Unlike a great many of his peers, Parkes had also been sustained by a religious faith that somehow had survived the war intact. On the other hand, he sensed acutely that if it were to be relevant in the establishment of a new and better world order, this faith would have to be thoroughly examined and probably reconfigured so as to yield new and relevant answers.

Oxford braced itself to absorb this high, perhaps battering tide of former soldiers eager to reconnect with their interrupted lives. The ancient seat of higher learning bulged with over four thousand undergraduates, many of whom didn't readily brook traditional sources of authority. In that first peacetime year, the prevailing atmosphere on the campus was markedly sober. What had been a carelessly privileged bastion of prankish and cranky high Victorianism before the war now sustained a more straitened and bracing atmosphere.[1] Hertford, one of the smallest colleges with little more than a hundred students, managed better than most to retain a semblance of pre-war collegiate intimacy.

The hearty intellectual appetite of the former soldiers in no way translated into servility. On the contrary, a democratic spirit of self-assertiveness soon prevailed. Parkes, for example, was not considered notably eccentric when he informed scholars E. A. Burroughs and J. D. Denniston that, feeling no urgency to prepare for exams at the moment, he wanted 'to work at things that interested me for their own sake'.[2] Notwithstanding inner reservations, the two tutors accepted Parkes' prescription without demur.

Parkes offers no overview of generational dissonance or of the unsettled cultural climate at Oxford nearly as graphic as Graves provides. Presenting a broader perspective, however, and on the whole a more compelling picture of transitional earnestness vying with traditional campus quietude, was a woman returnee from four years of war on the Continent:

> The swarming male undergraduates varied in type from the ex-officers ... on shortened courses who were determined to have a good time and forget, to the small but very articulate group of young writers such as Edmund Blunden, Charles Morgan, Louis Golding [and] Robert Graves ... who were seriously analyzing the effect of the War upon themselves and upon their world. Between these two extremes, large numbers of exhausted ex-soldiers pursued their War degrees with the dull-eyed determination of tired brains ... Whatever their type, one and all combined to create that 'eat-drink-and-be-merry-for-to-morrow-we-die' atmosphere which appears to have drifted from the trenches *via* Paris hotels and London night-clubs into the Oxford colleges.[3]

How should one reconcile these apparently contradictory perspectives? While the majority of the post-war students may still have been rather dronish, at first the more earnest of the ex-soldier scholars seem to set the prevailing tone. However, as the initial awe and uncertainty of the conservative dons receded, an inevitable counter-reaction seems to have set in:

> The ex-service men, who included scores of captains, majors, colonels, and even a one-armed twenty-five year old brigadier, insisted on their rights. At St John's they constituted themselves as a 'College Soviet' and successfully demanded

an entire revision of the scandalous catering system ... The elder dons, whom I had often seen during the War trembling in fear of an invasion ... and who then regarded all soldiers, myself included, as their noble saviours, now recovered their pre-War self-possession and haughtiness.[4]

Parkes, who had never abandoned his boyhood enthusiasm for architecture nor spurned his passion for painting, remarks that before going up to Oxford he had not completely made up his mind which profession to pursue, 'feeling that Oxford would give me the opportunity to reflect and decide'. Elsewhere, however, he confesses, 'when I returned to civilian life, it was with a fairly clear belief that I wanted to be ordained'.[5] When we recall his intimate familiarity with virtually every notable ecclesiastical structure in Britain and his moth-like attraction to the shrine at Canterbury, his idealization of his mother into frozen piety and his long-standing predilection for the company of the likes of Christine Ozanne, the Reverend David Lee-Elliott and Father Plater SJ. – 'the most canonizable saint I have ever known'[6] – is it any wonder that the inky arts of sketching and architectural draughtsmanship were superseded by clerical black? In retrospect, it is plain that his assumption of religious orders was virtually a foregone conclusion.

As for the choice of which course of study to pursue, although Parkes went through the agonizing motions of reaching a decision, this too seems to have been preordained. Evoking unawares the Jewish proscription on premature study of kabbala, young Parkes pronounced 'it was absurd for a man to pretend to be a student of philosophy before he was forty'. Upon taking a 'good second in Classical Mods – I was not fit enough to do the hard work which would have got a first' – Parkes settled comfortably into preparation for his lifelong career. 'I have,' he avers, 'never regretted that I preferred theology to the Greats.'[7] His comment that he was 'not fit enough to do the hard work', echoes an earlier remark that at Oxford he was 'rarely fit enough to do a full day's work'.[8] The picture that emerges is that at first the ex-soldier student was something of a semi-invalid, hobbled by residual childhood debility and suffering from painful physical and emotional war-caused afflictions.

At this critical juncture, in Hertford College chaplain 'Holy John' McLeod Campbell Parkes encountered an 'admirable' and

'excellent' figure who would serve as an embodiment of the ideal
Christian servant of mankind. Parkes recalls that Campbell
'quickly found out that I was thinking of ordination ... '[9] Little
surprise in that: Parkes probably let it drop at their first Sunday
morning encounter. He recalls a limerick – a subliterary form of
which he was excessively fond – which bespoke the candour,
probity and simplicity of the faith that Campbell embodied and
plainly inspired.

> The Chaplain of Hertford, called John
> Is a singular man for a Don;
> For he actually says,
> He believes what he prays,
> And preaches his sermons upon.

This piece of doggerel, remembered half a century later, raises
issues that, for obvious reasons, Parkes rarely deals with
frontally: the depth and wholeheartedness of his own Christian
faith – the *sine qua non* for his future struggles on behalf of the
Jewish people – and the hypocrisy which so wounded him when
encountered in the Church, academia and the general social
order.

With his superb classical training, Parkes excelled at Greek
and Latin in tutorials with Burroughs and Denniston. He recalls
with particular pleasure, however, his weekly meetings with
Cyril Emmet, a church historian who was also a leading ideologue
in the Christian Modernism Movement, cutting edge of the
liberal Protestantism of the day to which Parkes was instinctively
drawn. Originating among liberal Roman Catholic theologians
in France, Modernism's main following in England was to
be found among like-minded Anglicans who emphasized
autonomy and independence from traditional authority while
simultaneously seeking out new directions to render Christianity
relevant to the many who viewed it as discredited. The movement was particularly influential at Oxford where another of
its exponents, Dr H. D. A. Major, was principal of Ripon Hall
and editor of *The Modern Churchman*. One of Parkes' favorite
professors, he would serve on his undergraduate examination
committee.[10]

'Modernism,' Major stated in his best known work, 'consists
in the claims of the modern mind to determine what is true,

right and beautiful in the light of its own experience, even though its conclusions be in contradiction to those of tradition ... The intellectual task of Modernism is the criticism of the tradition in the light of research and enlarging experience, with the purpose of reformulating it and reinterpreting it to serve the needs of the present age.'[11]

Cyril Emmet took Major's mandate for innovation and timeliness a step further, fleshing out innocuous generalities with polemical verve.

> The advanced 'unorthodox' view of one generation often becomes the accepted orthodoxy of the next. It is quite true there is chaff mingled with the wheat. The theories of no single school or writer are accepted in their entirety, nor are they admitted universally. But they come in time to be accepted as legitimate. The denial of verbal Inspiration, the right to reinterpret the Bible 'like any other book', the questioning of the strict accuracy of some of its historical statements, the rationalising of some of its miracles, the recognition of myth and allegory, the rejection of traditional views of Atonement, of Eternal Punishment and Hell, the attempt to restate the Incarnation in terms of modern modes of thought such as these are the commonplace of every theological student to-day.[12]

This revisionist challenge to smugger, more sanctimonious and established forms of Protestantism defined the theologically radical climate that Parkes encountered and thoroughly embraced at Oxford. His inner need for spiritual renewal responded powerfully to these strivings for a newly relevant theology. Modernism was his natural métier; its impact was formative and would colour his thinking for decades to come. Just as its bracing spirit moulded a new approach to traditional Christianity, its avidity to challenge the received wisdom of the Church steered Parkes onto a track which would eventually lead him to groundbreaking conceptions of Judaism and the Jewish people.

Even with a figure of Emmet's eminence, whose thinking he highly respected, it was not like Parkes to play the timid acolyte. On the intellectual field of battle he always fought with tenacity in order to prevail. Because, for example, the prophecies of Second Isaiah were qualitatively more profound than his other writings, Emmet firmly held he could not have composed the Servant poems. In their weekly tutorials young Parkes, arguing mainly *analogia ad absurdum*, fought long and hard for the contrary position. What strikes the reader most is the pure delight he takes in recalling, to his own satisfaction at any rate, how utterly he vanquished his distinguished tutor.[13] Not for the first time do we encounter the irritating bravado with which the young theological student could comport himself as a controversialist.

These polemical jousts with Emmet, which both of them clearly relished, left a lasting impact. Parkes incorporated aspects of his retorts contra Emmet into the fabric his own, highly original theological *oeuvre*. He recalls, for example, that Emmet '... found most satisfaction in the definition of the three Persons [of God] as the Lover, the Loved and the Love. But an active person, a passive person, and an abstract principle cannot make anything adequate or comparable to the intentions of those who originally found the definition necessary ...'[14] When a decade later Parkes, with far more at stake, fully engaged the burning issues that would preoccupy him for the better part of a lifetime, no matter that the upshot of his research set him at odds with sacrosanct Christian truths and at cross-purposes with main-stream Christian activists, he would never waver. How grateful we are now for the probity, the stubborn persistence, the per-spicacity and the sheer brilliance of this at times infuriating polemicist who, yes, loved dearly to win.

Parkes took an impish delight in discovering that in selecting Early Christian Art and Architecture as his special subject he had stumbled upon a topic that, though included in the approved list, had not been selected by an undergraduate for at least twenty-eight years. In fact, nobody at Oxford was qualified to supervise it. As a result, for two terms the university was obligated both to hire an expert from the British Museum to tutor Parkes one day a week and later to locate a special exami-ner just for him. As Parkes, ever a stickler for obtaining his due according to the letter of the regulations, wickedly puts it, he turned out to be 'an expensive item' for Oxford.[15]

Scholarship came naturally to Parkes and the high-mindedness and idealism of the post-war Oxford community accorded with his native temperament. Nevertheless, Parkes' main concern at Oxford was not his studies *per se*. Once made cognizant of his young congregant's bent for Christian service, Campbell introduced him to the Student Christian Movement (SCM), a devotional, Christian service society then in full flowering. Parkes soon became an enthusiastic participant in a week-long campaign of talks and discussions that attracted hundreds of Oxford students. Among the major speakers were Baron von Hugel, W. Maltby and William Temple, a liberal, ecumenically minded, highly influential churchman, who was eventually elevated to the archbishop's seat in Canterbury (1942–44). He became Parkes' trusted mentor.

The necessity to rethink and revitalize the role of the Church in the modern world – the central theme of the week – struck such a resonant chord in Parkes that in 1921 he travelled to Glasgow to attend the SCM's missionary quadrennial.[16] However something about Glasgow – possibly an intuitive distaste for the parochialism of the missionary mentality – seems to have caused a certain recoil. Very soon afterwards Parkes shifted his energies to the League of Nations United (LNU), whose activities attracted many other members of the SCM as well. In those happy days,' Parkes comments,

> ... neither 'liberal' nor 'humanist' was a term of abuse, and humanist and committed Christians worked together over a wide area of life. Nor were we ashamed to work for the possibility of 'progress', nor, because we did speak of it, believe in it and work for it, were we utopians or shallow or superficial. It was a generation which had seen too much of the reality of war, and which saw too clearly the immense gaps in the Christian tradition in so far as human community was concerned, for it to be legitimate to call it 'starry eyed'.[17]

Elsewhere Parkes stated his reason for embracing the work of the LNU more succinctly: after the Armistice he was 'determined to work for a world in which war was impossible'.[18] The term before his Mods Parkes accepted an appointment as university secretary of the LNU, virtually a full-time administrative position.

Obviously, Parkes' plunge into social and political activism marked a dramatic change in orientation. Although polemical by temperament, neither his background nor education had previously indicated an inclination for direct engagement in public affairs or controversy. We recall Parkes observing earlier, for example, that before enlisting in the Army he had never even heard of pacifism or conscientious objection.[19] Later on, although he remarked that he accepted his post as gas officer because, more concerned with saving rather than destroying lives, 'it seemed the right path to follow', we also recall that at the time the job's chief appeal seemed to be the opportunity it afforded him to work at close quarters with an officer whom he much respected.

Parkes' political *naïveté* and relative passivity when in uniform are underscored when contrasted to the far more conspicuous posture taken at the time by some of his more politically exposed contemporaries. By 1917, Robert Graves recalls, he and his friend Siegfried Sassoon '… could no longer see the War as one between trade-rivals: its continuance seemed mainly a sacrifice of the idealistic younger generation to the stupidity and self-protective alarm of the elder'.[20] In July of that year Sassoon delivered to his commanding officer a statement of conscience entitled 'Finished with the War', a copy of which he sent to Graves.

> I am making this statement as an act of wilful defiance of military authority, because I believe the war is being deliberately prolonged by those who have the power to end it.
>
> I am a soldier, convinced that I am acting on behalf of soldiers. I believe that this war, upon which I entered as an act of defence and liberation, has now become a war of aggression and conquest …
>
> I have seen and endured the sufferings of the troops, and I can no longer be a party to prolong these sufferings for ends which I believe to be evil and unjust …[21]

Nothing remotely of the sort ever issued from Parkes when on active service. Although he implies that by the end of the war he considered himself a closet pacifist, '… I felt that I was not sufficiently detached to be able to take so momentous a decision [to declare himself] a conscientious objector after more than two years in the Army'.[22] The final phrase gives the show away: no matter how closely conscientious objection accorded with his inner feelings, to claim it would have appeared too self-serving for him to have carried it off successfully. In actuality, despite pacifist leanings, five years would pass before Parkes attained enough detachment and self-confidence even to allude to pacifism in a public forum. Moreover, shortly thereafter he was already edging away from its implications: 'More and more I was convinced that the attempt to create a pacifist nation, a whole nation which would voluntarily allow itself to be destroyed, was following a wrong line altogether.'[23]

In sum, although it would be years before Parkes satisfactorily conjoined his globalism with his Christian faith, at Oxford he totally embraced the internationalist creed as his own. For nearly a year Parkes devoted his time and considerable energy to making the LNU, which based its functioning upon the structure of the League of Nations in Geneva, both highly visible and very influential. Under his leadership, the LNU's International Assembly attracted many of Oxford's most gifted undergraduates. Further, the high seriousness of its well-researched and lively debates made LNU meetings, governed by meticulously balanced rules of procedure of Parkes' own devising, the most influential and popular forum at the university.

It was principally when speaking at public meetings in the villages and towns of the area that Parkes encountered at first hand the residual tide of public scepticism about the League: 'Yes, you're a nice, idealistic young chap but it won't work you know, the League of Nations letting in the wogs and all that.'[24] He soon became acutely sensitive to the depth of the post-war divide: whereas many of his generation had emerged from the war intent upon reconstructing and revitalizing the failed political structures that had led to catastrophe, the older generation blindly regarded the war as a temporary lapse in an otherwise viable system, the best, in fact, of all possible systems. They preferred to see the re-establishment of the *status quo ante*.

Parkes was now associating with important players from all the campus organizations, and he even anonymously contributed some not unclever verse to *Isis*, the major campus literary organ, which in 1922 named him as one of Oxford's 'Men of the Year'. The President of the Oxford branch of the LNU was the redoubtable Professor Gilbert Murray, a charismatic Oxford fixture who had widespread international contacts. Extending himself to the young Guernseyman, he introduced Parkes to the passing parade of notable visitors to Oxford.

Spreading his wings in an ever-wider orbit, one thing Parkes did not do, at least not noticeably, was to preen himself with a view to attracting any of Oxford's lovely, lively women students. A salient vacancy from Parkes' reminiscence of LNU days is Elizabeth Murray, the famous professor's radiant daughter, whom Parkes must have encountered very frequently. She was,

> ... wildly brilliant and fiercely in love with life ... [and shone] like a bright meteor amid the constellation of humbler stars at the League of Nations Union. Her eccentric clothes were untidy, and her straight black hair was often unkempt, but she strode like a young goddess through the Somerville students and condescended to notice very few of them outside a small group ...[25]

Eerily, with only minor transpositions, this description of the brunette goddess, who burnt out tragically young, closely adumbrates various observers' description of Parkes himself.[26]

Parkes claims that he enjoyed a number of elaborate academic hoaxes, such as a well-attended lecture about the Mexican Revolution delivered by a student posing as an American journalist. Parkes took himself too seriously and was too high-minded to perpetrate such japeries. When he wasn't dashing about the campus from one meeting to another, he was often flat on his back in a state of near-collapse. On one occasion he was so exhausted and befuddled that in the midst of changing into formal clothes for a dinner being held in his honour, he forgot why he had half-undressed and proceeded to go to bed.[27] Notwithstanding episodes of near-delirium, during this year of Parkes' emergence as a major performer on the Oxford stage we can recognize the strut and cut of the paradoxical figure that the world eventually would recognize: self-possessed, brilliant, argumentative, charming, infuriating, meticulous, progressive, painstaking, charismatic, full of hauteur and, in his spheres of expertise, absolutely indispensable.

Lacking sufficient funds to travel abroad, during his student summers Parkes vacationed with the Lee-Elliotts, sometimes at Maxstoke Castle, sometimes at their country cottage. Occasionally, often with an Oxford friend in tow, Parkes returned to Guernsey where he stayed with his father. For days on end he occupied himself by painting the seascape, the jagged rocks, the countryside, local churches or the island fortifications. Adept both at watercolours and charcoal drawings, he was, he realized, merely

a talented amateur but a decidedly dedicated one. Upon returning to Oxford, his pictures always sold briskly. Indeed, Parkes
pocketed enough from the proceeds of his summer pastime to
accumulate 'a very pleasant collection of Jacobean and eighteenth-
century furniture'.[28] Particularly since it testified to his own good
taste and sense of entitlement, Parkes took immense pleasure
in surrounding himself with graceful artefacts and historical
furnishings.

Of a piece with the Bungalow Ghost and his schoolboy success
at mental telepathy, Parkes' painting entailed yet another surprising and curious encounter with paranormal phenomena.
Although he never pauses to ponder long on the larger significance of these paranormal incursions into his life or just why
he seemed to act as a lightning rod for them, there is no question
that Parkes treated them all with healthy regard, greeting these
most curious experiences with inquisitive respect and no little
pleasure.

During one of his convalescent periods Miss Kleppe, the housekeeper of Ripon Hall, urged Parkes to turn out some pastels of
her native Norwegian scenery. Parkes protested it was scarcely
possible; until then he had never visited Norway. Still Kleppe
persisted, and she showed him many coloured postcards depicting spectacular fjords. Arguing for Parkes' susceptibility to older
women, Kleppe must have been most persuasive: Parkes'
memoir yields precious few instances of his changing his mind
about anything. In any event, a mysterious partnership evolved
between the simple, homesick housekeeper and the brilliant,
sickly undergraduate.

> I had to do them when she was in the room, and she had
> to imagine herself looking at the scene I was trying to
> transfer to my picture … I could say to her with complete
> certainty: 'you have stopped thinking about it', and if she
> left the room I had to stop. The last two I did were of her
> own island, and she had no picture for me to take as a basis.
> I had to do it entirely out of her mind. But some time later
> … I stood behind two Norwegian students who were
> identifying them one by one. When they came to the two
> of her island, they proceeded to identify it correctly.[29]

Exploiting their unique working relationship, this odd couple
ultimately executed nineteen scenes together.

At the close of his third year at Oxford, upon retiring from the chairmanship of the LNU, Parkes set about preparing for his theology exams in earnest, but controversy and distraction pursued him. His successor at the LNU had issued an invitation to a dozen German students to visit Oxford during the summer of 1923. Outraged, the rector of the city church led the charge: the invitation, he declared, was 'an offence against all decency, the mere mention of which shocked and disgusted him'. Parkes took it upon himself to respond in a letter to the *Oxford Chronicle* and that in turn drew fire from a journalist who misrepresented Parkes as 'a schoolboy attacking ex-servicemen ... the natural product of the pernicious teaching' of four well-known liberal clergymen – most notoriously, William Temple. For the rest of his days, it was a jibe that Parkes would delight in repeating.[30] Until Temple's death in 1944, he would remain one of Parkes' closest confidants and, especially in matters ecclesiastical, his most trusted advisor.

At an open debate of the LNU, who should mount the rostrum in support of the rector of the city church but young Evelyn Waugh, already self-assured, pawky and, although (or because) his mother's maiden name was Raban, already incipiently anti-semitic. Parkes then delivered a rebuttal. This extended brouhaha over the German students marks Parkes' full transition into a public figure and academic celebrity. Not content alone with the pleasures and toils of scholarship, Parkes, a polemicist who drew persistent fire and returned it with greater accuracy and redoubled force, would ever be attracted to controversy. In the end the LNU endorsed the invitation by a vote of 177 to 74, and the summer visit of the Germans passed uneventfully, but not, however, without an ill omen: Parkes received an anonymous death threat, the first of several that would cross his desk over the years.

However little (or much) one credits a reported antisemitic incident,[31] this public engagement with Waugh reminds us that it was at Oxford that Parkes was said to have overheard 'Jewboy' carelessly and loudly bantered from the hallway and underwent a defining epiphany. Lest the absence of any allusion to anti-semitism in Parkes' own account of those years lull us as to its prevalence, any one of several biographies of George Orwell or a riffle through his letters and journal entries would be highly instructive.[32] Orwell, then still Eric Blair, Parkes' younger contemporary, chose to go out to Burma instead of up to Oxford. He emerged from the same upper middle spectrum of society as the Guernseyman. In the secular arena, of course, he has long shone as a beacon of conscience and decency in a time of moral murkiness. Unlike Parkes, however, Orwell never transcended the antisemitic animus native to most young men in his circumstances and class but to which Parkes was entirely immune.

For raw antisemitism unsheathed from its genteel scabbard, little can match the impact of the familiar but shockingly scurrilous imagery of Eliot's 'Burbank with a Baedeker: Bleistein with a Cigar'. Originally published among Eliot's first collection of poems in 1920, its central stanzas still serve as a useful antidote to social amnesia, reminding us that in post-war Britain antisemitism, if not fully acceptable in its more crude, vulgar, nasty manifestations on every occasion, was generally well within the pale on most.

> But this or such was Bleistein's way:
> A saggy bending of the knees
> And elbows, with the palms turned out,
> Chicago Semite Viennese.
>
> A lustreless protrusive eye
> Stares from the protozoic slime
> At a perspective of Canaletto.
> The smoky candle end of time
>
> Declines. On the Rialto once.
> The rats are underneath the piles.
> The Jew is underneath the lot.
> Money in furs. The boatman smiles.[33]

As his examinations approached, Parkes' susceptibility to illness and physical affliction once again extracted him from the immediate necessity of conforming to regulations to which, in any case, he felt superior. After nearly a year of rigorous preparation, like a schoolboy who wills 'an upset stomach' so as to avoid the agony of taking a test, Parkes was felled by a schoolboy disease – measles. Typically, he transformed the postponement into a test of willpower.

Together with Parkes' physician, who represented the Faculty of Medicine, a procession of dons in full academic dress arrayed themselves at his bedside in order to verify that 'yes, Parkes had indeed come down with the measles'. When some weeks later he had recovered sufficiently to take his exams, they would afford him 'the final joy of [his] undergraduate life, that of flooring my examiners'. The single question they posed was how one might construct a dome? Parkes recalls gazing at his questioners 'with infinite compassion' and then responding, 'I cannot tell you that in a sentence or two. You must first tell me whether it is to be an in-centric or an ex-centric dome, and am I to construct it on a horizontal or a vertical axis?'[34]

Having routed his adversaries with élan and dispatch, Parkes was awarded a 'first'. Although several dons amply appreciated the special qualities of mind that underlay Parkes' wry humour and recalcitrant nature, others concluded that the sanctimonious, egoistical young scholar was simply insufferable. How pleased the latter contingent must have been finally to be quit of their 'expensive item'.

NOTES

1. Robert Graves, *Good-bye To All That* (New York: Anchor, 1989), p. 291.
2. James Parkes, *Voyage of Discoveries* (London: Victor Gollancz, 1969), p. 55.
3. Vera Brittain, *Testament of Youth, An Autobiographical Study of the Years 1900–1925* (London: Virago, 1978), pp. 497–98.
4. Graves, *Good-bye To All That*, pp. 291–92.
5. Parkes, *Voyage of Discoveries*, p. 52.
6. Ibid., p. 39.
7. Ibid., p. 55.
8. Ibid., p. 15.
9. Ibid., p. 58.
10. Robert A. Everett, *Christianity Without Anti-Semitism: James Parkes and the Jewish–Christian Encounter* (Oxford: Pergamon, 1993), p. 57.
11. H. D. A. Major, *English Modernism: Its Origins, Methods, and Aims* (Cambridge, MA: Harvard, 1927), pp. 193–94.
12. Cyril Emmet, *Conscience, Creeds, and Critics*, cited in Everett, op. cit., pp. 59–60.
13. Parkes, *Voyage of Discoveries*, pp. 55–56.
14. James Parkes, *God At Work In Science, Politics, and Human Life* (London: Putnam, 1952), p. 144.
15. Parkes, *Voyage of Discoveries*, pp. 56–57.
16. Ibid., pp. 58–59.
17. Ibid., p. 59.
18. James Parkes interviewed by Laurence Dobie in The *Guardian*, 28 March 1970, Parkes Archives, File MS 60/31/37.
19. *Vide* Chapter 9.
20. Robert Graves, *Good-bye To All That*, p. 260.
21. Ibid.
22. Parkes, *Voyage of Discoveries*, p. 41.
23. Ibid., pp. 84–85.
24. James Parkes interviewed by Laurence Dobie in The *Guardian*.
25. Brittain, *Testament of Youth*, p. 107.

26. *Vide* Chapter 24.
27. Parkes, *Voyage of Discoveries*, p. 64.
28. Ibid., p. 67.
29. Ibid., p. 68.
30. Ibid., pp. 64–65, ff.
31. Edith Ruth Weisz, interviewed by the author and Maggie Davidson in Cambridge, England, 28–29 August 2000. *Vide* Afterword for details.
32. *Vide* Jeffrey Meyers's *Orwell: Wintry Conscience of a Generation* (New York: Viking, 2000); and Gordon Bowker, *Inside George Orwell* (London: Macmillan, 2003).
33. T. S. Eliot, *Collected Poems, 1909–1962* (New York: Harcourt Brace, 1963), pp. 32–33.
34. Parkes, *Voyage of Discoveries*, p. 57.

13

Sand Castles

On the island I accepted that I should never learn how Friday lost his tongue, as I accepted that I should never learn how the apes crossed the sea. But what we can accept in life we cannot accept in history. To tell my story and be silent on Friday's tongue is no better than offering a book for sale with pages in it quietly left empty.[1]

Parkes and fellow-classman Harold Mulliner, to whom he had given measles, spent much of the summer of their matriculation immersed in an architectural fantasy. Day after splendid day they constructed elaborate sand castles on the strand of Alderney where the sand

> ... was excellent, fine and firm, so that one [might] built [sic] a three-storey keep of vaulted chambers ... If a building collapsed one rebuilt it in the period at which one was at that moment working. The 'show castle' completed, we chose two sites, and fortified them against each other ...[2]

The picture, a study in black and white, of the two Oxford companions passing their summer at the beach fully engaged in fabricating elaborate sand castles, shimmers with a wondrously keen sort of innocence. Might it carry intimations as well of another kind of 'excellent, fine and firm' idyll? Even if not corporeally palpable, given the context of their boyish absorption it almost certainly bears the burden of repressed emotion and lightly disguised sensuality. Early on in his own youthful memoir Robert Graves intermittently alludes to the strong allure of another schoolboy, of feelings overtly passionate but not yet explicitly sexual:

> In English preparatory and public schools romance is necessarily homosexual. The opposite sex is despised and treated as something obscene. Many boys never recover from this perversion. For every one born homosexual, at least ten

permanent pseudo-homosexuals are made by the public school system: nine of these ten as honourably chaste and sentimental as I was.[3]

Undoubtedly the strikingly handsome, well spoken, gracefully turned-out Guernseyman cut an attractive figure for other young men, and in his fashion he was indubitably drawn towards them. However the very guilelessness of his reminiscence of that Alderney summer of 'show castles' and comradeship, its charming unselfconsciousness, argues strongly against blatant physicality and even more unquestionably against calculated salaciousness. At least for the present, on balance it seems that Parkes' sexuality was, for the most part, sublimated. Diffused, it got rechannelled into his studies, his manifold collections, his social and political activism, his painting and his deepening sense of religious vocation. Which is to say that Parkes' sexuality was still mainly subterranean, a turbid force intimately harnessed to his idealism and the chivalric, medieval strain in his sensibility. It would not be inconsistent were he now consciously to strive for a kind of apotheosis through inner dedication to ideals of service and chastity.

The Oxford Parkes left behind no longer resembled the collection of Gothic sand piles under siege, hunkered down against an incoming tide of insistent lieutenants that it had been four years earlier. With muted regret Parkes alludes just once to a reversion to its former smugness and tranquillity. The International Assembly of the LNU, which Parkes had shepherded to such prestigious heights in the campus intellectual firmament, was 'too complex and mature a body for the much younger generation which followed the ex-service men and women for which it was devised'. Just two years after Parkes' tenure as its secretary had terminated, it had declined to near inanition.[4] As later recalled by Evelyn Waugh, at least on the surface Oxford in 1923 once again resembled an embalmed tableau of high-table immutability, high jinks and undisguised anti-feminism.

Oxford, in those days, was still a city of aquatint. In her spacious and quiet streets, men walked and spoke as they had done in Newman's days; her autumnal mists, her grey springtime, and the rare glory of her summer days ... when the chestnut was in flower and the bells rang out high and clear over her gables and cupolas, exhaled the vapours of a thousand years of learning. Here, discordantly, in Eights Week, came a rabble of womankind, some hundreds strong, twittering and fluttering over the cobbles and up the steps, sight-seeing and pleasure-seeking, drinking claret cups, eating cucumber sandwiches; pushed in punts about the river, herded in droves to the college barges; greeted in the Isis and in the Union by a sudden display of peculiar, facetious, wholly distressing Gilbert-and-Sullivan badinage, and by the peculiar choral effects in the college chapels.[5]

By his final term Parkes fully anticipated setting out in the near future upon a fairly traditional clerical career. He knew himself capable of gratifying, indeed of delighting worshippers at any parish in Britain and, if he put his mind to it, of swift elevation in the hierarchy of the Church of England. Moreover, he was notably pleased to be accepted by the Bishop of Lichfield, the chief town of the region where the Parkes family had its origins. Yet when tested, this pastoral vision of a country clerical seat proved to be another sand castle. Based upon his wide renown as a campus activist, in March of 1923 Parkes was approached and asked to join the staff of the Student Christian Movement. With scarcely a moment's hesitation, he accepted. How might this be understood?

True, during his final undergraduate year, necessarily devoting himself to his theological studies, Parkes' routine was more sedentary than formerly. One suspects that until then he had not fully appreciated how much sustenance he derived from his role as a public figure. The young man who in boyhood had been very much a loner had rapidly gravitated to the very vortex of Oxford's social and political whirl. Plainly, he now thrived on the hum, and the sense of purpose and craved the stimulation, the spotlight and the applause. Brilliant at both planning strategy and managing organizational detail, increasingly passionate about promoting an internationalist social agenda informed by modernist Christian humanism, Parkes' leadership, experience and panache provided him with the necessary credentials and confidence to succeed as a professional activist. When SCM offered him an opportunity, the assistant curacy in Lichfield didn't stand a chance.

Nevertheless, Parkes did not entirely lay aside his clerical aspirations, and he was much gratified when the Bishop of London offered to ordain him. The final hurdle he would have to negotiate was, not unreasonably, an examination. And yet this commonplace requirement somehow released the stopper that had contained the more petulant, unyielding, egoistical forces of Parkes' combustible personality. 'When I sat for the exam I found a set of mid-Victorian questions of which the first I read – a "gobbet" – indicated the kind of rubbish which was provocative to my extremely bad temper, for I had had to cancel a quite important piece of work to sit the exam.'[6]

Responding at times curtly, at other times frivolously, Parkes refused to mask his condescension at the encounter with his examiner, the newest avatar of his old headmaster. Later, summoned for a meeting with the bishop, Parkes was directed to a senior examining chaplain whose two-hour interrogation so exasperated the would-be cleric that 'on principle' he refused to retake the test. Exactly which 'principle' that was remains rather vague. Grandly retreating, Parkes took refuge with William Temple, at the time the Bishop of Manchester. Temple, Parkes recalls, could not decide who was the bigger fool, his young friend or the examining chaplain. In any event, the Bishop of Manchester employed his good offices with the Bishop of London, and in due course Parkes was ordained as a priest in the Church of England. Had it not been for this timely intercession, it is conceivable that Parkes might never have become a clergyman.[7]

Though not uncritical of Parkes' excesses and piques Temple, in the inter-war years already the most influential clergyman in Britain, would intercede on his younger friend's behalf on several similar occasions in the future. Seeing much of himself in Parkes, he would almost always acquiesce to his friend's version of reality. The touchstone of Temple's worldly, progressive, social and politically sensitive brand of theological liberalism was that 'the main field of revelation must always be in the field of men'.[8] His thinking had a strong appeal for his young friend.

> Temple's philosophy enshrined the belief ... that Christian morality was reflected in the pursuit of secular economic 'solutions'. The Christian notion of guilt ... embodied in the unease of comfortable, well-fed Anglican dignitaries, power-fully enforced the feeling of obligation which the possessing

classes and the better-off nations were beginning to entertain towards the deprived, at home and abroad.[9]

It is easy to fathom how for Anglicans of the stripe of Temple
and Parkes the British Labour Party would serve as a natural
political home.

Parkes' altercation with the Bishop of London may be viewed
as prototypical of the way Parkes conducted his professional life.
Ever in his own eyes 'a special case', as long as he found means
to insulate himself from the interference of meddlesome knaves
or fools, Parkes could function brilliantly within an organizational structure. However, when standard operating procedures
impinged upon his elevated sense of values or *amour propre*, as
eventually they inevitably did, Parkes reacted as though he were
oppressed by irrelevant, conventional, arbitrary rules that, he
would grant, might apply to ordinary men but certainly not to
himself. At times, Parkes was not above behaving like a royal
jackass.

Usually Parkes was fully aware that he had a friend in power
who might be relied upon to extract him from a particularly tight
corner. On the above occasion, it was the good Bishop Temple
who permitted Parkes to circumvent rules designed for more
ordinary men, to shield himself from retribution and even to
validate his slantwise view of reality. In fact, Parkes would never
really seriously come a cropper.

At £5 a year, Parkes was assigned to the curacy at St Stephen's
in Hampstead. While granting that 'his dear Vicar', Archdeacon
Sharpe, was a sincere, warm-hearted, devout Christian, Parkes
knew he could not work effectively with a cleric who preached
that 'it was not the duty … of the Church of England to call the
English people to make atonement and restitution, but to preach
Christ to other people so that they should forgive us without
making restitution'.[10]

Fortunately, just as in the nadir of his descent into a militarized
Wonderland Parkes had stumbled upon a figure with the humanity of Captain Trend, he now became closely associated with two
persons whom he came to respect profoundly. The two central
pillars of the SCM were the Reverend Tissington Tatlow, or simply
'T', who had served as its general secretary since 1903 and Zoë
Fairfield, Tatlow's long-time assistant. Both were dedicated Christians of his own progressive tendency. The former excelled at

training staff members, the latter at creative programming. 'Both,' Parkes concludes, 'were completely without any denominational narrowness; and the contribution they made to the developing ecumenicism of British Christianity was immeasurable.' Not alone their abilities and attitudes but 'their deep and unassuming religious sincerity', reminiscent of Oxford's 'Holy John' Campbell, earned them Parkes' immediate approbation and went far to cement his ties to the SCM.

Headquartered in London and equipped with a staff of forty whom Parkes calls 'a goodly company',[11] the SCM organized and ran outreach programmes at universities throughout Britain and Northern Ireland. Sponsors of workshops, conferences and support services for other student organizations, it mainly aimed to develop programmes and to promote young Christian leadership. Parkes was assigned the SCM's International Study section. Given such an area of responsibility, he was selected almost as a matter of course as one of the youngest members of the British Institute of International Affairs at London's Chatham House. This centre, since its inception in 1920 a prototype for the think-tanks of the future, may be conceived as something of a lush meadow whereon the foreign policy establishment grazed. Parkes' association with Chatham House would last for much of his life.

Over the ensuing decade, Parkes' travels on the international stage, at first for the SCM and later for other organizations, would more than compensate for all those summer vacations when he could not afford to travel abroad. In fact, in the highly specialized sphere of European educational and public affairs, Parkes soon became one of the best-informed and best-travelled young men in Britain when, that is, temporarily back from careering around the Continent, he actually was in Britain.

Parkes' first overseas assignment called for representing the SCM at a conference of the World's Student Christian Federation (WSCF). Convening in Heinrichsbad, a spa in eastern Switzerland, it marked the first post-war joint international forum to embrace French as well as German student organizations. Both in substance and in style, Parkes was struck by the contrast between SCM chapters in Britain and on the Continent. At subsequent international conclaves this yawning difference bedevilled Parkes and impaired the effectiveness of the SCM. Whereas the British chapters were, with the signal exception of the Roman Catholics, interdenominational, run democratically and open to all students who expressed a desire to investigate and deepen their understanding of Christianity, the German Movement of Christian Students (DCSV) was unabashedly evangelical, functioning primarily to serve the needs of its pietistic constituency.

Uncompromising, prolix and fixated on the efficacy of grace alone to attain salvation, the DCSV delegates generally succeeded in domineering SCM-sponsored meetings. Albeit a gross simplification, the formulistic opposition of head versus heart goes far towards defining the differing emphases of these countervailing Christian tendencies. As a result of his frustrations at the course of events in Heinrichsbad, Parkes reacted sharply against the dominant confessional stream of German Protestant theology that had sprung, as it were, full-fledged out of the theological broodings of Karl Barth. The German theologian's innate pessimism, his insistence upon the centrality of the sinful nature of man, and his refusal to countenance the possibility of any earthly melioration of man's condition – all inimical to Parkes – would embroil Barth and his followers in theological controversy with more liberal streams of Protestantism for decades to come.

Although Parkes' endorsement of liberal Christianity placed him squarely in the camp that de-emphasized immanent visitations of the Holy Spirit such as glossolalia – gift of tongues – as well as their soteriological efficacy, it would be wrong to conclude that he yielded the ground of spirituality to the Evangelicals. On the contrary, we recall the great lengths to which he went to relate an eighteen-year long tale of ghostly incursions and later how he dwelt upon a number of telepathic adventures. These intimate strongly that Parkes placed heightened value upon any manifestations that seemed to surpass the wildest imaginings of those who adhered to Horatian rationalism. Polemical elsewhere, in metapsychological matters Parkes' testimony is untainted by enthusiasm. His strictly reportorial tone inspires trust. The plain implication, of course, is that such encounters confirm the existence of a realm beyond mere 'philosophy'.

Deeply affected by the emotional coming together of the young French and Germans, Parkes, though not yet officially ordained, composed and read the English portion of the trilingual communion service, the culmination of their *rapprochement*. Of real consequence to young Parkes was not a 'living' at some curacy in Hampstead but communion between man and God, and engagement with these former enemies. Despite the intensity of his Barthian recoil, Heinrichsbad initiated what Parkes calls his 'somewhat odd clerical career, conducting strange services in strange places under strange language conditions'.[12] On the other hand, in the larger scheme of things Parkes' stirring spiritual experience was of lesser significance than the role he naturally assumed in his debut on the international stage. His intelligence and talents were immediately recognized, and he donned the mantle of leadership from the very start.

Far beyond the ken of the vast majority of his countrymen, Parkes comprehended the effects of post-war stress, disillusion and hopelessness on the students in Germany, a land whose people were overwhelmed by starvation, a worthless currency and moral isolation. Looking back, we know only too well that this would lead many students and ex-soldiers to flirt with a variety of desperate measures, among them suicide and anti-nomic radicalism. The latter, of course, would ultimately result in Germany's disastrous embrace of National Socialism. As fore-shadowed in his Oxford debate with Evelyn Waugh, from the beginning Parkes recognized the danger in isolating and humi-liating young Germans. Here, at the outset of his twelve-year career of organizing international conferences, Parkes adopted a strategy of forming coalitions and alliances that might neutralize the anti-German policies of the *Confédération Internationale des Etudiants* (CIE).

In effect, through his work for the SCM Parkes now became a citizen of the world. When he wasn't engaged in drawing up new resolutions, he was labouring behind the scenes to patch together viable compromises. As a member of the British Institute of Inter-national Affairs, he served as a knowledgeable conduit for the transmission of up-to-date intelligence about European univer-sities which, unlike their British counterparts, were intensely politicized. Beyond that Parkes was soon inducted as a visiting member of the executive of the National Union of Students (NUS) and he also maintained close contact with the LNU. Moreover, he frequently networked with the Committee for European Student Relief (ESR). Founded in 1921, it later rechristened itself the International Student Service (ISS). Together with the World University Service (WUS),it was an important organ for fund-raising in Britain.

The extent of the continental student crisis was so enormous that the role of these organizations was indispensable. In 1923–24 the ESR raised £80,000 with which it fed 30,000 students a day in Russia, then in the midst of a severe famine. Shortly thereafter, upon the complete collapse of the German economy another £50,000 was raised for its students. Parkes himself, to the tune of £2 per month, 'adopted' two impoverished German students. (Typically, on the grounds that feeding starving students had no connection with preaching the Gospel, the DCSV opposed this sort of personal initiative.) As months passed into years, Parkes would solidify his collegial role so broadly that his *bona fides* permitted him both to operate in and to cooperate with virtually every European student organization. Parkes soon developed into Britain's most effective tactician for dealing with the generally more sophisticated student operatives of the Continent.

In February of 1924, as a representative of the British chapter of the SCM, Parkes went to Norway for the Jubilee celebration of its SCM chapter. It goes unrecorded whether what he saw of the Norwegian countryside and seascape resembled the pastels he had painted a year earlier through the spooky agency of Miss Kleppe. Parkes' primary SCM duties now called for him to devise new study programmes in relation to international affairs and, either formally or informally, to implement their introduction into university curricula. The hot topics of the day were war and pacifism, the League of Nations, and problems of Africa and India. While noting only in passing his involvement in devotional retreats, Parkes takes particular pleasure in recalling the minor scandal he triggered when, high among his recommendations for Lenten reading, the cheeky cleric included a 'spiritual' text entitled *Imperialism and World Politics*.

Within Britain, Parkes' area of special responsibility for the SCM was Wales, a particularly happy choice for the young activist who ever since his boyhood had favoured the underdog. Familiar sounding sentiments issue from the Guernseyman. 'I was completely at home among the Welsh, feeling the affinity between my island and their mountains, each harbouring a small people with their own history and identity.'[13] Like the Norman-French, the Celtic stock of Wales had been engaged for centuries in a rearguard 'Kulturkampf' against an English ascendancy. Not language alone but religion also reinforced and insulated them. Their faith, with its deep-seated dissenter traditions, Wesleyan strains and full-throated hymn singing, was resonant with Old Testament undertones.

Although Parkes never drew so clear-cut an analogy between his native island's long-time inhabitants and the tribes of Israel, it is obvious that his identification with Wales and the Welsh strongly adumbrates his later affinity for Israel and the Jewish people. Uncannily, one of the Welsh students who attended a Parkes lecture at Aberystwyth that spring would resurface forty years later to play a key role in ensuring that his legacy of advocacy for the Jewish people would not suffer erosion from the tides of time.[14]

All of that, of course, was inconceivable in the summer of 1924, apogee of Parkes' early manhood. His heavy rucksack topped by sketchpad and crayons on his back, he set out on a long-deferred summer of solitary roaming in the European countryside and exploring its historic centres and byways. He was now twenty-seven. A photo of him from this period could have made a brilliant silent movie still. It depicts a lean figure of middling stature in a studiously romantic pose: hands on hips, elbows thrust out dramatically, a passionate stare directed towards the viewer. What strikes one most forcibly, beneath a set of bushy eyebrows, are the lively, penetrating, slate-blue eyes embedded within prominent cheekbones. A well-trimmed moustache framed by a short, rough-cut beard set off his even features, and he seems poised to smile amiably. Later recordings capture a voice that is soothingly unaffected but at the same time crisply cultivated.

The most surprising facet of the photo, however, is that Parkes' carpet of fine-spun, amber-tinted hair is entirely concealed by a meticulously knotted kaffiyeh. He could have been auditioning for the lead in *Lawrence of Arabia*. We are, in fact, beholding Parkes' 'New Look', for he had only recently heeded the counsel of a physician that he take a more proactive line in combating his recurring bouts of ill health by 'hardening himself'. Hence his style of apparel and the romantic air of many German students who dramatically defied the sunless, rainy northern clime by opening their collars and in all seasons scuffling about in their dusty sandals.[15]

Plainly, Parkes was taking considerable pains to appear as though he didn't care a fig what impression he made on the world. It is also perfectly transparent that he loved the dashing, devil-may-care image he projected when decked out in his informal, most un-British attire. In short, here stood what was by any standard an inordinately handsome, self-possessed, intelligent young man, who was amply endowed with social finesse and great reserves of charm. What he projected was a readiness to take on the world. In the background the camera, as cameras sometimes do, accidentally immortalized Parkes' perfect foil: a well-turned out stranger of around forty dressed in white shirt, tie and jacket, smirking as he throws the oddly attired, young Oxford graduate a frankly quizzical glance.

This photo subverts Parkes' official version of the summer of 1924 as an extension of his usual round of consultations and meetings. Somewhat offhandedly, he lets drop that 'in between the conferences, I also had some personal holidays'.[16] In fact, what is notable about this summer is that for the first time in his life Parkes was entirely free of the military harness, the pressure of examinations and the tensions with his father. While not neglecting to recount strategic intrigues at various conferences and clever manoeuvring about now musty issues in greater detail than anyone scores of years later could possibly care to hear, he relates far too little about the adventures of Jimmy Parkes off on his own on an unbuttoned continental holiday. To fill in the blanks, as earlier, we shall necessarily have recourse to our imagination.

But first, the official business. After attending meetings in Bavaria and Prussia, Parkes was present at a gathering in Warsaw where the central issue was the admission of Germany into the CIE. The opposing sides set liberal delegates from Britain and Sweden against hardliners from France, Belgium, Czechoslovakia and Poland. To help balance the two sides Parkes, applying what he irksomely labels his 'chameleonesque diversity', resorted to a bit of jiggery-pokery. Ukrainian students, prevented by the Poles from attending the conference, had vested the British with the right to represent them at the table. So at Warsaw, Parkes, ever the brilliant tactician, startled the assembly by speaking not only for the British delegation but, in his Oxford-accented tones, for the Ukrainian students as well.[17]

Among the many conferences he attended in the course of a decade, Warsaw is recalled mainly to illustrate his adroitness. However, and this is indicative, Parkes neglects to point to the real upshot of the controversy in Warsaw. In fact throughout his account of activities in the 1920s and 1930s, Parkes is singularly remiss at establishing the larger context. The indifference of British student organizations to the threat of German rearmament fairly closely mirrored the attitude of the British government.[18] It is far from definite whether a more moderate French posture towards the Germans, one that might have engendered in turn a lesser measure of resentment, would have made a substantial difference to the flow of European history. What we search for in vain in Parkes is an appreciation that the British SCM's generous stance towards the Germans may have proved as shortsighted or illusory as that taken by the French or the Poles. What is certain is that their SCM representatives were not amused by Parkes' star turn as a ventriloquist at Warsaw.

Armed with a list of names and addresses of friends and acquaintances whom he had encountered at endless conclaves, not to mention friends of friends, upon concluding his summer round of conferencing, Parkes was both keen and ripe to embrace new adventures. Firm details are sparse, conclusive data absent, but if until this period the preponderance of evidence suggests that Parkes' affective leanings had been either chastely sublimated or subtlety homoerotic, his account of this summer on the road suggests a tentative voyage of discovery into the regions of bisexuality. What one may safely infer from Parkes' account is that something of emotional consequence occurred in the course of that summer. If events in Prague did not proceed precisely as follows – which is a near certainty – something very much like them seems to have transpired. In the end, of course, it is entirely the reader's decision to suspend or to maintain disbelief in the following reconstruction.

Czech opposition to the 'Voice' of the Ukraine at Warsaw did not discourage Parkes from enjoying an iridescent week 'in the glorious city of Prague' where he suggestively dangles a tantalizing hint: '… a Czech lady revised my views of university precedence'.[19] Revised his views of *what*? To a certain extent, Parkes demystifies. His lady friend – perhaps his concierge – thought that since so many Americans passing through Prague had come from Oxford, the town surely must be located in America. Parkes spells out the transparent point: in the post-war world the Americans were inestimably richer and better travelled than the British or anyone else in the world.

Prague, of course, is generously endowed with more than

enough charms to play exotic mistress for anyone's idyll, all the more for an enthusiast of medieval history and architecture. Yet, silently echoing the earlier refusal to describe his experiences at the front lines,[20] Parkes spurns even a sidebar about the Charles Bridge or the city's splendid palaces. More puzzlingly still in view of Parkes' future preoccupation with European Jewry, he resists even a passing glance at Prague's uniquely intact medieval Jewish Quarter. That such a flat anecdote should be the chief upshot, indeed the only remembrance from that glorious week, leads one to wonder whether the real point was to serve as a disingenuous peg upon which to hang a grateful, private allusion to the anonymous lady of Prague.

Evidence is slim, yet if ever it was to be, this summer of 1924 was the time when the adventurous young man was ready and eager to indulge in new experiences. The very scantiness of his treatment of his 'glorious week' signals the possibility that he not only could have attracted the interest of an older, more experienced woman but that, under her tutelage, he could well have succumbed to her advances. It is, after all, far easier to imagine Parkes as the seduced than as the seducer. In sum, particularly in view of his prior history of close involvement with a succession of 'aunts', it seems not unreasonable to endorse the general notion that, at liberty in foreign fields, the dashing, handsome young activist fell into a brief affair with an older woman. If so, then let medieval Prague serve as a likely backdrop for Parkes' sexual experimentation or even initiation, a first or early step in gradual reorientation from what until then seems to have been feeble homoerotic assays.

Or the above perhaps did not happen at all. Built of hint and surmise, it represents a much-pondered conjecture about what was experienced by a footloose, twenty-seven-year-old man on his first solo adventure on the Continent. Like a distinguished scholar's recent seductive hypothesis that Shakespeare's rich characterization of Shylock derives in good measure from the likelihood that he bore witness to the grisly execution of Roderigo Lopez, the converso physician to Elizabeth I,[21] this unverified speculation about Parkes' escapade in Prague is offered to clarify our conception of his developmental process. Although no irrefutable evidence confirms that the passing liaison ever came to pass, if not in Prague then somewhere else in that summer of rapturous wandering something of the sort seems very likely to have occurred. Therefore, with all its insubstantiality, I shall leave my castle of sand to stand uneffaced, inviting even the most severe readers to consider its general lines. If they cannot endorse them, they are of course at liberty to drown its vaulted chambers in a tide of scepticism. I take heart, however, from recalling Harold Mulliner who, upon recovering from the measles, had gleaned so much by building skilfully out of sand, that in the end, he went on to take a first in History and would be especially commended by his examiners for his paper on medieval fortifications.

NOTES

1. J. M. Coetzee, *Foe* (London: Penguin Books, 1987), p. 67.
2. James Parkes, *Voyage of Discoveries* (London: Victor Gollancz, 1969), p. 67.
3. Robert Graves, *Good-bye To All That* (New York: Anchor, 1989), p. 19.
4. Parkes, *Voyage of Discoveries*, p. 62.
5. Evelyn Waugh, *Brideshead Revisited* (Boston: Little Brown, 1945), pp. 21–22.
6. Parkes, *Voyage of Discoveries*, p. 74.
7. Ibid., p. 75.
8. William Temple, *Nature, Man, and God* (London: Macmillan, 1960), p. 305.
9. Paul Johnson, *Modern Times: The World From The Twenties To The Nineties* (New York: Harper Perennial Edition, 1992), pp. 166–67.
10. Parkes, *Voyage of Discoveries*, p. 76, ff.
11. Ibid., p. 70.
12. Parkes, *Voyage of Discoveries*, p. 72, ff.
13. Ibid., p. 78.
14. *Vide* Chapter 33.
15. Parkes, *Voyage of Discoveries*, p. 82.
16. Ibid., p. 80.
17. Ibid., p. 81.
18. Johnson, *Modern Times*, pp. 138–39.
19. Parkes, *Voyage of Discoveries*, p. 80.
20. *Vide* Chapter 9.
21. Stephen Greenblatt, *Will in the World: How Shakespeare Became Shakespeare* (New York: Norton, 2004), pp. 256–87.

PART 3
ON THE CONTINENT

14

Watersheds

*Life is not what one lived, but what one remembers and how one remembers
it in order to recount it.*[1]

Upon his return to London at the close of the summer, Parkes
was soon fully engaged in fresh SCM assignments: preparing
and distributing study materials, travelling around in Wales, and,
in preparation for the major event of the SCM calendar, attending to organizational details for the Missionary Quadrennial due
to convene in Manchester in January. Although he soon fell ill,
he still managed to complete a considerable quantity of work
from his sick room and emerged just in time for the start of
Quadrennial. More than two thousand current and former
students attended.

As International Study secretary, dealing with foreign visitors
was one of Parkes' major responsibilities, and this led him to
befriend a Pastor Médard of the French SCM. Although Parkes'
hardy regimen of donning German-style dress had, he felt, 'done
marvels', he still suffered grievously from the damp, cold British
winter. Médard advised him to 'dry out' in the winter sun of
Provence.[2] This provided a splendid rationale for Parkes to play
the vagabond on the Continent as he had the previous summer.
Very shortly thereafter he headed south.

So began a long-drawn-out love affair with the triangle
bounded on the north by Montelimar, on the east by Cassis
and on the west by Carcassonne. I don't know how many
times I have been down to the magic triangle, always sleeping the first night at Avignon, always renewing the magic
of the South. I left the North, grey and damp, when the
train passed into the night as it swayed through Burgundy,
to find the South as one looked out in the morning at blue
sky and a branch of mimosa blowing across the window. I
came up once into the sun from the shady side of a long

hill to see the whole line of the Basses Alpes in a panorama
before me; and I understood, as never before, what the
psalmist meant when he spoke of the mountains and little
hills skipping. For as the clouds passed across them, there
were the high mountains slowly galumphing along like
dignified dowagers while, at their feet, the little hills skipped
merrily from sun to shadow and back again.'[3]

Such exuberance had not been voiced since Parkes' effusive
account of boyhood holidays on the primeval western shores of
Guernsey whose climate, if not as salubrious as that of southern
France, is considerably milder than Britain's. Similar to his earlier
description of the pebbly beaches and unspoiled reaches of his
native island,[4] his evocation of Provence is strikingly sensual.
What seems at first the awkward repetition of 'magic' and
'magical' actually marks the transformation of a geographical
region into an allegorized landscape, one suffused with a surfeit
of displaced sexual energy. 'Magic' is also charged with the
mystique of a chivalric ethos whose natural home has always
been France – and in France pre-eminently in Provence. Its landscape was imbued with the ideals of glory, honour and self-
sacrifice that had captured Parkes' heart as a schoolboy. Criss-
crossing this southern realm seemed to open the new, inner
channels not only of Parkes' store of high idealism but simultaneously of his hitherto mainly latent sensuality.

To substantiate this proposition, we shall repay Parkes' newest
flight of lyricism with close attention and a nuanced explica-
tion. From the outset, Parkes' declaration that his relationship
to Provence was 'a long-drawn out love affair' establishes an
emotional context that tends to corroborate the hypothesis that
he had indeed cut his first teeth sexually in 'a very brief love
affair' the preceding summer. We note that Provence, like Parkes'
beloved native island, is not merely triangular in shape but
specifically perceived as such. However, whereas Parkes' boyhood Guernsey was intrinsically associated with maternal values,
the triangular zone of Provence is implicitly charged with sexual
energy.

With all his necessaries packed tightly in a rucksack, Parkes
at first set out to explore on foot, 'for one could find a clean
bed in the humblest village', but soon took to pedalling along
the tree-lined, rural byways of Provence. At a later stage, his

1. Babies James and David on a settee

2. Three Parkes children sitting on a low wall, 1904

3. Annie Parkes

4. Henry Parkes

5. Jousting tournament staged at Delancey Park, St Peter Port in the early 1900s. Reproduced courtesy *Guernsey Press and Star*

6. Elizabeth College in the early 1900s

7. State-of-the-art tomato cultivation on Guernsey in the first decade of the twentieth century. Reproduced courtesy *Guernsey Press and Star*

8. Molly

9. David in uniform

10. James in uniform

11. Parkes seated on the left with members of the League of Nations Union at Oxford

12. Parkes, hand on hip, kaffiyah on head, 1932

13. Parkes in his reading chair in Geneva. In the background hang several of his watercolours and some antique candlesticks from his collection

14. 3 Grand Mezel is the building on the left. Parkes' flat was on the top floor directly above the lantern

15. American Church (Episcopal) of Geneva

meanderings acquired more direction, focus ... and phallic intention. They '... always ended at La Rolane, just outside of Marseilles, the delightful farmhouse where Mme Cru and her two daughters, Alice and Helène, lived. Helène was a keen member of the French [Student] Movement, and we had met at Heinrichsbad.'[5] As he recalls, with his descent southward his excitement would intensify as he accessed the magic triangle.

Mme Cru was born in Gloucestershire, very close to Oxford, no more than eighty miles east of the birthplace of Annie Parkes. Her husband had been a Protestant missionary. With such familiar points of reference, it is scarcely surprising that the young man bereft of his mother at the age of fourteen and subsequently taken up by a procession of older women, was naturally drawn to her as well as to her daughters, who, like himself, were half-orphaned.[6]

Parkes may indeed have understood as never before what the Psalmist meant when he spoke of the mountains and little hills skipping, but it is also evident that he hasn't a clue what he reveals by it. We recall that '... as the clouds passed across them, there were the high mountains slowly galumphing along like dignified dowagers while, at their feet, the little hills skipped merrily from sun to shadow and back again'. 'Dowager' precisely signifies widow. Fairly obviously, what the heavens disclose is a mimetic tableau wherein the slowly galumphing mountains represent the widow Cru presiding over a household consisting of daughters Alice and Helène, themselves symbolically the 'two merrily skipping hills' and each in turn metonymically distinguished by her own pair of merrily bouncing hills.

In the coming months, time and time again the tanned, handsome, road-weary but exhilarated young Englishman in search of improved health tumbled out of the North, his rucksack packed with fresh exploits to unload for the diversion of his receptive hosts. They shared engaging conversation over appetizing meals and long walks in the verdant countryside. Inverting the inner configuration of his own adolescent household, at La Rolane the surviving parent was not a disapproving father but a supportive mother whose loving acquiescence and indulgent presence almost surely abetted the dalliance and (she hoped) romantic ties between the promising, brilliant, good-looking twenty-eight-year-old Oxford graduate and one of her daughters.

Appropriately, all of the above was played out on the native soil of the wandering medieval troubadours out of whose 'ruck-sacks' was born the tradition of courtly love. Idealistic, genteel and pious, through a celebration that uneasily yoked honour and chaste devotion to adultery, courtly love in many of its versions dubiously supplanted the ideal of Christian celibacy with a carnal counterpart and an otherwise irreproachable but now approach-able lady. Of course the young man who as a boy had gazed in wonder at ceremonial medieval jousting tournaments and had thrilled to tales of *le Clameur de Haro* and medieval *Guernesiais* spoken as a living tongue, responded warmly to the vestiges of medievalism that he encountered in Provence.

Moreover, although no one would ever characterize James Parkes as unduly libidinous, neither is there reason to conclude that he was irretrievably homoerotic or irrevocably in thrall to the ideal of knightly chastity. On the contrary, on balance it seems far more probable that, in the course of his two to three years of journeying to that irresistibly desirable ménage, he did indeed dally with the affections of these nubile, young women. It does not seem likely that Mme Cru's bouillabaisse alone could account for the 'eleven or more' expeditions to La Rolane.[7] Given such a surfeit of opportunity and encouragement, what may have begun as a troubadour-sanctioned romantic dalliance almost certainly in the fullness of time graduated to a love affair with one of the Cru sisters. To think otherwise of the adventuring Parkes at this point in his life is to conceive a veritable monster of rectitude, a creature so bloodless as to beggar belief.

Parkes' affections may have wavered between the two sisters. 'Magic triangle,' after all, embraces not only the warm prize that excites the male imagination but the triadic character of the relationship that seems to have prevailed among the young per-sons. Intuition alone argues a tilt towards keen Helène, who later married and during the Second World War was active in the Resistance, rather than towards the more reclusive Alice, who would remain single for life.[8] To recapitulate then, beginning in the summer of 1924 Parkes, at the time quiescently bisexual but experimenting with his sexual identity, in all likelihood was involved in an exploratory affair at La Rolane that, given his temperament, developed into considerably more than fun and games.

The world of the flesh would always be a complicated busi-ness for Parkes. Nevertheless, putting aside the never marginal issue of his prowess, one feels warranted to draw the minimalist conclusion that during his late twenties Parkes was powerfully and erotically moved to journey to what loomed for him as the miraculously immanent, carnal triangle at La Rolane. Whether or not the reader finds every aspect of this close, analysis sufficiently penetrating, one hopes he will grant that Parkes aimed to penetrate to the very core of Provence, itself a surrogate for both his native island paradise and the biblical landscape of mountains and skipping streams described by the Psalmist. In short, in addition to his sexual involvement, his intense love affair with Provence and with its specific embodiment in Cruish corporeality also anticipates the most enduring love affair of Parkes' life: between himself and the Jewish people.

Although far better informed about France than most of its legions of visitors, Parkes, while footloose in Provence, seemed blissfully oblivious to the post-war trials of the French. True, inflation in the country was not nearly as devastating as in Germany, but still the French were also suffering from it. Inflation in France 'lasted much longer and was ultimately more corrosive of national morale ... Against the dollar, the franc in 1939 was only one seventieth of its 1913 value'.[9] For American and British tourists and expatriates, France between the wars was a bargain-basement cornucopia, 'but it was oppressive for the French who treated the erosion of their *rentes* and savings as an additional reason for having fewer children'.[10]

Moreover, on a tight budget but fortified with hard currency, Parkes displayed little sensitivity to the impact of the pound sterling's strength on the staggering French economy or on the feelings of the natives. In fact, his infatuation with France seems to have blinded him to most of its less seemly realities. His memoir takes no notice of the steady growth in power of the French nationalist *ultras*, of the popularity of monarchist poet Charles Maurras's *Action Française*, of French receptivity to bizarre racist and antisemitic theories, nor of the growing vulnerability of the Third Republic to fascism. Things had come to such a pass that at the time of the Stavisky scandal in 1933, one seasoned observer comments 'some kind of proto-fascist state would almost certainly have come into existence ... had Maurras given the signal for action'.[11]

Did Parkes not know that Maurras, 'the major counter-revolutionary writer during the Third Republic', was not only a native of Provence but had made it his base?[12] As he pedalled about his beloved *département*, perhaps the future historian was unaware of the populist upheavals that preceded the 1898 French national elections in Marseilles, just a few kilometres down the road from La Rolane, there had been virulent and violent antisemitic demonstrations. Perhaps he did not know that, as the Vichy regime would bear out fifteen years later, anti-Dreyfusard, anti-democratic, antisemitic sentiment was rapidly fermenting beneath the choppy surface of the Third Republic.[13] For all we can tell he was too charmed by the Provençal countryside, its heritage and *les belles Cru* to pay France's desperate realities due notice.

Political reflections of a different sort, however, were now beginning to isolate him from his SCM colleagues. Parkes was sensitive to inherent contradictions in the stance of the doctrinaire pacifists, in particular of those committed to the struggle for a just international order. As noted earlier, at least since the end of the war Parkes in principle had supported pacifism but, subsuming his views under a general endorsement for the strengthening of the peace-keeping role of the League of Nations, he had refrained from actually joining any pacifist organizations. Since the efficacy of pacifism in the real world was fatally compromised by the rise of Mussolini and then Hitler, in retrospect Parkes' inner reservations seem rather prescient.

Parkes' second dilemma, also theoretical in nature, was considerably more vexing to him personally: the more conferences, workshops and retreats he attended, the more conscious he grew of a growing void at the very heart of his activities, a hollowness that in his own eyes imperilled their integrity. In the absence of what he designated a meaningful 'theology of politics', Parkes was unable satisfactorily to connect his progressive political orientation to his Christian beliefs: '... I could find no solution, not even in discussion with William Temple, though it was he who always encouraged me to go on puzzling. To my colleagues in the SCM, I think I became something of a bore. Somehow I felt it must be tied up with our doctrine of the Trinity ...'[14] Over the years, this pivotal intuition would flicker but never entirely dim; in time it would play out in highly original reflections about the nature of the Personhood of the Trinity.

What is particularly instructive about Parkes' fixation on the nexus between political orientation and religious belief is the habit of mind it reveals. Intellectually rigorous, Parkes always strove for an integrative consistency that promised to resolve seeming contradictions at a higher level of synthesis. An inability to construct a web of connectedness between politics and metaphysics would not leave his mind at rest. His constantly exasperated colleagues labelled Parkes' theological agitation 'Jimmie's bee in his bonnet about God'. In a few years Parkes' focus would shift towards effecting reconciliation between the verities of the New Testament and the unterminated imperatives of the Old Testament. Rather than permitting him to rest comfortably in theological 'mysteries', Jimmie's 'Jewish bee' would sting his conscience mercilessly, in the end driving him towards the resolution of dissonance with a spate of strikingly original theological speculations.

In the summer of 1925 Parkes attended an ESR conference at Gex, very close to Geneva. Because the relief work for which the ESR had been founded four years earlier had become less urgent, a Committee of Two composed of Parkes and Bettina Warburg was appointed to make recommendations regarding its future. They proposed that the ESR gradually phase out its operations. For Parkes the immediate uproar of disapproval, particularly from Jews and other student minorities in Eastern Europe, was illuminating. He had not fully appreciated that, as the only European organization in which all student factions, groupings and nationalities met on an equal footing, the ESR provided a uniquely valuable forum for many of its participants. Beyond its relief activities, the very presence of the ESR on the international scene fulfilled a vital need.[15]

Reflecting changing conditions but still taking cognizance of the ESR's special role, a compromise solution was hammered out. The name of the organization would thenceforth be the International Student Service (ISS). However, with a nod towards its ethnic constituencies, the assembly also approved the Parkes–Warburg counterproposal for the establishment of a new Committee for Cultural Cooperation. In light of Parkes' imminent preoccupation with Jewish issues, it is passing strange that he refers to Bettina simply as the daughter of 'the great American banker', a strikingly circumspect locution for Paul Warburg whom Parkes also neglects to note was a prominent Jew, one highly visible in communal philanthropies such as the Joint Distribution Committee.

A similar muffling of an explicit Jewish connection tinges Parkes' recollection of one of the most spectacular public events of the era. While attending a conference Parkes had become acquainted with a German student who was a member of what Parkes understatedly characterizes as,

> ... a small group of very serious students, high minded, patriotic, and intellectually of the first water ... [who] ... with a kind of mystical exaltation very foreign to our calmer temperaments [out of despair decided] to assassinate the greatest man in Germany ... as a demonstration! Their choice was unhappily correct, and in the hour of their greatest need, their insane crime robbed Germany of the one man whose brilliant gifts might have rendered her enormous service, Dr Walter Rathenau.[16]

This dark 'mystical demonstration' made history on June 24, 1922.

While Parkes' repugnance is manifest, a queer aspect of his brief account is the care he takes to distinguish between condemnation of the crime and empathy with the desperation of the assassins. This makes a signal omission all the more puzzling. Scores of historians and political commentators have described the assassination of Walter Rathenau. Consider a typical rendering of the assassination that virtually sealed the fate first of Germany, then of Europe and, finally, of its Jews:

> [Rathenau] was an aristocratic revolutionary, an idealistic economic planner, a Jew who was a German patriot, a German patriot who was a liberal citizen of the world ... Rathenau and Hitler are two men who excited the imagination of the German masses to the utmost; the one by his ineffable culture, the other by his ineffable vileness.[17]

When one compares these various reports, Parkes' stands apart by neglecting to mention that Rathenau was a Jew. However Parkes must have realized that Rathenau was murdered not because of his brilliance, his moral character, his ethical qualities or even his prominence. As with *Wall Street Journal* correspondent Daniel Pearl, Rathenau was singled out for assassination primarily because he was publicly identified as a Jew.[18]

First with Warburg and then with Rathenau, Parkes' curious absent-mindedness about Jewishness may have been a conscious rhetorical tactic to suggest his distance from specifically Jewish issues at that time. It may even have served some long-forgotten expedient need. Contrariwise, recalling that his memoir was written in old age, the omission could also reflect the thoroughness of Parkes' subsequent immersion into a Jewish *Weltanshauung*. That is to say, writing as though he were actually a Jewish historian whose main target was a communal audience, perhaps Parkes assumed that the issue of the Jewishness of his better-known subjects could be taken for granted. In the end, neither of these explanations feels satisfactory. Perhaps the best ground upon which to rest is that the conference at Gex, which marked Parkes' first public involvement with an issue of specifically Jewish salience, planted a seed of concern which required a period of gestation in darkness before ripening into public and habitual commitment. Until that process came to full term, Parkes' memoir mimetically downplays explicitly Jewish signposts.

Another minor but pungent mystery also invites speculation: Bettina Warburg's nickname for Parkes was 'Flibberty', a sobriquet about which Parkes displays not a whit of curiosity. 'Flibbertigibbet', its closest cognate, calls to mind an irresponsible or silly person and vaguely suggests fecklessness or something akin to insubstantiality, attributes Parkes would not ordinarily admire and certainly not ones he would acknowledge in himself. So why might Warburg have found so earnest a young chap as Jimmy Parkes silly? Assuming the pet name echoes 'liberty' but sounds a mildly censorious note, it might have originated in a romantic overture which Parkes did not have the wit or wish to reciprocate. Finally, the name also evokes 'Liberty's,' a well-known, up-market London department store, very likely patronized by Warburg, which then featured a *beaux arts, fin de siècle* decor redolent of sexual indeterminacy. Perhaps Parkes was too much the flibbertigibbet for Bettina to pin down. If so, the nickname points toward Parkes' unresolved sexuality, an ineffable lightness in his being that he was not then – or ever really – prepared to confront directly.

Warburg was not alone in detecting a mercurial strain in Parkes as a young man. With all his butterfly-like flitting among what reads to a casual observer like a gaggle of interchangeable, self-important organizations all promoting similarly good works – the LNU, NUS, ESR, CIE, SCM and WSCF, and several other now-defunct bodies to which at various times he attached himself – one influential reviewer of *Voyage of Discoveries* thought this clerical advocate of internationalism, humanitarianism, peace and democratic cooperation a perfect example of a 'uni-dimensional organization man'.

> He never had a parish, but spent most of his working life in one high-minded international body after another, scurrying from capital to capital, making contacts, getting resolutions passed, summoning meetings. Indeed there were even moments when Muggeridge-like tremors began to possess me and I craved, in all this garrulity, of good wishes and brisk smiles, for something dark and poetical, deeply mystical, death-enhancing, for some sense of the wry, the really wicked, the mad, the effete, the complex, the subtle, the perverse.[19]

Overlooking small accuracies, this meretricious portrait entirely obscures the essential point. Among the 'shallow' attitudes embraced by Parkes one could cite a penchant for the reconciliation of former enemies and a detestation of anti-semitism. Beyond that, what the reviewer describes is the brilliant organization man Parkes might have become had he not chosen the life of a freelance scholar and fashioned himself into an original theologian, an anti-Nazi activist, a ground-breaking historian and a profound moralist who for the greater part of his creative and professional life was beholden to no organization whatsoever. Just how misleadingly wicked, mad, effete, complex, subtle, perverse can a reviewer be?

Gex was followed later in the summer of 1925 by another Swiss conference, a regional conclave of the World Student Christian Federation at Oberägeri. This was the first international conclave over which Parkes presided as chairman. Unusually for the period, the focus of the conference was the Jewish question itself; yet even more atypical of the WSCF, a Jewish student leader had been invited to present the Jewish perspective. It marked the first time that Parkes was constrained to deal front-ally with 'the Jewish problem': 'Hitherto it had just been one of the many contemporary problems of which I was aware. This conference made me aware of its violence and special quality'.[20] More than anyone could have anticipated, the Oberägeri conference signalled a watershed in Parkes' life, altering its course permanently.

This portentous occasion deserves a full airing. After Parkes opened the inaugural session of the conference on a hopeful, conciliatory note, the first scheduled speaker responded by delivering before the gathered delegates of the Central European Christian Movement a venomous, antisemitic diatribe. Even though Parkes had not yet embarked on his special research on the Jewish question or even adequately formulated the issue for himself, the former Secretary of the LNU, whose debates under his leadership had been organized with scrupulous attention to fairness, was appalled. Like all well-read Europeans of progressive tendencies, Parkes was fully conscious that the incendiary harangue was rife with 'false accusations and innuendos'.[21] Although the speech in question itself is untraceable, its all-too-familiar themes may easily be surmised: a Jewish conspiracy, in an advanced state of implementation, was planning to take over the world. It had to be stopped at all costs. Such is the basic plot of the notorious *Protocols of the Elders of Zion*. As Parkes would detail a few years later in his first book,[22] in spite of having been exposed repeatedly as a forgery, in the years immediately following the First World War *Protocols* had already achieved wide currency, first in Eastern Europe and later in the West.

When the speaker concluded his tirade, Parkes, in his maiden appearance in the chair, displayed stunningly heroic resolve, principled stubbornness, chutzpah, a new-found maturity and qualities of leadership one searches for in vain in the record of his years in the military. Outfacing the confounded, openly hostile assembly, he adamantly refused to recognize the next or any speaker until the opening oration, which Parkes declared wholly unacceptable as a fair and adequate introduction to the issue, had been entirely withdrawn. This threw the Central European delegates into pandemonium, and no one could have been more startled than the conference's token Jewish observer from Rumania. The minutes passed fitfully, the din only grew, but Parkes adamantly refused to 'listen to reason'. Standing upon his prerogative as chairman and virtually alone, a remarkably calm Parkes declared that the conference would end there and then unless the first speaker delivered a formal apology or unless he, Parkes, was forcibly removed from the chair.

What no one in the packed hall, except perhaps Parkes himself looking back on it later, could possibly have appreciated is that in stanching the flow of conference business, Parkes' passionate stand for fairness, truth and justice could well have proceeded from a sudden access to consciousness of submerged, youthful memory traces of Guernsey's *Clameur de Haro*. We recall that in the event of what was perceived to be a manifest act of injustice, an appeal to *le Clameur* automatically suspended public proceedings for twenty-four hours.[23] At Oberägeri, of course, such a delay would have been out of the question, but twenty minutes of behind-the-scene manoeuvrings were sufficient to prevail upon the reactionary keynote speaker to retake the floor. Pleading that he must have been misunderstood, the young man declared that his intent had truly not been antisemitic and, with something short of good grace, he reluctantly tendered an apology.

This transparent fiction provided Parkes with the fig leaf he needed in order to permit the conference to proceed. At this distance, the insincerity of the speaker's recantation is insignificant. What is of signal importance is that, when exposed at first hand to the poisonous malevolence of Eastern European antisemitism, Parkes acted with decisiveness, clarity and dispatch. Suddenly coming of age, he had outgrown the temporizing of his past. It bears mention, of course, that he thoroughly relished rising to the dramatic moment. Beyond histrionics however, his instinctive response, which threatened to wreck the entire conference, constituted a display of the decency and courage which from that time forth would characterize his involvement with the Jewish issue. Finally, it hardly seems accidental that Parkes' virile imposition of will and assertion of authority upon the assembly at Oberägeri overlapped with his serial voyages of sexual discovery down the valley of the Rhône to La Rolane.

From the very start Parkes felt drawn to defend the Jewish people for a variety of reasons, some conscious and highly principled, others perceived darkly at best. At no point, for example, does he offer any hint of self-awareness that might confirm the premise that his Guernsey background or Guernseyman identity prepared him for his self-appointed mission. On the contrary, he himself ever tended to view his 'Jewish bee' as something of a mystery. What Parkes did sense almost immediately, however, was that he was equipped, situated, motivated, and even destined to assume his extraordinary role as 'Paladin of the Jews'. In good time this would cause him to spearhead opposition to the Church's traditionally prestigious missionary activities among Jews. With his spontaneous rise to the occasion at Oberägeri, Parkes had discovered the higher purpose that would lend immense substance and meaning to his life. He never looked back.

After Oberägeri and subsequent meetings in Venice and Belgrade, Parkes attended a conference of the Russian Orthodox Church in Hopovo. Aspects of this gathering strongly appealed to a different side of his nature. Like the Rumanian Jew at Oberägeri, he was now the lone stranger, the only non-Russian in attendance. Although he understood not a word of the pre-breakfast service, which lasted for up to three hours, he found the Russian liturgy to be 'an overwhelming ... profound spiritual experience'.[24] This serves as an instructive reminder. Because Parkes' powers of reasoning were highly developed, it is tempting to de-emphasize, if not to scant entirely, his spiritual yearning upon which he comments little. However, as with his earlier experience at Heinrichsbad, Hopovo reminds us that one of the notable achievements of Parkes' life would be to establish and to maintain a finely calibrated balance between these complementary facets of his personality.

NOTES

1. Gabriel García Márquez, *Living to Tell the Tale*, translated by Edith Grossman (New York: Knopf, 2003), p. 1.
2. James Parkes, *Voyage of Discoveries* (London: Victor Gollancz, 1969), p. 79, ff.
3. Ibid., pp. 82–83.
4. *Vide* Chapters 1 and 2.
5. Ibid., p. 82.
6. Ibid., p. 83.
7. Ibid.
8. Ibid., p. 216.
9. André Bisson, *L'Inflation Française 1914–1952* (Paris, 1953), cited in Paul Johnson, *Modern Times: The World From The Twenties To The Nineties* (New York: Harper Perennial Edition, 1992), p. 141.
10. Johnson, *Modern Times*, p. 141.
11. Ibid.
12. Michael Curtis, *Verdict on Vichy* (New York: Arcade, 2002), p. 41.
13. Pierre Birnbaum, *The Anti-Semitic Moment: A Tour of France in 1898*, translated by Jane Todd (New York: Hill and Wang, 2003), p. 150, ff.
14. James Parkes, *Voyage of Discoveries* p. 84, ff.
15. Ibid., p. 86, ff.
16. Ibid., p. 73.

17. Sebastian Haffner, *Defying Hitler: A Memoir*, translated by Oliver Pretzel (London: Phoenix, 2003), pp. 40–41.
18. Noel Ascherson, 'Goodbye to Berlin', *New York Review of Books*, Vol. L, No. 6, 10 April 2003, p. 22.
19. Philip Toynbee, 'Champion of the Jews', *Observer*, 13 April 1969, Parkes Archives, File 60/7/36/5.
20. Parkes, *Voyage of Discoveries*, p. 87.
21. Ibid.
22. James Parkes, *The Jew and His Neighbour: A Study in the Causes of Antisemitism* (London: SCM Press, 1930).
23. *Vide* Chapter 4.
24. Parkes, *Voyage of Discoveries*, p. 88.

15
———

Perpetual Refreshment

In the spring of 1926 Parkes enthusiastically agreed to carry on with his work at the SCM for another three years. For a young man of his talents and temperament, careering around Europe from conference to conference where he frequently took centre stage among the other young leaders of a post-war generation, it was an ideal job. However, the first assignment of Parkes' second tour would keep him much closer to home: he took on what was '... unquestionably the most difficult job in the SCM',[1] the wardenship of the Student Movement House in the Blooms-bury district of London.

Charged with the task of devising innovative programmes both to facilitate interaction among disparate groups of overseas Christian students and to enable them to relate harmoniously with non-Christian students, Parkes' newest challenge was urgently hands-on: to keep the lid on a turbulent, potentially explosive brew. Working closely with Zoë Fairfield, Parkes demonstrated extraordinary talent in the roles of innovator, organizer and administrator. In order to bridge the gap between the residents and himself as warden, one of his first moves was to forge a close relationship with Thomas 'Len' Thomas, handy-man of the Student Movement House. A few years older than Parkes, Thomas provided the house warden with an invaluable channel of informal communication with the students. In contrast, Parkes found it impossible to work effectively with the House's ageing, interfering chairman. After a very stressful period, he employed the same tactic that had worked at Oberägeri – the threat of resignation. Parkes prevailed, and the obstructive chairman was removed.[2]

Although his work in London was tremendously time-consuming, Parkes continued to keep track of developments, especially Jewish developments, on the Continent. To no one's surprise, when the World Union of Jewish Students (WUJS) applied for membership to the ISS and turned to British student organizations for support, Parkes immediately warmed to the idea. Step by step, with no clear idea where it might lead, Parkes kept extending his involvement with the Jewish student question. Still, a confidential, handwritten report entitled 'The Situation of the Jewish Student' that he filed with the British SCM office in 1926 was less a testament to his expertise than to the dearth of knowledge of others. His conclusions confirmed that in France, as in every country where Jewish numbers were not limited by the imposition of a *numerus clausus*, Jews comprised a disproportionately high percentage of the student body. In contrast, at Poland's five universities, which imposed strict restrictions, the proportion of Jewish students did not exceed ten per cent, the same as that in the general population.[3]

In the winter of 1926, nearly a year after he had assumed his onerous duties as warden, Parkes was approached by the general secretary of the ISS. As noted earlier, this Geneva-based organization was an offshoot of the ESR, but its mandate was much broader. Parkes had been selected to coordinate its new venture in cultural cooperation, a most logical choice since Parkes at Gex had co-authored the proposal. At first he was thrilled by the opportunity, but his enthusiasm was short-lived: neither the position nor the programme was properly funded. If he accepted, it would be left to Parkes to raise the funds to implement it.

Except for his boyhood success as financier of the joint stock company composed of the three Parkes adolescents, he had never displayed notable talent or interest in this more tawdry side of internationalist idealism. In fact the conferences he had organized for the SCM invariably ran up substantial deficits. Parkes' new appointment, therefore, seemed likely to be aborted from the start until the intervention of a most unlikely *deus ex machina*, a pattern, by the way, that foreshadows the happy resolution of a number of his other cruxes in the future. Parkes, of course, tended to view these as timely intercessions of the Third Person (or 'channel') of *Deus* Himself.

At one of his occasional luncheon dates with Bettina Warburg, Parkes mentioned ruefully how for lack of financing the opportunity to implement the programme the two of them had devised at Gex was likely to slip through his fingers. Her response was immediate: 'If you're going to do that, Flibberty, you know the family will be responsible for your finances.'[4] It was a deal Flibberty could not turn down. Moreover, since Parkes was nothing if not a quick learner, the Warburg connection powerfully anticipates his *modus operandi* when, nearly a decade later, the time would come to move on from the ISS.

Parkes' subdued acknowledgement appeared in the introductory pamphlet he issued about ISS history and programmes: 'It is interesting to note that the entire finances of the Department were paid by a single American who had taken part in the original discussions of the meeting of cultural cooperation at the conference of 1925'.[5] Perhaps even more 'interesting' and 'noteworthy' is that, possibly complying with Warburg's wishes, Parkes dropped a veil over the identity of its chief benefactor. Additionally, or alternatively, he might have been tactfully aiming at concealing the new department's dependence upon Jewish funding, always a potentially sensitive matter.

Compounding obfuscation, Parkes also misleadingly alluded to the presence of the wrong member of 'the family' at Gex in 1925. This is not the last time mistaken identity would complicate the plot of Parkes' outward voyage. Before leaving London on his new assignment, he reached an agreement with handyman 'Len' Thomas: upon Parkes' return to England, Thomas would come to work as his manservant and general 'factotum'.[6] That seems straightforward enough, but when the time arrives, save that the denouement would entail unexpectedly serious consequences, we shall see that the tangle of misleading expectations and misidentification between the two of them could rival that of any Shakespearian comedy.[7]

Parkes spent all of March 1928, his first month as a full-time ISS staff member, in Prague, scene of his 'glorious week' during the summer of 1924. This time, occupying himself with sharpening his grasp of Central European political affairs and student matters, he lodged with the married sister of one of his SCM friends. Upon arriving in Geneva, Parkes rapidly established easy working relationships with the general secretary of the ISS, an Austrian named Kotschnig, his Welsh wife with whom Parkes was acquainted as a past SCM colleague, and Michel Poberezski, a Russian whose home base was Paris. Others later joined the staff, but these four comprised the administrative core of what turned out to be a lean and efficient operation.

Registered under Swiss law, the central purpose of the ISS, which was a non-membership organization, was to serve the needs of students, especially those under duress, anywhere in the world. Inevitably, however, its focus was European. The ISS's midsummer conferences were, we are informed, 'one of the big annual occasions in the student world, being a unique meeting of staff and students from many continents'.[8] At these festive gatherings, the ISS's annual programme was formulated and plans for its implementation by student representatives from all participating countries were discussed and approved. These annual get-togethers provided a young man with Parkes' ideals and abilities with both a highly receptive audience and the perfect stage upon which to perform.

Early that summer, still ebullient about the novelty and seemingly unlimited potential of his new position, Parkes established himself in cosmopolitan but cosy Geneva. The greater part of the foreign colony resided in the modern city, then as now a most expensive place to live. But it would not do for Parkes. Yielding to a penchant for aestheticism and drama, antiquarian tastes, and an islander's instinct to distance himself from the rootless anonymity of the city's international community, Parkes located ideal accommodation in *la Cité*, Calvin's compact hill town. The view of Geneva's famous lake from his top floor flat, which originally had been the servants' quarters of a bourgeois, sixteenth century dwelling, was splendid. His newcomer's sensibility – an eye for architectural purity and a taste for authenticity – responded keenly to his apartment's original appointments:

> I had wonderful ironwork on my doors, curly hinges, lovely key plates and latches, immense bolts and locks, all of which I cleaned and oiled. There was an enormous larch beam right across the flat nearly forty feet in length and ten inches in girth. In my work room it rested on two complex struts, one of which stood up from the floor on a wooden pillar.[9]

Carelessly elegant, 3 Grand Mezel was the exquisite antithesis of the haphazard, haunted, scruffy domicile where he passed his adolescence. For nearly seven years it would serve as Parkes' work-in-progress, his lair and his refuge. His hand-picked collection of Jacobean and eighteenth century period pieces – which had cost him considerable effort and a pretty penny to ship from Oxford – were dramatically offset by their late medieval trappings. No doubt for Parkes, taking possession of his sixteenth century redoubt against vulgarity was sheer bliss. Philosophically modernist, in the private sphere Parkes cultivated a connoisseur's disdain for modernity. As he puts it with precision, 'the beauty of my flat was a perpetual refreshment'.[10] Not a syllable is expended on the sanitary amenities at 3 Grand Mezel which, by Anglo-Saxon standards, were doubtless 'primitive'. Nevertheless, Parkes' situation in *la Cité* may be considered a hands-on, real-time 'study conference' in good taste and gracious living.

Establishing a sympathetic religious base in the Swiss centre did not proceed quite as smoothly. Parkes, in fact, was sharply jolted by an uncivil reception at the city's Anglican church. Its chaplain, vociferously disapproving of the progressive political line taken by the SCM, effectively consigned Parkes' seven years of bountiful toil in the field of student activism to irrelevancy if not utter damnation. Rebuffed by the local Anglican establishment, Parkes took refuge at Emmanuel Episcopal, the American Church of Geneva, where he was warmly welcomed by the Reverend Everett Smith. Parkes became a regular parishioner at Emmanuel, occasionally doing a turn as acting chaplain. Nevertheless, rejection by the chaplain of his home church foreshadowed seven lean, ecclesiastical years to come during which Parkes could count upon the support of few beyond Smith and his small band of American Christian expatriates.

During those first weeks at 3 Grand Mezel, Parkes had little time to enjoy his new home. He had to throw himself instead into the preparations for the big ISS July conference, that year to convene in Chartres. At this gathering Parkes' main objective would be to secure organizational endorsement for the implementation of cross-cultural study conferences for which, after all, he had been scouted. Preliminary to that, however, far more mundane organizational details fell within his purview. Since, for example, 'a bevy of British and American girls' would be arriving in Chartres,[11] it fell to him to negotiate with the concierge of the charming *lycée* where they were to be housed over the matter of the uncharming stench that emanated from its WCs. In a trice, a less foul facility was located, one that the English-speaking *jeune filles* would find inoffensive. Would that all of Parkes' crises in the coming months and years had yielded to resolution so readily.

In the evenings at Chartres, while smaller, more earnest contingents of this multinational congregation carried on debating issues raised during the daily sessions, the greater part transformed themselves into *philosophes du café*, seeking entertainment and fun. Unsurprisingly, at the morning sessions a great many turned up late and bleary-eyed. Parkes bore special responsibility for keeping all aspects of the conference moving smoothly, so organizational chores kept him very busy. Inasmuch as the centerpiece of the conference agenda – debate over a refined version of the programme Parkes and Warburg had hastily cobbled together three years earlier – won approval without difficulty, he could only have viewed the Chartres conference in an auspicious light.

It is curious that, in recalling those five days spent in Chartres as a young man, the elderly Anglican cleric, who as a boy had been such an enthusiast about medieval churches and cathedrals, could not rouse even perfunctory delight over the aesthetic qualities of the light that streamed through the cathedral's universally admired rose window. Nor would he deign to praise the splendid proportions or spiritual qualities of the fabled Gothic cathedral. As we shall discover, these omissions are characteristic.

Later that summer Parkes returned to Gex to attend a conclave under the auspices of the WSCF. Having earned universal respect for wielding such a stern gavel as chairman of the tumultuous 1925 WSCF gathering, Parkes was now invited to deliver the invocation and opening meditation. His pleasure in these token honours soon faded. The main speaker was Fritz Lieb, one of the closest associates of the conservative theologian Karl Barth, and the ensuing four days were fully devoted to an exposition of Barth's astringent, retrograde ideas about the Fall of Man. Confirming his repugnance upon first being exposed to Barth's ideas two years earlier at Heinrichsbad, Parkes remarks, 'It was my first encounter with the full blast of the abominable heresy of Barthianism'.[12]

What most infuriated the young English cleric about what was, after all, a highly traditional version of Christian theology was its exclusive emphasis on the depth of man's depravity and his radical incommensurability with God-the-Unfathomable. This not only undermined mankind's capacity for ameliorating political and social ills but released him from the responsibility of making the effort. 'The growing effect of Barth began to be pitifully and tragically evident in the students who came to international conferences from the Christian Student Movements influenced by him. All social and political striving was dead.'[13] In contrast, Parkes' more socially responsive, less supine style of liberal Christianity aimed to impel believers to assume personal responsibility for the promotion of God's plan of creation in the real world and urged them to work to allay social wrongs.

On this theological wrangle, history gives the nod decisively to Parkes. In just a few years widespread attachment to Barthianism would emasculate German Christianity root and branch, rendering it silent and overwhelmed in the face of the burgeoning threat of National Socialism. Not given to hyperbole, from the very start and without qualification Parkes viewed Barth's version of Christianity as 'an evil doctrine.' He would never waver from this verdict.

Parkes now channelled his fury over the doings at Gex in a new and fruitful direction: he spent much of the autumn and winter preparing an analytical essay *contra* Barthianism. This, his first foray into original theological speculation, was highly ambitious: it aimed at nothing less than a fresh approach to the mystery of the Holy Trinity which, as we recall, he had earlier intuited was the key to formulating a new 'theology of politics'. Two years later, he felt better prepared to deal with the issue. Parkes entertained unrealistically high hopes that the fruit of his arduous studies might help to stem the spread of Christian quietism which, like the rising tide at Alderney, threatened to undermine the solid foundation that supported all he had striven to achieve for nearly a decade, but to little avail. 'By the beginning of the thirties,' he later remarks, 'I was out of sympathy, not merely with the WSCF, but with the SCM itself in which the same [Barthian] influence was becoming paramount.'[14]

Zealously fulfilling his cross-cultural mandate, Parkes soon found himself fully engaged in organizing a perpetual round of student conferences throughout Europe. These kept him constantly on the road to the extent that in the course of seven years in Geneva, he recalls spending four uninterrupted weeks in *la Cité* only once.[15] Typically, these student gatherings attempted to increase mutual understanding by bringing together all sorts of disparate groups: there was a conference for students from Europe and the Pacific rim of Asia, a conference for students from Europe and India, a conference for students from new nation states, and so on. Under the guidance of panels of invited experts, carefully selected participants cocooned themselves for

up to a week at a time to engage in extensive study by day and
intensive socializing by night. In a way, these sessions anticipated
the teach-ins that flourished on American university campuses
in the 1960s.

One surmises that for Parkes the formal aspects of these
gatherings, which he conducted in the spirit of fair play as
embodied in the procedures of an English debating society, were
as important as their substance. Nevertheless, although each
conference brought together a unique mix of ingredients, to the
single participant who perforce had to attend them all, these
student stews came to taste much the same.

Moreover, while travel in moderation elicits fresh perspectives,
perpetual motion dulls them. Parkes' grinding schedule soon
exacted its inexorable toll of weariness and disillusion. Only six
months after starting to work in his dream position, Parkes was
already complaining that his day-to-day job was 'concerned
almost always with the ugliness men made of their common life'
– meaning not their so-called individual 'ordinary lives' but their
social life together. Attendance at 'assemblies which lasted a
whole week' wore him down both physically and spiritually. 'My
temper was usually exhausted by the end of the first day of the
committees, with the result that I was a burden to my colleagues
and myself for the rest of the week.'[16]

Growing increasingly impatient with his administrative duties,
Parkes brings to mind the unenviable man upon whom the genie
showers three wishes. The Warburg family bestowed Parkes with
the platform, the financing and the organizational authority to
implement the programme for cultural cooperation that he and
Bettina had concocted at Gex. However, these could not and
would not bring him anticipated pleasure or real satisfaction.

In sharp contrast, Parkes' vivid description of the delights of
meandering about the narrow streets of *la Cité*, of browsing in
its shops in the months before the onset of the Great Depression
is exuberant.

> Within two hundred yards of my flat I could get any article
> in gold, silver, copper, or iron made for me. I could get cloth
> woven for furnishing or for dress. I could get a dinner
> service made and painted. I could get furniture made or
> repaired. I could get jam or cakes or a whole dinner cooked
> for me; and in addition, for groceries, fruit, and so on I had

delightful little shops where I was served by the patron, and we knew each other by name.

Save for one necessity, Parkes could find everything he wanted under the sun in *la Cité*: for Gruyère, cheese that suited his pallet, the Guernsey gourmet was constrained to cross the French frontier at Annemasse.[17]

However, Parkes could not, with his fastidious taste, often splurge on antiques or superfluous services when negotiating in hard Swiss francs with yet harder local shopkeepers. His annual salary was £400,[18] roughly what his father earned in his greener years as an agriculturalist. Nevertheless, the relative strength of sterling elsewhere on the Continent and the acumen Parkes had developed as a collector during his acquisitive forays had sharpened his financial skills. Besides, as though sublimely certain of his own qualities or God's good favour, Parkes displayed little apprehension about money. An excerpt from a 1929 letter addressed to a close friend from his days at the Student Movement House reflects his 'worldliness': '... the standard of expenditure is to realize the Kingdom of God here and now (as well as in the future). [Therefore] we are justified in spending on luxuries: books, good pictures, theatre, beautiful furniture, flowers, holidays.'[19]

Whenever he felt dispirited or the urge to escape from Geneva overwhelmed him, Parkes crossed the frontier for more than conferences and cheese. Only fifty miles over the Alps sat Lyon from where he could easily cycle down the valley of the Rhône to indulge his passion for Provence and its amiable downriver residents. In addition, at regular intervals Parkes exploited a ready excuse for not detraining at Lyon. The ISS subsidized a student restaurant in Paris which was managed by a woman who could never seem to comprehend that the point of the operation was not to turn a profit but to fill the bellies of impecunious, Eastern European students. Since she persisted in cutting corners, Parkes had to put in an appearance in Paris fairly regularly to oversee the operation. He took delight in his absurdist exchanges with the devoted but seemingly dim-witted employee.[20]

Before returning to the Gare de Lyon, one imagines the young aesthete taking in some of the attractions of the city, then at its zenith as the unchallenged capital of the world of arts and letters.

One would think that during his many trips there the talented amateur draughtsman and watercolourist would have stopped to sketch along the banks of the Seine and visited the Louvres. Yet inexplicably, in his memoir Paris fares no better than Chartres or Prague.[21] Are we to credit these lapses to Parkes' single-mindedness, to the memoirist's editorial reticence, to negligence or even perhaps to the onset of his imminent, obsessive involvement with Jewish issues? At a more appropriate point, the import of these omissions will be addressed and explored.[22]

During the summer months Parkes regularly played host to visiting American students, a different group almost every weekend in fact. He made the most of it. Invitations were issued through the American Consul or the consulate wives, the YMCA arranged the catering and Parkes himself organized the evening's entertainment. The script he authored was tailor-made to inform and to impress. After a rendezvous in the modern city, all the way bantering impressively, he guided the earnest young tourists through the courtyards and passageways of *la Cité*.

> The culmination came with my candle-lit flat. When I had a full evening, it took sixty candles, all in ancient sticks and sconces. It was a unique occasion for most of the guests who could handle antiques and sit on furniture they ordinarily saw only in museums and show places … Lit with wax candles, and with all my old furniture, 3 Grand Mezel came to rank with Versailles as one of the places an American student tried to visit on a trip to Europe.[23]

Following a well-crafted programme, Parkes led his guests in an after-dinner discussion on a topic of current interest. With these untutored overseas visitors, he shamelessly revelled in his self-appointed role as cosmopolitan, worldly savant, spiritual advisor and cicerone. For this 3 Grand Mezel provided a brilliant *mise-en-scène* for its occupant to stage, direct and star in his very own *pièce de théâtre*, every week doing his one man show before a new, appreciative audience. We can hardly help but smile at Parkes' boyish delight in his offbeat performance – the hip pastor. Although his religious, political and ethical commitments cast Parkes both spiritually and intellectually in a decisively anti-Bloomsbury mould, his sensibility was fully responsive to the G. E. Moore–Lytton Strachey brand of aestheticism that was in

the ascendant in post-Edwardian Britain. With all its inconsis-
tencies, the figure Parkes cut in Geneva surpasses the sickly
schoolboy, the irresolute lieutenant, the neophyte lover and the
precocious scholar. Basically, this was James Parkes as he would
remain for the rest of his days.

If in physical stature the boyish cleric from Guernsey was no
taller than average, he carried himself with a sure, graceful,
aristocratic bearing. Certainly more than a few of his visitors
would have welcomed a sexual overture from this young man.
The question inevitably arises whether from time to time the professional organizer ever organized an assignation for himself
with some of the passing parade of nubile visitors to 3 Grand
Mezel. In short, did any admirers ever spend the night? The
likelihood seems slim, as long as Parkes embraced his twin roles
as official representative of the ISS and priest of the Church of
England. By the same token, one could fondly imagine that once
away from the domain of Calvin – in Provence, Prague or Paris,
on an exhilarating hiking or cycling expedition with a chosen
few of his increasingly younger contemporaries, or perhaps even
after a drearier than usual session at the conference table – that
at least on occasion Parkes deviated from the fine ethical line he
had drawn in the sand to negotiate for himself an exploratory,
consensual intimacy.

As if to put to the test his abstract faith in the goodness of the
human spirit Parkes, following his earlier practice when he lived
in Oxford, fought Barthianism in his own way: he left his key
with ISS colleagues who in his absence freely lent his flat to
anyone they saw fit. *Noblesse oblige*, as Parkes conceived it, was
well requited:

> During that time I never had any damage done to my
> furniture; on two occasions when a jug was broken, I only
> realized it when I found a new jug in its place; and I never
> lost a book. I never found the flat dirty on my return, and
> often only found out it had been used when I went to the
> office and they told me.[24]

No one failed the test. Parkes draws special attention to this rare
sign of the high potential of man at the personal level because
it contrasts so starkly with the public sphere whose political,
economic and social interstices were fast coming undone. More
and more the centre was slackening. Rather than heralding a

cessation to colonialism, the First World War had only stimulated the appetite of the Western imperialist powers. Worse, each successive crisis and failure of diplomacy rendered the League of Nations more powerless and of greater irrelevancy.

He had never lost a single book. However Parkes and the best of his generation had emerged from the Great War espousing much higher ambitions than that. They had been determined to create a more peaceful and a more just world. Their losses had not been offset by gains. Although nearly a decade earlier Parkes had served as Secretary of the LNU, during his lengthy period of residence in Geneva he alludes to the League of Nations on only two occasions and then merely to underscore its marginality.[25] By the turn of the calendar year, Parkes had not only grown visibly despondent over his administrative grind but also quietly despaired of the efficacy of most ISS activities. Indeed, what finally becomes clear is that the very effusiveness of Parkes' paean to 3 Grand Mezel is a reliable gauge of the depth of his disillusionment.

NOTES

1. James Parkes, *Voyage of Discoveries* (London, Victor Gollancz, 1969), p. 89.
2. Ibid., p. 89.
3. Haim Chertok, *Prisoner of Hope* (Hanover, NH: Brandeis University Press, 1996), p. 30.
4. Parkes, *Voyage of Discoveries*, p. 92.
5. James Parkes, *The Story of the International Student Service* (Oxford: ISS, 1940), p. 30, ff.
6. Parkes, *Voyage of Discoveries*, p. 129.
7. *Vide* Chapters 20 and 21.
8. Parkes, *Voyage of Discoveries*, p. 93.
9. Ibid., p. 96.
10. Ibid., p. 97.
11. Ibid., p. 93.
12. Ibid., p. 101, ff.
13. Ibid., p. 103.
14. Ibid., p. 105.
15. Ibid., p. 98.
16. Ibid.
17. Ibid., p. 97.
18. Ibid., p. 109.
19. Parkes Archives, File 60/17/3.
20. Parkes, *Voyage of Discoveries*, pp. 100–101.
21. *Vide* Chapter 13.
22. *Vide* Chapter 26.
23. Parkes, *Voyage of Discoveries*, p. 96.
24. Ibid., pp. 96–97.
25. Ibid., p. 105.

The Good Neighbour

The turn of the calendar year marked the beginning of what Parkes would later consider his 'real involvement in the Jewish question'.[1] If, however, due account be taken of his principled stand at Oberägeri in 1925, then 1929 might more accurately be viewed as his plunge into 'formal involvement'. In the interval between those years, restrictions and pressures on Jewish students across Europe intensified markedly. Fomented by nationalist political movements, particularly in Central and Eastern Europe antisemitic student thugs harassed and rioted against their Jewish classmates with increasing frequency and generally with impunity. Violence and bloodshed had become commonplace.

Given such chaotic conditions, most of the attendees at the ISS conference in Chartres in 1928 thought that Parkes' proposal that the assembly sponsor a conference aimed at improving understanding between representatives of these fiercely antagonistic groups was totally misguided. Nevertheless in this, his maiden appearance on the ISS podium, Parkes' earnestness and determination prevailed over the general sceptism. The Jewish-nationalist conference at Bierville would sorely test his administrative skills, first as an organizer and then as a facilitator. Merely to prevent it from aborting before it ever convened would require exquisite tact and meticulous planning, and once at the site, he would have to exercise vigilance to contain centrifugal pressures. There was even real potential for blood-letting.

In order to ensure the arrival of essential delegations, Parkes travelled to Warsaw, Bucharest and other major academic centres where tensions ran highest to wrest commitments from leaders of both factions that they would indeed turn up. To protect them from reprisals, Parkes gave each his personal assurance that their identities would remain confidential, that no resolutions would be passed and that no official report of the proceedings would ever be published. The single-minded aim of the conference was to open a safe channel of communication where none had previously existed and thereby to help defuse the incendiary atmosphere that prevailed on many European campuses.

Nestled deep within snow-filled woods, Bierville was a seventeenth-century chateau located five miles from the small city of Étampes, around thirty miles south of Paris. The venue was selected precisely because of its isolation and dearth of distractions. A final Machiavellian, or rather Parkesian twist: the conference site could boast only one properly heated assembly area, thus encouraging an uncommon propinquity, if not exactly cosiness, among the twenty-five edgy participants. Unlike earlier occasions when one could only wince at Parkes' celebration of his own cunning, this astute stroke rates a full measure of approbation.

When the final preliminary piece of the puzzle fell into place – delivery of kosher food from Paris – everything was ready for the arrival of the conferees. In January 1929 Parkes called the Bierville conference to order. Every one of the representatives who had promised to attend actually materialized, a high tribute to Parkes' standing in the international student community. For the next four days they argued, interrupted, postured, yelled, gesticulated and wrangled, but each time proceedings threatened to spiral out of control, they permitted themselves to be pacified by a transparent ploy that became something of a conference joke: ostensibly in order to translate a presentation, Parkes would announce a temporary postponement. After each break in pro-ceedings, tempers had cooled.

Even the major crisis of the week was turned to good effect. Parkes had scheduled a 'quiet cultural evening' featuring a presen-tation about Jewish mysticism by Josué Jehouda, a Swiss-Jewish novelist. The maladroit M. Jehouda rambled on so interminably that afterwards, as a unified body, the delegates delivered Parkes a collective ultimatum: an end to 'quiet cultural evenings'.

The long and short of it was that, to the astonishment of nearly everyone, the Bierville conference was immensely successful.

> Firstly the leaders of the two sides met each other personally, and actually heard from the other side what their claims and complaints were; and secondly ... the 'Christians' present heard very competent lectures on Jewish history and the

contemporary Jewish situation ... Moreover, both sides wanted ISS to continue the work of mutual understanding ...[2]

Thus at Bierville, both as a functionary and a conciliator, Parkes was notably effective. Alas, he could not know it would turn out to be the apogee of his career as a student organizer. However, like the second Gex conference, Bierville soon drove Parkes to his writing table. Although prior to the gathering he had located any number of Jewish scholars who were willing to lecture about Judaism, a search for a competent Christian scholar capable of discoursing on aspects of Jewish history and culture had proved fruitless. In the end, Parkes was directed by the ISS assembly to prepare himself to be its in-house expert on all aspects of the Jewish question 'in his spare time'.[3] Since the idea evidently originated with Parkes himself, it did not take much urging for him to accept to this new assignment with enthusiasm.

In fact all of Parkes' previous experience on Guernsey, in Flanders and at Oxford, now converging with deep foreboding about the vulnerability of Jewish students across Europe, came to a head in a powerful impulse to forge an authentic and informed connection with the Jewish people. More than he could know at the time, Parkes was travelling a well-worn road. At least since the time of the Jewish Emancipation in the eighteenth century, a similar recoil against antisemitism had triggered a philosemitic mind-set in other Christians and humanists as well. A brief excursus on Joyce and Beckett – Parkes' near contemporaries – would be instructive.

Like the Guernseyman, then living the life of an expatriate on the Continent, both self-exiled Irishmen, in their lives as in their writings, were unquestionably susceptible to a philosemitic tug. In the difficult decade to come their Jewish ties only intensified. In Paris during the Occupation, for example, Beckett joined a predominantly Jewish cell of the Underground and even took to wearing a Star of David. All three of these outsider-exiles spontaneously responded not only to rank injustice and the suffering of innocents but also to analogies between their personal narratives and the communal history of Europe's prototypical outsiders and exiles.

In their imaginative work, however, neither Irishman could

create recognizable or authentic Jews *qua* Jews. In this connection Beckett's allegorical *oeuvre* is so universalistic as to require no comment. As for Joyce, the marginality of his supreme 'Jewish' fiction has often been noted. *Ulysses*, with its focal (half) Jewish protagonist, first appeared during Parkes' third year at Oxford; although there is no record that he ever read it, at some point he could hardly have remained unaware of its general motive force and cultural impact.

> Bloom, the Jewish Everyman is not really Jewish – he is uncircumcised, and his first action in *Ulysses* is the purchase of a pork kidney for his breakfast. The authentic Jew, for Joyce as for many other writers and artists in this century, is that not-quite, non-Jewish Jew, the inhabitant of two worlds. This non-Jewish way of being Jewish is equivalent to the non-Irish way of being Irish signalled in Beckett's alleged answer when asked by a Frenchman who detected his foreign accent whether he was English: *'Au contraire'*, replied Beckett.[4]

Joyce's 'admirable Jew', like similar creations issuing from the philosemitic pens of other non-Jewish authors, projects a distorted mirror image of his own displacement from temporality and his native turf. Bloom embodies not only modernism's nostalgia for authenticity but also a corresponding affinity for instability. As will soon be clear, Parkes' embrace of philosemitism went deeper and carried him much closer to genuine Jewish experience. Internalized as an essential component of his Christian faith, energized not only by intensive thought and study but also by a widening involvement with a network of Jewish intimates, from this period onward 'Jewishness' served as one of the central planks of Parkes' cultural identity and the fulcrum of his active intellectual and affective life.

At the very outset, Parkes' serious engagement with Judaism entailed a paradoxical choice. Rather defensively, he pleads that the burden of so many other professional obligations militated against his carving out time for the acquisition of Hebrew. Unable to pursue this study in depth, Parkes opted to abandon even an attempt; perforce he would carry on with his programme of Jewish studies in translation. Regret for having to resort to second-best sources, which might sound inauthentic or even specious in others, in Parkes rings true enough. No scholar with such excellent Latin and Greek, not to mention passable French and serviceable German, could possibly underestimate the value of engaging historical texts in the original.

Nevertheless, no small irony attaches itself to Parkes' decision. Even as a youngster he had chuckled at the ineptitude of befuddled Guernsey magistrates in adjudicating cases on the basis of poorly translated Norman-French testimony. A few years hence, as an aide to James G. Macdonald, newly appointed Canadian High Commissioner of Refugees, Parkes would poke fun at his new boss for planning to introduce himself to French authorities as the *Haut Commissionaire de la Société des Nation,* that is, a common porter.[5] Even Joyce learned more Hebrew than Parkes ever would. How could he have misled himself into believing that reliance upon translations would adequately insulate him from occasional misreading or significant misinterpretation? How could he possibly have rested comfortably with a decision that would disable him from perusing original texts so vital to fulfilling his life's highest commitment?

Furthermore, Parkes must have been aware that his dependence upon translations meant that he was almost certainly disbarring himself from the possibility of obtaining an academic appointment in his chosen field at any major seat of learning. A thorough knowledge of Hebrew would inevitably be considered a prime prerequisite for anyone dealing so intimately with Jewish history. Indeed, his very reason for pursuing a doctorate in the first place – 'If I were going to get anywhere in so controversial and difficult an issue [antisemitism], I had to become *Herr Doktor*'[6] – applies equally to the desirability, indeed the necessity of the acquisition of Hebrew. Even as the Jewish reader of Parkes' total *oeuvre* is continually gratified at the adroitness of this Gentile in his presentation of both the substance and the spirit of Judaism, one is pained to see him commit such *faux pas* as inscribing *bar mitzvah* as *Barmitzvah,* an error that even an elementary acquaintance with Hebrew would have precluded.[7]

One cannot help wondering whether Parkes might have been inwardly uneasy, perhaps even apprehensive about mentally acclimatizing himself to Judaism through the tongue of the Jews as if intuiting that, more than anything else, Hebrew had the potential to put his Christian loyalty to the greatest test. Such a speculation may sound far-fetched, but it is in reality not all that implausible. Parkes, as we shall see, was extremely susceptible to all aspects of Jewish faith, thought and practice. Language and consciousness are, after all, virtually identical twins. Hebrew appears to have stood for him as a final, impermeable barrier, a non-negotiable hurdle which he instinctively sensed should not be cleared, a fence that, inverting Robert Frost's irony, actually did permit the unthreatening emergence of a very good neighbour.[8]

Beginning his autodidactic regimen with a six-month immersion in Heinrich Graetz's comprehensive *History of the Jews* punctuated with side-glances at Herbert Danby and Hermann Strack, two universally acknowledged Christian experts on Talmudic texts, Parkes pushed ahead steadily with his undertaking. Its scope was more than bookish. The preceding summer at Chartres Parkes had met up with Alexander Teich, a Zionist activist from Austria then serving as chairman of the WUJS. Drawn to one another, the two became fast friends. Since Teich's duties involved overseeing the welfare of impoverished Jewish students, he ran a kosher eating facility in Vienna, one of whose employees was, by the way, Anna Shikel Gruber, Hitler's mentally defective sister.[9] One may safely conjecture that among the friends' early conversational mainstays were the antics of refractory refectory employees. With Teich's active intercession, Parkes was able to extend his contacts with important Jewish student leaders throughout Poland, Hungary and Rumania.

As for Western Europe, Parkes set about systematically cultivating friendships with Jews sympathetic to his aims but he soon discovered that this would not be a simple exercise. 'I had not long been in the field when I was brought smartly up against the fact that any Jew automatically suspected an interested Christian of having missionary motives, and that he deeply resented the Christian attitude of superiority.'[10]

Persevering, at his home base in Geneva he soon won over Professor L. Hersch. Then in London he befriended Rabbi Dr Israel Mattuck, a liberal Jew, and Professor Herbert Loewe who in turn introduced him to Claude Montefiore, a major philanthropist as well as a significant liberal Jewish thinker. Of all his new Jewish companions, however, Parkes grew closest to Dr Charles Singer, Professor of Medicine at the University of London. When later in the decade Parkes returned to live in England, these and other friendships with Jews would ripen. It would be fair to say that henceforth Jews comprised a large proportion of Parkes' circle of intimates.

Meanwhile, still in the early stages of feeling his way into Judaism and Jewish history, Parkes became a habitué of Jewish booksellers in Paris, Berlin and Geneva. At a stroke this united his new-found fervour for Judaism and his enthusiasm for scholarship with his long-time avidity as a collector.[11] In remarkably short order Parkes' private collection of Jewish books and manuscripts could boast some extremely rare and valuable items. As early as 1933, after visiting with Parkes, Toronto's Rabbi Maurice Eisendrath wrote to friends about his 'splendid Jewish library', and of his frank astonishment that one 'so complete, so authentic, so massive was presided over by a Nordic gentleman'.[12] Eventually Parkes' collection would constitute the core of one of the most extensive Jewish libraries in Great Britain.[13]

Not only did Parkes' passion first for Jewish history and then for Judaism and Jews redirect his energy away from European and universal issues but they also served to revitalize him. In the process, however, he was subjected to new but all too predictable pressures.

> My colleagues were, in fact, just as busy for the work of ISS was growing steadily more difficult during those years of depression. It was no unusual thing for me to come back to Geneva for a few days, and to find the office was so busy that I had to engage a typist from one of the pools ...[14]

By the middle of 1929, hard-pressed to fulfil his extensive range of responsibilities on the conference circuit, Parkes was feeling increasingly stretched. Not only did his stays in Geneva grow shorter, but his occasional absences to visit with his father in Guernsey were also truncated. It seems that the more Parkes' interests gravitated towards patriarchal Judaism, the less he attended to his filial duties. Aside from simple logistics, one might possibly make something more of this. If the practical, worldly engineer father had never truly approved of his son's earlier vocational choices, how he would react to his latest enthusiasm comes as no surprise.[15]

Early that summer Parkes underwent an unpleasant encounter with the law in Dresden, the most active ISS centre in Germany. He and two young Anglican friends had arrived late for a service at the city's American Church. The chaplain, rather less hospitable than his counterpart in Geneva, refused them permission to celebrate Communion on their own because not only did Parkes sport a subversive beard and neglect to don a collar but, he was informed, his clerical licence was defective because it had been issued in England rather than in America. The three suspicious characters then retreated to a corner of the church and proceeded to pray quietly, but a vigilant caretaker soon delivered them into the hands of the police. The three soon confronted the on-duty magistrate.

Fortunately, only three months earlier Parkes had been feted at a civic luncheon attended not only by the city's *Bürgermeister* but also by the Minister of Education for Saxony who had personally presented Parkes with a gift of Dresden china for his outstanding service to German students during the period when the deutschmark had collapsed.[16] After a timely phone call, the young Anglicans were abruptly released from custody. Only then did Parkes learn that the American chaplain had accused them of plotting to steal the church's communion plate.

Parkes recalls this episode, the only time he was ever arrested, ostensibly as an ironic object lesson for Americans that they might be prevented from falling 'into the sin of *superbia*'.[17] However this incident also bears faint but distinct traces to Parkes' more distant past. We recall the tale of Farmer 'A', brought to dock before the bailiff of Guernsey for using witchcraft to transmit threatening letters to Farmer 'B'.[18] Both legal anecdotes turn on misunderstandings and false accusations, and both carry Kafkaesque undertones of the menacing vagaries of the law. Perhaps less problematically, it might have crossed Parkes' mind that had refugees or Jewish students fallen into the hands of the Dresden authorities, the upshot would not have been as expeditious nor, in retrospect, nearly as amusing.

The following month, Parkes' most signal contribution to the ISS's annual summer conference was his report on the embattled conditions faced by Jewish students in Eastern Europe, especially in Rumania and Hungary. On or near university campuses, he reported, they were often waylaid by nationalist student hooligans. Pitched battles and bloodied heads were commonplace. Less fortunate still were many young Jews who were excluded from attending university in their own country and unable to gain admittance to overburdened universities in the West. Anguished by the intensity of the prejudice against Jewish students, Parkes' considered response was a plan to place as many as possible into non-university positions, thus providing them with the means to survive temporarily in Paris, Amsterdam, or Brussels.[19]

Although well intentioned, at best this proposal could serve only as a palliative rather than as a genuine remedy for dealing with the growing crisis. As for Bierville, although as a conference it had been an unqualified success and had buoyed Parkes' spirits, it bore little actual fruit in the combat zones on Eastern European campuses. Moreover, it would be more than two years before a sequel could be staged. Parkes now began to realize the acute limitations of alleviating the Jewish student problem within the parameters of his duties for the ISS. Apart from that, the personal stakes were high because – and the irony was not lost on him – the meagreness of his success in fashioning an effective, proactive strategy to counter the effects of antisemitism tended to reinforce the very Barthian premises that he so reviled in principle. At times this frustrating impasse brought him close to tears, and he had to steel himself just to carry on with his regular work.

In the spring of 1930, in the absence of any short, competent English-language historical analysis of the roots of antisemitism, Parkes took it upon himself to produce one. This response is not surprising when one recalls the callow senior prefect who had presumptuously concluded that 'everything depended upon him[self]'.[20] Half a lifetime later, he drew a similar conclusion, but this time his assessment was sounder: he truly was the best situated, best motivated and most accomplished person for the task. Typically working late into the night, he threw himself into it totally; in the process, of course, he gradually threw off his depressive funk. By early summer, in a letter to a friend he remarked, 'I have been very busy writing about the Jewish question and giving rather little attention to the rest of my work.'[21]

Setting aside as many of his main responsibilities as he dared, in a matter of only three to four months Parkes typed the complete text of his new study. At least in part, one is tempted to attribute the demotic, commonsensical tone of *The Jew and His Neighbour* to its method of composition, but in fact Parkes had simply found his genuine voice, and his first book-length manuscript would serve as a prototype for many non-scholarly works to come. To his immense gratification, the Student Movement Press scheduled *The Jew and His Neighbour* for publication that October. Shortly thereafter, an American edition would appear. From the very midst of the Christian camp a new voice had issued an audacious challenge to the venerable tradition of Christian hostility towards the Jewish people.

Starting with an account of the Jewish dispersal under the Romans, Parkes' book methodically explores the religious, economic, political and racial components of antisemitism over the millennia. It affirms that, from any perspective, the Jewish people are innocent of every charge on their historic bill of indictment. They had not committed deicide, they did not kidnap and kill Christian children, they did not charge exorbitant interest, and they harboured no insidious designs on the Church's communion plate. Of their economic parasitism, for example, Parkes concluded, 'from this survey of Jews in many countries living under different conditions, we see that the narrowness which has characterized the life of European Jews cannot be specifically called Jewish'.[22]

More than anything else, Parkes focused on the scandal of Christianity's guilt for having invented and perpetuated the sin of antisemitism. Homing in on the religious-historical nexus at the font and source of the problem, Parkes explained,

> ... when the Church acquired power ... she used it to impress upon Jews, with the use of legal sanctions, the position which she believed already allotted them by Divine Pronouncement. It was a work of piety to humiliate them ... It is here the abnormality emerges for there was nothing in the actual conduct of the Jews which justified the theological presumptions and legal action of the Church.[23]

And then his polemical *coup de grâce*: 'The real evidence that the origin of antisemitism was *abnormal* is that it took the ordinary Christian almost a thousand years [that is, until the time of the Crusades] to be convinced of the reality of the theological picture' (emphasis added).

As for the specific source of antisemitic venom, it was, he charged, the Gospels themselves whose '... picture of the Pharisees is all that is taught of the origins of contemporary Jewish religion. The result is inevitably to create a dislike of the *modern* Jew ... since all their good qualities belong to the period before the Incarnation.'[24] Parkes was aware that his understated conclusion bore explosive implications: from the very start the instigator and chief perpetrator of the ongoing crime of anti-semitism, the prime villain of the piece, was none other than the Church itself.

Even though, strictly speaking, his findings were not original, Parkes' first book struck a powerful revisionist chord. In empha-sizing the causal link between Christianity and the most egregious forms of antisemitism, his conclusion was reinforced not only by mainline Jewish historiography but also by the key philosophers of the Enlightenment. Voltaire, for example, while he may have been obsessed with what he viewed as the repugnant features of contemporary Jewish life, ascribed them neither to racial defor-mation nor to Jewish religious practices themselves. Rather, as he perceptively acknowledged, they actually sprang from the effects of centuries of unjust Christian persecution.[25]

At first, Parkes' unique distinction lay as much in who he was as in what he had to say: a brilliant, earnest, devout Anglican clergyman driven by an inner urgency to explore, to confess and to rectify the shame and guilt of the Church for the ongoing crime of antisemitism. Having stumbled upon the area in which he could make not only the most significant but also the most conspicuous contribution to creating a better world, Parkes had the wit to recognize it. He appropriated antisemitism not as a researcher in quest of a topic of academic inquiry but as a crusader against a virulent evil that needed to be exposed and uprooted. As a believing Christian on a journey of self-discovery, he knew in his bones not only that without remorse there could be no true salvation but also that without knowledge there could be no remorse.

Properly perceived, *The Jew and His Neighbour*, is an Epistle to the Gentiles. Like the great majority of Parkes' writings, it issues from his anguish and his shame for the countless innocent victims who had suffered and were suffering still at the hands of his own community of faith. The underlying spirit of Parkes' mission was redemptive and prophetic. Aiming at the extirpation of the antisemitic malignancy from the body of Christianity, ultimately Parkes preached atonement for the enormity of Christian transgression of God's plan. Taking the burden of this failing upon his own shoulders, his labours represented an act of private contrition for collective sin. As he himself tragically appreciated, what he achieved in the greater world might be vastly incommensurate with the crimes he exposed; however, Parkes felt constrained to do all that he could, and his efforts graced his own life with nobility and higher purpose.

> Unlike any of his predecessors, Parkes did not come to the study of Judaism through contact with Jews, or through a scholarly interest in the background of the New Testament. His preoccupation with Judaism and the Jews, which was indistinguishable from the subsequent story of his life, arose directly out of his experience of antisemitism.[26]

Though narrowly conceived,[27] De Lange's observation succinctly clarifies the essential nature of Parkes' connection to the Jews as one which ultimately derived less from a gradual growth of sympathy or infusion of knowledge than a shock of recognition and an immediacy of identification. Parkes' indignation and his fury were intensely personal; they issued from a direct extension of his evolving understanding of himself. In short, Parkes responded to antisemitism not merely as an informed, fair-minded or even outraged Christian, but as if he were himself a Jew.[28]

To preclude any possible misunderstanding, unlike contemporary 'Messianic Jews' or 'Hebrew Christians', Parkes was scrupulous about maintaining distinctions vital to the integrity of adherents of both faiths. Habituated to viewing black as black and white as white, he eschewed muddle. What should be grasped, however, is that whenever Parkes reified the Jewishness of Jesus, as he consistently did, in scores of books and articles his aim was never merely to make an historical, technical or essentially anachronistic point. His essential insight was that antisemitism causes God to suffer today. In his life and career, Parkes took upon himself the burden of that suffering. His is a scholarship which, properly understood, seers the page as well as the soul.

Finally in this, his very first book, we already encounter an intuitive, fully-fledged appreciation of the centrality of Palestine for the Jewish people, a point Parkes will expand upon repeatedly in later studies. '[Zionism's] success or failure,' he remarks, 'will be of crucial importance to the whole future of the Jewish people, as well in its internal structure and psychology as in the attachment of others to it.' On the other hand, at this stage appropriating the Ahad Ha'am vision of cultural Zionism, Parkes also affirmed that '... Zionism loses a great deal of its importance unless it is careful to connect Palestine with the Jews elsewhere. This means that its primary value is as a great spiritual ideal.'[29] About the latter proposition, Parkes, like many others, would shift his position with time.

An emerging pattern is now clear: first in 1928–29 in defence of the principle of social and political activism, then in a book-length historical analysis of antisemitism, and shortly thereafter in a critique of the morality of missionary activity,[30] Parkes was taking the field less against the Nazi threat without than against the far more familiar foe within – his benighted fellow Christians. Meanwhile, riven by the excesses of nationalism, stricken with paralysis in the face of fascist triumphalism and the imminent rise of Hitler, battered to its foundations by the frenzy of capitalist greed that had spiralled down into the Great Depression, the world was blindly plummeting toward war.

In that summer of 1930 the ISS annual conference was convened in Oxford, its British headquarters and Parkes' old stamping ground. Nothing if not clever, Parkes had effectively lobbied for its selection as the conference site. This meant he could exploit the occasion to see his father and old friends on Guernsey, to visit former SCM and WSCF colleagues and to expand his circle of Jewish contacts in London. In Oxford, Parkes met with Gilbert Murray and other former mentors and also hand-delivered to the British ISS secretariat a confidential report on student organizations in Europe between 1926 and 1929.

Reflecting Parkes' frustration, the document, while couched diplomatically, was an indictment of the ISS and a personal apologia for bidding it farewell. Student organizations, he reported, espoused high ideals but in practice were politicized, much, he might have added, like the League of Nations itself (or its successor). In view of Parkes' good working relationship with his colleagues, the harshness of his report was surprising. Too often, Parkes concluded, student organizations had actually exacerbated poor relations among different groups of students, most particularly between Jewish students and other minorities. Given the terms of the ISS's primary mandate, most damningly of all his report brands its attempts at relief work a failure.[31] For anyone prepared to read between the lines, it was plain that Parkes would soon be moving on.

NOTES

1. James Parkes, *Voyage of Discoveries* (London, Victor Gollancz, 1969), p. 111.
2. Ibid., p. 114.
3. Ibid.
4. Steven Conner, in *The Jew in the Text: Modernity and the Construction of Identity*, eds Tamar Garb and Linda Nochlin (London: Thames and Hudson, 1995), p. 216.
5. Parkes, *Voyage of Discoveries*, pp, 108–109.
6. Ibid., p. 120.
7. Ibid., p. 150.
8. The title of Parkes' first book, published in 1930, would be *The Jew and His Neighbour: A Study in the Causes of anti-Semitism. Vide supra.*
9. Edith Ruth Weisz, interviewed by the author and Maggie Davidson in Cambridge, England, 28–29 August 2000.
10. Parkes, *Voyage of Discoveries*, pp. 115–16.
11. *Vide* Chapter 22.
12. Parkes Archives, File 60/33/3. Eisendrath's unconscious employment of Nazi jargon with his usage of 'Nordic' is telling.
13. *Vide* Chapter 33.
14. Parkes, *Voyage of Discoveries*, p. 115.
15. Ibid.
16. James Parkes letter to Archbishop Eber, 17 July 1929, Parkes Archives, File 60/17/3.
17. Parkes, *Voyage of Discoveries*, pp. 94–95, ff.
18. *Vide* Chapter 4.
19. James Parkes interview with Jewish Telegraphic Agency, August 1931, Parkes Archives, File 60/17/4.
20. *Vide* Chapter 7.
21. James Parkes letter to M. Wybenje, 25 June 1930, Parkes Archives, File 60/17/3.
22. James Parkes, *The Jew and His Neighbour, A Study in the Causes of Antisemitism* (London: SCM Press, l930), p. 55.
23. Ibid., pp. 63–64.
24. Ibid., pp. 80–81.
25. *Vide* Ronald Schechter, *Obstinate Hebrews: Representations of Jews in France, 1715–1815* (Berkeley: University of California Press, 2003).
26. Nicholas de Lange, 'James Parkes, A Centenary Lecture', in *Cultures of Ambivalence and Contempt: Studies in Jewish–Non-Jewish Relations*, eds Jones, Kushner and Pearce (London: Vallentine Mitchell, 1998), p. 34.
27. *Vide* Chapter 3.
28. *Vide* Irving Greenberg, *For the Sake of Heaven and Earth: The New Encounter Between Judaism and Christianity* (Philadelphia: Jewish Publication Society, 2004), p. 233: 'When Christians carry on their convenanted mission, are they members of the House of Israel? Are they in a parallel convenant or part of a single covenant alongside Jewry? Personally I believe ... Christians (... possibly also Muslims) may be deemed to be members of the people Israel, even though they practice different religions than Jewry does.' Rabbi Greenberg is fully aware that his views currently represent at best a tiny minority of those who position themselves within normative Judaism. Only time will tell whether it is an aberration or the cutting edge of a growing reappraisal of Christianity by adherents of Judaism. In any event, Parkes would have be immensely gratified had he encountered this generous echo, which approximates to his own inner feeling, emanating from the other direction.
29. Parkes, *The Jew and His Neighbour*, p. 172.
20. *Vide* Chapter 17.
31. Parkes Archives, File 60/17/3.

17

The Other Side of the Hedge

By the early months of 1929 Parkes had completed a draft of an article that distilled what he considered to be a creative approach to the mystery of the Trinity. Acutely conscious that any revisionism in this sensitive area would provoke controversy, he prudently solicited feedback from his closest clerical mentors. In a letter dated 3 March, Parkes sent William Temple, by then Archbishop of Manchester, a detailed summary of the development of his theological thought over the previous decade. Four weeks later a shorter letter that focused more narrowly on the Holy Spirit was dispatched to William Eber, Archbishop of York. The salutations clearly bespeak the warm, intimate nature of these relationships: Eber, for example, was addressed as 'dearly beloved Archbishop'; his reply of 17 April was directed to 'very dear Jimmy'.[1] No one perusing this correspondence could doubt either the depth of Parkes' Christian commitment or his determination to explore its implications, wherever they took him.

Encouraged by a positive reception from both bishops – which he construed as an Anglican episcopal imprimatur – Parkes circulated the working draft of his ruminations among his continental associates. Later that spring Parkes' much-vented reflections on the Trinity brought him an invitation to deliver a series of three lectures at the WSCF summer conference in Montreux. Parkes grew excited because the year before at Gex the dais of the WSCF conference had been exclusively given over to promulgating the theology of Karl Barth. Now the same forum was offering Parkes a golden opportunity to rebut that 'evil doctrine'.

Alas, at Montreux, Parkes' 'Politics and the Doctrine of the Trinity' created less than a sensation. Whereas for committed Barthians the yoking of theology to politics was *ipso facto* opprobrious – if not blasphemous – the pragmatic idealists from the Anglo-Saxon camp recoiled at any attempt to the Trinity political relevance. Parkes' ideas dropped with a thud between the two stools. In the end, the Montreux conference effectively spelled the end to Parkes' relations with the WSCF, and he decided prudently not to resurrect 'Politics' for another performance at that summer's ISS conference at Krems-on-Danube in Austria.[2]

True to character, however, Parkes did not let the matter quite lapse. Although intensely disappointed with the public reception to his first stab at linking the Trinity to a progressive political stance, Parkes had inaugurated a line of thought which in the coming decades he would pursue in a great torrent of theological articles and books.[3] Inasmuch as this early essay is seminal, a synoptic account of its main line of development follows.

While acknowledging that aspects of God are wholly other and for ever unknowable, Parkes insists that as Creator of the Universe, God cares about and bears responsibility for what He has wrought. He does not stand aloof from man and his concerns:

> God the Creator aspires toward 'the Kingdom of God' for all men. Only the community provides the sphere through which great men of spirit may work, e.g., Moses in the Court of Pharaoh. We make a mistake if we think of pre-Christians as the sphere only of the Holy Spirit. In the doctrine of the pre-existence of Christ, we have the insistence upon his activity in the world from the Creation. But we also make a mistake if we confuse His function with that of the Holy Spirit ... If we see this work of the Logos in the continual striving of the individual for the perfection of Himself, which is the response within man to that perfect pattern of humanity which is immanent in the world from the Creation and was revealed in Christ, we can trace it in the reaction against a purely negative form of mystery ... There is [therefore] no heavier atonement to be made than that of Christians to the Jews.
>
> Paralleling these two movements in human history – the search for the absolute and the search for self-perfection – is the search for corporate progress, the gradual growth of ordered community life; the insistence on the sanctity of the oath of treaties; the gradual enrichment in art, literature and philosophy, the evolution of the ideas of law and the extension of its control. All this I take to be the work of the Holy Spirit.[4]

This led Parkes to view President Woodrow Wilson's Fourteen Points and the League of Nations not merely as concrete manifestations of the activity of the Holy Spirit in the world,[5] but also propelled him into what some observers viewed as dubiously parochial positions. Parkes held, for example, that 'the English Labour Party is impregnated with Christian ideas and is constructive'.[6] Further, having by his own route arrived at an approximation of the Jewish conception of man's individual and communal co-responsibility with God for the healing of a creation that is of its nature incomplete or flawed – *tikkun olam* – Parkes proceeded to appropriate it whole in order to justify his humanistic conception of the Logos.

For Parkes, the participation of man as a social being, acting in his various communities, is essential to the fulfilment of God's plan for the redemption of the human condition. Indeed His involvement in Parkes' evolving conception of the operation of the Trinity, especially those aspects that refer to 'the gradual growth of orderly community life', is a vital key to comprehending the young cleric's theological embrace of central aspects of Judaism. As a matter of principle, from this period Parkes assiduously ceased to iterate the rubric 'God's only begotten son' in referring to Jesus. Neither in his public sermons nor in private prayers did he ever again voice this traditional locution, because it fundamentally offended his man-centered conception of the Trinity and of the dignity of all men and women as children of God.[7]

Even though Parkes could hardly feel gratified with the lukewarm response to the exposition of his metaphysical speculations, it still struck him that formulating his ideas had more life to it than imposing his will upon recalcitrant conferees. After five years of service as an SCM and ISS functionary, although the transition from frustrated student organizer and social activist to historian, theologian, and scholar had not yet crystallized, Parkes' future course was now set.

It is not clear whether Parkes was conscious of the parallel between his conception of the agency of the Creator and that of the divine afflatus that traditionally descends to inspire the Writer. However, energized by his new orientation, in rapid order he turned out two further pieces: 'Politics and the Person of Christ' and 'The Community and the Purpose of God'. Although neither was accepted for publication, they testify to his new-found intellectual excitement.

By the autumn, Parkes was again expending energy on two Jewish fronts: combating antisemitism on European campuses and his self-learning programme in Judaism. These complementary campaigns coalesced dramatically over the thorny issue of Christian outreach and the conversion of the Jews. With painfully good cause, Jewish sensitivity to their vulnerability has ever been acute; over time losses have been incalculable. Naturally, Jews treat Christian overtures with a high degree of suspicion. Since this more than any other controversy threatened to undermine Parkes' standing with the growing number of Jews in his orbit, its salience at this juncture of his life calls for careful exploration.

We recall that eight years earlier, as an undergraduate at Oxford, Parkes himself had enthusiastically attended the SCM's Missionary Quadrennial in Glasgow. At the time the notion that the missionary enterprise was fatally contaminated by an imperious, hegemonic mindset had certainly not occurred to the budding cleric. Traditionally, missionary work has always occupied a position of special honour among Christians. It is not unlikely that among the inspirational tales with which Annie Parkes regaled her impressionable younger son, not a few featured missionary families as selfless heroes and sometime martyrs in far-flung outposts of Asia, Africa, and Micronesia. We recall as well that Reverend Cru also had been a missionary.

As for the Jewish people, that ineradicably alien presence lodged within the bosom of Christendom, proselytizing campaigns to win them to the Gospel of Christ have been intermittently undertaken, at times vigorously, at times with circumspection, with the full theological sanction of every mainline Christian body. During the five years that he had toiled for the SCM, Parkes never hinted that he considered such Christian designs on Jews as a matter of controversy.

Towards the end of 1929 Conrad Hoffman was appointed First Secretary of the Committee on the Christian Approach to the Jew, a newly formed offshoot of the International Missionary Council. A professional acquaintance of Parkes', Hoffman had pre-eminently been selected for the post because his resolute efforts to alleviate their sufferings had earned him the respect of young Jews. Parkes himself had described Hoffman in glowing terms:

The General Secretary [of ESR] in these early days was Dr Conrad Hoffman, who had been working in German prisoner of war camps for the American YMCA. He almost lived in trains, returning to Geneva only to see what was in the cash box, and to dispatch all of it – to the great indignation of the office staff and the accountant – to the countries which he had been visiting, or was intending to visit.[8]

Hoffman, in short, projected an attractive, generous, selfless image to members of the very community that he was now assigned to attract to Christ. He felt no compunction about exploiting his reputation in the fulfilment of his new responsibilities. Like nearly all his associates, Hoffman viewed implementing his redemptive programme among the Jews as his highest Christian duty.

Meanwhile, pursuing his own agenda, Parkes' had only recently overcome his Jewish associates' suspicions about his true intentions. At the same time, he was on excellent terms with Hoffman. Might he not assume a neutral stance on Hoffman's latest, soul-gathering activities among the Jews? The scales fell from his eyes only when he informed Alexander Teich of Hoffman's new appointment: '... [Teich] just sat there and sobbed. 'But Conrad would not do that to us', he whispered, with tears running down his cheeks ... I began to understand what Jews felt about the Christian missionary approach.'

All at once, Parkes' new understanding moved him well beyond the realm of empathy. His close friend's visible distress totally disabused him of the possibility of maintaining a disinterested position. As never before, Parkes now appreciated the depths of Jewish abhorrence of bodies such as Hoffman's Committee on the Christian Approach to the Jews; he felt their repugnance wholeheartedly. The efficacy of Teich's tears provides unusual access to the inner workings of Parkes' sensibility, a matter which in due course will be investigated at greater length.[9] As if newly enlightened, Parkes now characterized the Committee's appointment of Hoffman as 'a naked piece of religious aggression'.[10]

It is hardly surprising that the majority of Parkes' Christian associates, including close friends, found his reaction puzzling, extreme, even bizarre. Only in the aftermath of the Shoah would most mainline, Western Christian confessions – most notably the

Roman Catholic Church – reappraise their traditional support for such missionary activity, and ban it as inappropriate, vulgar, indeed unchristian. Back in 1929 however, Hoffman naturally assumed that, if it ever came down to it, he could count upon the covert support and the good offices of his friend Jimmy Parkes, a tiller in the same fields of immortal souls. Incredibly, two full decades later Hoffman, still directing the Committee on the Christian Approach to the Jews, was not yet fully disabused. Hoffman could still disingenuously address his 'Dear Jimmy' with '… I am sorry that apparently my approach to the Jewish–Christian relationship does not seem to meet with your approval though I believe in reality we are closer together than seems the case at first sight.'[11]

His remark typifies the circularity of their polemical waltz. Hoffman complained of Parkes' '… implied accusation against the integrity of the friend [a Church of Scotland missionary in Israel] about whom I wrote'. A month later Parkes replied to his 'dear Con': 'Apart from the fact that I do not find his [the missionary's] evangelistic approach convincing, I find his statement … a ridiculous travesty of the fact, and constant innuendo. I cannot see how you can expect me voluntarily to meet its author'.[12] Behind a polite façade, cooperation between the two former friends had long ceased and relations had soured. As Parkes comments:

> I found it unsafe to express any opinion to him [Hoffman]. He would misquote it to the next man he met. When my first book [*The Jew and His Neighbour*] was in the press, he tried to get me to suppress it on the grounds that it would damage my reputation to publish a book which both laid the chief blame for medieval antisemitism on the Christian Church and, in discussing the remedies, made no reference to the necessary conversion of the Jews.[13]

Yet Hoffman could not have been more correct. Among most professional, mainstream Christians, Parkes' reputation was indeed much tarnished, and for the rest of his professional life he would be embroiled in similar epistolary controversies.

In 1930, for example, William Paton, another of Parkes' former SCM colleagues, was serving as Secretary of the International Missionary Council. He complained to Parkes that arguing that Jews should be exempted from missionary activity because they constituted an exception to the general run of other non-Christian religions 'undermined the whole claim of Christianity to be of universal significance'. When Parkes insisted that the unique genitive bond between Christianity and Judaism meant that the former's attitude towards Jews bore little relevance to its stance towards other non-Christians, he was brusquely advised, 'to go and read your Bible'. Even his dear friend Temple, Parkes noted ruefully, '... refused to agree that Judaism was so special a case that it justified special treatment in relation to Christian missionary activity'.[14] Sadly but correctly Parkes concluded, '... to evolve a new attitude to Jewish–Christian relations was to be a lonely job'.[15]

Like Parkes' impulsive, principled stand at the 1925 WSCF Conference in Oberägeri,[16] the missionary controversy decisively defined the crossing of another divide in the development of Parkes' thinking and in his reputation among his co-religionists. Separating himself from the common, broadly accepted run of Christian opinion, Parkes had irrevocably crossed his Rubicon to occupy *terra incognita*, and he knew it. He recognized that, albeit alone, this was his moment to take up a lance to fight for fairness, justice and repentance, the very sort of holy, personal crusade about which he had fantasized ever since boyhood. If he were up to the challenge, quite possibly it crossed his mind that it would redeem his equivocal performance in Flanders. An even more fundamental matter, however, was whether he could truly justify his solitary stand against normative Christian principles and practice even to himself.

In his heart, Parkes surely had to grant that Hoffman, Paton and others had made some seemingly reasonable points. It is far from obvious that the missionary work among Jews should be more 'naked [a] piece of religious aggression' than missionary work among South Sea islanders. Moreover, although the Gospels direct believers to spread the faith primarily among Gentiles, a glance at Paul's 'Epistle to the Hebrews' should disabuse anyone of any illusion that he provides the Jews with blanket immunity. Unless Parkes were prepared to rethink the underlying theological premises that buttressed Christianity's historical stance towards Judaism and to address them courageously, his objection to missionary work in the Jewish field could only be considered sentimental. To his credit, the newly launched

Paladin of the Jews neither flinched nor wavered; convinced of the correctness of his position, over the long haul he never wearied of bearing the lance that at times must have felt as heavy as a cross.

Upon reflection, it was inevitable that the inadmissibility of a Christian mission to the Jews should have been the cutting edge severing the priest from Guernsey from conventional Christian opinion and virtually exiling him to a St Helena of thought and action. It evokes a parallel polemic from the first century of the Common Era, one which Parkes himself later notes had awakened mainstream Judaism to the realization that Christianity was more than a harmless, inconsequential Jewish heresy. Projecting himself imaginatively into a Jewish frame of consciousness, Parkes conceived the complaint the Pharisees might have made against Paul and his sect to the Roman authorities in these suggestive terms:

> We are a peaceable community, and if a proselyte does join us from time to time, you have always looked the other way, for you know that by making him observe the Law we guarantee that he will be a good citizen. But this man spends all his time making proselytes out of anyone he meets, and does not enjoin upon them the keeping of the Law, in addition to the fact that they are not taken from the most reputable elements among the population, and some of them lead lives which we should never allow. When these people get into trouble, as they are sure to do, it is we who will be blamed for it, for they will call themselves Jews, and claim our privileges. But they know nothing about the Law on which their privileges are based and are even taught to despise it. We beg you to forbid this Paul to call himself a Jew, and to go on abusing our Law, and also to recognize that neither he nor his precious following have anything to do with us.[17]

By the end of the first century of the Common Era, Pauline Christianity adamantly refused to acknowledge either the integrity or continued validity of its mother faith. The inherent antisemitic thrust of Christianity devolved from its inner dynamic to define and to constitute itself as Judaism's legitimate successor. Catalyzed by his instinctive empathy with Teich's feeling of betrayal, in advance of all other significant Christian thinkers of the twentieth century, Parkes intuitively grasped the essential character of Judaism's eternal covenant with God. His controversy with Hoffman and Paton, colouring all his subsequent thinking about Jewish– Christian relations, very soon led him to undertake a seminal investigation into the historical origins of antisemitism. The result, which would appear five years later as *The Conflict of the Church and the Synagogue,* is a scholarly, ground-breaking *tour de force.* It unquestionably stands as Parkes' most enduring contribution to a radical reformulation of a fractious issue.

The following samplings from Parkes' many Epistles to the Missionaries exemplify the tenor and substance of his rearguard skirmishing with fellow clergy over the years. To the Reverend William Simpson of the Methodist Missionary Society, who urged Parkes to recognize that Judaism was in need of completion through its embrace of Christianity, Parkes responded that the two religions were 'two sides of the same whole ... I do not think I can be much use to you, for I must tell you quite frankly that I stand definitely on the other side of the hedge.'[18] But Parkes could sometimes be wrong. Nearly a decade later Simpson, having in the interim swallowed Parkes' argument whole, would assume the reins of the newly organized Council of Christians and Jews and would become one of Parkes closest friends and associates.

Equally instructive is a letter Parkes wrote just a day earlier to Zoë Fairfield, his long-time SCM friend whom he once characterized as possessing 'unassuming religious sincerity' and being blessed with 'ever-fresh imagination and intuition'.[19] Probably not for the first time, he directed one of his favourite arguments to the very sort of rare Christian from whom he craved moral support:

> I am more and more convinced that the separation of Judaism and Christianity has been the greatest tragedy in world history [because] each alone is insufficient. Judaism and Christianity are two parts of the same whole ... The Church needs as much from Orthodox Judaism as it can offer it.[20]

Over the ensuing years, although missionaries of every theological stripe attacked from all quarters, Parkes manfully held his ground. This was trench warfare for which he was ready. It is noteworthy that through it all he was unfailingly civil and good-tempered. Consider his urbane response to a letter from a Father McNabb:

> Miss Haldin has sent me your letter about my lecture, and asked me to reply to it. This, I admit, I am somewhat at a loss to do, for the assumption that in a discussion between 'Christians' and 'Jews' any non-Roman is to be classed as a Jew, and therefore not entitled to say 'we' of the medieval Church seems to me so quaintly impertinent that I suspect you have not expressed what you meant.[21]

A decade later, rebutting criticism from a missionary pamphleteer named Stevens, Parkes argued in a similarly cogent and unyielding vein:

> I never said that they [Sinai and Calvary] are alternatives. My whole theology is built on the belief that both are equally relevant to all, and that it is only in the recognition of the equal and permanent validity of the two that we can apprehend the purpose of God in creation … I have always made a complete distinction between the relation of Christianity to Judaism and its relation to any other religion whatever, based on the historical fact that Jesus was a Jew and his religion was Judaism.[22]

The polemic between Parkes and the platoons of missionaries did not wind down until late in the 1960s when, neither quarter having conceded an inch, Parkes dispatched a final volley from the other side of the hedge. Outraged by the activities earlier in the century of Christian 'baby-snatchers' among poor Jewish immigrants in London's East End, Parkes reiterated what was now an entrenched position:

> I do not believe that such things could happen if the attitude which we Christians had adopted toward Judaism and the Jews had been the will of God. They are irrefutable evidence of something fundamentally wrong, not just of the missionaries not being 'good' enough. They are as good as any other Christian group. There are only two possibilities. Either our estimate of Christianity is wrong or our estimate of Judaism is wrong. It is the latter which I have put forward.[23]

First in 1928–29 *contra* the advocates of Barthianism when Parkes claimed theological warrant for political activism, then in 1929–30 *contra* the missionaries in defence of the Jews, Parkes pitched his theological tent on high ground that he would fortify and staunchly defend for the rest of his career. A maverick embattled against his establishment Christian brethren, Parkes instinctively assumed a rebellious, anti-traditionalist stance. It stimulated his thinking, it propelled him into action, and it accorded with his personality. Parkes' well-researched, splendidly reasoned argumentation vanquishes any suspicion of posturing. Even his opponents had to grant that he acted out of firm conviction and his own hard-won understanding of the demands of Christian conscience.

In 1930, with the world once again plummeting irreversibly into chaos, Parkes the functionary, Parkes the team player, Parkes the deviser of programmes to promote reconciliation among opposing groups was more and more fading into the background. Expanding upon ideas he first broached in *The Jew and His Neighbour*, Parkes spun off several articles detailing the violent oppression of Jewish students in Eastern Europe.[24] He had written some short pieces on this subject previously, but these articles inaugurated a new stage in his professional life: he had good cause to think that they would appear in periodicals. Parkes had backed into what actually was his proper métier. From this point onwards Parkes would view himself primarily as a polemicist, an historian and a theologian engaged in producing a steady stream of books and articles aimed at redressing a historic injustice.

At the age of thirty-three Parkes the writer conjoined his most passionate concerns to his highly personal, ingratiating style. Entrenched on the other side of the hedge, Parkes was fully committed to carry on with the struggle against antisemitism over the very long haul.

NOTES

1. Parkes Archives, File No 60/8/1/1–5.
2. James Parkes, *Voyage of Discoveries* (London, Victor Gollancz, 1969), p. 111.
3. *Vide* Chapter 25.
4. James Parkes, 'The Trinity in International Affairs', 1929, University of Southampton, Parkes Archives, File 60/6/8/10/12, pp. 27–33. Taken from a later version of the same essay which frames the issues with greater clarity. Neither version was ever published.

5. Ibid., p. 24.
6. Ibid., p. 33.
7. Ruth Weyl in conversation with the author and Maggie Davidson in Rehovot, Israel, on 26 October 2003.
8. James Parkes, *The Story of the International Student Service* (Oxford: ISS, 1940), p. 3.
9. *Vide* Chapter 24.
10. Parkes, *Voyage of Discoveries*, p. 116.
11. Conrad Hoffman Letter to James Parkes dated 19 July 1949, Parkes Archives, File 60/17/8, f.
12. James Parkes Letter to Conrad Hoffman dated 31 August 1949, Ibid.
13. Parkes, *Voyage of Discoveries*, p. 117.
14. Ibid., pp. 209–10.
15. Ibid.
16. *Vide* Chapter 14.
17. James Parkes, *The Conflict of the Church and the Synagogue* (New York, Meridian and Jewish Publishing Society, 1961), pp. 67–68.
18. James Parkes Letter to W. W. Simpson dated 15 November 1933, Parkes Archives, File 60/17/8.
19. Parkes, *Voyage of Discoveries*, p. 70.
20. James Parkes Letter to Zoë Fairfield dated 14 November 1933, Parkes Archives, File 60/17/8/1.
21. James Parkes Letter to Reverend McNabb dated 14 April 1936, Parkes Archives, File 60/17/8/1.
22. James Parkes Letter to Stevens dated 3 December 1947, Parkes Archives, File 60/17/8/1.
23. James Parkes, *The Church of England Newspaper*, London: 2 May 1959, Parkes Archives, File MS 60/17/8.
24. James Parkes, 'The Jews and the Student Movement', *Student Christian Movement Journal*, 19 July 1930 and 'The Jewish Problem in Eastern Europe', WSCF, *Student World*, 1931, Parkes Archives, File 60/9/14.

18

Antisemites and Antimacassars

One evening soon after his return to Geneva, while 'contemplating with disgust' the prospect of the impending week's round of mainly pointless meetings, the disgruntled ISS functionary found himself gazing at a shop window that displayed some lovely tapestries and a great variety of coloured wool. Suddenly, Parkes was visited by the revelation that, as opposed to the vapid types whose speechifying left him stuporous,

> ... the people who bore with the committees best were the women who knitted. They did not talk when they had nothing to say. They had the uncanny faculty for seeing the way out of a dilemma in which the rest of the committee had got itself bogged down, and their dispositions remained sweet and sunny the whole week.[1]

On impulse, the newly enlightened proto-feminist entered the shop, purchased wool and canvas, and at once set about teaching himself to make a tea cosy. Uncommonly adept, in a remarkably short time Parkes was making tapestries for his antique chairs. By sheer chance he had stumbled upon a brilliant expedient for controlling his exasperation with witless blather. It is of course true that Englishmen, especially those with upper class connections or pretensions, enjoy a well earned a reputation for behavioral tics. Nevertheless what strikes us most vividly is Parkes' total lack of self-consciousness about taking up such a traditionally distaff-side pursuit.

Perhaps he had assumed that his new hobby would register simply as another of 'Jimmy's eccentricities'. Undeterred by the full glare of the public eye, his immediate and wholehearted embrace of a 'woman's activity' is nevertheless arresting. Given even *his* sexual reticence, Parkes could not have been entirely unaware that whatever its tranquillizing qualities his new pastime might broadcast a gender-related message. Moreover, especially when abiding some tedious speechifying, Parkes must have known that his unusual pastime was effectively upstaging the speaker. Yet the more his distracting antics irked some of his fellow conferees, the more Parkes' attachment to his new hobby grew. Indeed, like most of his intellectual or moral commitments, once embarked upon it would not only absorb Parkes' energies but also claim his affection for the rest of his life.

We note that Parkes' conspicuous 'coming out' as a needle worker coincided with his equally emphatic emergence as a powerful advocate for the increasingly hard-pressed Jewish students of Eastern Europe.[2] In some underground manner, could the gratification he took in designing antimacassars to drape over the graceful lines of his prized antique furnishings parallel his satisfaction in devising strategies for counteracting the designs of missionaries or antisemites? Perhaps there lurked behind this apparently frivolous linkage of disparate realms of experience something of the dazzling yoking of similitudes to startling effect indulged in famously by seventeenth century metaphysical poets such as George Herbert and John Donne.[3]

With another turn of the calendar year, Parkes returned to writing and produced two noteworthy theological essays. Domesticating the Deity in an ingratiating, old bachelor style reminiscent of Chesterton, their common theme was God's intimate concern and involvement in the everyday affairs of mankind.[4] In 'God and My Furniture' Parkes, surrounded by his own treasured antique tables and chairs, discoursed on the canons of goodly, godly interior design thus:

1) in order to achieve harmony, do not varnish woods;
2) avoid imitations and antique finishes;
3) eschew colour schemes;
4) forestall room domination by just one thing ('expel the egotist');
5) include one's treasured ornaments in the total picture; and
6) exile whatever jars one's sensibilities because one's home should reflect beauty and the Kingdom of God.[5]

Parkes could just as easily have been elucidating the spareness of his homely writing style as the elegance of his taste in home furnishings. However his lovingly decorated flat on Grand Mezel, he reminds us, served not alone as an aesthetic statement but also as a 'perpetual refreshment' spiritually.[6] During this turbulent, disruptive time in his life, the subtext of this essay gently proposes a prescription for spiritual hygiene. It recommends that one should strive to attain a state of interior harmony. Parkes' doxy on furniture seems designed to prod not only the reader but also its author in his more disquieted moments in the direction of emotional integration and authenticity.

It is not at all clear, however, that 'Item 4' in the above litany was ever applied with much determination, force or focus. None of Parkes' associates would have seriously quibbled with the assessment of a close friend who once described him as 'highly sentimental but very precise, very proud, and *very* arrogant'.[7] If Parkes ever did perform spiritual calisthenics aimed at specifically muzzling his will or exorcising the resident egoist, they were never so robust as to enable him to score more than momentary victories. Upon taking up his antisemitic lance, Parkes would always portray himself as the foremost champion in the field. Additionally, while there is considerable evidence to support this self-assessment, one would never guess from his own account that he hadn't filed an original patent on inter-communal collaboration or that he did not deem the culpability of Christianity for the sin of antisemitism his very own intellectual property.

We do well to remind ourselves that when Parkes was living in London in 1924, he was by his own account 'busy enough with the study groups, conferences and retreats which occupied my time'.[8] Yet among the conclaves he did not attend was the Conference on Economics and Citizenship, a gathering of British churchmen concerned with the ethical responsibilities of Christianity in a post-war world. That same spring Parkes seems also to have skipped the London Conference on Religions of Europe which focused on creedal pluralism. Yet later that same year 'the Social Service Committee of the Liberal Jewish Synagogue in London, moved by the consideration that "in spite of serious differences of belief Jews and Christians are at one in their desire to bring nearer the Kingdom of God on earth", ... convened the Conference of Jews and Christians to discuss "Religion as an Educational Force".'[9] Once again Parkes was in the ranks of the missing.

At this seminal gathering a working committee was formed that four years later would launch the still active Society of Jews and Christians.[10] It would espouse two eminently Parkesian aims:

first, to increase religious understanding and to promote good will and cooperation between Jews and Christians, with mutual respect for differences of faith and practice; and second, to combat religious intolerance.[11] In sum, during those post-war years Parkes was neither the only British churchman to enter the fray against antisemitism nor even among the very first. Once engaged, however, in very short order the unexpelled egoist certainly did propel himself to the forefront as the leading light of the movement.

'Revelation and the Duster', Parkes' other 'domestic essay', also argues for God's intimate involvement in the daily lives of men and women.

> The greater part of humanity is occupied with the everyday tasks of living, and apparently must be so. Therefore man is man, and in all the everyday tasks of living it should be possible to serve Him – and find Him. To the intellectual, the nature of God is often like the carrot held in front of the nose of the donkey – they can never be quite sure they will get there in the next step ... But life is not made up of intellectual problems, and there is a whole side of it when intellectual proofs do not really matter ...[12]

The pleasure Parkes took in composing these two essays is transparent. Indeed, they turned out to be the precursors of a number of popular, book-length theological probes that he would publish a decade later.[13]

In the spring of 1931, a second ISS Conference on Jewish issues was convened under Parkes' direction. Unlike Bierville where Spartan simplicities prevailed, this gathering was held in Nyon, a five star venue on the shores of Lake Geneva. The featured speakers were two prominent Jews: the illustrious Nahum Goldmann who later that year would chair the political committee at the seventeenth annual World Zionist Congress,[14] and Hermann Badt, 'the highest ranking Jewish civil servant in Germany'.[15]

The nationalist students produced their own star attraction, a leading Nazi theorist named Wilhelm Stapel who expounded in rich, scientific detail why the 'differentiated plasma' of Jews precluded their 'symbiosis with Germans'. Inspired by this twaddle, that very evening Parkes composed a plasmic jingle of his own to the tune of 'My Bonnie Lies Over the Ocean':

> My plasma is over the ocean
> My plasma is awful to see
> My plasma is all of a muddle
> Oh, who will differentiate me?

Unofficially adopted by the Jewish conferees as the conference anthem, it was also later picked up and adapted, as if to belie the impossibility of cultural symbiosis, by some of the Nazi students.[16]

Although there were relatively few disruptions at Nyon, no one could claim that the sessions achieved much to enhance mutual understanding. This lacklustre gathering played its part in persuading Parkes to pay closer heed to his sixth precept for home decoration – exile whatever jars one's sensibilities: Nyon would be the last Jewish-oriented conference Parkes would organize for the ISS.

Returning dispirited to his Geneva apartment, Parkes was buoyed by a fresh, entirely unexpected discovery that he intuited had to be more than merely fortuitous.

> When I originally found and rented the flat I had no special interest in the relations between Jews and Gentiles. Also at that time the study of medieval Geneva was incomplete. When several years after I had come to Grand Mezel a medieval map was compiled, I found that I was living in the bridge house between the Jewish ghetto and the Christian city.[17]

His dear friend Teich would label such a coincidence *besheert,* or an act of fate. For Parkes the mysterious workings of the 'third channel' of the Trinity were never far from his mind; they were viewed as an indication of the mysterious, ineffable agency of the Holy Spirit.

A visit to Poland then returned him to a more mundane affair at which he was a well-practiced technician: a situation that called for subterfuge in the service of producing a good end. Exploiting an invitation to Warsaw under the auspices of the Polish National Union of Students Parkes' real aim was to document the harrowing condition of Poland's Jewish university students. It would take six years, but eventually this investigation bore fruit in a short article, 'Notes on Bench Ghettoes in Polish Universities'.[18] For English readers, Parkes detailed for the first time how Aryan students in Polish universities had been assigned even-numbered rows and Jewish students odd-numbered rows, thereby segregating the Jews so as to render them more vulnerable to intimidation and physical assault. In 1937, the year after Parkes had returned to England, this article, co-signed by many others, inspired an open letter of protest in the British press.

As for the category of 'Christian Jews', the seating arrangement for these students at Polish universities was indeterminate, a problematic arrangement that echoed the amorphous status of their brethren under the skin, the 'Judeo-Christians' of Jerusalem near the end of the first century of the Common Era. Trapped between the twin hostilities of an intimidated, not yet ascendant Christianity and a beleaguered Judaism, 'rejected, first by the Church, in spite of their genuine belief in Jesus as the Messiah, and then by the Jews in spite of their loyalty to the Law, they [the Judeo-Christians] ceased to be a factor of any importance in the development of either Christianity or Judaism'.[19] Parkes concluded that '... there was no more tragic group in Christian history than these unhappy people.'

The Bishop of Jerusalem in that era was James, the brother of Jesus, a tragic figure to whom Parkes had felt close ever since boyhood. With the passage of time, he had come both wholeheartedly to embrace this apostle as a tormented precursor and anachronistically to view James's original Church of Jerusalem as one of his spiritual homes. Among the more sublime achievements of Parkes' intellectual life, in fact, is how well he comprehended the predicament of his first century namesake and derived inspiration from his experience. With consummate skill Parkes sympathetically interpreted the unhappy fate of the Judeo-Christians as exemplary rather than predictive. James' stance was instrumental in guiding Parkes towards a life of service to both Christians and Jews without prejudice to either confession.

Tellingly, Parkes remarks of the first century Judeo-Christians, 'they, who might have been the bridge between the Jewish and the Gentile world, must have suffered intensely at the developments on both sides which they were powerless to arrest'.[20] This soteriological identification both confirmed and reinforced one of Parkes' most potent conceptualizations of his earthly mission. In his more mystical moments Parkes came to perceive his very person as a living embodiment of a link that might reconnect the two covenanted traditions and communities of faith. That is to say, Judeo-Christians might have been what Parkes in his more grandiloquent moments imagined he might yet become, a living incarnation of the personhood of the bridge.

Other streams flowed out of Parkes' intimate, emotional ties with the early Judeo-Christians. Parkes' Geneva apartment, for example, was furnished not exclusively to provide a dwelling place but also to function as a sanctuary and private 'chapel'. In the glow and shadow cast by sixty lighted candles arrayed in tall, ancient sticks and sconces, weekly soirées cum 'communion services' aimed at fostering mutual understanding were conducted under Parkes' benign tutelage. Indeed, those evenings stand among Parkes' most memorable pastoral triumphs.

Transparently sincere, luminously brilliant, intermittently charismatic, in his self-appointed role as the binder of the schism that separated the two seminal faiths, Parkes now faced one of his most difficult challenges: how to maintain the trust of his Jewish friends while at the same time fending off marginalization from mainstream Christianity. It was a much tougher balancing act than impressing visiting American students. At Nyon, having witnessed how an honorific helped *Herr Doktor* Stapel obtain a respectable hearing even for claptrap, Parkes had again seen the importance of becoming *Herr Doktor* Parkes. Without the proper credentials, Parkes had good reason to believe that, particularly among his clerical colleagues, his eccentric view of the Jewish question could be too readily pigeonholed as beyond the pale.

Moreover, having reached his mid-thirties, Parkes was visibly wearying and increasingly disillusioned with his work. He did not look forward to turning into a superannuated, professional student functionary. For at least a year, certainly ever since the publication of *The Jew and His Neighbour*, the idea of obtaining a doctorate had been in the back of his mind. It certainly had immense appeal for his ego and his self-esteem, and, aside from satisfying his scholarly bent, a doctorate could open fresh professional avenues. Parkes knew exactly what he wanted to investigate. Touched upon superficially in his first book, the First Crusade had become something of a personal obsession. He wanted to unravel the mystery of why the worst violence against the Jews had erupted in regions where Jewish communities had been well established and where for many years Christians and Jews had coexisted in relative peace.[21]

The previous summer at Oxford Parkes had set the preliminary steps in motion. When he met Professor Murray and other
former tutors, he had discussed the feasibility of returning to
engage in serious historical research into the sources of 'the
Jewish Question'. Now, with his first book coming out in the
autumn and disillusionment with life as an organization man
ever growing, his desire to return to Oxford to earn his doctorate
took wings. Suddenly things began to fall into place with great
dispatch. An Oxford committee formally accepted *The Jew
and His Neighbour* as the equivalent of a first research degree;
Professor Maurice Powicke undertook to supervise his thesis;
Exeter College, with historic ties to Guernsey, awarded Parkes a
partial scholarship; and the ISS approved his request for leave
for each of the next three summers, the minimum residence
requirement for a Ph.D. candidate. Since the summertime conference was the centrepiece of the ISS year, this last concession
was no small matter.

Finally, a surprise ingredient materialized to spice Parkes'
academic pie: Helen Ellershaw, a friend from six years earlier,
when they had both worked as sub-wardens at the Student
Movement House, volunteered to come to Geneva at her own
expense to assist Parkes both with routine ISS duties and the
onerous chore of typing his thesis.[22] Edith Ruth Weisz, an astute
Parkes watcher for over a quarter of a century, characterizes
Ellershaw as 'an upper-class gentlewoman, a Quaker from a
Quaker village who had a private income and was crazy about
Parkes'.[23]

It is highly likely that Ellershaw did indeed harbour 'designs'
on the very eligible Reverend James Parkes. However, Parke
chose not to examine her intentions too closely. It has already
been noted that he was not above exploiting the expectations of
others for his own purposes. Hard pressed for both time and
money, Parkes could scarcely afford to refuse Ellershaw's
tempting proposal.

Since the two of them worked at close quarters over an extended period of time, at least at the start Parkes must have walked
a rather fine line. Whatever his true feelings, he had very good
cause not to dash Ellershaw's hopes utterly or prematurely. While
the degree of their intimacy is impossible to ascertain, one surmises that Parkes took care to avoid seriously compromising
himself. Ultimately, Ellershaw's editorial assistance would be

acknowledged in the routine fashion in the preface of the finished dissertation.

In view of future developments, the misfiring of Ellershaw's generous ploy seemed to hinge less upon her unsuitability for the role of Mrs James Parkes than on Parkes' emotional unreadiness for any permanent alliance. At this juncture Parkes' long sublimated sexuality was diffuse and feeble at best, his sexual identity still amorphous. Not many years thereafter, when 'Ellershaw II', another editorial assistant whose curriculum vitae and even physical appearance approximated that of 'Ellershaw I' presented herself as a connubial candidate, there would be a different outcome. The playing-out of this alternative script to a more successful consummation required both a more domesticated locale and clime and the fullness of time in which to ripen.[24]

In 1931, in the depths of the Depression and subject to the rigours of Prohibition, the ISS summer conference convened on the campus of Mount Holyoke College in Massachusetts. Parkes emerged from that gathering with a mandate to produce a handbook on international conferencing. His admirably comprehensive work on this recondite business appeared two years later.[25] Examining it, one would never guess that, although he would continue attending such gatherings for the rest of his days, Parkes was already much disillusioned with their efficacy. Plagued by mishap, the circulation of *International Conferencing* was more paltry than deserved.

The Mount Holyoke conference also yields a juicy anecdote about the earnest cleric as a party-goer, his coming out for his reader as a *bon vivant*. During a boating excursion off the Atlantic coast, Parkes' bosom companion Alexander Teich recalled never having been offered a greater variety of 'fruit juices'. Rockefeller, he said, was giving them the time of their lives. Suddenly, a great storm arose. Was Parkes, that erstwhile teetotaler, the Job of the party? Reminiscent of the gloriously sentimental sinking of the *Titanic*, '... all the passengers came on deck, held one another's hands, and sang "Abide With Me"'.[26] Parkes, as tipsy as the others, was right in his element.

NOTES

1. James Parkes, *Voyage of Discoveries* (London: Victor Gollancz, 1969), p. 98.
2. *Vide* Chapters 16 and 17.
3. Viz. the striking comparison from disparate realms of experience in Donne's 'The Dissolution' between the speaker's soul, which he wishes should expire so that it might be reunited with his dead mistress, to a speeding bullet that overtakes another fired earlier: 'As bullets flowen before/A latter bullet may o'rtake, the pouder being more.'
    Now kindly indulge a momentary flight of fancy. Had Parkes only mastered the art of knitting, we might well have pushed the question considerably further. What *could*, after all, have resonated with such a one who grew up on Guernsey around the turn of the century was just such a subconscious remnant, a memory trace or perhaps even a clear association of his subversive activity, with the ritualised jousting that had so dazzled him as a lad. These tournaments were part and parcel of the fabric of the island's enduring medieval tradition that had stimulated the lad's early daydreams of knighthood, the very stuff which would so amply feed Parke's later appropriation of the role of the Paladin of the Jews. In other words, Parkes would have devised not only a brilliant means of dispelling the boredom of the seasoned committeeman and of drawing vagrant eyes in his direction but also a strikingly apt piece of symbolic action which, in T. S. Eliot's immemorial phrase, operated as an 'objective correlative' for the bodying forth of his life's mission. Alas the Guernseyman never would learn to knit.
4. James Parkes, 'God and My Furniture', *Student Movement*, March 1931 and 'Revelation and a Duster', *Student Movement*, May 1931.
5. James Parkes, 'God and My Furniture', Parkes Archives, File 60/17/3.
6. Parkes, *Voyage of Discoveries*, p. 97.
7. Ruth Weyl in conversation with the author and Maggie Davidson in Rehovot, Israel, 26 October 2003.
8. Parkes, *Voyage of Discoveries*, p. 85.
19. W. W. Simpson and Ruth Weyl, *The Story of the International Council of Christians and Jews* (London: ICCJ, 1988), p. 15.
10. Recall that 1928 was the same year that Parkes urged a meeting between nationalist and Jewish student organizations in Chartres. *Vide* Chapter 15.
11. Simpson and Weyl, *The Story of the International Council of Christians and Jews*.
12. Parkes, 'Revelation and the Duster', p. 8.
13. *Vide* Chapter 25.
14. *Encyclopaedia Judaica*, Vol. 7 (Jerusalem: Keter, 1972), p. 723.
15. Ibid., Vol. 4, p. 75.
16. Parkes, *Voyage of Discoveries*, pp. 118–19.
17. Ibid., p. 135.
18. James Parkes, in *The Times*, 6 October 1937, Parkes Archives, File 60/17/4.
19. James Parkes, *The Conflict of the Church and the Synagogue* (New York: Meridian and Jewish Publishing Society, 1961), p. 92, ff.
20. Ibid.
21. Ibid., p. 120.
22. Parkes Archives, File 60/17/3.
23. Edith Ruth Weisz, interviewed by the author and Maggie Davidson in Cambridge, England, 28–29 August 2000.
24. *Vide* Chapter 26.
25. James Parkes, *International Conferencing* (London: ISS, 1933).
26. Edith Ruth Weisz, interviewed by the author and Maggie Davidson.

19

The Money Behind the Power Behind the Scholar Behind the Throne

Later in the summer of 1931, twelve years after he first went up to Oxford, Parkes returned to its immutable, reassuring precincts. At the time of his departure, the former Secretary of the LNU had been one of the best-known faces on campus. Strolling now along its familiar paths, Parkes occasionally stopped to greet a don, but none of the boyish-looking men he passed hailed him by name, the thirty-four year old who had enthusiastically committed himself to a clear plan of study.

With three consecutive summer sessions at his disposal, Parkes girded himself to march, like a thoroughly disciplined soldier, through the small forest of early church manuscripts in Greek and Latin. In *The Jew and His Neighbour* he had already intimated that, unlike later forms of antisemitism, the nature and the intensity of negative attitudes toward Jews among the ancients had fallen well within the normative range of the xenophobia exhibited towards other conquered peoples. Upon immersing himself in the sources, Parkes would soon grow more convinced than ever of the position flowing from that central insight: 'The universal, tenacious, malicious hatred [of Jews] … has no existence in historical fact. The generalizations of patristic writers quoted in support of the accusation have been wrongly interpreted.'[1]

Such radical revisionism would require thorough verification. Systematically and exhaustively, Parkes undertook to locate every comment the patristic fathers uttered about Jews and Jewish–Christian relations during the entire first eight centuries of the Common Era, transcribing each of them on to a separate index card. His thickening piles of cards, his newest 'collection', soon grew into his richest treasure trove. Almost

from the start Parkes uncovered compelling evidence to corroborate his ground-breaking thesis. He took particular note of
the process whereby, from one Church Council to the next, the
civil rights the Jews had come to take for granted and had
exercised as Roman citizens were incrementally circumscribed.
Over the course of centuries, the erosion of their position was
inexorable until, as Europe entered the early Middle Ages, Jews
qua Jews, except at the pleasure of local princes, enjoyed no rights
whatsoever. This, of course, rendered their compromised communal life increasingly vulnerable to incursions of violence.

Parkes was soon able to demonstrate,

> ... that the aetiological roots of antisemitism were traceable
> to the false and artificial division of Old Testament Israelites
> into the 'virtuous Hebrews', who were pre-Incarnation
> Christians [upon whom were heaped] all the praise and
> promise and the 'wicked Jews' [who] had all the crimes and
> denunciations. This interpretation was repeated again and
> again, in every possible variation, and in every century from
> the third onwards.[2]

In short, rather than any evil acts perpetrated by Jews, anti-
semitism was actually rooted in the mendacity of Christian
apologetics and the tendentiousness embedded in the fabric of
Christian theology. Parkes fully appreciated that his findings
would engender strong resistance.

At the same time, a careful reading of *The Jew and His Neighbour* renders suspect Parkes' claim to have been 'completely
unprepared for the discovery that the Christian Church, and the
Christian Church alone' was responsible for antisemitism, that
'most crippling sin of historic Christianity'.[3] In fact almost
every significant point made in *The Conflict of the Church and
the Synagogue* is prefigured in the earlier study.

During Parkes' first post-graduate sojourn at Oxford, W. A.
Visser t'Hooft, incoming General Secretary of the WSCF and a
figure of consequence in the entourage of Karl Barth, launched
a speaking tour of English theological schools in order to spread
his mentor's ideas. The appointment of a drum-beater for
Barthianism to the leadership of the WSCF effectively sealed
Parkes' alienation from that body. In galling contrast to the tepid
response Parkes had been accorded at Montreaux, to Parkes'

frank consternation t'Hooft was received in England like an emissary from a celebrated savant.

With a passing nod at external factors such as the Great Depression, the impotence of the League of Nations and the perdurability of white supremacy and imperialism, Parkes essays a tour d'horizon to elucidate why the Continent provided such fertile soil for the growth of Barthian triumphalism. 'All these things provide the background for the failure of theological nerve and the disgraceful collapse into pessimism of German Protestantism.'[4] He ruefully concludes, 'that the Protestant continent went Barthian is explicable; that Anglo-Saxon theologians succumbed to its evil influence is still an unexplained mystery'.[5]

Parkes had been away too long. He seems woefully out of touch with a number of factors almost any of which might have impelled the English to embrace Barthian despair: the British economy was fast losing its competitive edge; major industries reduced costs by lowering wages. This led in May 1926 to a general strike of all heavy industry and transportation. Its settlement was widely viewed by workers as a betrayal. In 1927 Stanley Baldwin's Conservative government passed the repressive Trade Disputes and Trade Union Act. With execrable timing, just a few months before the Wall Street crash, Labour regained power. By 1931, the level of British exports had fallen to less than half what it had been in 1929. Within a year, unemployment had risen from one to two-and-a-half million. The October elections produced a national convulsion: Labour's parliamentary contingent fell from 287 members to fewer than 50.[6]

Even discounting the background cacophony of one international crisis after another, this litany of domestic disorder sufficiently accounts for the readiness of English theological students to jettison the seemingly irrelevant style of progressive, socially active Christianity espoused by the post-war generation of liberal churchmen such as William Temple. Their receptivity to a theology emphasizing man's radical depravity, remoteness from an unfathomable Deity, and inward-gazing spirituality is not all that inexplicable.

With the main thrust of his energies channelled into his dissertation, Parkes turned out only one article that year, an analytical piece spun off from his doctoral research and published ironically enough in a missionary journal.[7] Three years later, the next and last time Parkes would appear in such an outlet, his stance was more abrasive.[8] Passing up the 1932 ISS Conference in Brno, Czechoslovakia, Parkes again hunkered down for a summer in his carrel in the bowels of the Bodleian. His only literary diversion, which also earned him a small but opportune fee, was to produce a translation of a French article dealing with student life in Vienna.[9]

Parkes returned to Geneva, but much disheartened by the dismal turn of public events and the impuissance of ISS programmes, he was actively considering resigning from the organization. However, Hitler's rise to power in January 1933 stayed his hand. It fell to Parkes, for example, to direct the relief activities of the ISS at the rising flood of impoverished Jewish, non-Aryan and Leftist students newly expelled from Germany. He could not justify the luxury of disengagement.

To cope with the immense scope of this emergency, substantial new funding was urgently needed. Parkes was dispatched to England where he first turned to Jewish businessman-philanthropist Simon Marks. Friendly but preoccupied, Marks steered Parkes to Israel Sieff, his brother-in-law and co-director of the Marks & Spencer retail empire. 'Talk to him,' Marks advised. 'It is just the same as talking to me.'[10] The brothers-in-law were both familiar with Parkes from having read *The Jew and His Neighbour*. Indeed, no better calling card could have been devised. Not only did Sieff respond immediately to his philo-semitic Christian caller's request that 'a considerable sum' be provided for refugee relief, but he also gave Parkes assurances that future support would be forthcoming. For his part, in his mental card file Parkes sorted 'Sieff' under 'magnanimity' but probably not yet with any self-regard in mind. Indeed, he could scarcely have conceived the degree to which this encounter with Sieff would bear upon his future welfare.

In London Parkes stayed with his old SCM friend, Tissington 'T' Tatlow. When he informed 'T' of the full range of anti-Jewish measures the Nazi regime had already implemented, Tatlow scoffed. Earlier that day he and the Archbishop of Canterbury had been assured by the German ambassador, Joachim von Ribbentrop, that accusations of persecution of German Jews by the new regime had been grossly exaggerated. The very next day the archbishop was scheduled to deliver a speech in the House of Lords in which he fully intended to broadcast von Ribbentrop's disinformation to the nation. The naïveté and gullibility of these senior churchmen genuinely shocked Parkes. From his attaché case he produced official texts of German anti-semitic legislation for his friend's perusal. Tatlow immediately arranged for Parkes to have an emergency audience the following morning. As a result, the archbishop abruptly cancelled his speech.[11]

Upon his return to Geneva, Parkes was confronted by a parallel situation: men of good will averting their eyes as long as possible from the ugly face of reality and in the process temporizing with evil. Of course, the catastrophic situation in Germany dominated everyone's thoughts. At the close of the previous summer's ISS conference, Professor Fritz Beck, the featured speaker, had calmly informed Parkes that the two of them probably would never meet again. His parting words were not intended to be melodramatic. A short time later, Parkes learned to his horror that a group of Nazis, several of Beck's own students, had murdered their teacher.[12]

Six months prior to Hitler's accession to power, the ISS had accepted an invitation to stage its 1933 summer conference in Kloster Ettal, a small town in Bavaria. Ironically Beck himself, at the time still hopeful that the organization could exercise a measure of moral leverage within the German universities, had been instrumental in the making of that decision. Now, however, the choice of Kloster Ettal precipitated rare discord among the permanent staff. After a series of lengthy, heated meetings, they arrived at a working compromise: Walter Kotschnig and another staffer would attend the conference in Bavaria, but Parkes and Michel Poberezski, adamantly refusing to set foot in Nazi-dominated Germany, would keep their distance. The four of them would meet up in Lichtenstein, site of the second half of the conference.

Like a groggy awakening after a deep wintry slumber, the German Lutheran Church and the confessing Evangelical churches were only now beginning to appreciate the true dimensions of the Nazi menace. Along with its traditional military caste, Germany's churches were the only corporate body which, had they the will, possessed the authority to challenge the implementation of Hitler's agenda. Under the mesmerizing spell of Karl Barth, however, both the Evangelicals and the Lutherans were emasculated. Even now disgracefully few from their ranks – most notably Martin Niemöller – began to provide shelter and

other assistance to persecuted German Jews.[13] With the acrid
smell of war already in the wind, that autumn Parkes surveyed
the doleful situation in an article wistfully entitled 'Peace'.[14]

With the onset of winter, Parkes' fund-raising activities for
refugee relief took him for the first time to North America where
he delivered a sermon at Toronto's Holy Blossom Synagogue. He
was already acquainted with Maurice Eisendrath, its illustrious
rabbi, one of a stream of Jewish visitors to Geneva with whom
Parkes had struck up a warm relationship. In fact, one would
infer from Parkes' recollections that his take on 'I never met a
man I didn't like' – signature theme of Will Rogers, America's
most popular humorist of the period – was 'I never met a Jew I
didn't like'. Occasions would arise later that would cause him to
recant such blanket philosemitism,[15] but at least until the 1950s
it points us absolutely in the right direction.

The wellspring of Parkes' respect for Judaism and Jews was
clear, natural and deep. One observer places Parkes '… in the
stream of religious philosemitism that flowed, albeit erratically,
from the beginnings of Christianity',[16] but this surely pales
his distinction. The truth is that one can think of no significant
Christian figure in the past century endowed with a comparably
instinctive rapport with Jews, real, breathing Jews, not the abstract
reifications who inhabit the mental worlds of both antisemites
and philosemites. Parkes' stance was really quite unique: he identified wholeheartedly and without reservation as a Christian with
the special fate of the Jewish people. Never labelling himself 'a
philosemite', he viewed himself as an appointed contemporary
link between the divided faiths that, as he repeatedly averred,
needed each other's vision to complement their own. Only then
could they fulfil God's plan on earth. Loving the Jewish people,
embracing and defending Jews as possessors of an authentic,
living spiritual legacy, this most Jewish of Christian clerics was
also the most christian. Truly, the man was *sui generis*.

During Parkes' stay in Canada, James G. MacDonald, newly
appointed High Commissioner for Refugees by the League of
Nations, invited him to serve as his advisor. Parkes protested that
he could not possibly consider such an offer until he located
funds for ISS refugee programmes. Immediately MacDonald
brokered a meeting for him with Felix Warburg, uncle to Bettina,
a contact that yielded a very substantial contribution. Pleased
but at the same time feeling uneasily beholden to MacDonald,

Parkes reluctantly accepted the appointment. They embarked for Europe on the *Ile de France*, flagship of the French fleet, but the times were not right for a luxury cruise. Parkes, generally not averse to creature comforts, could not in good conscience square using funds designated for refugee relief on a luxurious Atlantic crossing. His tenure as aide to the High Commissioner would be very short-lived.

Parkes arrived in Europe with something more than a fresh infusion of cash. He had been recruited for a very special mission. At a fund-raising meeting in New York organized by Rabbi Cyrus Adler, President of the Jewish Theological Seminary, Parkes was approached by a former ISS activist, of late in exile. The man was now an underground operative for Elsa Brandström, an elderly, Swedish-born advocate for refugees who still lived in Berlin. Her international eminence was such that the Nazis decided not to harass her publicly. In contrast to his aversion for working with MacDonald, Parkes readily agreed to serve as a continental conduit in a highly secret operation whose aim was spiriting refugees out of Germany.

Of course Parkes was fully aware that becoming a covert operative in Switzerland, where there was considerable pro-Nazi sentiment, would place him in real jeopardy. For the most part, however, he filed his potential peril under 'Christian duty' and greatly relished the adventure. A special code was devised: part of it was already in Brandström's hands; Parkes took the missing, complementary portion with him to 3 Grand Mezel. Parkes recalls: 'I was always one meal behind in my washing up. There was always a pile of dirty plates on the kitchen table. In the middle of that pile was a clean plate on which the code reposed.'[17]

After three years of intensive but exhilarating research, in the spring of 1934 Parkes submitted his 125,000-word dissertation to his thesis committee. The man who had composed *The Jew and His Neighbour* out of his head, as it were, had turned every sheet, scanned every word of the sixty-six folio volumes of *Lives of the Saints*.[18] His manuscript was embroidered with hundreds of footnotes, five indices and six appendices. In marked contrast to his chronic discontent with his ISS duties, he was vastly and justly proud of this achievement, obviously a labour of love and a major contribution to the knowledge of the period. His committee unhesitatingly recommended its acceptance in fulfilment of the requirements of a Ph.D., thus heralding the fledging of the Reverend Doctor Parkes.

Then, Oxford University Press declared its scrupulous adherence to its mindless house rule that dissertations should consist of no more than 60,000 words. If Parkes desired publication, he was enjoined to reduce his manuscript by at least half and to excise the scholarly apparatus with which it had been so gorgeously decorated. Yet more preposterously, even though within the time frame of Parkes' manuscript officially no Jews resided in England, he was directed to include a new section about the Jews of England. Once again Parkes bruised his heel falling down the rabbit hole. Stymied by this draconian idiocy, he beat a path to the Jews; on the spot London's Soncino Press accepted *The Conflict of the Church and the Synagogue: A Study in the Origins of Antisemitism* for publication. Taking into account that it would appear in the midst of the Depression, the scholarly study was to sell briskly, soon going into a second edition. It has since enjoyed the distinction of being frequently plagiarized and never out of print.[19]

Beyond the howls of conservative churchmen and the scowls of obdurate scholars who rejected Parkes' views out of hand, even critics predisposed to endorse Parkes' larger themes have framed serious objections to his study. Nicolas de Lange, for example, after noting that Parkes' lack of Hebrew often led him astray about Talmudic issues, properly took issue with the argument that the institution of the synagogue could be traced conclusively to the period when the Jews under Ezra returned to Palestine from their Babylonian exile. Less persuasively, de Lange also cavilled at Parkes' depiction of a fairly stark 'parting of the ways' of Christianity from Judaism around the end of the first century of the Common Era, arguing that the process was less absolute and more protracted.[20] Still, notwithstanding other divergences of view, few open-minded scholars could deny that Parkes' pioneering account of the fissure between Jews and Christians from the earliest period through the Dark Ages and up to the medieval period marked a true watershed.

While in London that summer dealing with editorial details, Parkes attended to another kind of business which seemed to offer good promise of securing his future wellbeing. Walter Koltschnig had heard that the Crane Foundation was interested in funding a Christian scholar with expertise in Jewish affairs. He arranged for him to meet its director George Antonius who, it soon transpired, just happened to be a personal friend of the Grand Mufti of Jerusalem. Antonius made Parkes an exceedingly generous proposition: for £1,200 a year (three times his ISS salary) in addition to perks such as the use of a house in Jerusalem and a substantial pension package, Parkes would serve as the foundation's 'Jewish expert'. In return for this generous stipend all that he needed to do was to submit whatever he wrote pertaining to Jews to the editorial supervision of the Crane Foundation. Immediately recognizing the proposal as 'more in the nature of a bribe than a serious opening for scholarly work',[21] Parkes stepped smartly away from an offer he could not afford not to refuse.

At the end of his triumphant summer, the happy but impecunious Dr Parkes returned to Geneva where he tendered his long-contemplated resignation to the ISS. It came as no surprise to his colleagues. Ever since the Nyon conference two years earlier, Parkes' trajectory had been clear. He did not, however, take the next logical step – an early return to England. Just as in Lowestoft at the close of the war, Parkes felt the weight of responsibilities that could not be dropped so precipitously. Aside from his undercover assignment as a contact for Elsa Brandströmm, older academics, students and all sorts of refugee professionals beat a steady path to 3 Grand Mezel where Parkes hosted a weekly open house for students. In addition, Parkes sheltered a Jewish refugee, covering his fees at the University of Geneva.

Now reduced to an annual income of around £150, Parkes carried on in Geneva on the cheap. It was, as he puts it, 'a difficult year,' but he continued with his extensive reading programme in Jewish history, took on the odd writing and translation assignment, and worked on the final revisions of his dissertation. In the midst of financial straits, it might have occurred to him that his situation somewhat parallelled the period when his widower father moved his family from Les Fauconnaires into the sunny, modest bungalow. Like his father, Parkes' Jewish boarder, who was supposed to keep the apartment tidy, was in fact notoriously inept at housework – '… he could not even wash up or make his bed without some completely unexpected disaster'. Incompetence had its advantages: there was little danger that the secret code concealed amidst the dirty plates would ever accidentally get deposited in the garbage. In any event, himself now seemingly on the cusp of confirmed bachelorhood, Parkes 'ended up a competent laundryman and sempster as well as cook'.[22]

This knotty relationship between past and present, father and son, abandonment and guilt, now becomes even tighter with complication. At the same time that his relative proficiency at housework reconnected Parkes with a boyhood role, the motif of the 'cook' inverts that association with a suggestive link to his father who, as we recall, in similar circumstances has also become 'a very good cook'.[23] A direct corollary of this duality is that the student, utterly devoted to his mother still in peril in Germany, also projects a dual character: in his deep attachment to his mother, the student enacted the part of Parkes as a boy but the refugee's ineptitude at housework links him to Henry Parkes. Furthermore, just as Parkes' father had always disparaged his son's estrangement from life's practicalities, Parkes soon began to criticize the practical abilities of his alter ego.

This doubling of identities is reinforced by the motif of abandonment: Parkes had endured 'abandonment' by his mother; the refugee student suffered from guilt for 'abandoning' his mother in Germany. While it is unlikely that Parkes was constantly conscious of the range or nature of these mirror images, that he was sensitive to their pressure is manifest. Beyond his generalized commitment to aid Jewish refugees, this net of special implication conspired to keep Parkes 'in exile' in Geneva long past the time when he might reasonably have departed. It could even be argued that the interpenetrability and reversibility of these elastic roles were a symbolic projection of Parkes' evolving identification of himself as a sort of refugee or, more poignantly, as a sort of Jew.

Viewed otherwise, whereas at a critical juncture Parkes' father had energetically relocated his family, his son's ambivalence disabled him from decisively moving back to England precisely because he then would have 'abandoned' his boarder, a Jewish version of himself. In sum, the intensity of his recent experiences, disclosures issuing out of scholarship converging with his long-time sympathetic identification with the fate of James the Just all encouraged Parkes to appropriate the sensibility of a twentieth-century incarnation of a first century Judeo-Christian, or a 'Christian Jew'.

At the same time, as if apprehensive that the wrong conclusion might be drawn from his dalliance with Jewishness – or even perhaps to put others off the scent – that very spring Parkes turned out 'Judaism, Jews, Antisemites: Thoughts of a Non-Jew'. It marked his first appearance in the pages of a Jewish journal.[24] The irony was that in spite of explicitly labelling himself a 'Non-Jew', Parkes' increasingly frequent appearances in Jewish journals reinforced his public image as a philosemite.[25]

Unsurprisingly, Parkes' maiden 'Jewish' article reiterated several of the themes he had had honed for his dissertation. Thereafter, aside from writing a second article for another Jewish journal,[26] Parkes grew preoccupied with research into the range of attitudes towards Jews evinced by the Gospels and the Pauline letters, a matter touched upon but left unresolved in his dissertation. Mainly composed in Geneva, this follow-up study, *Jesus, Paul and the Jews*, would be published the year after Parkes' return to England.

At the end of 1934 a remarkable public trial got under way in Bern. The Jewish community of the Swiss capital was trying to persuade the court to declare *The Protocols of the Elders of Zion* an obscene forgery and to prohibit its distribution. As it happens, Parkes had not long since purchased one of the rare extant copies of *Dialogue aux Enfers entre Montesqieu et Machiavel*, the original from which *The Protocols* had been adapted. During the course of the trial, a number of Swiss students, professing solicitude for Jews and a special interest in the pamphlet in Parkes' possession, made repeated visits to his flat. On each occasion Parkes received them graciously and responded openly to all their enquiries. We recall that Parkes has been aghast at the naïveté of the Archbishop of Canterbury. Especially after the murder of Fritz Beck, therefore, it is not easy to account for his own credulity. In short order he would have cause to regret it.[27]

At the start of the new year Parkes made a trip to Britain. Still in good, or good enough odour with a few Christian organizations, he travelled under the colours of the SCM. Much like t'Hooft four years earlier, his aim was to tour English and Welsh theological colleges in order to spread his word. The topic was one he was rapidly making his own: the historic dysfunctional relationship between Judaism and Christianity. Looking back, Parkes felt that he enjoyed little success. Considering that his heterodox slant undermined everything his listeners had ever been taught about Jews, there are no grounds to suspect him of undue humility. At every platform he was received with incomprehension if not outright abuse. Reinforcing the unpopularity of his theme was the off-putting figure Parkes cut at the lectern; at Swanwick he was remembered as '... striking in shorts and wearing sandals',[28] a Bohemian image not likely to ingratiate him with future clergymen.

One luminous exception to Parkes' string of ill-starred appearances was Birmingham, the home of his illustrious forebear Joseph Parkes, in his day also a champion of the Jewish cause.[29] After his presentation before the combined staffs of a group of area colleges, an Anglican professor enquired whether Parkes' views enjoyed the support of any 'recognized authority'. Parkes beamed. He had recently been staying with William Temple, then the Archbishop of York. The two friends both realized that Temple's rise within the Church hierarchy embodied precisely the kind of career that Parkes would never enjoy. Yet on most matters of substance, they were of one mind, and so Parkes could cite his well-positioned friend as feeling disposed to agree with the basic hypothesis that 'the separation of Christianity and Judaism was a schism which, like all schisms, left truth divided'.[30]

This homiletic response was received with an outburst of laughter. Parkes was mystified. His host then explained that the very preceding week Temple, speaking in Birmingham, had used those precise words. 'Then we heard it from the throne,' he said. 'Now we hear it from the power behind the throne.' 'The Power' could scarcely contain his delight.

Having snubbed Antonius' generous bribe on his previous stay in London, on this trip Parkes primed himself to make another entreaty to Israel Sieff. Unlike their previous encounter,[31] this appeal would be on his own behalf: Parkes had hit upon the idea of requesting a regular subsidy that would enable him to pursue his future research into the history of Jewish–Christian relations. After his exposition in Sieff's comfortable library, his host asked how long he thought the work would take. Sensing that success hinged upon the proper reply, Parkes hesitated.

> I wondered what answer I could give him. If I said five years, he might say it wasn't long enough. If I said ten, he could think it was too dear. So I gave him the honest answer. I said three hundred years. He laughed and said 'Good, I am prepared to help you. Had you said 'twenty-five years'

or 'in my life time' I would have told you to go away because you did not understand what you were talking about.[32]

Seven years older than Parkes, Israel Sieff occupied for the young scholar the middle station between a mysterious father figure and a solicitous older brother. The role he would play in Parkes' life as benign, Dickensian benefactor would ever be timely and for the most part constant. On several occasions Parkes makes it abundantly clear that, unlike Antonius, Sieff never threatened to influence the direction of his research, let alone to censor his writings. As far as it goes, his disclaimer is accurate. What Parkes never seemed to appreciate fully, however, was that Sieff intuited that he would never be given occasion to interfere with the young scholar's work. Having read *The Jew and His Neighbour* and now met Parkes, Sieff had excellent grounds to support Parkes' scholarly pursuits. Friend and philanthropist, Sieff was also a canny businessman and judge of character; he had every reason to believe that his modest investment in Parkes would pay high dividends for the Jewish people.

Parkes and Sieff were both conscious that the latter was fulfilling the traditional role of the disinterested Jewish benefactor. Just a few years earlier in Germany, for example, secular Zionist Salman Schocken, another department store magnate, 'who believed … the modern nation-state the Zionists were building in Palestine was in need of a mystical foundation, subsidized [Gershom] Scholem's explorations of previously ignored Jewish mystical thought for years'.[33] He also lent important support to the fountainhead of modern Hebrew fiction, Shmuel-Yosef Agnon. What was previously entirely unheard of, however, was that the beneficiary of Jewish largesse should be a prominent Christian clergyman. The sense of being co-conspirators in an unorthodox arrangement served to foster their growing intimacy.

Parkes' bond to Sieff also resonates with the spirit of George Eliot's *Daniel Deronda*, one of the very few works of fiction with which we may confidently presume Parkes was familiar. Eliot's novel extends parallel ties of affection between the eponymous hero and his two surrogate fathers – his wealthy, genteel foster father and Mordecai, a prophetic Jewish Zionist. It is evident that Parkes viewed himself as a kind of Deronda, his Jewish affinity (if not fully-fledged co-identity) at first unknown to everyone but emerging in the end like an irrepressible force of nature.[34]

Unlike his natural father, Sieff would not only sustain Parkes materially for many years, graciously affording him the leisure and liberty to pursue his intellectual and moral goals as he saw fit, but he would also be unstinting with his time and generous in bestowing sympathetic affection.

The Christian cleric and the Jewish philanthropist developed, in sum, an intimate and lasting friendship from which they both drew liberal benefits. At the same time, there was a canker residing at the very core of their relationship. The disparity between their respective conditions was truly vast. True, the two of them stood on an equal footing intellectually and they shared a mutual admiration for the other's moral fibre. As long as the friends implicitly concurred about how best to proceed in jointly combating antisemitism, the inequality of their conditions did not impinge upon their mutual regard. As we shall see, however, that would not always be the case, and the potential for a falling out was ever present. Aristotle, much admired by both men, clarifies their dilemma:

> ... and this is most manifest in the case of the gods; for they surpass us decisively in all good things. But it is clear also in the case of kings; for with them, too, men who are much their inferiors do not expect to be friends ... In such cases it is not possible to define exactly up to what point friends can remain friends; for much can be taken away and friendship remain, but when one party is removed to a great distance, as God is, the possibility of friendship ceases.[35]

Neither Parkes nor Sieff would ever evince the least desire that their friendship should cease. Nevertheless, at certain junctures money would try their relationship sorely.[36] Rather stridently and perhaps too insistently, Parkes avers,

> ... [he had] never been embarrassed by the fact that I have been financially dependent for most of my life. I suppose that trouble would have arisen ... had there been an attempt by my benefactors to say you shall do this, and you shall not do that, and on this issue this is your opinion. But, in fact, such a situation has never arisen. That a rich friend should help me financially to do something we both want to see done, has always seemed to me similar to a busy

friend giving me his time to help in the understanding of some problem of concern to both of us.[37] I am a debtor to my parents, my teachers, my contemporaries, and to the whole community and its history. I have no desire to set upon my tombstone, HIS MONEY AT LEAST WAS HIS OWN.[38]

Although Parkes had excellent grounds for feeling confident that posterity held in store a more appropriate encomium, his sensitivity to the accusation that he had sold himself to the Jews for thirty pieces of silver is all too manifest.

NOTES

1. James Parkes, *The Conflict of the Church and the Synagogue* (New York: Meridian and Jewish Publishing Society, 1961), p. 150.
2. James Parkes, *Voyage of Discoveries* (London: Victor Gollancz, 1969), p. 123.
3. Ibid.
4. Ibid., p. 105.
5. Ibid., p. 104.
6. R. K. Webb, *Modern England: From the 18th Century to the Present* (London: George Allen and Unwin, 1969), pp. 523–25.
7. James Parkes, 'The Nature of Anti-Semitism', *The Church Overseas, An Anglican Review of Missionary Thought and Work*, October 1932.
8. James Parkes, 'Can Christianity Be Detached from the Old Testament?' *East and West Review*, October 1935.
9. Parkes Archives, File 60/17/4.
10. Parkes, *Voyage of Discoveries*, pp. 105–106. An old hand at the art of the limerick, it's hard to imagine Parkes didn't have a go at larking about with 'Parkes' and 'Marks', 'Sieff' and 'relief'. If so, however, the lines have fallen between the cracks of memory.
11. Ibid., p. 106.
12. Ibid., p. 107.
13. Ibid., pp. 103 - 104.
14. James Parkes, 'Peace', *The Student Movement*, October 1933.
15. *Vide* Chapter 23.
16. Alan Edelstein, *An Unacknowledged Harmony: Philo-Semitism and the Survival of European Jewry* (Westport, CT: Greenwood Press, 1982), pp. 177–79.
17. James Parkes, *Voyage of Discoveries*, pp. 107–108.
18. Ibid., p. 122.
19. Ibid., p. 124.
20. Nicholas de Lange, 'James Parkes, A Centenary Lecture', in *Cultures of Ambivalence and Contempt: Studies in Jewish–Non-Jewish Relations*, eds Jones, Kushner and Pearce (London: Vallentine Mitchell, 1998), pp. 41–43. Also *vide* de Lange and John Gager, *The Origins of Antisemitism: Attitudes Toward Judaism in Pagan and Christian Antiquity* (Oxford: Oxford University Press, 1983).
21. Parkes, *Voyage of Discoveries*, p. 125.
22. Ibid., p. 109.
23. Ibid., p. 10.
24. James Parkes, *Jewish Review*, London, March–June, 1934.
25. Among themselves, less polite observers surely labelled Parkes a 'Jew-lover,', an epithet one suspects he smilingly embraced.

26. James Parkes, 'Quelque Reflexions sur la Conference Juive Mondiale', Swiss-Jewish Journal, September 1934.
27. Parkes, *Voyage of Discoveries*, pp. 126–27.
28. Venerable Whitton Davies, *Tributes in Memory of James William Parkes*, at Bournemouth Hebrew Congregation, 1981, University of Southampton, Parkes Archives.
29. *Vide* Chapter 3.
30. Parkes, *Voyage of Discoveries*, p. 128, f.
31. *Vide supra*.
32. James Parkes interviewed by Laurence Dobie, in The *Guardian*, 28 March 1970, Parkes Archives, File MS 60/31/37.
33. Amos Elon, 'Wise Survivors', *New York Review of Books*, 10 April 2003, p. 76.
34. The parallel of the natural gentility of Fielding's *Tom Jones* comes to mind.
35. Aristotle, *The Nicomachean Ethics*, translated and edited by David Ross (London: Oxford University Press, 1969), p. 192 ff.
36. *Vide* Chapters 31 and 34.
37. The example of the rich man with a surplus of money logically parallels not the busy man, who is short of time, but the man of leisure with time on his hands. Parkes is clearly unaware of the ineptness of his analogy which, inasmuch as it misstates Sieff's true position, ironically foreshadows a later misperception of his benefactor's true priorities.
38. Parkes, *Voyage of Discoveries*, pp. 190–91.

20

'Old Elizabethan Threatened'

Reminiscent of conundrums such as *The Turn of the Screw*, *Rashomon* and the recent, award-winning documentary film *Capturing the Friedmans*, getting a firm grip on what actually happened next is challenging. As with the elusive mystery of the Bungalow Ghost,[1] there seems little alternative but to deconstruct and reconstruct so as to make the best sense possible out of a baffling but indisputably important sequence of events in Parkes' life.

Seven years after having reached his original 'understanding' with 'Len' Thomas,[2] the former warden of the Student Movement House looked up the handyman who had served him so well. Parkes wanted to know whether Thomas was prepared to resume their former relationship by coming to serve him as a valet and general factotum. It is plain that Parkes had not maintained much if any contact with Thomas over the years; otherwise, he would not have had to enquire whether their 'understood thing'[3] would still be honoured seven years later.

On the face of it, there are any number of reasons why Thomas might have warmed to the idea of leaving his long-time job where he was at the beck and call of so many in the raucous Student Movement House and to go to work for the genteel Reverend Doctor Parkes. Equally plain is that after a seven-year hiatus, there are reasons why the cautious, sedentary Thomas, now the father of two small sons, might have hesitated. Hesitate, however, Thomas did not.

It is worth recalling that if there had been ambiguity or grounds for misunderstanding regarding their prior understanding, the two men were unequally matched as polemicists. In his frank eagerness to obtain Thomas's services Parkes, perhaps unthinkingly, might have led the handyman to feel that the two men had reached an implicit agreement that, if not legally enforceable, was still morally binding. Or perhaps Parkes withheld information that, seemingly only technically relevant, might have given Thomas undue cause for alarm, enough perhaps to cause him to reconsider their 'agreement'. Tentative, nevertheless these hypotheses go straight to the question of culpability, an issue that later comes strongly into play.

Whether Parkes considered the implementation of their 'understood thing' to be good for Thomas is not recorded, but if he had any reservations, they seem to have evaporated. Thomas was, after all, an adult and capable of reaching his own decisions. Whatever the event, Thomas almost immediately accepted Parkes' proposal that the two men rejoin forces. 'When he said "yes", I told him that I would take him back to Geneva to help me close the flat and pack up, but first I wanted to spend a few days in Guernsey with my father.'[4]

For reasons that will shortly become transparent, the exact sequence of these events is highly significant: first Thomas, confirming their original agreement, consented to work for Parkes; only then was he informed about accompanying his future employer to Geneva to help him in packing and closing the flat, and finally Parkes, pleased that his plans were proceeding smoothly, caught a boat to Guernsey. Shortly after his arrival, his father handed him a sheaf of letters that had arrived from his friends in Geneva. Most conveyed the same disturbing news: ever since his departure, 3 Grand Mezel had come under close police surveillance. Everyone thought that upon his return Parkes would very likely be subject to arrest. Several friends, whose past experience with the Swiss police had given them cause not to trust in their impartiality in dealing with foreigners, advised Parkes not to return to Geneva.

With his antique furniture and precious collection of Jewish books and journals in Geneva, not to mention a box of index cards representing hundreds of hours of work relating to *Jesus, Paul and the Jews* – his current project – it seemed out of the question to Parkes that he should not return. Not to return until the present danger had appreciably subsided may have sounded nominally more prudent but, Parkes reasoned, with European tensions only intensifying, there was no reason to believe delay would be beneficial. In any event, he really couldn't afford to wait. Therefore, believing himself in need of Thomas's assistance, it was clearly in Parkes' interest to minimize the possibility of danger in Geneva or even not to bring the matter up at all.

But, if Parkes did not himself learn about the potential danger until he had sifted through his packet of letters on Guernsey, how could he possibly be faulted for inadvertently deceiving his man? It transpires, however that Parkes' recollection of a highly significant detail is fatally flawed. Dated 29 March 1935, a letter was dispatched to Parkes by Walter Kotschnig, the selfsame chap who two years earlier had opted to convene an ISS conference in Nazi-dominated Bavaria and who a year earlier, apparently in all innocence, had benevolently steered Parkes to an interview with George Antonius of the antisemitic Crane Foundation. It was directed not to Guernsey but addressed to Parkes c/o Zoë Fairfield at the SCM office in London.[5] We may safely conclude therefore that Parkes was familiar with its contents before he sailed for Guernsey, which in turn means that he almost certainly was aware of the situation in Geneva before making his proposal to Thomas.

Unlike Parkes' other correspondents, Kotschnig reported that the police on the scene had actually been assigned to protect Parkes from danger. In view of the uncertainties of the situation, he strongly urged Parkes to send him a power of attorney so that he would be able 'to take any steps that might be necessary' until Parkes' return.[6] Which steps these might be is not initially clear, but given Kotschnig's dodgy record one would think that Parkes might have paused long and hard before accepting his reading of an ambiguous situation. Instead, because its general lines were in accord with Parkes' uncharacteristic bout of wishful thinking, he succumbed to the comforting delusion that bad things happen to others. Disregarding the advice of most of his Geneva friends, Parkes immediately took steps to comply with Kotschnig's suggestion.

Since Parkes had good reason to forget the precise sequence of events, his recollection thirty-five years later, although incorrect, could very well be genuine. His version does, after all, clear him of culpability for being less than forthright with Thomas about the position's prospective risks. After three decades, self-deception could easily have become ingrained and habitual. On the other hand, one cannot dismiss the possibility that in his memoir Parkes consciously perpetrated a seemingly inconsequential, face-saving deception, one carrying major ramifications.

From his father's solicitor Eugene Carey – if not the very lad Parkes had thwacked so resoundingly at Elizabeth College then certainly of the same clan – Parkes obtained a power of attorney.

Then two Guernseymen, in a burst of whimsy, proceeded to festoon it not only with the impressive seal of the Careys but also with the prominent-looking seal of Parkes' previously unmentioned great-grandfather. Finally, they 'garnished' it with the official medieval seal of the bailiwick of Guernsey. In the end it made for such a gaudily magnificent official document that, once in their hands, the Geneva police would refuse to relinquish it. The *plein pouvoir* did, however, serve its purpose: it enabled Kotschnig to learn that the authorities in Bern were acting on intelligence they had received that the *Eisene Front* – the Swiss Nazi organization – had been ordered by the German *Antisemitche Weltdienst* to liquidate James William Parkes as an enemy of the Third Reich. Those obsequious Swiss 'students' who for months had been loitering in his apartment just bubbling over with curiosity about his Jewish pamphlets – especially his copy of *The Protocols of the Elders of Zion* – were actually Nazi agents.[7]

Faced with an undeniably serious threat, Parkes' spirits perversely seemed only to soar! As though Nazi threats were an occasion for hilarity, the man now verifiably on Hitler's hit list joked about it with his solicitor.[8] Had Parkes forgotten the fate of Walter Rathenau or that two years earlier Fritz Beck had been murdered by Nazi students? From a certain slant Parkes' sangfroid could be viewed as admirable, even in a fashion typically British. More likely, however, it represented a kind of cheery whistling in the dark, an untimely defence mechanism to suppress the thought of very real danger so that he could get on with his foray to Geneva. With regard to himself this could be interpreted as simple foolhardiness. Was it not inexcusable, however, that he spared no thought for the welfare of his factotum? 'Len' Thomas was entirely left out of the equation.

Perhaps Parkes had concluded that inasmuch as it was he who was the actual target, Thomas would be in no real jeopardy, and that therefore there was no reason unnecessarily to rouse his anxiety by raising irrelevant spectres. Yet the experience, familiar to Parkes, of Herman Badt who in 1931 had spoken forcibly at the Nyon conference,[9] should certainly have disabused any rational person in 1935 of the notion that the Nazis would draw a distinction between their enemy and the servant of their enemy. Here is how a German national ruefully recalled the flight two years earlier of another important figure scheduled for assassination: 'On the 4th of March, a day before the [German] elections, their [Social Democratic] "strong man", the Prussian prime minister Otto Braun, drove across the Swiss frontier. He had prudently bought a small house in Ticino.'[10] In recounting the same episode, Parkes' emphasis is rather different:

> ... when none of his own staff would lift a finger to help him, Dr Badt donned his chauffeur's uniform, took the largest, most official car from the ministry, and drove Dr Braun and his wife through the night across the frontier ... In the morning Dr Badt was at his desk in the Ministry as though he had spent a quiet night in bed at home.[11]

Whereas in the first account Braun's close escape is cited as one of many instructive examples of the failure of German democratic leadership to withstand Nazi intimidation – if not its outright cravenness – Parkes ignores these aspects entirely in order to highlight Badt's 'contribution to the annals of German Jewry'.[12] It is as though at the time Parkes unconsciously avoided drawing the conclusion appropriate to his own situation. Badt knew better than to remain at his desk until the Nazis could draw their own conclusions about his role as Braun's 'chauffeur' in the affair: later that year he too fled the country – for Palestine.[13]

It was hardly a secret that even officers in the British Foreign Service professed Nazi sympathies. Did Parkes not suspect that some members of the Geneva police force had also been infected by Nazi ideology? Upon arrival at his flat with Thomas, should Parkes not have solicited outside protection for his remaining weeks in Geneva from some of his ISS connections or refugee friends? Until far too late, somehow he never thought it worth the bother. Parkes would like us to surmise that it never crossed his mind that he was in some measure responsible for bringing Thomas into the line of fire and, as the circumstantial evidence strongly argues, for never clearly apprising him of the true danger.

Ethically whether Parkes adequately informed Thomas about the risk awaiting them in Geneva matters enormously. Seven years earlier, after all, Thomas had not consented to sign on for a life-threatening job. Under the changed circumstances – Nazi assassins waiting in the wings counting as an important if not decisive new contingency – a married man with responsibilities could not be expected to feel bound by the conditions of such a prior 'understanding'. If Parkes secured Thomas's agreement to work for him prior to informing him about the need to travel to Geneva and thereafter grossly understated or totally withheld information about the danger awaiting them, then to some extent he was responsible for whatever befell his valet in Geneva. Thirty years later, however, Parkes was still in a state of denial.

One month to the day after Parkes had read Kotschnig's letter in London, a communication that trumped all the letters of warning that he received on Guernsey, the following headlines were spread across the front page of one of Guernsey's dailies:

OLD ELIZABETHAN THREATENED BY NAZIS
FLAT BURGLED, SERVANT KNOCKED OUT
WRITER WHO DENOUNCED ANTI-SEMITISM
REFUSED TO CARRY REVOLVER

These descending statements accurately reflect the paper's skewed, four-paragraph account of the affair. A 'threat' to the Old Elizabethan distorts what actually occurred. The flat, taking precedence over the condition of the servant, in fact was not burgled. At first glance Parkes' refusal to bear a weapon seems hardly relevant, but the article itself provides grist to gloss an old conflict: 'Mr Parkes urged his son to carry a revolver, as he had received threatening letters from German and Swiss Fascists, but he preferred to remain unarmed.'[14] Who other than Henry Parkes could possibly have been the source of that titbit? This is not surprising: that his son had never displayed much inclination to take his advice in no way diminished his father's capacity to give it or then tell the world 'I told him so'. Of course Parkes, armed with his splendiferous *plein pouvoir*, would pay little heed to his father.

On the other hand, just because the source of the counsel was 'bad old Henry Parkes' does not mean that we may simply discount it. It need not have been a revolver, but given the circumstances should and could Parkes not have taken some protective measures so that he and Thomas would not be so vulnerable?

Repaying close attention, Parkes' own recollection of 'the affair' is more nuanced than what appeared in the *Guernsey Star*.[15]

Thomas and I duly arrived in Geneva one Thursday evening. Shortly after we arrived the telephone rang. As soon as
I lifted the receiver and gave my name, the caller rang off.
We were proceeding in the best *whodunit* manner: it had
been ascertained that I had returned. Friday passed peacefully. On Saturday morning Thomas and I went to the
market. He was in his best suit, and walked beside me while
I did the bargaining and buying, since Thomas did not
speak French. Obviously we were identified during this
excursion, but the appointed thugs decided that Thomas
was the scholar and I was the *valet de chamber*.[16]

Could anyone blame the thugs for mistaking Thomas 'in his best
suit' for Parkes at large in his normal casual attire?
   The tableau of scholar and valet out together on a shopping
expedition at the Geneva market is highly evocative; it projects
a picture resonant with veiled significance and studied ambiguity.
A parallel text sheds oblique light on its potentialities:

> ... I sensed that everyone kept their eyes on the two lobster
> eaters, whom I heard variously described as master and
> man, two friends, relatives, or even brothers. Endlessly the
> pros and cons of these theories were advanced, and the dis-
> cussion filled the hall with a low murmur, even long after
> the table for two had been cleared and the first light of dawn
> was at the windows. No doubt it was above all the eccen-
> tricity of Cosmo, combined with the impeccable manners of
> Ambros, that had aroused the curiosity of the Deauville
> summer guests. And [as] their curiosity naturally grew,
> and the suspicions that were voiced waxed more audacious,
> the more the two friends contented themselves with each
> other's company ...[17]

   Similarly, Parkes and Thomas, the scholar and the valet, as if
acting in one accord on a morning's outing in Geneva, seem
entirely self-contained and insulated. Any onlooker would have
adduced the easy, natural intimacy of their relationship, if not
its precise nature, from their demeanour. This will be pursued
later because at this point, precipitated by yet another tumble
down the rabbit hole, the lights of rational and civilized behaviour
go out, ushering in a return to the world view of 'black and

white' that characterized Parkes' military years. This time the one who landed on his head was not Reverend Parkes; it was 'his man' Thomas.

> We were busy all the rest of Saturday. When my post came, I threw the envelopes with foreign stamps over to Thomas, since his younger son, Johnny, collected stamps. In the evening he said he would post my letters, and take a walk … I told Thomas that, as I was now a bourgeois with a valet, I would leave him to look after the dustbins [which late every night Parkes had been accustomed to carrying downstairs and depositing outside the front door for his elderly concierge].
>
> The next thing that I knew was that, an hour or so later, Thomas staggered into my room and collapsed dramatically at my feet. I rushed to the telephone, but my doctor was out. I had to call the police and ask for their doctor. He was clearly instructed before he came to deny that anything had happened. He examined Thomas on the floor and looked up brightly:
>
> 'It's influenza.'
>
> 'But my dear doctor, is it normal that a man should feel perfectly well, then suddenly fall unconscious, remain unconscious for between half an hour and an hour, recover consciousness saying that someone had hit him on the head with a ton of bricks, and all the time his temperature should remain perfectly normal?'
>
> Looking at me with owl-like wisdom he replied: '*Ah, la grippe vous savez, ça prend des formes diverses.*' I have kicked myself ever since for not being bright enough to ask whether this was the political form of influenza (grippe). During the whole of the vital period my policeman remained fast asleep in my best armchair outside my door. He refused to descend the stairs after Thomas had staggered in, on the grounds he had no electric torch …
>
> The British consulate was completely unhelpful, in fact rather offensive. The Geneva police, who detest affairs with a political undercurrent – and I sympathize with them in this – maintained that either Thomas had invented the whole thing, or that he had taken a young man down to the cellar for immoral purposes, and that the young man

had turned on him. In furtherance of this point of view the next morning a police officer arrived and informed me that, as there was clearly no need for any guard, the policeman was returning to more important duties. At least I could once more enjoy my best armchair!'[18]

If only to locate a substitute to perform his pastoral duties the following day at Emmanuel, Parkes rang the American consul who proved far more helpful than his British counterpart.[19]

On the ground that I was temporarily American chaplain, the consul took a semi-official interest, and was an invaluable counsellor. The American ladies provided Thomas with invalid food, and as soon as he was well enough, took him daily for a drive. The Swiss legal advisor of the consulate briefed me ... on how to establish that Thomas had actually been attacked, and drew up for him an official *plainte d'une aggression livrée sur moi par un inconnu!*[20]

Parkes carefully explains the significance of two artefacts: Thomas's wallet and his silver cigarette case. Awaiting his opportunity to mount the stairs, the attacker had hidden himself behind a bend in the stairwell. When Thomas descended with the dustbin, the thug, suspecting he was about to be discovered, bludgeoned him with a heavy object. Upon examining the unconscious man's pockets, the Nazi mugger discovered the autographs of a local football team and the envelopes, all addressed to Parkes and covered with foreign stamps, that Thomas had just pocketed for his younger son.

So there was just the name of a town, then a list of signatures – could they be the secret local anti-Nazi organization? There was no single item in the pocket book to identify Thomas ... The silver cigarette case lay beside the unconscious man. Each half of it was twisted out of shape, as if to make sure it didn't contain a secret lining.[21]

After the police interrogation, Parkes continues,

... the detective in charge of the case came up to me and confessed himself to be very puzzled. He wished to maintain the official view of the police that Thomas had invented it – possibly to explain a disreputable incident –

but he was honest enough to admit that Thomas had given his evidence as an honest man would. He was impressed by the fact that Thomas knew what he ought to know and was ignorant of what he ought not to know – assuming his story to be true ...

The detective was ... won [over] ... completely to the innocence of Thomas. But we never got any satisfaction out of the Geneva police. To the end they maintained that 'the incident' had never happened.[22]

Ironically, after rereading this extensive citation thirty years after the fact, we too cannot rest easy with 'the authorized version of the incident' as recollected by an Old Elizabethan threatened by, among other things, bad conscience. The following chapter pursues the investigation to its unresolved denouement.

NOTES

1. *Vide* Chapter 8.
2. *Vide* Chapter 14.
3. James Parkes, *Voyage of Discoveries* (London: Victor Gollancz, 1969), p. 129, ff.
4. Ibid.
5. Parkes Archives, File 60/31/28.
6. Parkes, *Voyage of Discoveries*, p. 129.
7. Ibid., pp. 129–30.
8. Ibid., p. 130.
9. *Vide* Chapter 18.
10. Sebastian Haffner, *Defying Hitler: A Memoir*, translated by Oliver Pretzel (London: Phoenix, 2003), p. 108.
11. Parkes, *Voyage of Discoveries*, p. 119.
12. Ibid.
13. *Encyclopaedia Judaica* (Jerusalem: Keter, 1972), Vol. 4, p. 77.
14. The *Guernsey Star*, 29 April 1935. p. 5. The headlines in that day's edition of the *Guernsey Evening Press* provide an interesting contrast. Marginally less melo-dramatic, they too give place of honour to the flat, which actually was not burgled, rather than to the injured manservant and add no remonstrative hint about the revolver: GUERNSEY CLERGYMAN MENACED BY NAZIS – FLAT BURGLED – MANSERVANT ATTACKED
15. A small but poignant irony which probably did not escape Parkes' notice: on the reverse side of the page in the *Guernsey Star* where the story of the assault in Geneva appeared, there is a large advertisement. It announces a forthcoming meeting of the Britain in Israel Society. Major Ord-Statter's lecture would be presented on Tuesday, 30 April at St Andrew's Hall. The Britain in Israel Society is an association of adherents to the quaint notion that the British are linear descendents of the ten lost tribes of Israel. In their ahistorical daftness, they have carried the radically antisemitic distinction between the 'cursed, evil Jews' and the 'good, Old Testament Hebrews' who were considered prototypical Christians, to its 'logical conclusion'. Hitler rode a variation on this theme to a logical conclusion of his own. The roots of this insidious disjunction, frequently descanted upon Parkes' writing, are embedded in the Gospels.

16. Parkes, *Voyage of Discoveries*, p. 130.
17. W. G. Sebald, *The Emigrants*, translated by Michael Hulse (New York: New Directions, 1996), p. 125.
18. James Parkes, *Voyage of Discoveries*, pp. 130–31.
19. Parkes Archives, File 60/31/28.
20. James Parkes, *Voyage of Discoveries*, pp. 131–32.
21. Ibid., pp. 132–33.
22. Ibid., p. 133.

PART 4
THE MATTER OF BARLEY

Doubting Thomas

A few days after the assault, Parkes was rung up by a reporter from the *Daily Telegraph*. Having been beaten up himself in Germany by a gang of Nazis, he experienced no difficulty in crediting Parkes' account of what had transpired in Geneva. Parkes said that since he did not wish unnecessarily to worry his father, a regular reader of the right-of-centre *Telegraph*, he requested the reporter 'to play the whole thing down as much as was consistent with his journalistic conscience'. The upshot was a typically errant spin in a long-flawed relationship: 'When I next got to Guernsey and told him [his father] all that had happened I found him very sceptical, and convinced that I was exaggerating a great deal. When I protested at his suspicion of my accuracy, he quoted at me the much reduced account – in the *Telegraph*.'[1]

The son who as an adolescent had secretly 'supplemented his [father's] housework while he was out shopping'[2] so that his deficiencies at housekeeping might not be exposed was the same son who as an adult was shielding his father from undue concern about his safety. The parent who had undermined his son's early ambitions and questioned his abilities was still the father who doubted his middle-aged son's veracity. However, not everyone greeted 'the Parkes' Version' with such scepticism. A card from Gilbert Murray posted to Geneva had much buoyed his spirits: 'I hope you are not upset. This is probably the greatest honour you will ever be paid. G.M.'[3]

Had the father satisfied himself with a glance at the headlines in the *Guernsey Star,* his son might have had an easier time of it. If not exactly mortified, Henry Parkes, his agnosticism intact and his conservatism fortified by the passage of time, was still mystified if not dismayed that his son had turned into a 'Denouncer of Antisemitism' and a 'Champion of the Jews'. In the mid-1930s not only much of Middle England but also the better part of the progressive wing of Christianity – James Parkes' natural terrain – still swallowed variations of the vision of the war-profiteering Jew 'underneath the lot' that T. S. Eliot, from his redoubt on the Royalist Right, had promulgated a decade earlier.

The following passage from one of Graham Greene's 'entertainments' is typical enough. In it he conjures up a crew fully worthy of the noxiousness spun out by J. Alfred Prufrock's alter ego. Far from being thought *outré*, it was considered well within the pale. Among a dozen or more other representative fictional portrayals of repulsive Jews of the era that come readily to mind, Greene's Sir Marcus could be matched by Hilaire Belloc's I. Z. Barnett in several novels, H. G. Wells' Sir Reuben Lichtenstein in *TonoBungay* (1909), and Wyndham Lewis's Archie Margolin in *The Apes of God* (1930).

> Sir Marcus [Director of Midland Steel] entered on the tips of his toes. He was a very old and a very sick man with a little wisp of white beard on his chin like chicken fluff. He gave the effect of having withered inside his clothes like a kernel in a nut. He spoke with the faintest foreign accent, and it was difficult to tell whether he was Levantine or of an Old English family.
>
> Sir Marcus read the tape prices. Armament Shares confirmed to rise, and with them steel ... It made no difference at all that the British government had stopped all export licences; the country itself was now absorbing more armaments than it had ever done since the peak year of Haig's assaults on the Hindenburg Line. Sir Marcus had many friends, in many countries; he wintered with them regularly at Cannes or in Soppelsa's yacht off Rhodes; he was the intimate friend of Mrs Cranbeim. It was now impossible to export arms, but it was still possible to export nickel or most of the other metals which were necessary to the arming of nations. Even when war was declared, Mrs Cranbeim was able to say quite definitely that evening, when the yacht pitched a little and Rosen was so distressingly sick over Mrs Ziffo's black satin, that the British government would not forbid the export of nickel to Switzerland and other neutral countries so long as British requirements were first met. So the future was very rosy indeed.[4]

Although he tried to maintain a cool façade, Parkes' final three weeks in Switzerland were extremely nerve-wracking, the very antithesis of his high-spirited sojourn on Guernsey.[5] Upon being declared well enough to travel by a 'nickelled' Swiss doctor, Thomas set off alone to England. Parkes, now visibly jittery, began attending to details of packing and shipping in earnest. He was not, however, entirely on his own. His German Jewish boarder had moved, but a Russian Jewish student, thankful for the help Parkes had extended to him in the past, insisted on helping him with packing and shipping details. More importantly, he slept at the foot of Parkes' bed to help assuage anxieties which were far from baseless. Every window of the flat on Grand Mezel, once a source of perpetual refreshment, could easily be accessed from the roof which itself adjoined the roofs of neighbouring buildings. Bravado much deflated, Parkes did not disdain the Russian Jew's reassuring presence. Three nerve-wracking weeks passed without incident; Parkes caught a train for Calais and was soon safely back in England.

For much of that summer Parkes laboured at establishing himself in his new home in the village of Barley.[6] Not quite at the foot of his bed but nevertheless still right at his side was 'Len' Thomas. He was, however, a different man. Now partially disabled, seriously emotionally disturbed and grievously wounded psychologically, Parkes' valet was under the care of Dr Augusta Bonnard, a psychiatrist much respected by Parkes since their days together at the Student Movement House. Her diagnosis was anything but reassuring:

> After some weeks she ... told me that Thomas was still in a dangerous state of mind. On the one hand he was attached to me but, on the other, he felt victimized by the appalling headaches which became his lot while I went scot-free. He laboured under the impulse actively to make me share the fate which, although intended for me, had instead been inflicted on him. It was a situation in which he might at any moment succumb to a brain-storm, and suddenly attack me, if only to repent it bitterly afterwards![7]

Particularly in his youth Parkes had been no stranger himself to appalling headaches, and, under normal circumstances, this would have given him a ready appreciation of the intensity of

Thomas's suffering. As the servant put it, however, Parkes now went 'scot-free' not only of headaches but, surprisingly enough, of self-reproach or any visible show of remorse. Thomas's obdurate, leaden bitterness and Parkes' opacity should be understood as reciprocal. Their interface invites careful exploration into the underlying nature of their relationship.

Had Thomas justification for feeling aggrieved, angry, and aggressive? As indicated earlier, reasons abounded. Some well founded, others spurious, all of them coagulated into a great lump that lodged itself in Thomas's craw. From his narrowed perspective, it was Parkes who had tossed him the incriminating envelopes, which, thus 'planted' in his pocket, had confirmed the misidentification of the apolitical servant as the undercover agent liaising between anti-Nazi operations in New York and Elsa Brandström in Berlin. Although irrational, at a deep level Thomas felt he had been 'set up' by Parkes to be his stand-in, to absorb the blows that were directed at him. Thomas wondered whether, in some way he could not fathom, Parkes had genuinely deserved them. In any event, he reasoned, certainly the priest deserved them more than he.

Tending to confirm his bill of grievances against his employer, when he sent Thomas out with the rubbish – at most a five-minute chore – Parkes somehow 'forgot' about him for almost an hour. During that time the servant lay unconscious and could easily have died. One minute 'master and man, two friends, relatives, or even brothers',[8] and the next one of them – the wrong one – was severely assaulted and would be permanently cursed with chronic, appalling headaches. The sheer injustice of it simply would not give Thomas a moment of peace.

Moreover, Thomas must have learned that, during the three weeks after his own departure from Geneva, Parkes had welcomed the friendly services of a bodyguard. Thomas now knew that Parkes had been aware that he was marked as a target for Nazi retribution. He wondered how it was possible that a man considered one of the best informed about the deadliness of the Nazi menace in all of England had not taken even minimal precautions to protect not himself alone but also his truly innocent manservant. Taking into account the collusion of certain elements of the Geneva police force with local Nazis, was this not an unforgivable lapse in judgment?

We remind ourselves that, as one astute observer put it, 'what an Englishman is hopeless at, but James Parkes was good at, is putting himself in the place of someone else'.[9] So how is it possible that Parkes was so insensitive when it came to the feelings of his victimized valet? Dr Bonnard spelled out to Parkes that his servant felt a grievance against his employer for unaccountably and unjustifiably placing him in jeopardy of his life. Now, although he still felt bound in conscience by his original verbal agreement with Parkes, Thomas found it hard to work, behave naturally or control his resentment in his employer's presence. Thomas, Bonnard went on, had to guard continually against the impulse to strike out, to inflict upon Parkes the very sort of beating which he had suffered and which, he felt his employer richly deserved.

However, the psychiatrist warned, were Parkes simply to dismiss Thomas from his service, the valet would likely never regain his equilibrium. In spite of the potential risk, she urged Parkes to retain Thomas in service until in his own good time he could bring himself to disclose his massive disappointment, confess his rage and the urge to harm Parkes, and himself request release from their 'understood thing'. As if newly awakened, to his great credit Parkes immediately saw his duty and unflinchingly assumed the accompanying risks. Yet another tense month would pass, which must have been a harrowing time for both men, before Thomas screwed up his courage, revealed his inner turmoil to his employer, and requested release from their near-fatal 'understanding'. Parkes was genuinely moved but, while expressing perfunctory regret, accepted his valet's resignation readily enough.

But now let us suggest an alternative to Parkes' remembered account. Let us assume that the perspicacious Bonnard, herself formerly acquainted with Thomas from the Student Movement House, was even more penetrating than Parkes fully appreciated. Let us assume that she understood that she was confronted not only by the repressed enmity of a victim but also by his employer's denial and repression of culpability. Let us suppose, then, that in her subtle, indirect fashion she was trying to enable Parkes to perceive a very different picture, one that he simply could not or would not grasp on his own.

If in her above diagnosis we were to substitute *le valet* for *le bourgeois* and vice versa, a reverse mirror image emerges, resembling one of those two-toned, trompe l'oeil illustrations designed for the amusement of children and the edification of psychologists. Because the eye-to-mind nexus habitually focuses on the picture's shaded portions, at first one perceives what appears to be, let us say, a monkey swinging from a branch; only after the passage of some minutes, after a shift of focus to the picture's uncoloured portions, does one suddenly perceive the unshaded outline of a camel under a palm tree. This well-known phenomenon, while commonplace, casts the psychiatrist's analysis in a different light, one that grants us a measure of latitude tentatively to deconstruct what Parkes 'remembers'.

As Thomas's alter ego, *Parkes* reciprocated his man's turmoil. He too now felt bound by their original agreement, and he too could neither feel nor behave naturally in the presence of the other. Moreover, if the embodiment of his discomfort were peremptorily dismissed, *Parkes* would never recover his equilibrium. The solution would be for Parkes to retain Thomas in service until he could come to grips with *his own* repressed guilt and acknowledge it by confessing to his valet that he, *Parkes*, had indeed acted irresponsibly. Upon expressing remorse and begging Thomas's forgiveness for the serious harm and pain that he had caused him, *Parkes*, demonstrating that he had started to come to terms with his guilt and was prepared to make amends, would exorcise his guilt and achieve atonement.

This speculative revision, which amounts in effect to an alternative diagnosis, is necessary because Parkes' sensory apparatus, out of tune with Bonnard's message, missed its implications. We already know which of them, the scholar or the valet, would make the first move. Neither at the time nor later could Parkes adjust his vision to perceive the camel under the palm tree or his ear to receive on Bonnard's wavelength. In recalling the entire interlude thirty years later, Parkes obviously still judged Thomas's implicit accusation of his employer's guilt and blameworthiness to be unfounded, a consequence of his former servant's pathology. Thomas's death in 1968 occurred during the composition of *Voyage of Discoveries*,[10] and so he never read Parkes' account of the episode.

Nevertheless, much like the secret code 'hidden' so conspicuously in view on its appointed clean plate amidst a pile of dirty dishes, in his account of this painful affair Parkes unawares planted at least one blatant, tell-tale clue in full view. As hyper-intrusive as Poe's famously purloined letter, it is very noticeable that the clergyman himself was blind, or in this instance deaf, to its presence.

Parkes concludes his narrative retrieval with the nonchalant remark that after it was all over, the two men remained 'good friends'.[11] Insoluble as the knot of anger that Thomas could not gulp down for several months, that commonplace portrayal of their relationship sticks in the mind. In fact, as if unconsciously to belie this spurious 'friendship', with the very next stroke of his pen Parkes observes that he did not see Thomas again for the next thirty years. They would exchange greetings cards at Christmas and nothing more. By no stretch of the imagination, in short, could the two be said to have remained 'good friends'.

However the perplexing question of what impelled him not only to conjure up an imaginary, ongoing relationship with 'his man' but also to proclaim it loudly in his autobiography refuses to fade. What lay behind this self-deceiving verbal camouflage was almost certainly Parkes' load of unacknowledged guilt. For years it hovered at the margins of consciousness like an assailant poised in the shadows, ready to pounce. Although troubled, Parkes could never bring himself to recognize and to acknowledge his proper share of culpability.

Reviewing the entire course of events, we must conclude that Thomas's bill of indictment is largely justified. At no point had Parkes clearly informed his man that entering his service might entail significant danger. Although his high-spirited antics with his solicitor back on Guernsey suggest that he concealed the true extent of his peril from himself, that scarcely excuses him from blame *vis-à-vis* his servant. And what, after all, is the expression 'good friends' but a mendacious locution often exploited as an expedient to conceal pain and to mitigate the sting of betrayal. One of its most standard contexts is, of course, the break-up of lovers when the initiating party applies it as balm to soothe a searing wound.

Had Parkes and Thomas been lovers in their days together at the Student Movement House? As in earlier reconstructions of Parkes' intimate relationships, it is impossible to demonstrate this with certainty. In fact, given the slackness of Parkes' store of sexual energy and the disingenuousness of his rendition, to conceive at all of their relationship quite as 'an affair' would be misleading. Nevertheless, it was real and sufficient enough to have excited in Parkes a romantic reverie that focused upon his lower class factotum. And in light of Thomas's sense of betrayal, the conceit had clearly been reciprocal. Their 'understanding', which both had been so loath to disavow utterly , was the equivalent of their troth. Moreover, enough had transpired between them not alone to have left Thomas feeling he had been bamboozled but to cause Parkes to replay their external relationship in a suggestive manner, as if, that is, they really had been lovers. Honing the sharpened edge of Occam, that minimum is all that is needed for us unequivocally to avow the presence of a force field charged with ambiguous expectations.

To recapitulate, only past intimacies and the promise of a more than merely professional attachment bears the burden, darkness, and intensity of Thomas's feelings of rejection and despair. Week after week the servant struggled in vain to comprehend why Parkes had returned to London to resume their connection only later to cast him among the ranks of the insulted and the injured. For Thomas it was simply inexplicable. After a time, he anachronistically came to view the Nazi thug as a surrogate for Parkes himself, inflicting blows that virtually emanated from his employer. This doubleness, a distant cognate of 'duplicity', points us towards the basic correctness of Thomas's intuition of betrayal. What the innocent servant could not possibly grasp was the ultimate source of that doubling and duplicity: he had been unwittingly thrust into a vital, supporting role in his employer's long-standing, indeed primal, psychodrama.

For Parkes, this difficult, murky interlude is best understood as a transitional stage in the working out of his sexual identity. As adumbrated earlier,[12] the template had been etched in childhood when Jimmy first projected himself powerfully into the early life and career of Jacob, the smarter but less favoured son of Isaac. At the age of thirty, a decade or more later than the point in time when his biblical forerunner had unhesitatingly renegotiated his bargain with Laban so as to earn the hand of Rachel by labouring for seven additional years, the slowly ripening cleric arrived at his own bargain or 'understanding' with 'Len' Thomas.

Passively colluding with these delaying stratagems, Parkes proceeded to perform his preordained part in his archetypal drama. Just like his biblical namesake, Parkes laboured for seven long, often dismal years in a foreign field. Then, something like a sleepwalker, Parkes returned to England to receive his due.

And just as in the tale from the *Book of Genesis,* upon his claiming his prize, the machinations of incarnate evil – Laban-cum-Hitlerian operatives – interceded to thwart the promised fruition of what is basically the pattern of a romantic *Bildungsroman.* Like a Jacob, too late Parkes sensed that something was amiss: instead of obtaining a Rachel, he was cheated with a Leah.[13]

What is deceptive is that during those intervening years, while Thomas had remained fixed and constant, it was Parkes who had been undergoing a silent change. His slow, awkward, wayward maturation out of a narrowly homoerotic personality now propelled him to participate with the working out of an archetypal pattern that, deviating from *Genesis,* would conspire in the forceful ejection of the innocent Thomas from his life. As with Jacob in Haran, it would take additional years of travail after his return to England before Parkes, undergoing yet another translation, would ride the dynamic of this biblical pattern to yet a higher stage of psychosexual integration.[14]

There remains, however, an unresolved question. Why was Parkes not able to admit any personal culpability in this affair? At the primary level of consciousness, not to mention of conscience, he knew that he had incurred Thomas's blame for having exposed him to danger, for not taking the blows that were properly his to take, and for 'forgetting' and leaving him unconscious for up to an hour. It seems most odd that the man who spent a lifetime pointing the finger of blame at Christianity for the sin of antisemitism could not admit his guilt. Even if it were insincere, Parkes could have manufactured it, knowing that an expression of responsibility might have helped to assuage a sick man's pain. In fact this very insensitivity argues the pressure on Parkes at this juncture of yet another, even more deeply repressed regressive, primal pattern.

Immediately after the assault in Geneva, Parkes' vain attempt 'to manage the news' to protect his father had misfired because Henry Parkes placed more credence in an alternative version that, ironically, had originally emanated from his son. This heuristic sequence parallels an early stage of Parkes' boyhood. Competitiveness, chronic disagreement, and frequent spatting with his older brother David, associated even then in his mind with the bigger, tougher Esau, would from time to time come to his father's attention. Henry Parkes would then want to know what had been going on. As with the failed assassination attempt, without outright lying, young Jimmy would naturally colour his version of the story to achieve maximum credibility in the eyes of his father. Of course the son who attempts to deceive his father pre-eminently evokes young Jacob and blind, elderly Isaac. Frustratingly, Henry Parkes almost always credited David's version of events. The younger boy's major consolation was that, given the family constellation, Annie Parkes – playing out the role of Rebecca – always tended to side with and to succour her younger son.

How precisely do these typological figures resonate in the affair in Geneva? As iterated above and in the previous chapter, Parkes and Thomas comported with each other in the fashion of 'master and man, two friends, relatives, or even brothers'. At once the manifest content of the scene in Geneva, newly fraught with a different dimension, dissolves into the primal scene. It now takes on all the earmarks of a perennial fraternal conflict. Although David Parkes had been dead for fifteen years, is it not plain that he subsisted in Parkes' consciousness as an Esau, a powerful, ever-dangerous, undying antagonist?

Beyond the ken of the central protagonists, perhaps sensed but not apprehended in all their dimensions by Bonnard, for Parkes the events in Geneva were overlaid, not just with the narrative conflict between Jacob and Laban. Equally powerfully they also merged with Parkes' childhood conflict with David/Esau, the older brother whose injury, removal and death he had a thousand times secretly, guiltily fantasized about in the privacy of his bedroom after once again having, he felt, been unfairly chastised or perhaps even physically punished by his father. Not even the death of David had curtailed the innate power of the subconscious wish that his brother should die. When he did, Parkes' sense of guilt would never be fully allayed. Inconclusive in itself but consistent with this analysis is that in all his travels Parkes never mentions even one visit to his brother's grave at Zonnebeke. No wonder he now displayed such obtuseness and insensitivity *vis-à-vis* Thomas, 'his brother', so that, fifty years later, this brilliant scholar's account of the affair still exhibits incomprehension of its larger significance.

In fact, even had Parkes been jarred into a fit of insight into his responsibility in the Thomas affair, it is unlikely that he would have confessed it publicly. With the notable exception of smilingly confessing himself 'a tyrant'[15] in his account of the

16. External view of Barley manor house, front

17. Barley, the dining room

18. Barley, the bedroom

19. Barley, lawns and rock garden

20. John McNeilage

21. James and Dorothy, wedding photo, August 1942

22. Parkes as John Hadham making radio broadcasts during the Second World War

23. Parkes with Sir Richard Acland, founder of Forward March, 1942

24. Parkes with Rabbi Maurice Eisendrath at Barley,
in the 1950s

25. Parkes

26. In his habit, Parkes reading

27. Parkes as an elderly man with Wickings and family of Patrick Rolleston

28. Parkes' gravesite

schoolboy reign of terror he had instigated as a senior prefect, Parkes seemed constitutionally incapable of seeing himself in the wrong. This blunting of the self-critical faculty, a process correlative to the nearly full eclipse of self-irony and a dearth of introspection, should be viewed not merely as irksome but as a palpable fault. It lends an authentic basis for Philip Toynbee's assertion that Parkes was,

> ... shallow in too many of his attitudes, impatient of everyone who differs from him about anything, and cocky to the point of insufferable boastfulness. Story after story is told of how James Parkes got the better of anyone who ever made any reservations about his high deserts.[16]

During the war, while the rest of Europe endured cataclysmic upheaval, Switzerland performed its perennial role as the 'neutral spectator'.[17] A decade later, Parkes would briefly return to Geneva on a nostalgic visit.[18] If only because he was now in the middle of his life's journey, he was much changed. His health increasingly troublesome but feeling less ambivalent about his sexuality, the tone he assumes in the latter half of *Voyage of Discoveries* is less edgy, less cocky, less boastful, and, yes, less insufferable.

NOTES

1. James Parkes, *Voyage of Discoveries* (London: Victor Gollancz, 1969), pp. 133–34, ff.
2. *Vide* Chapter 6.
3. Parkes, *Voyage of Discoveries*, p. 134.
4. Graham Greene, *This Gun for Hire* (New York: Viking, 1964), pp. 134, 139–40. Curiously, Britain's best-known 'Sir Marcus' was the son of Israel Sieff. He was knighted in 1980.
5. James Parkes, *Voyage of Discoveries*, p. 134.
6. *Vide* Chapter 22.
7. James Parkes, *Voyage of Discoveries*, pp. 134–35.
8. W. G. Sebald, *The Emigrants*, translated by Michael Hulse (New York: New Directions, 1996), *vide* Chapter 20.
9. Colin Richmond, 'Parkes, Prejudice, and the Middle Ages', in *Cultures of Ambivalence and Contempt: Studies in Jewish–Non-Jewish Relations*, eds Jones, Kushner and Pearce (London: Vallentine Mitchell, 1998), pp. 225–26.
10. Parkes, *Voyage of Discoveries*, pp. 134–35.
11. Ibid., p. 135, ff.
12. *Vide* Chapter 2.
13. Just as Thomas Thomas and Thomas 'Len' Thomas were in fact one and the same, the sisters may be usefully viewed as two faces or aspects of the selfsame personality.
14. Vide Chapter 26.

15. Parkes, *Voyage of Discoveries*, p. 20.
16. Philip Toynbee, 'Champion of the Jews', the *Observer*, 13 April 1969.
17. Only half a century later would its major banks, companies and government most reluctantly admit a degree of collusion with Nazi Germany.
18. *Vide* Chapter 31.

22

A Terribly Slummicky Small Holding

Although he did not view himself as an expatriate, by the close of 1935 Parkes was in fact rounding out a seven-year cycle of self-exile from England. Throughout this period he had worked incessantly to promote progressive principles and to put them into practice on the world's stage. He had acquitted himself forcefully and honourably in public forums, and could point to any number of student refugees who had been materially aided through his personal intervention. In the arena of non-governmental activism, Parkes may be said to have made his mark. On the other hand, he recognized very early on that embroidering his way through an endless succession of study conferences really did little to impede the rising tide of fascism, rearmament and antisemitism. Disappointed at the negligible success of the ISS in stemming the drift of the world into a maelstrom, Parkes for some years had appreciated that as a social activist he was teetering on the edge of burnout. Still he dallied and permitted external events to dictate his movements. In the end, the attempt on his life felt like the finger of fate, confirming the correctness of his decision to withdraw from the peripatetic pace of the Continent to the more sedentary life that awaited him in England. Moreover, even if he had wanted to dither longer, his drastically reduced income combined with an inflationary spurt of sterling *vis-à-vis* the Swiss franc would soon have forced his departure.[1]

In spite of the above misgivings, Parkes years in Geneva had been immensely fruitful. Not only had he earned the admiration of his peers, but he had also demonstrated that he could write with vigour and natural grace. His first two books had been marked by the intelligence and lucidity that would characterize virtually all his subsequent writings. Gratified by their ready reception, Parkes was supremely confident of his abilities and conscious of the far-reaching nature of the task he had undertaken. In short, by the end of his sojourn in Geneva Parkes' intellectual pursuits and ethical compass had coalesced into a clear sense of purpose. Newly fortified by assurances from Israel Sieff, at thirty-nine Parkes was eager to establish himself in a stimulating and amenable working environment.

Never for a moment did Parkes contemplate returning to his island birthplace, but he had not decided where in England he should live. A vital requirement was access to a major library. Having on many occasions proudly declared himself 'a country-man' and sensitive to the desirability of maintaining prophylactic distance from '... storm centres of my [Jewish–Christian] problem',[2] Parkes eliminated London and its environs out of hand. As for the familiar precincts of Oxford, his claim that he had already exhausted many of the resources of the Bodleian sounds specious. The overriding reason for his rejection of Oxford was more likely the perfectly human impulse to start afresh in a new setting.

'I had already discovered,' he informs us, 'the pleasant line of bracing hills south of the city of Cambridge and it was there that I looked for a house, and found one in Barley.'[3] In addition to proximity to that ancient seat of learning, an altogether for-tuitous meeting with the major local personage helped to tip the balance in its favour. Taken together, it seemed as though the university, the propitious encounter and those rolling hills, like a topographical arrow, were pointing Parkes straight towards Barley and nowhere else. Once that was settled in his mind, in very short order he located and arranged a down payment on a suitable house. It was a run-down, spacious, 450-year-old place on a large plot of land that he would call home for the next three decades.

> It had a vast [Elizabethan] chimney in the centre, with three stacks. It had no documentary history but, as I became familiar with every inch of it, I realized it was basically a late medieval manor house of the simplest kind, consisting of a hall on one side of a chimney, and on the other a solar sleeping room, and a kitchen with huge hearth below it. Later ages had added dairy and cellar, divided the hall into a long parlour with two bedrooms above, and finally turned the parlour into drawing room and dining room ... In the

19th century it had declined into being two cottages, but when I bought it it was a terribly slummicky small holding with two and a half acres of misused land.[4]

At the start, the restoration of this 'late medieval manor house of the simplest kind' and its surrounding 'two and a half acres of misused land' would absorb every ounce of energy that Parkes could salvage from his other obligations. Whereas the glittering flat in Geneva had focused Parkes' shaping powers, within a narrow scope inspiring him to polish a small but perfect diamond, the manor house at Barley afforded him far greater play to exercise his architectonic powers. Indeed throughout this initial period of repatriation, fashioning his 'terribly slummicky small holding' into a more solid, ampler image of himself became almost an obsession.

> Thomas and I spent much of the summer of 1935 on the house and garden, both of which needed enormous attention. I put in two bath rooms and drainage for just over a hundred pounds. I had a big barn and a granary which gave me a garage, and all the store room I wanted. The garden was full of debris and ill-built sheds, pig styes and fowl houses. By the winter the house had begun to reveal some of the charm which had been hidden in its previous existence, and its rooms were beginning to be lined with the bookcases which ultimately became the main 'wall-paper' throughout.[5]

Who could not warm to this antiquarian's delight upon making the discovery that his manor house was shielded from the elements by thousands of original, Tudor-period roof tiles? After the experience of 3 Grand Mezel, Parkes' attention to authenticity and meticulous detail is hardly surprising. Still, his perfectionist's approach to cabinetmaking and his endless enthusiasm for the task at hand are revealing: 'He carved every door himself,' Edith Weisz recalls. 'Made them very beautifully. It was an amazing task. Every square inch had to be in the right style.' She continued,

> Parkes had a workshop, a barn opposite the cottage where he worked. He went to immense trouble to find original

materials, for example panelling for the cottage. He was one of the first not to paint these so that they would retain their original charm. All the house was similarly refurbished. Iron work was carefully reproduced. Bookshelves were never regular. The house had narrow corridors, so he cut a hole and built an area for hanging coats. He ordered a job lot of doors which had to be especially shipped from Geneva. He even bestowed a name to the master bedroom suggesting that it was very grand indeed. All the bedrooms were equipped with bells to summon the staff. His manservant lived in a little cottage a few houses down the road.[6]

Weisz, née Teich, had appeared on the Barley scene as a little six-year old refugee; she spent her first three months living with her parents in Parkes' home and over the years she visited it again on many occasions. Her description of its interior is graphic and precise:

> … a small bedroom with a little cupboard in the wall for small things and Parkes' collection of brass candlesticks. Books covered all the walls of the library which had a fireplace and a large desk. Just outside the window was a rose garden. The Elizabethan chimney had three different openings. In an old converted toolshed, Doris [Wilkinson] worked. A bell was connected to the house so that Parkes could call her in. The study had many books and a bust of Parkes' fine head was placed in the very centre of the room, i.e. a little to the side of the fireplace on a high pedestal facing the door so that the first thing you saw on entering was his head.[7]

Aided initially by Thomas, out of doors Parkes cut down and uprooted dozens of trees in what had been a chaotically over-planted orchard. The wood was chopped and stacked for the coming winter. Parkes modestly grants he was 'not inexperienced in garden making. It had been a main hobby ever since my work had made me live in cities, and I had made a number of gardens for my friends.' At Barley he could adorn his hobby with magnanimity: 'all the levels needed changing, but I kept an acre for an orchard, gave half an acre to the village for gardens of three cottages the Parish Trust owned on the edge of my land

... and had an acre left to landscape into lawn, herb garden, rock garden, herbaceous borders and vegetable garden.'[8]

Hour after hour, inch after inch, with attention to detail, the fastidious, newly established Lord of the Manor forged an intimate connection to his new estate. His currency was sweat and acts of civic liberality. All the while Parkes still intermittently suffered from Dupuytren's contractions in one foot, a permanent legacy from the trenches of Flanders. In the immediate postwar years two operations had failed to relieve the condition,[9] so much of the time Parkes was laying out his intricate garden in the style of a medieval monastery, he was suffering from excruciating pain. 'There were lots of paths so he could always walk around the garden. Parkes himself laid out the paths and planted a great many trees, especially apple trees. He also grew lots of vegetables.'[10]

Factoring in demands on his time for research and writing, the number of hours and the degree of attention Parkes devoted to his manor house and its grounds were prodigious. Over this period ambitious domestic projects with his own two hands were not merely an economy, but became a true passion, a reaction perhaps to a decade of immersion in social and humanitarian activities. One concludes that Parkes positively relished his innumerable hours of Voltairean labour, blisters and perspiration, acquired in the course of cultivating his own garden.

Yet attention to his house and property should not be viewed primarily as self-indulgence. Beyond its transformation into a 'gracious domicile', his restored home served Parkes as a visible embodiment of his philosophy of life if not his metaphysics. Discounting his pain, Parkes adhered to the six precepts for goodly and godly interior design of mind and dwelling place that he had originally enunciated in 'God and My Furniture'.[11] As with the books he would in time write, he firmly believed that a man's house and its furnishings should reflect the grace, beauty and truth inherent in the Kingdom of God. No less than Thoreau's cabin at Walden Pond, Parkes' manor house at Barley may best be comprehended as a symbolic embodiment of the man himself.[12]

As Parkes now entered upon his maturity, one is struck by the unconscious motivations that sustained his intention to spend the greater part of his adult life as a latter-day squire of a medieval manor house enclosed by faux monastic grounds.

Taking possession of this Barley abode was akin to accessing those blessed fourteen years of boyhood at gloomy Rohais before his mother died, save that now Parkes was not merely the son of a falconer but the Lord of the Manor himself. At times it must have crossed his mind that in appropriating and refurbishing such a venerable house, the dreamy-headed, impractical son had in his own way and in his own good time surpassed the worldly success of his 'practical' father who, by the way, seems not to have bothered to come to visit his son at Barley before the opportunity would be foreclosed by the German occupation of the Channel Islands.

Equally resonant, Parkes had acquired his property and the status it entailed under the extended aegis of Annie Bell Parkes. Before making the purchase, Parkes had sought out the opinion of Sackville Bell, a solicitor and an uncle on his mother's side. When appraising the property Bell was accompanied by a properties' 'expert' who, as Parkes delightedly recalls, 'was wrong on every point such as the ownership of the tumbling down boundary walls, and gave me a bill for eight guineas and a certificate that adultery had not been committed in the bedrooms. I had forgotten that my uncle had become an enthusiastic spiritualist.'[13] As we shall see, doubts would soon arise about the expert's acumen concerning intramural doings in the upstairs rooms. As for a propensity towards one or another form of spiritualism, which Parkes also shared, it was plainly a legacy from the Bells. Fortunately, the spiritualist uncle was well heeled; it was he who provided Parkes with the down payment for the property.

Parkes mentions that his house could boast no documentary history, its deeds having been destroyed in a fire many years earlier, but he knew more about its origins than he was prepared to reveal in a memoir inscribed as 'a silver wedding present' to his wife. The original draft of the manuscript of *Voyage of Discoveries* contains the following entry:

> It was one of four manor houses of this village for in that part of East Anglia, the village is older than the manor, and the manor little more than a free-hold farm. It had begun just as part of a great noble's estate but in the 14th century a yeoman named Hoare had acquired it, and his family owned it for nearly a century. It had been known as 'The Old Hore's House'.[14]

It is a pity that Parkes saw fit to delete this fascinating titbit because it camouflages an important symbolic dimension inherent in his physical exertions: the instrumentality of love, sweat and devotion of the metaphorical bridegroom in transforming the slummicky compound into a beautiful bridal bower. In a remarkably short time, Parkes accomplished this small miracle of restoration. Working with surpassing dedication, he lovingly ploughed and sowed his land. Like a beautiful woman who had gone to seed, the Old Hore was reborn as a lovely, innocent lass. Like the Prophet Hosea with his slatternly wife Gomer, Parkes rejuvenated his whorish wife and made her like new. Unrecorded is whether Parkes framed and hung the eight guinea certificate on a bedroom wall in the upper floor of the house.

Of course the style of life appropriate for a feudal manor would be impossible without its complementary roster of servants. Even with modest means, in the past Parkes had usually contrived to retain one or more persons in his service: his 'batman' in the Army, his Norwegian housekeeper at Hertford College, Helen Ellershaw and the occasional penurious student refugee in Geneva, and, most dolefully, 'Len' Thomas. There would soon be an entirely new supportive retinue. To Parkes, keeping up appearances had always been important. In this he diverged sharply from the path of his father who, when funds had grown scarce, had dismissed his only servant and 'courageously' opted 'to be comfortable'.[15]

Parkes too chose 'comfort', but in certain respects his notion of ease and wellbeing was less conventional than his father's. At odds with the philosophy that informs 'God and My Furniture' but consistent with the adoption of a seigneurial air, Parkes affected to be notoriously indifferent to clothing. While chairing an ISS conference in Leicester in 1941, for example, he displayed no sign of unease wearing a shirt one of whose sleeves was conspicuously torn.[16] His sense of entitlement sprang from a view of himself as a 'natural aristocrat' who, when not attired in his clerical collar and cassock, felt free to set his own standards of attire. In contrast to negligent posturing with his apparel, Parkes' physical surroundings in Barley assumed a potent, symbolically charged dimension. Service to mankind and spiritual service to God justified, he felt, the expenditure of a disproportionate share of his limited funds on his surroundings because an appropriate setting facilitated participation in the Kingdom of God in the here and now.[17]

Meanwhile, there was no shortage of trouble in paradise. As spelled out earlier, during those first weeks after Parkes' return 'Len' Thomas toiled sullenly at the renovations and garden projects all the while nursing an unappeasable resentment. Knowing that the bitter factotum posed a clear and real danger, Parkes could not help imagining that at any moment, overcome by rage and incomprehension, the malcontent might splatter his brains with a single swing of a spade or hammer. At the same time, it was far from certain that Swiss Nazis or their British sympathizers, of which there were legion, did not still have designs upon his life. The danger was greatest late at night when, after attending meetings in London, Parkes perforce drove back to Barley alone. Fortunately, police patrols routinely monitored Parkes' movements, and the local constabulary kept a sharp eye out for known British fascists. Their surveillance even extended to the protection of Parkes' European visitors. At the dockside the police generally required other passengers to remain on board until Parkes' visitors could discreetly be delivered into his hands.[18]

To assist him in his work, Parkes had urgent need of a personal secretary to handle his correspondence and accounts. He soon found 'a local youngster', Kenneth Dodkin, who over the course of the years evolved from an error-prone novice into a highly competent secretary, ultimately metamorphosing into 'a wonderful colleague'.[19] The vacuum left by Thomas's departure proved more intractable, and several applicants fell short of the mark. Then John McNeilage turned up to work as cook and household servant. For the next twenty-nine years he would be an essential fixture in the Parkes' household.[20]

Parkes also acquired a research assistant, Hermann Eschelbacher, 'who later englished his name into Ashbrook'.[21] Before coming to England, Eschelbacher had worked in a bookshop in Germany; he would prove useful to Parkes in locating local Jewish histories and antisemitic tracts and pamphlets that were widely scattered in European bookshops. Within a relatively short time Parkes' collection had grown to 2,000 items, many of them rare. While pursuing his research for *The Jew in the Medieval Community*, which appeared in 1938, Parkes took particular pleasure in mining resources from his own bookshelves. This led one observer to opine that, 'for Parkes, the books and his own writings were not ends in themselves; they were to be utilized for practical purposes. Indeed, he saw them as an extension of his day-to-day work in the 1930s, in a variety of areas aimed at helping the Jewish cause as persecution of the Jews mounted.'[22]

Since the major share of Parkes' writings and public activities would increasingly be undertaken in the service of the Jewish people, Parkes' enthusiasm for Jewish materials obviously had enormous practical utility. Nevertheless, to conclude that any of his several collections were not simultaneously ends in themselves certainly overshoots the mark. One need look no further than at those treasured brass candlesticks in the wall cupboards to appreciate that Parkes as a collector had never outgrown that lonely island boy smitten by an unappeasable craving for ecclesiastical photos and early Guernsey coinage. Until his retirement, Parkes would remain a compulsive collector, and even then he would be single-minded in arranging for the appropriate disposition of his prized assemblages.

If we bear in mind that in addition to their intrinsic value the accumulation of disparate items into 'collections' which may then be lovingly organized, fondled, and proudly displayed also functions as an emotional proxy for inner needs, then Parkes' boyhood *manqué* in a late Victorian enclave goes far towards explicating the psychological roots of his appetite for a great many very particular things. As one observer commented, '[late Victorians] expressed their need to grasp at stability in a world of radical transformation'.[23] This phrasing is redolent of Parkes' own words when he described the distant, forever-lost era of his Guernsey boyhood as 'a world of stable currency and falling prices'.[24]

In his unfinished study about the arcades of Paris, Walter Benjamin's probing analysis of the psychology of the collector is equally suggestive:

> ... perhaps the most deeply hidden motive of a person who collects can be described this way: he takes up the struggle against dispersion. Right from the start, the great collector is struck by the confusion, the scatter, in which the things of the world are found ... The collector ... brings together what belongs together ... by keeping in mind their affinities.[25]

Paralleling the activity of the scholar in perceiving hidden affinities amidst multiplicity and randomness, the compulsive collector struggles to appropriate and to fashion a smaller, parallel cosmos out of the appearance of chaos.

While one appreciates this determination and inner strength to 'take up the struggle', of even greater importance is a proper recognition of the depths of inner dissatisfaction and despair which set this process in motion in the first place. Underscoring this aspect John Baxter, himself an inveterate book collector, comments on the relationship between collectors and gender: 'Almost all collectors are male. A few women collect, but in an entirely different way from men.'[26] Another observer then points out that Baxter, unlike his collector wife,

> ... was never interested in a complete collection. He never concentrated on one particular subject and was always starting new [book] collections: by writer, time period, prizes won or any other category. The closer it is to completion, the less a collection interests a collector until, when he has everything, often he will sell it and turn to some other writer. The whole point of collection is the thrill of acquisition, which must be maximized and maintained at all costs.[27]

Therefore, Parkes' several collections should also be understood symbolically. Like the outsized manor house itself, for Parkes the thrill of the chase and the excitement of acquisition acted as surrogates for the pursuit of money, power or sexual pleasure. Only a rigid utilitarianism would insist that the rehabilitation of his terribly slummicky holding and endowing it with rare artefacts issued out of sheer vanity or self-indulgence. At the same time, when one takes into account the mortgage payments, current expenses, renovation costs and salaries for McNeilage, Dobkin, Eschelbacher and a charwoman, they certainly did entail a disproportionate expenditure for a man of modest means.

All this accentuates Parkes' dependence on the generosity of Israel M. Sieff. Here's how he deals with this most delicate matter.

> ... I.M.S. was reasonable about the inevitability of expenditure growing. But I never asked him for more than the minimum on which I could manage, for calls upon him were

far more than most non-Jewish millionaires would attempt
to meet, and I was always conscious of the unfairness of a
Jewish friend having to provide the necessary funds for
fighting against the non-Jewish, in fact Christian, sin of anti-
semitism ... Every development was discussed both with
William Temple and with I.M.S. – who were incidentally
well known to each other – and I could not have had a more
generous or understanding backer than the latter ... I always
stayed with him when I went to London, and conversations
late into the night before the woodfire in his delightful
library turned on most of the deep things of life as seen in
Judaism and Christianity.[28]

Notice how Parkes subsumes his financial dependence under
the mantle and glow of his intimacy with Sieff. His account makes
their friendship sound very much like one between equals, one
reflecting pleasure and mutuality, which in salient respects it
certainly was, but not in all. That this idyllic tableau by the fireside conceals a silent undercurrent will, in due course, become
painfully evident.[29] What Parkes did not anticipate was that
Hitler's war on the Jews would lead to a dramatic increase both
in levels of taxation and the needs of the Jewish people in Europe
and Palestine. Even a man as wealthy and munificent as Israel
Sieff could not continue to subsidize his dear friend at the level
to which he had become accustomed.[30]

Nevertheless, even when saddled with an increasing burden
of expense, Parkes never ceased to perceive his manor house as
essential, not alone for his scholarly activities but for his greater
wellbeing. Beyond serving as a workplace and a showplace for
his several minor collections, his establishment was gradually
transformed into a major repository of Jewish books and historical
pamphlets, the sorting and resorting of which, according to his
one-time secretary, was a task without end.[31] Along with writing,
creating these parallel, smaller, rational orders out of the chaos
of dispersion was one of Parkes' most gratifying pleasures. Both
intellectual and quasi-sensual, for Parkes the activity imitated
God's work of creation. By emending an imperfect corner of it,
Parkes performed God's work on earth. Symbolically, for Parkes
the act of collecting very closely approximated the Jewish *mitzvah*
of *tikkun olam*, the commandment enjoining mankind to work
unceasingly to heal the flaws in God's creation.

NOTES

1. James Parkes, *Voyage of Discoveries* (London: Victor Gollancz, 1969), p. 110.
2. Ibid., p. 129, ff.
3. *Vide* Chapter 26.
4. Parkes, *Voyage of Discoveries*, pp. 136–37.
5. Ibid., p. 137.
6. Edith Ruth Weisz, interviewed by the author and Maggie Davidson in Cambridge, England, 28–29 August 2000.
7. Ibid.
8. Parkes, *Voyage of Discoveries*, pp. 137–38.
9. Ibid., p. 153.
10. Edith Ruth Weisz, interviewed by the author and Maggie Davidson.
11. *Vide* Chapter 18.
12. Although Parkes' aesthetic of home furnishings was very nearly the antithesis of that espoused by Henry David Thoreau, his vital concern with his immediate environment and interior design, both for themselves and as symbols of divinity, is reminiscent of that shown by the great American apostle of simplicity and self-sufficiency. Both men proceeded with conscious deliberation to implement their theories in their real lives. Oddly enough, by different routes, furniture also led each of them to discourse upon the meaning of sacrament in the everyday affairs of mankind. *Vide* Henry David Thoreau, *Walden; or, Life in the Woods* (New York: Rinehart, 1959), pp. 53–56.
13. Parkes, *Voyage of Discoveries*, p. 137.
14. Parkes Archives, File MS 60/7/36/1.
15. *Vide* Chapter 6.
16. Alison Elias interviewed by the author and Maggie Davidson in Cambridge, England, 29 August 2000.
17. *Vide* 'James Parkes letter to Eleanor' in Chapter 15.
18. Parkes, *Voyage of Discoveries*, p. 136.
19. Ibid., p. 139.
20. Ibid., p. 138
21. Ibid., p. 139.
22. Tony Kushner, 'Independence and Integrity: The Vision of James Parkes and David Kessler to Transform Prejudice into Understanding', in *Noblesse Oblige: Essays in Honour of David Kessler*, ed. Alan D. Crown (London: Vallentine Mitchell, 1998), p. 98.
23. John D. Rosenberg, 'Victoria's Secrets', *New York Review of Books*, Vol. L, No. 6, 10 April 2003, p. 56.
24. *Vide* Chapter 1.
25. Walter Benjamin, cited by Charles Simac in his review of *Joseph Cornell: Master of Dreams*, *New York Review of Books*, 24 October 2002, p. 14.
26. John Baxter, *A Pound of Paper: Confessions of a Book Addict* (New York: Doubleday, 2003).
27. Michael Handelzalts, Tel Aviv, *Ha'Aretz*, Section B, 11 July 2003, p. 12.
28. Parkes, *Voyage of Discoveries*, pp. 140–41.
29. *Vide* Chapters 31 and 34.
30. Parkes, *Voyage of Discoveries*, p. 166.
31. Doris Wilkinson interviewed by the author and Maggie Davidson, in Barley, 2 September 2000.

23

The 'Jewish Scholar'

Cambridge was most accommodating to Parkes. When St John's College accepted him as a member of its Senior Common Room, it paved the way for the Oxford man to be awarded a Cambridge degree. 'Being modest, I asked them only to make me an M.A., holding that it was absurd to be a double Doctor of Philosophy.'[1] In time Parkes would change his tune about that, but the primary purpose of this degree was less decorative than instrumental: to ensure access to the university library and especially the right to bring books back to his Barley study. In addition to a bit of bragging about his modesty, it is noteworthy that Parkes did not find it absurd that two of his closest friends, William Temple and Charles Singer, had each been awarded three doctorates from Oxford, the only men, he informs us, ever so distinguished.[2]

While friendship with Temple went back, of course, to Parkes' first years at Oxford, Singer was part of the Jewish circle that Parkes had begun cultivating soon after the 1929 Bierville conference, the springboard of his serious involvement with Judaism.[3] On coming to England, Parkes' design was to penetrate two distinct, traditionally close-knit communities. The ambivalence felt by local villagers to overtures from Parkes will be explored in the following chapter, but with the Jews his success was far less equivocal. His already established intimacy with Israel Sieff testifies to the good will and trust Parkes was capable of inspiring in Jewish notables. Social ambiance according with intellectual and moral commitment, only a short while after his return this Church of England priest was hobnobbing with the elite of British Jewry.

The renewal of close ties with Singer, recently retired to the coast of Cornwall, commenced very soon after his return. Parkes acknowledged Singer as both an intellectual mentor and a moral guide, a giant of a man whom Parkes extols as 'one of the wisest as well as the most learned men I ever met'.[4] Son of an Orthodox rabbi and a Professor of the History of Science at the University of London, Singer '... found in Humanism a profoundly spiritual interpretation of life involving the necessity of absolute freedom in the pursuit of truth'.[5] Parkes would later appropriate humanism as a metaphysical category of his own.[6] What Parkes most admired about his friend, however, were his passion for social justice, his robust ethical activism and his solidarity with Jews under duress anywhere and everywhere.

On one occasion, when discussing the heavy financial burden on the Jewish community brought about by the arrival of so many refugees, Parkes records Singer murmuring, '... more to himself than to me, "Yes, I can rarely meet my communal obligations with less than a third of my income".' Parkes commented: 'I have never met a Christian who considered his "communal obligation" on that scale.'[7] Without identifying its source, which would have much embarrassed his friend, Parkes incorporated Singer's aside into the text of his forthcoming book.[8] If 'Holy John' Campbell most fully incarnated Parkes' conception of Christian faith, of all his contemporaries Singer best exemplified his ideal of moral perfection.

Parkes also resumed his close association with two of London's central Jewish personages, both of them first encountered in his Geneva days: Rabbi Israel Mattuck, and Herbert Loewe, a professor at Oxford and Cambridge. The latter figure Parkes canonizes as 'a veritable saint of Torah'.[9] As for Mattuck, he is eulogized as 'by far the best lecturer to a Christian audience on the traditional values of Judaism I ever encountered'.[10] Community leaders Neville Laski and A. G. Brotman, respectively president and secretary of Britain's Jewish Board of Deputies, worked closely with the Anglican scholar and urged him to undertake a book that would expose *The Protocols of the Elders of Zion* as a forgery.

At the same time Parkes began to spend a good deal of time among ordinary Jews under duress, working with anti-fascist activists in London's East End where Jewish stores were targeted and Jews were sometimes attacked by Sir Oswald Mosley's Black Shirts. In November of 1936 Parkes incorporated his reflections on these street experiences in 'Anti-Semitism in the East End', a fascinating piece of reportage which never saw publication. A few months later Mattuck passed along a morsel he'd heard from a congregant: a fascist had accused the Jews of the attempt on Parkes' life.[11] What dismayed Parkes most about this piece of lunacy was that it confirmed that even in London the Nazis were still monitoring his movements.[12]

Although the distance between Barley and London was not excessive, especially in foul weather it was an irksome and dangerous journey. To relieve Parkes' mind as well as to assist him materially, the Society of Christians and Jews, a small, mainly academic group that supported Jewish–Christian clubs in the East End, now provided him with a flat for use during the winter months. This also enabled Parkes to offer temporary hospitality in London to a number of refugees whose desperation sometimes moved him to tears.[13]

When it came to the question of refugees, Parkes did not spare the feelings of his apathetic or hard-hearted fellow Christians.[14] To the Bishop of Chichester, for example, he dispatched a highly irate letter complaining about the lack of response of Britain's Roman Catholics to appeals for aid. As tactically adroit as ever, Parkes emphasized the aspect of the crisis most likely to touch the conscience of the Bishop: grave concern over the fate of Europe's 'non-Aryan Christians'.

Among his newer Jewish friends, Parkes over time would draw closest to Louis Rabinowitz, or 'Rab', who later enjoyed a highly distinguished career as a rabbi and scholar. Ten years Parkes' junior, in the course of writing his dissertation Rabinowitz was a frequent visitor to Barley and often consulted with his unofficial mentor. He was particularly surprised to learn that Parkes was not the only 'Jewish scholar' in the village. In fact Barley's major personage was Dr Redcliffe Salaman, a stalwart of the 'Anglo-Jewish aristocracy'.

Actually, it was less than strictly fortuitous that Salaman and Parkes should reside in the same tiny Cambridgeshire seat. When it first appeared, *The Conflict of the Church and the Synagogue* had so impressed Salaman that he invited its author to visit him and discuss it. That was Parkes' maiden visit to Barley. Much taken by the quaintness of the village and its proximity to Cambridge, the author of *The Jew and His Neighbour* determined upon settling in the neighbourhood of such a learned and personable Jewish figure. Salaman had been a notable scientist, in fact the world's highest-ranking expert on the homely potato. In his retirement, he established himself in Barley's stateliest dwelling – its 'mansion on the hill'.[15]

The increasing dynamic driving Parkes' immersion in a Jewish

milieu is complex. Facets of it were keenly felt; others Parkes
barely sensed. We do well to recall again that the youthful outsider had as a boy yearned for acceptance as a bona fide native
of Guernsey. His linguistic deficiencies sabotaged this desire,
confirming that notwithstanding his touching sincerity, his
Guernsey pedigree was inauthentic. Inevitably, the allure of
Guernsey gradually paled, and by this period it no longer exercised the grip on his imagination associated with a homeland.
Consequently, one way of grasping Parkes' unusual emotional
attachment to the Jewish people is as displacement of his
unrequited childhood passion.

Already explored at length were Parkes' curiously weak
grounds for eschewing Hebrew, a decision which paralleled his
boyhood recoil from *Guernesiais*.[16] Similarly, his alienation from
Hebrew operated as a self-imposed brake on the very possibility
of sliding into the embrace of Judaism. However something
deeper than Parkes' Christian conviction was operative here. No
matter how powerfully Parkes responded to the Jewish ideal of
the realization of a just and a holy community, the inner rationale
underlying his personal mission for the Jews precluded the path
of circumcision. Only as a practising Christian could Parkes
possibly take upon himself the sins of historic Christianity or
seek atonement for specifically Christian sins. In other words, a
transference of confessional loyalties would have undermined
the fundamental logic of his life's work: to make amends for the
trespasses done to his Lord's people by his Lord's followers.

This stinger at the core of, to paraphrase his old SCM friends,
'Jimmie's Jewish bee in his bonnet' may be addressed from a
different angle. Parkes' attitude towards the House of Israel and
his 'slummicky small holding' at Barley were symmetrical. In
both spheres Parkes played out a symbolically charged personal
drama in which he assumed a soteriological role. Renovated
through heroic labour, both the dwelling and the grounds of the
'Old Hore's House' had been redeemed and born again into a
new life. Similarly, for the better part of a lifetime of devotion
and exertion, Parkes toiled to redeem a fallen Christianity from
the burden of its 'whorish' past and the incalculable crimes it
had committed against the Jewish people.

In this connection the key to Parkes' Christian sensibility was
his acute consciousness of the Jewishness of Jesus. Given his
heightened sensitivity to Jewish suffering, it was inevitable that

he would associate the figure on the cross with the terrible pain and suffering of the people from which he had sprung. Marc Chagall's series of paintings of the crucified Jew of Eastern Europe spring to mind as a parallel example except, of course, for Parkes the very faith which claimed his loyalty had itself instituted the Passion of the Jewish people and executed it most cruelly. Such was the paradoxical crux that precipitated Parkes' decision to assume that burden himself. Beyond making reparations, his goal was to move the parent and child faiths on to the path of genuine reconciliation.

In part to mitigate what he feared might sound like smarmy obsequiousness, Parkes recalls three occasions when, as he delicately puts it, Jewish friends and associates displayed 'some awkward qualities'. Conjointly, they might be captioned the perils of an unreconstructed conference leader among the Chosen People. Once, when Chatham House tried to organize a number of discussion groups dealing with the perilous situation facing Jews on the Continent – a project Parkes thought long overdue – he was approached to provide names of Jewish members likely to make a positive contribution to the programme. Yet more discreetly, thereafter he was asked to provide the names of Jews who 'from the noblest motives of passionate conviction, would wreck any group of people who did not think exactly like themselves'.[17] Parkes rashly complied. When some of the 'rejectees' got wind of their exclusion, as of course they would, the entire project was fatally compromised.

Another time, when Parkes himself attempted to organize private monthly luncheons between select groups of Jews and Gentiles 'to discuss any subject either side might wish to raise', although the latter were enthusiastic, the wariness of prospective Jewish participants undermined the idea. But the most frustrating occasion, this at the initiative of Israel Sieff, must have been when Parkes and two brothers named Martin worked long and hard to prepare broadsheets dealing with 'cultural, historical and contemporary aspects of Jewry'. These were specimen copies for what was supposed to be a new periodical intended for circulation among influential Gentiles. To Parkes' utter dismay, without warning or explanation Sieff, who of course was underwriting the project, simply pulled the plug.

Parkes' incidental writings during the late 1930s were relatively sparse. The nature of the organs in which they appeared is of greater interest than the content of the articles: in March 1936, for example, *The Jewish Academy* printed 'Post-War Antisemitism in Light of the Resignation of James G. MacDonald', whose departure from the public scene pleased Parkes more than the article admitted;[18] in *Social Credit Quarterly* for June 1936 appeared 'Church and Usury', a spin-off from research for *The Jew in the Medieval Community;* and finally Parkes composed a piece on what would be his touchstone for the next forty years – Jewish– Christian relations. Curiously, it was never published. As is evident, Parkes had virtually ceased to appear in mainstream Anglo-Christian journals.

Parkes was making his stand, on the hitherto untested ground of the 'Independent Christian, Jewish Scholar'. However the squire of Old Hore's House had neither independent means nor was he in any conventional way 'Jewish'. Moreover, despite his collar, for many co-religionists his heterodox views jeopardized his standing as a one hundred per cent 'kosher Christian'. As a result, his position was inherently unstable, and he would be '... an isolated figure in the British Christian world, and not least in his own Church of England, for most of his career.'[19] In fact, with the exception of Viscountess Stansgate, during the late 1930s no new Gentile friend surfaces in his memoir. Notwithstanding his efforts, and to Parkes' deep chagrin, significant Christian concern about the plight of the Jews would develop only when the situation had reached a terrible pass:

> It was not until the latter part of 1942, when evidence of the Nazi extermination programme received widespread exposure in Britain, that the Council of Jews and Christians, partly through Parkes' constant campaigning, came into existence to register protest at this unprecedented mass murder.[20]

Jesus, Paul and the Jews, Parkes' first book-length study to appear following his return to England, was published in 1936. Composed mostly during his final months in Geneva, it is a splendid, undervalued study to which Herbert Loewe contributed a fine Introduction. Parkes speculates that it was probably 'the first book by a Christian writer on Jesus and Paul which had a Foreword by an orthodox Jew'.[21] The book's overall theme is competently summarized in what to date remains the only book-length study of Parkes' theological thought:

Parkes took issue in this book with the Christian claim that the Jews had rejected Jesus, arguing instead that they have rejected Gospel accounts of the Life of Jesus and the exaggeration of Jewish failings and the distortion of their religion. He also faults Paul for giving a completely false picture of Judaism. He used the book to attack 'biblical theologians', whom he believed to be perpetuating the mistaken idea that the Church does not share the Old Testament but has exclusive right to it and its interpretation.[22]

Given the organizational and existential crises that the Apostle Paul had to overcome, Parkes' portrayal of the organizing genius of Christianity was not unsympathetic. At the same time, his indictment of Paul's basic strategy is clear-eyed and keen:

> Both Jesus and Paul lived within the Jewish way of life; both criticized the place which the ceremonial law and the interpretation of the Pharisees were coming to occupy in Judaism. The differences between them are explicable by the difference in their situation. Paul was living primarily in the Hellenic world; Jesus in the Judaic. It is wrong therefore to say that there is a fundamental contradiction between Jesus and Paul. But Paul must be held primarily responsible for the fact that instead of a gradual and peaceful development without schism, a violent break between the two faiths took place.[23]

It is early in this work that Parkes most explicitly staked out his dramatic claim to speak as his generation's primary bearer of Christian conscience:

> ... [that] the Gospels as a complete source or a study of the Pharisees are quite inadequate it is not possible to deny. That its picture of the 'Law' describes no known form of Judaism is equally certain ... If it is true that the picture of Judaism, which (with the Gospels and Epistles for basis) has been consistently given since the second century, is in reality unjust to the Jews, then the reparation which the Christian Church owes to Judaism is one so terrible that it is not possible to calculate it. For from this conception springs the whole growth of anti-Semitism, and the age-long tragedy of the Jewish people.[24]

Although certain details have been challenged and much new, subsequent data has been brought to bear, Parkes' first three books – *The Jew and His Neighbour, The Conflict of the Church and the Synagogue*, and, *Jesus, Paul and the Jews* – offer what is arguably the twentieth century's most comprehensive case for the culpability of the Christian Church in initiating, sanctioning and promoting the radical evil of antisemitism over the centuries.

In contrast to the vaporous, obscurantist tradition of German theological and philosophical discourse, Parkes' Anglo-Saxon, 'plain style' rhetoric is engagingly tactile, direct, and transparent. Indeed, he is so lucid that one would suppose that, short of insincerity or sheer perversity, a misconstruction of his meaning would be impossible. Not so. A typical example of misreading by a respected scholar is one Jewish historian's blinkered take on Parkes' *nostra culpa:* 'But Parkes raised the spectre of Christian guilt only to quickly dispel it, arguing already by page 13 that Jesus was in fact "the Messiah" and therefore "in the right" in his disputes with the Pharisees.'[25] One wonders whether to laugh or weep.

Aside from hosting intimate weekend gatherings of scholars at his home, from 1936 until the outbreak of the war Parkes qua scholar was preoccupied with researching and composing *The Jew in the Medieval Community: A Study of His Political and Economic Situation.* This work was projected as an extension into the Middle Ages of the historical account that Parkes had traced for the preceding centuries in *The Conflict of the Church and the Synagogue.* Parkes' new monograph focused on the status of European Jewry as chartered property of ruling princes in a number of countries and on the ramifications of the economic role the Church foisted upon the Jews as society's licenced usurers.[26]

For Parkes himself, the most illuminating aspect of his new work lay in the differing approaches of the two religions to lending money. In contrast to the '... absurd and disastrous perambulations of Christian scholasticism ... [usury] was thoroughly discussed by medieval rabbis, and was an occupation which, if no other was available, could be followed by an honourable man ... It gave me some initial insight into the fact that I was not going to find Judaism "just the same as Christianity but without Christ".'[27] Two by-products of his new findings were published during 1937 in, as was now usual,

Jewish-oriented journals: 'Rome, Pagan, Christian' in *Judaism and Christianity,* and 'The Jewish Money-Lender and the Character of English Jewry in Their Historical Setting' in the *Journal of the Jewish Historical Society of England.*

Parkes was both fascinated and appalled to discover that the most pernicious calumniators against the Jews, those who invented and spread the most gruesome blood libel accusations that led directly to the deaths of tens of thousands were Jewish converts to Christianity.[28] In the conclusion to *The Jew in the Medieval Community,* however, he did not flinch from excoriating the Church itself, which over the centuries had systematically stripped Jews of the rights they once had enjoyed as Roman citizens, for the lion's share of the blame for antisemitism:

> The Jew became what circumstances made him: his main, almost his only responsibility in the creation of those circumstances was his desire to remain loyal to his Judaism. It was Christendom which decided that the price of that loyalty should be psychological and social degradation.[29]

Upon the completion of this splendid study, Parkes immediately embarked upon a companion work. It aimed at exploring aspects of the deleterious impact of the Church and of the general populace upon Jews that he had been unable to integrate into the earlier study.[30] Around the same time Parkes' first book, *The Jew and His Neighbour,* came out in a new edition. All things considered, James Parkes had now established himself as the leading English-language authority on the history and current status of Jewish-Christian relations. He was, as it were, on an intellectual roll: zealous to redeem Christian history and atone for Jewish suffering, an inner dynamic was propelling him from project to project, from strength to strength.

It was at this juncture, in retrospect the apogee of his scholarly career, that Parkes was approached by his former mentor Gilbert Murray, then editor of the popular Home Library series, with a proposal to produce a very short book for popular consumption. The topic was perennial but achingly contemporary – 'The Jewish Question'. Yielding to Murray's blandishments, Parkes laid aside the task he had set for himself earlier, and in less than a year he turned out a slim volume.

Parkes' aim was to continue his historical project with three further volumes on the Church and the People in the Middle Ages, the post-medieval developments (including the Reformation, Christian Hebraism, the Protestant missions, Deism), and the immediate background to antisemitism as it emerged in the nineteenth century. This project was sadly interrupted by the war, and not resumed subsequently.[31] Not only did Parkes never manage to recover the inner momentum required to carry on with his original plan,[32] but the Home Library diversion became something of a pattern for the future: his creativity now tended to flow into lesser streams and eddies.

The Jewish Problem in the Modern World, the book produced at Murray's behest, presents a schematized, highly readable but not especially original account of the causes and nature of 'the problem'. Parkes divided his analysis into pre-war and post-war segments. Part One offers an abridged account of historic Christian intolerance, its confrontation and neutralization in Western Europe by the liberal tide of the Emancipation, and then the shock and recoil of the Dreyfus Affair. As though common sense could be brought to bear successfully on so irrational a business as antisemitism, Part Two pleads for a humane and rational response: 'Whatever the feeling about individual Jews, it is difficult to see how anyone can sincerely see in a people so harassed, and so impotent to avert whatever fate may have in store for them, the secret would-be rulers, the universal menace to Gentile society.'[33]

One winces to see reference in 1939 to 'whatever fate may have in store' for the Jewish people. Although Parkes had always declined to plunder the Barthian depths of the human heart, he had nevertheless stared long and hard at the rough, howling beast that resided there and which soon would ravage and devour its incredulous prey. For years he had described, analyzed and incessantly warned about this denizen of the dark forest of European imagination, but of course even he could not envisage the enormity of what fate held in store for European Jewry.

In his summing up of a poisonous decade, Parkes once again reminded his readers that '... in any civilization which is founded on moral precepts, antisemitism is a measure not of Jewish failing, but of Gentile failure'.[34] Indeed, looking back with grief at the calamity that engulfed the Jewish people, one marvels that even at that late stage Parkes could labour under the illusion that such a reminder would make a difference in a world gone numb. In tandem with the 'Jewish problem', we might also acknowledge the 'Parkes syndrome': a refusal to grant that that long night of barbarism could not be checked by right reason, good will, faith in God or brilliant scholarship. With the world paralyzed by the resurgence of atavistic gods, all that Parkes most believed in now proved impotent and as irrelevant as memories of summer conferences or candlelight soirées in *la cité* of Geneva. The 'abominable heresy of Barthianism',[35] with its obsessive focus on Adam's Fall, helped to ensure that man's sinful obduracy would be a self-fulfilling phenomenon. In its obtuse way, however, one wonders whether it did it not more adequately mirror the growing abyss than the unreconstructed liberalism that informed the thought and writings of the world's most distinguished independent Jewish Christian scholar.

It is noteworthy that *The Jewish Problem* reiterates the positive approach to Zionism that Parkes had earlier staked out in *The Jew and His Neighbour*. Well before the onset of the Shoah, Parkes had grasped the essentials of the two-pronged argument for the necessity and legitimacy of the establishment of the Jewish State in the only place in the world where it could possibly take root: 'Although Palestine ceased to be home of the bulk of the Jewish people nearly two thousand years ago, it has never lost its appeal to their emotions, and the land itself has never lacked some Jewish population.' Significantly qualifying his warm enthusiasm for the rebirth of a Jewish State, however, Parkes also presciently cautioned that 'in the final analysis the success of the National Home must be based on harmonious Jewish–Arab relations, whatever the price at which they are achieved'.[36]

NOTES

1. James Parkes, *Voyage of Discoveries* (London: Victor Gollancz, 1969), pp. 138–39.
2. Ibid., pp. 145–46.
3. *Vide* Chapter 16.
4. Ibid., p. 145.
5. James Parkes interviewed by Laurence Dobie in the *Guardian*, 28 March 1970.
6. *Vide* Chapters 25 and 30.
7. Parkes, *Voyage of Discoveries*, p. 146. Parkes and probably Singer as well were unaware that Jewish law, striving for balance, prohibits giving more than twenty per cent of one's income to charity. *Vide Small Acts of Kindness: Striving for Derech Eretz in Everyday Life*, by Shalom Freedman (Jerusalem: Urim, 2004), p. 139.
8. James Parkes, *The Jewish Problem in the Modern World* (London: Thornton and Butterworth, Home Library, 1939), p. 246.
9. Parkes, *Voyage of Discoveries*, p. 123.
10. Ibid., p. 145.

11. Israel Mattuck letter to James Parkes, 27 April 1937, Parkes Archives, File 60/31/28.
12. Ibid.
13. Minutes, Society of Christians and Jews, 20 January 1939, Parkes Archives, File 60/15/76.
14. James Parkes letters 14 June and 19 July 1938, Parkes Archives, File 60/16/51.
15. Parkes, *Voyage of Discoveries*, p. 136.
16. *Vide* Chapter 16.
17. Parkes, *Voyage of Discoveries*, pp. 147, ff.
18. *Vide* Chapter 19.
19. Tony Kushner, 'Independence and Integrity: The Vision of James Parkes and David Kessler to Transform Prejudice into Understanding', in *Noblesse Oblige: Essays in Honour of David Kessler*, ed. Alan D. Crown (London: Vallentine Mitchell, 1998), p. 98.
20. Ibid.
21. Parkes, *Voyage of Discoveries*, p. 126.
22. Robert Everett, *Christianity With Anti-Semitism: James Parkes and the Jewish–Christian Encounter* (Oxford: Pergamon, 1993), p. 26.
23. James Parkes, *Jesus, Paul and the Jews* (London: Student Christian Movement Press, 1936), p. 107.
24. Ibid., p. 12.
25. Robert Wolfe, *Christianity in Perspective* (New York: Memory Books, 1987), p. 8.
26. James Parkes, *The Jew in the Medieval Community: A Study of His Political and Economic Situation* (London: Soncino, 1938).
27. Parkes, *Voyage of Discoveries*, p. 141.
28. Ibid., pp. 139–40.
29. Parkes, *The Jew in the Medieval Community*, p. 387.
30. Ibid., p. 386.
31. Nicolas de Lange, 'James Parkes, A Centenary Lecture,', *Cultures of Ambivalence and Contempt: Studies in Jewish–Non-Jewish Relations,* Ed Jones, Kushner and Pearce (London: Vallentine Mitchell, 1998), p. 33.
32. Parkes, *Voyage of Discoveries*, p. 141.
33. Parkes, *The Jewish Problem in the Modern World*, p. 141.
34. Ibid., p. 248.
35. Parkes, *Voyage of Discoveries*, p. 222.
36. Parkes, *The Jewish Problem in the Modern World*, pp. 204, 233.

24

Citizen Parkes versus the 'Man of Feeling'

Whenever he set aside his shovel, his pen, his ill-concealed apprehensions, and his Jewish commitments, Parkes took special delight in fulfilling his obligations as an active participant in the daily life of Barley. He had not envisaged the village exclusively as a scholarly retreat; on the contrary, just as though he were a resident of a rural hamlet in the vicinity of ancient Thebes or Athens, Parkes conceived of it as his polis, a focus that for the first time would afford the historian a proper stage on which to perform a full range of civic roles. And indeed, he would treat these responsibilities very seriously, exercising at the micro-level the same organizing skills he had developed at Oxford and had honed as a professional activist on the Continent.

Predictably, the handsome bachelor-vicar cut a wide swath on the village scene. At times the number of public duties assumed by Parkes extended so widely that they threatened to overflow their banks and swamp his other commitments. Nevertheless, he was immensely gratified to be brought into meaningful contact with almost every inhabitant of Barley. As detailed earlier, as a youngster he yearned to be accepted by others as a bona fide child of Guernsey as much as if he had been born a Carey or an Ozanne. Now, on returning from years abroad to the English roots of his mother especially, he was ready to stake not only his felicity but in great measure his identity on Barley becoming his home, with all that the word entailed. To earn the village's approbation, he was prepared to work very hard and very diligently.

After only a few months on the scene, Citizen Parkes assumed management of the Church-run primary school. He functioned as its official correspondent, a task that in reality no one else wanted to take on. Soon thereafter, under the chairmanship of Redcliffe Salaman, Parkes served as a member of the parish council and two years later was elevated to the post of vice-chairman. After the Chamberlain–Hitler fiasco in Munich in 1938, Parkes also took on special responsibility for the organization of Barley's air defences as well as for the negotiation of 'treaties' with surrounding villages to cover every sort of contingency. In order to place children evacuated from London with suitable families, out of his hat Parkes fashioned 'The Cats' Club', an association of local women who throughout the war years would perform invaluably.[1]

Since his conspicuous arrival in the summer of 1935, any observer taking the measure of Parkes' range of activities and leadership would conclude that Barley had gained greatly from his selfless presence. By any standard Parkes was an ideal local citizen. Ironically, this itself inspired ripples of potential conflict. Noting an earlier understated complaint that 'not all of my Jewish friends were of the level of Singer and Montefiore',[2] one wonders, how well the clerical interloper from Guernsey really got along with his Jewish neighbour, the chairman of the local council. On this point one Barley resident observed that Salaman, jealous of his reigning position as Barley's leading light, occasionally displayed signs of resentment over the newcomer's panache and instant prestige. 'Probably both wanted to be the Squire of the Village,' she opined.[3]

On closer inspection, apart from minor differences that inevitably arise between fellow committee members, nothing suggests the presence of serious tension between the two neighbours who, as it happened, were very close politically – 'both Parkes and Dr Salaman, the "brains of the village" were left-wing'.[4] Parkes' autobiography alludes to four separate occasions on which the two men worked together. Three of them deal with village matters, one with a Jewish-related issue; not a hint of discord is recorded.[5] Moreover, in the mind of the villagers, the two were viewed as a close team and even, in the outlandish 'Barley Rectory Affair', as co-conspirators in larceny.[6]

Certainly Salaman, more than twenty years Parkes' senior, enjoyed his role as the most exalted local personage, and Parkes too craved his own fair share of adulation. However, he also genuinely respected Salaman's abilities, and he took care to show him appropriate deference as the unofficial but popularly anointed 'Village Squire'. In any event, to garner prestige Parkes could always lean upon his many outside activities and associations.

Principally as an expert in Jewish–Christian relations, he was in demand to lecture before Christian and Jewish audiences the length and breadth of Britain. Soon after returning from Geneva, Parkes became an active member of the Jewish Historical Society, and in 1949 he would be invited to serve a two-year term as its president, only the second Gentile ever so honoured.[7]

The Church was yet another arena in which Salaman and Parkes did not compete. From his first months in Barley Parkes maintained high visibility in his role as a vicar, becoming a licensed preacher for the Diocese of St Albans and filling in whenever the need arose either locally or in a neighbouring parish.[8] During the war, when Barley lacked a permanent rector, Parkes assumed major responsibilities for maintaining regular services while at the same time preaching at many of the area's Congregational churches.[9] Moreover, he frequently acted as chaplain at the annual conference of the Auxiliary Movement, a social action offshoot of the SCM, as well as working with Zoë Fairfield to establish a devotional Christian centre aimed at promoting social change in areas on the outskirts of London.[10]

By the late 1930s Parkes had also become a peripheral but provocative presence in academia where he never shrank from the opportunity *embêter* either *la bourgeoisie* or their donnish cousins. In 1939, for example, he was invited by Oxford University to deliver its annual McBride sermon, one endowed 'with an especial view to confute the arguments of Jewish commentators and to promote the conversion to Christianity of the ancient people of God'.[11] Parkes outrageously exploited his chance to turn the purpose of the sermon on its head: in 'Christianity and the Conversion of the Jews' he argued against traditional efforts of missionary societies to convert Jews. Scandalizing many, it is uncertain whether Parkes' uncompromising revisionism gained even one convert that day. Three decades later, however, he still took take justifiable pride in his subversive sermon which concluded on this admonitory note:

> The men of the historic church were no less Christian, no less filled with missionary zeal than those who would set out today along the paths they trod to retrieve the consequences of their errors ... They failed, and did incredible harm because what they did was not the will of God. They believed themselves possessed of the whole truth, setting

out to convert those who lacked it. In both beliefs they were
in error ... We have failed to convert the Jews, and we shall
always fail, because it is not the will of God that they shall
become Gentile Christians; antisemitism has failed to destroy
the Jews, because it is not the will of God that essential parts
of His revelation should perish. Our immediate duty to the
Jew is to do all in our power to make the world safe for him
to be a Jew.[12]

These lines shimmer with personal resonance. Parkes had
remained in frequent contact with Alexander Teich, his companion from Vienna, who shed tears of anguish and betrayal
when Christian associates unexpectedly displayed a ravenous
appetite to save Jewish souls.[13] After the Anschluss in March 1938,
Teich's personal situation became far more hazardous. Parkes
immediately initiated procedures to sponsor his friend's passage
to Britain, but before learning how Teich had fared, he himself
had to set sail for North America. His top priorities were to
discourse on the evils of antisemitism and to lobby Canadian
authorities to admit a far greater number of refugee professionals
from Germany. Upon arrival, he wired Kenneth Dodkin for
word of Teich as well as of the family of Hermann Eschelbocher.
His secretary's terse reply imparts a feel for the anxieties of the
period: 'Alexander worried but family alright. Hermann's father
arrested. No knowledge of whereabouts. Miss Wood-Leigh
asks should Cambridge Refugee Committee try to get family to
England.'[14]

Later that year Teich arrived in England; Parkes welcomed
him eagerly into his Barley home. Shortly thereafter Parkes
'invited' Teich's wife and six-year-old daughter as well. Meanwhile Eschelbocher's parents also reached England and stayed
for a while with Redcliffe Salaman. In August 1939, a few weeks
before Hitler and Stalin gorged on Eastern Europe, Teich's wife
and daughter also reached England.[15] The Eschelbochers and the
Teichs were among the nearly 50,000 German and Austrian
refugees who arrived in Britain between 1933 and 1945, of whom
around ninety per cent were Jews.

At the same time that it was extending this life-saving
hospitality, Britain, ever sensitive to Arab pressure, was sharply
restricting Jewish emigration to Palestine. Until the outbreak of
the war, although the attitude of the British government towards

Jewish refugees has been characterized as 'cautiously welcoming', in fact it genuinely welcomed only those Jews 'who had achieved distinction whether in pure science, applied science such as medicine or technical industry, music or art'. Despite guarantees from the British Jewish community to absorb the costs of accommodation and maintenance in full, immigration restrictions were never relaxed; in fact it was decided that 'certain further restrictions should be added in order to strengthen controls'.[16]

Additionally, over this period Parkes became deeply involved in saving Jews from a less publicized but, in his eyes, an equally insidious menace. Foreseeing the imminent Nazi occupation, hundreds of Czech Jewish parents tearfully bid their children farewell at the railway station in Prague as part of the *kinder-transport* programme. They were entrusting their children to volunteer British families, perfect strangers. Although many host families were scrupulous in respecting the Jewish heritage of their charges, other less sensitive sponsors routinely took Jewish children in their care to weekly church services. Far worse was the ambush that awaited children unfortunate enough to be delivered into the hands of Christians intent upon saving their immortal souls. No one in England could feel this affront more personally than James Parkes. For many months he devoted countless hours to tracing Czech Jewish youngsters and prising them out of the clutches of these unconscionable zealots.[17] In tandem with these tireless efforts, Parkes became active in the creation of the National Council for the Rescue of Victims of Nazi Terror.[18]

Obviously, no one could belabour Parkes with the accusation that he was among 'those [British] who rescue Jews almost always … not out of love for them but out of hatred for their persecutors'.[19] On the other hand, Parkes' judgment as to the motivations of others was not infallible. In 1940, for example, he was asked to work with Malcolm Macdonald, the Colonial Secretary, on the formulation of British policy in Palestine. With uncommon obtuseness, Parkes refused to acknowledge that, as an outspoken Zionist, his appointment was sheer window-dressing. In fact, he was singularly ineffective in influencing the views of his former Oxford classmate who in short order proceeded to issue two notoriously one-sided white papers that, taken together, effectively repudiated the promise of British support for the establishment of a Jewish homeland in Palestine.

Compounding his ineffectuality, Parkes publicly defended Macdonald from charges of one-sidedness and anti-Zionism, thereby lending credence to Macdonald's hollow claim that the white papers were intended '... to be only the formal opening of a policy seeking direct agreement with Arab rulers and leaders in Palestine on a development which would be fair to both Arabs and Jews'.[20] That is certainly not how they appeared to most seasoned Jewish observers.

> Originally he [Macdonald] had, he said, been opposed to the idea of an Arab veto on immigration but the intransigent attitude of some members of the Jewish delegation had made him realize that so long as the Jews had the British government behind them, they would never meet the Arabs halfway.[21]

Macdonald now proposed that a maximum of 75,000 Jewish immigrants be admitted over a period of five years, a scandalously inadequate figure. This was peremptorily rejected not only by the Jewish but also by the Arab delegation which 'insisted upon total cessation of Jewish immigration'.[22]

This is a singular instance of Parkes' clubbability and incipient snobbery eclipsing his good sense. Soon afterwards, however, his defence of Macdonald would be repaid. At the behest of Lady Reading, Parkes interceded with the Secretary over the fate of German-Jewish youngsters trapped in Norway after the Nazis overran that country. Macdonald's handling of an earlier appeal had led Reading to conclude that he was 'nothing better than a murderer'.[23] Within forty-eight hours of Parkes' intervention, however, Macdonald informed him of the safe transport of the youngsters to Sweden. Nevertheless, why Parkes should have concluded that Macdonald's positive response to the plea of an old classmate exonerated him of charges of antisemitism or anti-Zionism is difficult to fathom.

Fortunately for Parkes, among Britain's 'better' classes eccentricity has long been considered a sanctioned quasi-virtue. If Parkes struck his fellow Barleyites as idiosyncratic, as indeed in his day so had Salaman Redcliffe, such was his entitlement. At the same time one wonders how the ordinary villagers actually did perceive the eccentric, scholarly, charming, philosemitic, globetrotting, public-spirited parson in their midst. Abridged and minimally emended for readability, a few unmediated voices provide direct testimony. A certain degree of seeming irrelevancy has been retained because it underscores the village perspective. The first speaker is the daughter of Alexander Teich who, arriving on the local scene as a child, adopted a thoroughly Barley perspective.

'We told the authorities', she recalls, 'that we were going for a holiday and took one suitcase each. James and Dad met us at Dover.'[24] Parkes piled the reunited family into his small car and drove to Barley where a few weeks later the little girl celebrated her seventh birthday. The Teichs lived with Parkes for three months at which point they relocated to a nearby cottage. Sixty-one years later, here is how the little girl who grew to adulthood in Barley remembers 'Uncle James'. Any resemblance between Parkes and the actor Peter O'Toole is probably intentional.

> He was very posh, both socially and academically. He spoke a beautiful English in an exquisite, upper-class voice, and he had the habits and manners of an English gentleman. He was a bachelor with a full life and lots of friends. He was one of the very few people in the village with a car – an MG. It was always open-roofed, and he was always bronzed. He was extremely eccentric. No formal dress. He dressed like a hippy: sandals, open shirts (often torn!), with short sleeves and shorts. Occasionally he preached in the local church in his Church of England cassock. He always looked dishevelled but was always clean. He had brilliantly blond, tousled hair; very big, clear blue eyes; a straight, beautiful nose and a flashing smile. What a wonderful mane of hair he had! He was always aware of his splendid appearance, enjoying knowing he was handsome. He would tilt his head just a little to the side. An actor could not have pulled it off better. Yes, he knew exactly what impression he was making.
>
> He was very dashing. There was nothing effeminate about his appearance. Ladies fell for him violently. The vicar's sister, for example, threw herself at him. But he kept aloof from all of them. He was a passionate and creative gardener. In his yard he installed a pond which he stocked with goldfish and frogs. In order to remind my father of his native Austria, he let wild strawberries grow along with plums,

greengages, and many other varieties of fruits and vegetables. Everything that Parkes grew, he shared.

He could easily have been an artist. He had a very romantic disposition and had travelled all over Europe. He particularly loved walking in the mountains. Every day he did a sketch which, like his watercolours and pencil drawings, were delicate. He also made petit-point cushions. As for music though, he would sometimes boast 'I haven't got an ear'. Probably he had only been exposed to church music. With Parkes in residence, the village attracted a steady stream of cultivated, interesting people and numerous writers. I especially remember the arrival of Alberto Moravia.

James was a great gourmet and enjoyed fine wine. He often cooked for himself, but he also had a lovely man-servant, John McNeilage, a Scotsman who'd been in the Army in India and whose idea of festive 'haute cuisine' was curry! Parkes was really a stickler about his food. He expected it to be hot, good, and on time. He would discuss what he wanted to eat with McNeilage days in advance. He was also snobbish about wine; it was all part of his persona as an upper-class English gentleman bachelor.[25]

We recall that Parkes' apartment in Geneva had also borne witness both to his refinement and to his pretentiousness. That there was little of the ascetic in his make-up is corroborated by Zvi Werblowsky, an Israeli friend of over thirty years. 'James introduced me to some of the finest wines. I remember once at the Atheneum Club a certain Alsatian. It was splendid.'[26] Another friend recalls an 'expression would light up James's handsome face when he poured the wine at dinner. His beaming in so artless a way was made possible by a standing order he had worked out with a London merchant who agreed to keep his clientele supplied with very good French wines at no higher than "seven and six" per bottle.'[27] Although Parkes was charming and generous, Weisz also notes:

> Sometimes he could be very self-important and peremptory; he did not suffer fools gladly. I remember him getting angry about misinterpretations of the Old Testament, e.g. the real

meaning of 'an eye for an eye ...' or attributing 'Love thy neighbour like thyself' to Jesus when in fact it was really Jewish. No, he definitely was not a gentle, benign person, and some parts of him seemed distant and cold. He never spoke about his parents or siblings. He would freeze at the very mention of his mother's death.[28]

Werblowsky also remarks upon Parkes' fathomless reserve in matters pertaining to his upbringing: 'Unlike many of my friends, James never spoke about his family. To this day I have no idea what his father did.'[29]

Reacting somewhat excessively to Parkes' reticence, Weisz concludes her sketch with contradictory assessments of his emotional make-up. Taken together, however, they do point towards the paradox of the man.

> He seemed not to have any 'personal' feelings. He felt most at home with the poor maiden sister of a vicar called the Reverend Gardiner. Gardiner had been caught abusing children and Parkes, trying to avert scandal, had smoothed things over and assumed his duties. Gardiner's sister, who was very ugly, adored Parkes. He loved animals very much and had a dog called Shanda. He was always happy to explain the name's derivation to those worthy of the effort: 'He was *Ratza Shanda*, or from 'a race of disgrace'.
>
> Parkes gave me books to read – the first was a story book by Kipling – but he never kissed or hugged me, which would have been more normal. He was always 'the chaste knight' in shining armour, giving away his wild strawberries, sharing everything. Years later, after I was married, I came to visit James with my three-year-old daughter Rachel. On leaving Rachel threw her arms around his neck and clung to him. Parkes was very moved.[30]

In her eagerness to be forthcoming and 'objective', Weisz sometimes marginalizes the truly essential: the warm humanity, the open-handed generosity and the remarkable kindness of the man who plucked the Teichs from the jaws of the Shoah and invited them into his home. Far more telling than a desire to cover up unpleasantness was the ready compassion Parkes extended to the lugubrious vicar. Though not without occasional lapses, throughout his life Parkes conscientiously sought the means and generally found them to neutralize his psychological tics and behavioural eccentricities so that he might rise above them through acts of kindness and humanity.

Werblowsky also underscores Parkes' broad streak of sentimentality:

> He could get very emotional. When talking about Christian persecution of Jews over the centuries, he would not uncommonly burst into tears. When the two of us met, we would warmly embrace. It was very 'unEnglish', and the older he got, the more likely he was to break abruptly into tears. I often wondered whether his weepiness somehow had something to do with his being a Channel Islander.[31]

Similar perplexity is reported by others: 'I remember watching Parkes give a talk at Bar-Ilan University in the fall of 1967, not long after Israel's massive triumph in the Six-Day War. Tears flooded his eyes. He could hardly get his words out without sobbing: "Israel is what the whole world's been awaiting," he sobbed.'[32] Or again, recalling a lecture on 'Jewish History and the Holocaust' delivered to a crowded audience in Bournemouth, one observer '… was greatly moved by the sincerity of his words which frequently brought *him* to tears …' (original emphasis).[33]

Although Weisz's remark about Parkes' desiccated affective life was intended only narrowly, the larger impression it conveys is surely wrong-headed. We notice how warmly Parkes embraced Werblowsky, and Weisz herself observes how much he was moved by her daughter's impulsive show of affection. Plainly, she overstates Parkes' superficial dearth of 'personal feelings'. In fact not only did Parkes weep with remarkable frequency but we also recall his vulnerability to the crying of others. It was Alexander Teich's total loss of composure which first illuminated for Parkes 'what Jews felt about the Christian missionary approach'.[34] Parkes' appropriation of Teich's inner agony as though it were his own is extraordinary. Over the course of time, the depth and intensity of this Anglican priest's empathy with Jewish suffering led him not merely to respond forcefully to the plight of Jews but, with an astonishing lack of self-consciousness, to speak, feel and react as if he himself were a Jew.

Werblowsky's speculation about a link between Parkes' origins and his weepiness, on first hearing rather strained, bears closer examination. Possibly Guernsey's long-time remoteness from the mores and traditions of the English 'mainland' combined with its living vestiges of the island's medieval heritage, meant that the affective texture of the lives of its natives at the turn of the century actually did differ markedly from that of the English. Aspects of the litigious social context and the emotional climate of Chaucer's fourteenth century England are highly suggestive both in relation to the Guernsey of Parkes' boyhood and to the man himself.

> Property and inheritance were abiding concerns – obsessions really – in the late Middle Ages, especially among the merchant class to which the Chaucers belonged; and armed seizure, kidnapping, and trumped up lawsuits were not uncommon ways to gain possession of them. Englishmen of Chaucer's day were not like stereotypical stiff-upper-lip English of modern times, who are the children of the Enlightenment and the Empire; they were more like their Norman forebears, hot-tempered and given to extremes when among equals (they cultivated reserve before inferiors or superiors). They wept freely in public, flew into rages, swore copious and imaginative oaths, carried on almost operatic blood feuds and endless legal battles.[35]

Moreover, although for many it marked the Guernseyman as downright peculiar, Parkes' 'unEnglish' emotional outbursts remind us of a time when pathos was widely recognized by English artists, poets, aristocrats and other taste-setters as a sign of heightened sensibility and intensity of feeling, a natural 'correlative' for sincerity and 'authenticity'. Eighteenth century readers were accustomed to a heavy diet of sentiment, often verging on sentimentality, as delivered forth by Richardson, Goethe and a battalion of lesser pre-Romantics. Although bathetic excess was brilliantly satirized by the novelist Laurence Sterne, ultimately even he embraced it. Yorick, the eccentric narrator of Sterne's *A Sentimental Journey*, shares an uncommon number of evocative points with the dashing, petit-pointing Parkes. Both 'characters' are pastors, both are ingenuous beguilers of the fair sex, both fall under the dreamy spell of the Knight of la Mancha, and both are often and publicly overcome by their emotions. The following tear-stained passage is typical.

> I felt a damp upon my spirits, as I am going to add, that in my last return through Calais, upon inquiring after Father Lorenzo, I heard he had been dead near three months, and was buried, not in his convent, but, according to his desire, in a little cemetery belonging to it, about two leagues off. I had a strong desire to see where they had laid him – when upon pulling out his little horn box, as I sat by his grave, and plucking up a nettle or two at the head of it, which had no business to grow there, they all struck together so forcibly upon my affections, that I burst into a flood of tears. But I am as weak as a woman; and I beg the world not to smile, but pity me.[36]

Like Yorick, rather than merely posturing, Parkes was frequently hostage to unchecked emotions and in thrall to feelings of shared humanity. In many ways Parkes was an avatar of a 'Man of Feeling', a throwback to a plangent, throbbing strain in English sensibility that reached its apogee in the eighteenth century but which, both publicly and privately, still subsists behind the English traditional reserve. The whole point of the proverbial British stiff upper lip is to provide a bulwark against succumbing to this deep-seated strain of sentimentality. Clement Attlee, for example, declared that during the 1930s he met Churchill at the House of Commons, and the latter recalled what was being inflicted on the Jews, all the time 'with tears pouring down his cheeks'.[37] This weakness, if weakness it be, emerges most conspicuously in the affection many Britons famously displays toward their pets.[38]

As with Churchill, all the more so with Parkes: whenever tapped or trapped, his inner feelings positively overflowed their banks. Even Parkes' insouciance with his clothing,[39] while surely an affectation of superiority, conforms to the late eighteenth century 'type' depicted in many portraits of dreamy-eyed young men in a state of dishabille so emotionally absorbed in the landscape or spiritual meditation that they simply could not bothered with their appearance. Earlier we identified one source of this surfeit of feeling in the unresolved trauma Parkes underwent in his boyhood. His mother's early death registered not only as a loss and bereavement but also as a kind of abandonment. For the rest of his life Parkes felt himself vulnerable to a loss of composure; in fact so susceptible was he that he took special care to avoid topics of conversation that might trigger a loss of self-control. As repeatedly seen, he was often less than successful.

As well as performing some housekeeping chores, Doris Wilkinson, to this day a resident of Barley, also worked in Parkes' home as his secretary during the late 1930s and early 1940s. Reinforcing most points made by Weisz, qualifying several, here follows her detailed recollection of his household:

> This was Parkes' daily round: he got up about 8 a.m. Breakfast was prepared by Dorothy [his wife]. John [McNeilage] would arrive early and get the coal fire going in his study. John would take the mail to him in his study on a silver salver. Pausing at 10.30 for his coffee with newspaper, he worked at his desk until lunchtime. Afterward, he would rest in his study for one hour, not to be disturbed. I went to the house mornings, working mostly with Dorothy. I helped to unpack and to sort his books. His office was upstairs in the house. The books were mostly downstairs in 'the men's club', a building next to the house. He was a charming man, always very hospitable, but at first his state of dress caused a furore. He usually wore sandals and shorts. It was a strange costume for us Barley kids to see. Parkes was very good-looking, and he knew it. Barley, don't forget, was a village of farmers along with a large number of retired people; we'd never seen anyone with a manservant before. The villagers were in awe of him. He took an active part in the village Church of England school. Sometimes Parkes would come to the school on Monday morning to give a little lesson or lead prayers with the children. There was lots of poverty in the village. When Sam [her future husband] won a scholarship to go away to school, Parkes presented him with a book.
>
> He seemed very idiosyncratic to us: every day John had to press *The Times* before taking it in to him. Nobody was allowed to read it before him. He liked to get his own way. He was precisely punctual, and he liked his cars. He had little Corgi dogs and used to go with Dorothy for long walks in the fields, both of them using tall walking sticks with

clefts. He was also very funny about the washing up. Everything had to be done in a certain sequence. One time I
washed a spoon and put it down to drain 'the wrong way.'
He was very perturbed. The spoon had to be laid flat.
Also, he was very sensitive to criticism. Once there was a
gentleman who came to help him catalogue his library. His
personality clashed with that of his new assistant who
accused Parkes of living in an ivory tower. After just two
weeks the man was sent packing.'[40]

Her husband added his own impressions:

He could talk well at any level. He was a member of the
Athenaeum Club in London, but he talked especially well
to kids. He never looked as though he was bored talking to
them. The man just oozed charm. He did a lot of work for
the local school. At one time Parkes drove an Austin 7; at
another point he had an MG. Later, when Dorothy was
working there, Lizzie Green sometimes drove the two of
them around in a hired car from Dreighton's Garage.[41]

Finally, a postscript from a villager who functioned as an activist
in the ISS during the early 1940s succinctly complements much
of the above: 'In Barley in those days only Salaman, the local
doctor, and Parkes had cars. Parkes was strong-minded and
always very full of talk. He scattered his thoughts very widely.'[42]
These accounts converge at several suggestive points: Parkes'
consciousness of his extraordinary good looks, the studious non-
chalance of his attire, his insistence on driving (or being driven
in) flashy automobiles, and not merely the queerness of his
ways but his proud attachment to them. Friendly, generous and
bookish but also guarded and peculiar, as a model citizen Parkes
made a major splash, as a man of feeling, minor splashes.

Still, as both a valued member of local society and a local
eccentric, as both hospitable and aloof, as both a clerical insider
and a perennial outsider, Parkes thirty-year struggle for full
acceptance by the villagers can only be considered a qualified
success. Poignantly, his efforts were never crowned with
the reward and the privileges he craved most: to be 'one of us'.
Despite his invaluable service to the community and notwithstanding his special gift for communicating with children, he did
not seem to inspire much genuine affection in the breasts of his

fellow villagers, not even in the little girl who knew him as 'Uncle James'. In her unpublished *Autobiography*, Dorothy Wickings justly concluded that although her husband's assistance was often sought – such as when he set up a clinic in his scullery to combat an outbreak of impetigo whose source was evacuees from London, or in the education of evacuee children – he ever remained 'an enigma to the villagers'.[43]

NOTES

1. James Parkes, *Voyage of Discoveries*, p. 153.
2. Ibid., p. 148.
3. Edith Ruth Weisz, interviewed by the author and Maggie Davidson in Cambridge, England, 28–29 August 2000.
4. Doris Wilkinson interviewed by the author and Maggie Davidson in Barley, 2 September 2000.
5. Parkes, *Voyage of Discoveries*, pp. 153, 167–69, 171.
6. *Vide* Chapter 27.
7. Parkes, *Voyage of Discoveries*, p. 210.
8. Ibid., pp. 153–54.
9. Ibid., p. 171.
10. Ibid., pp. 148–49.
11. Rose G. Lewis, 'James Parkes: Christianity Without Anti-Semitism', *Midstream*, January 1981.
12. Parkes Archives, File 60/17/10/1.
13. *Vide* Chapter 17.
14. Ibid., p. 151, ff.
15. Dorothy Wickings Parkes, *Autobiography*, an undated seventy-page account which from internal evidence was composed in the Parkeses' retirement at Iwerne Minster after 1964. Parkes Archives, File 60/33/3.
16. Bernard Wasserstein, 'The British Government and German Immigration 1933–1945', *The Nazi Holocaust: Bystanders to the Holocaust*, Vol. 8, ed. Michael R. Marrus (London: Meckler, 1989), pp. 396–99.
17. Parkes, *Voyage of Discoveries*, pp. 149–50.
18. Tony Kushner, 'Independence and Integrity: The Vision of James Parkes and David Kessler to Transform Prejudice into Understanding', in *Noblesse Oblige: Essays in Honour of David Kessler*, ed. Alan D. Crown (London: Vallentine Mitchell, 1998), p. 99.
19. Noel Ascherson, 'The Remains of Der Tag', *New York Review of Books*, 29 March 2001, p. 44.
20. Parkes, *Voyage of Discoveries*, p. 152.
21. Walter Laqueur, *A History of Zionism* (New York: Holt, Rinehart, and Winston, 1972), p. 526.
22. Ibid., p. 527.
23. Parkes, *Voyage of Discoveries*, p. 152, ff.
24. Ruth Edith Weisz in a letter to the author dated 18 September 2000.
25. Ruth Edith Weisz interviewed by the author and Maggie Davidson.
26. Zvi Werblowsky, Professor Emeritus of Comparative Religion at Hebrew University, interviewed by the author and Maggie Davidson in Jerusalem, 16 November 2003.
27. A. Roy Eckhardt, 'In Memoriam: James Parkes', *Journal of Ecumenical Studies*, 9:1 (Winter 1982).
28. Ruth Edith Weisz interviewed by the author and Maggie Davidson.

29. Zvi Werblowsky interviewed by the author and Maggie Davidson.
30. Ruth Edith Weisz interviewed by the author and Maggie Davidson. That little girl grew up to become a talented, very well-known stage and film actress.
31. Zvi Werblowsky interviewed by the author and Maggie Davidson.
32. Harold Fisch, Emeritus Professor of English, Bar-Ilan University, Ramat Gan. Telephone conversation with the author, October 2001.
33. Jonah Indech, 'James William Parkes', *Tributes in Memory of James William Parkes*, at Bournemouth, 1981, p. 11, University of Southampton, Parkes Archives.
34. *Vide* Chapter 17.
35. Donald R. Howard, *Chaucer, His Life, His World, His Work* (New York: Dutton, 1987), p. 5.
36. Laurence Sterne, *A Sentimental Journey Through France and Italy* (Reading, PA: Spencer Press, 1937), pp. 23–24.
37. Michael J. Cohen, 'Churchill and the Jews: The Holocaust', *The Nazi Holocaust: Bystanders to the Holocaust*, Vol 8, ed. Michael Marrus (London: Meckler, 1989), pp. 333, 339–48. Unlike Parkes, the tears Churchill shed for the sufferings of the Jews did not cause him to act on their behalf when he had the opportunity. As Cohen spells out all too clearly, during the war Churchill (like Roosevelt) keep entirely aloof from specifically Jewish concerns as though the Shoah were not being relentlessly prosecuted on his watch.
38. The name of Parkes' pet dog was Shanda. Derived from the Yiddish for *shame*, Parkes almost certainly picked it up from Teich; the name probably sprang from the young dog's deplorable toilet habits. Also possible is that by naming his pet Shanda Parkes intended to evoke the sweetness so winningly and unwittingly embodied by Toby in Sterne's *Tristram Shandy*. If so, we are reminded again that the conventional portrait of the Englishman as stiff-lipped and buttoned down is belied by atavistic, historically powerful currents of emotion, which Parkes himself displayed on many occasions.
39. *Vide* Chapter 22.
40. Doris Wilkinson interviewed by the author and Maggie Davidson.
41. Sam Wilkinson interviewed by the author and Maggie Davidson in Barley on 2 September 2000.
42. Alison Elias interviewed by the author and Maggie Davidson in Cambridge, England, 29 August 2000.
43. Dorothy Wickings Parkes, *Autobiography*. Henceforth, in order to avoid the appearance of condescension of 'Dorothy' or the potential confusion of 'Parkes', generally she will be referred to as 'Wickings'.

25

What's in a Name?

Marking the debut of Parkes' genial alter ego, radical theologian John Hadham, Penguin published *Good God* as a 'Special on Religion' in the spring of 1940. Parkes traces Hadham's origins to nearly two decades earlier when he was secretary of the SCM.[1] This is a bit misleading: internal evidence points to the 1928 WSCF summer conference at Gex as the time when inner disquiet bubbled over into a Hadhamite direction, and that was six months after Parkes had resigned from the SCM. Catalyzed by a visceral repugnance to the Barthian juggernaut that had overwhelmed the convocation at Gex, Parkes felt impelled to pen 'Politics and the Doctrine of the Trinity',[2] a seminal statement that served as a kind of prologue for a closely-linked pair of essays – 'God and My Furniture' and 'Revelation and a Duster'. Both composed in the spring of 1929, these two pieces spawned concepts that would be germinal to books by 'John Hadham'.[3]

Throughout the 1930s Parkes focused almost exclusively on research and writing about Jewish–Christian relations and on implementing programmes aimed at alleviating the sufferings of refugees. Thus for a decade, further work on the nature and activity of the Godhead was deferred; nevertheless, all the while Parkes' thoughts were quietly gestating. They would reach full term in the spring of 1939, and the midwife was none other than Israel Sieff.

> We had been discussing religion and one of us – I forget which – had spoken of the difficulty of the ordinary man seeing a real God in the now archaic language and thought of both our religions. I then told him that I had long wanted to write a book for a general audience called *Sketches of the Character of God* in which I did not theologise or seek to prove that God existed, but simply described his activities as I would those of the prime minister.[4]

One is struck by how Parkes' directness and aversion for abstruse terminology in his discourse about God and God's ways parallels the matter-of-fact, non-polemical approach that characterized his earlier pair of essays in domestic theology and even his account of the Bungalow Ghost.[5] Eschewing ontological speculation, Parkes' rhetorical strategy falls naturally into the plain-speaking, British empirical tradition.

Before approaching Sieff, Parkes had already shown *Sketches* to two clerical colleagues whose opinions he valued highly; each unconditionally advised him to recast it fundamentally arguing that a theological work stripped of metaphysical speculation would be considered simplistic and puerile. In striking contrast, Sieff was positively ebullient: "'But James,'" he said, "'you must write it. Go and do it.'"[6] This was all that Parkes needed to hear. The irony that the Jewish benefactor should act as the catalyst for the emergence of the Reverend John Hadham, Christian theologian, was lost on neither man.

In truth, it is scarcely surprising that Parkes' root idea resonated so powerfully with Sieff. Unlike normative Christian theology, Jewish speculation traditionally does not probe long or hard into the existence or nature of God: generally the former is simply assumed whereas the latter is considered beyond man's ken. Moreover, by God's 'activities' Parkes principally intended whatever one might reasonably infer that God expected of His creatures in their everyday relations with their Creator and in their dealings with each other. It was natural that Sieff would warm to such a Buberian leitmotif, as little could be closer to the spirit of Judaism. Thereupon, with Sieff's encouragement – later he would also provide Parkes with a typist and even exert pressure on a hesitant publisher – in the summer of 1939 Parkes set out to compose *Sketches*, rechristened as *Good God*.

The book's two operative assumptions are that God has a plan for the world and, since He is intelligent, reasonable and responsible, He remains vitally interested in how well man is fulfilling his part in the grand design. There is nothing especially new in these formulations. Shunning both French speculativeness and German murkiness, exuding temperance and common sense, Parkes reifies a highly accessible theological construct of a God who comports Himself much like a fair-minded, well-educated English gentleman:

So far as I know, there is nothing God dislikes more than that kind of humbug which cloaks itself in false reverence. I am convinced that so far from adopting an attitude that we are not to criticize or examine His activities, He welcomes the frankest attempts to understand who He is and what He is doing. In fact it is perfectly obvious that if He were so easily offended and of so sensitive a dignity as many religious persons assert, He would have closed down this particular planet a long time ago.[7]

As in the earlier 'domestic essays',[8] Parkes marshalled evidence of God's active presence not from miracles but rather from His benign involvement in common, everyday events of life. Parkes had not spent a decade toiling in the vineyards of Judaism for nothing: that God may be addressed so informally and directly, that He is susceptible to passionately reasoned argumentation and that He seeks man's active collaboration in the fulfilment of His plan for the universe are quintessential Jewish concepts. No wonder that when *Good God* appeared in 1940 Sieff would find it 'one of the most exciting experiences that I have had'. He sensed instinctively that 'it seems to answer a lot of questions which people are now seeking [sic].'[9] Naturally, in the absence of authorial signposts, the specifically Jewish provenance of Hadham's thought entirely escaped the notice of the over-whelming majority of its enthusiastic readers.

In the main, however, the reviewers were nonplussed. One traced its central ideas to the influence of William Temple: 'It is not surprising that Temple would like Hadham's works since they reflect a good deal of Temple's theological ideas ... Many of the themes discussed at these lectures – the Trinity, the Kingdom of God, progress and revelation, God and the ordinary, Christo-centric theology – are discussed once more in greater detail.'[10] The archbishop himself made no claim upon the book, but his praise could not have been more unqualified: Hadham's book was 'the most important contribution to theology for the past fifty years'.[11] Parkes himself, of course, was fully aware that he had fused Christian theological concepts and 'Jewish' sensibility, and he is on record as having felt he had written 'a pioneering book'.[12]

This first Penguin 'Special on Religion' became a publishing phenomenon. Appearing in June, after an erratic start interest grew and sales soared: over three hundred copies a week were sold in July; the following month, as the Blitz over London accelerated, so did the sales of *Good God*. The Army added it to the list of titles that it distributed to POWs in Germany.[13] By the time the wartime paper shortage short-circuited book production, *Good God* had sold over 100,000 copies. Moreover, following upon its success, *God in a World at War*, a companion volume appearing that autumn, sold close to 75,000 copies. The Reverend John Hadham was launched as a clerical celebrity.[14]

But who was 'John Hadham' and why had Parkes resorted to a pseudonym in the first place? His explanation to Penguin was that since 'James Parkes' was already enmeshed in the touchy area of antisemitism, 'he didn't want to get his controversies mixed. One of his Jewish friends persuaded him to start his career as John Hadham'.[15] Since the second statement is both ambiguous in itself and strictly speaking a *non sequitur*, this 'explanation' leaves much to be desired. The matter is muddled by a different or perhaps complementary response twenty-five years later when Parkes provides a detailed account of Hadham's origins that playfully mocks his ingrained streak of pretentiousness:

> ... I wanted one [a name] that was not an existing name of someone else. So I went through the names of all the neighbouring villages in the London Telephone Directory until I found one that was euphonious but not in that collection of surnames which surely covered every family name in the country. So I came to be *Hadham* ...[16]

This is supported by an entry in his wife's *Autobiography*: 'the name "John Hadham" was chosen almost at random from the telephone directory for Much Hadham in spring of 1940'.[17] Unfortunately, since Dorothy Wickings did not meet her future husband until the following year, her 'recollection' has no independent basis. Years later Parkes would tell a friend that 'the surname was inspired by love of the Hadham villages of Hertfordshire'.[18]

All in all, Parkes various explanations raise as many questions as they purport to answer. Let us back up a little to Parkes' so sensible-sounding proclamation that, like an Orthodox Jew who assiduously avoids wearing articles of clothing woven from two different natural materials or eating meat with dairy products at the same sitting, 'he didn't want to get his controversies mixed'. In other words, consonant with his penchant for orderliness, Parkes is endorsing the wisdom of keeping methodology and the differing modes of thought appropriate to the historian and theologian as discrete as possible:

> By definition, theologians cannot be historians, certainly not trustworthy ones. History must be written without fear or favour, without prejudice or misconceptions. Any *idée fixe*, any religious axiom that may interfere with logical analysis must be rejected out of hand'.[19]

On the other hand, if the main point is to prevent mis-apprehension, it does not take a prophet to foresee that even as a temporary stay against 'confusion' a pseudonym harbours the seed of future complication.

Recall in addition Parkes' initial assertion that 'one of his Jewish friends persuaded him to start his career as John Hadham'. That friend, of course, would have been Israel Sieff, but except to assuage concerns voiced by Parkes himself, why would Sieff have urged his friend to adopt a *nom de plume*? Furthermore, it is already apparent that Sieff did not propose the specific name that Parkes' ultimately decided on. We may safely conclude, there-fore, that in this matter recourse to Sieff is something of a red herring.

For a more satisfactory explanation of why the man who had never before hidden from the spotlight now opted for conceal-ment, we turn again turn to the manifold associations between a boy named Jimmy, a scholar named James, Old Testament Jacob and New Testament James.[20] To these we now conjoin Israel Sieff. During their many evenings of free flowing conversation at the fireside, it is conceivable that the idea occurred to either that they were at least nominally avatars of the biblical Jacob (that is, James) and his alter ego Israel. This most fortuitous convergence of the Jew and Christian – two sides of the same 'Adam' and together embodying complementary roles in God's plan – goes right to the core of Parkes' primal theological insight. Having noted the 'coincidence' of names, it is likely that Parkes attached some significance to it. Although, for reasons that will later be explored at length, Parkes, masks Sieff as 'I.M.S.', deliberately obscuring the connection, this only has the perverse effect of drawing attention to it.[21]

Biblical exegetes have long commented upon how the God-mandated name change from Jacob to Israel marks the Jewish patriarch's passage from the cheeky, spoiled younger son of Rebecca to his role as progenitor of the Jewish people, that is, the Children of Israel.[22] What is germane here is that Jacob's readiness for his appointed mission is first signalled and later confirmed by the embrace of his new name. At the age of forty-three, without any clear-cut rejection of his former activism or scholarship – because this certainly was not the case – Parkes now shifted his attention to a frontal consideration of what God expected of him. Closely matching the newly launched Jacob, Parkes in turn responded in parallel fashion: with a new name.

Had Parkes chosen to adopt 'Israel Hadham' as a pseudonym, it would have been symbolically appropriate. After all, in his fashion Parkes had already chosen 'Israel' a decade earlier when he accepted his prophetic mission not 'to' but 'for' the Jewish people. However, not only did the personhood of Israel Sieff make such a moniker inexpedient, but even for Parkes it would been a shade *outré*. Instead, for reasons Parkes himself seems never fully to have appreciated, he chose to be retrofitted as John Hadham, explaining:

> The Christian name *John* was for family reasons. It is a forbidden name for a Parkes for the last John Parkes sold the land on which we had lived for generations near Dudley because, so the family legend goes, he disliked his relations … I had no ambition to be a coal-owning millionaire, so I became a *John*.[23]

Like Jacob/Israel, 'John Hadham' enjambs two radically contrary tendencies. Parkes' 'Hadham yarn', over the years one of his favourites anecdotes, explains both too little and almost everything. More than anything else in Parkes' immediate orbit, what Hadham adumbrates is *Chatham*, the left-leaning, progressive London centre for social and intellectual engagement which he regularly frequented. Both the place and the experience certainly registered as a positive in his psyche. 'John', on the other hand, was a name 'forbidden for a Parkes … so as soon as I ceased to be a Parkes, I became a John'.[24] So in the constellation of the Parkeses, John was an outlaw, a manipulative coal-baron, the serpent who choreographed his own family's eviction from their ancestral garden: in short, the incarnation of exploitation and betrayal.

Moreover, among early Christians the rantings of two notoriously Jew-despising Johns – the Apostle and Chrystosom – were for Parkes a canker on the body of Christianity, the font of the worst sort of poisonous, calumnious, antisemitic rhetoric. For more than a decade Parkes had been labouring to extirpate this sinful excrescence from Christian discourse. Notwithstanding the countervailing sanctity emanating from the nimbus of 'Holy John' Campbell and, as we shall see in the following chapter, an ambiguous glow emanating from yet another John, on balance 'John' bore assertively disruptive, seditious, repugnant associations.

As expanded upon earlier[25] for nascent Christianity the antithesis of John was James, the Judaizing head of the Jerusalem Church. Conflating the two, fanatically antisemitic biblical Johns with his own avaricious, coal-baron relation – whose spirit he kept at bay but never fully expelled from his psyche – Parkes unconsciously aimed to neutralize their power by yoking them to 'Hadham/Chatham', that is, a force for progressive modernism. In Parkes' first major thrust into the popular arena, this intrinsic, creative tension would prove a major source of John Hadham's appeal.

Parkes was only too aware that one of his major weaknesses was a craving for adulation. He knew himself to be a showboat and highly susceptible to flattery. Redux 'Little Hadham':

> ... So I came to be *Hadham*, which had also the advantage that supposing a bishop bore down on me in full sail in the Athenaeum to which I had just been elected, and said: 'I suppose you think you are Much Hadham,' I could reply, 'No, my Lord, I'm Little Hadham.'[26]

The manifest point is that the reborn man disdains greatness and espouses modesty. We note ruefully, however, that in the very telling Parkes cannot resist drawing gratuitous attention to the prestigious club to which he had recently been elected. The assumption of a pseudonym may temper a character flaw, but ingrained immodesty is not so easily routed.

Parkes took a lively interest in Hadham's sales and royalties. What with the runaway success of his first two Hadhams for Penguin and Sieff smoothing the way with practical arrangements, one might have thought that, if only temporarily, Parkes' chronic financial duress would have receded. This did not transpire. A typical invoice from Penguin, dated 10 April 1941, runs as follows: between 20 March and end of 1940, 62,873 copies of *Good God* were sold at £1 per copy, accruing to its author all of £62.17. Minus a £50 advance, this yielded a grand total of £12.17. Using the same formula, over the same period 45,153 copies of *God In A World At War* added a paltry £4.17 to Parkes' coffers.[27] In sum, over this period the total royalties of the bestselling John Hadham amounted to less than £175.[28] These were not the best of times for a freelancer to fill his larder and set his table.

In a letter to Penguin's Miss Frost, Parkes enquired how well sales of *Good God* compared to those of *Things That Go Bang in the Night,* a rival exercise in popular theology concocted by the Bishop of Woolwich.[29] Subverting the pieties of a Woolwich with his pared-down, theological statement for Everyman, Hadham harboured more grandiose ambitions. He aimed,

> ... to break free from a parochial interpretation of God and His revelation without falling into syncretism. It is a Christian theology which argues for God's ability to act outside of Christian experience, a theology which considers the human–Divine encounter in personal and corporate life more essential to God's plan for His creation than the dogmas and interpretations that arise from such encounters. Finally, it is one which takes the human side of the encounter as seriously as the divine. In it all, one can discover a new Christian view of Judaism, and appreciate other religious traditions as well.[30]

A less pedestrian, more illuminating approach, one that comments not on the book's manifest content but on its psychological sources, issued from Parkes himself:

> Comments on *Good God* come from his own three-fold character:
> a. James Parkes, student of Judaism and Jews,
> b. the Rev. JW Parkes, ordinary Anglican parson,

c. John Hadham: All the teachings of Jesus were Pharisaic and he was attacking the corruption from within, not condemning it root and branch from without.[31]

We may confidently correlate the above three-fold manner of self-understanding with Parkes' earlier thinking on the nature of the three persons of the Godhead, or, as he came to prefer, the three 'modes of activity' of the Holy Trinity. The first two manifestly parallel the traditional personhood of the Christian Trinity, immanent in the activities of James Parkes the (Jewish) Father and the Reverend J. W. Parkes the (Christian) Son. As for the Reverend John Hadham – Anglican divine extraordinary – he would personify the Holy Spirit acting from the body of the Church and criticizing 'the Movement from within, *not* condemning it root and branch from without.'[32]

This theme of self-reflective activity leading to renewal, one largely overlooked by Everett, is struck much more insistently in *Between God and Man*, sequel to the first two Hadham books. Writing about his aims for his third public appearance in the guise of Hadham, Parkes disclosed that he wanted 'to try if possible to make people see how responsible the Protestant movement which led to Barth is also leading to Hitler. For Hitler is Barth's "word made flesh" and could not be anything else. When a Church goes mystogogic and "other", a civilization will do the same.'[33] Properly understood, it is apparent that masked as John Hadham, Parkes had embarked upon a mission that he conceived of as 'prophetic'.

The broad appeal of the first two 'Penguin' Specials also led Parkes to compose a series of Hadhamite articles for the *St Martin's Review* – six in 1941, six more in 1942, and the final two in 1943. These pieces stressed the theological importance of everyday life and ordinary events:

> The real essence of the Church lies not in a supposed inerrancy of doctrine, not in Divine authority, but in the membership of ordinary people, living ordinary lives in the palace, in the village, in the slum. For it is in the haunts of ordinary men that God needs men and women who combine ordinary vocations and ordinary interests with the extra something that arises from faith which responds to the calls of service and the demands of sacrifice ...[34]

As Hadham, Parkes reached an even wider audience through a series of eight radio broadcasts for the BBC Home Service. His introductory talk struck a universal chord.

> The need of men today is for a God in whom they can find wisdom, not one whose dominant characteristic is power ... What would make an appeal would be the statement that the Cross involves an out-and-out acceptance of responsibility by God for all the suffering and anguish, the failure and despair in the world which God made without our consent, and into which He placed us without our having the power to determine the conditions. This would have more meaning than the proclamation of the selective redemption of those who believe in Him.[35]

This same reassuring theme was struck repeatedly in the Hadham books: 'God's whole title to our unbounded admiration and affection rests on the fact that He has accepted responsibility and under terms which He set in man's presence'. Or again: 'God will not be satisfied until His world reaches its perfect development.'[36]

On several occasions during these broadcasts, Parkes' reluctance to 'accept responsibility', or rather his propensity for raising hackles, broke through his benign persona. Very early in the war, for example, when Hadham was intoning a prayer for countries which had been deprived of their freedom, he impoliticly included Estonia, Latvia and Lithuania among his list of slave states that yearned to breathe the air of freedom. This triggered a *cause célèbre* that briefly threatened to fray relations between Great Britain and its Soviet wartime ally.

Hadham's tactics in a second tiff with the BBC bureaucracy were reminiscent of the guerilla campaigns Parkes had launched against headmaster Penney and the Sittingbourne Colonelcy.[37] Taking his cue from J. B. Priestly, who on one of his highly popular BBC broadcasts had spoken of the need for a post-war 'radical reconstruction' of society, Hadham impishly,

> ... took the six parables of the Kingdom of Heaven and used the word 'Reconstruction' instead. Reprimanded for mixing 'politics and religion', Hadham was informed that on 'the British Broadcasting Corporation you cannot mention Jesus and reconstruction in the same sentence.'

'May I mention them in succeeding sentences?'
'I have no instructions on that head' … and the interview terminated. Those who knew of this conversation
enjoyed Saturday morning. I managed never to get 'Jesus'
and 'Reconstruction' on the same side of a single full stop.[38]

In 1941, a new publisher encouraged Parkes to turn out yet
another title as Hadham. Inasmuch as Parkes was always eager
to combat retrograde traditionalists of the stripe of the Bishop of
Woolwich and since the prospect of royalties was ever welcome,
Hadham undertook to write *Between God and Man*. Appearing a
year later in the very darkest moments of the war, this new text
argued for 'the gradual development of religion, the creativity
of its forms in each age, and then the tremendous need for a
reformulation in the idiom of our own day'.[39] Far more polemical,
indeed more feisty and 'Jacobite' than the first two Hadhams,
Between God and Man did not succeed in conveying the message
of forbearance and reassurance that a war-weary people (and its
publisher) had been anticipating.

Undaunted, that May Parkes donned his collar to disseminate
the book's central theme in the annual university sermon at
Cambridge. Alas, his reception that day was equally muted.[40]
Even more disheartening was the tepid reaction he received at
what should have been a friendly forum: a conference on Church
reform convened by William Temple at Malvern. With remarkable suddenness, first Hadham and then Parkes had gone out of
vogue. Although the editors of *The Christian Frontier Movement*
still printed his writings on Judaism, Parkes' hammering on about
Church reform was now unwelcome.

Then came yet another setback. Initiating the BBC's religious
broadcast series for 1943, a puckish Reverend John Hadham,
sounding increasingly like the Reverend James Parkes, could not
resist tweaking the noses of his entrenched clerical opposition:

I began by saying 'I do not believe that those who have
ceased to worship in the churches or the chapels of this
country will ever return to take part in normal services
offered today,' continuing, 'they will not be brought back
by the kind of tinkering with the services that is all that
progressive elements in the churches have attempted so
far.' The Church of England turned its screws; Hadham

was told he would not be invited again to speak over the airwaves.[41]

Parkes' third Hadham 'Special' for Penguin was scheduled to appear the following year. Sensing correctly that *God and Social Progress,* Penguin's preferred title, would lend the book a sectarian cast, Parkes insisted upon changing it to *God and Human Progress.*[42] In retrospect, the original title might actually have hyped the book's disappointing sales. This, the final Hadham of the current series, presented an '... historical sketch of human development, of the first Christian civilization whose death pangs in the agony of war we were then witnessing, and of the challenge of a new attempt in the reconstruction after the war'. It closed with an announcement that could not have been better calculated to irritate many of the very readers who earlier had warmed to *Good God:* 'In many fields [Christians] would have to sit at the feet of those they denounced as humanists.'[43]

This provocation could issue only from someone 'unafraid to expose the Bible to the scrutiny of human reason. He [Parkes] often cited Temple saying "Revelation is an event; its interpretation is our responsibility".'[44] Although he elicited little public approval, Parkes *qua* Hadham eloquently and consistently enunciated the Christian humanist position:

> Modern liberal and religious scholarship ... and the whole of human knowledge and experience has become capable of being illuminated by the same light – the light of the objective search for truth ... For just as the intellect of men works from a hypothesis in the intellectual field with which the intellect can deal, so the emotional side of man, the spirit in man, is entitled to work from a hypothesis in the spiritual field. In each field men have to discover by experience whether the hypothesis is tenable or not. Only in one case the experience can be demonstrated intellectually and in the other, though conclusive to the individual concerned, it is incapable of 'scientific' demonstration or contradiction. It can be communicated in its own field, that of emotional, personal experience.[45]

Parkes was surely thinking here of what he considered irrefutable examples of 'emotional truths' recalcitrant to scientific demonstration from his personal experience: for example, the Norwegian landscapes that, emanating from the mind of Miss Kleppe, had taken such confident possession of his draughts-man's hand.[46]

An interesting sidelight: in a letter to Penguin's Miss Frost, Parkes voiced a complaint. 'The main mistake in the proofs is that the printer has insisted throughout in giving "he", "him", etc. a capital when applied to God according to the conventional manner. These were not in the mss. and I would like them out. But, on the other hand, if that means extra delays in these days I am willing to sacrifice the principle.'[47]

Even though it only concerned the issue of whether or not to capitalize 'he' and 'him', that Parkes was willing 'to sacrifice the principle' was a new departure. After four years in the spotlight, John Hadham was dropping out of sight. Might, however, Parkes' softness on capitalization portend the future return of a less truculent Hadhamite persona?

NOTES

1. James Parkes, *Voyage of Discoveries* (London: Victor Gollancz, 1969), p. 156.
2. *Vide* Chapter 15.
3. *Vide* Chapter 17.
4. Parkes, *Voyage of Discoveries*, p. 156.
5. *Vide* Chapter 8.
6. Parkes, *Voyage of Discoveries*, p.156.
7. John Hadham, *Good God* (Harmondsworth: Penguin Books, 1940), p. 6.
8. *Vide supra.*
9. Israel Sieff letter to James Parkes, 25 October 1939, Parkes Archives, File 60/6/1/2.
10. Robert A. Everett, *Christianity Without Anti-Semitism: James Parkes and the Jewish–Christian Encounter* (Oxford: Pergamon, 1993), p. 36.
11. Parkes, *Voyage of Discoveries*, p. 159.
12. Dorothy Wickings Parkes, *Autobiography*, Parkes Archives, File 60/33/3.
13. Christine Knowles, Head of British POW Book and Game Fund, letter to James Parkes, 5 September 1940, Parkes Archives, File 60/6/1/2.
14. Parkes, *Voyage of Discoveries*, pp. 158–59.
15. James Parkes letter to Penguin Books, Parkes Archives, File 60/6/1/2.
16. Parkes, *Voyage of Discoveries*, p. 158.
17. Dorothy Wickings Parkes, *Autobiography*.
18. A. Roy Eckhardt, 'In Memorium: James Parkes', *Journal of Ecumenical Studies*, 19:1 (Winter 1982).
19. Moshe Aberbach, 'A Puzzle Penetrated', *Midstream*, Vol. XXXXII, No. 2 (February–March 1996), p. 34.
20. *Vide* Chapters 2, 7 and 10.
21. *Vide* Chapter 34.
22. The transition is not, of course, absolutely clean. Depending upon emotional response to changing circumstances, patriarchal Israel over the course of the later narrative at times reverts to tricksy Jacob.
23. Parkes, *Voyage of Discoveries*, p. 158.

24. Ibid.
25. *Vide* Chapter 18.
26. *Vide supra*.
27. Penguin Books invoice, Parkes Archives, File 60/1/2.
28. Parkes, *Voyage of Discoveries*, p. 159.
29. Parkes Archives, 4 April 1941, File 60/6/1/2.
30. Everett, *Christianity Without Anti-Semitism*, pp. 104–105.
31. James Parkes letter to Eunice Frost, 16 July 1940, Parkes Archives, File 60/6/1/2.
32. James Parkes, *God at Work In Science, Politics, and Human Life* (London: Putnam, 1952), p. 64.
33. James Parkes letter to Walter Kotschnig, 2 January 1942, Parkes Archives, File 60/16/4–19.
34. John Hadham, 'The God We Believe In', *St Martin's Review*, April–September 1941, pp. 602–607, cited by Everett, *Christianity Without Anti-Semitism*, p. 301.
35. John Hadham, 'The Parson in the Pew', BBC series 'Worship and Life', in *The Listener*, 1942, cited by Everett, *Christianity Without Anti-Semitism*, p. 301.
36. Hadham, *Good God*, pp. 56, 74.
37. *Vide* Chapters 7 and 11.
38. Parkes, *Voyage of Discoveries*, pp. 160–61.
39. John Hadham, *Between God and Man* (London: Longmans Green, 1942), cited in Parkes, *Voyage of Discoveries*, p. 163.
40. Parkes, *Voyage of Discoveries*, p. 163.
41. Ibid., pp. 164–65.
42. James Parkes Letter to Eunice Frost, 13 August 1943, Parkes Archives, File 60/6/1/2.
43. John Hadham, cited in Parkes, *Voyage of Discoveries* p. 165.
44. Everett, *Christianity Without Anti-Semitism*, p. 151.
45. John Hadham, *God and Human Progress* (Harmondsworth: Penguin Books, 1944), pp. 59, 80.
46. *Vide* Chapter 12.
47. James Parkes letter to Eunice Frost, 14 October 1943, Parkes Archives File 60/6/1/2/.

26

Stopgap

Back from the lake, at Montreux, stretches the wide deep gorge or ravine, on one side of which, on a little plateau, this hotel is planted. Into the gorge, above, below, you can plunge to your heart's content. Along its bottom rolls the famous course of a little mountain river, hurrying down to the lake.[1]

In August of 1942 James Parkes took Dorothy Wickings as his bride. All of Barley was initially struck dumb by the suddenness of their pell-mell courtship. While of course wishing the newly-weds well, by the time of their nuptials – nine months after the announcement of their engagement – the bemused villagers had long found their tongues and were still sharing private constructions on the seemingly improbable merger. With minor variations, the consensus was decidedly anti-romantic. As if insensible to the surrounding din, Parkes placidly proclaims that his marriage 'started a most happy partnership which is still prospering while I write this. To marry a scholar of forty-five with a reputation (deserved) for being difficult requires considerable courage, courage which it naturally took some time to turn into pleasure – and custom!'[2]

How did this unforeseen alliance come to pass? One approach to this mystery would be to ground it in a parallel context: how did Parkes generally arrive at similarly major sorts of decisions? We turn again to his earlier capitulation to the seductive charms of Barley: 'I had already discovered the pleasant line of bracing hills south of the city [of Cambridge], and it was there that I looked for a house, and found one in Barley.'[3]

As seen earlier, the above is misleading. Just as though Barley had always been his predestined portion, Parkes did not so much discover the village as did the village – in the person of Dr Salaman – through his writings stumble across him. Drawn by those pleasant hills, it seemed to Parkes that their shadow upon the landscape were the very finger of fate pointing him in the direction of homely, ordinary Barley. Unresistingly, he acquiesced to its bidding. Since his future wife was, by all accounts, a notably unprepossessing woman, might not something of the same sort of fatalism have been operant when it came to his 'choosing' her? An oblique prologue to this investigation necessitates a brief digression.

In W. G. Sebald's fictionalized memoir that was cited earlier, we espy a character peering out through the window of a Swiss train. Later, upon recalling glacial Jungfrauloch 'gleaming snow white in the midst of summer', he and his father hike to the crest of Grammont:

> All the noontide of that blue-skied day in August I lay beside father on the mountaintop, gazing down into the even deeper blue of the lake, at the country across the lake, over to the faint silhouette of the Jura range, at the bright towns on the far bank, and at St Gingolph, immediately below us but visible in a shaft of shadow perhaps as fifteen hundred metres deep.[4]

We know that Parkes loved to take lengthy walks in the same mountains described by Sebald. Earlier Weisz observed that, sketchpad and colours at the ready, Parkes turned out a landscape practically every day. Even allowing for exaggeration, it is strange that *Voyage of Discoveries* never pauses to comment on gorges, crests or cloud-piercing peaks. This omission may seem minor, but, like Conan Doyle's famous non-barking dog, it bears a heavier burden of meaning once we begin to enumerate similar 'oversights'. After, for example, spending almost a week at Montreux, Parkes offers not a single word extolling its magnificent view. Or again is it not perverse to behold the beauty of Lake Geneva from one's sitting-room window for six years and never once remark upon it? In all that time, Parkes records no emotional transport, no inspiration, nothing sentient.

We may conclude that perhaps Parkes was afflicted by some kind of 'Swiss problem', but what of his silence on visiting the cathedral at Chartres?[5] What is one to make of the nearly perfect blank we find filed under 'Parkes in Paris', a place we know he visited frequently? There is not one word about the city's physical beauty or cultural attractions. He makes no mention of London, either, where he actually lived after leaving Oxford and later visited on innumerable occasions.

The antithesis of reticence can be found, of course, in Parkes' encounter with Provence.

> Where but in Provence ... would it be possible to find, unannounced by any written or illustrated advertisement, *on an eleventh visit* to the region: A Cathedral of the time of Charlemagne – at S. Paul Trois Chateaux. A Cistercian Abbey, complete with all its thirteenth century buildings, but now a farm – at Silvacane. The largest renaissance chateau in the south of France – at Grignan?[6]

It seems that the chief point for Parkes was that the effulgence of the Alps and the treasure-troves of Paris, New York, and London had already been celebrated *ad nauseam* by hundreds of youthful explorers from the provinces and an equal number of elderly memoirists. If absences reflect anything, his earlier abnegation as a memoirist of the trenches of Flanders is of a piece with the same proud habit of mind. It offended his amour propre to render redundant notice to attractions whose charms one might expect to find 'announced by any written or illustrated advertisement'. This intellectual tic may be viewed as a residue of the arrogant, insufferable schoolboy. Like another cantankerous 'countryman', a celebrated American poet who was his older contemporary, Parkes also skirted the broad, too well travelled highway. We may even detect a residue of the same tendency in his enthusiasm for taking up a lance for the honour of all Christendom in his lonely, self-appointed role as Paladin of the Jews.

In sum, Parkes' transport of joy over the hidden gold of Provence draws its vitality from the same source as his avidity as a collector. Exhilaration issues from the rapture of fresh discovery, recognition of the unappreciated, a touch of inverted snobbery, and the unearthing of overlooked qualities in something – or someone – very new or very old. Such is the habit of mind that links S. Paul Trois Chateaux to antique brass candlesticks and to Parkes' spirited acquiescence to the proposition that the charmless Miss Wickings should indeed be his destiny-appointed bride.

Who was Dorothy Wickings? Her grandfather had been an architect, a profession that always exercised appeal for Parkes. Along with Scandinavian antecedents, her lineage included Irish and Italian forebears. Her father was a Freemason. Whenever the father and daughter met, instead of embracing they shook hands in accordance with masonic rite. He would then enquire, 'How old is your grandmother?' For Parkes this formality evoked the recondite opacities that *les Guernesiaises* paraded before undiscerning English magistrates. Until seriously injured in a road accident, as a young woman Wickings was active in dramatic societies. Upon recovering, she took a job as a typist for Lloyds of London.[7]

Remembering her well, the villagers, are grudgingly complimentary.

> Dorothy was an extremely big woman, slightly taller and considerably broader than he. She was something of a middle-class battleaxe. With a high-pitched laugh, she could be a jolly good companion. She was upper-middle class. Like him, she spoke very good English. Although she had taken no degree and was not very intellectual, she became one with living with him. Dorothy was very capable: nice, no-nonsense, a brilliant secretary, bossy in the nicest way, kindly, and boring. She did all his library work, typed his letters, etc.[8]

Wickings's replacement as secretary to the Press and Publicity Committee of the Christian Council for Refugees from Germany and Central Europe provides colourful confirmation: 'Romantic involvement at that stage? Not really. She looked very much like Margaret Rutherford, the actress, and was not very attractive, let alone feminine. A cigarette permanently dangling from a corner of her mouth, nicotine-stained from abuse. Don't get me wrong … I became very fond of Dorothy Wickings, enjoyed her company and was treated with unfailing kindness and generosity …'[9]

In and of themselves, 'capable', 'nice' and 'kindly' would scarcely have breached the heavily fortified barricades to capture Parkes' heart. Far more telling were character and convictions. A professed pacifist, in her youth Wickings joined the Peace Pledge Union and the China Campaign Committee. During the inter-war period, when she realized that her employer was engaged in insuring armaments, she refused on principle to type any letters that dealt with the sale of arms to Germany.

Her boss was not 'understanding'; she was forced to resign.[10] We recognize in her the very sort of principled obduracy that Parkes would instinctively respect.

Born in 1900, Wickings was part of a generation of women for whom the impact of the First World War outlasted the close of hostilities. So many soldiers had been slaughtered that the number of single women far exceeded the number of available men. 'This excessive female population was habitually described, none too flatteringly, as "superfluous" ... An agitation over their mere existence began with the census of the late summer of 1921, and during the "Silly Season" of that year their position became a favourite topic with the Stunt press ...'[11] With the passage of two more decades, this unattractive, no-nonsense woman had surely resigned herself to spinsterhood – but then she saw her chance.

A parallel account of the unlikely taking of a spinster-bride by an eccentric parson down from Oriel College, Oxford, is curiously illuminating.

> He whirled before the wind of her contrary mind, spinning like a top. He was not offended by her donnish walk, the loudness of her voice, the fact that she had large hands, and that they had freckles on them already. She was large-boned, but this was not the sort of thing he noticed, either to like or dislike. He had no eye for the physical at all and could meet you four times and still not recognize your face ... So he did not notice the freckles. He knew she had flaxen hair, but if he had been asked the colour of her eyes he would have had to guess. He saw her face, in memory, with that gentle formlessness, all the details made soft by feeling, with which a one-year-old is said to perceive its mother. He saw her ideas though, like a garden in profusion, and so it was, he imagined, with her ideas and arguments.[12]

It seems only reasonable to presume that for each vicar's besotted sister, wealthy Quaker typist or far wealthier Warburg heiress, we may infer ten other would-be admirers. Yet the debonair, handsome, intellectual bachelor, who over the years had been so adroit at fending off the advances of predatory women, succumbed not to good looks, status or wealth but to the prim probity and scanty charms of 'a middle-class battleaxe' cursed with an irritatingly high-pitched laugh. Parkes must have noticed that Dorothy Wickings was universally considered unappealing and unfeminine but, as with the parson from Oriel, fundamentally this simply did not signify. When Parkes looked at her, 'he saw her ideas … like a garden in profusion'. Given Parkes' own priorities, convictions, disposition, scriptural and other special needs – perhaps the greatest of which was a capacity for limitless adulation – far from a deficiency, Wickings's very plainness took on an advantageous light.

Could the conjunction of these two smokers of high principles be filed, in the end, under 'true love'? Before venturing to penetrate this greatest of human enigmas, it is instructive to circle round the mystery by interweaving their separate accounts of how they got together in the first place. Discrepancies, both major and minor, have of course been retained.

They first met late in 1941 at a Chatham House forum in which Parkes had been a featured participant. Afterwards they were introduced by a sister-in-law of Parkes' cousin, the Bishop of Chichester. While chattering with Chichester at Chatham, Parkes heart-rendingly announced that his secretary had just abandoned him, and that he '… was desperately looking for secretarial help'.[13] It is most unlikely that there had been any design in that. Nevertheless, highly impressed by Parkes' performance or his anguish or his good looks, Miss Wickings saw her responsibility or her opportunity or perhaps just a chance for a brief diversion in the countryside. She impulsively rejoined that she just might see her way clear to spend a little time at Barley as 'a stopgap' and thereby alleviate his immediate distress.

Now Wickings played a not unimportant role in the affairs of Bloomsbury House. She had, for example, been a founding member of the 'Thursday Group' of Jews and Christians which, like almost all refugee agencies in the city, was headquartered there.[14] Assuring her superior at the Press and Publicity Office of the Christian Council for Refugees that she would return to London after a week, that she was merely helping the harassed clergyman get through a difficult patch, on 4 November Wickings boarded a northbound train to join someone she knew might be 'a very difficult man to work with'. By the end of that week, she had already tendered her resignation to the CCR.

Recognizing that it sounded 'unreasonable to leave her post in order to work with James Parkes', she maintained that it would be 'valuable to the cause of the refugees and the Jews'.[15] This flimsy rationalization is undermined by Parkes who comments that, with the coming of the war,

> ... refugee work was gradually shutting down, and Wickings had had her full measure of the blitz from the beginning. She had either travelled up and down between London and [her residence in] Hildenborough daily, or she had slept in London, and often spent evenings at Phyllis Gershom's club in Stepney for Jewish girls in the East End. Presenting herself as a 'stopgap', she arrived in Barley in November 1941.[16]

Taken together, however, these two accounts constitute a reasonably consistent record of their first meeting. Nevertheless, a somewhat contradictory, not easily dismissed alternative recollection is offered by Ruth Weyl: ' I remember quite distinctly that one day James called [the Reverend] W. W. [Simpson] very upset. His secretary had recently left him, and he was desperate to find a replacement. Could my husband possibly lend him someone from the Christian Council of Refugees as a stopgap? He sent him Dorothy. She never returned.'[17]

The salient difference between the synoptic account of the Parkeses and the more disinterested Weyl recollection is that in the former, after some stagey action by Parkes, it is Wickings who initiates 'the plot'; in the latter, however, at least at the start, she is a supporting player in the schemes of others. There are important zones of congruence – everyone agrees on 'stopgap,' and 'desperation' – but one wonders whether the mutually exclusive aspects of these narratives may be reconciled. For now, however, let us adhere to Parkesian virtues – every index card and teacup in its appointed place – and hold off until the players are properly positioned.

When Wickings first arrived at Barley manor she recalls entering upon a heterogeneous but small household: Grace Gardiner ('the excellent sister of our very unsatisfactory rector'[18]), an evacuated schoolmistress and an evacuee whose aunt lived in the village.[19] Parkes' inventory is more thorough.

> When Dorothy Wickings came, it still left a small bedroom available on my side of the house, and Grace installed in it a 'houseboy' of great wit and humour ... who had been

billeted on an aunt in the village. Wickings occupied the room which had been inhabited by the Zoellner's [*sic*], a German refugee couple whose house had been destroyed in the blitz and whom Parkes had taken in. There was also Grace herself as well as a housekeeper.[20]

Before she could possibly ascend to the station of 'Mrs Parkes', Miss Wickings first had to dispatch the rector's sister who, with the exodus to war of McNeilage, only months earlier had installed herself in Parkes' manor and made herself indispensable. Early in the autumn, for example, working side by side for hours, the two of them had cooked hundreds of pounds of jam from bruised plums and greengages for a nearby charitable facility. Wickings proved a brilliant tactician. Unloosing a blitzkrieg, she sent the 'excellent Grace' packing after only a week, and just 'a few months later' she and Parkes were engaged to be married.[21]

Wondering what triggered the engagement leads us to conjecture just how proactive Wickings might have been. It is easy enough to imagine the two of them encountering one another, like a Ruth and a Boaz, in the middle of the night in the manor house hallway or kitchen. As likely occurred between their biblical counterparts, did Wickings's machinations set in motion a successful seduction of her new employer? We cannot know, but even if their new-found intimacy were not definitively erotic, the key point may be inferred from later events: she persuaded him that whatever had transpired had been profoundly personal enough to imply a level of mutual commitment. In other words a real or purported breach of intimacy effectively constituted itself as the moral equivalent of seduction. On his part the passive Parkes, and this is critical, yielded to her interpretation of events. Once words had been extracted that could be construed as entailing an obligation – we recall how Parkes had once fatally burdened 'Len' Thomas with the weight of a 'moral obligation' – Wickings judged that she could rely upon Parkes' splendid Christian–Jewish conscience 'to do the right thing'.

Their formal engagement, of course, set village tongues wagging. It also necessitated a new housing arrangement. Although as Parkes' secretary Wickings had occupied a room in the manor itself, propriety dictated that the future mistress of the establishment now take up temporary residence in an outbuilding which the village took to calling 'the wedding cottage'. Until they were man and wife, the two no longer would sleep under the one roof.[22]

So now, assuming it reflects on at least a fair portion of the truth, how might Weyl's recollection be conflated with those of Wickings and Parkes? One resolution commends itself. If the most problematic element – Wickings's decisiveness – is transposed from the occasion of their first encounter at Chatham House to the period of their whirlwind courtship, it all makes a kind of sense. Precisely what occurred between the two of them to precipitate so rapidly the ungainly Wickings from spinsterhood to prospective marriage is unclear, but that in the course of that first week at Barley the future Mrs James Parkes outmanoeuvred Grace and was well advanced in plotting Parkes' future capitulation is all but certain.

> Our wedding took place just eight weeks after our engagement. Parkes asked his great friend Temple [by then Archbishop of Canterbury] to marry us, but Hitler was thought [to be] preparing to invade East Anglia in 1942, and in any event on the day fixed for the wedding Temple had to christen a Royal baby.[23]

In place of Temple the bride's regular vicar undertook to marry the two of them in Hildenborough, her home town in Kent. She chose to omit to promise her obedience, but this was in no way ominous. The Church of England had recently determined that the vow was optional; its omission represented a show of Wickings' and Parkes' joint support for the principle of liturgical reform. Similarly, the couple decided not to pray for 'the heritage and gift of children' but rather, following an alternative approved in 1928, that the bride might be 'a follower of holy and godly matrons'.

A peculiar transposition in Parkes' account gives one considerable pause. 'I got down to Hildenborough,' he recalls, 'with John as my best man, to be greeted on the platform by Dorothy's small nephew.'[24] The above context makes it perfectly clear that Parkes is referring to his man McNeilage. 'Dorothy Wickings,' he continues, 'was not a stranger to either James or John – she naughtily told the vicar that she wanted to bring along her 'two fiancés' to make arrangements.'

As though Parkes were momentarily possessed by the antic spirit of Laurence Sterne, his usage here carries a teasing, sexual connotation. Moreover, as if suddenly unhinged, Parkes ceases to allude to McNeilage, for he then recalls that he presented his bride with a silver wedding ring 'because I had no money to buy a gold one'. The ring had been fashioned from a Georgian tea-spoon by a London jeweller. The same Jewish craftsman had also fashioned 'John Hadham's engagement ring [because] Dorothy had required one from each of her fiancés'. Intending McNeilage, Parkes refers instead to Hadham. McNeilage has drifted off his syntactical screen, and yet just one paragraph later Parkes again tunes him in: 'Shortly after we got married John came back to us and took over the main charge of the house ...'[25]

This most queer logomachic Johannine slide from McNeilage to Hadham and back to McNeilage is not merely confusing, but, with a nod to Freud, fraught with consequential import. Bearing in mind that McNeilage initially had served as an understudy for the role originally played by 'Len' Thomas, who himself had once played Parkes' alter ego and might have been his lover, then the conflation of the two Johns at this pivotal juncture in Parkes' life makes a kind of psychological sense. On the verge of his marriage, Parkes unconsciously subsumed Thomas – his first 'fiancé', in this scene disguised as John McNeilage – into the identity of *John* Hadham, another of Parkes' *Doppelgängers* and, in the above context, the second 'fiancé'. This slip of the pen or lingual elision may be interpreted variously but perhaps most pertinently as disclosing an inner readiness to enter upon a new stage in his long deferred process of maturation.

The symbolic return from the depths of Parkes' unconscious of 'the two Thomases' ('Len' and 'Tom') in the guise of 'the two Johns' occurring at the very point of his marriage shifts the focus from why, of all available partners, Parkes chose to marry Dorothy Wickings to the more fundamental question of why he permitted himself to collude with Wickings's transparent manoeuvres and to marry at all. One fruitful avenue into this fascinating matter is to view it as yet one more manifestation of pressure in 'real time' of Parkes' deep-seated internalization of the typological pattern set by Jacob-the-Patriarch.[26]

The interval between Parkes' departure from Geneva in 1935 – the inception of this current phase of the archetypal 'Jacobite' pattern – and its culmination in Hildenborough in 1942, comprises seven years. Such, of course, is the requisite time Jacob had contracted with Laban to discharge his obligation for the hand of Rachel. His agreement to care and nurture the flocks of Laban, resurrected for Parkes as Hitler, got displaced on the helpless Jewish refugees of Europe. At the age of forty-five, after fourteen long years – seven in exile followed, after a 'near-death' and 'rebirth' experience in Geneva, by seven more at Barley – Parkes had undergone his full measure of psychosexual toil.

In parallel fashion, like a Jacob upon his arrival in Haran, the immediacy of Parkes' response to Wickings derived in large measure from her parallel activity as the shepherdess. That is to say, he was inwardly primed to recognize his predestined bride as she watered her flock at the well. It was clearly propitious, to him a kind of sign, that for years Wickings too had been succouring refugees, the same displaced sheep that so engaged Parkes' conscientious devotion.

Not Grace and neither Helen nor Bettina but Dorothy alone could successfully propel herself into Parkes' internal psychodrama, not because Parkes was enraptured by her charms or, as the villagers jokingly bantered, that he really sought free secretarial services, but because she unknowingly bore the proper talismanic signs. Wickings materialized at precisely the point of peripeteia, the juncture when Parkes was psychologically primed to fulfil a seemingly foreordained denouement. To what if any degree Parkes apprehended the agency of this archetypal pattern is unknowable and ultimately immaterial. Most probably it acted on his consciousness like an irresistable subterranean undertow. What is critical is that when he felt its impingement, he responded without hesitation.

For her own reasons, declining 'to obey' her husband, Wickings uncannily cooperated in playing out the role of typological Rachel who, against Jacob's wishes, wilfully stole her father's idols. She played the part of the 'disobedient wife'. Furthermore, she also functions tropically by simultaneously reflecting the central issue of the biblical narrative. Abstaining from children reinforces Wickings's purchase on what was, until her barrenness was assuaged, Rachel's prototypical attribute. At the same time, the couple's decision to suspend the biblical mandate to increase and multiply by refraining from 'the heritage and gift of children' was both convenient and conscientious: 'We should have liked children but – in view of our special work, the agony of the

Second World War and the refugees and the holocaust – we felt we were called to work together but not to produce a family.'[27]

The Parkeses would have found the following fictional parallel apposite: 'The Strattons had not children and, given the chaste nature of their embraces, had no reason to have any. They thought this a civilized arrangement. They had reached it, with relief, on their wedding night and felt no temptation to change their minds.'[28] On the other hand, given the gravity of the Parkeses' commitments, there is no reason to view with sceptism their claim that pressures issuing from 'their special work' and the impact of the Shoah actually did impinge upon their thinking in this matter.

There is a final twist on this playing out of synchronous lives as though one were attuned to the unsounded music of the other. Taken together, these two, seven-year cycles lent shape to Parkes' personal life in the period between his joining the ISS staff in 1928 until his marriage in 1942. They may be viewed as corresponding to the first fourteen years of his life, Edenic in memory if not actuality, which ended so abruptly with the death of his mother. In disguised form, this indelible loss burst out of sub-consciousness into symbolic action when Parkes loudly vented his anguish and desperation at the desertion of his secretary. It was remitted only when he happened upon a wholly admirable replacement who, to all appearances, would serve as an admirable asexual surrogate for his long-departed mother.

As for the period between the ages of fourteen and thirty-one during which Parkes was feeling out the contours of his 'Jacobite' paradigm, these years passed under the aegis of the Bungalow Ghost, a primal force of nature (and psyche). If we may take this 'elemental' with some seriousness, apart from demanding its proper due as the spirit of the cromlech, it seems additionally to have emanated from the spirit of his dead mother. Appeased by Parkes' sense of mission to the Jews, the ghost retired from the scene to watch and wait, but only with the advent of Dorothy Wickings was the spirit of Annie Parkes fully propitiated. At forty-five, having attained maturity seventeen years later than his patriarchal analogue, Parkes had fulfilled a biblical pattern that might best be characterized as the 'hard labour of exile'.

The wedding reception was held in Barley's medieval town hall. In his ceremonial address, Redcliffe Salaman feted the bride with unintentionally doubled-edged praise: 'It took a Viking to

capture our James,' he intoned.[29] Salaman also invoked eight
facets of Parkes' personality, of which Wickings could later retrieve
only five: 'scholar, cleric, gardener, writer, and embroiderer, and
now he has taken one over eight by becoming a husband.'[30] The
couple honeymooned at the home of Charles and Dorothea Singer
in Kilmarth, 'a delightful seventeenth century dower house overlooking St Austell's Bay in Cornwall'. With East Anglia under
constant threat of German invasion, the Parkeses resorted to
Kilmarth again and again to relax and to refresh themselves.[31]

How did the villagers perceive the odd pair as newly-
weds? Edith Weisz's rambling, condescending, but representative account follows.

> She adored him and was terribly possessive. Often keeping
> no more than only a yard away, she wouldn't let him out
> of her sight. She said she thought he was the 'Messiah.' Yes,
> the Messiah! It was genuine, stifling adoration. Of course
> she mothered him and organized his life, made herself
> his absolute right-hand man. On the other hand, he often
> resented Dorothy's bossiness. I remember that they often
> discussed what he wanted to eat days in advance. Dorothy
> kowtowed to him; she tolerated a lot. Fairly frequently I
> overheard him getting 'impatient' with Dorothy. She was,
> after all, his intellectual inferior. He was so beautiful and
> had such a smooth voice, that sometimes it seemed to me
> that I could see him cringing when Dorothy laughed too
> loudly.
>
> All in all, it was more a marriage of convenience and
> friendship than of passion. My father and I doubted they
> ever kissed on the mouth, and they probably had no sex. I
> think it's doubtful whether he ever screwed anyone but
> certainly not a woman. Yes, they certainly were devoted to
> each other, but the joke went around, 'now he won't have
> to pay her any more'. This was quite apart from the worldly
> hilarity among the more sophisticated people in village over
> their marriage: 'What', they wondered, 'will he do with
> her'?[32]

Weisz's jaundiced view of their marital relationship is succinctly corroborated by others. Back in Wickings's old bailiwick
in London, such was the incredulous reaction:

> One day, not very long after Dorothy had gone to work for
> James at Barley, W. W. [Simpson] burst into our office,
> shaking with uncontrollable mirth. 'Do you want to know
> the latest news?', he said, between gasps, 'Dorothy is going
> to marry James'. We were truly stunned, rolling about
> laughing … I am not being snide but the two were such
> unlikely candidates for marriage, the three of us in the office
> that day simply could not credit it.[33]

Several decades later, the considered judgment of another
acute observer was that 'Dorothy loved James; James tolerated
Dorothy'. As for Parkes' proclivities: 'James could have been
bisexual, but more probably he was homosexual or, in the tradition of Christian aestheticism and its peculiar association of
sexuality with sin, entirely asexual. They slept, I think, in separate
bedrooms.'[34] Detectable errors in some accounts argue a degree
of caution: 'In those days we didn't talk about such matters
publicly, but many of us just assumed that Parkes and his man
McNeilage had a homosexual relationship. After all, they lived
together in that big house for years.'[35] In fact, very shortly after
starting to work for Parkes, McNeilage married a village girl with
whom he lived in a nearby cottage.[36]

A villager long intimate with the Parkes household supports
another of Weisz' observations: 'Dorothy's relationship to James
was mother-to-son.'[37] Although a simplification, it is not far
from the mark. Settling upon a bride with whom he anticipated
intimate relations would play little if any role may be viewed as
a rather elegant solution for what otherwise might have posed
the insuperable dilemma of symbolic incest.

At least some of the suppositions of the villagers may be
dismissed as patently baseless. Was Wickings, like the oddly
matched partner of another James, Joyce's Nora Barnacle, Parkes'
'intellectual inferior'? Certainly not to the point of mutual embarrassment. In fact one rather astute observer from outside Barley
viewed her intellectual capacities in a rather flattering light: 'His
wife Dorothy was personable, active, intelligent, and took an
active part in our conversations. She made pottery, often giving
pieces to me and my wife as gifts.'[38] Another found her clever,
witty and rather good company.[39] At the same time, she was
much dismayed when she recalled the manner in which Parkes
treated his wife in company:

Once, when she sat down on one of his precious, embroidered antique chairs, he shouted at her to get up at once. Another time, after he had set the luncheon table with beautiful glasses, Dorothy served sherry. He told her off in no uncertain terms: 'Sherry doesn't go in these glasses. Go and get the wine!' Since Dorothy was not a very attractive person, she probably didn't mind how poorly she was treated. Whereas he was always impeccably got up, she had no sense of colour. Her clothes and appearance were slovenly and unclean. I never could enter the kitchen or bathrooms of their house. Once James told my husband that one reason he liked me was that my lipstick matched my dress.[40]

Overall, Wickings was undeniably highly principled, obstinate, capable, and unconditionally devoted to the alleviation of suffering in the world: not a mean curriculum vitae for the likes of James Parkes. Was theirs merely a marriage of convenience? This underestimates Wickings, a formidable woman of conviction in her own right, one capable of exciting both the admiration and the imagination of a man of Parkes' temperament. It did not take him long to apprehend the special qualities of the selfless helpmate and adoring acolyte that she would remain throughout their union. True, Parkes addressed her rudely and was deemed by others to exploit her. There is no indication, however, that he genuinely considered her his inferior or intended to wound her with his condescension. Nor do we sense that she herself inwardly recoiled at her husband's demeanour. If Parkes could not forthrightly declare that he was in love with her, if even his silver anniversary present inscribed 'To Dorothy' omits 'With Love', if he often displayed impatience with her vulgarity and slovenliness, if he at times wearied of her servility, still the stream of genuine respect and admiration between them ran very deep.

As we recall, Parkes from the very start tellingly declares about his marriage that 'it naturally took some time [for courage] to turn into pleasure – and custom!'[41] One wonders how long it took for the couple to enjoy a degree of conjugal satisfaction. Weisz, who discounts the possibility that as in the case of Parkes' contemporary Stephen Spender, homosexual episodes may be confined to an earlier chapter of one's life, seems to think never.

Weyl is less dogmatic but her view is even more austere, leaning towards celibacy or asexuality. Based largely on external appearances, Roth simply could not conceive of them as lovers. The truth may indeed reside somewhere within the above triangulation: although Parkes assuredly was not a roaring heterosexual, neither could he ever be accused of blatant homosexuality. Abstinence seems his most characteristic posture.

Parkes' previous experience, admittedly meagre, seems to have embraced both genders. Moreover, that he himself confesses initial ineptitude or even dysfunction in itself strongly argues the likelihood of melioration. In short, many close observers may just have underestimated 'Messiah's' capacity to appropriate some of the more customary joys of the connubial state. In sum, the opinions of onlookers cannot be construed as the last word on the private behaviour of the Reverend and Mrs Parkes; what is highly probable is that they reflect not only the biases of the observers but also a dearth of imagination.

We do well to recall that the mystery of the marital relationship, especially one between ostensibly unequal partners, runs very deep. There is no reason to conclude that Wickings's lack of physical beauty reflected a weak libido. Aside from the above, later textual hints suggest that over the passage of time Parkes may have developed into a modestly animated, closet heterosexual.[42] This possibility brings to mind Boswell's sane judgment about the connection between Samuel Johnson and Mrs Thrale, his own famously unhandsome, conjugal battleaxe, one hacked out of the same classic mould as Margaret Rutherford:

> To argue from her being much older than Johnson, or any other circumstances, that he could not really love her, is absurd: for love is not a subject of reasoning, but of feeling, and therefore there are no common principles upon which one can persuade another concerning it. Every man feels for himself, and knows how he is affected by particular qualities in the person he admires, the impressions of which are too minute and delicate to be substantiated in language.[43]

NOTES

1. Henry James, letter to Mrs Henry James Sr, 28 June 1869, *Henry James, Selected Letters*, ed. Leon Edel (Cambridge, MA: Belknap, Harvard University Press, 1974), p. 41.
2. James Parkes, *Voyage of Discoveries* (London: Victor Gollancz, 1969), p. 176.
3. Ibid., p. 129.
4. W. G. Sebald, *The Emigrants* (New York: New Directions, 1996), pp. 172–73.
5. *Vide* Chapter 15.
6. Parkes, *Voyage of Discoveries*, p. 83.
7. Dorothy Wickings, *Autobiography*, Parkes Archive, File 60/33/3.
8. Edith Ruth Weisz, interviewed by the author and Maggie Davidson in Cambridge, England, 28 August 2000.
9. Letter to the author from Ellen Roth, 10 October 2003.
10. Wickings, *Autobiography*.
11. Vera Brittain, *Testament of Youth* (London: Virago, 1978), p. 527.
12. Peter Carey, *Oscar and Lucinda* (London: Faber and Faber, 1988), pp. 47–48.
13. Parkes, *Voyage of Discoveries*, p. 177.
14. Ibid., pp. 176–77.
15. Wickings, *Autobiography*.
16. Parkes, *Voyage of Discoveries*, p. 177.
17. Ruth Weyl, Interview.
18. Parkes, *Voyage of Discoveries*, p. 173.
19. Wickings, *Autobiography*.
20. Parkes, *Voyage of Discoveries*, p. 174.
21. Wickings, *Autobiography*.
22. Weisz, interview.
23. Wickings, *Autobiography*.
24. Parkes, *Voyage of Discoveries*, p. 176, ff.
25. Ibid., p. 177.
26. *Vide* Chapters 2, 7, 10, 21, and 25.
27. Wickings, *Autobiography*.
28. Carey, *Oscar and Lucinda*, p. 48.
29. Weisz, interview.
30. Wickings, *Autobiography*.
31. Parkes, *Voyage of Discoveries*, p. 145.
32. Weisz, interview.
33. Ellen Roth, letter to the author, 10 October 2003.
34. Ruth Weyl, interview.
35. Conversation between Ellen Roth and author, London, 22 July 2004.
36. Parkes, *Voyage of Discoveries*, p. 138.
37. Doris Wilkinson, interviewed by author and Maggie Davidson in Barley, 2 September 2000.
38. Zvi Werblowsky, interviewed by author and Maggie Davidson in Jerusalem, 16 November 2003.
39. Weyl, interview.
40. Ibid.
41. Parkes, *Voyage of Discoveries*, p. 176.
42. *Vide* Chapter 29.
43. James Boswell, *Life of Johnson*, ed. George Birkbeck Hill and L. F. Powell (London: Oxford University Press, 1934), Vol. 1, p. 235.

27

Sound to the Bottom
of the Skip

At twenty-seven Parkes had blithely turned his back on a normal clerical living. At thirty-seven he had confidently put aside the temptations of a regular academic career. At forty-five, still very much a freelancer, he was confronted by new uncertainties. Wickings, Hadham and Hitler respectively had delivered unto him a first marriage, an alternative identity and a second war with Germany. Then he was dealt a disagreeable jolt from an unexpected quarter – Israel Sieff.

Starting in 1933, when the first wave of several hundred Jewish refugees reached Britain, the Anglo-Jewish community had taken it upon itself to guarantee their resettlement and maintenance. As this burden grew, meeting that obligation had become increasingly onerous. After five years the Jewish community informed the Home Secretary that it was experiencing difficulties and 'intimated that they cannot extend this undertaking to new arrivals ...' Nevertheless, 'the community's guarantee was maintained until after the outbreak of the war in spite of the fact that the numbers arriving were more than ten times the original estimate'.[1]

We recall that Charles Singer was donating up to one third of his income to bear 'his fair share' of the burden. Increasingly, however, the financial load was shifting to the very wealthy. At some point it was unavoidable that this would impact upon Parkes, and with the start of hostilities, Israel Sieff was forced to suspend his monthly subsidy to the historian. Encumbered by far greater material and personal obligations than formerly, Parkes was constrained to admit that the economic stays that had buttressed his youthful, quixotic choices were coming undone. Like one of the artfully crenulated sand castles he used to construct on the beach at Alderney, his manor house and the style of life it sustained might yet crumble.

With the collapse of the tomato market, Henry Parkes, at approximately the age of his grown son, had faced a comparable challenge: newly widowed, he had been obliged to keep his family and household afloat through difficult, choppy economic waters. His recourse, as his son had put it so delicately, was 'courageously' to sell *Les Fauconnaires*, fire all the servants and move his children to the straitened self-sufficiencies of life in a bungalow. 'Opting for comfort,' he chose to descend from the upper middle-class to a respectable but definitely lower social echelon.

His son, having late in life taken a wife, was now pressed by an equally compelling set of restraints. Although the first two Hadham books had been *bona fide* bestsellers, they had yielded precious little cash. Adopting a strategy seemingly opposite to his father's, Parkes 'courageously' opted to stay put. Even had he been able to sell the Old Hore's House and move into a more modest dwelling, he would have resisted. Still, the survival strategies of son and father were not grossly dissimilar. With a much-reduced staff of servants and the help of his new bride, Parkes the son like Parkes the father also practised the Thoreauvian arts of making-do and self-sufficiency. Parkes' account of carrying on under the stresses of straitened circumstances in time of war evokes the 'normal' heroism often associated with most other Britons under the inspired leadership of Churchill.

For survival, the Parkes household was thrown back upon its natural resources and native ingenuity.

> The first market after the war broke out I sent a quarter of ton of perfect apples to be sold [in Royston, the nearest market town]. The whole lot made one shilling and six pence, and I paid the auctioneer more than ten shillings to sell them! And I had to pay the same amount for carriage to the market.[2]

Storing what he could, with the harvest of 1942 Parkes tried his luck again at Royston. The results were even more dismal. Upon recounting his tale of woe one evening to Israel Sieff, as if miraculously Parkes was once again delivered from the toils of indigence: '"But James, why don't you sell it to us?", asked Sieff. 'I did not then know that Marks and Spencer had started a produce department, but thereafter I sold everything to them. The change was fantastic.'[3]

Parkes volunteered to serve as a conduit for marketing surplus apples and plums of other local fruit growers. 'Give them to me,' Parkes urged. 'I'll sell them for you. Only you must promise they are sound fruit to the bottom of the skip. I haven't time to reweigh and repack.' Everything was delivered to the bins of Marks & Spencer. How gratified Henry Parkes would have been to hear this familiar strain from his son's Guernsey boyhood echo forth again. Parkes' agricultural endeavours yielded him in the neighbourhood of £20 annually.

The Parkeses' other exploitable resource was Old Hore. Like Henry Parkes during the First World War, for the duration of the conflict his son rented out some of its rooms.

> Fortunately the house could be very easily adapted for evacuees, as it had two staircases and two bath rooms ... I moved my bed down to my work room, kept my bedroom for a secretary (if I was ever to have one), and was able to turn a sitting room, with three bedrooms and a bath room reached by their own staircase, over to various people from London ... That still left us with a large kitchen and a common dining room.[4]

Wickings pulled her considerable weight. Early in the war, before conclusive word of the magnitude of the Shoah had reached ears in the West, Chatham House had commissioned Parkes among a team of experts to prepare papers for a hypothetical peace conference. Inevitably, his main foci were antisemitism and Palestine. Parkes implored Sieff to provide clerical assistance for the project. With her husband in America, this time it was Rebecca Sieff who rode to the rescue by authorizing Wickings the sum of £250 annually, exactly her former salary at the Christian Council for Refugees, for secretarial services. Beyond that, the couple could depend absolutely only on Parkes' private income – £3.10 per year. With exemplary understatement, the only salaried member of the household commented uncomplainingly that during the war years they had 'very little money'.[5]

Barley, surrounded by small airfields, was frequently overflown by German air runs because 'those who funked going into London, where the ack-ack fire was fierce, dropped their bombs in our neighbourhood'.[6] Fortunately, the village suffered no casualties, but the local Air Raid Precaution Corps (ARP) would be called out on nearly a hundred occasions. Parkes, whose property abutted the village school grounds, pulled down all his fences so that fathers of the schoolchildren could dig protective trenches in his orchard. In case of a sudden emergency, the children could then take cover quickly. What else might they take? Reminiscent of his anti-Barthian vaunt about books 'unborrowed' from his Geneva flat bespeaking the goodness of man,[7] Parkes delivers a 'Parable of the Plums': 'I told them that, in return, they were on their honour not to steal my fruit. I don't believe I lost a single plum from them, or from the London evacuees when they came, during the whole of the war.'[8]

Making-do and pitching-in, reigning virtues of wartime Britain, served to break down class barriers and to infuse those years of shared hardship with Churchillian determination and a sense of larger purpose. Parkes' 'Cats' Club'[9] placed over one hundred child evacuees: Redcliffe Salaman himself took in twenty-five children; the rectory housed a dozen more.[10] Parkes, who throughout the war served as chairman of the village school, was intimately involved with the wellbeing of children. Particularly concerned with the integration of refugees in local schools in the district, he proudly recalls swaying reluctant officials to open the door of a new high school in a nearby town to evacuee youngsters and to the friends they had made among the Barley children.[11]

When a large number of evacuees developed impetigo, Parkes converted his newly built scullery into a temporary clinic where the children were repeatedly scrubbed with soap and hot water. In fact, since …

> … baths were almost non-existent in our corner of the village … on one or two days a week we had a succession of bathers to our two bath rooms. We never had any trouble with them, and they never left the bath rooms dirty and wet. 'What, never? Well, hardly ever.'[12]

Why Lerner and Loewe now? First books, then plums and fences, and now bathrooms demonstrate that had he ever acted on the recurrent passing fancy to take a regular living in a parish, the Reverend Dr Parkes, with his bent for upbeat homiletics, would surely have delighted his parishioners, those, that is, that he didn't offend. More pointedly, Parkes' temporary resort to

My Fair Lady at this juncture is especially appropriate. His light-hearted, self-directed irony, rare elsewhere in his memoir, mirrors the popular mood of war-time England. As noted by many observers, the pressures of war imbued the nation with collective purpose, and the virtues of sharing and self-sacrifice promoted a sense of fraternity. At the same juncture that he recollects these years of anxiety and hardship, Parkes reminds us that the working title for his 'Autobiography' had been *A Life Enjoyed.*[13]

Prominent among the steady stream of visitors to Barley during the war was Rabbi Louis Rabinowitz – portmanteau 'Rab' – who turned up at any time of the day or night. Although he had been appointed as the Jewish chaplain for most of eastern England, the Army neglected to provide him with a vehicle. For extended periods, Parkes loaned his car to his friend, no minor gesture for an avid motorist who loved his car so much.

For Parkes, as for a great many Britons, these topsy-turvy times bred a mood of gritty satisfaction. Uplift, even a chastened elation prevailed. They also yield by far the most amusing anecdote in Parkes' entire repertoire.

> The doodle bugs in the last stages of the war brought us again to the situation where total strangers came to the door and asked if they could stay with us for a week or a fortnight. The oddest of them were two sisters whom we christened 'the bitch and the beldame'. The 'bitch' found us as odd as we found her, but she added an immortal phrase to our repertoire. Because of the shortage of fuel, baths were fairly strictly rationed at the time, and it was her turn to have one. I asked her if she would like one and she replied: 'May as well, mayn't I. Saves the trouble of washing, huh?'[14]

At other times, of course, the poverty pinched painfully. An income based upon apples, plums and rents, mostly nominal, rendered the Lord of the Manor penurious. The level of apprehension may be gauged from a politely grim exchange with Conrad Hoffman, Parkes' long-time adversary on the playing fields of Christian controversy.

> Dear Jimmy,
> It took a very long time for your manuscript entitled 'Jesus, an Enemy of the Jews' to reach me. I have read it

with interest but doubt whether we can publish the same. Apparently, various friends in Britain have also had the opportunity to read the manuscript and in three cases, have commented thereupon, expressing the opinion that it is not the type of material that we of the International Missionary Council's Committee on the Christian Approach to the Jews should publish ...[15]

A few weeks later Parkes dispatched his reply:

Dear Con,
I am sorry that you do not now find the material I sent what you wanted. But I don't think that affects the issue that you owe me £100 which I should be glad to receive as soon as possible. You approached me to write a pamphlet for you, and you had every opportunity of knowing my approach to the subject since we have both talked about it and I have published a book on it [*Jesus, Paul and the Jews*]. Had this been a commercial approach, I should of course have had a contract from you before I wrote. In view of our previous relations, I relied upon your word ... If your choice of author was a bad one that is surely your affair ... I am sorry to write like this, but as you know I am entirely dependent upon my earnings and I would not for one moment have dreamed of writing for you as a speculation. I wrote in response to a quite definite request from you and on an equally definite understanding that my work should be paid for.[16]

Of course Hoffman considered Parkes' views about missionaries beyond the pale, but how could he not have foreseen that they would be? At the same time, how could their author not have known that they would be anathema to their recipient? No record can be found to indicate whether the perennial chairman of the IMCCCAJ did eventually pay the £100 fee for the article he had commissioned. Although Parkes was fairly desperate to earn a fee he was not nearly desperate enough to compromise his position.

That 'an intelligent man' like Parkes had undertaken to run a manor house while earning an income more appropriate for a cottage bewildered Ernest Westmore, manager of Parkes' 'finances' ever since he first came to Barley in 1935. It took

Westmore nine years, but in 1944 he finally gathered the nerve to voice his consternation. Parkes' response is illuminating.

> It was only for the work I was doing that I ever bought a house of eight rooms instead of moving into much smaller accommodations that a 'single' author would need. For nothing smaller would house the library, the mass of archives, periodicals, documents, and what not which are here for consultation, or rooms for people of all sorts who come to consult them.'[17]

This apologia conveniently neglects mentioning that, like his cars, the Old Hore's House served not merely as a repository of collections and higher aspirations but also satisfied a deep-rooted yearning for status and social acceptance.

'The Barley Rectory Affair', a truly bizarre episode, underscores the exigencies of the times. In 1942 Parkes was accused of aiding Redcliffe Salaman in 'climbing into the church roof to steal beams for repairing cottages he owned in the village'.[18] This allegation, rivalled for sheer preposterousness only by the occasion in 1929 when Parkes had been accused of plotting to steal the communion plate in Dresden,[19] argues a powerful undercurrent of nativist resentment against the two left-leaning 'Brains of Barley'. Notwithstanding their tireless, public-spirited efforts or Parkes' personal intercession with the director of Marks & Spencer that so benefited Barley's orchardmen, at bottom the two were still resented 'interlopers' who had no real warrant to be meddling in, let alone running local affairs. In the election of 1945, when the country at large was expelling Churchill and the Conservatives from power, Barley booted Labourites Salaman and Parkes off the parish council, returning in their stead two more representative 'labourers': with a fine sense of irony, the village selected Salaman's gardener and McNeilage, Parkes's manservant.[20]

As mentioned earlier, what with three books between 1940 and 1942 and his articles and popular broadcasts, the decade had commenced with the Reverend John Hadham high in the saddle. As for the Reverend James Parkes, gentleman scholar, he was deeply engaged in researching the sources of *The Protocols of the Elders of Zion* at the behest of the Jewish Board of Deputies. Diverted by burgeoning obligations and other activities, at the time Parkes did not get around to publishing anything concerning his current research. His most fascinating discovery was a pamphlet dated 1840, the time of the Damascus ritual murder libel, in which several distinguished converts from Judaism publicly gave it the lie. This was the first time in the gloomy history of antisemitism that this sort of thing had ever occurred.[21]

Throughout this period Parkes *qua* historian maintained a complete file on the activities of the Barley-area Christian families who aided the influx of impoverished Jewish outsiders whom the war had thrust into their midst. When the authorities warned Barley that it lay at the epicentre of the area where the Germans were most likely to stage an air drop, Parkes took it with the seriousness one might expect of one who had no doubt that his name appeared in Nazi files. Fearful that his file of local Righteous Gentiles might fall into German hands, Parkes notes that he destroyed it.[22] Wickings's version, written closer to the time, differs: she records that her husband buried all letters and documents naming persons who had taken in Jewish children.[23] In this instance, Wickings's specificity gets the nod for a higher degree of probability. For a historian wilfully to destroy raw data is just one step away from sacrilege.

The upheavals of war engendered a number of promising, independent, progressive social movements in Britain. In that respect the early 1940s felt to Parkes much like the early 1920s all over again, and, as he had then, he succumbed to the temptations of idealism and progressivism.[24] In March 1941, Parkes enlisted in Sir Richard Acland's Forward March movement, a loosely structured organization which often gave rise to prolonged moments of *déjà vu*. In spite of the militaristic aura of its name, Acland's movement saw itself as spearheading the restructuring of society on a new basis, one in which creative, non-exploitative relationships might form and prosper.[25] It inaugurates one of Parkes' interludes of ambivalence and equivocal conduct that one must strain hard to perceive with any clarity.

Less than a year after its founding, Forward March merged with a rival organization called Common Wealth that, spawned and then precipitously abandoned by J. B. Priestley, was in something of a muddle. Parkes was invited to join its national committee, and in December 1942, because of so much backbiting among its would-be leaders, he was catapulted into the

role of its national chairman. Wickings, who now saw considerably less of her new husband than formerly, felt he'd been
asked to assume the chair chiefly because he was a clergyman:
'It was a safe cover for the organization'.[26] Ego commingling with
noblesse oblige, Parkes allowed the internal needs of Common
Wealth to prevail over common sense. After all, did he not strongly
favour Common Wealth's ostensible goal, the revitalization and
democratization of British society? If only as a compromise
choice, why should he not function as its chairman? Inevitably,
it wasn't long before Parkes found himself expending vast
amounts of time scuttling to and dashing from countless mainly
sterile meetings and mediating between hostile personalities.
All too soon he would ascertain the answers to his rhetorical
questions.

A year later, at a meeting in Manchester, R. W. Mackay, a figure
whom Parkes characterizes as 'ambitious, autocratic [and]
unscrupulous', besmirched Parkes' reputation in a sharp attack.
Thereafter MacKay had himself installed as the new general
secretary with enhanced powers. Deciding that a protracted
leadership struggle 'would prove fatal to the movement', Parkes,
taking a leaf out of Priestley's book, abruptly withdrew from all
involvement with Common Wealth. He did not say a word in
public in his own defence.[27]

Was this strategic withdrawal, desertion from the field or perhaps a little of both? This time Parkes felt constrained to justify
himself before a very select audience by composing an apologia
for his actions. Aiming to draw together the irreconcilable ambitions of Acland and acting secretary Jackson Newman, Parkes
explains that he had set out to work with both men. Acland he
viewed as '… a would-be dictator – poor at collaboration, he
would divide people instantly into black and white'. Worse by
far, Parkes found Newman, 'a man of much lower calibre … an
ambitious little trickster, trying all the time to play one of us
against the others …'[28] Fixated on the 'ambitious little trickster',
Parkes seriously underestimated the cunning of the ambitious
big trickster just behind the scenes – R. W. MacKay.

Perhaps the most interesting aspect of these personality assessments is how they unconsciously resonate with earlier ones. As
a soldier returned from the front, 'black and white' is precisely
the simplistic taxonomy Parkes had employed to describe the
world he encountered behind the lines and the critical manner

in which he typically assessed situations and personalities. On the other hand, especially in the years prior to his coming of age in Geneva – until 'he found himself' or his better self – one all too easily imagines others describing Parkes himself as something of 'an ambitious little trickster'.[29]

As much as anything, what actually precipitated Parkes' decampment was his naïveté. He had invited members of the overworked CW staff to journey up to Barley for weekends of rest and relaxation in order to remove themselves from the CW pressure chamber. Shoptalk, however, most notably about Newman's manoeuvrings and Mackay's relations with women staff members, could not be banished merely by a wave of the host's wand. This recurring state of affairs rendered Parkes vulnerable to charges that the real purpose of the weekends in the country was to allow him to pump the staff for information.

If to a certain extent Parkes' 'strategic withdrawal' reflected understated anxiety about being publicly discredited and exposed to *shanda*, it is surely also true that, as Wickings put it, 'the breakdown of the Commonwealth [*sic*] from the ideals of Forward March grieved' both of the Parkeses.[30] On balance, Parkes' resignation accorded with a just and proper recognition of his real priorities. He desperately needed to distance himself from the corrosive infighting that made a mockery of the ideal of 'restructuring of society on a new basis'. From a larger perspective, the 'Reverend Safe Cover' had been little more than the 'Reverend Stopgap'. Outfoxed by MacKay, feeling 'framed', refusing to grant even a modicum of truth to the allegations, Parkes, given the Hades-sent opportunity of MacKay's *Putsch*, was inwardly relieved to slink away from his sticky entanglement.

Parkes promised himself never again to become similarly inveigled into joining, or to be enmeshed, in an organization. 'What, never? Well, hardly ever'. That very year, in fact, Parkes helped to give birth to an entirely different sort of association, one with narrower but better conceived and articulated goals springing from his clearest vision of social regeneration. Moreover none of its founders conceived of it as a stepping-stone for personal aggrandizement. One sunny, summer afternoon, under a pear tree at Barley, prominent members of the two broad Western faiths met to launch the Council of Christians and Jews. For its national secretary they selected the Reverend W. W. Simpson, a Methodist cleric and the same man who nine years earlier had so vehemently opposed Parkes on the issue of missionary outreach to Jews.[31] Parkes wrote:

> I was often asked in its early days whether I did not think that *I* should have been invited to fill the post which I had done so much to bring into existence. My reply always was that I would have wrecked the Council in a month. Nor can I disagree with those who consider this estimate of my patience and diplomacy rather exaggerated, and who consider that a week is the maximum I would have borne the frustrations, the necessary compromises, the dilatory verbosity, which W. W. [Simpson] has surmounted with unruffled patience for a generation – and still looks relatively young in spite of it![32]

Over the years 'W. W.' became one of Parkes' closest friends and most trusted associates. In marked contrast to all the defunct organizations of the era, the CCJ today functions as a viable body, so indispensable that, had it ceased to exist, it would surely have to be reinvented.

Parkes recounts a monitory tale that illustrates, particularly during periods of social disruption, just how vital the role of the CCJ in the fabric of British society has been. A number of times during the war there were sporadic outbreaks of antisemitism throughout East Anglia and Hertfordshire. The secretary of the Jewish Board of Deputies appealed to Parkes and the CCJ to investigate a fantastic complaint it had received from one village: Jewish expectant mothers who had been evacuated and now lived among them were in fact prostitutes who 'immediately put on their war paint to seduce the innocent countrymen'.[33]

Taking immediate note of incongruities in this tale, Parkes,

> ... made straight for the vicar of Bishop's Stortford. I learned from him that Bishop's Stortford had received no evacuees ... but there was a crying scandal ... in the neighbouring village of Ugley ... I pursued the story for the best part of the day from Ugley to Stansted Mountfichet, from thence to Manuden, from Manuden to Widdington, from Widdington to Newport, and so on. In every case the scandal was firmly believed in, but it never had happened in that actual village ...[34]

Around the same time word began to filter to the West about the extent and enormity of the Shoah. The grim irony was that a great many inhabitants of Britain's Bishop's Stortfords, Ugleys, Liverpools and Hulls preferred not to credit what they heard.[35]

At this juncture Parkes turned out two poignant and timely articles, both plainly originating from a tortured conscience. Among a stream of similar pieces in the early 1940s, these stand out. In January 1943 'The Massacre of the Jews' issued an impassioned plea for Britain to admit all Jews who reached safety in Turkey. The choice, as Parkes put it, lay between 'future vengeance or present help'. In the second piece, 'Christianity and Jewry' (22 July, 1943) Parkes, connecting the dots and drawing unequivocal conclusions, laid the blame for the onset of the Shoah at the door of the Church: 'I am not exaggerating – Christian responsibility for the whole thing. The Christian Church is the creator of antisemitism.'[36] However both articles were so provocatively out of keeping with wartime British opinion that neither ever saw publication.

In May of 1944 Parkes published 'I Talk to Two Audiences: Meditation of a Christian on Judaism, Meditation on Judaism from the Outside' in a Jewish journal. In it he averred, 'I am not a controversialist, though I am an orthodox Christian. [It does not follow, however, that] I must desire to convert the Jews from the present form of their religion to the present form of mine.' In short, Parkes fully accepted Judaism as a 'civilization whose central message is not salvation but a way of life' and reaffirmed that 'the Incarnation in Torah is equal to the Incarnation of Jesus. Christianity has not comprehended the significance that Jesus was a Jew, that his religion was Judaism.'[37] At every opportunity affirming his solidarity with Jews and Judaism, later that year he attended a conference of American Jewish Chaplains in London.[38]

With the war drawing to a close, Penguin published *An Enemy of the People: Antisemitism* in its 'World Affairs' series. This slim, eloquent work represented a distillation of many years of Parkes' thought and research. Starting with the late nineteenth century, Parkes sketched a concise account of how antisemitism had been exploited for political purposes by the governments of the major European states. Turning to Nazi Germany, he illustrated how antisemitism 'was woven into every strand of thought and action' and took on an independent life of its own.[39] The real heart of the book, however, was a crystalline chapter entitled 'Psychology and Sociology of Antisemitism'. The man who had devoted ...

> ... a wearying day careering from village to village in the Cambridgeshire countryside had accumulated enviable expertise in the aetiology of antisemitism. His analysis detailed how 'Hitler created a world-wide feeling of insecurity ... In such times the sense of danger causes a group to coalesce and close its ranks; and its fears make it look with suspicion on the outsider.'[40]

An early chapter of Parkes' new study traced *The Protocols of the Elders of Zion* to a pamphlet entitled 'The Mystery of Jewry', a 'farrago of nonsense' that was forged and first promulgated by Tsarist agents stationed in Paris in 1895. Sergei Nilus edited its first printed edition in 1905, but the full story of its genesis remained, Parkes remarked, 'completely shrouded by mystery'.[41] Parkes was later contacted by Henri Rollin, an elderly French historian who specialized in the covert influence of Russia on European politics in the years preceding the First World War. Rollin informed Parkes that the author of the *Protocols* was a certain Elie de Cyon who first obliquely adumbrated its theme in *L'Apocalypse de Notre Temps*.

The Nazis thought that they had succeeded in destroying all copies of de Cyon's book. Before Rollin himself could return to Paris to try to convince de Cyon's widow to release the papers which would have verified his discovery, he died, but not before informing Parkes where he had hidden several copies of de Cyon's pernicious forgery. In addition to his scholarly interest in this matter, we recall that Parkes' involvement with the *Protocols* also bore a personal dimension.[42] Immediately after the war, with the help of Alfred Wiener, the director of London's Jewish Information Institute, Parkes located and secured copies of Rollin's work for his own collection.[43]

'The Elimination of Antisemitism', the concluding chapter of *An Enemy of the People,* reflects Parkes' familiarity with Rollin's work, but it also reveals the limitations of even Parkes' mastery of his lifelong subject. 'However controversial the Palestinian question may be,' he declared, 'it cannot be dodged. Jewish interest in the country is not merely sentimental ... Palestine [needs to be] made capable of fulfilling the needs of large numbers of Jews.'[44] Had Parkes uncritically accepted the classical Zionist proposition that antisemitism would, like the Marxist conception of the capitalist state, wither away when Jews constituted themselves as a normal people living in a normal state? A superficial reading of *An Enemy of the People* gave some people this impression. Recent history, however, lends support to an inversion of this thesis. In any event, with or without a Jewish state, the last half-century has demonstrated the perdurability, the tenacity, and the protean nature of the 'Jewish problem'.

In contrast to the dubious aspects of his service during the First World War, Parkes could recall his performance on the home front during the Second World War confident that he had acquitted himself very well. This time he felt no compulsion to skip over whatever happened at the 'bottom of the skip'; even his father would have had no grounds for fault. Over and beyond his duties and obligations, Parkes had been reasonably productive as a writer. Unfortunately, these years were also punctuated by several false starts and misfires. In contrast to the focus and momentum of the previous decade, we are struck by the diffusion of Parkes' scholarly energies.

The privations of the wartime years – shortages of petrol, eggs, paper, virtually everything and anything that consumers craved – cast a pall over the publishing trade. Nevertheless, when *An Enemy of the People* appeared in an American edition, for a change it netted Parkes a fair profit.[45]

For the most part, the publishing fate of *The Emergence of the Jewish Problem* may be viewed as emblematic. Originally commissioned by Chatham House, then much postponed, it was a very long time in preparation. When finally completed, the directors of Chatham House found it too biased in favour of a Jewish national home to countenance publishing it under its trendy logo. It would appear a year after the end of the war under the prestigious imprint of Oxford University Press, but this made for an even sadder show. In-house displeasure with Parkes' Zionist theme effectively sabotaged efforts actually to market their own book. When Parkes made an inquiry, the publisher reported selling all of seventy-five copies in America! Even more curiously, in England the title was listed as 'out of print' before it was ever distributed to bookshops. Oxford University Press could not even bring itself to deliver a few mock-ups to its distraught author.[46] Saves the trouble of shredding, huh!

NOTES

1. Bernard Wasserstein, 'The British Government and German Immigration 1933–1945', in *The Nazi Holocaust: Bystanders to the Holocaust*, Vol. 8, ed. Michael R. Marrus (London: Meckler, 1989), pp. 397, 400, ff.
2. James Parkes, *Voyages of Discoveries* (London: Victor Gollancz, 1969), p. 169.
3. Ibid., p. 170, ff.
4. Ibid., p. 166.
5. Dorothy Wickings Parkes, *Autobiography*, Parkes Archives, File 60/33/3.
6. Parkes, *Voyages of Discoveries*, p. 167.
7. *Vide* Chapter 15.
8. Parkes, *Voyages of Discoveries*, p. 167.
9. *Vide* Chapter 24.
10. Parkes, *Voyages of Discoveries*, p. 167.
11. Ibid., pp. 168–69.
12. Ibid., p. 168. Apart from a passing reference to James Bond, this impetigo outbreak occasions the only allusion to popular culture in Parkes' memoir.
13. Ibid., p. 181.
14. Ibid., p. 186.
15. Conrad Hoffman letter to James Parkes, Parkes Archives, 22 July 1941, File 60/17/8.
16. James Parkes letter to Conrad Hoffman, File 60/17/8.
17. Parkes letter to Ernest Westmore, Parkes Archives, File 60/33/3.
18. Parkes Archives, File 60/33/3.
19. *Vide* Chapter 16.
20. Dorothy Wickings Parkes, *Autobiography*, p. 48, Parkes Archives, File 60/33/3.
21. Entitled 'Antisemitism', it was republished in 1945. Parkes Archives, File 60/9/7/2.
22. James Parkes, *Voyages of Discoveries*, pp. 141–42.
23. Dorothy Wickings Parkes, *Autobiography*.
24. *Vide* Chapter 12.
25. Parkes, *Voyages of Discoveries*, pp. 182–83, ff.
26. Dorothy Wickings Parkes, *Autobiography*.
27. Parkes, *Voyages of Discoveries*, pp. 183–84.
28. James Parkes, *Apologia pro vita mea in rebus publicis versata 1942*. Parkes Archives, File 60/4/1, f.
29. *Vide* Chapter 11.
30. Dorothy Wickings Parkes, *Autobiography*.
31. *Vide* Chapter 17.
32. Parkes, *Voyages of Discoveries*, p. 175.
33. Ibid., p. 172.
34. Ibid., p. 173.
35. One passingly notes a further irony here. For the villagers, credence in a tale about predatory Jewish women exercising special powers was plainly rooted in the atavistic survival of a belief in witchcraft. Parkes displays no consciousness of any tension between a benign tolerance for the quaint survival of this folk tradition on his native Guernsey and his alacrity at its recrudescence among English villagers many years later.
36. James Parkes, 'Christianity and Jewry', 22 July 1943, Parkes Archives, File 60/9/5.
37. James Parkes, 'I Talk to Two Audiences: Meditation of a Christian on Judaism, Meditation on Judaism from the Outside', May 1944, *The Metsudah*, Parkes Archives, File 60/9/5/12.
38. Parkes Archives, File 60/9/20.
39. James Parkes, *An Enemy of the People: Antisemitism* (Hammondsworth: Penguin, 1945), p. 56.

40. Ibid., p. 93.
41. Ibid., pp. 36–37.
42. *Vide* Chapter 19.
43. Parkes, *Voyages of Discoveries,,* p. 143.
44. Parkes, *An Enemy of the People*, p. 131. By 'Palestine', Parkes was of course referring to the Jewish homeland.
45. Parkes, *Voyages of Discoveries*, p. 181.
46. Ibid., p. 180.

PART 5
POST-WAR

28

Paradise Lost,
Palestine Regained

After centuries of relative isolation, the Channel Islands sidled unenthusiastically back on to the world's stage in June 1940 as the only British soil to undergo the trials of enemy occupation. Because the German high command considered these tiny island specks a trial run for the later conquest of Britain, unlike the fate of lands overrun in Eastern Europe, theirs was a 'soft' subjugation. Nevertheless, Hitler expended an extravagant amount of manpower and considerable *matériel* to fortify their defences against an anticipated British offensive.

The British assault never materialized. Just as though their fate roused no greater concern in British breasts than that of Jews at Auschwitz, the islanders, who by the last year of the war were practically starving, were utterly overlooked. Communication between the Islands and Britain was so erratic that after Germany finally capitulated, the Allies had no idea whether the occupying force even knew it, and there was real apprehension that it might choose to fight on alone.[1]

Like Rochefort, the Saint-Nazaire pocket west of Nantes, and other bypassed German strongholds along the coast of France,[2] the Channel Islands were not liberated until after the surrender of the German general staff on 7 May. The following day two small landing parties set out from Plymouth, one for Jersey, the other for Guernsey to ascertain the situation. Only on 12 May did a British force land on Guernsey and quarter the German commander-in-chief for the islands as a prisoner on H.M.S. *Faulkner*.[3]

Several weeks later Parkes boarded a packet boat at Southampton for the five-hour trip to Guernsey. He lodged at a guesthouse that during the war had been requisitioned as a German officers' club. A year earlier he had been informed that his father had died. Clearly, the Germans never did connect

the old man with his nettlesome son's anti-Nazi activities.[4]
During the war Henry Parkes had boarded with a family in
the Foulin district of St Peter Port. Parkes' only personal channel for maintaining contact with his father was the Red Cross.
For reasons of caution, he fictitiously attached himself to the
English branch of the family of his father's landlady who now
recounted to Parkes his father's final days and directed him to
his grave.

Henry Parkes had buried all copies of books authored by his
son in his possession, and throughout the Occupation expressly
instructed his landlady not to communicate with him by means
of her family. These were, all things considered, prudent measures. The sire of such an early and conspicuous anti-Nazi activist
was, after all, surely at risk. All the same, the picture of an ageing
father disinclined to assume the relatively minor risk of occasionally sending a coded communication to his only surviving son
while simultaneously burying evidence of his very existence is
profoundly disturbing. To Parkes it could only have been hurtful.
So long separated in so many ways, in the end Parkes experienced
as much relief as sorrow at the passing of the figure who had
occupied a central place in his psychic universe. At the same
time, a piece of himself had died as well.

An unobtrusive detail suggests the persistence of Parkes'
latent hostility towards his father. Early during the Occupation
Henry Parkes' birthplace on the 'mainland' assumed potentially
dire implications. In September 1941, in retaliation for British
internment of German nationals in Iran, Hitler personally ordered
the deportation of large numbers of British-born residents of the
Channel Islands to internment camps in Germany. Originally
only those between the ages of sixteen and seventy had been
targeted, but by the time this order was executed a year later
– as long as they safely could, the German authorities on the
Channel Islands had procrastinated – criteria for removal to
Germany no longer explicitly excluded the elderly.[5]

In September 1942, with just a single day's notice, 825
Guerneysites readied themselves for deportation to Germany.
Early in 1943 a smaller party followed.[6] Henry Parkes, then
in his seventies, was not among the deportees, arguing that a
combination of age and poor health rendered him ineligible or
unfit to travel. Still, according to the letter of the regulations, he
had certainly been in peril. As if absentmindedly, Parkes neglects

to mention his father's vulnerability to a most unpleasant contingency.

Despite, or rather because of their chequered relationship, it is hard to imagine that Parkes had not at times fantasized some sort of final *rapprochement*. Both circumstances and the fixed posture of the protagonists militated against this final act ever being played. Like a biblical Isaac, Henry Parkes died quietly off-stage. Instead of a blessing, he bequeathed his son a small inheritance. Since the total earnings of the Parkes household during 1946–47 would come to exactly £713,[7] this proved most welcome. In fact this modest windfall would secure the couple's financial independence for close to two years, a welcome salve for consciences that were keyed to the needs and tribulations of the world's Jews: '... it would have been shameful for two Christians,' Parkes muses, 'to keep a nice safe nest egg to themselves and live on Jewish funds when they did not need to.'[8]

When not settling his father's affairs, Parkes visited the Ozannes, the Careys and a few other old acquaintances. He had already absorbed a full account of the years of Occupation from a special edition of the *Guernsey Evening Press,* but now he heard first-hand about the stress and extreme hardship of those final months of Occupation.

> Pathetic evidence of the enfeebled state of the island at the time of his [Parkes' father's] death was given by the granite tombstone over my mother's grave where he had been buried. The grave was on a steep slope in Foulon cemetery, and the undertaker had been able to dislodge the stone, which had then rolled down the hill, but the men were too weak to pick it up or roll it uphill again.[9]

Parkes also sensed intimations of internecine friction arising out of the equivocal conduct of some islanders during the Occupation. This tension would plague relations on the island for a long time to come.

An ugly, largely repressed story of how the Channel Islanders dealt with the handful of Jews in their midst was played out between June 1940 and May 1945. Even at the time Parkes doubtless apprehended some of it, but he could not have read a scholarly narrative of those years until Cruickshank's *The German Occupation of the Channel Islands* appeared in 1975.

Even its laundered pages revealed enough to have given the Guernseyman reason to weep, but an unblinking report on the attitudes and behaviour displayed by the Islanders towards their Jews would not be published until after Parkes' death. Had he seen it, he would have been enraged. In any account of his life, Parkes unquestionably would have sanctioned a brief historical excursus on this matter.

The majority of Jews from the Channel Islands were evacuated to Britain in June 1940, barely a week before the onset of the Occupation, but only a small minority of other islanders joined them. The departure proceeded quite differently on the two large islands. Alexander Coutanche, bailiff of Jersey, urged Jerseyites to remain, and only 6,600 out of 50,000 of them left for Britain. In contrast, Victor Carey, new on the job as bailiff of Guernsey, took no clear line; 17,000 out of 42,000 Guernseyites fled to Britain.[10]

In October 1940, when anti-Jewish legislation was introduced in Vichy and Occupied France, the *Feldkommandantur* of the Channel Islands presented the local authorities with a parallel list of anti-Jewish measures. Cruickshank opines soberly that the islanders '... could have turned the anti-Jewish laws into a test case. There were few Jews left in the Islands, and little was at stake, except a principle. If the Islanders had refused to register the legislation it would have been promulgated by decree, but at least they would have made a stand.'[11]

In his unpublished memoirs Major Sherwill, Guernsey's attorney general, recorded that 'he had satisfied himself that the few Guernsey Jews had all gone – although in fact at this time there were still four Jewesses resident in Guernsey'. He then added,

> I felt ashamed that I did not do something by way of protest to the Germans: a vital principle was at stake even if no human being in Guernsey was actually affected. The honour of refusing to concur fell to Sir Abraham Lainé who, when called on as a Jurat to vote on the matter, openly and categorically refused his assent and stated his grave objections to such a measure.[12]

At least Sherwill's moral faculty had not totally atrophied. There is no reason to doubt the genuineness of his repugnance at the supine endorsement of Nazi racist regulations by his island's own representatives. Moreover, with the lives of two captured British soldiers, both of them Guernseymen, lying in the balance, one is tempted to extend a measure of sympathetic understanding for the *Jurat*'s choosing to avoid quibbling over what appeared to be a hypothetical principle. At a later stage, however, when Jewish *Todt* workers were shipped to Guernsey to be worked to death, the legislation that island authorities themselves had so ignominiously authorized assumed a different complexion.

Although Cruickshank refers to the free hand he was given to write the story of that turbulent period, that his account was commissioned by the Committees of the States of Guernsey and Jersey in order to commemorate the twenty-fifth year of their islands' liberation plainly affected the result. Focusing exclusively on the qualms of Major Sherwill and Sir Abraham Lainé, the historian threw a blanket of silence over the equivocal role played by Guernsey's chief official – Bailiff Victor Carey. While not without considerable merit, unlike Parkes' partially subsidized works, Cruickshank's was tainted at the source and was in every sense of the word an 'official history'.

Appearing ten years after Parkes' death, a later study by Peter King provides a useful corrective to Cruickshank.

> Of the four Jewish women who remained on the island two, both natives of Austria, worked as hospital employees. They apparently had stolen away to France before the deportations and were never subsequently traced. The other two, Elizabet Fink Duquemin, another Austrian, and Elda Bauer Brouard from Italy, had married native Guernseymen. They were included among the 800 Guernsey residents who were deported to Germany in September 1942. Unlike them, however, the Jewish women were retransported to Auschwitz where they were murdered in the gas chambers.
>
> Just how diligent had Carey been in maintaining surveillance over these Jewish women for the Nazi authorities? The answer was rather slow in surfacing. Although official indices indicated that throughout the war Guernsey maintained records about Jewish matters, at the time Cruickshank was researching his history they mysteriously seemed to have vanished. However a book that Solomon Steckoll published privately in 1982, included a small fragment of

the administrative correspondence of the Guernsey Controlling Committee. Although the letters are few they are extremely important. There is no reason to think they differ in tone from those destroyed and their tone is conciliatory in the extreme.[13]

What exactly is revealed? In October 1940, a Herr Brosch enquired about a list of Jews living on Guernsey and Sark that had earlier been requested.[14] In sharp contrast to his protests to the German authorities regarding the deportation of islanders, on this matter Carey responded obsequiously: 'I can assure you that there will be no delay, so far as I am concerned, in furnishing you with the information that you require.' Just two days later, Carey informed Brosch that the list was ready. Later still, now on his own initiative, he transmitted the two Jewish women's bank statements to the Germans and gratuitously ordered Duquemin and Brouard not to enter any Guernsey restaurants.[15] Despite his craven pusillanimity, after the war Victor Carey would be awarded a knighthood.

If anything, the grovelling of senior officials on Jersey was even more contemptible. When twelve Jersey Jews complied with the locally approved directive that all Jews come forward to be registered, 'island officials made meticulous inquiries into their ancestry'. Much like the Vichy regime on the European mainland, which 'took the initiative in framing [racial] definitions [of who is a Jew] even broader than those used by German authorities and without subjection to German pressure',[16] officials on Jersey banned their Jewish population from all public places, subjected them to special curfews, and allowed them to shop only during one hour in the afternoons. In 1943 an unspecified number of Jersey's Jews were deported to their deaths.[17]

Not merely did no one publicly protest this reprehensible treatment of their Jewish neighbours, but Jersey cannot point to the words or deeds of a single native to salvage even a shred of local honour. None of the island's residents suffered pangs of conscience like Major Sherwill or could boast of the mettle of Sir Abraham Lainé. Worse still was the mendacity. After the war Alexander Coutanche had the gall to claim that during the war Jersey's Jews had not suffered. Like Victor Carey, he along with Duret Aubin, Jersey's attorney general, were duly knighted for their diligent service. Only in 1995 did a file that the Jersey

Archive Service long maintained 'had been overlooked among miscellaneous records' reveal the scandalous extent of the close local collaboration with the Nazis on Jewish matters.[18]

Today around forty Jews reside on Jersey; they support a Reform congregation. According to the same resourceful Jewish resident of Guernsey who not long ago invoked *le Clameur de Haro*,[19] at present three Jewish families and a smattering of singles permanently reside on that island.[20] Guernsey has never attracted enough Jews to support organized communal life.

Those five years of Occupation left a bitter legacy, cleaving Guernsey into opposing camps, each burdened with accusations and recriminations. Even when this writer first visited the island in 1995, he heard stories about old-timers who harboured resentment and personal grudges against persons or families who had 'cooperated' too enthusiastically with the Germans. On several future occasions Parkes would holiday with Wickings on Guernsey and Sark.[21] Still, upon departing from the unhappy, post-war island, so altered from memories of his boyhood Eden, aside from periodic visits to his parents' gravesites Parkes would feel no compelling reason ever to return to his birthplace.

On returning to Barley after his brief sojourn, Parkes set about revising two of his earlier books: Oxford University Press expressed interest in a new edition of *The Jewish Problem in the Modern World*, which had originally appeared in 1939, and the Allied governments of Occupation requested a German translation of *An Enemy of the People: Antisemitism*. Although this latter had seemed a very good idea to all concerned, sales were only moderate. As Parkes put it later, 'it was still too soon for the German people to face the terrible realities of the Final Solution'.[22]

Shortly thereafter, an Italian publisher obtained permission from OUP to translate the revised version of *The Jewish Problem in the Modern World*, but a new impasse emerged: it included a controversial updated section on the Jews in Palestine. As Parkes puts it, 'I wrote of [Foreign Secretary Ernest Bevin's anti-Zionist] policy with a great moderation, but without concealing my disagreement and regret'. This was not good enough for Oxford, a publisher that Parkes, with excellent cause, came to hold in contempt. It insisted that he rewrite the offensive passages because they were tantamount to 'fouling the British nest abroad'. Parkes balked. In the end, on the reverse side of the title page of the Italian edition was printed Oxford's timorous disclaimer of responsibility for Parkes' views about Palestine.[23]

These editorial tasks precipitated what for Parkes would be a new turn, or rather a return. During the war years his energies had largely been channelled into civic and political work appropriate to a public-spirited resident of a land threatened by attack. In exemplary fashion the Reverend J. W. Parkes, Anglican parson, performed his Christian and his christian duties, the latter subsuming Jewish-related activities such as accommodating refugees and launching the Council of Christians and Jews. In a way, Parkes' other persona – the Reverend John Hadham, genial, progressive Christian thinker – had temporarily supplanted his progenitor. With Hadham's 'retirement' and the fresh opportunities afforded by an end to hostilities, the field was clear for the resurrection of James Parkes, 'Jewish historian' and defender of the Jewish people.

His fresh look at the ill-fated *Emergence of the Jewish Problem, 1878–1939* persuaded Parkes to pursue again his original plan of producing a sequel that would trace geopolitical developments in the Middle East up to the outbreak of the Second World War. There followed a characteristic round of Machiavellian antics of the sort that seem endemic to the publishing trade. When Parkes realized 'it would be absolutely essential ... to visit Palestine for myself if I was to undertake the second volume,' he approached his old friends at left-leaning Chatham House. 'In actual fact,' he explains, 'the book never came under serious consideration, but it was through Chatham House pulling the appropriate strings that Dorothy and I were able to set out in March 1946 on the *Strathnaver* for a visit to Palestine which lasted nearly three months.'[24]

The couple, graced with an official invitation to visit Palestine as guests of the Jewish Agency, was elated by the prospect of a very grand tour of a very small land. Whether the Agency was genuinely deceived is uncertain,[25] but it made little difference. Parkes had testified for the partition of Palestine into Jewish and Arab states before the Anglo-American Committee in February.[26] The Agency judged correctly that, one way or another, bringing him to Palestine would reap positive gains for the Zionist cause.

Before sailing, Parkes remobilized his car for active duty and, again through connections, obtained enough rationed petrol actually to drive it. In order to prepare themselves for their visit to the Jewish homeland, the Parkeses wanted to make a spirited swing through Britain's Zionist hinterland. It was, Parkes mentions, Wickings' very first extensive driving tour. From Bedfordshire and Warwickshire to St Asaph in North Wales, the two of them touched base at the rural training centres where young Jews were preparing themselves for living on a kibbutz. They encountered scores of idealistic Jews who were strongly imbued with collectivist principles. While accustoming themselves to the knotty joys of group living, the young people also became acquainted with the rudiments of agriculture. Eager to join comrades already living in Palestine, they shared their enthusiasm with the middle-aged, curious, indeed most curious Christian visitors. Two years later the couple would be deeply touched upon learning that the young pioneers at St Asaph had been totally annihilated during the War of Independence.[27]

Parkes had reason to be pleased with himself. He had successfully parlayed his urge to update *The Emergence of the Jewish Problem* into a plum assignment as a V.I.P. After five wartime years of insular confinement – if we discount his North American speaking tour in 1938, actually more like a full decade of rustication – he was positively itching to sail forth again into the wider world. Israel Sieff secured passage for the couple on a ship filled with troops from the Sixth Airbourne Division heading for duty in Palestine. While Wickings shared a cabin with another woman, Parkes bunked in a cabin with thirty soldiers.[28]

Apart from the presence of his wife, a boon travelling companion, for Parkes 1946 was turning out to be 1924 revisited. The sea journey left him positively rejuvenated. He was abroad, at liberty, and positively flourishing. Even arrival at Port Said in the teeth of a sandstorm did nothing to dim the couple's gritty enthusiasm. Sorely confronted by temptation at Qantara, their first stop, they enthusiastically succumbed. Eggs, virtually unavailable in Britain since the start of the war, were piled high at market stalls. They surfeited themselves on omelettes and tangerines.[29]

They stopped next in Rehovot where they were hosted by Prof. Chaim Weizmann and his wife Vera. It was the first of several meetings between the couples in the coming months. On his return to England, Parkes would send Weizmann some tactical pointers on how best to reply to the British government about the recommendations of the Anglo-American Committee:

a) Most urgent is admission of 100,000 Jewish refugees.
b) Absorption of the 100,000 will engage the energies of many now engaged in terrorism against the British.
c) Jewish Agency would be prepared to discuss modification of Land Regulations.[30]

Also staying with the Weizmanns was Sir Simon Marks. This turned out to be a most fortunate encounter for Parkes as Marks grandly took it upon himself to cover all of the historian's book purchases in Palestine. It is hard to imagine a gesture more likely to endear one to Parkes for all eternity. As with eggs and tangerines, so too with books: Jerusalem's second-hand bookshops were glutted with a wartime accumulation, and Parkes' overindulgence would set Sir Simon back to the tune of many hundreds of pounds.[31]

Finally arriving in the Holy City, the couple was set up in upmarket quarters in the fashionable Rehavia district, a frequent meeting ground for British officials, Jewish Agency members and Hebrew University academics. However their first Sunday in the Holy Land was neither for socializing nor for divine service. Rousted early in the morning by Gershon Agronsky, the founder and first editor of the *Jerusalem Post,* they hurtled north out of Jerusalem in the direction of Metulla, the northernmost point in the country. En route they passed through Nablus, Jenin, Tiberias, and skirted the Sea of Galilee at Safed. Turning west, they saw Nazareth, Hadera, Ramle, and the Mediterranean coast – all in all an expedition of over three hundred miles. Apart from the island landscape of his boyhood, Parkes' enthusiasm for the Palestinian countryside can be compared only to the ardour of the footloose young Guernseyman set upon wandering the length and breadth of Provence.

The couple would be even more impressed by visits to over thirty kibbutzim in all parts of the land. Disdaining reliance upon their guide's rehearsed explanations and standard anecdotes, they insisted upon spending the better part of every day speaking to residents and figuring out for themselves how communal social, economic, and political arrangements operated in practice. Several times they re-encountered young English Jews whom they had met in their peregrinations around Britain. Particularly beguiled by the kibbutzim of the Modern Orthodox Movement, they spent their longest stretch of time at two of their collective settlements: one near the Sea of Galilee, the other in the Etzion bloc of settlements, just south of Bethlehem.

Wickings, better than her husband at recording concrete impressions, was captivated by the country. She was smitten by the staff and youngsters at a girls' agricultural school and found celebrating Passover on Kibbutz Deganya Aleph – especially 'The Song of Songs' sung in Hebrew – 'a wonderful experience'. She was moved at Kibbutz Kfar Blum, founded by English immigrants, which was in mourning over the death of an infant, and she was deeply touched by the sensitivity shown to Holocaust survivors at Kibbutz Deganya Bet.[32] Hannah Chisuck's rehabilitation programme with orphans in a children's village at Ben-Shemen, Helena Kagan's work with children of all the communities in Jerusalem, the dedication of pioneering residents of the new city of Holon in carting barrow-loads of earth to make themselves gardens – Wickings' journal is punctuated with praise and wonder at the achievements of the pioneering society.[33] Topping it all, she even spotted copies of *Good God* for sale in bookshops in Jerusalem.

Parkes, meanwhile, had entrée to virtually everyone worth talking to, and the British cleric charmed them all save, true to form, for one notable exception – Bishop Stewart, the Anglican prelate of the city. Stewart, who spoke fluent Arabic but not a word of Hebrew, consistently took the Arab view of the conflict; nevertheless, Parkes granted, he '... tried his best to be fair to the various aspects of the work of Jerusalem ... [which] included Christian–Jewish relationships as well as Christian–Arab relationships'.[34] When Parkes unwisely let slip that the Jewish Agency had paid his fare, the Bishop scornfully rejoined: 'That is a pity, Dr Parkes.' He also fended off Parkes' offer to officiate at any Anglican church in the country for the Easter holiday.

During that first, hectic week in the country, Parkes also met Dr Judah Magnes, the chancellor of Hebrew University, and throughout his stay he enjoyed long meals, talks and walks with many HU professors. He spent, for example, an entire day talking with philosopher Martin Buber at his flat, an experience, Parkes hints, in some ways reminiscent of the fried eggs at Qantara: while affirming that *I and Thou* 'had created a new epoch in philosophical thinking of universal significance', Parkes also comments that 'Buber's thought is nearly always most penetrating at its briefest'.[35] Nevertheless, Parkes credits his exchange with Buber for helping him to resolve a long-term quandary: how could Christianity genuinely save individual souls while at the same time making such a wreckage of civilization?

It was during this visit to Palestine that Parkes arrived at a clear recognition that would inform much of his mature theological thinking: by its separation from Judaism, Christianity had lost a vital dimension.[36] Reshaping an idea he had first conceived and launched in London in 1944 at a conference of American chaplains, in his Hebrew University lectures Parkes '... affirmed the equality of the two religions, their need of each other, and the impossibility of either absorbing the other.'[37] Particularly by religiously observant academics this truly radical formulation, a natural extension of his previous ideas, was received with enormous excitement. A perennial outsider in the British Christian establishment, among the Jewish intellectual elite of Palestine Parkes was accorded the respect due an intellectual of the first rank. The prophet away from home was, of course, inordinately gratified.

Beyond university circles, Parkes was granted ready access to the Jewish political leadership as well. He encountered Histadrut Labour leaders Golda Myerson (Meir) and Itzhak Ben-Zvi in Tel Aviv and spoke on many occasions with Moshe Shertok (Sharett), later the State of Israel's first foreign minister and second prime minister. He chatted as well with the suave Sharett's charismatic opposite – Dayan, the other Moshe. The dashing Dayan had recently returned from the United States where he had undergone eye surgery. The only significant public figure Parkes seems not to have met was David Ben-Gurion.

Parkes spent considerable time conferring with British administrators who felt stretched to the limit by the intractability of the conflict. What struck him was how few of these careerists had any appreciation of what lay behind the Jewish perspective on the Palestine conflict. Parkes did his best to fill in the gaps in their education. Missing from Parkes' recollections is any effort to interact with local Arab leadership; nor does it seems that the Anglican cleric was particularly inspired by visits to any of the usual Christian pilgrim sites. To all intents and purposes, Parkes' three-month visit to Palestine not merely confirmed but intensified his identification with the Zionist cause.

One final encounter in Jerusalem that would affect Parkes' immediate future bears mention: during his activist days in

Geneva, Parkes had met the American Reform leader, Rabbi Stephen Wise. Meeting again in Jerusalem, Wise invited Parkes to deliver the prestigious Charles William Eliot lectures at the Jewish Institute of Religion in New York that December. Parkes accepted on the spot. Wickings in particular was immensely excited at the prospect of her first transatlantic trip. Before that, however, a more immediate transportation affair lay before them: obtaining passage back to Britain seemed quite impossible. After much ado, they secured places aboard a military air transport for what would be his wife's first flight ever. Since weight was a critical factor, their baggage would have to come separately, so it would be some while before Parkes' would unpack and lovingly sort his most recent acquisitions for his book collection at Barley.

NOTES

1. Charles Cruickshank, *The German Occupation of the Channel Islands: The Official History of the Occupation Years* (Guernsey: The Guernsey Press, 1975), p. 260, ff.
2. Robert Gildea, *Marianne in Chains: Daily Life in the Heart of France During the German Occupation* (New York: Metropolitan, Holt, 2002), pp. 350–52.
3. Ibid., p. 298. Also *vide* Chapter 36.
4. James Parkes, *Voyage of Discoveries* (London: Victor Gollancz, 1969), pp. 187–88.
5. Cruickshank, *The German Occupation of the Channel Islands*, p. 218, ff.
6. Asa Briggs, *The Channel Islands: Liberation and Occupation, 1940–1945* (London: Batsford and the Imperial War Museum, 1995), p. 56.
7. Dorothy Wickings Parkes, *Autobiography*, Parkes Archives, File 60/33/3.
8. Parkes, *Voyage of Discoveries*, p. 191.
9. Ibid., pp. 187–88.
10. Cruickshank, *The German Occupation of the Channel Islands*, pp. 58–59.
11. Ibid., p. 113.
12. Ibid.
13. Peter King, *The Channel Islands War* (London: Robert Hale, 1991), p. 153, ff.
14. Ibid. The two Jewish women on Sark managed to evade registration temporarily, but eventually they too suffered the fate of Guernsey's Jewish women.
15. King, *The Channel Islands War*, p. 154.
16. Michael Curtis, *Verdict on Vichy* (New York: Arcade, 2003), p. 113.
17. Madeline Bunting, *Manchester Guardian Weekly*, 19 April 1995, p. 7.
18. Ibid.
19. *Vide* Chapter 4.
20. Paul Moed in conversation with the author on Guernsey, July 1995.
21. Parkes, *Voyage of Discoveries*, p. 215.
22. Ibid., p. 188.
23. Ibid., pp. 188–89.
24. Ibid., p. 189.
25. For the period in question, the official archives of the Jewish Agency have not yet been catalogued.
26. James Parkes, Parkes Archives, File 60/9/6/15.
27. Dorothy Wickings Parkes, *Autobiography*, Parkes Archives, File 60/33/3.
28. Parkes, *Voyage of Discoveries*, pp. 189–90.
29. Dorothy Wickings Parkes, *Autobiography*, Parkes Archives, File 60/33/3.

30. James Parkes letter to Chaim Weizmann, 24 May 1946, Parkes Archives, File 60/17/42.
31. Parkes, *Voyage of Discoveries*, p. 190, ff.
32. Dorothy Wickings Parkes, *Autobiography*, Parkes Archives, File 60/33/3.
33. Parkes, *Voyage of Discoveries*, pp. 195–96.
34. Venerable Whitton Davies, *Tributes in Memory of James William Parkes* at Bournemouth Hebrew Congregation, Southampton, 1981, Parkes Archives.
35. Parkes, *Voyage of Discoveries*, p. 193.
36. Parkes Archives, File 60/17/42.
37. Parkes, *Voyage of Discoveries*, p. 192, ff.

29

He Also Speaks as a Jew

Early in 1947, immediately upon his return from Palestine, Parkes set to work *not* on pushing *The Emergence of the Jewish Problem, 1878–1939* chronologically forward – his original plan – but on backdating it. By the time it would reach print in 1949 as *A History of Palestine From 135 A.D. to Modern Times*, its origins would effectively be fully masked. In the midst of these editorial toils, Parkes received an urgent appeal from the government's Bureau of Current Affairs to produce a pamphlet on Palestine for immediate distribution to British military personnel. Seizing what seemed a splendid opportunity not merely for an easy fee but also to reach a critical audience, Parkes unhesitatingly complied. His aim, as he recalls, was to strike a scrupulously balanced approach to the subject, but that certainly was not what the Bureau could have anticipated or desired. Indeed, in the entire affair it is difficult to decide which of the parties acted with a greater degree of perversity.

In the first place, one wonders how a government agency fixed upon James Parkes, of all people, to turn out a hatchet job on Zionism. Of course it rejected Parkes' 'pro-Zionist' pamphlet out of hand. If Parkes had given the matter the least bit of thought, he would have guessed that what the Attlee government craved was 'a description of Zionism [that] should at every point arouse hostility or contempt'.[1] In the end the Bureau found someone else to cook up a hastily produced tract in accord with the pro-Arabist leanings of Ernest Bevin. But that was not the end of the matter. Parkes alerted his Jewish friends at the War Office to the situation, and they in turn succeeded in suppressing most of its intended circulation.

When not revising old copy, turning out pamphlets or jousting with bureaucrats, Parkes was seriously preoccupied with preparing the series of lectures he would deliver that winter at the Jewish Institute of Religion. Zestfully exploiting the rich, new resources he had recently snatched up from overstocked

Jerusalem bookshops, his thrust was to clarify and further develop the ideas he had fielded with such success in his lectures at Hebrew University. His goal was to disclose a multifaceted, relevant and vital Judaism, the very antithesis of the empty husk or withered limb depicted in the Gospels, Paul's Epistles and the writings of the Church Fathers.[2] The countryman-scholar aimed to dig deep beneath the surface among the twisted, half-hidden roots that still nourished the perennial conflict between Judaism and Christianity.

His choice of topic was not haphazard. As if the rise of Nazism had taught the world nothing, an insidious, grotesque distortion of Judaism was once more abroad in the land having achieved general currency and legitimatization through the immense success of Arnold Toynbee's series, *A Study of History*. Parkes aimed to neutralize the effect of Toynbee's flawed, unenlightened insistence that Judaism was nothing more than 'a fossil of Syriac civilization' utterly refuting his pernicious premise about the nature of Judaism.[3] In fact the two historians had known each other for a number of years, and on occasion Parkes had hosted Toynbee at Barley. However just as he refused to allow fundamental differences to blight his relationship with Conrad Hoffman – at least not utterly – Parkes now strove to maintain at least a façade of cordial relations with Toynbee.[4]

In his introduction to the Eliot lectures, Parkes succinctly and provocatively personalized his argument:

> I speak as a Christian, as one who believes in the essential truth of fundamental Christian doctrine, but in a sense I also speak as a Jew. That is, I speak on the basis of believing Judaism also to be true – as true as Christianity … Both religions are true. Neither is simply an incomplete form of the other; and I do not desire to see either disappear, even by conversion to the other … Sinai and Calvary [are] two closely interlocked and complementary stages of a single divine plan … In Judaism and Christianity together the 'I–Thou' relationship of a free creation is ultimately fulfilled. But in each is an essential part fulfilment, and until there appears the way by which they can fulfil the two together without losing their own essential nature, each must fulfil its own part.[5]

Later, focusing again on the specifically Pauline points of stress that led to the historical divergence between the faiths, Parkes reiterated,

> ... conflict between Jesus and the Pharisees [was] not based on the 'un-Jewishness' of the teachings of Jesus, but on the rejection of contemporary developments in Pharisaic inter-pretation ... It is wrong to say there is a fundamental contradiction between Jesus and Paul. But Paul himself must be held primarily responsible for the fact that instead of a gradual and peaceful development without schism, a violent break between the two faiths took place. It cannot be said too often or too strongly that antisemitism is a Gentile, and pre-eminently a Christian problem. It is not a Jewish problem.[6]

For anyone closely following the development of Parkes' thought, these are not unfamiliar ideas, but their articulation is now more precise. Even more than half a century later, for not a few thought-ful, mainstream Christians they remain deeply disturbing notions.

Parkes concluded his lecture notes with a summary of the con-trasting bases of the two faiths and their subsequent dynamic:

> The Christian assumed that the religious man would act aright, and did not trouble continually to explore and to teach him the nature of right action. Judaism assumed that right acting men would believe aright, and did not trouble continually to argue with them about the nature or activities of God.[7]

Note that whereas for Parkes praxis that follows normative Christian belief entails a critical blind spot, shortcomings devolving from basic Jewish assumptions about man's relation to God, if shortcomings indeed they be, are relatively benign.

Far less premeditated than his public remarks or published discourse, however, Parkes' correspondence over this period discloses an example of what at first glance might be construed as open-mindedness but on further consideration appears to be an atavistic tic. His correspondent recalls a lecture in which Parkes 'incidentally stated that although it is absurd to think that the Jewish religion ever demanded the use of human blood for

religious purposes, yet it is certainly possible that individual
Jews did use human blood for the purpose of witchcraft'.[8] Instead
of exploiting the opportunity to clear the air by treating this
notion dismissively as one might have expected, the man who
sought to quash the rumour that Jewish women were engaged
in witchcraft displays a shocking residual receptivity to its
implications: 'I have never been sure that the ritual murder
accusation is untrue, *as a ritual murder accusation involving Judaism*
covers the facts as completely as Jewish opinion suggests' (italics
supplied).[9]

As James Shapiro, an astute cultural commentator, has plain-
tively queried: 'Why have these English writers continued to find
this myth so irresistible?'[10] He locates the vitality of this hoary
canard in the symbolic slide from circumcision to castration to
sexual indeterminacy that governs, for example, Shakespeare's
multifaceted exploitation of the pound of flesh in *The Merchant
of Venice*. Embedded in the English psyche, it seems that not even
a James Parkes was fully immune to this dangerous twaddle.

Far less *outré* was Parkes' fecund conception of Judaism as a
procreative religion, fresh aspects of which surfaced during the
course of his research for the Eliot lectures. Especially palatable
for an audience of Reform Jews, this motif would later develop
into one of his central themes: 'Judaism was just as much a missionary religion as Christianity. True, it did not attempt to make
converts of individual Christians, but in every society in which
Jews were admitted to citizenship they sought to mould the life
of the community one stage nearer to the messianic ideal.'[11] One
can only speculate how Parkes might have reacted to the resurgence of a more aggressive Judaism which, inverting Parkes'
'trickle-down' model of its societal mission, had reverted to the
pre-Christian era approach of actively reaching out for potential
converts. In recent years some voices, especially in the Diaspora,
alarmed by Jewish demographic trends, have outspokenly
endorsed such a strategy.

The time came round for the couple's American adventure.
However space on transatlantic transports in the winter of 1946
was still so limited that it took the intervention of the American
ambassador to obtain passage for the Reverend and Mrs James
Parkes. Along with a shipload of British war brides and babies,
the two sailed in December. On arriving in Manhattan, they glee-
fully took temporary possession of Rabbi Stephen Wise's luxury

apartment overlooking Central Park, as the rabbi was then out of the country. Ever strapped for ready cash, the couple had grown accustomed to sharp fluctuations of fortune. When travelling, their style of accommodation depended entirely upon the magnanimity of whoever was footing the bill.

As always, Parkes' first order of business in a new city was to locate a suitable, Anglican-affiliated church. He stumbled upon one just around the corner from Wise's apartment, and the spiky Guernseyman took care not to scandalize the Episcopalian rector. In contrast to previous travails among doughty Anglicans on overseas duty in Geneva, Dresden, and Jerusalem, in Manhattan the friend of the esteemed Rabbi Wise was received with conspicuous honour – and then accorded honours. Upon completion of his Eliot lectures, the Jewish Institute of Religion conferred an honorary doctorate on its distinguished visitor. Eighteen months later the JIR, which today enjoys a kind of half-life existence under the auspices of the Yeshiva University's Center for Jewish History, merged with Hebrew Union College in Cincinnati, flagship institution for the Reform Movement and the next stop on Parkes' tour.[12]

Apart from his early days in Geneva, when he was forced to skim odd francs from his exiguous salary in order to purchase rare items for his Jewish library, Parkes could reliably depend upon the generosity of benefactors such as Sir Simon Marks in Jerusalem. In North America, Maurice Blinken stepped forward to cover his acquisitions. In short, with substantially more than a little help from his friends, Parkes' collection enjoyed steady, if not spectacular growth. In breadth, of course, it could not begin to compare with the Judaica collection at Hebrew Union College, but when Parkes requested that a number of books and pamphlets which he planned to mention in his lecture be put on display, the HUC librarian could not oblige him. It was then, Parkes warrants, that he was struck powerfully by a realization of the real worth of his own Jewish collection that sat on his bookshelves in Barley.[13]

In fact, Parkes exaggerates his Cincinnati epiphany, as he must have had earlier intimations that his collection of printed Jewish material was of world class standing. Nevertheless, this confirmation was most welcome. The accommodation of this auspicious collection had, like the tail that wags the dog, significantly affected his choice of residence when he returned to

England in 1935. Constantly growing, transcending its strictly functional purposes, bearer of the Parkes name, it would with the passage of time play an increasingly important role in determining his future plans as well.[14]

At the University of Chicago the views of the visiting British theologian were received with great interest, and arrangements were made for publication of the Eliot Lectures by the university's prestigious press. All in all, this was another heady time for Parkes. In Britain a maverick clergyman, an unaffiliated scholar and an outspoken philosemite, Parkes was too exotic to be fully respectable. Both in Palestine and America, however, the Reverend Doctor James W. Parkes was a much-esteemed historian-theologian, an intellectual celebrity of the first order.

Of course America has its own way of treating visiting luminaries. An unusually self-deprecating Parkes recalls an unctuous radio presenter in Chicago who concluded their interview thus: 'You hear what a kick I got out of talking to Dr James Parkes. I get just the same kick out of X's shaving cream, the whisker-wilting shaving cream.'[15] Getting her own kicks off-mike, Wickings laughed herself silly.

Following a stopover in Buffalo and a detour to gaze at the weirdly static, frozen falls at Niagara, the jolly pair arrived in Manhattan where they very soon grew accustomed to another kind of creamy kick. After long days of copying, typing, and editing manuscripts, the two adjourned nightly to a *gemütlich café* on West 72nd Street where they sipped nightcaps of Viennese coffee *mit shlag* accompanied by delectable cheesecake. This had turned out to be Parkes' most gratifying lecture tour in another respect as well: his earnings much exceeded expectations. He earned enough, in fact, for them 'to do up the house' upon their return to Barley.[16]

On their voyage home on the *America*, we are informed that Wickings underwent her first Atlantic gale.[17] This otherwise pointless titbit caps a series of other 'Debuts for Dorothy' in 1946. It was perhaps the case that at this time emotional and physical intimacy was heightened also. That is to say, if four years earlier Charles Singer's commodious Cornwall home, a place filled with 'wisdom and knowledge and of true spiritual refreshment',[18] had imbued their official honeymoon with an Apollonian aura, only now does intimacy and sensual exuberance seem genuinely to suffuse their relationship.

Emerging from the shadow of wartime rationing, discarding the grey cape of spectral John Hadham, enthralled by Jewish renewal in Palestine, feted in Manhattan and Chicago, invigorated by his increasingly dear travelling companion's enthusiasm and delight, most remarkably even temporarily solvent, Parkes in 1946 had gone from strength to strength. It can only be viewed as a year of triumphal rejuvenescence. Predictably, its glow would fade soon enough.

Reinstalled at Barley, in addition to hosting the usual stream of interesting visitors and supervising household renovations, with the turn of the year Parkes again plunged into his Palestine project: a two thousand year history of the land that would give due account to the presence and claims of Jews, Christians and Muslims. As Parkes viewed it, historic Palestine rested upon a tripod of these monotheistic religions; it would always be inextricably bound to them all. His methodology was unchanged from the days of researching his dissertation nearly two decades earlier at Oxford: after painstakingly transcribing each note on a separate index card, he then arranged, shuffled and reshuffled until a clear, unambiguous, persuasive and verifiable pattern gradually emerged. After tracing the history of each religion's strand of occupation, Parkes found their intermingling all the more fascinating. It will come as no surprise that in the end he concluded 'the Jewish story out-topped both [of the others] in its hidden splendour'.[19]

Was this, as his critics would have it, a foregone rather than a fully justified conclusion? Perhaps. Nevertheless Parkes does decisively shatter the distorted, Christian-generated image of 'Jewish exile' that for so long permeated both sectarian and secular thinking about the course of Jewish history. His revisionist touch is both delicate and persuasive:

> Through every century there came [to Palestine] a steady and unrecorded trickle which at least kept a few communities in existence, and made it possible, from time to time, for more important numbers to come ... At times it must have sunk to very few thousands; but though the community of indigenous Jews, who could claim that their ancestors had never known exile, dwindled to a single village by the nineteenth century [i.e., Pekin in the Upper Galilee], there had grown up in its place a community ...

which represented almost all the Jewries of the world ...
which was supported in its need by all the communities in
the world, and which was regarded by Jews everywhere as
peculiarly blessed because it lived upon the holy soil itself.[20]

Perhaps what made life most sweet for Parkes during these
immediate post-war years at Barley was the steady diet of
recognition he was now accorded by Jewish friends, community
worthies and organizations.

If most men are conventionally driven by a craving for money,
power or love, Parkes' sights had always been on another plane:
the service of God by working for the general betterment of
mankind, the contrition and reform of the Church, the alleviation of the misunderstanding of Judaism and the suffering of the
Jews, and the reconciliation of the two faiths. He had taken great
risks, and he flourished best on a steady diet of recognition of
his efforts and achievement. In a sense, Parkes had been wooing
the Jews for years. Imagine his elation when in 1949 he learned
of his elevation to the presidency of the Jewish Historical Society,
only the second Gentile ever to be so honoured.[21] In his own
mind nothing could be quite as gratifying as the love and high
regard of his adoptive community.

The following year Parkes was designated the society's official
representative for the twenty-fifth anniversary ceremonies commemorating the founding of Hebrew University. Playing out his
role in Jerusalem with pride and enthusiasm, Parkes' pleasure
would not be unalloyed. Onlookers could not possibly know that
all the while he was somberly stepping in time to the measured
processional, the visitor from England was being soundly tongue-
lashed by an American Orthodox rabbi with whom he happened
to be paired. With every footfall, the rabbi *sotto voce* lambasted
Anglo-Jewry for sinking so low as to have chosen an Anglican
priest as its representative. Given the occasion, unable to launch
even a weak defence, this was one time when Parkes could not
get the better of an adversary.[22]

Throughout the late 1940s and early 1950s the Parkeses went
off together on a number of overseas excursions, most notably
in 1950 for their 'unforgettable Spring holiday in Sark'[23] and the
following year for seven nostalgic weeks on the Continent
where, mainly nosing about Provence, Parkes caught up with
the adventures of the Cru sisters under the heel of Vichy and

the Occupation.²⁴ That trip ended with a week-long stay in Strasbourg where, again in his capacity as president of the Jewish Historical Society, Parkes 'opened the *Année Culturelle* of the Jewish community'. Parkes recollects needing assistance to render his lecture 'into good French' and reports with pride that he 'was able to sustain a long discussion afterwards'.²⁵ This comes as a surprise; in spite of his Guernsey upbringing and six years' residence in Geneva, Parkes' French turns out to have been less than fully fluent.

Most of the couple's excursions were, of course, closer to home and of much shorter duration. Mainly they poked around the old churches and cemeteries, antique shops and bookshops in venerable villages along England's eastern coast. In addition, Parkes fairly frequently took off by himself on brief trips abroad to attend various conferences. In 1947, for example, he was present at the International Conference of the Council of Christians and Jews in Seelisberg, Switzerland, and a year later attended its annual gathering in Freiburg, Germany. The following spring he would be off in Switzerland for a few weeks, yet again with his embroidery and without his wife.²⁶ Similar gatherings convened nearer to home: in 1948, a few months after returning from Switzerland, Parkes was numbered among the 120 participants at a Socialist Christian Conference at Church House, Westminster, an affair that was closed to the press.²⁷

In fact Parkes' engagement calendar was perpetually marked by a meeting the next day, two more the following week in London, half a dozen around Britain during the following month, and a trip abroad in three months' time. After decades of crocheting his way through endless hours of talk at countless gatherings of various groups, as much out of habit as conviction Parkes was still soldiering on. One wonders at the indefatigability, tenacity, and resolution of the man. In spite of chronic disappointment, frequent *déjà vu* and bouts of ennui, what seems really to have impelled Parkes to carry on was the unquenchable hope that the next conference would be the one that really made a difference. Beyond this ingrained optimism, we do well to remember there was no slicker professional in the field: after all, Parkes was the author of *International Conferencing*, the most comprehensive insider's handbook on the subject.

Another local storm demonstrates that Parkes had not lost his edge. During the war he had served as the chairman of Barley's school; in its aftermath, he assumed responsibility for steering the school's adaptation to the post-war Education Act. A heated controversy developed. Parkes had refused to accept a majority decision of the school board that it should retain a connection with the local parish. He felt justified in circumventing strict democratic procedure because that decision violated what were now mandated disestablishmentarian procedures. The irony of the situation was evident to all. Resisting diocesan pressures, the Reverend Parkes held out firmly for secularist control. To his visible satisfaction, at a parish meeting with all the children's parents in attendance, his argument prevailed: it was unanimously decided that the school should realign itself from church to public control.

'This provoked a grin from the county educational authorities later, when one of them visited me and explained that they proposed to have an acre of my orchard for a proper playground which the Church could never have afforded.' The visitor, certain that Parkes must now regret his public-spirited stance, did not know his man. Without missing a beat, Parkes informed the nonplussed official that he,

> ... entirely agreed that the school should have it, but that, as chairman of the managers, [he] insisted that the owner of the property must [first] modernize his sewage system ... The county was able to satisfy both the chairman and the owner, and the acre passed to the school, giving it room for additional buildings, better sanitation, and a reasonable playground.[28]

Here we see shades of the Machiavellian whippersnapper who a quarter of a century before had acted at one and the same time as acting company officer and as adjutant, and who earlier had served simultaneously as gas officer and the schizoid 'personal me'.[29] In fact Parkes was rarely more delighted than when he could pull off a caper of this sort, not just for its own sake but especially in the service of some higher principle. We recall that at a conference in Warsaw, the same young man had cheekily represented both the British and the Ukrainian delegations.[30] In this playful division of personality we can perceive an adumbration of Parkes' most dramatic moment of self-revelation: when the distinguished Christian cleric had the wit, the courage and the bald-faced chutzpah to proclaim openly at the Jewish Institute of Religion, 'I also speak as a Jew'. After a delay of several months, was this not in effect Parkes' daring but precise *ésprit de escalier* retort to the assault of the Orthodox rabbi who had badgered him in the Hebrew University processional? His commitment to a multiplicity of identities in the name of the density of truth was not merely grasped but self-consciously affirmed.

Unexpectedly, we find ourselves confronting Parkes' primal myth of himself, one fashioned in early adolescence and reminiscent of the dualities of a Walter Mitty, an Old Testament Jacob or even a Clark Kent: the sickly, feeble island boy whose imagination choreographed epic romances in which he played the role of the knight who rights the wrongs of the world. Later in life this figure morphed into either the cleric who, as the situation dictates, assumes or dramatically lays aside his cassock or the debonair double agent in his elegant lair in Geneva. He is Parkes, aka John Hadham, almost certainly the only Gentile in the world who could not only publicly address a Jewish audience 'also as a Jew' but also reap applause for his audacity. Parkes loved the excitement, the drama and the inherent danger that accompanied enacting a double role. Some of his early parts were minor, some later ones more important, but when he finally discovered his proper métier on the world's stage, James Parkes did not fail to perform all his appointed parts with conviction and panache.

More arresting both for Parkes and his readers than an Alberto Moravia or the other distinguished personages who made their way to Barley in this period was a shadowy figure he and Wickings allegorically dubbed 'The Old Man of the Road'. Paradoxically, this anonymous wraith was so self-effacing and humble that he grew all the more conspicuous:

> Some tragedy early in life had turned him into a 'tramp', and he had been on the road since the First World War. He took great pride in keeping himself clean; he knew that he could have a bed in our 'garden house' when he wanted, that he could come to us when he felt ill, and there would always be a meal for him … He loved the country, would tell of its beauty and bring Dorothy some offering of flowers or fruit culled on his way. His visits continued until he was

too old for the road, and we found a place for him where
he died peacefully and well loved ...[31]

Apart from the obvious, just why was Parkes so taken with
this Wordsworthian spectre who had so touchingly withdrawn
from life's hurly-burly? The allusion to the First World War provides the telling clue. Where so many had been slaughtered
Parkes had survived, but not unscathed. We recall that after his
demobilization it was many months before he had sufficiently
readjusted to civilian life and was psychologically fit to go up to
Oxford.[32] Like Jake Barnes or Nick Adams, Parkes never recovered
from his own agonizing wartime disability – Dupuytren's contracture. Now afflicting his hands as well as his feet, it was at
times so painful that he had to resort to typing manuscripts with
the top of a pencil clasped in a fist he could not unclench.[33]
Dupuytren's served additionally as a natural symbol for his
enduring emotional and psychological contracture. In short,
hunching perennially not far beneath a suave, unruffled surface,
'The Old Man of the Road' embodied yet another of Parkes'
personae – a permanently wounded self.

Beyond the Old Man's unspoken tragedy, another clue to his
special appeal lies in his incessant wandering – his homelessness,
a condition that resonates with one of Parkes' central boyhood
anxieties.[34] Remarkably, this most rare Gentile, who had earned
the right to speak as a credentialled Jew, seems oblivious not only
to these personal echoes but even to the patent correspondence
between 'The Old Man of the Road' and Ahasuerus, the Jewish
Wanderer. Parkes' Abrahamic hospitality decisively undermines
the instrumentality of the myth of Ahasuerus, the homeless,
prototypical alien that medieval Christianity had fathered and
fastened as a crab-like curse to the underside of the Jewish
psyche. As the following excerpt from a classic modern Hebrew
text suggests, what Parkes may not have clearly apprehended,
his imagination had nevertheless grasped instinctively:

At midnight the girl fell into a deep sleep and dreamed she
was wandering on a lonely path. She lifted up her eyes and
saw an old man walking slowly toward her. He was carrying
a heavy burden and leaning on a staff. At first, fear shook
her very soul and she could not move. But she summoned
up her courage, and went up to him and asked who he was.

The ancient answered her saying, 'I am a Hebrew and we are walking in exile'.[35]

Fittingly, and in no small measure through Parkes' heroic efforts, in his own lifetime mainstream Christianity would jettison the meta-historical premises that had sustained the myth of the Wandering Jew. Not only was the charge of deicide exposed and dropped as a malicious and utterly spurious calumny, but the political events of 1948 spectacularly validated Parkes' thesis when, by both undoing and fulfilling history, the Jewish people proudly re-established themselves as an independent polity in their ancient homeland.

NOTES

1. James Parkes, *Voyage of Discoveries* (London: Victor Gollancz, 1969), p. 198, ff.
2. *Vide* Chapter 28.
3. Parkes Archives, File 60/9/20.
4. Parkes, *Voyage of Discoveries*, p. 178.
5. James Parkes, *Judaism and Christianity* (Chicago: University of Chicago, 1948), pp. 18–19.
6. Ibid., pp. 69–70, 107.
7. Ibid., p. 178.
8. M. J. Richman letter to James Parkes, 10 April 1946, Parkes Archives, File 60/17/42.
9. Ibid.
10. James Shapiro, *Shakespeare and the Jews* (New York: Columbia University Press, 1996), p. 102, ff.
11. Parkes, *Voyage of Discoveries*, p. 200.
12. Michael Terry, Head of Dorot Jewish Division, New York Public Library, communication in January 2003.
13. Parkes, *Voyage of Discoveries*, pp. 201–202.
14. *Vide* Chapter 32.
15. Parkes, *Voyage of Discoveries*, p. 202.
16. Ibid., p. 205.
17. Ibid., p. 204.
18. Ibid., p. 186.
19. Ibid., p. 207.
20. James Parkes, *A History of Palestine from 135 A.D. to Modern Times* (London: Victor Gollancz, 1949), pp. 191–92.
21. Parkes, *Voyage of Discoveries*, p. 210, ff. The first Gentile president of the Society was Canon Henry Paine Stokes (1849–1931), a medievalist who served between 1914 and 1916.
22. Ibid., p. 210.
23. *Vide* Chapter 5.
24. Dorothy Wickings Parkes, *Autobiography*, Parkes Archives, File 60/33/3.
25. Parkes, *Voyage of Discoveries*, pp. 216–17.
26. Dorothy Wickings Parkes, letter to a friend, Parkes Archives, File 60/16/689.
27. Parkes Archives, File 60/15/72.
28. Parkes, *Voyage of Discoveries*, p. 213.
29. *Vide* Chapter 11.
30. *Vide* Chapter 13.
31. James Parkes, *Voyage of Discoveries*, p. 215.

32. *Vide* Chapter 11.
33. A. Roy Eckhardt, 'In Memoriam, James Parkes', *Journal of Ecumenical Studies* (Winter 1982).
34. *Vide* Chapter 1.
35. M. Y. Berdichevsky, 'Miriam', from *Miriam and Other Stories*, translated by A. S. Super, introduction by Avner Holtzman (New Milford, CT: Toby Press, 2004), p. 247.

Embattled

A photograph taken in 1954 at the Board of Registry in Hampstead, where Parkes was serving as a witness at the civil marriage of his Israeli friend Zvi Werblowsky, depicts the clergyman as a dapper, robust, surprisingly portly chap, cigarette lightly poised between his fingers. His expression fortifies the impression that in the post-war decade his life in Barley was abundantly filled with intellectual refinements and provincial pleasures. There is something to this. He and Wickings for example, were enthusiastic participants in the Duodecimos, a high-minded local society that met monthly at the homes of its members. At each gathering a 'Duo' would deliver a serious, well-researched paper on a subject of his or her choice for everyone's mutual edification.[1] Over and above the learned discussions, Parkes revelled in the congenial social ambiance afforded by this typically provincial English social edifice; like play-reading groups, the Duodecimo Society was amateur but not amateurish.

However, appearances are often misleading. The fact of the matter was that with each passing year the glow of contentment emanating from the triumphs of 1946, Parkes' post-war *annus mirabilis*, grew progressively dim, its protective insulation increasingly threadbare. It was around 1950 that he first conceived of the notion of encompassing the activities of his manor house in an organizational framework that would be altogether more permanent and grandiose. Inevitably, he initiated vague, preliminary feelers to Israel Sieff about the idea. Had it in later years ever crossed Parkes' mind, he would have thought the contrast between the unpretentious success of the Duodecimo Society and the frustrations that would harry his campaign to reorganize his establishment at Barley dreadfully demoralizing.

Furthermore, one would anticipate that during these years of his prime the Reverend Dr Parkes, not long since fêted as a distinguished visiting dignitary in Palestine and an ecclesiastical lion among the New York Episcopal elite, would have straightforwardly negotiated a satisfactory niche for himself in the life of the village parish. During the war, after all, he was perhaps the pivotal figure on the local scene. Now, returned to his home turf, the charismatic prophet abroad found himself treated by the Church *Dégagé* or Retaliatory as a cross between a leper and a loose cannon.

> After the rector who had been there when I originally came had retired in disgrace ... the bishop planted on us a retired missionary to the Jews, who had never been in charge of a parish in his life, who had never lived in the country, and who announced from the very beginning that he regarded the parish as a pension, not as a field in which to work.[2]

Hard on the heels of the installation of this sore provocation, an episode occurred that crystallized the sort of proactive, pastoral role in the world that Parkes felt the Church should be urgently pursuing instead of its usual passive, smug or spiteful disengagement from pressing human problems.

> An affair in the neighbourhood acted, I grieve to say, to increase my prejudices against the Anglican bureaucratic structure. We heard by accident that a bachelor parson, whom we did not know, had been convicted of homosexual intentions. I went to see him. I found him alone in a vast rectory. Nobody had been near him for nearly a week (he was from the dominions and had no relatives in England) and he possessed five pounds in the world. I took him home. We sent him off to Belgium for a holiday with friends, and then he came back to us. He was too hurt and shocked to let me tell any of the authorities he was with us, and it was six weeks before diocesan or suffragan bishop, archdeacon or rural dean made any enquiry as to what happened to him. A diocese so big that such a thing could happen is, to me, an intolerable outrage.[3]

There but for the grace of God went Parkes himself? Perhaps something of the sort actually crossed his mind, but as on an earlier occasions when he had compassionately intervened with higher authorities or when he succoured one of his confrères under duress,[4] the issue for Parkes, at least ostensibly, was not sexual morality *per se* but the ignoble impact of the Church's retrograde diocesan system. At the same time, even Parkes was not so impervious to public opinion as to be unaware that some of his closest associates harboured suspicions about his own sexual proclivities.

As in the affair of the disgraced Reverend Gardiner, fear of exposure and anxiety about *shanda* – whether warranted or not – ever lurked. In this current instance, the rigidity of the diocesan system might have expediently served as a screen for the veiled intromission of homosexuality into his memoir. What helped to defang the potential for personal risk was that it was not Parkes alone but the Reverend and Mrs Parkes together who lent support to the woebegone bachelor parson. What is true for politicians is all the more so for clergymen: customarily, wives serve as useful accessories.

Almost every Sunday Parkes, garbed in clerical habit, celebrated Communion and preached at one or another nearby church, wherever in fact there happened to be a temporary vacancy. Effectively, at home he was 'completely excommunicated'.[5] Not for the first time shunned by other Christian pastors Parkes, much like the banished, archetypal Jew set awandering for the heinousness of his sin, had himself taken to the road, a displaced parson. This internal exile adumbrated aggravated relations between Parkes and mainstream Christianity for decades to come.

In 1949 Parkes published a damning review of a new study by Jakob Jocz, a converted Jew. He particularly faulted Jocz's strict adherence to 'the heresy of Dr Karl Barth' and his distorted or meagre understanding of Judaism:

> Dr Jocz shows no knowledge of the Yavne reformation, or the real meaning of the growth of rabbinic Judaism. He refers to Judaism again and again as 'tribalism' ... and speaks constantly of the 'subordination of the religion to nationalism' as characterizing the whole work of the rabbis. At no point does he make any contact with the conception that God works through, and speaks to, the community as well as to the individual.[6]

Although Jocz could scarcely have been pleased, he paid Parkes the tribute of taking his words '... very seriously, and he did not hesitate to praise Parkes for his battle against antisemitism. He paid Parkes the extreme compliment that 'his theology [was] pervasive and influential within the Churches of Great Britain and America and that it need[ed] to be continually dealt with by those who hold opposing ideas'.[7] If only, the castaway clergyman thought ruefully, Jocz's assessment of the widespread acceptance of his ideas were true.

This encounter between Parkes and Jocz turned out to be merely a preliminary skirmish; with a score to settle, Jocz soon supplanted Conrad Hoffman as Parkes' foremost antagonist and principal nemesis within the camp of Christian traditionalism, in a sense his Jewish–Christian allotrope. It would be a ten-year scrap played out in various denominational journals, a polemical joust of words between the James who was a Jacob versus the Jakob who was a James. It more closely resembled trench warfare than a chivalric tournament: neither side was capable of making more than a temporary, negligible advance.[8]

For his part Parkes indefatigably launched numerous epistles to the Christians. Constantly trumpeting his perennial theme of the eternal validity of Judaism, it would not be very long before Parkes' revisionism rendered him *tref* to the editors of a good many of the more conservative Christian organs. By 1959 Parkes gratefully welcomed reinforcements from the liberal Protestant camp in the person of the eminent theologian Reinhold Niebuhr who had declared that the Church's missionary activities '... are wrong not only because they are futile and have little fruit to boast for their exertions. They are wrong because the two faiths, despite differences, are sufficiently alike for the Jew to find God more easily in terms of his own religious heritage ...'[9] Or rather, not failing to note that Niebuhr's position was 'pragmatic' whereas his own was 'theological',[10] it was Parkes who had leapt to the defence of Niebuhr when he came under sharp fire from pro-missionary forces spearheaded by the Reverend George Stevens.

This last duel precipitated yet another round in a protracted struggle: 'are Missions to the Jews Justified?' Arguing for the negative, the redoubtable Reverend Dr James Parkes' opening flourish establishes his withering, declamatory tone:

Dear Mr Stevens,
No, I will not answer your question, because I am not prepared to admit that an answer is necessary. My faith in

Christ does not need the prop of a conception of Judaism and an attitude to the Jews which as a scholar I know to be false.[11]

By this time Parkes' recapitulation of the entire affair – the only sort of capitulation he ever would make – had appeared in a Jewish organ.[12]

Whenever Parkes could now command a Christian platform, his role *par excellence* was that of the insider-outsider, a rare, two-way viaduct capable of transmitting Jewish insight and conveying Christian remorse for open-minded Christian and Jewish audiences. The following titles suggest his range: in *The Christian News-Letter*, 'The Issue in Palestine' and 'The Emergence of Israel'; in *The Modern Churchman* 'A Living Faith', 'The Religious Situation in Jewry' and 'Progressive Judaism'; and in *St Martin's Review*, 'The Permanence of Sinai as God's Revelation'.[13]

Responses from the traditionalist camp to these philosemitic soundings were wildly discordant. Parkes generally ignored the more hysterical fulminations, but whenever approached in what he sensed was the genuine spirit of Christian dialogue, no one could be more forthcoming and even-tempered. Typical is this patient rejoinder to a missionary stalwart:

> I cannot identify with God the natural consequences of a sustained policy initiated by Christian apologists in the second century, and carried out consistently by the Church from the moment in the fourth century she had the power to embody her theological view of the Jews in the legislation of the Roman Empire and the subsequent Christian states of Europe.
>
> Among the many views of the Messiah prevalent at the time, nobody expected One who would make a challenge to each individual, Jew and Gentile, separately and who would be accepted only by individual personal surrender. Whatever view they held (and this includes the apostles) they expected mass acceptance, first of Jews then of Gentiles. When the mass acceptance did not come, they quite wrongly announced that there had been a mass rejection, and the whole of our traditional theology about the Jews is based on that unhappy error. The historical fact is that there was no mass rejection; Jews were being converted steadily to Jesus as the Christ all through the first century.[14]

In all fairness, the traditionalists' perception of Parkes and the
Council of Christians and Jews as dangerous to their interests
was essentially correct. If not effectively routed, their views
had the potential of undermining the rationale for missionary
efforts among Jews, traditionally the most prestigious of all
Christian outreach enterprises. Hence Parkes was surprised
when in March 1949 he received an invitation to present the
view from the other side of the hedge to a missionary assemblage
convening at an Ecumenical Institute in Celigny, Switzerland.
The upshot of this descent into the lion's den was foreordained:
'I did so, but I really had no common ground on which to base
a discussion with the almost wholly Barthian assembly and its
biblical fundamentalism.'[15]

Fortunately, as Christian editors grew increasingly wary,
Jewish editors, most notably David Kessler, opened their doors
all the wider. 'In early November 1948, Kessler asked if he could
"exploit his friendship" with Parkes for an article in the *Jewish
Chronicle* on the creation of the State of Israel, which appeared
at the end of the month. Thereafter Kessler commissioned him
to write a series of articles and reviews ...'[16] For an ordained cleric
in the Church of England, Parkes had attained an unprecedented
position among the Jews of Britain, and he had earned it.

> [He was] one of only a handful of British church leaders
> who not only supported the new State [of Israel] but
> regarded it as an exciting development in which Jews would
> be reinvigorated inside and outside of Israel. Even most
> Gentiles on the Council of Christians and Jews had difficulty
> in coming to terms with the reality of Jewish power in the
> Holy Land.[17]

Diminished access to Church publications was far from Parkes'
sole or even major professional problem. To his chagrin, progress
on his book-length projects proceeded no more smoothly than
it had during the wartime years. On his return to England from
the trip to Israel in 1949, the London Zionist Council commissioned him to write a short volume about Jerusalem. In contrast
to his irritating involvement a few years earlier with the Bureau
of Current Affairs, his Zionist contact, Bertha Urdang, was '...
almost unique in the field of Jewish public relations in that she
realized that, if one wants to presents a case to a Gentile, one

should get a Gentile to do it! *The Story of Jerusalem* which resulted from our discussions went into two editions and was extensively used in the new Israeli embassies.'[18]

At first this sounds very positive, but it turns out that in the end Parkes' succinct but splendid work was rejected by the Jewish Agency. Instead they chose to distribute a rival booklet on the Holy City, one so blatantly propagandist that it could not possibly recommend itself to any reader not already fully committed to Zionism. Parkes' work had been effectively shut out from the greater share of its natural market. To this day the State of Israel displays singularly painful ineptitude in the arena of public relations.

Dismayed but resolute as ever, Parkes a year later wrote and himself distributed several hundred copies of *Israel: Intrusion or Fulfilment?*, a brief polemic that situated the rebirth of the Jewish state within an historical perspective while both justifying and celebrating its establishment. For a change this publication generated a fairly lively response, one which would encourage Parkes to set to work on a scholarly, book-length study of the same theme. From another quarter as well, Parkes was encouraged to proceed apace:

> By the early 1950s, James Parkes was in great need of a supportive publisher. Interest in anti-Semitism was declining, and his increasing focus on Israel alienated him from the academic and general world. As he wrote to David Kessler in November 1951, 'I can say with all due modesty that I am one of the few chief writers on the Jewish question; but it is uphill work, and I need all the additional backing I can get.' Kessler encouraged Parkes to write *End of an Exile: Israel, the Jews, and the Gentile World* when Parkes had been somewhat depressed by the apparent impossibility of getting it published.[19]

End of an Exile appeared in 1954 but, like so much of Parkes' later output, it was less successful than he had anticipated. Then, as though his skills were not already wilting, owing to what seemed to many a surfeit of *Yiddishkeit*[20] and Zionist froth, Parkes suffered yet another diversion. In the wake of the establishment of the State of Israel in 1948, he decided to undertake a thorough study of the Arab refugee problem. He was particularly fascinated with the question of why so many Arabs abandoned their homes 'when they would have been able to sabotage the new Jewish state simply by staying put'.[21] To this day, of course, this issue remains unresolved, and is still hotly debated by propagandists, politicians, and historians.[22]

Just at the point when Parkes was poised to launch into this study, he received an urgent appeal from his close friend and frequent polemical ally W. W. Simpson. On behalf of the World Council of Churches, at that moment meeting in Beirut for the purpose of strengthening its links to the Palestinian refugees, Simpson urged Parkes to delay publishing anything on the subject. It would be, he was assured, only a temporary postponement, and the Council promised to remain in contact. Regrettably, Parkes acceded to his friend's request and would honour his word to the WCC. 'Needless to say,' he bemoans, 'the promise was not kept, and the opportunity was lost, for I got involved in other things.'[23]

This telltale excuse resurrects the image of the Reverend 'Flibberty' Parkes who was increasingly adrift in a post-war slump. At least temporarily, he seemed to have misplaced the assiduity and focus necessary to carry a major, new work to successful completion. Twenty years later Parkes would still be maintaining that he had isolated the fundamental explanation for Palestinian behaviour in 1948 in the traditional conflict between the psychology of the fellahin versus that of the Bedouin, an ahistorical theory so specious as to suggest that his accession to Simpson's plea was less a reason for deferring the project than a pretext for derailing it. Meanwhile, over the ensuing years ties between the World Council of Churches and the Palestinian refugees had grown so firmly knotted that the world's churchmen had long abandoned any pretence to impartiality.

At a distance of fifty additional years, another disquieting dispute that certainly would have drawn Parkes' close scrutiny exudes a sense of *déjà vu*: Mel Gibson's inflammatory film *The Passion of the Christ* released in 2004. When in 1953 Parkes learned that the director Carl Dreyer was planning a retrograde version of the last days of Jesus, he unleashed a flurry of letters in a campaign to persuade the Danish director to allow the Pharisees – the Jewish intellectual milieu from which Parkes believed Jesus himself to have sprung – to play a more affirmative role than they are customarily accorded. Whether he consciously preferred dramatic effect to historical verisimilitude or simply chose to ignore the impassioned pleas of the English parson, Dreyer was unmoved.[24]

Throughout this nettlesome period, muddle and even comic ineptitude bedevilled Parkes, who during the war years had been efficient even in pedestrian matters. Offered the responsibility of organizing the Barley branch of the Labour party, Parkes regretfully declined because he was too busy. 'All we could do was to give up time at elections for speaking in the constituency, and help with the car on polling day. But here we proved to have a genius for picking up people who wanted a car ride, but had neglected to see that their names were on the register.'[25]

After the failure of *God and Human Progress* in 1944, John Hadham had stolen silently into the shadows. This does not, of course, mean that Parkes had forsaken theological speculation. On the contrary, as he himself puts it, 'during the period of "lean and busy years", when my main Jewish interest was focused on Palestine and Israel, the religious puzzles and experiences of many decades began to fall into place'.[26] While this indeed may be true, one also surmises that, with his way forward looking somewhat murky, Parkes' loss of momentum in advancing his Jewish theme was instrumental in causing him to view this as a propitious time for resurrecting the straw man under whose banner he had inhaled his last whiff of popular success in Britain – the Reverend John Hadham.

'Co-authored' by the team of James Parkes and John Hadham, the March–May 1950 issue of the *St Martin's Review* featured an article entitled 'Politics and Pacifism'. The collaboration was a particularly deft *jeu d'espirit* by our spiritual Jew; it was destined to be the only formal joint effort by Parkes and Hadham to reach print. Unlike *Good God* and *God in a World At War*, the thrust of Parkes' newest foray into theology aimed to harmonize Judaism with Christianity rather than the other way round.

Later that year, in a lengthy essay, Parkes fused his ideas about Judaism with his conceptualizations about the Trinity whose origins date back to 1929. The result, 'God and His Creation', was another co-production of the Reverends James and John. They make for a stimulating amalgam.[27]

In a description of how God intervenes in the doings of the world, in place of the agency of the traditional three 'persons' of God Parkes substituted three 'channels', a term less loaded

with controversy. Through man, Parkes maintained, God channels His thought into his three active roles: a) a member of
concentric communities, b) a person in himself (a mystery) and
c) a worker for good or a searcher after truth. Parkes then
correlated Judaism with the first role, Christianity with the
second and scientific humanism with the third. These three
avenues, he asserted, are, each in its own sphere, equally valid
and important. A curious but significant paradox, however, is
that laws governing one function are not compelling in the
others; for example, man as a social being is not necessarily
governed by democratic constraints, for as a searching individual
he also has to make decisions on his own. Paradox, Parkes concluded, is an integral aspect of Creation.

Unfortunately, when soon after its inception the Church
erroneously insisted that Jesus alone was the answer to every
question, it neglected the full implications of the other two
discrete and equally operative channels that mediate between
man and God: man as a seeker and man as an individual.

> At Sinai, God revealed himself to man as a social being. With
> the Incarnation, revelation descended to man as a person.
> Man as a searcher by definition cannot give answers in
> advance. The tragedy of Christianity has been in its attempt
> to make the second revelation override the first and a
> condition of the third. But Judaism has preserved the first,
> and Christians still need to learn it from the Jews. The third
> we all need to consider together. The three have to be held
> together in a creative balance, indissolubly one in quality
> and purpose as we believe to be the triune nature of God.
> Only in this way shall we begin to see answers to the world's
> needs.[28]

Never published as an independent essay, 'God and His
Creation' encapsulates an argument that in 1952 informed a new
Hadhamite text. Rather than funnelling its text through Hadham,
however, at the misguided insistence of its publisher *God At Work
in Science, Politics and Human Life* materialized through the
'channel' of James Parkes. Working his way to this new synthesis
was extremely gratifying for Parkes personally. Unsurprisingly,
however, this latest synthesis of Parkes' thinking '... was, so far
as sales went, a complete flop'. Parkes improbably implies that

this may be ascribed partly to his having masked a Hadham product in the cloak of Parkes, but he is later constrained to admit that 'I am sure there are deeper reasons why I cannot convey to others the satisfaction and excitement that it is to me to see the vision of God in terms of the restatement of the Trinity',[29] and he was correct. In 1940, among countless admirers of *Good God*, Israel Sieff had been inspired by its author's free-flowing sense of discovery; however, while no less visionary, Parkes' 1952 reconceptualization of God 'in terms of the restatement of the Trinity' felt more didactic. Not very likely to interest a Jewish audience, alienating much of its Christian readership, at the time it could appeal only to relatively few.

Indeed, when we consider the book's concrete suggestions for structural reform of the Anglican Church, we are constrained to grant that Parkes did seem out of touch with reality. He urged, for example, that the Church should pattern itself on the model of the early rabbinic academies, which were in *'continual session*, engaged in *continual revision*, peopled by members of the highest available *intellectual understanding*, together with the most varied *experience of the life of the community*, and insisting upon the *complete responsibility* of men themselves for their decisions' (original emphases).[30]

Parkes' wistfulness over his latest failure verges on self-pity. It betrays how high his hopes had been that *God At Work* might, reversing his string of failures, re-enact the startling success of *Good God*. Visibly bruised by years of manning the journalistic barricades, he had lost his popular touch along with a substantial portion of his income potential. In 1956 Parkes in turn approached Penguin, Weidenfeld & Nicolson, George Allen and Unwin with a proposal to publish a revised edition of *Good God*. Each turned him down.[31] Their instincts were sound; ten years later, when the SCM Press issued an updated edition of *Good God* highlighting Parkes' Trinitarian speculations, it too would fail to garner an appreciative audience.[32] The last laugh, however, may yet belong to Parkes. Fifty years further down the ecumenical road, his stimulating ruminations now seem to have struck a resonant chord in some of our boldest and most stimulating contemporary theologians.[33]

NOTES

1. James Parkes, *Voyage of Discoveries* (London: Victor Gollancz, 1969), p. 215.
2. Ibid., p. 214.
3. Ibid., p. 214–15. The only earlier allusion to homosexuality in his memoir occurred when Parkes discounted the suspicions of the Geneva police concerning 'Len' Thomas's motivations. *Vide* Chapter 20.
4. *Vide* Chapter 24.
5. Parkes, *Voyage of Discoveries*, p. 214.
6. James Parkes, Review of *The Jewish People and Jesus Christ* in the *Jewish Chronicle*, November 1949.
7. Robert Everett, *Christianity Without Anti-Semitism: James Parkes and the Jewish–Christian Encounter* (Oxford: Pergamon, 1993), p. 274.
8. Curiously, on the symbolic level of this publicly played out struggle between what may be viewed as two facets of Parkes' sensibility, orthography allies him with his grandmother Catherine, or the Old Testament, and Jocz with Parkes' mother Annie Katherine, or the New Testament.
9. Everett, *Christianity Without Anti-Semitism*, p. 45.
10. James Parkes letter to Marcel Simon cited in Everett, *Christianity Without Anti-Semitism*, p. 46.
11. James Parkes, *The Church of England Newspaper*, 24 April 1959, p. 11, Parkes Archives, File 60/17/8.
12. James Parkes, 'Missions to the Jews, A Theological Dispute', *Jewish Chronicle*, 27 November 1959, p. 11.
13. Everett, *Christianity Without Anti-Semitism*, pp. 323–24.
14. James Parkes letter to H. L. Ellison, Parkes Archives, File 60/17/8.
15. Parkes, *Voyage of Discoveries*, p. 209.
16. Tony Kushner, 'Independence and Integrity: The Vision of James Parkes and David Kessler to Transform Prejudice into Understanding', in *Noblesse Oblige: Essays in Honour of David Kessler*, edited by Alan D. Crown (London: Vallentine Mitchell, 1998), p. 98.
17. Ibid., pp. 100–101.
18. Parkes, *Voyage of Discoveries*, pp. 210–11.
19. Kushner, 'Independence and Integrity', p. 100.
20. Jewish learning.
21. Parkes, *Voyage of Discoveries*, p. 212, ff.
22. *Vide* Meron Benvenisti, *Sacred Landscape: The Buried History of the Holy Land Since 1948* (Berkeley: University of California, 2000), pp. 144–228; and Benny Morris, *Righteous Victims: A History of the Zionist–Arab Conflict, 1881–1999* (New York: Knopf, 1999), pp. 252–62, for authoritative accounts of the origins of the Arab refugee problem.
23. Parkes, *Voyage of Discoveries*, p. 212.
24. James Parkes letters to Carl Dreyer, Parkes Archives, File 60/17/51. Before the film was released, it was reported that Gibson, responding to focus groups and Jewish critics, would cut a controversial scene dealing with Jews from his film. In fact no 'scene about Jews' was consigned to the cutting room floor. The extent of Gibson's 'concession' was to delete Caiaphas's saying 'His blood be on us, and our children', a spurious interpolation into the Gospels which over the centuries has engendered so much Jewish suffering. In the year 2000 even the Oberammergau festival finally deleted this incendiary line from its cycle of passion plays. (Stuart Schoffman, 'The Gospel According to Gibson', *Jerusalem Report*, Vol. XIV, No. 24, 22 March 2004, p. 41.)
25. Parkes, *Voyage of Discoveries*, p. 215.
26. Ibid., p. 223.
27. *Vide* Chapter 17.
28. James Parkes, 'God and His Creation', Parkes Archives, File 60/8/12: 1–2.
29. Parkes, *Voyage of Discoveries*, p. 225.
30. James Parkes, *God At Work in Science, Politics, and Human Life* (London: Putnam, 1952), p. 166.

31. Parkes Archives, File 60/6/1/2.
32. Parkes, *Voyage of Discoveries*, p. 225.
33. Irving Greenberg, *For the Sake of Heaven and Earth: The New Encounter Between Judaism and Christianity* (Philadelphia: Jewish Publication Society, 2004), pp. 145–61.

Hand-to-Mouth

Parkes now felt himself growing older in step with the century. Looking out upon the world from the vantage of his middle fifties, he confronted a broad, broken field pockmarked by chronic political upheaval and scarred by social disequilibrium. Before fizzling out, post-war hopes for healing and a fresh start had lasted for only a brief moment. Where once a line of trenches had divided Europe, now the Iron Curtain split the entire world in two. Mankind had not begun seriously to contemplate what had been wrought at Hiroshima or by the Shoah. At the same time, whenever he looked back Parkes was acutely conscious that his own 'career' was faltering, his own way forward at an impasse. Indeed, at times he had to struggle to ward off despondency.

It was just at this juncture that a new direction opened. While its advent was unanticipated, its cause, agency and operation are far from inexplicable. As Parkes recounts, '... at this period when I was arguing for the equality of Judaism and Humanism with Christianity ... we were thrust into a series of experiences which compelled us to recognize that it was a larger view of God, not a smaller view of Christianity, which had to be put forward'. Upon reading *Good God*, he tells us, a young woman suffering from both tuberculosis and cancer took it into her head that '... if she could put herself into the hands of John Hadham, God would give her healing. It was her faith, not mine or Dorothy's which effected the cure, but the cure was effected.'[1]

As if propelled by an outside force, a phenomenon we have noted before, Parkes was '... thrust into a series of [new] experiences' Not actively solicited, at first entertained hesitantly, Parkes' 'new direction' was soon embraced with enthusiasm. This readiness to accept his therapeutic role did not issue from a vacuum. Already for several decades Parkes had been pondering a broader conception of the Godhead and the means God employs to interact with His Creation. He was therefore well primed to receive this 'gift' of the Holy Spirit. Indeed, Parkes' personal experience as a healer directly parallels that of his ailing reader who, as if driven by a powerful suggestion emanating from outside herself, 'took it into her head ... [to] put herself into the hands of John Hadham'.

We recall that as a young man at Hopovo Parkes had responded profoundly to the spell of the Russian Orthodox liturgy,[2] and that an unassuming but deep well of spirituality always nourished both his scholarly and his political ventures. Like repeated visitations from the spectral 'Elemental of the Cromlech,' the efficacy of the laying-on-of-hands strongly confirmed the spiritual basis of reality. Moreover, although Parkes disclaims any connection between his own faith in God and the power of his new gift, elsewhere he asserts quite the contrary: '... but He demanded the same self-surrender in healer and healed that He demanded in His preaching and His parables'[3] – that is, gifts of the spirit are extended to all but may only be exploited by those prepared to receive them. In short, Parkes' signal success in promoting a 'cure' for the dying woman paralleled a corollary process in the healer as well: self-ministration engendered by reaffirmation of faith.

The passage that recounts how, inspired by Hadham, the sick woman was healed by Parkes contains a curious error. Even though it came to print via the 'channel' of 'James Parkes', it is obvious that that the sick woman had just finished reading not *Good God*, which first appeared in 1940, but the recently published *God at Work in Science, Politics and Human Life* (1952).[4] Unlike the earlier work, it was this later book that emphasized the healing spirit of God as a power proceeding from a specifically Christian dispensation.

> He spoke to the hearts and minds of men, calling them sons of a heavenly Father; but He spoke also to their bodies. During various periods the Church regarded His miracles of healing as something belonging to a past age, which they did not expect to repeat ... Today, with a new humility, we are discovering that the healing spirit of God can speak directly to the matter of our bodies, as to the diseases of our minds. Spiritual healing within the churches, and psychosomatic 'medicine' in the clinics and surgeries, are feeling after the power which rests on the unity of all creation within the spiritual dynamic of the Creator.[5]

With another nod to Freud, so startling a slip – an author mistaking one of his offspring for another – signifies something of moment. Does it not suggest that Parkes fervently yearned that *God at Work* should indeed be another *Good God*? His ill-suppressed, guilt-tinged complaint was surely that had God only worked as hard for *God at Work* as He had done good for *Good God*, it would have done wonders to stabilize its God-smitten author's financial duress. In sum, while Parkes always depreciated money as a value in itself, this timely slip of the pen reveals just how acutely the lack of it preyed upon his mind.

Their inspirational encounter with the ailing woman efficiently nudged both the Parkeses into the embrace of the ascendant healing movement within the Church of England.

> There was no doubt in our minds that, if the Jewish work were to collapse, we would go with a sense of gratitude for the past and excitement for the future, into some aspect of that pioneering renewal of the twentieth century. Dorothy and I both agreed at the end that the Jewish work could and should go on, and must be my main preoccupation, but that left her free to give a good deal of her time, and to identify herself more fully, with the healing movement. She became a member of the international and inter-denominational Order of St Luke the Physician and brought continual refreshment in the contacts thus made ...[6]

While never, of course, an overriding consideration, a significant aspect of Parkes' 'Jewish work' that should never be entirely discounted was there alone had he struck a long-term, workable vein of ore that actually helped to settle the daily bills. It was therefore only expedient that the Parkeses should divide forces in such fashion. Nevertheless, even to have broached the possibility that his 'Jewish work' might at some point collapse would have been inconceivable a few years earlier . It tellingly reflects Parkes' unsettled state of mind. Although he was too committed and far too stubborn ever to accede to such a break-down, the choice of words is oddly proleptic. Within a year not his work but Parkes himself would undergo a physical collapse.

Early in 1953 a shift in Parkes' fortunes seemed in the offing. The American Reform leader, Rabbi Maurice Eisendrath extended an invitation to participate in a study group soon to travel

to Jerusalem in order to investigate Israel's tangled religious
situation. The two men had first met in Geneva in 1933, making
Eisendrath one of Parkes' 'oldest Jewish friend[s]'.[7] Keen to return
to the Jewish State, and generally sympathetic with the Reform
perspective, Parkes readily accepted. However, while attending
a conference six weeks before the scheduled sailing, Parkes
suddenly felt a sharp blow to his chest. Rushed to hospital, he
underwent emergency cardiac surgery. After a trauma of this
nature, six weeks is scarcely time enough to recover one's full
strength. Nevertheless, such was Parkes' eagerness to return to
Israel that, dismissing the advice of his doctors, after just a month
he declared himself strong enough to complete his convalescence at sea. Auguring well, he in fact arrived at Haifa feeling
relatively fit.

Fifteen years after the event, Parkes recalls enjoying 'a very
interesting trip', which, for no clear reason, made him moderately
optimistic about the prospects for Israel's religious liberalization.
In fact, he presents Israel's religious situation somewhat misleadingly: '[The] country paradoxically guaranteed and practised
complete religious freedom for Christians and Muslims, but
the only form of Judaism tolerated was an extremely religious
orthodoxy.'[8] The actual situation, essentially unchanged from
fifty years ago, is more complicated: although the State of Israel
grants special status and privileges to Orthodoxy, it tolerates all
forms of Judaism. Moreover, the variety of practice within
Orthodoxy is far broader than meets the uninitiated eye. Under-
cutting Parkes' assertion, the so-called 'ultra-Orthodox' themselves frequently complain of discrimination and second class
treatment at the hands of the State.

None too wisely, Eisendrath invited his still recuperating friend
to undertake an extensive lecture tour of America that winter.
The proposed circuit would plunk Parkes down among assemblies
not only of Reform Jews but also of Christian clergy interested
in past, current and future relations between Judaism and Christianity. This latter audience, both men agreed, would provide a
tailor-made platform for the rhetorical and fund-raising talents
of the Reverend James Parkes. Dorothy and James deliberated
the wisdom and the dangers of such an undertaking as measured against its potential benefits. What tipped the balance
was the strong likelihood of earning enough to enable them to
return to England with the means to resuscitate what otherwise

increasingly looked to be their stillborn hopes regarding their 'reorganization'.

When, one wonders, had Parkes' intense yearning to father a Jewish–Christian Institute at Barley fully taken root? How had a manor house, initially conceived as a gracious home, a commodious workplace, and a suitable repository for Parkes' several collections, gradually evolved into the locus of a grandiose *idée fixe*? As Parkes recalls,

> While I wrote books and articles, and was frequently away for conferences, lectures, and committee meetings, John McNeilage ran the house and exercised general control of the vegetable garden, surrendering the reins to Dorothy for the evening meal. Dorothy was responsible for the whole secretarial and filing work, as well as being hostess to a continual series of guests. It was only by the competence and generosity of these two 'legs of the tripod' that Barley remained upright until the mid-fifties. Financially we spent all that was realizable from my inheritance, and then relied on I.M.S.[9]

In fact, paralleling how prior to 1948 the Zionist enterprise in Palestine had already created the essential, functional organs of a shadow state-in-waiting, thanks to the largesse of its sole benefactor, the operation at Barley had for some time been functioning as a virtually independent institution.

Parkes' gratifying epiphany in Cincinnati had only formally confirmed what he long had sensed: the Jewish collection he had been assiduously nurturing for fifteen years contained many irreplaceable items, and it was of great value.[10] A seed of an idea that had been germinating ever since Parkes' return to England suddenly crystallized into a full-blown vision. From a certain perspective prosaic, in the eyes of its beholder the Barley Centre for Jewish–Christian Relations was suffused with ethereal splendour. The manor house would be transformed into an officially recognized, properly funded, ongoing foundation, a countryside version of Chatham House devoted to research and conferences – but with a difference. Its particular, indeed exclusive focus would be the promotion of understanding and reconciliation between the two consanguineous faiths long divided by schism. Transmogrified, the manor house with its unique resources and agreeable surroundings would be an avatar of 3 Grand Mezel: an articulate, contemporary bridge-house linking Judaism and Christianity.

Parkes' devotion to shepherding his vision to fruition was reinforced by a personal, indeed intimate consideration which he could never quite bring himself to admit. Childless, and stung more than he outwardly admitted by the failure of all but one of his last eight titles to find a substantial audience, Parkes now concentrated the full force of his personality and sublimated desire upon siring an institutional structure that would not only perpetuate his life's work but also bear his name.

'James,' remarked the wife of one of his closest friends, 'was a man of faith and deeply devout, but that did not prevent him from being arrogant and very vain. The first thing he looked for in the newspaper was his own name being mentioned in book reviews, and he was very disappointed at not finding it.'[11] However, on opening a newspaper what author does not turn first to its book pages and whose eyes do not feast on reports of his latest work? In Parkes' case, however, the indictment is somewhat weightier. Indeed, even his greatest admirers are unanimous in attesting to a deep and broad streak of vainglory, a noteworthy chink in the armour of an anti-establishment maverick who steadfastly avoided professional encumbrances and jealously guarded his intellectual independence.

It seemed very droll to many of his friends and colleagues that, at the onset of serious illness and his decline into old age, Parkes should so energetically strive to morph into a foundation. Not for him the anonymity of the artisans who fashioned the cathedral at Chartres. The man with principles so astringent that in his benedictions he scrupled to refer to Jesus as 'God's only begotten son'[12] passionately lusted after a private conceit which, he felt in his heart, God would forgive: his work should be perpetuated in his own name.

Where should Parkes turn to secure the means to realize this dream? The answer was glaringly obvious. Half in blame, half in admiration, not for nothing did one of Parkes' closest associates comment, 'including his wife and his closest friends, James knew how to exploit people'.[13] Since he always viewed his aims in a noble light, he of course did not conceive of his manoeuvring in these terms. Still, the charge harbours a large measure of unquestionable validity.

At the same time, and not for the first time, he self-consciously takes pains to remind us, Parkes was acutely sensitive to the equivocal position of a Christian who repeatedly seeks financial support from a Jew so that he might better discharge his duties as a Christian.[14] He had always been inwardly embarrassed and extremely reluctant to solicit more than a minimal level of support from Israel Sieff. Nevertheless, he was now a man armed with a vision. At first tentatively, then with more insistence, Parkes urged his friend to treat the project with appropriate seriousness. However, again and again, Parkes' feelers came to nothing. The director of Marks & Spencer was unfailingly polite, at times even mildly encouraging, but in the end he was mainly noncommittal and unforthcoming.

Months passed and then a year and then years; the frustrated couple expended more and more of their time and energy at the grinding, disheartening task of winning a sympathetic hearing elsewhere. In 1953, for example, fatalistic but far from stoical, Parkes matter-of-factly let drop to Lady Stansgate, an associate in the field of Jewish–Christian relations, that he was on the verge of insolvency. As if distracted, he bemoaned that his library was not likely to survive his demise intact. As he anticipated, Stansgate conferred with others, most notably their mutual friend Victor Gollancz, the publisher who in 1948 had published the British edition of Parkes' *Judaism and Christianity*.[15] Although Gollancz had nothing to offer at the time, some years later he would be helpful.

Such undignified thrashing about for the means to flesh out his project without the involvement of Sieff gradually sapped Parkes' spirit and went far towards depleting his limited store of energy. Since what had started as a self-evident desideratum – the metamorphosis of his tripodic household into a solidly established edifice – had become a fully-fledged private obsession, at times he very nearly succumbed to despair. After years of effort, his visionary foundation was still unfunded and unfounded. A 'long holiday in my beloved Provence' in 1951 was preceded by a spell of crashing headaches and crushing, all-encompassing fatigue: '... we were both so tired that we took advantage of the falling in of an insurance policy of Dorothy's ...'[16] Beyond immersion in nostalgia, the understood purpose of this trip was to distance James and Dorothy from an intractable situation.

Serving as a catalyst, it was Eisendrath's invitation to tour America in 1954 that brought a long-simmering impasse to the boil. Parkes suddenly apprehended that the tripod on its own simply could not sustain the weight of the Barley operation any longer. To all intents and purposes, his fresh assessment constituted a *cri de coeur*. Parkes had,

> … no secretarial help, no room for files and archives except, metaphorically, under the bed, and no certainty from one day to another … In addition to books, the collection of pamphlets and periodicals continued to grow and to demand substantial space, and the mere record of my activities in the field of Jewish–Christian relations covered twenty-five years.[17]

Then there occurred yet another adventitious event, perhaps even the figurative straw that broke the camel's back. Wickings's eighty-year old mother had recently come to live at Barley. Parkes remarks that, provided with a 'toy house' of her own in the orchard, she was no bother and could be 'as independent as she wanted'.[18] How much or how little that actually was goes unsaid. In any event, on his return from a meeting in France and spurred on by his wife's open concern for his health, Parkes was firmly resolved to brook no further equivocation. Early one evening he peremptorily turned up at the comfortable study of his long-term benefactor. Only a change of heart could render the ordeal of a mid-winter American tour unnecessary.

However, it was not to be. Although Sieff did prop Parkes up with enough cash to enable the construction of an additional office and the engagement of another secretary, once again he avoided dealing with the main business: the legal incorporation and long-term financial underwriting of a Barley Centre for Jewish–Christian Relations.[19] Parkes was satisfied that he had done his best. The only way forward was to proceed with his American tour.

It was now September 1953. Still far from fully fit, as a prologue to his return in December, Parkes flew to the States to make advance arrangements. He contacted every Christian organization that sponsored ongoing programmes or interest groups in the Middle East.

The ignorance of Israel was as complete as [their] identification with the refugees. A Quaker lady ... explained to
me that, if they did not identify their opinions completely
with those of the refugees, they would not be allowed
to work in the camps. This hideous and destructive moral
cowardice was common to Catholics, Protestants and
Quakers.[20]

Excepting American Evangelicals, who on the whole today are
wholeheartedly committed to the official Israeli narrative, the
perspective of Quakers and mainstream Protestant confessions
remains unchanged.

When Parkes returned to London, the Israeli Ambassador
suggested that he incorporate material about Israel into his
lectures. If Parkes was an authority on anything, however, it was
the programmed range of response of Christian audiences to
Jewish-related issues. He knew that nothing short of 'a fully
prepared and whole-time campaign would do any good, and
that could not be combined with ... theological lecturing'.[21] Moreover, he was only too sensible that, due largely to his own long-
standing opposition to the missionary activity among Jews, his
ability to extract funds from Christians had been much compromised; he had distanced himself from the core community
of professing Christians who attend church on Sunday and make
out cheques to good causes. The rebirth of a Jewish State and
especially Jewish control over Christian holy sites in Jerusalem
were extremely difficult nuggets for most of them to digest, and
an institute to improve Jewish–Christian relations could not rank
very high on their religious agenda.

The marathon tour got under way in January, in the very
depths of winter. In order to achieve his aim – the maximum
harvest for his exertions – Parkes committed himself to a punish-
ing schedule. Starting in New York, remaining in most cities only
overnight, the couple plane-hopped across the continent. Their
westerly path cut an arc across the centre of the country: New
Jersey, Philadelphia, Washington, Nashville, Dallas, Kansas City,
and Los Angeles. After a jog north to San Francisco, they then
traced a more elliptical trajectory to the East Coast: Milwaukee,
Chicago, Cincinnati, Detroit, Buffalo, Rochester, Boston and New
York again. For a man of his years and physical condition, this
was a veritable Via Dolorosa.

Everywhere Parkes took up the heavy burden of 'explaining to his Christian brethren [how and why] their views of Judaism ... were theologically an intolerable offence to their Jewish neighbours ... I can say quite objectively that there was then no other Christian clergyman in existence who would even have tried to perform such a task.'[22] In truth, for his attempt to enlighten Christians as to why and how contemporary Judaism was not merely an irrelevant, incomplete form of Christianity, no amount of praise would be immoderate. At every stop the couple was greeted by strange faces and a new round of hand-shakes. They had to deal as best they could with hastily eaten or over-generous meals and sharp changes in weather. The demanding schedule, even had they been twenty years younger, would have been extremely taxing.

It proved, of course, too severe a strain for the constitution of the fifty-seven-year-old clergyman only recently discharged from hospital. After successfully delivering the most important presentation of the entire tour – the Gilkey Lecture at the University of Chicago[23] – Parkes first temporarily lost his voice and then, in freezing weather, underwent a physical collapse. Simultaneously he sustained an anxiety attack at the very notion of spending another night in a hotel (from which he was rescued by the hospitality of a local rabbi). In short, Parkes was once again a very sick man and very far from home.

Compounding matters, he was also a very stubborn man. Instead of cancelling the rest of the tour, overruling his wife's pleas he rose too soon from his bed. At the next stop following his presentation he collapsed yet again, but recovering suffi-ciently, still he pushed on to city after city. When they finally arrived in New York, Parkes was in a state of total exhaustion. As if waiting in the wings, mortality obliquely announced its presence: the couple was informed of the death of Dorothy's mother. Yet even then only the adamancy of a Manhattan physician forestalled Parkes from delivering his final round of lectures.

Booked by Eisendrath in first class berths on the *Ile de France*, Parkes' favourite liner, the couple sailed back to England. Yet, displaying truly remarkable resiliency, on a wave of vinaceous splendour and gastronomic glory at sea Parkes' spirits and strength seemed restored. It would only be a short-lived reprieve. Very soon after their arrival in England, reality again hit hard. In terms of its overriding objective, the trip to America had been an abysmal failure.

> We had returned with some eight thousand dollars, to find that nothing had been done in our absence to turn us into some kind of institute to which we could hand over the money. In spite of the efforts of Mr Westmore [Parkes' accountant], we lost a large part of it in super-tax. Then followed an agonizing time, I.M.S. was really too busy to give sufficient thought to our problems to make a sensible decision possible. He was also involved in too many demands to give us the minimum financial help we needed. We struggled on for a year, not knowing from month to month whether we would have to close.[24]

Erroneously postdating the onset of an extended period of despair, one close observer characterized it problematically: '... in the early 1960s, Parkes was becoming increasingly bitter, but was still determined in his idealistic way that his life's work would not end with him'.[25] Parkes was perhaps bitter and idealistic, but he was still definitely determined.

In June, however, yet another bout of ill health eclipsed all immediate thought of the Institute. This time diagnosed with a cerebral spasm, an exquisitely painful and very persistent condition, Parkes once again found himself in a hospital. Upon his discharge several weeks later Sieff, now truly alarmed by his friend's frailty, dispatched the couple off on holiday to Switzerland. Beyond assuaging any twinges of guilt, of course, his primary aim was to help Parkes regain his strength and to restore his drooping spirits. Additionally, however, one cannot help but wonder whether, wearying at last of endless hints about the unborn Barley enterprise, for his own peace of mind Sieff also factored in the benefits of shipping the weakened cleric out of the country for a spell.

Parkes led Wickings through the narrow, familiar streets of *la Cité* to Grand Mezel. From the outside, at first glance Number 3, on whose top-floor flat Parkes had so doted but which in the end was so eager to flee, looked exactly the same.[26] Closer inspection revealed another reality: 'On the way back I showed Dorothy Geneva, but found that nothing was left of my flat except the outside walls. The whole inside of the house with its dignified eighteenth century interiors ... had been swept away and replaced by three beastly little boxes ... on each floor.'[27] The old 'bridge house' had been gutted; the new one, despite his best efforts, was yet stillborn. Ill, weary and now chronically depressed, Parkes existed in a state of limbo, his spirits at their lowest ebb perhaps since his service as a soldier in the trenches.

Somehow yet another year ground past, and Parkes still could not move or persuade Sieff to act. Fully five years had now elapsed since, during an earlier interlude of wallowing in the Slough of Despond, the Parkeses had decamped to Provence on the proceeds of her insurance policy. It too had provided respite only temporarily and had brought their vision no closer to fulfilment. Her poignant rendering of their frustrations and how it might be banished by a mere touch of their benefactor's magic wand appeared in a letter Wickings addressed to a friend.

> We have come to a turning point in our lives. For one thing our capital is exhausted now and we have to find out whether it will be possible either to expand our work – or pack up on it and take a parish ... If we can do it, we want to turn Barley into the Institute we have longed for – that of Jewish–Christian relations ... We want to build a library and a secretary's room here – and get a good secretary. We should like to dig up the orchard and turn it into a campus where students of the Institute could stay ... We hope that to do this we may become a Foundation – with American capital – with three main interests: a) God at work as approached by both religions, b) a bridge for Arab–Jewish relations, c) liberal theological approaches in both Christianity and Judaism.[28]

Then, in the autumn of 1955 at a point when things could hardly have seemed less promising, the ice began to thaw. For good reason, however, Parkes' pleasure was much subdued. 'I.M.S. was at last having steps taken to put the work [Barley] in institutional form, but,' Parkes added ruefully, 'it looked less and less likely that I would be able to profit from the decision which we had hoped for more than ten years earlier.'[29]

Rushed to hospital yet again after another coronary thrombosis, Parkes was informed that his chances of survival were barely fifty per cent. Although he survived, in the ensuing months he would be rushed to hospital in critical condition twice more.

In the end the one-time feeble Guernsey youngster, battered and toughened by so much adversity, would endure a dozen or more periods of hospitalization. Still his 'unfinished business' stiffened his will to live.

Then there was a denouement that might be labelled 'What Goes Round, Comes Round' or, in a more spiritual key, 'Faith Rewarded'. After one of Parkes' homecomings from hospital, with the couple living virtually hand-to-mouth, Wickings was ordered by her husband's physician to pack him off south for the winter; otherwise, she was told, he would not live to see the spring. Exceedingly reluctant to turn again to Sieff for assistance, at this critical juncture, a *deus ex machina* manifested herself: Mrs Salomons, Wickings's old friend, dispatched the couple a letter containing a cheque for two hundred pounds.

'We spent the winter in Menton, in the diocese of my old SCM colleague, Tom Craske, then bishop of Gibraltar; and I received from him the laying-on-of hands. It was not until the late spring that, much restored, I returned to England by easy stages ... after enjoying stays with friends in Marseille, Lyon, Dijon, and Paris.'[30] Notwithstanding his heterodox tendencies and his bouts of desperation, Parkes, we remind ourselves again, was a man of profound Christian faith. He does not even speculate whether the wintering on the Côte d'Azur would in and of itself have restored him to a semblance of good health.

NOTES

1. James Parkes, *Voyage of Discoveries* (London: Victor Gollancz, 1969), p. 224.
2. *Vide* Chapter 14.
3. James Parkes, *God at Work In Science, Politics and Human Life* (London: Putnam, 1952), p. 91.
4. Ibid., the Foreword names the four titles that Parkes penned under the name of John Hadham and declares that *God at Work* is, 'in a way a continuation of the line of thought of those volumes'.
5. Ibid., pp. 91–92.
6. Parkes, *Voyage of Discoveries*, pp. 224–25.
7. Ibid., p. 229.
8. Ibid., p. 217, ff.
9. Ibid., p. 208.
10. *Vide* Chapter 29.
11. Ruth Weyl interviewed by the author and Maggie Davidson in Rehovot, Israel, 26 October 2003.
12. *Vide* Chapter 17.
13. Ruth Weyl interviewed by the author and Maggie Davidson.
14. Parkes, *Voyage of Discoveries*, pp. 190–91.
15. David Wedgwood Benn, son of Lady Stansgate, letter to the author, 1 October 2003.

16. Parkes, *Voyage of Discoveries*, p. 216.
17. Ibid, pp. 217–18.
18. Ibid, p. 218.
19. Ibid.
20. Ibid.
21. Ibid., p. 219.
22. Ibid., p. 220.
23. James Parkes, *The Concept of a Chosen People in Judaism and Christianity* (New York: UAHC Press, 1954).
24. Parkes, *Voyage of Discoveries*, p. 221.
25. Tony Kushner, 'Independence and Integrity: The Vision of James Parkes and David Kessler to Transform Prejudice into Understanding', in *Noblesse Oblige: Essays in Honour of David Kessler*, edited by Alan D. Crown (London: Vallentine Mitchell, 1998), p. 104.
26. James Parkes, Parkes Archives, File 60/31/28.
27. Ibid.
28. Dorothy Wickings Parkes, letter to Else Rosenberg, 31 August 1955, Parkes Archives, File 60/16/689.
29. Parkes, *Voyage of Discoveries*, p. 222.
30. Ibid.

32

Parkes Ltd

From the mid-1950s onwards, either a serious relapse or the threat of one constantly clouded Parkes' horizon, but the old campaigner against antisemitism now basked in the glow of Sieff's explicit promise to fund the Jewish–Christian Institute. After a year of further delay, during which time he remained largely bedridden, Parkes received the word he had been awaiting for over a decade. Finally, Israel Sieff had got around to laying his munificent hands on the dream of a very sick friend: '... in the middle of these distresses, on 9 August 1956, a week after I had started having coronary thromboses, we at last became *The Parkes Library Limited,* a company created for charitable purposes, and registered under the Board of Trade'.[1] *Mirabile dictu.* Even in the midst of his excitement, however, Parkes could not suppress the churlish thought that he might never rise from his sick bed with the energy to function effectively as its director.

For its entire first year as a legal entity, during which time Parkes was either totally incapacitated or a semi-invalid, the operative term of the newly incorporated body was 'limited'. It took Sieff that long to set in motion a dinner at the Savoy to launch the project before a roomful of potential donors. Sieff himself delivered what Parkes considered '... a brilliant speech, not merely on my work, but on the long-term necessity for it.'[2] Sieff knew his old friend well: warm appreciation for a life-time of high achievement was the most potent restorative for the ailing scholar. Over and above such public recognition, material tribute flowed freely from this chosen congregation of guests and admirers. It would yield Parkes a secure income for the first time in his life as well as modest proceeds for the perpetuation of the work of the Library.

A year later a follow-up fund-raiser convened in order to expand the activities of both the Parkes Library and the Wiener Jewish Library. The latter, a parallel institution head-quartered in London, had originated in 1934 as the Jewish

Central Information Office in Amsterdam, an activist body for battling antisemitism as well as a repository of information about National Socialism. Alfred Wiener, who transferred it to London in 1939, was now older and even more frail than Parkes. At the fund-raising dinner David Kessler proposed an operational merger of the two institutions. Although the idea had obvious merit Parkes, who had waited so long for his own Library to spring into existence as an independent entity, was unimpressed. 'It was not,' he notes, 'really a very sensible project because I had somewhat doubtful strength to run my own work, and certainly could not spend several days a week in London running the Wiener Library.'[3]

Parkes was assuredly correct, but even had he been at full strength it is certain he would not have enthusiastically compromised the integrity of the eponymous Centre for which he had so long pined and struggled. In the end both libraries retained their separate identities, but a working relationship was successfully forged. Leonard Montefiore, President of the Wiener Library, generously insisted that all the proceeds of the joint dinner should go to the Parkes Library.[4] With newfound revenues at his disposal, Parkes' health improved markedly. He expanded the Library's premises so that its several collections might be housed more comfortably, and he was able to hire additional secretarial help. Moreover, a competent part-time librarian volunteered his services.

Comprising of men and women of high accomplishment and stature, a board of governors for the Library was organized, all distinguished players from Parkes' past: Professors Alexander Altmann of Brandeis University, David Daube of Oxford, Marcel Simon of Strasbourg, and Zvi Werblowsky of Hebrew University; Lady Stansgate, Ambassador Eliahu Elath, David Kessler, Rabbi Eisendrath, Charles Singer, and Carlisle Witton-Davies, chairman of the Council of Christians and Jews whom Parkes had befriended in Jerusalem in 1946. Inevitably, Israel Sieff assumed the chairmanship. All in all, the board was a varied, competent, well-connected body.

With the coming to fruition of his dream, one might have guessed that the dreamer would be pleased. But when it came to the matter of the Library, Parkes' glass was perennially half empty: 'We were not able to persuade I.M.S. to bring into existence ... a competent finance committee which could also plan expansion and look after the succession when I was ready to retire.'[5] Nor did he succeed in locating the means with which to employ a deputy who might share the burdens of administering the institution he had not only conceived, but also, after terrific labour pangs, delivered into the world.

After another lengthy stay at Cambridge's Addenbrooke's Hospital, on his return to Barley yet another of Parkes' chronic problems seemed to be moving at last towards a happy resolution. While he was away, Dorothy had become a member of St Edward's, a parish church in Cambridge proper. It was an independent-minded congregation, a so-called 'peculiar' closely associated with reform-minded local Anglicans and removed from the jurisdiction of the local bishop. Finding both the parish church and its chaplain, the Reverend Arthur Dowle, much to his liking, Parkes officially joined as well. In a setting that resonated with the spirit of his college days, Parkes had encountered in Dowle another incarnation of Oxford's 'Holy John' Campbell. 'We found there all the fellowship which we had lacked at Barley', he recalls with the inner satisfaction of a man who had at last come to rest. 'I used to preach for him and usually read the lessons. When we brought one of our visitors with us, he used to introduce them [sic] to the congregation with a natural and overflowing affection ...'[6]

At a point in life when he no longer had the strength to scurry from parish to parish like an Old Man of the Road, Parkes, or rather Wickings, had uncovered a spiritual home peculiar to his needs and a vicar who suited his personal taste and theological disposition, and none too soon. Far more sedentary than in former years, Parkes had to expend considerable energy just to fight off one bodily malfunction after another. A letter dated 26 July 1958, for example, alluded to his having been ill for two years with double pneumonia and a coronary thrombosis.[7]

This poor health inevitably much curtailed Parkes' scholarly and journalistic output. He did turn out 'The Separation of Church and Synagogue' for the *Liberal Jewish Monthly* in January 1955, 'The Present State of Jewish–Christian Relations' for *Conservative Judaism* in the Winter of 1956, and for the Autumn/Winter 1957 issue of *Jewish Heritage* 'The Jewish Contribution to Civilization', but these and others like them were in reality short jottings and updates that he could dash off on a good afternoon. What they led to, however, was a nuanced extension of his earlier thinking:

Parkes now maintained that rabbinic Judaism and traditional Christianity had evolved in parallel fashion on separate but equal tracks. 'In fact,' he argued, 'there is no argument for the divine guidance of Jewry which is not an equally valid argument for Christendom, and there is no argument for a divine guidance of Christendom which is not equally valid for Judaism.'[8]

Parkes' most seductive development of this theme, 'The Chosen People', appeared in a regional American academic journal, a new departure for him. A reasonable conjecture is that during his onerous American tour two years earlier an editor who heard him speak in Nashville or Dallas had invited Parkes to submit a piece on this frequent sticking point for Gentiles. The result is one of his most successful and sympathetic explorations of a widely misunderstood aspect of the essence of Judaism. Its conclusion is vintage Parkes:

> From their beginnings Judaism and Christianity were differ-ent kinds of religions. Christianity faced the world as 'a way of salvation' for the elect out of every nation. Judaism stood as a way of life for a single elect nation. It was a natural consequence of its divine calling that Christianity, in the fulfilment of its mission, should define ever more closely that faith the acceptance of which insured salvation. But it was an equally natural consequence of its own peculiar mission that Judaism, in seeking to call the whole nation to its high responsibility, should define ever more closely the way in which to live so as to maintain the identity and obedience of the chosen people.[9]

The cogency of Parkes' argument lends implicit endorsement to his wife's sense that what kept him out of hospital during this period was his inner determination to develop implications that flowed out of the beguiling symmetry between the faiths. David Kessler published them in 1960 as *The Foundations of Judaism and Christianity*; upon its appearance, Parkes was chosen as the subject of a profile in the *Observer*. There can be no doubt that enhanced public recognition always contributed materially to Parkes' general state of wellbeing.

Albeit on a very limited scale, soon after its founding the Parkes Library itself took to publishing. In 1956 it issued a pamphlet Parkes had written about the Library itself, the first in

a series of reprints to be issued in a distinctive format. Like
'Jewish–Christian Relations in England', originally published in
1960 by the Jewish Historical Society, these largely consisted of
Parkes' own lectures or articles. Also included, however, were
reprints of works by Jules Isaac, Raphael Loewe, Maurice
Eisendrath, and others of comparable stature in the field of
interfaith relations. One reprint, 'The Meaning of Eichmann' by
David Astor, 'set in train a whole series of events culminating in
the creation, linked with Sussex University, of an institute
directed by Norman Cohn on The Psychopathology of Politics'.[10]
At Parkes' behest, Cohn then took over and finished Parkes'
never-completed work on *The Protocols of the Elders of Zion*. This
exemplified the sort of synergy that Parkes had hoped the
Library would facilitate.

From 1957 until the appearance of 'Christendom and the
Synagogue' in *Frontier's* Winter 1959 issue except for one short
piece in the *Jewish Chronicle*, Parkes, entirely undone by weakness
and ill health, did not publish anything. Thereafter however,
confounding the expectations of his physicians, he bounced back
with astonishing vigour. Parkes' rebound happened to coincide
with an upsurge in worldwide antisemitism. This led him to
suggest that Penguin reissue a revised edition of *An Enemy of the
People*. Sceptical about public interest in what seemed to its editors
a tired subject, Penguin countered by commissioning a 'Pelican'
edition on the history of the Jewish People.

The specifications for his new book were daunting: from
Abraham to the founding of the State of Israel, a running account
of the entire span of Jewish history in eighty thousand words.
In that narrow frame Parkes was 'to produce a leisurely and
unhurried survey'. As he explains,

> I first planned the titles of the chapters, then considered
> whether they told a simple or a complex story, allotted
> them so many words, and juggled with the words until
> the total came to eighty thousand ... My secretary, as
> she took each section, counted it and came back to me
> reporting 'you are seven words in hand' or 'you are five
> words over'.[11]

The meticulous planning involved in implementing this work
seemed to energize him nearly as much as the substance of the

work itself. It was the very sort of writer's game that Parkes, that inveterate index card strategist, loved to play and was one that he was confident he could win.

Parkes' finicky streak must at times have driven his secretary to distraction. We do well to recall that like his prudishness, his fussiness over detail was an enduring aspect of the personality, which played schoolboy martinet tyrannizing the younger boys at Elizabeth College when they strayed even an inch from the school regulations. In later years, if his wife were not at his elbow precisely at the moment when he wanted her, in or out of company he would bellow '*Daar-or-THEE!*' at the top of his voice, and he would often rudely chastise her over some minor indiscretion.[12] This is also the same pernickety chap who insisted that his copy of *The Times* should appear each morning not merely folded correctly but also ironed, and who instructed his servants on the correct method of draining washed teaspoons: they should be placed concave side down in order to drain properly.[13]

In short, the older Parkes grew, the less he tried to conceal his obsessive personality. At the same time, it is worth pondering that it took just such a punctilious type even to contemplate the discharging of Christianity's burden of guilt *vis-à-vis* the Jewish people by assuming the squaring of those historic accounts as a personal responsibility.

When Parkes was invited by Hebrew University in 1960 to address the Third International Congress of Jewish Studies in Jerusalem between 24 July and 2 August, he seized the chance; it would mean he could also conduct fresh research for his work-in-progress on Jewish history. It was his fourth visit to the country. At the final evening's plenary session, Parkes delivered a lecture entitled 'Religion and Peoplehood in the History of the Diaspora'.

Among Parkes' more disquieting findings in Israel were the troubling circumstances of the country's Protestant communities. From Archbishop Appleton, a friend and theological ally, he learned that the '... Anglican Archbishopric is in Jordan and Protestant Churches are scattered with little control over its "wild men".'[14] Later in the decade, when Archbishop McGuiness, a reactionary who was very hostile to Jewish interests, replaced Appleton, this chaotic disarray only intensified.

Parkes' most significant encounter was with young Peter Schneider, an Anglican chaplain in Jerusalem (not, in deference to Greek Orthodox sensibilities, 'of' Jerusalem) who acted as official advisor to the archbishop on Israeli religious affairs. Born a Jew but baptized as a child, Schneider was an ardent worker in the field of Arab–Jewish reconciliation.[15] He had formerly served as chaplain of Fitzwilliam College, Cambridge, 'but after nine years fewer and fewer remembered him'.[16] Drawn to one another, almost at once the two clerics established a close relationship.

Schneider, considered by his associates somewhat unstable, enthusiastically adopted Parkes' reformist perspective and came to be considered Parkes' disciple, perhaps even something of a surrogate son – certainly the closest to a spiritual son Parkes would ever have. Parkes equipped the young cleric with letters of introduction in Jerusalem, where the Parkes name was golden,[17] aided him in raising funds for his activist work, and did not neglect to warn him about Archbishop McGuiness: 'He is a most insinuating and dangerous person … and his ultimate ambition is a new missionary campaign to convert the Jews.'[18] Schneider, in turn, kept Parkes abreast of Jewish and Anglican matters in Jerusalem. His mentor at Barley would feel the young canon's early death as a grievous loss.

All things considered, for Parkes' spirit the Israeli interlude had been tonic. Back in England, he was soon again ticking off words for his *History*. Who at this point should arise from the shadows of oblivion but the seemingly indestructible 'Holy John' Hadham. Parkes had been asked to contribute to Gollancz's *Common Sense* series of books. Not one to decline an assignment, he interrupted his historical research, and in very short order 'Hadham' had turned out *Common Sense and Religion*. Until this point Parkes had entirely neglected the role of the Eastern religions in God's scheme for man's salvation. Inspired by the largeness of conception of the Gollancz series, now for the first time Parkes tried to incorporate Buddhism and Hinduism into his comprehensive vision. The result was less than successful.

Common Sense did, however, provide him with a fresh opportunity to reconcile what some had felt in *God at Work*, a 'Hadham' which had appeared under the 'pseudonym' of Parkes',[19] was an ambiguous relationship among his three cardinal virtues: love, truth and righteousness. Now nine years later, instead of positing a kind of static equipoise among them, he envisioned a vital dialectic. All three, he asserted, were essential for man's salvation, and the tension among them was now understood as 'creative'. A parallel resolution embraced similar distinctions in the activity of the three channels (or 'persons') of the Godhead. These were, for Parkes, the 'essential fuel with which the Creator ensured the development of his creation'.[20]

A History of the Jewish People appeared in 1962. Shortly thereafter it was translated into Dutch, Italian and Spanish. Parkes' real achievement with this book was not merely the technical miracle of producing a free-flowing, accurate, well-proportioned account of Jewish history in 80,000 words; more than any other English-language overview, Parkes' retrospective on Jewish history reflected his strongly Zionist bearings.

> It enabled me to put before the reader a perspective which could only be achieved by decades of more detailed study and writing. In particular, it gave me the opportunity of breaking with the Graetz–Roth tradition of treating the history of the Jews in the Middle East as episodic and concentrating attention on Europe. In relation to the length of the book, I paid much more attention to Palestine and the neighbouring countries than my predecessors.[21]

Parkes also took inordinate pride in being only the fourth Christian scholar ever to have attempted such a synthesis of Jewish history.

The following year, reacting strongly to the allegations of Arab propagandists and their academic sympathizers that Jews were basically Europeans alien to the Middle East – that is, a foreign, colonialist incursion into an Arab land – within the limits of his strength Parkes still carried his lance for the rights of the Jewish people in the region. In the autumn of 1963 he addressed the Anglo–Israel Association in London on 'The Continuity of Jewish Life in the Middle East'. Parkes demonstrated the absurdity of the regnant Arab narrative by pointing out that 'more than half the Jews in Israel were in their family background and tradition even more rooted in the countries of the Middle East and North Africa than the Arabs themselves – who only erupted from the [Arabian] peninsula in the seventh Christian century'. Six months later he hammered home the same theme in the annual Brodetsky Memorial Lecture at Leeds University.[22]

Having turned out two new titles in the space of two years,

hardly skipping a beat the resurgent scholar submitted to David
Kessler a proposal for a third book: an updated revised version
of *An Enemy of the People*. The upshot was that within a year it
too would be published under the imprint of Kessler's publishing house, Vallentine Mitchell. In short, in his early sixties Parkes
had ceased to comport himself like a man who hovered on the
brink of death. Furthermore, no longer a conceptual foundling,
the Parkes Library Ltd was now a proper foundation with an
enviable niche in the world of ecumenical scholarship. Although
far from robust or in the best of health, Parkes had adroitly
guided its development ever since its formal establishment in
1956. It would be both his legacy and his spiritual heir.

What then actually transpired within the precincts of the
Parkes Library? Deploying domestic detail in the spirit of the
Flemish masters, the Parkes' Christmas letter from 1963 paints a
tableau filled with a variety of figures pursuing purposeful
activity:

> We have one scholar – from America – working in the Hall
> on material from our periodicals; another in the Garden
> House – from Jerusalem – writing a book on the present
> confrontation between Judaism and Christianity; a third
> – from Germany – in the South Room preparing for
> publication by Gollancz her wonderful broadcasts on her
> life before, through and after the Nazi period. A fourth is
> occupying a corner of my workroom checking rabbinic
> references to a German work which he is translating for an
> English publisher. Dorothy is correcting the galley proofs of
> two publications due to appear this winter. And I am busy
> on my next book! You will see I refer to *the Hall* and the
> *Garden House*. The Hall is the big Club house next door
> which was idle and which we lease. We have all our
> periodicals there as well as our three offices. The Garden
> House is the old granary which we restored in 1961 with
> sitting room, bedroom and utility room.[23]

This scholarly pastorale fulfilled the greater part of Parkes'
fondest hopes for Barley, Ltd. He had excellent reason to feel a
sense of contentment and satisfaction. It was Parkes, for example,
who shepherded the manuscript by Else Rosenfeld – the 'scholar'
in the South Room – to Victor Gollancz and on to bestsellerdom
as *The Four Lives of Elsbeth Rosenfeld*. Moreover, as noted earlier,

Parkes himself seemed regenerated. A qualitative difference, however, may easily be detected: the impetus for writing two of his most recent books had issued not from a personal agenda but from the needs of publishers, and the third volume was actually a revision of an earlier work. Although Parkes worked contentedly and steadily, the falling off in creativity that had become noticeable around the time of the Second World War was all the more conspicuous. If not bone dry, the well of originality had been much drained. Noting the same decline, a close friend gives it a capricious spin:

> After the 1950s, Parkes went into a kind of eclipse [because] the Jewish world became obsessed with the importance of the Pope, hence with Roman Catholicism. With the end of the Mandate, there was less interest in Anglican prelates, especially since so many of them were pro-Arab. Further, it gravely disappointed him that he didn't get the credit in the public eye that he felt he deserved for helping to bring about this volte-face in the Church. People always mentioned that the Pope was influenced by Jules Isaac and Malcolm Hay, but few people mentioned Parkes any more.[24]

It is certainly true that with the end of the war and the unspeakable revelations about the Shoah, among intellectuals on the Continent antisemitism, a field whose fundamental ground had been broken by Parkes, suddenly became hot.

> Books such as Marcel Simon's *Versus Israel* (1948), Léon Poliakov's *Histoire de l'Antisémitisme* (1955), and Jules Isaac's *Genése de l'Antisémitisme*, all of which are in agreement with his thesis, have achieved classic status ... *Faith and Fratricide* (1974) by the radical American Catholic theologian Rosemary Reuther has made even more impact in the English-speaking world, though it has aroused a good deal of controversy.[25]

Blatantly overlooked, Parkes had genuine cause for professional jealousy and for nursing a measure of resentment. Even Jean-Paul Sartre's superficial *Antisemite and Jew*, which appeared in English in 1976, would make a major splash in trendy intellectual waters.[26] By the early 1990s *Anti-Semitism: The Longest Hatred* by the distinguished Israeli scholar Robert Wistrich omitted Parkes' name from the hundreds of entries in his selected bibliography.

Superannuated and superfluous, eclipsed by the Pope and the Roman Catholic Church, clearly increasingly embittered by the neglect of some of his peers, especially those on the Continent, deeply disturbed about what it foreboded about the perpetuation of his life's work, the silver-haired clergyman was undergoing a complex psychological crisis that his memoir camouflages behind a façade of geniality. In one respect his inner quandary reflected the very fact of 'retirement', a symbolic step that brings everyone significantly closer to the end of his journey. A man of Parkes' steadfast faith, however, rather than closing the door to further discoveries anticipates that death grants access to the greatest mystery of all. Ageing alone, therefore, hardly accounts for the severity of his inner turmoil.

Nor would heightened public consciousness of the centrality of the Roman Catholic Church within Christendom in and of itself render Parkes sombre or morbid. To a certain extent it is true that, as Werblowsky notes, the Jewish world was now looking elsewhere, and this impacted on Parkes' *amour propre*. Nevertheless, the Anglican priest who also spoke as a Jew responded to the dramatic and rapid alteration in Catholic attitudes towards the Jewish people with much the same subdued gratification as the rest of 'the Jewish world'. The ascension to the papacy in 1958 of John XXIII, who personally had given aid and succour to Jews during the war, had much to do with altered Jewish perceptions. Although John died in 1963, *Nostra Aetate,* his enduring legacy, would be promulgated by his successor, Pope Paul VI, in 1965.

On the one hand, Parkes notes that '… as late as 1961 an Irish Catholic priest could find a publisher to print … another outrageous work in which Jews are made subtly responsible for the whole history of antisemitism',[27] at the same time, Parkes established excellent relations with Father Paul Demann of the Jerusalem-based order of *les Pères de Sion*. Like its more active counterpart, *les Soeurs de Notre Dame de Sion,* several of whom Parkes also got to know well, *les Pères* are devoted to spreading a sympathetic understanding of Judaism. Within Britain the Dominicans, the order that had taken such a prominent role in the Inquisition, took the lead in organizing an annual Catholic–Jewish conference.

Indeed, it seems that in its incapacity to realize self-renewal and its hesitancy in approaching Jews in a spirit of reconciliation and understanding, the Anglican hierarchy, as timorous in its attitudes and behaviour as during the First World War,[28] was playing the turtle to the Roman hare. Parkes comments:

> ... today it would be unthinkable to plan any Jewish–Christian encounter in which one did not expect full Catholic cooperation ... Roman Catholic scholars ... may still drop bricks. The change is that nobody, Jew or Christian, doubts their integrity and the sincerity of their determination to write a new page in the relations of the two religions.[29]

Yet, having devoted the better part of his lifetime to the service of the Jewish people and to salvaging the honour of the Christian conscience, Parkes' true payment had always been appreciation and praise. For whatever cause when, as it seemed to him, this just recompense disproportionately deflected to Pope John XXIII and his Church, in spite of himself Parkes felt the slight as ingratitude. At times the man was genuinely in great spiritual pain. Compounding his disgruntlement and mortification, Parkes pondered why at this advanced stage of the journey the burden of perpetuating his life's work still rested so heavily upon his own shoulders.

Little of this inner stress surfaced in Parkes' Christmas letter of 1963, but by now he was tetchier and more short-tempered than formerly and altogether much more difficult to live with. Parkes had now passed sixty-five, the symbolic threshold of old age. Although he could point to a life of high achievement and international accolades, the very success of the Centre for Jewish–Christian Relations, later the Parkes Library, made him terribly uneasy. In the autumn John McNeilage announced that he could not carry out his household duties very much longer. One leg of the tripod upon which the entire operation stood would soon hobble away. If in truth Parkes was indispensable to its operation, how would it carry on without him? And what then the fate of his precious collection? When another man might have rested content, on the brink of retirement, indecision bedevilled the historian; indeed, he was soon precipitated into the throes of a profound depression.

NOTES

1. James Parkes, *Voyage of Discoveries* (London: Victor Gollancz, 1969), p. 222.
2. Ibid., p. 228.
3. Ibid.
4. Ibid., p. 229.
5. Ibid.
6. Ibid., p. 233.
7. James Parkes, Parkes Archives, File 60/31/2.
8. Parkes, *Voyage of Discoveries*, pp. 229–30, ff.
9. James Parkes, 'The Chosen People', *Georgia Review*, Vol. 9, No. I (Spring 1955), pp. 45–55.
10. Parkes, *Voyage of Discoveries*, pp. 230–31.
11. Ibid., p. 231.
12. Ellen Roth interviewed by the author in London, 22 July 2004.
13. *Vide* Chapter 24.
14. Archbishop Appleton letter to James Parkes, Parkes Archives, File 60/ 31/37.
15. Zvi Werblowsky interviewed by the author and Maggie Davidson, Jerusalem, 16 November 2003.
16. Parkes Archives, File 60/16/79.
17. Parkes Archives, File 60/33/19.
18. James Parkes letter to Peter Schneider, 11 July 1968, Parkes Archives, File 60/16/79.
19. *Vide* Chapter 31, Footnote 4.
20. Parkes, *Voyage of Discoveries*, pp. 226–27.
21. Ibid., 231–32.
22. Robert A. Everett, *Christianity Without Anti-Semitism: James Parkes and the Jewish–Christian Encounter* (Oxford: Pergamon, 1993), pp. 278–309, 330.
23. Parkes, *Voyage of Discoveries*, p. 237, ff. Notably absent is any reference to activity relating to Arab–Jewish reconciliation, the second of Wickings' three stated aims for the Centre. *Vide* Chapter 31.
24. Zvi Werblowsky interviewed by the author and Maggie Davidson.
25. Nicholas de Lange, 'James Parkes, A Centenary Lecture', in *Cultures of Ambivalence and Contempt*: *Studies in Jewish–Non-Jewish Relations*, eds Jones, Kushner and Pearce (London: Vallentine Mitchell, 1998), pp. 36–37.
26. In part reflecting his general mood, in a review in the *New Republic* (December 1948) after a preliminary nod in the direction of the famous existentialist's 'good intentions', Parkes savaged Sartre's *Antisemite and Jew*. 'Mr Sartre reveals in this study the inadequacy of [his] method of public psychoanalysis to the examination of sociological problems, and its complete sterility when it comes to discuss what action can be taken. And indeed when Mr Sartre at the end comes down to these matters, the result is hesitant, banal and unconvincing.
27. Parkes, *Voyage of Discoveries*, pp. 233–34.
28. *Vide* Chapter 10.
29. Parkes, *Voyage of Discoveries*, p. 235.

PART 6
THE MATTER OF IWERNE MINSTER

33

'A Life Enjoyed'

The bird would cease and be as other birds
But that he knows in singing not to sing.
The question that he frames in all but words
Is what to make of a diminished thing.[1]

The year was 1963 and Parkes was now sixty-seven. On the brink of retirement, his crisis of indecision over the disposition of the Parkes Library was impacting on his much-debilitated physical condition. The choice seemed to lie between reconstituting the collection primarily as a reference facility or continuing it mainly as a centre for ongoing scholarly activity. If the former, then even though it would flicker as but a faint star among far more prestigious constellations, Parkes conceded that for maximum benefit it should be relocated in London. If the more *engagé* role were embraced, true to the instincts of a lifetime he strongly preferred a venue at a distance from the distractions of the capital.

Ideally, Parkes would have liked to cement an association between the Parkes Library and Cambridge University; however the reaction to his overtures was disappointing. Were it to receive his collection, Cambridge held out scant hope that it would retain its integrity. An image of the dismembered contents of the Parkes Library melting away repelled him. Along with his trove of personal writings, his Jewish Collection, nurtured so lovingly from humble beginnings in the early 1930s, constituted an integral component of his spiritual legacy. As in the Solomonic parable, the thought of its corporeal dissolution struck him as almost unbearable.

At the same time the Institute at Barley had been as it were co-sired, if only *in vitro*, by Israel Sieff. At this trying juncture the Library's *éminence grise*, acting in what he considered his old friend's best interests, exacerbated his distress immeasurably. With neither Parkes' knowledge nor his consent, Sieff brokered a deal with the provost of University College, London, one of his battalion of close friends, for the transfer of the entire Parkes Library to the capital.[2] When it reached Parkes' ears that his dearest treasure had been contracted to lie within the guarded vaults of the library of University College, accessible solely to those granted special authorization, he was outraged. It would be difficult to resolve whether the arrangement itself or Sieff's presumption vexed him the more.

In any event, the upshot was that a freshly galvanized Parkes energetically countermanded Sieff's *fait accompli,* in the process driving a painful wedge between himself and his well-intentioned chairman of the board. In superseding Parkes' authority in the final disposition of the Library, his benefactor could not possibly have realized what it would evoke for his friend: the high-handedness of Henry Parkes who had repeatedly and provocatively disposed of any possessions his son left behind on his return to Oxford.[3] There had always been a filial dimension to the relationship between Parkes and Sieff, a very Sir Hugo Mallinger[4] to Parkes' Deronda. At his best Sieff was the embodiment of an idealized parental figure, one whose vital divergence from Parkes' natural father was founded upon their mutual respect. Now that his paternal role had suddenly drifted into paternalism, Sieff triggered not merely opposition to his plan for the Jewish books but a highly personalized reaction. Parkes saw only one way forward: 'I felt obliged to ask him to resign the chairmanship he had assumed when first the institution was established.'[5]

This episode also activated what had been a less salient aspect of the relationship between the two. As well as a father figure, Sieff embodied the parallel role of an idealization of Parkes' older, long-dead brother. From this perspective, his betrayal in the affair of the Library took on a deeply ironic and far more sinister cast, one traditionally associated with Judas.

Parkes goes on to declare that some months later 'it was a great happiness to us that we could forget the past and renew our previous relations before we actually left Barley'.[6] Although a fine sentiment, this is reminiscent of his remarking after the breach with 'Len' Thomas that the two of them 'remained good friends'. One gravely doubts, after what for Parkes was so grievous a betrayal of trust, that his relationship with Sieff could ever genuinely be restored to its former intimacy. The sentiment stood only because the press of circumstance never again would strain it. In effect, then, at this critical juncture in his life, Parkes fired his 'Jewish father' and disavowed his 'Jewish brother', a symbolic double banishment that later would bear a most curious consequence.[7]

With his official retirement looming ever closer, Parkes could devise no better recourse for dealing with his dearest treasure than to pack it up and put it in temporary storage. At this point Fate, or perhaps the Holy Spirit, interceded. On this occasion the *deus ex machina* spoke with a Welsh accent. After delivering the 1963 Montefiore Lecture at the University of London, Parkes was invited to attend the following year's winter convocation which would convene at the University of Southampton. Ten months later, therefore, we find him idly chatting at a reception following the evening's presentation when he heard an unfamiliar voice from the other side of the room call out in his direction: 'I THOUGHT IT WOULD BE JIMMY.'

Parkes was pleasantly startled by the approach of a bluff stranger who identified himself as a student at Aberystwyth in 1924 when Parkes, then a novice travelling secretary for the SCM, had made a memorable presentation. Over the years that impressionable student had risen in life to become the irrepressible vice-chancellor of the University of Southampton.[8]

At a meeting the following morning, the Welshman offered the Guernseyman a deal he could not refuse: except for the relatively few items Parkes wanted closer at hand, the entire Parkes Library, including special gems such as a Jewish book printed in 1475 and a pamphlet dating from 1493, would be bestowed upon the library of the University of Southampton. Thus enriched, this institution contracted to maintain the Parkes Library intact as a living collection. Further, the University would fund a Parkes Research Fellowship in the field of Jewish/non-Jewish relations. On Parkes obtaining the approval of his board of governors, early in 1964, after operating for eight years, the Parkes Library Ltd ceased to function as an independent entity. It rested with its founder and former director to arrange for the shipment of the collection to Southampton where it would be consolidated with the far more modest Jewish library of Claude Montefiore, president of Southampton College in its pre-university days.[9]

Having divested himself of the pleasures and burdens of stewardship over a great treasure, Parkes felt free officially to 'retire'. The Parkeses had already spent the better part of a week poking about the countryside of Wiltshire and Dorset in search of a likely village. Had he been chiefly interested in salubrious breezes and mild winters, theoretically Parkes might have entertained the notion of a return to Guernsey. Although he had over the years nurtured a few friendships with islanders, in fact the possibility never arose. Once the Parkes Library had found a permanent repository in Southampton, easy access to its precincts was a non-negotiable priority. Even after his retirement Parkes, as he might have done for his own child, would still be manoeuvring for its aggrandizement. For example, as late as 1973 he was trying, albeit unsuccessfully, to exploit the bestowal of the Munk Award as leverage to transform the Parkes Library into 'a proper Institute'.[10]

Moreover, although Parkes always enthusiastically endorsed a romanticized affirmation of his roots, an equivocal subtext clouded the official legend. Overridingly self-conscious, somewhat skewed recollections of the simple folk and rugged sea coast of an idyllic land, Parkes' Guernsey would always be ineradicably shadowed by irreparable loss and private desolation. The inner logic of the plot of his lifeline militated against any full circle 'return of the native'. Far more suitable than a shock of confrontation half a century later with scenes of his boyhood, which given the post-war surge in Guernsey's property values he could ill have afforded anyway, was the insulation of his redoubt in Dorset.

In a fashion, the ageing, slightly stooped figure continued to tread in the path of the patriarch Jacob who would also die outside the borders of his land of birth. There was a difference, however, for in the end Jacob's sons would repatriate his bones to the homeland his heart had never abandoned. But in this unravelling of Parkes' final skein of years, more than his namesake, Parkes now evokes the greatest of all Paladins of the Jews. Despite his non-Jewish upbringing, like the Anglican scholar the orphaned Moses – also in his prime, also with reluctance – spoke also as a Jew. At the end of his days, he could no more than gaze off in the direction of the land of his dreams which, while not distant, was now proscribed.

In scouting about for a new home in the vicinity of Southampton, one of Parkes' major considerations was to take up residence within the jurisdiction of a spiritually congenial bishop, one with

whom he might manage to avoid feuding. Given Parkes' professional needs, his prickly personality and the ecclesiastical
humiliation he had undergone during his latter years at Barley,
this was plainly sagacious. The play of fortune turned up the
Reverend Joe Fison, a friendly acquaintance who had served as
a chaplain in Jerusalem during the Second World War. He was
now Bishop Fison with jurisdiction for the diocese of Salisbury,
Wiltshire, which, fortuitously enough, embraced all the saturnine
Hardy Country lying north and west of Southampton. Similarly,
the choice of a particular village hinged upon locating a local
vicar for whom both Parkes and his wife might feel a measure
of warmth and respect. That eliminated a great many locales out
of hand.

Steered by Fison to the village of Iwerne Minster, the two of
them attended a communion service at which the Reverend Rex
Wells officiated. They responded immediately to Wells' sensitivity and special deftness in bringing 'parish problems and
personal needs into the service'.[11] On the spot the couple arrived
at a firm decision. By happy chance – though at this point
perhaps even sceptics might detect the agency of some higher
power – a cottage belonging to Wells' churchwarden was on the
market. With little ado, in March 1964 they purchased the house
on the High Street in the village where they would live out the
remainder of their days.

West of Southampton in the county of Dorset, not far from
the town of Blandford Forum, Iwerne Minster remains today
a small, attractive hamlet on the River Iwerne (pronounced
'Youwern'). Or, as Parkes himself more picturesquely puts it:
'Iwerne Minster is a pleasant village, nestling under the western
heights of Cranborne Chase, a village of cows and pigs and their
attendants in the first and second degree, of Clayesmore School
– and of retired persons like ourselves.'[12] In short, it was a quiet,
peaceful place with obvious intrinsic appeal for the elderly
scholar-cleric who relished the sobriquet of 'countryman'.

However, the arrival at Barley of the librarian of the University of Southampton who, naturally enough, wished to appraise
his valuable, new acquisitions at first hand, precipitated a sudden
crisis. Overcome by the realization that the time for his actual
departure from Barley was fast drawing nigh, that the life he
loved was to change utterly and irrevocably, Parkes sank into
depression. He simply could not contemplate leaving the home

into which so much of his life had been poured. As on several
past occasions of a similar nature, he suddenly made himself
extremely scarce. Or, as he puts it more blandly: 'I deliberately
left all the final clearance to John McNeilage, so that the memories
which Dorothy has of the house are of it in a relatively normal
state, with its beauty of floors, beams, and furnishings.'[13]

Memories which *Dorothy* had of the house! Parkes' tortured
syntax exposes his inner turmoil. It is true that, after more than
two decades in residence, Dorothy Wickings too had grown very
attached to her home at Barley. However, it is manifest that by
far the greater share of delicate feelings that needed sparing
were Parkes' own. By all accounts he was a deeply sentimental
man who frequently was seen to weep copiously in public.[14] To
delegate responsibility for the final clearance of the premises to
McNeilage as a manoeuvre to protect his wife's easily bruised
sensibilities is a woefully transparent ruse, a self-conscious,
misguided effort to put an acceptable face on private anguish.
Is it plain that Parkes was deeply embarrassed by the eruption
of 'unmanly' feelings.

This sleight of hand bears yet other dimensions. Once again
we recall Parkes' failure to acknowledge guilt or responsibility
in the Thomas affair. Just as Thomas absorbed the bruising
intended for his employer, Parkes was now conscious that not
Thomas's successor McNeilage but he himself should have been
overseeing the packing and shipping details and in his own
person absorbing the emotional blows that accompany this rite
of passage. Not only did Parkes sense that at this juncture the
delegation to someone else of responsibility for attending to his
beloved collection was bad form, but also the whole business
almost certainly resurrected never resolved feelings appertaining
to his 'man' Thomas and the leave-taking from Geneva three
decades earlier when we recall that once before Parkes could not
quite bring himself to attend to the 'dirty work'.

That he was in his own eyes not man enough to finesse the
situation appropriately goes entirely unremarked upon in *Voyage
of Discoveries*. The ceremonies of departure from Barley so
unnerved Parkes, in fact, that, he resorted to a pattern of avoid-
ance behaviour that brought him to the verge of emotional
prostration. In the months after his Library no longer lined the
bookshelves of the manor house, redolent of another time,
another place, Parkes absconded, a deserter from a scene of

devastation he could not bear to survey. At first the couple took up residence in the cottage that had until her death been inhabited by old Mrs Wickings, but even then he simply could not bear guiding prospective purchasers through the vacant, echoing rooms of the manor house that had served as the intimate backdrop for his life of service and of privilege. Thereupon Parkes prevailed upon his neighbours Sam and Doris Wilkinson to move into the manor for several months. Until the property was sold, it fell to the Wilkinsons to show the house and grounds to potential buyers.[15]

In sum, first resorting to McNeilage, then ducking behind the Wilkinsons, when it came actually to performing the normal and necessary chores and duties, incumbent upon their departure from home, Parkes faltered. Reminiscent of his boyhood terror of homelessness and later of the trenches, he was just not up to it. In a fit of weakness Parkes devised his unchivalrous dodge: a highly dubious show of conjugal delicacy that presumed to spare his wife's feelings on confronting a devastation that evoked echoes of Ypres Salient.

At the same time, throughout this agonizing period of transition Parkes remained surprisingly productive. Exploiting a school building as a temporary study, he turned out short pieces for the Ecclesiastical History Society and the Jewish Historical Society as well as an upbeat essay by Hadham entitled 'God's Great Canvas' for a journal in Wales. He also brought *The Five Roots of Israel* to press for Kessler at Vallentine Mitchell. Still Parkes was moody, his nerves taut, and he felt incapable of performing the usual ceremonies of departure. What saved him was an unexpected, seemingly godsent, invitation to visit Israel. The ostensible purpose of the trip was to study how well the recent influx of Sephardic Jews was adapting to a new society. In fact the greater part of this mass wave of immigration had crested a full decade earlier, and Parkes himself had already devoted considerable attention to the subject in *A History of the Jewish People* (1962).[16] The excursion's real impetus was to put time and distance between Parkes and his former Barley home.

In August, on their return to England, the couple headed straight for Iwerne Minster to take up residence in their new cottage and to enter upon this new and final stage of their lives. True to form, Parkes at once set to work refashioning the modest domicile in his own image. Indoors he turned his attention to minor carpentry, but out of doors he was more typically ambitious, completely redesigning the garden which had been much neglected by the previous owner,

> ... alter[ing] its levels and its main axis [because the garden] should be visually effective from the kitchen when we are washing up, and from the one window which looks over the whole of our vast estate. We are Dorset landowners to the extent of one-fourteenth of an acre, just a convenient size to retire to.[17]

The self-deprecating tone of this description should not deafen us to its bittersweet undercurrent: 'a convenient size to retire to,' conforms to the many travails and diminutions that define the process of ageing. Could Parkes adjust to Yeats' paltry, tattered country of the elderly with half the good grace that at least some of the Sephardim were successfully adapting to their new land?

Like promotional hype for a gilded retirement, Parkes in *Voyage of Discoveries* labels this episode 'A Life Enjoyed'. The move did not seem yet to have radically affected the nature of his activities. Parkes carried on with some writing, travel and occasional lecturing. Furthermore, his new home was soon orderly enough to receive visitors. One summer afternoon, for example, Ruth Weisz, who had arrived in Barley as a refugee schoolgirl of six around the time of the inception of the 'idea' of the manor house, drove down with two daughters of her own to meet 'Uncle James'.[18] Another August visitor to Iwerne Minster vividly recalls his jovial host 'captivating our children Paula and Steve with tales of a mischievous "impersonating Elemental" that dwelt in his boyhood homestead of Guernsey'.[19] Particularly when one recalls how close Parkes had been to dying several times and how debilitated he had grown over a period of years, at least on the surface those early months and years at Iwerne Minster were enjoyable enough.

As will be discussed from another angle in the ensuing chapter, before *A Life Enjoyed* was abandoned in favour of *Voyage of Discoveries*, Parkes originally intended it to serve as the title for the memoir as a whole. Even were it applied solely to this initial period of retirement, however, 'A Life Enjoyed' would emit a scent of evasiveness and falsification. Apart from its entirely unsuitable overtone of hedonism, Parkes' life was, like most lives, a very mixed affair. He himself was, of course, familiar with Aristotle's commentary on this point:

> Now if we must see the end and only then call a man happy, not as being happy but as having been so before, surely this is a paradox ... because we have assumed happiness to be something permanent and by no means easily changed, while a single man may suffer many turns of fortune's wheel. For clearly if we were to keep pace with his fortunes, we should often call the same man happy and again wretched, making the happy man out to be a chameleon and insecurely based.[20]

Notwithstanding its reduced estate, a house of his own with a pleasing view of a patch of garden were critical elements for sustaining Parkes' peace of mind and self-image as a countryman scholar. Still lacking, however, was a most critical element for his wellbeing. Later that autumn Parkes begged his old friend Simpson to drive to Barley to pick up and to deliver to Iwerne Minister cartons containing books he had selected to accompany him into retirement. Simpson's widow recalls the journey well:

> The move was difficult, a major event. Driving down to Iwerne for lunch, Bill [Simpson] was almost hysterical with apprehension because haywagons in the road delayed the journey, and you could *never* be late to lunch with James. He was very proud of his cottage garden and indicated which colours were best to look at. He set the table for lunch. He was very precise. He explained where everything in the house had come from. When I remarked upon the lovely cups, James showed me how to place one sideways inside of the other to ensure that they wouldn't accidentally break.[21]

Closely parallelling the early months at Barley thirty years earlier when he periodically took sanctuary from the physical demands of his estate by retreating to the hushed precincts of Cambridge, Parkes now established a second base in Southampton. At first he spent considerable time at the Hartley Library, unpacking, arranging and then lovingly rearranging his old friends on the waiting shelves. Each book spoke to him not only of a particular time, a definite place and the exact details of its purchase but also of the exquisite elation that accompanied its acquisition. Although in the end he had succeeded in keeping the collection intact, a dimension of melancholy attached itself to these pilgrimages to Southampton.

In the midst of this labour of love, Parkes mused over the summer some sixty years earlier when a lonely adolescent had volunteered to clean and catalogue all the books in the Elizabeth College library. He recalled the friendship the shy, lonely adolescent forged with William Rolleston, the history master who chose to assist him. Engaged again at much the same task after so long an interval, he reflected upon how good a show he had made of the intervening years. For the most part, Parkes certainly had reason for contentment and, especially during this early phase at Iwerne, he visited Southampton and his collection fairly regularly.

In 1965 Parkes attended the annual conference of the Council of Christians and Jews, convening that year in Cambridge; it was his final session as a member of its governing board. In the course of the year he composed three short pieces and one substantial article: 'The Bible, the World, and the Trinity', the lead piece in the January number of the *Journal of the Bible and Religion*. Then came a surprising development: a sectarian publishing house in the United States issued a bowdlerized edition of *Good God*. This set Parkes in quest of fulfilling every old man's fondest dream: to recreate some of the successes of his youth.

In such disingenuous wise he brought the idea of producing a revised, proper edition of *Good God* to the attention of the director of the SCM Press:

> Though just as personally 'orthodox' as [Bishop] Woolwich, I am far more radical, because I have *lived* among the people he admits the preaching of the Church cannot reach: Jews, atheists, agnostics, and so on ... Consequently, I am far more concerned that this challenge to the full use of the Trinitarian revelation be put to the present world than that it be put by or even refer to James Parkes or John Hadham.[22]

Things, he asserted, had changed in forty years. If the Church's traditional theology was still as 'blinkered' as ever, at least more churchmen were aware of it.

The churches now realize that a Christo-centric religion does not now and never will again meet the whole of human need ... Man a social being, lives by righteousness and justice ... and righteousness and justice always belong to the realm of the attainable, not to the personal realm of the infinite and the unattainable ... The whole set of emotions connected with the idea that 'God sent his son' seemed to me already in 1939 to be repellant. That is why I always speak of 'God-in-a-human-life'.[23]

Parkes' proposal carried the day; a third version of *Good God* appeared that very September. Little could do more to enhance the retirement or to intensify the gratification of its author's 'life enjoyed'.

Also appearing in 1966 were two brief Parkes articles about Israel as well as a proleptic piece about the power of Christian healing; in the following year he turned out two signature pieces on Jewish–Christian relations, a major examination of the millennial idea in Judaism for the *Jewish Journal of Sociology*, and an update on the Middle East conflict. On a modest roll as a writer, Parkes was thwarted in another sphere. Early in 1967 he tried to persuade the CCJ to establish the Autonomous Committee for Peace in the Middle East. It would, he remarks, have been 'expensive' because its activities would have called for full-page notices in the national press.[24] This turned out to be a decisive consideration: the idea never got off the ground.

In June Parkes shared in the universal jubilation of the Jewish world over Israel's lightning victory in the Six-Day War. Thereupon he accepted an invitation to address a Jewish conference in Toronto in September and, taking full advantage of a surge of uncommon vitality, even tempted fate by undertaking the rigours of yet another journey to Israel. He had been invited there to address a special convocation at Bar-Ilan University. Located just outside of Tel-Aviv, it is the only university in Israel that functions under religious auspices.[25]

In Israel Parkes confronted a people who, basking in the triumphal glow of having thoroughly defeated their enemies – or so it seemed – were vaingloriously swarming over their much-expanded boundaries. It was this reflex of hubris that, nullifying residual Shoah guilt, has so altered the way Israel is perceived by most Europeans and many North Americans. At first little sensing this change in perception, many Israelis behaved as if typecast for brashness and boorishness. While of course partaking in the mood of elation, the elderly, visiting cleric could not help but sympathize with the diminished estate of the remaining Arabs. He was himself a Dorset landowner 'to the extent of one-fourteenth of an acre'. Far better than his hosts Parkes understood that a Jewish State dominated by the tribe of Gulliver would be most inconvenient for the promotion of peace either with themselves or with their neighbours.[26]

There were several religious sites Parkes wanted to visit on what, for all he knew, would be his final visit to the Holy Land. One site that he approached with deep ambivalence was the Church of the Holy Sepulchre in Jerusalem, Christianity's holiest and most disputatious site. By special permission of the Greek Orthodox Church, which claims by far the majority of Christian adherents in the country, Church of England clerics are permitted to celebrate the Eucharist at a single altar located in an obscure corner of the poorly lit building. As Parkes approached the designated place, he was overwhelmed by the scandal and enormity of the internecine contentiousness so powerfully reified by the dismemberment of the church into warring Christian fiefdoms. Repulsed more than he could bear, crashing into several chairs along the way, once again he fled the scene.[27]

On his return to England, Parkes produced several articles aimed at counteracting the unalloyed one-sidedness of *Israel and the Arabs*, Maxime Rodinson's highly influential pro-Arab polemic that Penguin had recently published.[28] However the most intriguing project on his plate was a suggestion from Victor Gollancz that the time was appropriate for him to consider composing his memoirs. As the publisher had anticipated, Parkes instantly warmed to the offer. After all, it dealt with a topic very dear to his heart.

NOTES

1. Robert Frost, from 'The Oven Bird', *American Literature*, Vol. 2, edited by Poirier and Vance (Boston: Little, Brown, 1970), p. 519.
2. James Parkes, *Voyage of Discoveries* (London: Victor Gollancz, 1969), p. 239.
3. *Vide* Chapter 11.
4. Daniel Deronda's 'Uncle'.
5. Parkes, *Voyage of Discoveries*, p. 240.
6. Ibid., p. 241.
7. *Vide* Chapter 34.

8. Parkes, *Voyage of Discoveries*, pp. 240–41.
9. Ibid., p. 241.
10. James Parkes, letter to the editor of *Every Echo*, 24 November 1973, Parkes Archive, File 60/33/19.
11. Parkes, *Voyage of Discoveries*, p. 241.
12. Ibid., p. 242.
13. Ibid.
14. *Vide* Chapter 24.
15. Edith Ruth Weisz, interviewed by the author and Maggie Davidson in Cambridge, England, 28–29 August 2000.
16. *Vide* Chapter 32.
17. Parkes, *Voyage of Discoveries*, p. 243.
18. Dorothy Wickings Parkes, *Autobiography*, Parkes Archives, File 60/33/3.
19. Roy A. Eckhardt, 'In Memoriam James Parkes, 1896–1981', *Journal of Ecumenical Studies*, 19:1 (Winter 1982).
20. Aristotle, *The Nicomachean Ethics*, translated and edited by David Ross (London: Oxford University Press, 1969), p. 20.
21. Ruth Weyl interviewed by the author and Maggie Davidson in Rehovot, Israel, 26 October 2003.
22. James Parkes, letter to the Reverend David Edwards, 1 February 1966, Parkes Archives, File 60/6/1.
23. Ibid.
24. James Parkes, *Voyage of Discoveries*, pp. 244–45.
25. Harold Fisch interviewed by the author by telephone, 10 October 2001.
26. James Parkes, *Voyage of Discoveries*, pp. 244–45.
27. Zvi Werblowsky, interviewed by the author and Maggie Davidson in Jerusalem, 16 November 2003.
28. Parkes Archives, File 60/16/79.

34

An Anniversary Present

*Borges referred to anything put into words as a 'fiction'. We are all fiction
makers, he reminds us, from the fictions we cobble together to explain our
days to the larger fictions we assemble to make sense of our lives.*[1]

True to the habits of a lifetime, James Parkes maintained a meticulous file of correspondence and drafts of all his writings.
Displaying, however, little talent for introspection, the historian
rarely stirred the embers of his own past. If, misled by the title
of his autobiography, we anticipate that the Reverend Dr Parkes
would draw inspiration from Saint Augustine, we err. He kept
no journal of his passing days and years. Zvi Werblowsky, Ruth
Weyl and other friends have no recollection of his ever alluding
to his parents, brother, or sister or of his reminiscing about his
boyhood. To spice his social discourse Parkes, unlike most ageing
raconteurs, rarely made withdrawals from the deepest deposits
of memory – Guernsey, Ypres, Oxford.

At least until he moved to Geneva and was struck dumb –
and then wise – by antisemitism, an impermeable barrier
sealed his youth in the deeper crevices of consciousness. Banish-
ing the more problematic facets of his past insulated Parkes from
their doleful influence at the cost of self-alienation. This was
hardly an ideal mindset for someone who at the age of seventy-
three and unpracticed in introspection undertakes to write his
autobiography.

> Writing about your past is like blundering through your
> house with lights fused, a hand flailing for points of refer-
> ence. You locate the stolid wardrobe, and its door swings
> open at your touch, opening on the cavern of darkness
> within. Your hand touches glass, you think it is a mirror, but
> it is the window. There are obstacles to bump and trip you,
> but what is more disconcerting is a sudden empty space,
> where you can't find a handhold and you know that you
> are stranded in the dark.[2]

Had Parkes, as Borges remarks in the above epigraph, been driven by an inner fury to explain his days and years, had he quested after a Northwest Passage to link the old scholar with the boy on the beach or the subaltern in the trenches to the expatriate activist, he would have risked being stranded on a distant shore. But basically Parkes was only fulfilling a publisher's assignment, doing homework. If he did sporadically make landfall, as often as not he mistook America for India or Iceland.

Parkes' *Voyage* is more of a breezy cruise than a conscious probe into mysterious depths and nothing at all like the disorienting bout of private terror conjured up by the above commentator. Were Parkes ever aware of having mistaken a window for mirror, he took pains to conceal it. As an antidote, a seasoned writer's nuanced description of the art of autobiography serves as a corrective:

> Memoirs are not lives, but texts alluding to lives. The technique of memoir resembles that of fiction: selection, distillation, dramatization. Inevitably, much is omitted. Inevitably, much is distorted. Memories are notoriously unreliable, particularly in individuals prone to mythmaking and the settling of old scores, which may be all of us.[3]

It takes some doing to reconcile the protagonist, half-blinded and stumbling like a dreamy intruder in an unfamiliar house that shockingly bears his name, with the helmsman in full technical control of the passage. By turns, both formulations are correct and both are incomplete. If one resounds with the sensibility of overheated Romanticism, the other reflects the Enlightenment filtered through post-Modernist lenses; in short, Poe versus Dr Johnson.

Although the journeys undertaken by the memoirist and his reader are spatially co-terminus, they are temporally disjunctive. This reflects not contradictory but complementary orders of experience. We only give Parkes his due to grant that much of the skill of the navigator resides in smoothing out bumps for his passengers. Cushioned by his placid tone and veneer of self-assurance, we never feel ourselves endangered by high waves lapping over the bulkhead or in imminent peril of being swept overboard. Parkes never imagined we might have wanted it otherwise. Only upon reflection are we jarred by textual omissions and serial discontinuities which, taken together, subtly affect our sense of the inner man behind the composed, strikingly handsome face.

Little in *Voyage of Discoveries* recalls the ironic perspective that informs Joyce's self-portrait as Stephen Daedalus. In Parkes' meanderings around Provence, for example, we hear that the young traveller was enthralled by the twelfth century Cistercian Abbey of Silvacane.[4] Did he never find his way to Carpentras where a fourteenth century synagogue still stands or to the medieval Jewish quarters of Draguignan, Manosque, or Petuis, most venerable of all French Jewish communities? If not, should the ageing champion of the Jews not have found that droll or at least noteworthy? If so, should we conclude that they left no impression? What strikes us is not the young man's excusable ignorance of Provence's powerful Jewish resonance but the old scholar's insensibility to its potential and his failure to exploit it. Because Parkes seems profoundly unaware of the comic provincialism and naïveté of the twenty-eight-year-old backpacker, his 'Portrait of the Historian-Priest as a Young Man' engages us little.

Parkes is explicit about his autobiographical aims only once. When insulted by the shoddy treatment he was accorded by Oxford University Press, he reports that he aimed to add a row of bricks to already tall defensive ramparts.

> It is no part of my intention in this record to moan over the number of times I found myself 'on the wrong side of the fence' for failing to live up to the attitudes expected of a Christian cleric or a 'non-Jewish' scholar. I was naturally accused of being a partisan, or being in the pocket of the Jews, and so on. But I started the work itself with my eyes open, and the original title I chose for this story was *A Life Enjoyed*. Moreover, I have never written on any aspect of the question without doing my very best to understand all the issues and both of the sides involved.[5]

The open-eyed 'work itself' in the above refers, of course, to the central mission of Parkes' life: to carry a lance as a Christian Champion against the Serpent of Antisemitism. In context, the effortless segue into *A Life Enjoyed* proclaims an intention of projecting the mythos of a life positively overflowing with the satisfactions of manly, intellectual engagement. Moreover, by inscribing the book to his wife as 'A Silver Wedding Present', Parkes armed himself with a structural rationalization, a built-in justification for detouring around matters that might derogate from the spirit of celebration.

There were, of course, more than a few readers who found much to admire in Parkes' navigational skill:

> When I read his autobiography – *Voyage of Discoveries* – I learnt a lot more about his life ... I found in the events he described and in the way he described them the same boyish curiosity, enthusiasm, and irrepressible fun. He adored deflating pompous people, teasing the self-important, cutting through mystification and deception, and at the same time he was always ready to stand up for the underdog, for the unfortunate or oppressed, and had an unquestioning faith in goodness and truth. These characteristics ... kept him young and fresh and greatly loved to the end of his long life, and they prevented him from ever becoming over-earnest or pompous himself.

'I do recommend the autobiography,' continues the above commentator, emphatic syntax betraying awareness that he was bucking a trend. 'It makes fascinating and very entertaining reading.'[6]

However both Parkes and Wickings were sensible to general dissatisfaction with the book: 'To some *Voyage of Discoveries* was "disappointing" because it was deficient in "personal touches".'[7] In fact Parkes' memoir abounds in too many personal touches for its own good. What it lacks is personal insight, a shortcoming not be confused with moral or ethical obtuseness; nor does it diminish Parkes' achievement as an historian and ethical template for a whole generation. Unwitting irony attends Wickings' judgment that 'in a sense it [the book] ... is a version of *Gulliver's Travels* – and I have been a fellow traveller'.[8]

Although construing Parkes' work differently from the above fellow travellers, as far as it goes we concur in the judgment that *Voyage of Discoveries* is a fascinating, entertaining excursion that does drop anchor at nearly all the major ports of call in his life. It is jumbled with bric-a-brac and riddled with significant omissions and unconscious distortions, and infrequently, it is even unreliable. Inverting one of the above prescriptions, less than Parkes doing an impersonation of a self-possessed memoirist, it is his critical reader who, ever groping for handholds, discovers himself at times careering about the deck, at times on hands and knees, as he strives to reconstruct the elusive, all the more instructive gaps in the record. Alone among Parkes' books, this is a text that warms to deconstructive caresses.

Let us readdress Parkes' much meditated choice of title, *Voyage of Discoveries*. The elision of plural and singular terms is not merely queer but singularly infelicitous. Its only saving grace is that either of Parkes' discarded contenders – *Voyage of Explorations* and *A Life Enjoyed* – would have been clumsier still. The only thing that *A Life Enjoyed* reflects is an old man in Dorset persuading himself how he must have felt.[9]

But just when we are on the verge of consigning Parkes' *Voyage* to superficiality, a tremor causes the entire artifice to wobble disclosing a startling slant of playfulness and complication. Could there after all inhere in *Voyage* facets devised mainly for self-gratification or additionally, perhaps, for the pleasure of Parkes' wife? Were this the case, we would have to revise previous estimates not only of the author's craftiness but also of his innermost loyalties.

We pause at length, therefore, over a most curious business: the transfiguration of Israel Marcus (Moses) Sieff, Parkes' great Jewish friend and benefactor but also his occasional tormentor and, almost inevitably, Dorothy Wickings Parkes' unacknowledged rival. As expounded earlier Sieff, seven years Parkes' senior, functioning for him like a fusion of older brother and foster father,[10] is consistently referred to as 'I.M.S.'. Peculiar at first, the reader soon adjusts to the practice because, at times confusingly, Parkes' text is peppered with scores of initialled abbreviations. All but two of these initials signify institutional bodies such as the Student Christian Movement which appears dozens of times as SCM. Similarly, ISS stands in for the International Student Service on at least twenty occasions. Had Parkes not proceeded thus, his text would have been sluggish and a great deal lengthier.

However, this is not the case with the non-institutional 'I.M.S.' which, we also note, actually occupies slightly more space on the page than 'Sieff'. Apparently self-conscious about treating such a dear old friend with unexpected flippancy, on Sieff's first appearance Parkes volunteers a semblance of an explanation: 'As Israel Sieff comes into the story a good deal and as "Israel" by itself is liable to ambiguity he appears henceforth by the initials "I.M.S.".'[11] The reader readily grants the superficially plausible premise provisional credence. Only later are suspicions aroused that Parkes' 'explanation' is most likely a ruse.

Shortly after the Second World War America's National Weather Bureau began personifying hurricanes. One year it announced that it planned to name the ninth storm of the autumn season 'Israel'. However, on receiving warnings that some people would associate the havoc wrought by the storm with the Jewish State, it replaced 'Israel' with a different 'I' name. Unlike that atypical situation, however, at no time or place in Parkes' memoir does the context raise the remotest doubt whether 'Israel' would refer to the millionaire or to the Jewish State – it would never have been an issue.

In conversation Sieff always answered to 'Israel', and over the years he always signed his letters to Parkes as 'Israel'. It was simply his name. Moreover, Parkes always addressed his friend in correspondence as 'My dear Israel'. A flimsy but at least comprehensible reason for resorting to initials, paralleling this author's use of 'Wickings', could have been to prevent the reader from even momentarily mistaking one Sieff for another. However, apart from a single appearance by Sieff's wife Rebecca, on no occasion are other Sieffs featured in Parkes' text. Furthermore, Parkes identifies all his other close friends by surname. If Archbishop William Temple, again and again, could appear just as 'Temple', then it would be reasonable to expect that Israel Sieff would appear as 'Sieff'.

Could Parkes possibly have conceived that the man with whom he had conducted so many intimate conversations before the wood fire long into the night and who lived on for three years after the publication of *Voyage of Discoveries* would be passive, unmoved or even pleased by seeing himself depicted in such impersonal, indeed discourteous guise, as though at bottom he were less a man than some international agency? Did he think that tri-syllabic 'I.M.S.' somehow aggrandized monosyllabic 'Sieff' or that it sounded more deferential? Might Parkes have been aping the manner in which Sieff signed his business memos? Upon consideration, none of these conjectures is even remotely credible.

Moreover, apart from one passing reference to W. W. Simpson as 'W. W.', only one other figure, the publisher Victor Gollancz, is accorded such cavalier treatment. While performing textually mainly in his own name, on several occasions Gollancz surfaces as 'V. G.', usage adumbrating 'Very Good', thereby exuding a positive vibration. As for the SCM director Tissington Tatlow, it is true that he is generally referred to as 'T.', but this for good reason: his friends actually addressed him as 'T'. Nothing of the sort was the case with Lord Sieff.

We might rest easy with the conclusion that Parkes' recourse to 'I.M.S.' was a harmless, insignificant quirk or at worst a bit of faulty judgment. However the surprising impact of the forty or more appearances of 'I.M.S.' strewn through the latter half of Parkes' memoir, an average of one for every fourth page – like the trompe d'oeil of servant and master that we were obliged to squint at to decipher[12] – plays more and more on the reader's consciousness until they assume an alternative significance of their own, albeit one collaterally related to 'Sieff'.

We recall that at one time Parkes displayed a penchant for playing with words. The son of a fancier of limericks, he was himself an accomplished quipster one of whose limericks had been published;[13] his plasma jingle had carried the day at Nyon.[14] If we entertain the hypothesis that Parkes' peculiar employment of 'I.M.S' represented an exercise in wit and ingenuity, what possible significance might it have carried?

Let us suppose that in the twilight of his life the cleric scholar, in the process of summing up its shape and meaning, wished *to his own satisfaction* definitively to quash the persistent, vexing suspicion that his rapprochement to Judaism had in some way compromised his Christian identity, loyalty or conviction. To that end he resolved to sound, or rather to sight, a subtly contrapuntal theme *pianissimo* across the pages of his book.

On the penultimate page of *Voyage of Discoveries* Parkes plays a reprise of an old motif:

> The attempt of the 'new' Christians to build a *'Jesus-centricity'* into a satisfying religion accentuates rather than diminishes the inadequacy of our [Church's] previous *Christo*-centricity … [Neither version of Christianity can access] the spiritual dynamic and insights and relevant experience of Judaism … or Humanism …[15]

Now here's the crux: at the same time Parkes was consistently arguing for an expansion of the Church's vistas, a subterranean, spiritual strain of his own temperament led him to become a licensed practitioner of the laying-on-of hands; that is, he embraced a form of 'neo–Christian' spirituality. At odds with himself, might Parkes not have devised a cryptic means for charging his silvery, 'progressive' text with a countervailing, secondary layer of significance, one which effectively reaffirmed the primacy of his undeviating faith in Jesus as his personal messiah: Jesus Hominum Salvator, or 'I H S'? If this Jewish reader's attention was caught by a catenation of typographical blips, a textual tremor that converted seemingly innocuous 'I.M.S.' into a heavenly-laden cipher, would the Reverend Dr Parkes have been oblivious to the overlay of 'I.H.S', or Dorothy Wickings, his handmaiden in laying-on-of hands? Would Temple too not have responded to it?

It is true that Parkes rarely alludes to English poets in his writings. Tennyson was mentioned earlier, and Parkes' article 'Peace' (1933) was launched with a nod to Browning, but these are exceptions. Nevertheless, although not notably fond of contemporary literature, neither was Parkes untutored in his native tongue. It is, in fact, quite inconceivable that he was unfamiliar with the works of George Herbert, the seventeenth-century Anglican divine, all of whose verse conveys a densely worked out expression of intense Christian piety. A Cambridge man, Herbert's confessional poetry earned the special affection not only of James Parkes but also of King James I.

One of Herbert's favourite stratagems, most noticeable in his cruciform-shaped verse, was to concretize his themes by rendering them immanent typographically. In 'Easter-wings', for example, the shape of his poetic line on the page visually embodies its spiritual meaning: pertinently, when the poem is viewed sideways it assumes the form of an open pair of butterfly wings. In like manner we note that the 'M' from 'I.M.S.', by a trick of perception, may simultaneously be viewed as projecting the shadowy flutter of wings of salvation. This might sound far-fetched today, but this mode of discernment was second nature to seventeenth century priests and metaphysical poets. It would also have been especially appropriate for the metaphysical agent of Geneva who had hidden his secret code on the one clean plate amidst a pile of dirty dishes.

Our conjecture is that Parkes felt confident that, although his old friend might wince at the trivialization or even sub-current of animus implicit in being rendered as a triad of capital letters, he would almost certainly not divine its deeper intent. And even if he guessed, Parkes knew that Sieff was too much the Jewish gentleman ever to allude to it. By the time his memoir reached publication, Parkes would be in his retirement and no longer dependent upon subsidies. Moreover, he met his former bene-factor much less frequently than formerly. In any event, Parkes could always resort to the hollow explanation that he had incorporated into his text.

But what could have led Parkes to employ Israel Moses Sieff as a vehicle to impart an encoded affidavit of his own firm and enduring Christian faith? Once we recognize that for Parkes his Jewish benefactor had become the very embodiment of 'the Synagogue', or the Jewish establishment, it is not so very com-plicated. Probably more than any other man on earth, Parkes had not only delved into the inexorability of the divorce between historic Christianity and Judaism but regretted it the most pro-foundly. It is all the more ironic, therefore, that he could not utterly escape its dynamic in the personal sphere. Paralleling the rupture between the faiths that he had described so perceptively Parkes, who had relied materially and psychologically upon Sieff for so long, could not resist that very process. With a stroke of wit, he symbolically severed himself not only from decades of subservience but from the man as well.

Parkes, after all, had been the eternal suppliant, Sieff the perpetual source of bounty. Although each had tactfully nego-tiated his part, inevitably a residue of resentment emanated from the imbalance. Because the delicate issue had so long been circumvented, this salient aspect of their relationship had frozen into sterile posturing. Ethically indefensible, intellectually shaky, like Christianity's historic redeployment and declaration of independence, Parkes' covert resort to 'metaphysical' tactics proved psychologically irresistible.

Circumstances had silently corroded their friendship. In the course of their long relationship Parkes, responding to an inner need to demonstrate how profitably Sieff's 'investment' had paid off, frequently felt impelled 'to render accounts' to his benefactor. Upon the publication of *Judaism and Christianity*, for example, Parkes testified that his book was '... the first statement from the

Christian side that Judaism was not an inferior religion, lacking something Christianity has, while Christianity has everything Judaism offers'.[16] With good grace Sieff readily granted in turn that both the quality and the quantity of Parkes' output had matched or exceeded all expectations.

It should also be recalled that Parkes' disappointment with his benefactor, of necessity muted or repressed, had on occasion become acute. At an advanced stage of development, abruptly and without explanation Sieff pulled the plug on the plan to publish broadsheets about 'cultural, historical and contemporary aspects of Jewry' for a distinguished Gentile audience. Parkes reaction grimly understates his frustration: 'It was an interesting project, and I was very sorry when "I.M.S." decided to abandon it; for ignorance of things Jewish is one of the most potent allies of antisemitism.'[17] This was far from the only occasion when the two men's fundamentally unequal footing emerged nakedly from behind its heavily embroidered façade of mutuality.

By the far greatest irritant, of course, was Sieff's provocative dithering over Parkes' grandest ambition – the institutionalization of the Barley Centre for Christian-Jewish Relations. As already spelled out,[18] both men were exquisitely aware that it lay within Sieff's power to bring Parkes' noble vision to realization, but the Jewish businessman vacillated, prevaricated, and pleaded the press of circumstance for almost ten years. Parkes might have been led to conclude that Sieff was fending him off or playing him for a fool. Sensing his friend's disquiet about the project, it pained Parkes even to raise the matter. In this connection, a letter he addressed to a prominent London rabbi strikes a poignant note: 'That which struck me in attending synagogue – and this includes orthodox as well as progressive – is the large place that is given to affirmation and praise, and the relatively small place to petition and supplication.'[19]

Yet for nearly a decade, this pertinacious cleric could not let an encounter slide past without tendering a politic petition or a subtle supplication to his wealthy friend. At times Parkes' exasperation and repressed rage drove him past distraction. Given the unequal nature of their relationship, Parkes could scarcely vent his frustration on Sieff. Sharpened by humiliation, a brew of futility and bewilderment simmered in his heart.

As remarked above, only saints are immune to the settling of old scores, and not all of them. Parkes certainly did not aim to

inflict real injury upon Israel Sieff; nevertheless, to salve an open
wound that had been festering for a great many years, between
the unwashed pages of *Voyage of Discoveries* he seems to have
encrypted a coded, unobtrusive, non-lethal statement of exclusive Christian affirmation – and of private retaliation.

One cannot help but wonder why Sieff had not years earlier
performed the service he would execute only after his friend had
sustained a major heart attack. After all, even if at times just
barely, he had not failed to keep the Barley Tripod afloat. Yet
months passed into years and then a full decade and still Parkes
could not succeed in concentrating Sieff's mind on the task at
hand: authorization of the formal, legal and financial necessaries
that would bring the Parkes Library, Ltd. into existence.

Unacknowledged by either man, the fact is that both actually
cloudily apprehended what lay behind Sieff's inaction. He had
originally undertaken to subsidize a brilliant, young Christian
scholar's work on behalf of the Jews 'for about three hundred
years'.[20] Each man kept his part of the bargain scrupulously, but
when it came to the Barley Centre for Christian-Jewish Relations,
Sieff felt that Parkes had exceeded the terms of their original
mandate. True, Sieff would not voice his objections, but it is plain
that from the start he considered Parkes' vision a gratuitous,
unwelcome imposition on his sufferance, and quite possibly,
especially given his friend's failing health, a piece of folly.

Can we maintain without a shadow of a doubt that Parkes
consciously conceived and pulled off the aforesaid coup of
devotional *double entendre*? Before responding directly, we do
well again to bear in mind that while not Parkes' final book,
Voyage of Discoveries does constitute a kind of a summing up.
Although he may in some ways have considered himself a
'Christian Jew' and although he was sincerely accepted in all but
the most traditional Jewish circles as a much-honoured, much-
treasured associate member of the tribe, virtually 'one of us', the
sly iteration of faith sprinkled liberally on the palimpsest of
Voyage of Discoveries constitutes a reaffirmation of the overriding
primacy of Parkes' Christian faith. Existing only for those with
the eyes to see and the ears to hear, it goes without saying that
it contradicts nothing Parkes ever wrote or said about the eternal
validity of the Jewish faith.

It is most probable that, while initially wayward and fortuitous,
'I.M.S.' triggered a consciousness of unforeseen potentialities

that appealed to the more jaunty side of Parkes' nature. Seeing little if any harm in it, he proceeded to embrace them with relish. This combination of scrupulousness, deep spirituality and adolescent naughtiness bespeaks the very essence of the man. At the same time, as with earlier ruminations over Parkes' exploratory sexual ventures, it is clear that neither absolute credence nor unqualified disbelief can be firmly attached to these speculations. Virginia Woolf addressed this issue of credibility most judiciously:

> ... when a subject is highly controversial ... one cannot hope to tell the truth. One can only show how one came to hold whatever opinion one does hold. One can only give one's audience the chance of drawing their own conclusions as they observe the limitations, the prejudices, the idiosyncrasies of the speaker.[21]

Whatever its genesis, inherent in the title Parkes finally chose are intrinsic grounds that legitimize and endorse not only acts of 'self-discovery' – which unfortunately are all too few – but also 'discoveries' by fellow voyagers on the same passage. Especially for the latter, the issue of intentionality is largely moot. After all, Parkes' anniversary gift was bestowed not upon his wife alone. Once its queer textual quiver is felt, his readers can hardly be expected to efface its effect.

Where lie the most serious grounds for disappointment with *Voyage of Discoveries*? This act of retrieval and reconstruction presented Parkes with a final opportunity not merely to wrestle his dark angel to a draw but to extract a meaningful concession. Instead of this self-confrontation, Parkes retreated to the banality, superficiality and essential falseness of *A Life Enjoyed*. Parkes redeemed himself from futility and impotence through his profound relation to the Jewish people. It enabled him to strike and maintain a stalwart, even heroic pose throughout his maturity. The man within, however, remained deeply and permanently fractured.

Perhaps the age of seventy-three is not the ideal time for a man to make major revisions in the script that has brought him safely to a wintry port. On the other hand, is there a better moment? If the conscientious clergyman-historian delivered himself of a hearty, self-indulgent narrative, it is partly because he assumed that this would satisfy the expectations of a reasonably sympathetic audience. Outwitting himself, the canny historian was clearly mistaken. He did not so much artfully trim his sails as persevere in his habitual practice of hedging his interior world with good cheer and thorny shrubbery. Given the confessional spirit of our age, however, most readers, like most parishioners, crave banal reassurance less than the laying-on-of hands; that is, direct revelation. On this ground Parkes' unreflective log sorely disappoints. As at several earlier critical junctures in his life, in crafting his autobiography Parkes effectively deserted the field to produce a *Voyage of Evasions*.

NOTES

1. Alastair Reid, 'You Can Go Home Again', *New York Review of Books*, Vol. LI, No. 1, 15 January 2004, p. 21.
2. Hilary Mantel cited by Joyce Carol Oates, 'Stranded in the Dark', *New York Review of Books*, Vol. I, No. 16, 23 October 2003, p. 23.
3. Oates, 'Stranded in the Dark', Ibid.
4. James Parkes, *Voyage of Discoveries* (London: Victor Gollancz, 1969), p. 83.
5. Ibid., pp. 180–81.
6. Nicholas de Lange, 'James Parkes, A Centenary Lecture', in *Cultures of Ambivalence and Contempt: Studies in Jewish–Non-Jewish Relations*, eds Jones, Kushner and Pearce (London: Vallentine Mitchell, 1998).
7. Dorothy Wickings Parkes, *Autobiography*, Parkes Archives, File 60/33/3.
8. Dorothy Wickings Parkes, letter to Hugh Harris of the *Jewish Chronicle*, 4 April 1968, Parkes Archives, File 60/7/36/2.
9. *Vide* Chapter 33.
10. *Vide* Chapter 19.
11. Parkes, *Voyage of Discoveries*, p. 106.
12. *Vide* Chapter 20.
13. *Vide* Chapter 12.
14. *Vide* Chapter 18.
15. Parkes, *Voyage of Discoveries*, p. 249.
16. James Parkes, letter to Israel Sieff, 14 August 1952, Parkes Archives, File 60/17/51.
17. Parkes, *Voyage of Discoveries*, p. 148.
18. *Vide* Chapter 30.
19. James Parkes, letter to Rabbi Leslie Edgar, London's Liberal Jewish Synagogue, 20 October 1952, Parkes Archives, File 60/17/51.
20. *Vide* Chapter 19.
21. Virginia Woolf, *A Room of One's Own* (Harmondsworth: Penguin, 1970), p. 6.

35

The Old Boy

He could not have looked less like a great scholar or campaigner. He was a smallish, rather stooping figure, with a fine head of white hair and expressive, bushy eyebrows. His eyes were beautiful – gentle yet penetrating and full of life. His voice was low and purring (in his last years it faded out completely), and he spoke with hardly a pause, about every subject under the sun. Everything he mentioned came to life, and his sentences were punctuated by little questions and succinct judgments which gave a very lively air to his conversation. There was actually something very boyish in his manner, although he was in his seventies.

Later, when I used to visit him at his delightful cottage in the unspoilt Dorset village of Iwerne Minster, and saw the miniature garden he had created, the path of ancient bricks he had laid himself, the collection of English brass candlesticks on which he had made himself a leading authority, I realised more fully what I had only glimpsed in that first meeting in the Senior Common Room at Southampton – that he was in a way a child who had refused to grow up.[1]

So runs an admiring and indeed admirable mini-portrait of James Parkes at the close of 1969. Never attractive to Parkes was the broad, conventional highway: of family, of career, or of caution. At least as early as his ritual combat with headmaster Penney over the Open Scholarship exam, he had wagered his life on the risky premise that he would succeed only on his own terms. All that he valued and genuinely needed to sustain his high but far from extravagant opinion of his own abilities had been the corroboration of an elite of superior persons, later of Chosen People. As he turned seventy-three, the sickly orphan from Guernsey, having sailed through rough seas, was conscious of having won his chief wager with life.

Rightly, the above observer emphasizes Parkes' boyishness. For all of his days he maintained the stance of a puckish sprite at odds with the careerist, materialistic world of grown-ups. In his unreconstructed inner world, Peter Pan in the guise of Don Quixote never stopped tilting with the world's Hooks, Barths and Hitlers. This is not too whimsical; on the contrary, Parkes as earnest Don Pan rings with deadly accuracy. For the perennial paladin there was but one villain with a thousand faces. If in his old age Parkes seemed more content, it was not because he imagined that the Hooks had been banished for ever or the Hitlers permanently vanquished. With much justice he did feel, however, that in his day he had inflicted some timely blows of his own.

In March 1970, their first class passage on the *Anotria* charged to the account of Marks & Spencer, Parkes and Wickings sailed off on yet another sojourn to Israel, this one for three weeks. Parkes had been invited to deliver a series of lectures at Beit Berl, the think tank of Israel's Labour Party which at the time still exercised hegemony over all the central institutions of the young country. He knew this would certainly be his final trip to the country where he had so many friends and admirers and which, unlike Switzerland in an earlier period, had truly become a second homeland.

The visitors were put up at the 'very English home – fireplace, garden, four o'clock tea – of Anglican Archbishop George Appleton in Jerusalem' in whose study Parkes was interviewed by a reporter from the *Jerusalem Post*. 'Five times in Jewish history of the past 1,500 years,' Parkes declared portentously, 'the life of the whole people had come to a crisis and every time that crisis has been resolved by the little community in Eretz Israel.'[2] But Parkes' role had never been merely to play background music to accompany Israeli triumphalism: 'The West Bank', he declared without qualification, 'should be returned by Israel to Arab control.' His historical perspective has, of course, turned out to be accurate, but at the time few Israelis were prepared to heed the prophetic warnings of Professor Yeshayahu Leibowitz let alone those of James Parkes. Ironically, Parkes' grasp of Jewish history was at this juncture firmer than of his own. In response to a query, he informed his interviewer that this was his sixth visit to the country. It was in fact his seventh.[3]

His lecture at Beit Berl on 14 April was principally about current tensions between Christianity and Judaism, but his most memorable remarks touched upon a different conflict. Although more oblique about the Arab role, and in a lower register for those attuned to his message, he struck much the same chord:

There is no solution for the future which could claim to be 'just' except one which recognizes that it [Palestine] has never been naturally the house of a single people, and that there has never been a substantial change of population corresponding to a change of masters. It is a country in which three peoples, of three religions, are inextricably mingled. The vital fact is that there has never been a period in Palestinian history ... in which the Jewish population was not as extensive as could possibly find the most meagre living on the sacred soil.[4]

The above themes would also permeate *Whose Land?, A History of the Peoples of Palestine*, issued as a Pelican 'Original' later that year.[5] 'Original', in this instance, is something of a misnomer because the text is actually an updated version of *A History of the Jewish People* which had first appeared in 1961. Similarly, 1970 saw the publication of an American edition of *The Emergence of the Jewish Problem, 1878–1939* that had first come out in 1946. Surely more gratifying for Parkes was overseeing new editions of *The Conflict of the Church and the Synagogue* and *The Jew in the Medieval Community*, seminal works from his most fertile period. The general pattern, however, is all too clear: after *Voyage of Discoveries*, no genuinely original books would appear.

It is noteworthy that in his revised conclusion to *Whose Land?* Parkes abandoned the pleasing symmetry of '... three peoples, of three religions, are inextricably mingled ...' in favour of the more nuanced 'two peoples, of three religions ...' a downsized but actually knottier formulation that he first employed in a letter to the editor of *The Tablet* early in December 1973 and again to the Editor of *The Times* later that month. With these missives he had hoped to neutralize the irksome, well-worn accusation that James Parkes could easily be pigeonholed, hence discounted, as merely a Zionist propagandist.[6] In aiming at 'evenhandedness', however, Parkes was neither the first nor the last commentator who succeeded mainly in angering the central parties to the dispute. Wildly overreacting, at least one of his Zionist friends unfairly characterized the *The Times* letter as 'a stab in the back'.[7]

In view of Parkes' patchy record with ecclesiastical officialdom in the Holy City, he had reason to feel particularly pleased on the morning of 21 April. Under the auspices of the Anglican archbishopric, he donned his cassock and solemnly ascended the pulpit of Jerusalem's St George's Cathedral. Adapting his tone but not his tenor to the occasion, he preached the urgent need for Christian re-evaluation of Judaism.

It is the greatest tragedy of the first two millennia of Christian history that the apostolic age convinced itself that it had replaced Judaism. What it failed to notice was that Judaism … was tailored to the natural community which one entered by birth to the nation, where applicable to the state. The Christians were preaching a religion of the elect from every nation, a community which one entered by choice. So the church created a false antithesis between 'law' and 'gospel'.[8]

On his return to England, still in fine fettle and high dudgeon, Parkes dispatched a characteristic sally to his travel agent. The majority of the passengers on the *Anotria* had been Holocaust survivors: 'The film that was provided for their "pleasure",' Parkes objected, 'was an absolutely bloody picture of torture and murder of Red Indians destroying a white settlement and the massacre of soldiers who came to relieve it. Anything more beastly to revive old memories I cannot imagine.'[9] No reply either from the agent or the Adriatic Lines survives.

In 1970 Parkes initiated a correspondence with a number of distant relations – the only sort he had – persons who in the past had chiefly figured on his Christmas mailing list. Why suddenly in his retirement did Parkeses on every continent now bulk large among his concerns? Nostalgia and sentimentality apart, there was another pressing reason. Now that his collection of Judaica had been most satisfactorily housed and with mortality looming ever closer, the childless cleric's mind turned to the serious consideration of whom to bequeath the remainder of his possessions of value. This, is turn, triggered a collateral interest in family history. A letter directed to the Institute of Civil Engineers, for example, requested information about William Parkes, the grandfather who had designed the naval harbour at Alderney.[10]

Parkes resumed contact with Barrie Parkes, a cousin in Melbourne who, as an airman in the Australian Air Force during the Second World War, had made Barley his base away from base.[11] Parkes wanted his cousin to know that 'he has left him in [his] will a small group of Parkes portraits … as well as some water colours by Annie Parkes'.[12] A few weeks later he dispatched a letter to Basil Parkes, another Australian cousin: '… I wish you did not live so far away,' Parkes bemoaned, 'as if you were closer I gladly would share with you Mother's picture of Freiburg by sending it to and fro. It was the very first of her pictures which she gave me when I was quite small because I loved cathedrals so.' These rare allusions to his mother suggest a keenness to set in order not only his estate but his mental state as well. His intensive campaign of family outreach next extended to a kinswoman, 'Cousin Pam' in Geneva, of all places, where she was just commencing her university studies. Offered one of his etchings, her reply indicated that she was 'most pleased to accept it'.[13]

Above and beyond determining which cousin on what continent might most appropriately be bestowed this or that etching, it is plain that in old age Parkes was taking genuine pleasure in rekindling these family connections. We are reminded of the opening pages of his memoir when he felt constrained to present his bona fides as a true 'native son' of the Channel Islands by evoking his local antecedents, some of them ludicrously remote.[14] With Death pacing the corridor and his posthumous reputation in the balance, the Parkes cousinhood assumed renewed significance. Parkes considered his etchings and portraits small pieces of himself which, in the right hands, might serve as tokens of survival; that is, vessels through which he might one day be spiritually resurrected as the great-great-great uncle of Parkeses yet unborn.

However gratifying the renewal of ties of kinship and the suitable disposition of his property, they could not displace the old intoxication of bequeathing his ideas and thoughts to the widest possible audience. The *Jewish Chronicle* continued to serve as his main outlet for relatively brief pieces. Longer articles, most of them dealing with the Jewish–Arab conflict, appeared in the *New Middle East* (June 1970), the *Journal of Ecumenical Studies* (Fall 1970), and the *Modern Churchman* (October 1970). Parkes also turned his hand to writing a number of entries on Christian themes for the forthcoming edition of *Encyclopaedia Judaica*.[15]

The following year, however, saw a major shift of topical focus from Israel and Jewish–Christian relations to matters relating to health and spirituality. As seen earlier, both as a donor and a recipient, for some time Parkes had been actively engaged in the Christian healing movement. As though, for example, it were a common enough activity, one of Wickings's letters remarks, 'tomorrow we go to him [a friend] for James to administer the laying-on-of hands to him [together] with his own cleric'.[16] Throughout this period Parkes' correspondence is replete with references to spiritual healing, and a great mass of printed material about this sacramental function clutters his files.

If all else failed, the Parkes Library in Southampton would always provide him with a dependable public forum. Under the auspices of its 'New Theology for a New Age' series, in 1972 he delivered the ninth annual Montefiore Lecture. 'Religious Experience and the Perils of Interpretation' reiterated many of Parkes' favourite themes: the ongoing validity and relevance of religious Modernism, a doctrine which had informed his intellectual posture ever since his student years at Oxford; the virtues and desirability of religious pluralism; and contemporary man's urgent need for a creative reinterpretation of the Bible.[17] Aimed at counteracting Christianity's chronic divisiveness, Parkes, in rhetoric that curiously echoes William Faulkner's 1950 Nobel Prize address in Stockholm,[18] emphasized not only the essential unity of Christianity but also a progressive, humanistic agenda for mankind.

> I am encouraged to demand a human co-operation which over-rides traditional differences and antagonisms, because I am convinced that today we can only interpret our religious experience in terms of a responsible and intelligent Creator who is equally committed to the whole of creation ... There needs to be a new understanding of co-operation across historic barriers ... Such an interpretation is obviously as perilous as those of previous ages, but there is no safe way forward ... But for those who interpret life in theistic terms and for those who do not, it will be a co-operation [in] which all human qualities of intellect, of insight, and of imagination, will be stretched to the full, as much as qualities usually associated with religion – love, compassion, sacrifice. But it is in such co-operation that we shall begin to discover the range and capacities of adult man.[19]

In 'Judaism and the Jewish People', an address he delivered in Southampton the following year – his final public appearance of any consequence – Parkes characteristically embraced both religions to which he gave fealty. Insisting 'it is the Messianic claim, rather than the character or teaching of Jesus of Nazareth, which separates Jew from Christian today', he went on to argue that when Jesus proclaimed,

... change your ways of looking at life and the Kingdom of God is around you, *not* that a world war was coming at the End of Days, which was John the Baptist's message and is often conflated with [that of] Jesus whose life leaves us uncertain as to his divinity. He never makes the claim uncategorically, which suggests the deliberate activity of an intelligent Creator Who safeguards the freedom of his creation.[20]

Later that summer Parkes returned to the business of dispersing pieces of his legacy among the far-flung Parkes clan. A letter dispatched to his cousin in Melbourne constituted a playful summing up: 'I now have degrees or fellowships of six universities in three countries, which seems an adequate supply for a fellow who has never taught at any one of the universities. Still, it keeps up the family reputation.'[21] As he details his high rate of success at installing his collections in havens most likely to maintain them securely and intact, it suddenly becomes clear that Parkes' preoccupation with bequeathing his estate issues from the same conscientious mindset that, upon appreciating that the covenant between God and the People of Israel had never been abrogated, applied all the force and talent at its disposal to expedite the restoration to the Jews of their promised patrimony, the Land of Israel.

In addition to disburdening himself of his library, retirement to a cosy cottage exacted an additional toll: save for a few personal favourites, Parkes' collection of over two hundred brass candlesticks also needed a proper repository. Unlike the Jewish collection, a solution for housing these antiques was expeditiously located: a museum in Birmingham, a city with ancient ties to the Parkes family, was pleased to receive them.[22] As for the hoard of church and cathedral illustrations, first locating and then relocating it in a safe harbour would test all Parkes' patience, persistence and powers of clemency. From inception to dispersion, the chequered history of this vast pictorial accumulation is, in its way, as instructive as that of his Jewish library. It makes for a sad and cautionary tale.

Back in 1928, when Parkes was preparing to depart from England for Geneva, his picture collection comprised some 5,000 illustrations and postcards. On the reverse side of many of these, in his careful hand Parkes had inscribed detailed notations. On the postcard of one French cathedral, for instance, he entered data relating to its main arcade, arches, vaulting, apse, clerestory windows, great windows, triforium and aisles. Realizing that such a collection might have substantial worth, Parkes consulted Professor Charles Reilly of the University of Liverpool, at that time the most distinguished school of architecture in Britain. Warmly welcoming such a prospective acquisition, Reilly urged that the entire collection be sent to Liverpool on a 'long-term loan'.

However Parkes' childhood pursuit was not so easily put to rest. During his six years of travelling about the Continent, the availability of a vast new store of postcards of churches rekindled the native avidity of a born collector. Starting anew, Parkes obsessively added to his collection. By 1935, he had accumulated 10,000 additional items which, over the course of six years, averages around five items per day. In the end, the exigencies of storage space at Barley precipitated another 'Conflict of the Church and the Synagogue'. In 1940, his Jewish collection and professional orientation clearly being first among his priorities, Parkes deposited this vast addendum to his church architecture collection with Liverpool's School of Architecture 'at the request of its professor'.[23]

A quarter of a century later, on Parkes' retirement to Iwerne Minster and his vigorous campaign to set his affairs in order, he wrote to Liverpool about his on-loan collection of 15,000 pictures. 'To my dismay they replied they did not know what "loan" I was talking about ...' – Parkes was stunned. Unwittingly, the University of Liverpool's School of Architecture had assumed a most ambiguous role in Parkes' inner economy. It had husbanded his collection with all the care and respect that Henry Parkes had accorded whichever of his son's possessions had been left 'on loan' on Guernsey whenever he returned to Oxford.[24] It was only after two years of further correspondence that '... the University accepted their responsibility for a loan made to their School of Architecture'.[25]

Any reasonable observer would surely grant that Parkes had exemplary grounds for seeking out a worthier recipient of his magnanimity. Largely because of the presence of family members on the scene, he selected the Faculty of Architecture at the University of Melbourne and assumed that at last the distasteful business with the University of Liverpool was at an end. Only when he was making ready to ship the collection to Australia did Parkes discover that parts of it had been cannibalized for use in courses at the university. Over 1,500 items still were 'missing'.

A letter earlier in the year from Parkes to the Faculty of Architecture in Melbourne mentioned that all but a relatively small number of photographs – those reported 'missing' by the University of Liverpool – had been dispatched to Australia.[26] It was only in 1973, eight years and endless letters later, that most of the missing items mysteriously materialized. Although one conjectures that some academic had swallowed them whole for use in his courses and regurgitated them upon his own retirement, no explanation was issued. Only later did the aggrieved but unremitting historian receive a letter of apology. Thereafter he shipped the remaining twelve boxes to their final resting place in Australia.

Perhaps the most remarkable aspect of this sorry affair is the admirable even-temperedness Parkes displayed throughout his dealings with Liverpool. He informed the university authorities in no uncertain terms that he would grant them no rest until the matter was resolved to his satisfaction. At the same time, in spite of provocation, Parkes never gave way to anger over the sloppiness and ingratitude with which his generosity had been repaid. Were it ever to be published, the Parkes–Liverpool file, comprising dozens of letters, would constitute an exemplary text on the virtues of Christian fortitude and humility.

Parkes fought tenaciously to keep his several collections intact. He had invested in them not only an immense amount of time and energy but also a relatively high proportion of his modest personal resources. His accumulations of Jewish books, of church pictures and of candlesticks embodied, each in its way, a degree of perfection unrealizable in more mundane spheres of activity. Thousands of items had been lovingly selected and set into a meaningful, dynamic relation to others of their kind. For Parkes the pursuit of these 'hobbies' had constituted another instance of *imitatio Deo*, emulation of the creative activity of God who aims to realize the highest possible degree of order. In fact, recalling the central thematic thrust of the poems of Wallace Stevens, what Parkes' collections symbolically projected was a reification of the very idea of order. Untainted by the intrusive presence of others, each of Parkes' collections represented a lovingly proportioned projection cast in the shape of his mind.

The struggle for unity transcended any personal considerations for Parkes; it was metaphysical. The idea of dividing any of his prized assemblages was an operational metaphor for submission to entropy, that is, the cosmic victory of pure evil. Moreover, in their new locations his collections retained the name if not the very the anima of James Parkes. Their fragmentation would have given rise to emotional agony, evoking nothing less than dismemberment. Most particularly, Parkes' collection of 15,000 items connected with the Church seems to have been emotionally imbued with a measure of sanctity, a kind of immanent materialization of the mystical body of Christ. Only elevation to this dimension seems consonant with Parkes' heroic perseverance to maintain its integrity in suitable fashion. In this connection we recall Parkes' headlong flight from the Church of the Holy Sepulchre whose 'dismemberment' he found so viscerally repulsive.[27]

In November 1973, *The Times Literary Supplement* returned a Parkes submission entitled 'The Problem Inherent in Man Becoming God'. Acutely sensitive to not being in vogue, Parkes was more disappointed than he admitted.[28] After 1973 Parkes did not publish any new books; nor, except for a smattering of short pieces – none of any consequence – did he contribute anything of originality to religious or scholarly journals. Among his final published articles, 'Israel in the Middle East Complex' appeared in Glasgow's *Jewish Echo* on 4 May 1973;[29] later in the year his final introduction to a new book appeared.[30] All too plainly, things were winding down.

Rather than new work of his own, *faute de mieux* the book review became Parkes chosen avenue of expression. Despite a streak of fussiness, he proved to be a splendid reviewer. In fact, late in life his response to the works of others in the field of Jewish–Christian historical relations reveals the temper of the man better than most of his other writings. When Parkes encountered work he considered of genuine merit, while he rarely overlooked its failings, he could be a sweet Old Boy. However, whenever he came across slipshod scholarship or superficial thinking, neither reputation nor decorum could protect the perpetrator from his acid pen.

Parkes' 1973 review of *Faith and Fratricide* by Rosemary Reuther, with an introduction by Gregory Baum, exemplifies the former. After acknowledging the book's considerable merit,

Parkes does not scant its deficiencies: 'It is easy to miss the importance of this book ... [which] has no index and no bibliography. In addition the style is verbose and obscure. But ... Professors Baum and Reuther write as Roman Catholics, and admit that the roots of antisemitism lie squarely in the writings of the New Testament itself.'[31] Far more wholeheartedly, in the same year Parkes conferred glowing praise upon *Jesus the Jew* by Geza Vermes: 'In a field as well-trodden as New Testament exegesis, it is extremely rare to encounter a new book which can be described as epoch-making. But no lesser word would adequately reflect the importance of *Jesus the Jew*.'[32]

Then there was Parkes at the barricades, in defence of high seriousness scourging the famous for their fatuity or foolishness. In 1973 Parkes dealt in such manner with *The Jews in the Roman World* by the well-known classical historian Michael Grant. 'That Grant has made himself familiar with Roman history is obvious; that he has made himself familiar with the Jewish half of his object is, unfortunately, more open to doubt.' Less gentle by half was his 1975 laceration of *The Crucifixion of the Jews* by Franklin Littel, a theologian of international reputation: 'The relationship of Christendom and Christian theology to Judaism and the Jewish People is too fundamental an issue for a reader ever to waste time in complimentary clichés. This is a badly produced book, and written, I imagine, too hastily and in too emotional a whirlwind.'[33] It is in a score of such reviews that we engage the man as remembered best by the intimates of his later years.

In July 1974 *Search for a Dialogue, A Conversation with James Parkes* was videotaped in Southampton for an American television network. The only visual record of Parkes in a public performance, it deserves careful scrutiny. Even at seventy-seven, the former star Oxford debater proved a formidable polemicist. Indeed, at times Parkes' incisiveness verged on testiness. Obviously expecting a friendly chat with a benevolent clergyman-scholar, the urbane interviewer George Watson found himself continually thrust on to the defensive and repeatedly bested by a feisty old curmudgeon. Inasmuch as three observers of Parkes independently have reported that their old friend 'did not suffer fools gladly', it may be inferred they were echoing a sentiment Parkes took delight in attributing to himself.[34] We shall soon see why.

Watson began by enquiring whether 'antisemitism today

remains a threat to peace'. As if his interlocutor were slightly dimwitted, Parkes responded:

> Oh, I think it certainly does. I think it will, among the Christian world, until the churches recognize that, at the moment, the New Testament has no positive attitude to the existence of Judaism and Jews as contemporaries ... In the same way, there is no recognition by Arabs as Moslems of the permanent place of Jews in the life of the Middle East ....[35]

Watson assayed a paraphrase: 'So you're saying, if I understand you, that Christians have a blind spot about Judaism, and Arabs have a blind spot about other religions.' Watson did not 'understand', or at least not to Parkes' satisfaction. The pugnacious historian emended: '... about Jews ... I mean if you want to make the contrast to the Christian blind spot about Judaism, Arabs have a blind spot about Jews.' Moments later Watson suggested that what Parkes really meant was that 'no one should regard it [the Holy Land] as the special preserve of any particular religion.' Parkes would not cooperate: 'If you see it as a "special preserve", yes, they [the Jews] should regard it as a special, a very special responsibility that they are there, but they are not exclusively owners of it. That's the point.' Gamely, Watson again risked a paraphrase: 'You mean there are many paths towards the same goal?' Sensing his interviewer had trivialized his meaning, Parkes rejoined: 'There are many paths, but they don't all lead to the same goal.'[36]

For a while things proceeded in a more temperate fashion until Watson wondered aloud whether secular governments had failed in their roles. He had blundered into a minefield.

> Parkes: Well, isn't that obvious?
> Watson: Well, granted they haven't done so well, but ...
> Parkes: Hang it all, there have been two world wars in my lifetime and we're under threat of a third ...
> Watson: [incredulously] But could some sort of a – you're not suggesting that some sort of theocratic system might do better, are you?
> Parkes: I'm not suggesting a theocracy in the sense of a world run by clergy. Heaven prevent it! But I think the

world's religions have got to recognize that an intelligent
and responsible Creator wants them to govern the world
properly.
Watson: You don't believe that he [man] is indelibly tainted
with some original sin that would …
Parkes: Oh, no, no …[37]

The more flummoxed grew Watson, the more ebullient grew
Parkes, relishing both the discomfiture of his foil and his thirty
minutes of international exposure. In search of a dialogue
Watson, lightly armoured for the tournament, proved more of a
jester than a jouster. Age had not visibly moderated Parkes'
earnestness about himself or his Jewish mission to the Christians.
Moreover, as we shall see, on occasion he could certainly become
solemn about ritual and ceremony.

Throughout this period a steady stream of guests continued
to descend upon the cottage at Iwerne Minster. Chock-a-block
with Parkes' favourite antiques brought from Barley, it came to
be referred to as 'Little Barley'.[38] In 1974 Parkes invited W. W.
Simpson down to Little Barley together with Ruth Weyl, widow
of a German-born Israeli lawyer. The two had recently decided
to merge their lives and fortunes. After greeting them in the
garden, Parkes escorted the couple ceremoniously into the
cottage, now festive from tapers aglow in the vestiges of his
collection of candlesticks and sconces. To the stupefaction of the
couple, in an atmosphere redolent of a chapel, Parkes took it
upon himself to solemnize the new partnership with a brief
interfaith marriage service. 'He was,' Weyl recalls, 'very serious
about it.'[39]

Afterwards, examining the candlesticks and some of Parkes'
favourite cups, Weyl remarked that she too just couldn't resist
beautiful things. That provided their host with a cue to expound
'The Parable of the Cups', a lesson in housewifery for the edification of the honeymooners. Gloriously unconscious of any *double
entendre*, Parkes demonstrated his time-tested method for securing cups from breakage: 'One cup should always be inserted
inside the other and the two lain sideways on the shelf.'[40]

Finally, a matter that would not have been worth the mentioning were it not for a misleading impression in the above
epigraph. Subverting ceremonial gestures of elegance, Simpson
and Weyl soon grew disagreeably aware of the prevailing

slovenliness of 'Little Barley'. In fact, with the exception of his adolescence at the bungalow on Guernsey, housekeeping *per se* had never been one of Parkes' particular strengths. At 'Old Barley' John McNeilage had kept the inner precincts of the establishment reasonably tidy and clean. Even before age and infirmity had exacted their toll, Wickings had never been enthusiastic about keeping house. With her now at the helm, sanitary conditions in the kitchen, bathroom and elsewhere had deteriorated to such an extent that guests not infrequently departed from the 'delightful cottage' sooner than anticipated.

When in his Geneva days Parkes had encountered odoriferous facilities, he had negotiated means to ameliorate the situation.[41] It was a blessing that in his decline the Old Boy no longer seemed to notice the need.

NOTES

1. Nicolas de Lange, 'Unforgettable Characters', No. 1, University of Southampton, Parkes Archives, File 60/24/9.
2. Abraham Rabinovich, 'Expert on the Poison Gas of Anti-Semitism', interview with James Parkes, the *Jerusalem Post*, 24 April 1970.
3. After his first visit in 1946, Parkes returned in 1949, 1953, 1960, 1964, 1967 and finally in 1970.
4. James Parkes, Beit Berl Lecture, 14 April 1970, Parkes Archives, File 60/31/37.
5. *Vide* Chapter 32.
6. James Parkes, letters to editors of *The Tablet* and *The Times*, December 1973, Parkes Archives, File 60/33/19.
7. Zvi Werblowsky, interviewed by the author and Maggie Davidson, Jerusalem, 16 November 2003.
8. James Parkes, sermon in Jerusalem, 21 April 1970, Parkes Archives, File 60/33/19.
9. James Parkes, letter to R. Burt, Parkes Archives, File 60/31/4/70.
10. James Parkes, letter to Institute of Civil Engineers, 21 March 1970, Parkes Archives, File 60/31/4/70.
11. James Parkes, *Voyage of Discoveries* (London: Victor Gollancz, 1970), p. 176.
12. James Parkes, letter to Barrie Parkes, Parkes Archives, File 60/31/2.
13. Pamela Parkes, letter to James Parkes, Parkes Archives, File 60/31/2.
14. Parkes, *Voyage of Discoveries*, pp. 9–10.
15. Robert A. Everett, *Christianity Without Anti-Semitism: James Parkes and the Jewish–Christian Encounter* (Oxford: Pergamon, 1993), p. 332.
16. Dorothy Wickings Parkes, letter to a friend, 2 November 1971, Parkes Archives, File 60/33/47.
17. Everett, *Christianity Without Anti-Semitism*, p. 332.
18. *Vide* extensive footnote 20 in Chapter 36.
19. Everett, *Christianity Without Anti-Semitism*, pp. 153–54.
20. James Parkes, 'Judaism and the Jewish People', 1973, Parkes Archives, File 60/31/57.
21. James Parkes, letter to Barrie Parkes, 18 August 1972, Parkes Archives, File 60/33/19.
22. *Vide* Chapter 3.
23. James Parkes, letter to University of Melbourne, 2 November 1973, Parkes Archives, File 60/4/2.

24. *Vide* Chapter 11.
25. James Parkes, letter to University of Melbourne, Parkes Archives, 60/9/19/1.
26. Ibid.
27. *Vide* Chapter 33.
28. Letter from the editor of *The Times Literary Supplement* to James Parkes, November 1973, Parkes Archives, File 60/33/19.
29. As if scripted by an old-fashioned dramatist of 'well-made' plays, this lends to Parkes' career a kind of mechanical symmetry. Recall that he made his debut as a 'public man' in 1921 at a missionary conference in Glasgow. Now fifty-two years later he bows off the public stage in a Glasgow Jewish journal.
30. John Oesterreicher, *Jerusalem the Free* (London: Anglo-Israel Association, 1973).
31. James Parkes, review of *Faith and Fratricide*, Rosemary Reuther, 1973, Parkes Archives, File 60/33/19.
32. James Parkes, review of *Jesus the Jew*, Geza Vermes, 1973. A sidelight, amusing to Parkes, much less so to Vermes: in his review Parkes assumed that Vermes was a Jewish convert to Christianity. As far this went, this was accurate, but Parkes was unaware that later in life Vermes had returned to the Jewish fold. He vigorously protested Parkes' error. Parkes responded: 'So as a most Jewish Christian, I salute Dr Vermes, a brother, who is a most Christian Jew.'
33. James Parkes, review of *The Crucifixion of the Jews*, Franklin Little, 1975, Parkes Archives, File 60/33/19.
34. Ruth Edith Weisz and Ruth Weyl earlier and W.D. Davies in the following chapter.
35. James Parkes and George Watson, 'Search for a Dialogue, A Conversation with James Parkes', July 1974, Parkes Archives, File 60/33/19. ABC television broadcast this 'match-of-the-week' six months later one Sunday morning in January 1975.
36. Ibid.
37. Ibid.
38. Ruth Weyl interviewed by the author and Maggie Davidson in Rehovot, Israel, 26 October 2003.
39. Ibid.
40. *Vide* Chapter 33.
41. *Vide* Chapter 15.

36

Final Acts

Time past and time future
What might have been and what has been
Point to one end, which is always present.[1]

Long before the death of his father, the trajectory of Parkes' life
had overshot his first home. Later, after a few post-war excursions to Guernsey, Sark and Alderney, the thread connecting him
to his native islands became even more attenuated. In his late
seventies, however, the very act of composing *Voyage of Discoveries*
triggered an emotional recoil. After nearly a decade of gradual
adjustment to the placid rhythms of Iwerne Minster, from time
to time Parkes now would catch his mind *in flagrante delicto*
sailing round to its Byzantium. Parkes even turned out a piece
of pure nostalgia for the annual journal of The Guernsey Society.[2]

Unlike the Guernsey coastline, the beaches of Dorset are
ringed with cliffs that date back 180 million years. Great sections
of the ridged cliffs have collapsed into the sand, and other parts
seem poised to give way at the next storm or onset of high tide.
Along the seafront, miniscule ammonites and tribolites are abundant, and the patient eye easily detects fossilized fish and even
larger creatures that were prevalent here fifty million years ago
during the Jurassic and Cretaceous periods. The past comes grit-
tily alive between ones fingers and toes. In fair weather, strolling
along the strand when he was down on the coast, Parkes would
pause. Gazing over the waves, enveloped in a tide of apparition
and memory, he cast his eye southwards towards his first home
where so much of the man he was had been formed. Sometimes
he thought he sensed a presence beyond the horizon, even, he
fancied, a gentle but palpable tug on the line. At those rare
moments it seemed as though the arching years collapsed into
a pile of shards, and time itself contracted into a pinpoint of light
that beckoned him to dive and yield as though, like David and
Molly, he were a fish in the water.

Were he to stare long and hard enough across the sea, were he to will it, in those foreshortened moments of conflated time, space and consciousness, might he catch a glimpse of the boy who with so much yearning and expectation had once looked off in the direction of England? As if lovingly bound to the eye of the beholder by a thread of Thou-and-I, could the eye of the lad see anything of himself in the sometimes genial, sometimes testy old man, the retired clergyman scholar of Iwerne Minster? Who could possibly have anticipated that his pilgrimage would have led him so inexorably not only to defend the Jews but even to identify himself publicly as one of them?

When composing *Voyage of Discoveries*, miscalculation, the temptations of nostalgia, and the pitfall of self-justification had not infrequently blurred Parkes' retrospective focus. Like the prevailing weather of the south coast, unimpeded periods of self-perception through the mists and the clouds were rare and intermittent. So long embattled, had he not fought hard and played his part courageously? Had he not conscientiously disdained the pursuit of treasure or indulgence in pleasure for its own sake? Had he not aimed higher, at the truth, at service to mankind, and at atonement for perhaps the greatest of all historic acts of injustice? Realizing these aspirations comprised the real substance of Parkes' 'life enjoyed'.

True, he had trained himself not to expatiate upon his inglorious chapters. More than anyone could possibly have guessed, the old man was acutely conscious of his shortcomings; he knew he was far from being the 'Messiah' his wife had proclaimed him in former times. Nevertheless, he had kept faith with the heroic aspirations of the boy who, trailing two steps behind his brother, could fleetingly be glimpsed scampering along the rocks at the Bay of Rocquaine and in the coves and inlets at Vazon.

Parkes' final link to Guernsey was also his first and his best – the Ozanne family. Christine, the 'cousin' who on many awkward occasions rescued him from boyhood sloughs of melancholy, had passed from the scene. However, John Ozanne, a former classmate, still lived in St Martin Parish, and in 1973 Parkes responded warmly to a friendly letter from his daughter enquiring after his health. Bearing a postmark from 1975, in a final address to 'Dear Jimmy' John thanked his friend for having sent Clem, his philatelist grandson, 'an interesting stamp'.[3] Smiling to himself, the old man remembered a vivid image of the boy who would burn with anticipation at the arrival of the postman. Would a card from far off, magical England arrive to fill a critical gap in his collection of churches? At the same time he smothered a vagrant thought of another young stamp collector from the past, son of the one-time factotum whose days had, through his master's miscalculation, been blighted by chronic, blinding headaches.

One day, fatigued when he returned from a solitary walk, a glance at his unpruned roses forced Parkes to the realization that he and Dorothy had grown too frail to maintain the garden satisfactorily or even to keep the cottage reasonably clean and tidy. When he made enquiries at a nearby boarding school about a young girl to do part-time work, he made an unusual request: if possible, she should be 'a Guernsey girl'. The headmistress smiled: just fourteen, Lucy Brouard, dark-haired and pretty, away from home for the first time, should fit the bill admirably. Hired to come by the cottage one afternoon a week, her main tasks were to weed the garden, prune the roses, and help Parkes to sort, dust and straighten the books that were jammed on to a wall of shelves. The modest cottage, she recalled, was made to seem smaller by the clutter of pictures and objects from many places, and it was also disagreeably musty.

The teenager's duties were simple enough, but her mild-looking employer was pernickety and unpredictably short-tempered. 'He was very particular about those books,' she recollected. 'The spines of all of them had to be exactly level.'[4] During her first weeks of employment Brouard, inexperienced at gardening, over-pruned the roses. In a flash Parkes grew furious, frightening her with his shouts until tears welled first in her eyes, and then in his.

Photos bear out that the figure recalled by Brouard had declined dramatically from the vigorous warrior who only two years earlier had bested George Watson on ABC television. Beset by searingly painful sieges of Dupuytren's contracture, Parkes now often experienced difficulty in walking. Moreover the voice of the formerly brilliant performer at the lectern was now at times reduced to a scarcely audible mumble. Then again Brouard also recalls that, true to her given name, she sometimes acted as a light-bearer. Parkes eagerly anticipated her arrival and was often jolly. He took particular pleasure in showing her one of his recent pastels or watercolours of the seaside and in recounting tales from his boyhood on Guernsey.

Old Mrs Parkes, on the other hand, was off-putting, even a touch 'odd'. She made much, for example, of being endowed with extra-sensory gifts. Brouard also sensed that she, unlike her employer, was never truly pleased by her presence. Merely for the sake of 'the servant girl', the old woman would not trouble herself with niceties like inserting her false teeth. This boorishness, however, did not much disturb Brouard because it was clear that Parkes ruled the roost. 'Especially when it snowed, he liked to have his tea served on time and on trays. One thing that his wife did enjoy was her piece of cake; there would always be a piece for me as well.'[5] Early in 1976, after two years of service, Brouard ceased to work for the old couple.

For March of that year Parkes' files disclose a letter to a Mr R. F. Hoare, a fervent believer in the authenticity of the Holy Shroud of Turin. Doubtless aware that disabusing R. F. Hoare of his views could seriously deplete his limited store of energy, the great campaigner of the past put him off with just a polite demur.[6] Nevertheless, ever sensitive to the density and the persistence of the past, the brief exchange teased the great historian's imagination. Here at Iwerne Minster he was targeted by a man who quite possibly was connected to the very yeoman in whose fourteenth-century manor Parkes had once resided – Barley's 'Old Hore's House'.[7]

How improbable that two Hoares should have so impinged upon his pristine life. Did this hint, he wondered, at mysterious, even paranormal, agencies of an altogether different order than the sort that so strongly appealed to Hoare? How many times had Parkes felt constrained to refute the charge that being subsidized by Israel Sieff was tantamount to intellectual whoring for the Jews?

In April, when the old couple refigured their wills to factor in the effects of inflation, they discovered that they would have less to bequeath to their beneficiaries than previously thought.[8] Two decades earlier, when they were nearly impoverished, such a problem could not have arisen. The following year Parkes was again in touch with Cousin Barrie in Australia, this time about landscaping: a gap in the family tree.[9] The feeble old man still painted, still enjoyed his roses, still took pleasure in his regular tea and his irregular visitors, and had grown reconciled to the dimming and narrowing of his world. As always, the most dependable anodyne was a convincing display of public recognition.

Later that year, the library of the University of Southampton published a bibliography of *The Printed Works of James Parkes*. Visibly pleased, Parkes smiled wryly when he noted that it had been edited by a Mr D. A. Pennie. This surprised him hardly at all. After all, if out of the shrouded past an Old Hore could materialize in a new guise to supplant or possibly even to redeem his boyhood nemesis, why shouldn't an 'elemental' surrogate of bad old headmaster Penney now turn up as Mr D. A. Pennie? It was as though, as the end of his days neared, an antic Bungalow Ghost had resurfaced to, as it were, knot the looser threads of Parkes' life into whimsical, jokey patterns, all the while daring the old scholar to penetrate their meaning. Unlike the days of his youth, however, there now was no one with whom Parkes could exhaustively debate the genuineness and significance of these manifestations. Wickings lost patience for it early in the game.

The closer he got to marking his eighth decade, the less the increasingly feeble old man left Iwerne Minster.

> The last time I saw him was in July 1977, also in Southampton ... Parkes had celebrated his 80th birthday the previous December, and, although frail, he attended the gathering of the International Council of Christians and Jews, as usual attended by his faithful helpmate Dorothy. All the speakers paid tribute to his pioneering work and influence, but the Friday evening was devoted to a special tribute, with messages of greeting from all over the world and friendly reminiscences by those present. Suddenly and unexpectedly James himself stood to speak. He was evidently deeply moved by the occasion, but his voice was too faint to be heard. Miraculously, someone produced a microphone, and with its help he made a short speech of thanks. Finally emotion got the better of him, and his words tailed off into tears.[10]

Among those attending that celebration was a delegation of admirers from Israel led by the chairman of the Jerusalem Council of Christians and Jews. He paints a picture of Parkes' startling loss of control even direr than we encounter above:

> The truth is that Parkes utterly broke down under the strain of the occasion. From the start he seemed on the verge of

collapse, and several times some people had to prop him up. In response to every speaker's words of tribute, he wept. In the end, his tears fell copiously. I, for one, felt very bad about the scene.[11]

The next year Parkes resumed a correspondence with Margaret Bell, a cousin on his mother's side. Recovering from yet another stay in hospital, he gamely tried to assuage her anxiety about his condition. When he was twenty, he recalled, he had been hospitalized for a far lengthier period. His doctors then ordained that he 'couldn't possibly live more than three years'.[12] Parkes was thinking, of course, of the time when, evacuated from Flanders suffering from exposure to gas and trench foot, he'd been installed for months in a military hospital in London. How could it not have struck him that the selfsame prognosis that at twenty had sounded a death knell at eighty-one would have chimed a reprieve?

Issuing from complementary aspects of his personality, two pieces appeared in 1976: 'Jewish Mysticism'[13] and 'Christianity, Jewish History and Antisemitism'.[14] Though his body was failing, his mind was still exercised by the two central intellectual interests of his lifetime: the relationship of Christianity to Judaism and God's plan for His Creation – or, in another key, the reconciliation of James Parkes and John Hadham.

Three years later Parkes composed his last essay – 'Judaism and Christianity: Their Tasks and Their Relations in the Present Phase of the Evolving World'. What were the final thoughts about this, his signature theme? Taking a broad, non-sectarian perspective, in characteristic phrases Parkes affirmed, 'the inevitability of a religion like Judaism, and that it must be equal in permanence and significance with Christianity'. He reiterated his long-held view that God worked 'through three channels rather than through three personae.' And, most percipiently, he declared that Jewish missionary activity,

> ... is as persistent as that of Christianity, though different because it is coherent with the Judaism which the Jewish people have evolved. Wherever Jews are citizens, you will find them far more numerous than their proportion of the population would lead one to expect in every concern for social betterment and reform – in other words, concerned

with the missionary task of bringing the Gentile world
nearer to the Messianic age.[15]

In the summer of 1981, very close to three years since his
previous visit, James Parkes was again in hospital. For over sixty
years he had contrived to forestall a hanging – the sentence his
old headmaster had pronounced over the head of the young
troublemaker – but, like a long-deferred curse, the prognosis
of the military doctors now finally hit the mark. Occupying a
nearby hospital bed, also very seriously ill, lay his wife of thirty-
nine years.

Shortly before the end, W. W. Simpson and Ruth Weyl arrived
to bid farewell to their dying friend. They recognized all too
well that for decades Parkes had been feeling unappreciated,
bypassed and much aggrieved. With Death impatiently tapping
his fingers, the bedridden man was reconciled to mortality but
not, it seemed, to anonymity.[16] In the past the clergyman had
paid tribute to the high value Judaism places on the good deeds
– *mitzvot* – that are performed for their own sake. For example
Jews hold that contributing to the upkeep of the poor, an act of
justice rather than of charity, is most meritorious when performed in secret. Alas, the old man's ego was just not up to it.
'James cried his eyes out not because he was nearing death, but
because people were no longer reading his books. His name, he
felt, was no longer being mentioned.'[17]

We have freely dilated upon episodes for which, as the end
drew near, Parkes could and perhaps should have divined serious
grounds for shame, guilt or remorse. There seemed to be none
of that. Nor was there any evident anxiety about what might
normally be anticipated of a Church of England clergyman on
the verge of dying: the state of his immortal soul. Instead we
find Parkes concerned with the verdict of posterity and crestfallen over the unfairness of his diminished reputation. In recompense, in a fashion, for his wedding service, Weyl performed an
'interfaith' version of Jewish last rites: she reassured the distraught scholar that he would live on through his good deeds
and that his name would survive through the permanent value
of his writings.[18]

A few weeks later, completing an eighty-four year voyage
James William Parkes, the vicar who also spoke as a Jew, made
his final discovery. His voyage over, on 10 August 1981, he

delivered himself into the hands of his Saviour. He was buried in the shadow of the St Mary's, Iwerne Minster's parish church where several years later Dorothy Wickings would also be laid to rest.

Shortly after Parkes' death, a ceremony was held to honour his memory at the Hebrew Congregation of Bournemouth, the nearest Jewish congregation to Iwerne Minster. The principal speaker offered the following considered evaluation of the man.

> I should like to pay tribute to his great kindness and generosity which I sought from James on more than one occasion, [and] I should like to defend James from an accusation I have heard levelled against him, namely, arrogance. Brilliance and arrogance. I believe that his forthrightness and his considerable expertise in the field of Jewish–Christian understanding, and perhaps also his manner of speaking, may have given some the impression that he thought he knew all the answers. Certainly he knew most of them! Neither did he suffer fools gladly, and sometimes perhaps he did not hesitate to give a questioner a quick retort, but I am sure that this meant no unkindness.[19]

One doubts that George Watson would have borne quite the same witness as the above speaker, but if his acquaintanceship with Parkes was too brief for him to testify to the kindlier side of the man, ours certainly has not been. As seen repeatedly, almost any victim of ill treatment could feel confident of a sympathetic reception at the door of James Parkes.

As the above encomium infers, Parkes, like all complex figures, was flawed and paradoxical. In order to triumph over frailty and illness, his older brother's natural precedence, the premature loss of his mother and his father's disregard,[20] from early childhood he had constructed a romanticized self-image behind which his more vulnerable self might shelter. As a young man at Elizabeth College, this public persona fostered assertiveness and egocentricity. Although in certain circumstances, such as on the bloody fields of Flanders, his bifurcated personality was unsustainable, in the end it proved remarkably resilient. Indeed, once Parkes discovered his true vocation, it would serve him splendidly.

Of course at times Parkes could be petty, callous or insensitive,[21] not to mention self-indulgent and vain: it is difficult to banish the image of that 'bust of Parkes' fine head ... placed in the very centre of the room ... so that the first thing you saw on entering was his head'.[22] For good reason, he was not given to self-reflection. On the other hand, diverging sharply from the chilly aloofness of D. H. Lawrence,[23] one of his least apposite alter egos, Parkes was truly great in conscience and magnificent in compassion, a man of feeling given not to tears alone but to decisive, effective action. Notwithstanding defects of personality, his character was sound to the bottom of the skip.

The sickly, weepy adolescent – the loner and outsider – brilliantly reinvented himself as an irreverent toff who rode and strode as a knight errant, a priestly crusader and an historian *engagé*. If James Parkes may be viewed as the most steadfast and effective defender of the Jewish people to emerge from Gentile ranks in the twentieth century, then it is no great stretch to extend that judgment to any century. For over fifty years, he never lost focus or faltered in determination in pursuit of what he had the wit and courage to recognize as the 'main thing', the overriding purpose of his life – his christian, Christian's duty to render justice to the Jewish people. In the process he became one of the authentic intellectual and ethical heroes of our time.

We do well to remember that before Parkes the 'healthy-minded' Christian response to antisemitism closely approximated the spirit of a Gallic shrug. True, the enormity of the Shoah has resonated profoundly, but even today the feeling in many quarters is that the statute of limitations, which has long over-taken the massacres at York, at Worms and at Kishinev, is winding down for Kielce, Vichy, and Auschwitz as well. To the depths of his being, Parkes exclaimed loudly and persistently that it indeed had not. John Chrysostom, the *auto-da-fé*, the ritual murder libel and the *Protocols of the Elders of Zion* had ploughed and furrowed the essential ground and rationalized the barbarism that led directly to the Shoah. Christianity itself was in the dock. In order genuinely to atone for its sins against the Jewish people, Parkes believed, it must reform itself, abjure itself, and confess itself not alone or even primarily through its own sacramental modalities but, following traditional Jewish practice, face to face with its victims.

Recognizing in liberal Jewish values the finest expression of mankind's potential for communal greatness and social redemption, Parkes identified himself unreservedly with the people who propounded them. Parkes' chief ideological animus was never scepticism, which in fact he valued highly, but radical Christian pessimism, or Barthianism with its crippling emphasis on man's innately fallen nature. In the very final pages of *Voyage of Discoveries* he was still excoriating that 'pernicious doctrine'.[24]

Parkes appropriated what, after Rabbi Hillel the Elder's dictum that prohibits doing unto one's neighbour what is hateful to oneself, many consider the cardinal precept of Jewish ethical conscience: 'It is not up to you to complete the work, yet you are not free to desist from it.'[25] He ruminated long and hard over deep, seemingly intrinsic flaws in God's Creation. By exhaustively chronicling the unvarnished historical record of Christian attitudes and actions that came to a crescendo with the Shoah, Parkes picked up both the lance and the cross. In the process, he saved himself from the cosmic despair that he so despised in the theology of Karl Barth. Before there was a Bishop Desmond Tutu of Capetown there was the Reverend Dr James Parkes of Barley, a representative just man for our times whose life work constitutes a one-man commission for truth and reconciliation.

Although he instinctively gravitated towards the Jewish ideal of the realization of a just and a holy community, Parkes was exquisitely conscious that he could never himself become a Jew in the normative sense. His moveable home, the rock upon which he raised his tent, was his Christian faith, and his aim was to make amends as a Christian for the trespasses done to his Lord's people by his Lord's followers. Nevertheless, accused of being *ganz verjudet*, Parkes graciously and wholeheartedly pleaded guilty as charged, extenuated, however, by an essential caveat: 'it has not made me wish to deny or modify one single positive aspect of my traditional Christianity ... Open dialogue between oneself and others lies at the heart of Creation.'[26]

On the other hand, for one who could not possibly become a Jew, Parkes made good on his claim, indeed his vaunt, that as a Christian he had every right also to speak as one, that is, to take his stand in the world as a sort of Jew. Short of circumcision itself, his voyage brought this confessing Christian as close as possible to anchoring himself within the harbour of Judaism, the faith of his Lord. In works such as *The Jew and His Neighbour* (1931), *Judaism and Christianity* (1948), *End of An Exile* (1954) and *A History of the Jewish People* (1962), Parkes got Judaism remarkably right. An outsider insider, he was *sui generis*.

It is not merely that in reading his books and articles one does not stumble over gaffes on Jewish ritual, wince over inadvertent Christological introjections or shudder over historical blunders. Unique among Gentile scholars or so-called philosemites was Parkes' pitch-perfect internalization of the spirit of Jewish modes of thought and tradition, a comprehension from the inside, as it were, that is positively uncanny. For a Jew to read Parkes on Judaism or the meaning of the State of Israel is like being recognized at last for his inner self. After so much ignorance, distortion, malignity and,well-intentioned pandering, this is extraordinarily gratifying. A Jewish friend who knew Parkes intimately fleshes out much the same sentiment:

> James was one of the few Christians who did not make me feel uncomfortable with his philosemitism. He could get angry with Jews. As a Jew you could feel fine with him. You could curse Jews or Christians or even Israel. You could be yourself. He was genuine. His affinity for the Jews was profound and genuine. It has to do with Jewish suffering, his respect for the Jewish openness and affirmation of life, its questioning stance toward experience. He was both an honest historian and a man of faith.[27]

In 1969, in the first flush of response to the promulgation of *Nostra Aetate,* a group of Catholic and Protestant clergymen in the Boston area initiated a series of meetings aimed at fashioning a statement that would 'eliminate the erroneous portrayal of Jews as unfaithful deicides, accursed by God; expunge the teaching of contempt; [and] revise Christian doctrine about Jews and Judaism'.[28] This highly sensitive assignment would occupy some of the best theological minds of the generation for more than thirty years. Signed by twenty-two leading Christian theologians and ecumenists, only in 2002 was 'A Sacred Obligation: Rethinking Christian Faith in Relation to Judaism and the Jewish People' finally issued.

This watershed statement makes ten major declarations. Quintessentially Parkesian, their headings may stand as a succinct, remarkably adequate summary of his fundamental beliefs about the relationship between Christians and Jews.

1) God's covenant with the Jewish people endures for ever;
2) Jesus of Nazareth lived and died as a faithful Jew;

3) Ancient rivalries must not define Christian–Jewish relations today; 4) Judaism is a living faith, enriched by many centuries of development; 5) The Bible both connects and separates Christians and Jews; 6) Affirming God's enduring covenant with the Jewish people has consequences for Christian understanding of salvation; 7) Christians should not target Jews for conversion; 8) Christian worship that teaches contempt for Judaism dishonours God; 9) We affirm the importance of the land of Israel for the life of the Jewish people; 10) Christians should work with Jews for the healing of the world.[29]

Nearly seventy years after the publication of *The Conflict of the Church and the Synagogue*, the progressive Christian world had caught up with the vision intuited, delineated and actively promoted by the pioneering cleric and historian from Guernsey.

As for the body of Parkes' work, it may be justly characterized by the term Parkes himself had employed in acclaiming the achievement Geza Vermes, a 'fellow Jewish scholar' whom he admired inordinately – epoch-making. The influence and recognition of his achievement is bound only to grow with time. James Parkes did not aspire to be '*Messiah*' or even a prophet, but he was a rare avatar of the classic *ger tsedek*, the Righteous Gentile of Jewish tradition. In his everyday life, where and when it really counted, he comported himself as nothing less than a true *mensch*.

NOTES

1. T.S. Eliot, 'Burnt Norton' (1935), from 'The Four Quartets', *Collected Poems 1909–1962* (New York: Harcourt, Brace, & World, 1963), p. 176.
2. James Parkes, 'Holidays in My Childhood', St Peter Port: *The Guernsey Society Journal*, August 1976, Parkes Archives, File 60/33/92/81.
3. James Parkes, letter to John Ozanne, 1975, Parkes Archives, File 60/31/3.
4. Lucy Brouard interviewed by the author and Maggie Davidson, St Peter Port, Guernsey, August 2000.
5. Ibid.
6. James Parkes, letter to R. F. Hoare, March 1976, Parkes Archives, File 60/31/57.
7. *Vide* Chapter 22.
8. Parkes Archives, File 60/16/52.
9. James Parkes, letter to Barrie Parkes, May 1977, Parkes Archives, File 60/31/2.
10. Nicolas de Lange, 'Unforgettable Character', Pamphlet No. 1, University of Southampton, Parkes Archives.
11. Dr Joseph Emanuel of Jerusalem interviewed by the author by telephone, December, 2003.
12. James Parkes, letter to Margaret Bell, 1978, Parkes Archives, File 60/16/52.

13. James Parkes, *The Church's Fellowship for Psychical and Spiritual Studies Quarterly Review*, London: No. 87, Spring 1976, pp. 9–13.
14. James Parkes, Southampton, The Parkes Library, 1976.
15. James Parkes, 'Judaism and Christianity: Their Tasks and Their Relations in the Present Phase of the Evolving World', October 1978, Parkes Archives, File 60/9/19/24, pp. 1, 3 and 4.
16. *Vide* Chapter 32.
17. Ruth Weyl interviewed by the author and Maggie Davidson in Rehovot, Israel, 26 October 2003.
18. On his deathbed, a traditional Jew confesses his sins to his Maker.
19. The Venerable Whitton Davies, *Tributes in Memory of James William Parkes*, Bournemouth Hebrew Congregation, 1981, University of Southampton, Parkes Archives.
20. This final allusion to Parkes' father triggers a flight of fancy, an indulgent, whimsical excursus that returns us to beginnings: 'In the centre of the island of Guernsey is the parish of St Andrew. At the eastern end is the Manor of Rohais. My father was the falconer of the Manor, and I was born at Les Fauconnaires in December 1896.' For Parkes, an historian with an ear for undertone, this incantatory opening evoked an abiding sense of history as a haunting presence capable of making claims, sometimes urgent ones, upon the present moment. A compulsive reader of *The Times*, he could hardly have been unaware that the Noble Prize for Literature had been awarded to the American novelist William Faulkner. The chances seem excellent that the attention of the son of the falconer of the Manor of Rohais quickened. Upon skimming a potted account of Faulkner's life and work, he surely would have noted with interest that, like the works of James Parkes, Faulkner's *oeuvre* was haunted by the thematic presence and pressure of the past. In different ways, both men were committed to chronicling the complex intricacies of their imbrication. Admittedly, differences between the two men are equally striking. Although each hit his stride professionally during the early 1930s, Parkes' literary taste was far too Victorian to imagine him settling down some evening to sound the depths of *The Sound and the Fury* or the furies of *Absalom!, Absalom!* On Faulkner's side, of all major twentieth-century American novelists, he evinced perhaps the least interest in Jews. By 1950, the falconer of the Manor of Rohais had been dead for six years. The Bungalow Ghost had long since retired. Nevertheless, although it is a prodigious stretch from Les Fauconnaires to Mississippi mannerist we note that the two men were born the same year. Moreover, like Parkes, Faulkner also spent many critical years as a resident of Oxford, a Mississippi college town as remote from metropolitan centres as the bailiwick of Guernsey or the villages of Barley and Iwerne Minster. Not only had he spent the greater part of seven years at Oxford, but Parkes also had his memorable encounter with the Prague woman who firmly maintained that most itinerant Americans hailed from Oxford (*vide* Chapter 13). These coincidental congeries could well have excited Parkes' imagination enough to lead him to scan the new laureate's brief but widely circulated Nobel address, arguably the most decorous in the history of the ceremony. In that splendid oration, Faulkner extolled the capacity of the spirit of man to exercise compassion, endurance, and forgiveness, the very notes Parkes had begun to strike shortly after the First World War. Echoing T. S. Eliot, he passionately held that the past was never dead, a truism to which Parkes lent his enthusiastic assent. Moreover, consonant with Parkes' liberalism, Faulkner unashamedly proclaimed his belief that the spirit of man would not merely endure but that in the end it would prevail. In 1945, the year after the death of Henry Parkes, the spirit of man finally prevailed over tyranny on Guernsey. Appositely, the vessel that received the surrender of Admiral Hüffmeier, thereby officially liberating the island after more than five years of Occupation was the HMS *Faulkner* (*vide* Chapter 28). In the absence of evidence pointing toward reconciliation between Parkes and his father, we are left with a frustrating sense of a lost opportunity, of a stalemate in which both men colluded for over sixty years. Yet Parkes was no believer in meaningless 'coincidence'. Given his attitude of open-mindedness towards the world of

spirits, might he, through a trick worthy of Elliot O'Donnell's 'elementals' (*vide* Chapter 8), not have felt an intimation of the disinterested agency of William Faulkner interceding between himself and his father the falconer to negotiate their mutual forbearance? *Pace* Hoare and Penney (*vide supra*), one must merely conceive that the technocratic, impersonated father had been transfigured into the countryman humanist from Mississippi. In such fashion, would it really be so outrageous tentatively to propose that an 'elemental' of a chastened Henry Parkes appealed to the uncompromising spirit of his son to yield to the spirit of forgiveness and that, under the aegis of 'William Faulkner', an end to hostilities between son and father may have been effected? Although this strains credulity, depending on the predilections of the reader, let sentiment or sentimentality either be rebuffed or suffered gladly.

21. *Vide* Chapters 20 and 21 in particular.
22. Edith Ruth Weisz, interviewed by the author and Maggie Davidson in Cambridge, England, 28–29 August 2000.
23. *Vide* Chapter 2.
24. James Parkes, *Voyage of Discoveries* (London: Victor Gollancz, 1969), p. 247, ff.
25. Rabbi Tarphon, *Chapters of the Fathers*, edited and translated by Samson Raphael Hirsch, introduction by Rabbi Joseph Breuer (Jerusalem: Feldheim, 1972), pp. 'c'.
26. Parkes Archives, File: 60/8/12.
27. Ruth Weyl interviewed by the author and Maggie Davidson in Rehovot, Israel, 26 October 2003.
28. 'Symposium: A New Christian Document on Christian–Jewish Relations', *Midstream*, Vol. XXXXIX, No. 1 (January 2003), p. 3.
29. Ibid., pp. 3–4.

Aims and Methodology:
An Afterword

You can define a net in one of two ways, depending upon your point of view. Normally you would say it is a meshed instrument designed to catch fish. But you could with no great injury to logic, reverse the image and define a net as a jocular lexicographer with a biography. The trawling net fills, then the biographer hauls it in, sorts, throws back, stores, fillets and sells. Yet consider what he doesn't catch: there is always far more of that.[1]

For more than two decades since Parkes' death, only one book-length study dealing with his thought has appeared.[2] There was no biography. Yet, as noted by Colin Richmond, 'there is a particular need for an account of Parkes' life because his autobiography is so unassuming it reveals virtually nothing about a great English visionary, an eccentric not only because he went "against the grain" but because he was also an activist, one for whom thinking was not enough'.[3] *He Also Spoke as a Jew* aims to fill that void for our generation.

Parkes published *Voyage of Discoveries*, his 'unassuming autobiography,' in 1969. Notwithstanding its transparent deficiencies, Parkes' jauntily reconstituted log of his 'voyage out' fairly reliably charts his external passage through life. The ageing chronicler felt no desire and little imperative to play the artful dodger or intellectual chameleon. While at points evasive, his memoir, a heretofore untapped but rich vein of personal recollection, displays little of the wilful falsification of detail, obfuscation or urgency to promote an ideological agenda often encountered in recent years in autobiographical writings of problematic personages such as, say, Arthur Koestler or Edward Said.[4]

To a great extent, however, one must agree among others with Richmond that Parkes did himself a disservice in not producing a more reflective account of his life, one commensurate with his originality and ground-breaking achievement. At critical junctures we have often been disconcerted by idiosyncratic anecdotes, many of them patently self-serving and not notably amusing. Clearly Parkes is unaware of rhetorical complexities inherent in depicting a young man pointing forward in time and simultaneously an ageing historian peering through its rear-view mirror. Still, this very ingenuousness may be richly exploited, its artlessness turned to advantage. Turning Richmond's 'virtually nothing' on its head, even this maligned memoir's smarmy inscription – 'To Dorothy, a Silver Wedding Present' – may be trawled for a surprisingly abundant yield. Thus have I treated *Voyage of Discoveries* like a pristine sandbox, its natural surface yet undisturbed by earlier deconstructivist pokes, narratological strokes or other post-modernist probes.

Drawn to this investigation by frank admiration and raw curiosity about the man, I have not in the least felt tempted to trim my subject's nose hairs or to sanitize his inner pockets. Little, in fact, would have been more be more counter-productive to my aims. Moreover, I take solace in the certainty that, although at points Parkes would have differed markedly and tenaciously with my reading of his motivations, he would surely have found some of my 'excesses' amusing and strongly approved of my recoil from hagiographic impulses.

The challenge was to tease from the recalcitrant pages of *Voyage of Discoveries,* from hints in his other writings, from remarks in his voluminous correspondence, and from the testimony of his surviving friends and acquaintances a truly satisfactory solution to the mystery of how the lad from Guernsey became Champion of the Jews. Parkes himself may be cited as strongly encouraging such a line of investigation. Using the *nom de plume* John Hadham, in his first theological study Parkes referred to the birthplace of Jesus in these suggestive terms:

> The choice of time and environment is at first astonishing – an obscure artisan family in a subject province of the great empire of Rome among a despised people, far from the great centres of culture, science and philosophy, which embellished the greatest empire the world had yet known. It is only by looking back that we can see its aptness.[5]

The patent irony, of course, is that the historian capable of demonstrating great clarity of vision in discerning Jesus within his social and spiritual context in Galilee turned astigmatic as a septuagenarian directing his gaze at himself growing up on turn-of-the-century Guernsey. On the other hand, it would be rash to conclude that lacunae in Parkes' memoir imply that pertinent but unaddressed issues never arose in his mind. On the contrary, it is more prudent to assume that a man of his searching intelligence mulled endlessly over the factors and circumstances that led him to trace so curious a course. Nevertheless, Parkes chose not to delve into the matter very deeply in print. For his summing-up, he chose instead the conceit of an 'anniversary gift' for his wife, burnishing his life story to such a fine gloss that he clearly intended its lustre should outshine the faint glow emitted by painful or embarrassing embers from the past.

An important methodological issue remains to be broached. At every stage in the course of this excavation, I have tried to be guided by two considerations: first, to provide a plausible account of the implausible emergence of this eminent Christian historian with so close an affinity for Judaism and the Jewish people from such improbable origins; and second, to ascertain how outer and inner events led him to marshal his extraordinary scholarly and polemical gifts in a life-long campaign in defence of the Jews from obloquy, calumny and ultimately genocide. Confronted by vacancies and a dearth of sources, at times I have felt constrained to join the dots and fill in the blanks myself. This obviously entails risk; nevertheless, in order to paint a recognizable portrait, I believe that, consistent with the available evidence, it is the writer's responsibility to provide the reader with the fruits of his long-considered speculation. I anticipate that some readers will have concluded that at points I surmise too much. In my defence, I have tried to be scrupulous in clearly distinguishing fact from speculation, thereby enabling the attentive reader to draw his own conclusions.

I think it instructive to conclude these remarks with an illustration of the sort of seductive pitfall that confronts any biographer of James Parkes. A would-be proleptic moment from his days as an Oxford undergraduate is reported by Edith Weisz, acquainted with the cleric for over twenty-five years. From inside his room, Parkes overheard a loud, supercilious voice prattling in the outside corridor, '*He's only a Jewboy!*' 'From that moment on,' Weisz recalls him saying, 'I knew that I must delve into this.'[6]

What a splendidly apt occurrence, such an opportune recollection. Taken together, they purport to identify the genitive nub of Parkes' life-long obsession with championing the Jews. In actuality, this reported incident is so overdetermined that it raises more doubts than it assuages.

First of all, at the time Parkes could not have been unacquainted with Jews and antisemitism. If prior to Oxford encounters with Jews were, while probable, only conjectural, at Oxford it is certain that Parkes frequently met Jewish undergraduates and could not have been insensible to the social barriers they faced. Looking back on his year as secretary of the League of Nations Union for example, he recalls that for reasons both of fairness and an approximation of verisimilitude he preferred that in debate Palestine be represented by a Jewish student and Iraq by an Arab.[7] Parkes, therefore, not only had many encounters with Oxford 'Jewboys', but, since the context guaranteed a shared internationalist stance, most were almost certainly amiable.

Especially since Weisz's recollections are generally reliable,[8] the linking of Parkes' firm resolution to investigate the phenomenon of antisemitism to his repugnance at overhearing a banal Jewish slur seems not unreasonable. Nevertheless, the absence of any allusion to such a watershed episode in the text of *Voyage of Discoveries* casts prima facie doubt upon its authenticity. In fact, Parkes' own account of those years at Oxford points in the opposite direction: 'My Oxford background had been conventional. I had … no reason to ask myself whether our relationship to Jews and Judaism was something different from the relationship of Christianity to any other religion.'[9]

Later Parkes indicates it was only at an international conference in 1925, two years after his graduation from Oxford, that he first became conscious of the 'violence' and 'special quality' of the Jewish problem.[10] Later still he cites 1929 as 'the beginning of my real involvement in the Jewish question'.[11] 'Involvement' implies a considerably more intense engagement than 'consciousness.' Although these terms are far from mutually exclusive, they do suggest the difficulty, if not the impossibility, of confidently linking complex decisions, rife with ramification, to improbably apt 'smoking guns'.

How, then, do we account for Parkes' reputed remembrance at Oxford? In his middle years, in the course of lecturing before many audiences, Parkes was repeatedly constrained to account for his life-long absorption with the Jewish question. Jewish audiences in particular queried him about this matter *ad nauseam*.

Especially since he was not inclined to disentangle the intellectual components of his 'philosemitism' from its knotty emotional strands, the issue had become an utterly predictable, banal and burdensome business for him. One surmises that Parkes inevitably fashioned a number of set piece responses to negotiate the matter expeditiously. One of his favourite sound bites, for example, was 'there is no heavier atonement to be made than that of the Christian to the Jew'.[12]

These explanations do little more than dance around the question. What his audience really wanted to understand was less 'how' than 'why him'? How did it happen that the Reverend James Parkes of all people should have assumed the mantle of Paladin of the Jews? The mystery of Parkes' commitment to radical goodness, paralleling in its fashion the corresponding mystery of Hitler's radical evil, is tantalizing for we sense that were we only able to unlock its secret, to expose its root, that it might disclose one of the vital components of the human personality. In the end we too often yield to the temptation of resting with 'the' answer, whereas, bereft of context, one decisive turning point could not possibly make any real sense. How many would-be expositors of Hitler's obsessive hatred have traced it to a supposed indignity, affront or insult suffered at the hands of a Jewish schoolmate, art dealer, or doctor?

However, the specificity of the putative 'Jewboy Episode' argues that it may have had a basis. There is nothing inherently improbable in it, and insistent prodding may indeed have momentarily dislodged a memory trace from some inner recess of Parkes' psyche. It could not have been the first time – nor the last – that Parkes had overheard this snivelly slur, one once so prevalent in class-conscious Britain; nor is it improbable that there could have been a particular occasion when the arrogance, insolence, and unfairness of it – especially its unfairness – should have arrested his attention.

On the other hand, antisemitism was such a pervasive aspect of British society of the period that even were this hypothesis not subverted by other statements in *Voyage of Discoveries*, it beggars common sense to imagine that such an unsingular incident should of itself have moved Parkes to become acutely conscious of the 'special quality of the Jewish problem'. Even assuming that Parkes may have actually said something of the sort to assuage his interlocutor's need for a straightforward, easily comprehensible answer, one concludes that as a definitive illumination of Parkes' deeper motivations or decision-making processes it may safely be dismissed.

This study issues from a personal imperative not only to demystify but also to repay what had grown into a debt of honour. As he himself feared might happen, today James Parkes, one of the intellectual and spiritual heroes of the twentieth century, goes relatively unheralded. Yet the man was pivotal in initiating the movement to redress the historical evils inflicted upon Jews in the name of Christianity. It seems therefore only just and proper that it should fall to a Jewish writer and, yes, an Israeli writer, to labour to undo and annul the scandal of what Colin Richmond has labelled, with characteristic understatement, Parkes' 'unfortunate neglect'.[13]

As Julian Barnes remarks, however, neither the seine nor the fisherman can ever be fine enough. Even before this work sees light, I too look forward with much anticipation to future hauls by other hands.

Haim Chertok
Beersheva 2006

NOTES

1. Julian Barnes, *Flaubert's Parrot* (London: Picador, 1984), p. 38.
2. Robert A. Everett, *Christianity Without Anti-Semitism. Campaigner Against Anti-semitism*, Colin Richmond, biography of Parkes, was released in 2005 under the imprint of Vallentine Mitchell.
3. Colin Richmond, 'Parkes, Prejudice, and the Middle Ages', p.241. Had I been aware that Richmond himself was contemplating filling this gap, I probably would not have undertaken it myself.
4. *Vide* David Cesarani's effective dissection of fact from fancy in *Arthur Koestler: The Homeless Mind*, 1998 and Justus Reid Weiner's *emendation du text* '"My Beautiful Old House" and Other Fabrications by Edward Said', *Commentary*, September 1999.
5. James Parkes, *God At Work in Science, Politics, and Human Life* (London: Putnam, 1952), p. 51.
6. Edith Weisz, interviewed by the author and Maggie Davidson in Cambridge, 28 August 2000.
7. James Parkes, 'The Way Forward', delivered at a Colloquium at Southampton, June 1977, Parkes Archives, File 60/33/92/86.
8. *Vide* Chapters 22, 24 and 26.
9. James Parkes, *Voyage of Discoveries* (London: Victor Gollancz, 1969), p. 116.
10. Ibid., p. 87.
11. Ibid., p. 111.
12. James Parkes, 'The Trinity in International Affairs', 1929, University of Southampton, Parkes Archives, File 60/6/8/10/12, p. 27.
13. *Vide supra.*

Bibliography

BOOKS and PAMPHLETS CITED IN TEXT

Aristotle, *The Nicomachean Ethics*, translated and edited by David Ross (London: Oxford University Press, 1969)

Astor, David, *The Meaning of Eichmann* (Barley: The Parkes Library, 1960)

Augustine, *Confessions*, translated and introduced by R. S. Pine-Coffin (Harmondsworth: Penguin Classics, 1982)

Barker, Pat, *The Ghost Road* (New York: Dutton, 1995)

Barnes, Julian, *Cross Channel* (London: Picador, 1996)

Barnes, Julian, *Flaubert's Parrot* (London: Picador, 1984)

Baxter, John, *A Pound of Paper: Confessions of a Book Addict* (New York: Doubleday, 2003)

Bayley, John, *The Power of Delight, A Lifetime in Literature: Essays 1962–2002* (New York: W. W. Norton, 2005)

Be'er, Haim, *The Pure Element of Time* (Hanover, NH: University Press of New England/Brandeis University, 2003)

Benvenisti, Meron, *Sacred Landscape: The Buried History of the Holy Land Since 1948* (Berkeley: University of California, 2000)

Berdichevsky, M. Y., *Miriam and Other Stories*, translated by A. S. Super, introduction by Avner Holtzman (New Milford CT: Toby Press, 2004)

Birnbaum, Pierre, *The Anti-Semitic Moment: A Tour of France in 1898*, translated by Jane Todd (New York: Hill and Wang, 2003)

Bisson, André *L'Inflation Française 1914–1952* (Paris: Sirey, 1953)

Boswell, James, *Life of Johnson*, Vol. 1, edited by George Birkbeck Hill and L. F. Powell (London: Oxford University Press, 1934)

Bowker, Gordon, *Inside George Orwell* (London: Macmillan, 2003)

Briggs, Asa, *The Channel Islands: Liberation and Occupation, 1940–1945* (London: Batsford and the Imperial War Museum, 1995)

Brittain, Vera, *Testament of Youth, An Autobiographical Study of the Years 1900–1925* (London: Virago, 1978)

Carey, Peter, *Illywhacker* (London: Faber and Faber, 1988)

Carey, Peter, *Oscar and Lucinda* (London: Faber and Faber, 1988)

Cesarani, David, *Arthur Koestler, The Homeless Mind* (London: Vintage 1999)

Chapters [Sayings] of the Fathers, edited and translated by Samson Raphael Hirsch, introduction by Rabbi Joseph Breuer (Jerusalem: Feldheim, 1972)

Chertok, Haim, *Prisoner of Hope* (Hanover, NH: Brandeis University Press, 1996)

Coetzee, J. M., *Foe* (Harmondsworth: Penguin Books, 1987)

Cohn, Norman, *Warrant for Genocide: The Myth of the Jewish World Conspiracy and* the Protocols of the Elders of Zion (New York: Harper & Row, 1966)

Conner, Steven in *The Jew in the Text: Modernity and the Construction of Identity*, edited by Tamar Garb and Linda Nochlin (London: Thames and Hudson, 1995)

Cruickshank, Charles, *The German Occupation of the Channel Islands: The Official History of the Occupation Years* (Guernsey: The Guernsey Press, 1975)

Curtis, Michael, *Verdict on Vichy* (New York: Arcade, 2002)

Edelstein, Alan, *An Unacknowledged Harmony: Philo-Semitism and the Survival of European Jewry* (Westport CN: Greenwood Press, 1982)

Eliot, George, *Daniel Deronda*, two volumes (London: Dent, Everyman's Library, 1964)

Eliot, T. S., *Collected Poems, 1909-1962* (New York: Harcourt Brace, 1963)

Emmet, Cyril, *Conscience, Creeds and Critics* (London: Macmillan, 1918)

Everett, Robert, A., *Christianity Without Anti-Semitism: James Parkes and the Jewish–Christian Encounter* (Oxford: Pergamon, 1993)

Fackenheim, Emil, *The Jewish Return into History: Reflections in the Age of Auschwitz and a New Jerusalem* (NewYork: 1978)

Forster, E. M., *The Longest Journey* (London: Oxford University Press, 1960)

Freedman, Shalom, *Small Acts of Kindness: Striving for Derech Eretz in Everyday Life* (Jerusalem: Urim, 2004)

Gager, John and Nicolas de Lange, *The Origins of Antisemitism: Attitudes Toward Judaism in Pagan and Christian Antiquity* (Oxford: Oxford University Press, 1983)

Garb, Tamar and Linda Nochlin, eds, *The Jew in the Text: Modernity and the Construction of Identity* (London: Thames and Hudson, 1995)

Gardiner, Helen, Ed., *The Metaphysical Poets* (Harmondsworth: Penguin Books, 1957)

Garis, Marie de, *St Pierre du Bois: The Story of a Guernsey Parish and Its People* (St Peter Port: The Guernsey Herald, 1990)

Gibbs, Philip, *Realities of War*, Vol. I (London: Hutchinson, 1938)

Gildea, Robert, *Marianne in Chains: Daily Life in the Heart of France During the German Occupation* (New York: Metropolitan, Holt, 2002)

Graetz, Heinrich, *The History of the Jews*, six volumes (Philadelphia: Jewish Publication Society, 1941)

Grant, Michael, *Jews in the Roman World* (London: Weidenfeld and Nicolson, 1973)

Graves, Robert, *Good-bye To All That* (New York: Anchor, 1989)

Greenberg, Irving, *For the Sake of Heaven and Earth: The New Encounter Between Judaism and Christianity* (Philadelphia: Jewish Publication Society, 2004)

Greenblatt, Stephen, *Will in the World: How Shakespeare Became Shakespeare* (New York: Norton, 2004)

Greene, Graham, *This Gun for Hire* (New York: Viking, 1964)

Haffner, Sebastian, *Defying Hitler: A Memoir*, translated by Oliver Pretzel (London: Phoenix, 2003)

Hamel, Leo, *The Musings of Memory* (St Peter Port: Guernsey Press, 1981)

Hart, B. H. Liddell, *The Real War, 1914-1918* (Boston: Little, Brown & Co, 1930)

Herbert, George in *The Metaphysical Poets*, edited by Helen Gardner, Harmondsworth: Penguin Books, 1957)

Howard, Donald R., *Chaucer, His Life, His World, His Work* (New York: Dutton, 1987)

Hugo, G. W. J. L, *Guernsey As It Used To Be* (St Peter Port: Guernsey Star Gazette, 1933)

Isaac, Jules, *Genèse de l'antisémitisme* (Paris: Calmann-Lévy, 1956)

James, Henry, letter to Mrs Henry James, Sr dated 28 June 1869, *Henry James, Selected Letters*, edited by Leon Edel (Cambridge MA: Belknap, Harvard University Press, 1974)

Johnson, Paul, *Modern Times: The World From The Twenties To The Nineties* (New York: Harper Perennial Edition, 1992)

Johnston, Peter, *A Short History of Guernsey* (St Peter Port: Guernsey Press, 1994)

Joyce, James, *Ulysses* (Harmondsworth: Penguin Edition, 1960)

King, Peter, *The Channel Islands War* (London: Robert Hale, 1991)

Laqueur, Walter, *A History of Zionism* (New York: Holt, Rinehart, and Winston, 1972)

Littel, Franklin, *The Crucifixion of the Jews* (New York: Harper & Row, 1975)

Machon, Nick, *Guernsey As It Was* (St Peter Port: Guernsey Press, n.d.)

Machon, Nick, *More Guernsey As It Was* St Peter Port: Guernsey Press, 1987)

Major, H. D. A., *English Modernism: Its Origins, Methods, and Aims* (Cambridge MA: Harvard, 1927)

Márquez, Gabriel García, *Living to Tell the Tale*, translated by Edith Grossman (New York: Knopf, 2003)

Mellinkoff, Ruth, *Outcasts: Signs of Otherness in Northern European Art of the Later Middle Ages*, two volumes (Berkeley: University of California, 1993)

Meyers, Jeffrey, *D. H. Lawrence: A Biography* (New York: Random House, 1992)

Meyers, Jeffrey, *Orwell: Wintry Conscience of a Generation* (New York: Viking, 2000)

Mishnah, The, translated by Herbert Danby (Oxford: Oxford University Press, 1933)

Morris, Benny, *Righteous Victims: A History of the Zionist–Arab Conflict, 1881–1999* (New York: Knopf, 1999)

Nilius, Sergei, ed, *The Protocols of the Elders of Zion* (St Petersburg, 1905)

O'Donnell, Elliot, *Family Ghosts and Ghostly Phenomena* (London: Dutton, 1934)

Oesterreicher, John, *Jerusalem the Free* (London: Anglo-Israel Association, 1973)

Poliakov, Léon, *The History of Anti-Semitism: From the Time of Christ to the Court Jews* (New York: Viking Press, 1965)

Reeder, Roberta, *Anna Akhmatova: Poet and Prophet* (New York: Saint Martin's Press, 1994)

Reuther, Rosemary, *Faith and Fratricide: The Theological Roots of Antisemitism* (New York: Seabury Press, 1974)

Rodinson, Maxime, *Israel and the Arabs* (Harmondsworth: Penguin, 1967)

Rosenfeld, Elsbeth, *The Four Lives of Elsbeth Rosenfeld* (London: Victor Gollancz, 1962)

Sartre, Jean–Paul, *Antisemite and Jew* (New York: Schocken, 1948)

Schechter, Ronald, *Obstinate Hebrews: Representations of Jews in France, 1715-1815* (Berkeley: University of California Press, 2003)

Sebald, W. G., *The Emigrants*, translated by Michael Hulse (New York: New Directions, 1996)

Simon, Marcel, *Versus Israël: etude sur les relation entre chrétiens et juifs dans l'empire romain* (Paris: E. Boccard 1948)

Shapiro, James, *Shakespeare and the Jews* (New York: Columbia University Press) 1996)

Sterne, Laurence, *A Sentimental Journey Through France and Italy* (Reading PA: Spencer Press, 1937)

Stevens, Wallace, *Poems*, selected by Samuel French Morse (New York: Vintage, 1959)

Strack, Hermann, *Introduction to the Talmud and Midrash* (Minneapolis: Fortress, 1992)

Sykes, Christopher, *Orde Wingate* (London: Collins, 1959)

Temple, William, *Nature, Man, and God* (London: MacMillan, 1960)

Thoreau, Henry David, *Walden or, Life in the Woods* (New York: Rinehart, 1959)

Vermes, Geza, *Jesus the Jew: A Historian's Reading of the Gospels* (New York: Macmillan, 1973)

Waugh, Evelyn, *Brideshead Revisited* (Boston: Little Brown & Co, 1945)

Webb, R. K., *Modern England: From the 18th Century to the Present* (London: George Allen and Unwin, 1969)

Wickings (Parkes), Dorothy *Autobiography*, unpublished, Southampton, Parkes Archives

Wistrich, Robert S., *Anti-Semitism: The Longest Hatred* (London: Thames Mandarin, 1991)

Wolfe, Robert, *Christianity in Perspective* (New York: Memory Books, 1987)

Woolf, Virginia, *A Room of One's Own* (Harmondsworth: Penguin, 1970)

ARTICLES CITED IN TEXT

Aberbach, Moshe, 'A Puzzle Penetrated,' *Midstream*, Vol. XXXXII, No. 2, February/March 1996

Ascherson, Noel, 'Goodbye to Berlin', *The New York Review of Books*, 10 April 2003

Ascherson, Noel, 'The Remains of Der Tag,' *The New York Review of Books*, 29 March 2001

Benjamin, Walter, cited by Charles Simac in his review of *Joseph Cornell: Master of Dreams*, *The New York Reviews of Books*, 24 October 2002

Bunting, Madeline, *Manchester Guardian Weekly*, 19 April 1995

Cohen, Michael J., 'Churchill and the Jews: The Holocaust', *The Nazi Holocaust: Bystanders to the Holocaust*, Vol. 8, edited by Michael R. Marrus (London: Meckler, 1989)

Conner, Steven in *The Jew in the Text: Modernity and the Construction of Identity*, Eds. Tamar Garb and Linda Nochlin (London: Thames and Hudson, 1995)

Duffy, Michael, 'Weapons of War', Internet website for First World War, April 2003

Eckhardt, A. Roy, 'In Memoriam: James Parkes', *Journal of Ecumenical Studies*, 19: 1, Winter 1982

Elon, Amos, 'Wise Survivors', *The New York Review of Books*, 10 April 2003

Fackenheim, Emil, 'Post-Holocaust Anti-Jewishness' in *World Jewry and the State of Israel*, ed. Moshe Davis (New York: Arno Press, 1977)

Faulkner, William, Nobel Prize address, Stockholm, 1950

'Guernsey,' Internet website, October 2002

Guernsey Evening Press, St Peter Port, 13 October 1917

Guernsey Star, The and *The Guernsey Evening Press*, St Peter Port, 29 April 1935

Handelzalts, Michael, Tel Aviv, *Ha'Aretz*, Section B, 11 July 2003

Indech, Jonah, 'James William Parkes', Tributes in Memory of James William Parkes at Bournemouth Hebrew Congregation, 1981, University of Southampton, Parkes Archives

Kushner, Tony, 'Independence and Integrity: The Vision of James Parkes and David Kessler to Transform Prejudice into Understanding' in *Noblesse Oblige: Essays in Honour of David Kessler*, edited by Alan D. Crown (London: Vallentine Mitchell, 1998)

Lange, Nicholas de, 'James Parkes, A Centenary Lecture' in *Cultures of Ambivalence and Contempt: Studies in Jewish–Non-Jewish Relations*, Eds Jones, Kushner and Pearce (London: Vallentine Mitchell, 1998)

Lange, Nicolas de, 'Unforgettable Characters,' No. 1, University of Southampton, Parkes Archives

Lewis, Rose G., 'James Parkes, Christianity Without Anti-Semitism', *Midstream*, January 1981

Mantel, Hilary, cited by Joyce Carol Oates, 'Stranded in the Dark', *The New York Review of Books*, 23 October 2003

Pannet, Peter, 'Searching for the Man Who Hitler Feared', *The Guernsey Press*, 16 September 2000

Reid, Alastair, 'You Can Go Home Again', *The New York Review of Books*, 15 January 2004.

Richmond, Colin, 'Parkes, Prejudice, and the Middle Ages', in *Cultures of Ambivalence and Contempt: Studies in Jewish-Non-Jewish Relations*, Eds Jones, Kushner and Pearce (London: Vallentine Mitchell, 1998)

Rosenberg, John D., 'Victoria's Secrets', *The New York Review of Books*, 10 April 2003

Schoffman, Stuart, 'The Gospel According to Gibson', *Jerusalem Report*, 22 March 2004

Simac, Charles, 'Archive of Horror', *The New York Review of Books*, Vol. L, No. 7, 1 May 2003

Simpson, W. W. and Ruth Weyl, *The Story of the International Council of Christians and Jews* (London: ICCJ, 1988)

'Symposium: A New Christian Document on Christian–Jewish Relations', *Midstream*, Vol. XXXXIX, No. 1, January 2003

Toynbee, Philip, 'Champion of the Jews', *Observer*, 13 April 1969

'Trench Foot', Internet website of Indiana Hand Center, May 2003

Vermes, Geza, *Jesus the Jew: A Historian's Reading of the Gospels* (New York: Macmillan, 1973)

Wasserstein, Bernard, 'The British Government and German Immigration 1933–1945', in *The Nazi Holocaust: Bystanders to the Holocaust*, Vol. 8, ed. by Michael R. Marrus (London: Meckler, 1989)

Weiner, Justus Reid, '"My Beautiful Old House" and Other Fabrications by Edward Said', Commentary, September 1999

Whitton–Davies, Carlyle from *Tributes in Memory of James William Parkes* at Bournemouth Hebrew Congregation, 1981, University of Southampton, Parkes Archives

BOOKS and PAMPHLETS BY JAMES PARKES CITED IN TEXT

Between God and Man, under pseudonym of John Hadham (London: Longmans Green, 1942)

Common Sense and Religion, under pseudonym of John Hadham (London: Victor Gollancz, 1961)

Concept of a Chosen People in Judaism and Christianity, The (New York: U.A.H.C. Press, 1954)

Conflict of the Church and the Synagogue, The (New York: Meridian and Jewish Publishing Society, 1961)

End of an Exile: Israel, Jews, and the Gentile World (London: Vallentine Mitchell, 1954)

Enemy of the People, An: Antisemitism (Hammondsworth: Penguin, 1945)

Five Roots of Israel, The (London: Vallentine Mitchell, 1964)

Foundations of Judaism and Christianity, The (London: Vallentine Mitchell, 1960)

God and Human Progress, under pseudonym of John Hadham (Harmondsworth: Penguin Books, 1944)

God at Work In Science, Politics, and Human Life (London: Putnam, 1952)

Good God, under pseudonym of John Hadham (Harmondsworth: Penguin Books, 1940)

History of the Jewish People, A (Harmondsworth: Penguin Books, 1962)

History of Palestine from 135 A.D. to Modern Times, A (London: Victor Gollancz, 1949)

International Conferencing (London: International Student Service, 1933)

Israel: Intrusion or Fulfilment? (London: privately printed, 1950)

Jewish–Christian Relations in England (London: Jewish Historical Society, 1960)

Jesus, Paul and the Jews (London: Student Christian Movement Press, 1936)

Jew and His Neighbour, The: A Study in the Causes of Antisemitism (London: SCM Press, 1930)

Jew in the Medieval Community, The: A Study of His Political and Economic Situation (London: Soncino, 1938)

Jewish Problem in the Modern World, The (London: Thornton and Butterworth, The Home Library, 1939)

Judaism and Christianity (Chicago: University of Chicago, 1948)

Parkes Library, The (Barley: Parkes Library, 1956)

Story of the International Student Service, The (Oxford: ISS, 1940)

Story of Jerusalem, The (London: Cresset Press, 1949)

Voyages of Discoveries: Autobiography (London: Victor Gollancz, 1969)

Whose Land?, A History of the Peoples of Palestine (Harmondsworth: Pelican, Penguin Books, 1970)

ARTICLES and LECTURES BY JAMES PARKES CITED IN TEXT

'*Apologia pro vita mea in rebus publicis versata*', 1942, University of Southampton Archives, File 60/4/1

'Bible, the World, and the Trinity, The', *The Journal of the Bible and Religion*, January 1966

'Bungalow Ghost, The', *Publication of La Société Guernesiaise*, St Peter Port: September 1965

'Can Christianity Be Detached from the Old Testament?' *East and West Review*, October 1935.

'Christendom and the Synagogue', *Frontier*, London: Vol. 2, No. 4, Winter 1959

'Christianity, Jewish History, and Antisemitism'. Southampton, The Parkes Library, 1976

'Chosen People, The', *The Georgia Review*, Vol. 9, No. I, Spring 1955

'Continuity of Jewish Life in the Middle East, The', London: Anglo-Israel Association, 1963

'Demobilization: The Situation Made Clear', *Punch*, 26 February 1919

'Emergence of Israel, The', *The Christian News-Letter*, 25 May 1949

'God and His Creation', co-authored by John Hadham, unpublished, University of Southampton, Parkes Archives, File 60/8/12: 1–2

'God and My Furniture', *Student Movement*, March 1931

'God We Believe In, The', under pseudonym of John Hadham, *St Martin's Review*, April–September 1941

'Holidays in My Childhood', St Peter Port: *The Guernsey Society Journal*, August 1976

'Issue in Palestine, The', *The Christian News-Letter*, 7 August 1946

'I Talk to Two Audiences: Meditation of a Christian on Judaism, Meditation on Judaism from the Outside', *The Metsudah*, 1944

'I Walk Round My Library', February 1977, unpublished, University of Southampton, Parkes Archives, File 60/9/19/20

'Jewish Contribution to Civilization, The', *Jewish Heritage*, Fall/Winter 1957

'Jewish Mysticism', *The Church's Fellowship for Psychical and Spiritual Studies Quarterly Review*, London: No. 87, Spring 1976

'Jewish Problem in Eastern Europe, The', WSCF, *Student World*, 1931

'Jews and the Student Movement, The', *Student Christian Movement Journal*, 19 July 1930

'Jews, Christians, and the World of Tomorrow', 1968, University of Southampton, Parkes Archives, File 60/8/12

'Judaism and Christianity', *European Judaism*, Vol. 13, No. 1, Autumn 1979

'Judaism and Christianity: Their Tasks and Their Relations in the Present Phase of the Evolving World', October 1978, Parkes Archives, File 60/9/19/24

'Judaism and the Jewish People', Montefiore Lecture, University of Southampton, 1973, Parkes Archives

'Judaism, Jews, Antisemites: Thoughts of a Non-Jew', *Jewish Review*, London, March–June 1934

'Letter to the Editor', *Guernsey Magazine*,' 11 May 1977

'Living Faith, A', *The Modern Churchman*, 1948

'My Collection of Architectural Photographs', 1975, unpublished, University of Southampton, Parkes Archives, File 60/9/19/1

'Missionaries and Jews', *The Church of England Newspaper*, London: 2 May 1959

'Missions to the Jews, A Theological Dispute', *The Jewish Chronicle*, 27 November 1959

'Nature of Anti-Semitism, The', *The Church Overseas, An Anglican Review of Missionary Thought and Work*, October 1932

'Notes on Bench Ghettoes in Polish Universities', *The London Times*, 6 October 1937

'Parson in the Pew, The', under pseudonym John Hadham, BBC series 'Worship and Life' in *The Listener*, 1942

'Peace', *The Student Movement*, October 1933

'Permanence of Sinai as God's Revelation, The', *St Martin's Review*, August–November 1949

'Politics and Pacifism', co-authored by John Hadham, *St Martin's Review*, March–May 1950

'Present State of Jewish–Christian Relations, The', *Conservative Judaism*, Winter 1956

'Progressive Judaism', *The Modern Churchman*, September 1953

'Quelque Reflexions sur la Conference Juive Mondiale', *Swiss-Jewish Journal*, September 1934

'Religion and Peoplehood in the History of the Diaspora', Jerusalem, Third International Congress of Jewish Studies, 2 August 1960

'Religious Experience and the Perils of Interpretation', Montefiore Lecture, University of Southampton, 1972, Parkes Archives

'Religious Situation in Jewry, The', *The Modern Churchman*, June 1952

'Revelation and a Duster', *Student Movement*, May 1931

'*Jewish People and Jesus Christ, The*', reviewed in *The Jewish Chronicle*, November 1949

'Separation of Church and Synagogue, The', *Liberal Jewish Monthly*, January 1955

'Trinity in International Affairs, The', 1929, University of Southampton, unpublished, Parkes Archives, File 60/6/8/10/12

'Way Forward, The', delivered at Southampton, June 1977, University of Southampton, Parkes Archives, File 60/33/92/86

INTERVIEWS

Angell, Nick, January 2003, as reported by Philip Rankilor

Bichard, Keith, January 2003, as reported by Philip Rankilor

Brouard, Lucy, in conversation with the author and Maggie Davidson, St Peter Port, Guernsey, August 2000, ff.

Elias, Alison, interviewed by the author and Maggie Davidson in Cambridge, 29 August 2000

Emanuel, Joseph, of Jerusalem interviewed by telephone by the author, December, 2003

Fisch, Harold, interviewed by telephone by the author, 10 October 2001

Parkes, James, interviewed by Laurence Dobie in the *Guardian*, 28 March 1970

Parkes, James, interviewed in *Jewish Telegraphic Agency*, August 1931

Parkes, James, interviewed by Abraham Rabinovich, 'Expert on the Poison Gas of Anti-Semitism',*The Jerusalem Post*, 24 April 1970

Roth, Ellen, interviewed by the author in London, 22 July 2004

Senior Prefects interviewed by the author and Maggie Davidson at Elizabeth College, St Peter Port, 1 September 2000

'Search for a Dialogue, A Conversation with James Parkes', ABC television programme hosted by George Watson, July 1974, University of Southampton, Parkes Archives

Tomlinson, Harry, as reported by Philip Rankilor, October 2002.

Weisz, Edith Ruth, interviewed by the author and Maggie Davidson in Cambridge, England, 28–29 August 2000

Werblowsky, Zvi, interviewed by the author and Maggie Davidson, 16 November 2003

Weyl, Ruth, interviewed by the author and Maggie Davidson, Rehovot, Israel, 26 October 2003

Wilkinson, Doris and Sam, interviewed by the author and Maggie Davidson in Barley, 2 September 2000

ARCHIVES and REFERENCE

Commonwealth War Graves Commission, Internet website, Spring 2003

Elizabeth [College] Annual, The, St Peter Port: 1915

Elizabeth College Register, edited by Brigadier-General D.H. Drake-Brockman, Volume II, 1874–1911 (St Peter Port: The Star and Gazette, 1931)

Encyclopædia Judaica (Jerusalem: Keter, 1972)

Greffe Registry at the Royal Court, St Peter Port, Guernsey

Minutes, Society of Christians and Jews, London

Official Guernsey Census: Report on the Census of Population and Households for 2001, St. Peter Port: States of Guernsey, 2002

Parkes Archives, University of Southampton

Index

Thoreau, Henry David, 267–8, 274, 335
Thrale, Mrs, 332
tikkun olam (mending of creation), 48, 200–1, 274, 470, 475
Toynbee, Arnold, 50, 368
Toynbee, Philip, 168, 261
Trend, Captain, 118–19, 134, 146
trompe d'oeil, 255–6, 442–4, 446
Tutu, Desmond (Bishop), 473

Unitarianism, 80
universities, colleges (selected), Bar-Ilan, 296, 433; Brandeis, 409; Chicago, 372, 403; Geneva, 229, 453; Hebrew Union College, 371; Jewish Theological Seminary, 227; Leeds, 415; Liverpool, 456–7; London, 191, 276–7, 424, 425; Melbourne, 456–7; Sussex, 412; Yeshiva, 371
Urdang, Bertha, 387
usury, 282–3

Vermes, Geza, 459, 463
Voltaire (François Marie Arouet), 195, 267

Wales (and the Welsh), 150–1, 159, 175, 232, 361, 425, 429
Wandering Jew, the, 377–80, 379, 383
Warburg Family (Bettina, Paul, Felix), 165–8, 174–5, 180, 227, 321, 327
Watson, George, 459–61, 466, 471
Waugh, Evelyn, 138, 143, 149
Weisz, Edith, 218, 266–7, 290, 293–6, 300, 318, 329–30, 430, 481–2
Weisz, Rachel, 296, 430
Weizmann, Chaim and Vera, 361–2
Wells, H. G., 252
Wells, Rev. Rex, 427
Werblowsky, Prof. Zvi, 294–5, 330–2, 381, 409, 418, 436, 451
West Family, 97, 125
Westmore, Ernest, 339, 404
Weyl, Ruth, 108, 323, 330, 331, 399, 431, 436, 461, 470
Wickings, Dorothy (JWP's wife), 317–35; America, 370, 372; *Autobiography*, 301, 306; Barley routine, 299–300; boorish, 467; candidate for matrimony, 320–3, 326–7; Centre for Jewish–Christian Relations, 410, 420; Christian faith, 394, 396; Common Wealth, 342; compassionate, 383; conjugal relations, 329–30, 332, 372; courtship, 322–5; co-worker, 383, 405, 416; 'debuts', 361, 365, 372; decisive, 322–3, 324, 325; deference to husband, 329, 331, 413, 468; Duocedimo, 381; early years, 319–20; earnings, 336; Ellershaw redux, 219; engagement, 324–5; exploited, 399; final resting place, 471;

frustration, 405; good judgment, 331, 341–2, 343; healing movement, 394, 396, 443, 453; homely, 319, 320–2, 331, 332; ill, 470; impatient, 468; insurance benefits, 401, 405; mother, 401, 403, 429; old age, 467; on the Continent, 404–5, 406; personality, 320, 331; political commitment, 320, 322, 323, 343; protective, 383, 397, 401, 403, 406; retirement, 425; St Edwards parish, 410; scapegoat, 428–9; secretarial skills, 299, 320, 327, 336, 372, 416; Sieff's 'rival', 440; slovenly, 462; surrogate mother, 328, 330; travelling companion, 46, 359, 361–3, 365, 372–5, 404, 406, 443, 450, 468; *Voyage of Discoveries*, 438–40, 443, 447, 480; wedding, 317, 325–8, 329
Wiener, Alfred, 346, 409
Wiener Jewish Library, 408–9
Wilkinson, Doris and Sam, 266, 273, 299–300, 429
William IV, 5
Wilson, Woodrow, 201
Wingate, General Orde, 21
Wise, Rabbi Stephen, 365, 370–1
Wistrich, Robert, 417
Witton-Davies, Rev. Carlisle, 409, 471
Wood-Leigh, Miss, 290
Woolf, Virginia, 447
Woolwich, Bishop of, 310, 432
Wordsworth, William, 378
World Student Christian Federation (WSCF), 147, 159–69, 178, 179, 197, 199–200, 205, 222, 303
World Union of Jewish Students (WUJS), 174–5, 190
World War I *see* First World War
World War II *see* Second World War

Yeats, William Butler, 430, 464
Ypres Salient, brothel at Bethune, 106; carnage, 91, 118, 429; 'curtain of silence', 98, 101, 319, 429, 436; death of David Parkes, 116; Etaple 'Bull Ring', 98; gas warfare, 97; Messines Ridge, 109

Zionism, Ahad Ha'am, 197; Alexander Teich, 190; Anglo-American Committee, 360–2; Barley likened to Jewish Agency, 398; British, 361; British policy, 291; Chaim Weizmann, 361–2; Christian, 21; *Daniel Deronda*, 233–4; Jewish normalcy, 346–7; London Zionist Council, 386; mystical basis, 233; Nahum Goldmann, 214; Salman Schocken, 233; State of Israel, 296, 362–5